CARSWELL

PRINCIPLES OF CANADIAN INCOME TAX LAW

Ninth Edition

JINYAN LI
Professor, Osgoode Hall Law School
York University

JOANNE MAGEE
Associate Professor of Income Tax Law
York University

and

J. SCOTT WILKIE
Distinguished Professor of Practice, Osgoode Hall Law School
York University
Partner, Blake, Cassels & Graydon LLP

 **THOMSON REUTERS**

A cataloguing record for this publication is available from Library and Archives Canada.

ISBN 978-0-7798-8081-2

Printed in Canada by Thomson Reuters

TELL US HOW WE'RE DOING
Scan the QR code to the right with your smartphone to send your comments regarding our products and services. Free QR Code Readers are available from your mobile device app store. You can also email us at feedback.legaltaxcanada@tr.com

 THOMSON REUTERS

THOMSON REUTERS CANADA, A DIVISION OF THOMSON REUTERS CANADA LIMITED

One Corporate Plaza
2075 Kennedy Road
Toronto, Ontario
M1T 3V4

Customer Support
1-416-609-3800 (Toronto & International)
1-800-387-5164 (Toll Free Canada & U.S.)
Fax 1-416-298-5082 (Toronto)
Fax 1-877-750-9041 (Toll Free Canada Only)
Email CustomerSupport.LegalTaxCanada@TR.com

DEDICATION

This edition of *Principles of Canadian Income Tax Law* marks a change in more than the law it chronicles and explains. The team of authors is also changing. Professor Peter Hogg is passing the responsibility for his formative contribution to Canadian tax learning to his two continuing co-authors and a new one. Even so, Peter's influence on the tax law and, importantly, how it is understood and applied, is enduring. In this and successive editions, Peter continues to inspire us. We admire him, have been shaped and influenced by him, and hope that our students will benefit from Peter's insights.

This book originated as a set of lecture notes prepared by Peter, as a student of the law himself and for his own students — a hallmark of his academic commitment and humility. In keeping with his passionate and rigorous scholarship spurred by irrepressible curiosity about legal institutions, he sought to learn, understand and teach Canadian income tax law with as much attention to the system of the law as to its technical complexities. "System" matters to Peter. We operate within a legal system. Its elements exist to achieve objectives that, in one way or another, influence or contain behavior in order to permit civil and orderly coexistence. The tax law and supporting fiscal policy, developed and framed to reflect, direct and fund our collective consumption as citizens, is a particularly important example of this conception of the legal system.

As his more well-known constitutional scholarship indicates, Peter strives to test and question the law as he grapples with it. He is not satisfied merely to communicate intricate subjects in their original complexity. Implicit in all his work is a standard that few achieve. A communicator does not actually understand a subject unless he or she is able to distill it to its essence and then convey it in ways that are accessible and comprehensible to a non-expert, and contextual with respect to the legal, policy and practical environments that are "real life". Peter is such a communicator. In all his scholarship and teaching, he has sought to simplify, to discover the threads of a system in their weave, with the seamless elegance that only true masters achieve; *Principles of Canadian Income Tax Law* reflects this. We hope we are up to meeting Peter's standards and the aspirations he had for this book.

We know Peter will continue to be identified with this book even though he is no longer on its marquee. We will continue to be inspired by him. This edition is dedicated to Peter.

Jinyan Li
Joanne Magee
J. Scott Wilkie
Toronto
August 31, 2017

PREFACE

This is the ninth edition of Principles of *Canadian Income Tax Law*. The eighth edition was published in 2013 and the usual pace of change in the world of income tax has necessitated a further revision of the text.

The book originated as a set of lecture notes prepared by Professor Peter Hogg for his course in Income Tax Law at the Osgoode Hall Law School of York University. The notes were handed out to students, and were revised from time to time. In order to help convert the notes into a book, Professor Hogg enlisted the aid of Professor Joanne Magee, who teaches income tax to accounting students at the Faculty of Liberal Arts and Professional Studies of York University. She joined the project in 1994, and participated in an extensive rewriting. The final versions of the first and second editions were a joint product. Over time, Professor Hogg stopped being an active participant in the writing of subsequent editions. In the third edition, Ted Cook, now Director, Tax Legislation Division, Department of Finance Canada, became a co-author. Since the fourth edition, Jinyan Li has been a co-author and has undertaken significant restructuring and rewriting of the book. In this ninth edition, Scott Wilkie has become a co-author and Professor Hogg is relinquishing his formal role, although his objectives and influence are evident throughout the book.

Principles of Canadian Income Tax Law is an introduction to income tax. The ninth edition contains a single chapter on corporations, partnerships and trusts and has been updated and rewritten to improve its usefulness to readers: students, professors, lawyers and the judiciary. The book is designed for students doing their first course in income tax law and can be supplemented with other readings, court decisions and problem material. It should also be useful for lawyers who need a refresher in the basic principles of Canadian income tax. We hope as well that it will be useful to courts, especially when they have to deal with fundamental issues, and are delighted that the work has been cited in a number of decisions of the Supreme Court of Canada.

Taxation by its nature is an amalgam of rules, and just as important as the "rules" are the "reasons for the rules", which permeate their meaning and application. As with previous editions, this new edition attempts to disentangle complex statutory provisions by focusing on fundamental principles. That means the ideas of the income tax system, the policies that underlie the system, and the major features of the system. Income tax law is portrayed as a rational system. There is a reason for everything, and we always try to explain what that reason is. The law is never portrayed as a set of purposeless technicalities. The approach is not merely descriptive. Alternative ideas and policies are examined, and the provisions of the *Income Tax Act* and the case law are evaluated critically in light of our conceptions of sound tax policy.

The book is progressive. The early chapters assume an intelligent reader who has no knowledge of tax or accounting concepts, and little of commercial matters. As ideas are explained and information provided, the chapters become more demanding. The book is intended to be an aid to learning rather than a reference work. However, the detailed Table of Contents, the Table of Cases and the Index should make it easy for the non-continuous reader to find what he or she is looking for.

We have tried to avoid the complex abstractions with which the *Income Tax Act* is replete. Our language is as simple, concrete and non-technical as our capability and the nature of the subject permitted. Obviously, a lot of detail is unavoidable, but the minutiae of the subject are avoided or, where they are necessary for accuracy, are relegated to footnotes. Difficult numerical examples are avoided, although simple numerical illustrations are used from time to time to explain a concept. The book is designed to be easy to read.

We have had the good fortune to work in environments that encourage and facilitate the writing of a text such as this one. The book reflects not only the patience and support of those with whom we come into contact as teachers, researchers and practitioners, but also the insights they offer, even unwittingly, by their own experiences with Canadian tax law.

In previous editions, we have been helped by comments from Brian Arnold, Bob Beam, Neil Brooks, Larry Chapman, Joe Frankovic, Warren Grover, Doug Hartkorn, Thaddeus Hwong, Rick Krever, John Macintosh, Alan Macnaughton, Joel Nitikman, Lisa Philipps, Pearl Schusheim, Sandra Scott, Lee St. Aubin, Graham Turner, Scott Wilkie and Bonnie Zelman. Earlier editions also benefited tremendously from updating and editing contributions by Osgoode Hall Law School students Simon Cheung, Stephen Ji and Robert Watkins, as well as Denise Elliott, Joanne Gort, Simon Leith and Aihua (Charlotte) Wu. The editing, printing and production of this edition went smoothly thanks to Grant Daly at Thomson Reuters, who oversaw the project, and Cheryl Finch, the Thomson Reuters freelance editor whose skill, care, insights and suggestions improved our writing and helped make our messages clearer.

The authors dedicate their contributions to this book to their spouses and children.

Jinyan Li
Joanne Magee
J. Scott Wilkie
Toronto
August 31, 2017

ABOUT THE AUTHORS

Jinyan Li joined Osgoode Hall Law School in 1999 and served as Interim Dean from 2009-2010. She is a co-director of the Professional LL.M in Tax Law. She also teaches as an adjunct faculty at the Tax Program at the University of Sydney, Australia. Before coming to Osgoode, she taught tax law at the University of Western Ontario, Faculty of Law (1991-1999). She was awarded a Queen Elizabeth II Diamond Jubilee Medal for her contributions to the community. She has published widely in the areas of tax law and policy, comparative taxation, and Chinese taxation. Her recent work includes *Income Tax at 100 Years: Essays and Reflections on the Income War Tax Act* (2017) (Li, Wilkie and Chapman, eds.); contribution to a United Nations Base Erosion and Profit Shifting project; and *International Taxation in China: A Contextualized Analysis; and International Taxation in Canada* (Li, Cockfield and Wilkie). She is a co-editor of "Current Tax Readings" of the Canadian Tax Foundation's *Canadian Tax Journal* and a correspondent for the *Bulletin for International Taxation*. She is a former Governor of the Canadian Tax Foundation. In one of her recent expert advisory roles she served as a member of the Expert Advisory Group to the Minister of Finance, Canada on reviewing the tax system (2016-2017).

Joanne Magee joined York University in 1991. She is a frequent speaker and writer on issues of income tax law, tax policy and tax planning, and update editor of *Insight into Canadian Income Tax*. She is cross-appointed to the School of Administrative Studies (where she is Coordinator of Income Tax Law Courses) and the School of Public Policy and Administration (where she is Undergraduate Program Director). Joanne is a former Acting Dean and Associate Dean (1999-2007) and School Director (2007-2010) at York University, and a former Governor of the Canadian Tax Foundation. She is a Fellow of CPA Ontario and of the Financial Planning Standards Council and is a recipient of a Province of Ontario Volunteer Service Award. Over the years, Joanne has served on a wide variety of committees, councils and boards at York, at the Institute of Chartered Accountants of Ontario, at the Canadian Institute of Chartered Accountants, and in the community. She is currently a member of CPA Canada's Income Tax Education Committee.

J. Scott Wilkie is Distinguished Professor of Practice and the 2017/2018 James L. Lewtas Professor at Osgoode Hall Law School, where he is also a co-director of the Professional LL.M. in Tax Law. Scott is also a tax partner at Blake, Cassels & Graydon LLP. He is associated with the Vienna University of Economics and Business where he teaches a course in trade and tax policy (WTO and Tax Policy), and consults with and assists its Masters and Doctoral students. He is also an Executive Fellow, University of Calgary School of Public Policy. Scott is the Vice-Chair, Permanent Scientific Committee, International Fiscal Association and serves on the Board of Trustees of the International Bureau of Fiscal Documentation. Formerly, he has served as the Chair and a Governor of the Canadian Tax Foundation, co-editor of the Canadian Tax Foundation's *Canadian Tax Journal*, co-Chair and Tax Section Liaison of the Tax Committee of the American Bar Association International Law Section, chair of the Canadian Bar Association National Tax Section and, in that role, co-Chair of the Joint Committee on Taxation of the Canadian Bar Association and CPA Canada. Scott served as a public policy adviser for the Canadian E-Business Opportunities Roundtable and the Canadian E-Business Initiative, and participated in the work of the Minister of National Revenue's E-Commerce Advisory Panel on the international tax aspects of e-commerce. Scott participated as a member of the Organisation for Economic Co-operation and Development's Business Advisory Group for Business Restructurings; additionally, for many years, he has made contributions to various international tax and tax policy discussions in relation to project work conducted by the OECD and, recently, the United Nations Committee of Experts on International Cooperation in Tax Matters. In 2012, Scott was awarded a Queen Elizabeth II Diamond Jubilee Medal to recognize his significant contributions to the work of the Canadian Tax Foundation. He was awarded lifetime membership for service to the Canadian Tax Foundation in 2011 and in 2016 was an inaugural recipient of the Canadian Tax Foundation CTF Lifetime Contribution Award.

LIST OF CHAPTERS

For detailed table of contents, see page xi.

CONTENTS

CONTENTS

CONTENTS

CONTENTS

CONTENTS

CONTENTS

CONTENTS

CONTENTS

CONTENTS

CONTENTS

CONTENTS

CONTENTS

CONTENTS

CONTENTS

CONTENTS

TABLE OF CASES

Table of Cases

Table of Cases

Table of Cases

1
INCOME TAX LAW

1.1 — Introduction

A tax is "a levy, enforceable by law imposed under the authority of a legislature, imposed by a public body and levied for a public purpose".[1] Income tax is levied on "income".[2]

The income tax plays a pivotal and important role in funding public expenditures associated with collective consumption of "public goods" for the "public good" and directing economic activity to sustain and enrich a country's economy according to the social welfare choices made through the political process. It is the most important source of government revenues in Canada.[3] It is also a major mechanism of indirect government funding, as it uses hundreds of different tax expenditures to motivate taxpayers to engage in activities that are deemed beneficial to society and provide relief to Canadians in particular circumstances.

What constitutes "income" is not always obvious, although a clue emerges from a simple syllabic examination of the word. "In" and "come" suggest that income is "something" arising from or flowing out of a "place" that remains intact. As something separate from that "place", income becomes independently at the disposal of

---

[1] *Kempe v. R.*, [2001] 1 C.T.C. 2060 (T.C.C. [Informal Procedure]) at para. 9, citing *Lawson v. Interior Tree Fruit and Vegetable Committee of Direction*, [1931] S.C.R. 357.

[2] *London County Council v. Attorney General* (1899), 4 T.C. 265 (Eng. Q.B.) (per Lord Macnaghten of the Privy Council).

[3] See heading 1.2(a) — Revenue to finance public spending, below.

the "recipient" who "receives" it. Conceptually, this is fine. But a system for sustaining the fiscal needs of a country must be reliable and predictable and perceived to be fair.

An income tax system must have legislation with rules. But it is a mistake to think that the formulation and application of income tax law is just a simple mathematical exercise using words and legal forms. Words do not necessarily have a self-evident meaning. As is the case with words generally, the meaning of words used in legislation is influenced by the context in which the words arise. Words are used as threads in the legislative fabric in which they are woven. In tax legislation, words are woven to achieve a fiscal and legislative purpose. Their context and purpose are just as important as their textual meaning. As well, because of its accessory nature, income tax law is dependent on principles and concepts in general law unless and until the tax legislation grows its own deeming rules.[4]

Although the income tax is not a "new" kind of levy, other means of taxation that were less direct and less personal were certainly tried first. The modern origins of the income tax may be found in England around 1800 at the time of the Napoleonic wars.[5] The United States developed the modern antecedent of the Canadian income tax in the next hundred years, first influencing the development of the tax at the provincial level and, later, at the federal level in 1917.[6] Over the years, the theoretical notion of "income" as a justification and base for taxation was refined as the capacity of "income" to flow and be redirected (by the ingenuity and constructs of taxpayers) became evident and the government evaluated and reacted to gaps and problems in the system according to prevailing fiscal objectives and constraints.

This chapter provides an overview of the key functions of Canadian income tax, the sources of income tax law, the principles of statutory interpretation, the basic structure of the income tax system, and some basic income tax terminology and concepts.

---

[4] See M. Milet & C. Sheridan, "The Income Tax Act as 'Accessory': A Modern Re-Examination" in J. Li, J.S. Wilkie & L. Chapman, eds., *Income Tax at 100 Years: Essays and Reflections on the Centennial of the Income War Tax Act* (Toronto: Canadian Tax Foundation) [forthcoming in 2017] at 13:1.

[5] See John F. Avery Jones, "The Sources of Addington's Income Tax" in Peter Harris & Dominic de Cogan, eds., *Studies in the History of Tax Law*, vol. 7 (Oxford: Hart Publishing, 2015) at 1.

[6] C. Campbell & R. Raizenne, "The 1917 Income War Tax Act: Origins and Enactment" in Li, Wilkie & Chapman, *supra* note 4 at 2:1; J. Wilson, "Canada's Corporate Income Tax: The First Ten Years (1917–1927)" in Li, Wilkie & Chapman, *supra* note 4 at 7:1 and S. Wilkie, "Three Spirits of Canadian Corporate Income Tax: The Relic, the Remnant, and the Reflection" in Li, Wilkie & Chapman, *supra* note 4 at 8:1.

1.2 — Roles of the income tax

(a) — Revenue to finance public spending

The main purpose of the income tax is to raise revenue to finance government spending. Paying for government spending is, of course, the purpose of every tax, but the income tax has been the most important source of Canadian government revenue for over 60 years.[7] In the 2015-2016 fiscal year, federal income tax payable by individuals, corporations and non-residents yielded approximately 79 per cent of the federal government's total revenues and 65 per cent of its total budgetary revenues. The government's 2017 budget projects this pattern to continue through to 2021-2022. The next most important sources of revenue in 2015-2016 are the federal goods and services tax (approximately 14 per cent) and employment insurance premiums (8.7 per cent).[8] The income tax tends to be the most important source of revenue for Canadian provinces.

Government spending is the collective consumption of public goods that we, acting collectively through the political process, decide to consume in relation to a particular standard of civility and living that might be referred to as our social welfare choices. In that respect, we pay all taxes to ourselves — into a common pool from which expenditures are made according to our collective "national family budget". We entrust the exercise of establishing our spending and related economic priorities to Parliament, assisted by its officials primarily in the Department of Finance and the Canada Revenue Agency (the "CRA"). This perception of income tax as the cost of collective consumption is important to bear in mind as we interpret income tax legislation (and evaluate interpretations of income tax legislation), particularly those provisions dealing with tax avoidance.

(b) — Redistribution of income

The income tax serves a critical redistributive function (the mitigation of unequal distribution of income in society through redistribution). The income tax is framed by and funds the social welfare choices that are the marks of what we consider to represent a civilized life. When we study income tax with these considerations in mind, we discover the reasons that not all countries' income tax systems are the same even though many of them respond to similar influences: their tax systems reflect their "way of life" or their social welfare choices, as well as their capacities to satisfy them based on their economic resources.

---

[7] J. Li & S. Wilkie, "Celebrating the Centennial of the Income War Tax Act, 1917: The Future by the Light of 100 Candles" in Li, Wilkie & Chapman, *supra* note 4 at 1:1.

[8] Canada, Department of Finance, *Building a Strong Middle Class, Budget 2017* (Ottawa: 2017) Annex 1 at 252, Table A1.6. The figures for 2015-2016 are as follows, in billions: total revenues ($295.5), personal income tax ($144.9), corporate income tax ($41.4), GST ($33.0) and EI ($23.1). Non-resident income taxes ($6.5), a combination of personal and corporate taxes, are disclosed separately from personal and corporate income taxes.

In Canada and other Western democracies, income is primarily distributed through market exchanges and the outcome is often considered unjust or unfair by modern societies. The income tax, especially the personal income tax, is used to help redistribute social income in order to mitigate the unequal distribution. Taxes are collected from high-income earners at progressive rates (i.e., the higher the income, the higher the tax rate) and used to finance social programs that tend to primarily benefit lower-income earners. Although the appropriate level of redistribution can be debated theoretically and politically, there is no denial that personal income tax is the only tax in Canada that is progressive and functions as the main instrument of redistribution.

(c) — Regulation of private activity

All governments use tax policy to regulate private activities in order to promote certain economic and social policies. This is evident, for example, during election campaigns and budget debates. Fundamental social and economic judgments are made in deciding who to tax, what to tax, and when. Tax subsidies — although they are not described as subsidies — are used to specifically promote activities, such as environmental protection, home ownership, retirement savings, post-secondary education, research and development, natural resource exploration and exploitation and entrepreneurship.

These tax subsidies are referred to as "tax expenditures" because they are government expenditures on programs that are delivered through tax reductions and exemptions; but as such, they are not mysterious — "we" collectively make these expenditures to "buy" goods and services that enrich our collective social and economic experience. To simplify — probably oversimplify — we go to the "market" together and make purchases for ourselves and each other, in both cases motivated by the underlying self-interest that political, social and economic choices reflect. Our tax expenditures are what we spend when, in a more prosaic moment, we pay the cashier for our groceries. The tax revenue forfeited is the tax expenditure — in effect expenditures that we enlist citizens to make by engaging in the activities that generate relief from tax that otherwise would be due. These activities serve the "collective self-interest". As with the redistribution function, the regulatory function of taxation is controversial and discussed further in Chapter 2.

1.3 — Income tax law

(a) — The *Income Tax Act*

(i) — *History*[9]

The Canadian federal income tax is imposed by the *Income Tax Act* (the "*ITA*").[10] The federal government first imposed an income tax in 1917 by enacting the *In-*

---

[9] See Campbell & Raizenne, *supra* note 6; Wilson, *supra* note 6; Wilkie, *supra* note 6.

[10] R.S.C. 1985 (5th Supp.), c. 1 [*ITA*].

come War Tax Act, 1917 during World War I.[11] The tax was supposed to be a temporary wartime measure because it was accepted that the field of direct taxation should be left to the provinces. But as the income tax was proven to be a reliable source of government revenue, the temporary tax became permanent after the war: in 1948, the word "War" was dropped and the Act was renamed the *"Income Tax Act"*.[12] The current statute was initially enacted in 1971,[13] and came into force at the beginning of 1972.

The original income tax legislation and supporting regulations introduced in 1917 comprised a mere 20 pages. The current *ITA* (including historical references, various annotations, proposed amendments and regulations) runs for over 2000 pages (in small print and on two-column pages).[14] The print version weighs more than a kilogram![15]

In addition to an increase in length and resulting complexity, there have also been major changes in the style of legislative drafting. The 1917 legislation was drafted in broad, generally-worded provisions. The 1972 tax reform[16] and subsequent amendments reflect a high degree of detail and technical complexity. Recent legislative drafting has also included the use of algebraic formulae. The change in statutory style has been caused by several factors, including: aggressive tax planning, an increase in the complexity of income-earning transactions because of growth in cross-border activities, advances in technology and the rise of e-commerce; the use of income tax legislation by the government as a fiscal policy instrument; legislative overrule of judicial interpretation of the statute; and the use of statutory anti-avoidance rules as new avoidance transactions become known to the government.

(ii) — Current structure

The *ITA* is divided into parts: Part I contains the provisions that levy the ordinary income tax on individuals, corporations, or trusts and on income earned through partnerships; Parts I.1 to XIV levy a variety of special taxes that supplement or complement the ordinary income tax; Part XV provides for administration and enforcement; Parts XVI and XVI.1 deal with tax avoidance; Part XVII addresses interpretation, providing definitions of many of the terms used in the statute; and Parts XVIII and XIX deal with new reporting standards for international financial holdings involving financial institutions and for multinational business enterprises, in both cases to facilitate the sharing of information among countries' tax authori-

---

[11] S.C. 1917, c. 28.

[12] S.C. 1948, c. 52.

[13] S.C. 1970-71-72, c. 63 (Royal Assent December 23, 1971), which enacted the substance of the statute, although it did not wholly repeal the previous Act. Now the *ITA, supra* note 10.

[14] E.g., David M. Sherman, *Practitioner's Income Tax Act, 2017*, 51st ed. (Toronto: Carswell, 2017).

[15] *Ipsco Inc. v. R.*, [2002] 2 C.T.C. 2907, 2002 D.T.C. 1421 (T.C.C.) at para. 26.

[16] See Chapter 2 at heading 2.2(c) — Tax reform of 1971 and the Carter Report.

ties with respect to international influences on their tax bases and tax reporting by their taxpayers.

Part I is further divided into 10 "Divisions", identified by capital letters A to J. Division B and Division E are separated yet further into "subdivisions", identified by lower case letters. The basic provisions are contained in Divisions A to E. Division A (Liability for Tax) consists of a single section (section 2).

Division B (Computation of Income) prescribes the rules for the measurement of a taxpayer's income, which is commonly described as net income because it is net of deductions (other than the Division C deductions). Division B starts with section 3, which defines the income of a taxpayer for a taxation year as including, among other things, the taxpayer's "income for the year from each office, employment, business and property" (paragraph 3(a)). Division B then goes on to supply detailed rules for the computation of income from these sources: subdivision a provides the rules for income from an office or employment; subdivision b provides the rules for income from a business or property; subdivision c provides the rules for capital gains; and subdivisions d and e provide for a miscellaneous group of other sources of income and other deductions. There are several further subdivisions, each of which will be addressed in due course.

Division C sets out rules for the determination of taxable income. Taxable income is calculated by taking a taxpayer's income under Division B and subtracting the deductions and adding the additions allowed by Division C. Division C deductions include those for social assistance receipts, certain employee stock option benefits, part of the benefit arising from home relocation loans, charitable donations made by a corporation, exempt capital gains on qualified farm properties and shares of qualified small business corporations, losses incurred in other years, inter-corporate dividends, and income of part-time residents. Most individuals have no Division C deductions, which means that their "income" is the same as their "taxable income".

Division D prescribes the rules for the determination of taxable income earned in Canada by non-residents. Division E prescribes the rules for the computation of tax, including tax rates and credits.

Tax practitioners commonly refer to some specific areas of the *ITA* by their Part, Division, or subdivision. Some of the more common designations include Division C (deductions in computing taxable income), subdivision e (statutory deductions in computing income), Part I tax (basic income tax), and Part XIII tax (withholding taxes imposed on investment income earned in Canada by non-residents).

The Act contains over 269 sections (sections continue to be added as required to give effect to evolving tax policy and resulting legislation). Sections are often further broken down into subsections, paragraphs, subparagraphs, clauses, and subclauses. A unique numbering system is used to refer to each layer of the hierarchy. This is illustrated by subclause 44(1)(e)(i)(A)(II) which is in subdivision c, Division B of Part I:

Part	I	(Roman numerals)
Division	B	(capital letters)
Subdivision	c	(lower case letters)

Section	44	(Arabic numerals)
Subsection	(1)	(Arabic numerals in brackets)
Paragraph	(e)	(lower case letters in brackets)
Subparagraph	(i)	(lower case Roman numerals in brackets)
Clause	(A)	(capital letters in brackets)
Subclause	(I)	(Roman numerals in brackets)

In referring to a provision of the *ITA*, the key is usually the section number. For example, the above-mentioned provision could be cited as section 44(1)(e)(i)(A)(II). Alternatively, it could be cited as subclause 44(1)(e)(i)(A)(II). Where a section is cited, it is unnecessary to include the Part, Division, or subdivision, since the section numbers run consecutively and do not begin again with each new subdivision, Division, or Part.

(iii) — Legislative process

The Department of Finance is responsible for tax policy, which includes formulating amendments to the *ITA*. Amendments are introduced into Parliament by the Minister of Finance. These amendments are not necessarily announced in the Minister's annual budget. Recent practice has been for the Minister to introduce a separate technical bill dealing with technical deficiencies in the *ITA* and areas of perceived abuse. Press releases sometimes announce changes to the *ITA* when a single area is being targeted and there is a need for immediate action. Sometimes these technical changes are significant changes of policy, but, for the most part, they deal with particular fact situations and small numbers of taxpayers. It is usually the budget that is the source of major policy initiatives and substantive changes to the *ITA*.

The Minister of Finance presents a budget to Parliament each year, usually in February or March. The budget provides an estimate of the government's revenues and expenditures for the next financial year, which starts on April 1. Because of the significance of income taxes for the revenue side, the budget usually proposes a set of changes to the *ITA*. These proposals, along with the rest of the budget, are held in strict secrecy until the date of the Minister's presentation of the budget to Parliament. The reason for secrecy is to prevent taxpayers from anticipating the changes and taking avoidance measures or otherwise profiting from the proposals. When the budget is presented, the changes in the *ITA* are normally proposed to be effective as of the budget date for the same reason.

The Department of Finance is also responsible for starting the legislative process in amending the *ITA*. The Act is amended frequently. A "notice of ways and means motion to amend the *Income Tax Act*" is prepared by the Department of Finance. This document lists and describes all of the amendments to the *ITA* that have been proposed. The notice of ways and means motion is followed by legislation in draft form. Since 1983, the Department of Finance has followed the practice of issuing explanatory notes (or technical notes) to accompany the draft legislation. This material is helpful in explaining the purpose of amendments, which are often exceedingly difficult (even for tax professionals) to understand on their own. The purpose of issuing the legislation initially in draft form is to provide an opportunity for the tax community to comment on the legislation. In fact, commentary is received and sometimes does lead to changes in the legislation.

Eventually, a bill amending the *ITA* is introduced into the House of Commons by the Minister of Finance. That bill then follows the normal legislative process, which includes scrutiny by standing committees of both the House of Commons and the Senate, and in due course the bill is enacted into law. The amending Act will usually make many of its provisions retroactive to the date when the changes were first publicly announced (in the budget or elsewhere).

Although it is generally accepted that it is unfair to apply a new law to transactions that were complete by the time of the law's announcement, the government has made a few retroactive amendments as a legislative response to court decisions that it did not agree with.[17] For example, a series of amendments to the general anti-avoidance rule ("GAAR") in section 245 were announced in 2004 and enacted in 2005 but were effective retroactively to September 12, 1988, which was the effective date of the GAAR.[18] Since the time elapsed from the date of the budget or other announcement to the date of enactment is sometimes more than a year, the tax proposals of one budget may not be implemented by the time of the next budget (usually 12 months later). When amendments that are proposed to be retroactive to the date of the budget have not been enacted by the time that the income tax return forms have to be printed, the proposed changes are simply incorporated into the forms on the (normally safe) assumption that the changes will eventually be enacted[19] and will be retroactive. The taxpayer is, of course, not legally bound to comply with amendments that have not been enacted by the time that a return is filed, but compliance is the course of prudence that is followed by nearly all taxpayers.

While the *ITA* is the primary source of tax law, there are other sources of tax law as well, including those that strictly may not have legal effect but are nevertheless considered to be worthy of consideration in interpreting and applying the law. These sources help establish the meaning of provisions of the *ITA* or the implementation of the Act. The CRA[20] also publishes administrative interpretation and commentary on the law, which is not a source of law but very useful to taxpayers.[21]

---

[17] E.g., s. 10(1.01) was announced on December 20, 1995 as the legislative response to *Friesen v. R.*, [1995] 2 C.T.C. 369, 95 D.T.C. 5551 (S.C.C.) [*Friesen*].

[18] They were a legislative response to *Rousseau-Houle v. R.*, 2006 D.T.C. 3181 (T.C.C.) and *Fredette v. R.*, [2001] 3 C.T.C. 2468, 2001 D.T.C. 621 (T.C.C.).

[19] This assumption does not necessarily hold in the case of a minority government.

[20] The CRA is discussed in more detail at heading 1.5(e)(i) — The Canada Revenue Agency, below.

[21] Several commercial publishers have searchable electronic databases that include the various sources of law as well as commentary by the CRA and others.

(b) — Income tax application rules

The *Income Tax Application Rules, 1971* ("ITARs")[22] were enacted in 1971, along with the present Act. They consist of transitional rules, which were needed to shift from the old Act to the new one. As time passes, the ITARs steadily lose their significance, but some of the rules are still relevant. For example, the ITARs have to be used in order to calculate a capital gain on the disposition of property that was acquired before 1972 (the year when capital gains first became taxable).

(c) — Income tax regulations

The *Income Tax Regulations* (the "Regulations")[23] are introduced under authority conferred by section 221 of the *ITA*. Section 221 provides, among other things, that the Governor in Council may make regulations "prescribing anything that, by this Act, is to be prescribed or is to be determined or regulated by regulation".[24] The *ITA* makes frequent reference to "prescribed forms", "prescribed amounts", and so on. The word "prescribed" is the signal to look for a provision in the Regulations. The Regulations contain much of the detail of income tax law. Since they do not have to be enacted by Parliament, they can be changed much more easily than the *ITA*. However, they have the same force of law as the Act itself.

(d) — Tax treaties

A bilateral tax treaty is an agreement entered into by two countries to coordinate the tax treatment of cross-border transactions. Canada has entered into tax treaties with more than 90 countries, the most important of which is the Canada-United States Tax Convention.[25] Canadian tax treaties are mostly based on the Organisation for Economic Co-operation and Development ("OECD") Model Tax Convention.[26]

A tax treaty is part of Canadian law.[27] The purpose that is commonly recited in each tax treaty is to avoid double taxation and to prevent fiscal evasion. But, in

---

[22] R.S.C. 1985 (5th Supp.), c. 2.

[23] C.R.C., c. 945.

[24] *ITA*, *supra* note 10, s. 221

[25] Canada-United States Convention with Respect to Taxes on Income and on Capital, 26 September 1980 (entered into force 16 August 1984). It was first concluded in 1942. The current treaty was signed in 1980, came into effect in 1984 and has been amended by several protocols, the most recent of which was the fifth protocol concluded in 2007.

[26] Organisation for Economic Co-operation and Development, *Model Tax Convention on Income and on Capital 2014 (Full Version)*, 9th ed. (Paris: OECD Publishing, 2015). The Model Tax Convention, which is updated on a regular basis, has been important for decades as it has facilitated the growth of bilateral tax treaties between different countries. For the full text of the convention, see <http://www.oecd-ilibrary.org/taxation/model-tax-convention-on-income-and-on-capital-2015-full-version_9789264239081-en>.

[27] According to public international law governing treaties, governments may enter into agreements that bind them in the sense that the agreements are legally effective although not

fact, treaties have two other singular purposes, which persist from the earliest modern tax treaties. The first purpose is to allocate taxing rights between the treaty partners according to certain norms that direct how sovereign tax jurisdictions should be prepared to accommodate each other's entitlements to tax associated with the notions of "residence" of taxpayers and "source" of income. The second purpose is to provide for the exchange of information between the treaty partners so that their allocated taxing rights can be administered. Treaties, of course, have other elements including provisions directed to resolving disputes and therefore (it is hoped) avoiding double tax.

Unlike the *ITA*, tax treaties do not charge tax. Treaties are fundamentally relieving in nature as they reduce taxes imposed under domestic law. Each treaty makes some changes to the *ITA* in its application to taxpayers covered by the treaty. In the event of any inconsistency between the treaty and domestic law (other than the *Income Tax Conventions Interpretation Act*),[28] generally the terms of the treaty are to prevail. The *Income Tax Conventions Interpretation Act* is a domestic statute that governs the interpretation of Canadian tax treaties. Its purpose is broadly twofold: first, to provide for an established understanding of undefined treaty terms on an ambulatory rather than static basis (i.e., according to the prevailing law, not constrained by what the law may have been when the treaty entered into force), and, second, to refine and clarify the scope of a treaty as developments occur in domestic law (notably judicial decisions).[29]

In addition to tax treaties, Canada has a number of Tax Information Exchange Agreements ("TIEAs") with countries that do not have a tax treaty with Canada. The main purpose of TIEAs is to enable Canada to obtain tax information from the tax authorities of the other country. In the absence of such an agreement, a sovereign country has no legal obligation to share tax information with another country in order to assist the tax enforcement of that other country.

---

subjected to Parliamentary enactment. According to Canadian constitutional law, an international tax treaty is required to be ratified by Parliament for it to be effective in altering the provisions or application of domestic law, including tax legislation. The enactment to implement a treaty is introduced in the Senate of Canada, because it comprises a pre-existing agreement of the government and because tax treaties usually are not seen as revenue-generating legislation. (Revenue-generating legislation must commence its Parliamentary journey in the House of Commons.) After the Senate votes to adopt the agreement, it proceeds to the House of Commons where the procedure to ratify the treaty is completed. The Canadian Parliament implements the treaty by enacting a short statute which provides that the treaty has the force of law in Canada; the full text of the treaty is appended to the statute as a schedule. After each treaty has been ratified by both countries, it is effective according to its terms.

[28] R.S.C. 1985, c. I-4 [*ITCIA*].

[29] See, e.g., *Stickel v. M.N.R.*, [1972] C.T.C. 210, 72 D.T.C. 6178 (Fed. T.D.); reversed [1973] C.T.C. 202, 73 D.T.C. 5178 (Fed. C.A.); affirmed [1974] C.T.C. 416, 74 T.T.C. 6268 (S.C.C.) [*Stickel*], discussed at heading (h)(i) — General information and interpretative guidance, below.

Tax treaties serve an important function of "intersecting" Canada's tax system and other countries' system. Intersection of countries' sovereign tax systems and the latent tension attributable to those countries' persona as national economic actors is what commonly is described as the "international tax system". However, the "international tax system" is not a system at all. The international features of each country's tax system are most accurately understood as an agglomeration of what might broadly be referred to as the country's "hard" tax system and "soft" international law. Canada's hard tax system includes its domestic tax law, the private law platforms and tax treaties and customary public international law. "Soft" international law is comprised of a quilt of "international" guidance, interpretations, model provisions, best practices and "norms" of various kinds, all of which are manifestations of inter-nation cooperation developed by countries and their representatives through institutions such as the OECD and the United Nations. The OECD Model Tax Convention and Commentaries are examples of "soft" law. The OECD's recent initiatives to stem international tax avoidance have been important, as they have increased the systemic interactions among countries as well as the sharing of information and best practices.

(e) — Case law

Case law is an important source of tax law. Income tax liability is created solely by statute and many of the provisions of the *ITA* have never been the subject of any judicial decision. However, there are topics upon which the Act is silent, incomplete, or unclear, and which have given rise to many judicial decisions. The most frequently litigated issues include whether:

- a person is a resident of Canada;
- income is from employment or from a business;
- a profit on the sale of property is a capital gain or income from a business;
- certain types of expenses are deductible from income;
- losses from unprofitable ventures are fully deductible from other income;
- generally accepted accounting principles apply to the computation of income from a business;
- an interest expense is currently deductible; and
- any anti-avoidance rules are applicable.

(f) — Provincial income tax statutes

Each province also has an income tax act, and provincial income taxes are a significant impost, typically adding about 50 per cent to an individual's tax bill, depending on the province. The federal government has entered into tax collection agreements with most provinces. Under these agreements, the federal government collects the provincial tax, and, in return, each province agrees to accept most of the rules of the federal Act for the measurement of income (or the "tax base") and sets its own provincial rates of tax and tax credits for its residents. Therefore, provincial income tax acts are generally quite short and simple (and uninformative). A province that has not entered into a tax collection agreement needs to provide for the collection of the provincial tax by the provincial government. With respect to the personal income tax, all provinces except Quebec have entered into tax collection agreements. At the time of writing, all provinces except Quebec and Alberta have entered into corporate tax collection agreements.

(g) — Private law

The Act relies implicitly on the general law, especially the law of contract and property. For example, the person who is liable to pay tax on income is normally the person who has the legal right to receive the income; the existence and nature of that right will depend upon the law of the province in which the income is payable. Whether a person is an employee, independent contractor, partner, agent, beneficiary of a trust, or shareholder of a corporation will usually have an effect on tax liability and will turn on concepts contained in general law. A tax problem often contains issues of federal income tax law combined with issues of general law.

(h) — Administrative publications

The CRA provides an extensive and valuable commentary on the law and how it is administered, both on its website and in the forms and reference documents (which are available on its website). The reference documents include information circulars, interpretation bulletins, income tax folios and informational guides.[30] Aside from some of the forms that are prescribed by regulation, CRA publications do not have the force of law. However, they are exceptionally valuable secondary sources. The CRA also issues "advance rulings" in respect of a specific taxpayer's proposed transactions.

(i) — General information and interpretative guidance

The CRA publishes information circulars ("ICs")[31] to provide information on administrative and procedural matters, and interpretation bulletins ("ITs") to explain its interpretation of specific provisions of the *ITA*.[32] The CRA also provides a writ-

---

[30] When information circulars and interpretation bulletins are revised, the revision is indicated by "R" after the original number of the circular or bulletin. CRA folios and informational guides also indicate the date of the last update, but not in the title or number.

[31] Information circulars ("ICs") used to be published in hard copies. The CRA has archived many circulars, but over 50 remain current. Two information circulars also provide detailed commentary on the law: Canada Revenue Agency, Information Circular IC-88-2, "General Anti-Avoidance Rule" (1988) and Canada Revenue Agency, Information Circular IC-01-1, "Third-Party Civil Penalties" (2001).

[32] The CRA originally published hard-copy interpretation bulletins ("ITs") to explain its interpretation of many of the provisions of the *ITA*; it later published hard-copy Income Tax Technical News ("ITTNs") in order to provide updates on a more timely basis. The current income tax folios ("Folios") are a web-based publication that is replacing ITs and ITTNs with more up-to-date searchable information. The Folios are organized by subject matter and each chapter is identified by the series (S), the folio (F) and the chapter (C) number: for

ten technical interpretation upon the request of a taxpayer.[33] The CRA's policy is to assess taxpayers in accordance with the positions stated in its publications, which reflect the law as understood by the CRA.[34]

In practice, the taxpayer is usually safe in relying upon a CRA publication as being an accurate and up-to-date account of the CRA's view of the law for circumstances that fairly could be said to be within the contemplation of the CRA when it expressed its view. However, CRA publications are not like regulations, which are authorized by the *ITA* and, accordingly, have the force of law. The *ITA* is silent about CRA publications and it is clear that they do not have the force of law. In the past, the courts have looked at CRA publications as a persuasive aid to interpretation,[35] but the courts are not bound by the CRA's opinions, and do not always follow them.[36]

It must always be remembered that the applicability of the CRA's general statements inevitably will be affected by a taxpayer's circumstances. It cannot be taken for granted that a statement of general application about the law necessarily reflects how the law would or should be applied in the particular case. Where a taxpayer's circumstances reasonably can be considered to be of an "ordinary course" nature in relation to the law, general statements by the CRA may well reflect expected outcomes. On the other hand, general statements cannot fairly be relied on as conclusive statements of interpretation where a taxpayer's circumstances are complex and it is unlikely the tax authorities could possibly have had circumstances like those in

---

example, S1-F1-C1 is the Medical Expense Credit chapter. As Folio chapters are published, the ITs and/or ITTNs updated by that chapter are cancelled. At the time of writing, over 30 chapters have been published and several have been updated since their original publication. Any ITs and ITTNs that have not been archived, cancelled or replaced by income tax folios are still considered to be current CRA interpretations of the law up to their publication date.

[33] The CRA's policy and procedures with respect to rulings and technical interpretations, including the circumstances in which a ruling or technical interpretation will not be issued, are outlined in a CRA information circular: Canada, Information Circular IC-70-6R7, "Advance Income Tax Rulings and Technical Interpretations" (2016). The CRA's technical interpretation is different from an advance ruling in that it is a generic statement about the CRA's interpretation of specific provisions of the Act. The CRA's technical interpretation might not extend to all situations and is not determinative of the tax treatment of a specific taxpayer's situation.

[34] When the CRA wants to announce its opinion on a new provision of the *ITA* or a recent judicial decision, or to announce a change in its interpretation of an existing provision, it often does so at public conferences (such as the Canadian Tax Foundation's annual conference), by press release and/or by posting an announcement on its website. As discussed at heading 1.3(h)(ii) — Advance rulings, below (note 41 *infra*, and accompanying text), the CRA's views on particular interpretations and applications of the Act are also generally available in its published rulings and technical interpretations, which are disseminated electronically by commercial publishers.

[35] See e.g., *Nowegijick v. R.*, [1983] C.T.C. 20, 83 D.T.C. 5041 (S.C.C.) at para. 28.

[36] See e.g., *Southside Car Market v. R.*, [1982] C.T.C. 214, 82 D.T.C. 6179 (Fed. T.D.).

mind; it still may be the case that the interpretations are reliable, but the CRA could hardly be estopped from taking a more refined view if the circumstances themselves are "out of the ordinary course".

Even the CRA itself is not bound to follow its own publications, although it nearly always does so. It is well-established that the doctrine of estoppel does not preclude the CRA from issuing an assessment that is inconsistent with a previously published statement, or with a previous assessment, even when the taxpayer has relied upon the CRA's opinions as to the legal position.[37] In the rare case where the CRA departs from its own published position in assessing a taxpayer's return, the court will uphold the assessment if it concludes that the assessment is correct in law, notwithstanding the inconsistency.[38] In *Stickel v. M.N.R.* (1973),[39] the Minister had assessed the taxpayer on a basis that contradicted the applicable interpretation bulletin upon which the taxpayer had relied. The Federal Court — Trial Division rejected the taxpayer's argument that the Crown was estopped, and upheld the assessment.[40] The decision was reversed by the Federal Court of Appeal, not on the ground of estoppel, but on the ground that the interpretation bulletin, not the assessment, was the correct interpretation of the law.

(ii) — Advance rulings

At the request of taxpayers, the Rulings Directorate of the CRA will issue a written advance ruling (for a fee). The purpose of a ruling is to explain how the CRA will assess a specific transaction that is contemplated by a specific taxpayer. The CRA states that a ruling is binding on the CRA (subject to various caveats).[41] As such, a ruling is different from the CRA's general interpretation of the *ITA*, as it provides the requesting taxpayer with a more secure opinion as to the precise tax consequences of a proposed transaction. The CRA releases all rulings in "severed form" to commercial publishers by omitting the names and other details (which may include material facts) to preserve the anonymity of the taxpayer.[42] As such, other

---

[37] *Liberty & Co. v. C.I.R.* (1930), 12 T.C. 630 p. 639 [T.C.]; *Woon v. M.N.R.*, [1950] C.T.C. 263, 50 D.T.C. 871 (Can. Ex. Ct.) [*Woon*]; *M.N.R. v. Inland Industries* (1971), [1972] C.T.C. 27, 72 D.T.C. 6013 (S.C.C.); and *Gibbon v. R.*, [1977] C.T.C. 334, 77 D.T.C. 5193 (Fed. T.D.).

[38] See e.g., *74712 Alberta v. R.*, [1994] 2 C.T.C. 191, 94 D.T.C. 6392 (Fed. T.D.); affirmed [1997] 2 C.T.C. 30, 97 D.T.C. 5126 (Fed. C.A.).

[39] *Stickel, supra* note 29.

[40] *Ibid.*

[41] IC-70-6R7, *supra* note 33 at para. 14.

[42] The policy is referred to in IC-70-6R7, *supra* note 33 at Appendix E. Although commercial publishers usually make rulings and technical interpretations available for a fee (as part of a subscription), documents issued since October 2012 are available for free at <taxinterpretations.com>. These documents are not available under the *Access to Information Act* because publishers pay for the documents: see *Access to Information Act*, R.S.C. 1985, c. A-1, s. 68(a).

taxpayers have to exercise caution in relying on them. The CRA's view of the law may also have changed since the ruling was given.

However, in the unlikely event that the CRA did decide to assess the specific taxpayer in violation of a ruling, the CRA would not be estopped by its ruling. In *Woon v. M.N.R.* (1950),[43] the taxpayer had obtained an informal ruling as to the tax consequences of a dividend-stripping scheme. Relying on the ruling, the taxpayer carried out the scheme, but the Minister assessed him for a tax liability far in excess of that stipulated in the ruling. The Court held that the assessment was correct in law, and that the Minister could not be estopped by the earlier ruling from applying the law correctly.

1.4 — Interpreting the Act

(a) — Statutory interpretation

As mentioned above, income tax law is entirely statutory in origin and the *ITA* is the primary statute. Case law is important to the understanding of (and, in some situations, establishing the meaning of) various provisions of the *ITA* but it does not create any tax liability. Moreover, some decisions have been overruled by statutory amendments both to the Act and the Regulations.[44] As detailed as the provisions of the *ITA* are, their meaning is often unclear or open to different interpretations. Thus, learning to interpret the *ITA* is crucial to understanding tax law.

The skill of statutory interpretation is crucial not only to lawyers practising tax law, but also to lawyers in general. Statutory interpretation skills are important to the practice of law, as most lawyers spend much more time working with legislative materials and judicial treatment of those materials than working with common law jurisprudence. Since the *ITA* is one of the most complex statutes in the land, tax law is perfect for learning the skill of statutory interpretation.

The general principle of statutory interpretation is that "the words of an Act are to be read in their entire context and in their grammatical and ordinary sense harmoniously with the scheme of the Act, the object of the Act, and the intention of Parlia-

---

[43] *Woon, supra* note 37.

[44] See, e.g., *Friesen, supra* note 18; *Shell Canada Ltd. v. R.*, [1999] 4 C.T.C. 313, 99 D.T.C. 5669 (S.C.C.) [*Shell*]; *Royal Bank v. Sparrow Electric Corp*, [1997] 97 D.T.C. 5089 (S.C.C.); and *Canada v. Craig*, [2012] 5 C.T.C. 205, 2012 D.T.C. 5115 (Eng.), 2012 D.T.C. 5116 (Fr.) (S.C.C.). For an example of the opposite situation (i.e., a statute being amended because of a case law decision), see s. 4.3 of the *ITCIA, supra* note 28, which was enacted as a response to *Garron Family Trust (Trustee of) v. R*, [2012] 3 C.T.C. 265, 2012 D.T.C. 5063 (Eng.), 2012 D.T.C. 5064 (Fr.) (S.C.C.), to ensure that the application of rules under s. 94 of the *ITA* was not effectively defeated by how a tax treaty would determine a trust's residence. The *Garron* case (also reported as *Fundy Settlement v. Canada*) is discussed in Chapter 3 at heading 3.4 — Residence of trust.

ment".[45] As discussed in more detail in Chapter 16, the Supreme Court of Canada refers to this as the "textual, contextual and purposive" approach.[46]

(b) — Statutory language

The language of the *ITA* is often difficult to comprehend fully. Contrary to many people's suspicions, the Act is not written deliberately to confuse. Unfortunately, it often has that effect. There are several factors that contribute to the difficulty in understanding the *ITA*:[47]

1. *The sheer size of the statute.* This fact alone makes its interpretation a daunting task. There are also many cross-references and related provisions that add further complexity.

2. *The lack of statutory definitions.* Although the *ITA* contains some definitions, the majority of terms in the Act are undefined and their meaning has to be found in non-tax law and/or in judicial decisions.

3. *The complex commercial and social reality upon which taxes are imposed.* The legal, commercial, accounting and social circumstances in which income is earned must be examined in order to understand the tax implications.

4. *The doctrine of supremacy of legislature.* The overriding attitude of the judiciary is that the *ITA* comes first. Even when a provision of the Act is unworkable or undesirable from a policy perspective, the courts will not rewrite the law. The Supreme Court of Canada has stated in several cases that it is the Supreme Court, not the supreme legislature.

5. *Elusive legislative intent.* Where legislative intent is relevant to the interpretation of a provision, such intent is often difficult to discern by simply reading the statute.

6. *The use of precise language.* The *ITA* is intended to apply to more than 20 million taxpayers, many of whom are willing to exploit any linguistic imprecision to their benefit — to find a loophole, in popular parlance. The drafters of the Act attempt to use precise language in order to minimize loopholes. Many of the provisions in the *ITA* are limitations or restrictions involving two or more variables. Expressing such concepts algebraically would be more direct; using words to accomplish this task instead is often quite cumbersome.

---

[45] Elmer A. Driedger, *Construction of Statutes*, 2nd ed. (Toronto: Butterworths, 1983) at 87, cited in *Stubart Investments Ltd v. R.*, [1984] C.T.C. 294, 84 D.T.C. 6305 (S.C.C.) [*Stubart*] at para. 61.

[46] *Canada Trustco Mortgage Co. v. Canada*, [2005] 2 S.C.R. 601, [2005] 5 C.T.C. 215, 2005 D.T.C. 5523 (Eng.), 2005 D.T.C. 5547 (Fr.) (S.C.C.) [*Canada Trustco*] at paras. 10, 11.

[47] See *Friesen, supra* note 17.

7. *Drafting conventions.* Each provision (expressed in a subsection or section) is one sentence long. This convention causes difficulty in statutory interpretation. For example, the one sentence in subsection 95(2) (which deems income from the specified activities as either falling within the foreign accrual property income regime or falling outside it) has over 6,000 words and comprises more than 7 pages.

(c) — Interpretation tips

The best way of learning how to interpret the *ITA* is, of course, to read it. Reading the *ITA* is not easy, and is often intimidating. It is, thus, tempting to turn to secondary sources for help. Although sometimes useful, this is not a sufficient substitute for understanding the *ITA*, given the number and breadth of amendments and revisions to the Act each year. The following interpretation tips might be helpful:

1. *Keep in mind the following presumptions.* every word has a meaning; the same words have the same meaning(s); and different words have different meanings.

2. *Be familiar with the context.* When reading a provision of the *ITA*, one should always observe where it is located in the structure of the Act. There is a basic logic to the structure of the *ITA*, and a familiarity with this structure greatly assists in understanding individual provisions. Also, when reading a provision, always start from the beginning of the subsection (or section) where the complete sentence begins. One should also note the various levels of paragraphing within each provision, their relationship to one another, and the functions they serve. Read the provision completely; do not jump to conclusions.

3. *Be familiar with defined terms.* When reading the *ITA*, it is important to watch for defined terms. They are found in subsection 248(1) and many other places in the Act. A defined meaning trumps an ordinary meaning. Some terms are defined for the purpose of the *ITA*. Other terms are defined for the purpose of a particular segment of the Act. The scope of a definition is limited by the words introducing it. Therefore, definitional provisions should be read very carefully. In addition, it is important to be alert for hidden definitions; terms in a particular section may be defined in the same section, or in a separate section or part of the Act.

4. *Learn the word patterns.* There are some commonly used words and phrases in the *ITA*. Examples include "the total of [A] and [B]" (indicating addition), "the amount by which [A] exceeds [B]" (indicating subtraction), "that proportion of . . . that [A] is of [B]" (expressing a fraction A/B), "the lesser of [A] and [B]" (indicating a maximum limit), "the greater of [A] and [B]" (indicating a minimum). These word patterns are used to give structure to the provision.[48]

---

[48] For further detail, see T. Cook, *Canadian Tax Research: A Practical Guide*, 5th ed. (Toronto: Carswell, 2010).

5. *Do not overlook small words such as "and" and "or".* There is a world of difference between these two words. The word "and" is used as a conjunctive. Where "and" is used in respect of tests that must be satisfied, all of the tests must be satisfied before the resulting rules apply. In contrast, the word "or" is used as a disjunctive. If any one of the conditions set out is met, the resulting rules will apply. However, in certain contexts, the word "or" can also be a conjunctive. An example is the use of "or" between paragraphs 6(6)(a) and (b). The resulting rules (tax-free treatment of payment in respect of employment at special work sites or remote locations) apply if the condition in one or both (a) and (b) are met.

6. *Skip over non-essential words.* Words in each provision of the *ITA* generally fall into one of two categories: essential, operative words that give rise to the rule; and non-essential words that are simply verbiage used to make the legislation consistent and airtight. Being able to skip over the non-essential words makes it easier to understand the provision. The best way of doing this is to scan the whole provision first and then highlight the essential words.

7. *Find the basic rule.* The provisions of the *ITA* often have limitations and exceptions, but every provision has a basic rule and that basic rule is meant to achieve a purpose. It is, thus, important to extract the basic rule from the provision and know what limitations and exceptions should be taken into account in a particular factual context. One should guard against permitting the language of the provision to carry greater or lesser weight than was intended; in that vein, it should be understood that interpreting legislation requires taking account of a) its text, b) the context of the text, and c) the purpose of the provision the text of which is being interpreted in its context. While the "text, context and purpose" approach to interpreting and applying the *ITA* is closely identified with the Supreme Court of Canada's seminal decision on the "General Anti-Avoidance Rule" in section 245 of the Act, interpreting legislation has always involved these features.[49]

1.5 — Structure of the income tax system

An income tax has three principal requirements. First, there must be a "tax subject": "who" is accountable to pay tax? Second, there must be a "tax base" taking account of the private law to which tax law is an accessory:[50] "what" are the manifestations of "value" (the economic gains, the items of property and the activities

---

[49] See, in particular, *Canada Trustco, supra* note 46; and *Copthorne Holdings Ltd. v. The Queen*, [2011] 3 S.C.R. 721, [2012] 2 C.T.C. 29, 2012 D.T.C. 5006 (Fr.), 2012 D.T.C. 5007 (Eng.) (S.C.C.).

[50] *The Queen v. Lagueux & Freres Inc.*, 74 DTC 6569, [1974] CTC 687 (FCTD); Milet & Sheridan, *supra* note 4.

that give rise to income) in relation to the tax subject? Third, there must be a "tax realization event": "what" event or action "unlocks" the value that generates income and "when" did it occur? Timing is, indeed, a fundamental aspect of income taxation, affecting not only when income is considered to arise or be earned but also when the law expects it to be reported.

The *ITA* is organized to provide rules to deal with the above questions systematically:

- who is liable for tax;
- what is the tax base;
- when is tax payable (timing, tax accounting period);
- how much tax is payable (rates and credits); and
- how are taxes collected (tax administration)?

Tax policy decisions affect the answer to each of these questions and are discussed in more detail in Chapter 2.

(a) — Liability for tax

(i) — Person

Subsection 2(1) provides: "An income tax shall be paid, as required by this Act, on the taxable income for each taxation year of every person resident in Canada at any time in the year".[51] A taxpayer under the *ITA* is, thus, a "person", not a family or a marital unit. Subsection 248(1) defines a "person" to include a corporation and "executors, administrators or other legal representative of such a person" and defines a "taxpayer" to include "any person whether or not liable to pay tax".[52]

Because an "individual" is defined in subsection 248(1) to mean "a person other than a corporation" and a trust is taxed as an individual under subsection 104(2), an individual for income tax purposes includes a trust as well as a human being. In other words, human beings, trusts and corporations are all persons and, thus, taxpayers under the *ITA*. A partnership, on the other hand, is a legal entity that is not a person or taxpayer under the Act.

Subsection 2(3), which is discussed in Chapter 3, refines the scope of this charge for non-residents of Canada (subject to modifications arising from the application of Canada's tax treaties).

(ii) — Residence

The notion of "residence" is crucial to the determination of a person's tax liability under the *ITA*. Whether a person is a Canadian resident determines whether the person is taxable in Canada on income earned from outside Canada. Only Canadian residents are liable to tax on their worldwide income, and non-residents are taxable

---

[51] *ITA, supra* note 10, s. 2(1).

[52] *Ibid.*, s. 248(1) "person", "taxpayer".

only on their Canadian-source income. Furthermore, the residence status of an individual determines whether income from investment (such as dividends, interest, and rents) is taxable at progressive rates (in the case of residents) or flat or zero rates (in the case of non-residents). This is explained in more detail in Chapter 3.

(b) — Tax base

(i) — Concept of income

A tax base is the base upon which a tax is levied. Functionally, it measures a taxpayer's ability to pay tax. Technically, the tax base under the *ITA* is "taxable income".[53] "Taxable income", in turn, is based on "income" as computed under section 3 (sometimes called Division B "net income") because a taxpayer's "taxable income" is the taxpayer's "income" minus the deductions permitted by Division C of Part I of the Act. Section 4 requires income to be tracked according to its quality — as business, employment, property or gain income — and where it is earned.

Conceptually, sections 2, 3 and 4 provide the basic structure for the tax system. With sections 2 and 4 dealing with two of the three basic questions (the "tax subject" and the "tax object"), section 3 takes over[54] to compute the income, relying on many other specific provisions of the *ITA*.

"Income" is not a defined term, and the question of what items constitute income for tax purposes, and thereby form part of the tax base, is one of the major problems of income tax policy. As discussed in Chapter 4, not all economic gains or receipts are income. Inheritances, personal gifts, and gambling winnings are not taxed as income, whereas wages, business profits, and income from investments (such as dividends, interest and rents) are taxable.

(ii) — Measurement of income

The measurement of income consumes most of Part I of the *ITA*. Division B contains these specific rules. In general, in the absence of statutory overrides, accounting principles are relevant in determining when an item is included or deducted in computing income from a business or property, which is the main type of income earned by corporations and partnerships.

Tax accounting is, thus, important because, ultimately, taxpayers need to determine a specific number for their tax liability. Complex tax rules and policies must be reduced to a number. Many law students may regard tax accounting problems as merely mechanical exercises necessary to calculate profit. Accounting problems, however, frequently present some of the most difficult theoretical and policy issues in income taxation. Two taxpayers who have the same economic income and who

---

[53] This is for both residents (ss. 2(1) and (2)) and non-residents (s. 2(3)). As explained in Chapter 3, a unique withholding tax regime in Part XIII of the *ITA* applies to various kinds of property income earned by non-residents of Canada.

[54] In the case of non-residents, the same rule applies to the targeted Canadian-source income with refinements under section 115.

engage in the same transactions may have different taxable income and tax liabilities, depending *only* on how they account for the income.

(iii) — Assignment of income

Whose income is it? This is an important question because the *ITA* imposes tax on each individual at progressive rates. Taxpayers can achieve significant tax savings through shifting income from high-tax family members to low-tax individuals by way of intra-family gifts or using an entity, such as a corporation.

In general, the question "whose income is it?" is easily answered:

- income from employment or personal services (e.g., wages, salaries, service fees) is earned by the person who renders the services;

- income from property (e.g., dividend, interest, rent, royalties) is earned by the owner of the property;

- income from the sale of property is earned by the owner of the property; and

- income from a business is earned by the owner of the business.

When income is assigned or redirected to another person, the *ITA* contains a number of anti-avoidance rules that may apply.

(c) — Timing and accounting period

(i) — Taxation year

Income tax is calculated and paid annually, on the basis of a taxpayer's income for a taxation year. Subsection 249(1) defines "taxation year" as "(a) in the case of a corporation, a fiscal period, and (b) in the case of an individual, a calendar year".[55] This definition introduces the concept of a fiscal period, which is the taxation year of a corporation.[56] A fiscal period can be any twelve-month period, and, thus, it may not be the calendar year. The taxation year of an individual is a calendar year. Unlike a corporation, an individual has no choice as to the period for which income is to be reported for tax purposes: the period from January 1 to December 31 is the taxation year.

(ii) — Income fluctuation

When a taxpayer's income fluctuates from year to year, the progressive rate structure exacts a heavier total tax than it does from the same total amount of income earned in a multi-year period in fairly even annual amounts. For example, taxpayer A, who earns $20,000 in Year 1 and $70,000 in Year 2, will find that his or her tax bill for the two years is more than $1,000 higher than that of taxpayer B, who earns $45,000 in Year 1 and $45,000 in Year 2. Yet both taxpayers have earned the same

---

[55] *ITA, supra* note 10, s. 249(1).

[56] The meaning of taxation year for corporations, partnerships and trusts is discussed in Chapter 14.

amount of income (i.e., $90,000) in the two-year period. The discrepancy in tax treatment arises from the measurement of income in annual periods. If income were measured in two-year periods, then the amount of tax payable by each taxpayer would be the same.

There are two possible measures of relief available to taxpayers with fluctuating income. One measure is averaging, which (generally speaking) takes the change in income and allocates it over a period of years. Averaging was allowed under the *ITA* until 1988. The rationale for abolishing averaging was that the broader tax brackets and lower rates of tax that were introduced in the tax reform of 1988 would diminish the adverse impact of fluctuating income, and that the *ITA* would be simpler without such complexities.

Another measure of relief is loss carryovers. Since 1988, this has been the only relief available. Loss carryover rules in the *ITA* form an exception to the annual measurement of income because they enable a taxpayer who has incurred a loss in one year to carry the loss over to another year and deduct it against the income for that year. The policy reason for loss carryovers is much the same as the policy reason for averaging. There is no magic to the requirement that income be measured in watertight annual compartments, and there is force in the argument that only net income over a reasonable period of years should be taxed.[57]

(d) — Tax payable

(i) — Rates

Once a taxpayer's annual taxable income is computed, the next issue is the application of the relevant rates to this amount in order to calculate the taxpayer's tax payable. Sections 117 and 123 of the *ITA* set out the federal rates applicable to individuals and corporations, respectively. The rates of personal income tax are progressive (15 to 33 per cent) and the brackets are adjusted annually for inflation. For 2017, the brackets are as follows:

Taxable bracket	Tax on base amount and excess
up to $45,916	15%
over $45,916 up to $91,831	$6,887 + 20.5% on the next $45,915
over $91,831 up to $142,353	$16,300 + 26% on the next $50,522
over $142,353 up to $202,800	$29,436 + 29% on the next $60,447
over $202,800	$46,965 + 33% on the remainder

Corporate income tax rates, on the other hand, are flat. The general rate in 2017 is 15 per cent but three other rates may apply to certain types of income earned by private corporations.[58]

---

[57] For a discussion of loss deductions and carryovers, see Chapter 12 at heading 12.3 — Taxable income.

[58] For a discussion of personal and corporate tax rates, see Chapter 12 at heading 12.4 — Tax rates, and Chapter 14. Corporations other than "Canadian-controlled private corpora-

In addition to the federal rates of tax imposed by the *ITA*, taxpayers must also pay provincial income tax. Provinces set their own rates, but most use a tax base very similar to that determined under the federal statute.

(ii) — Credits

A tax credit is a deduction in computing tax payable. Tax credits are used to provide incentives on grounds of social and economic policy. Personal tax credits are provided in sections 118 to 118.95 of the *ITA*. The three most significant credits are the basic personal credit, the spouse or common-law partner credit and the spouse equivalent (or eligible dependant) credit. Other personal credits include credits for other dependants, medical expenses and charitable donations. The *ITA* also provides credits for corporations.[59] The tax policy debate on the use of tax credits and a more detailed description of the major personal credits can be found in Chapter 12.

(iii) — Computation of tax liability

The computation of federal tax liability involves four basic steps.

1. Compute income from each source namely, income from an office or employment, income from business, income from property, income from other sources, and taxable capital gains (net of any allowable capital losses). Costs and expenses incurred in earning income are deductible.

2. Compute net income under section 3. At this stage, income from each of the sources is added together. From the aggregated amount, the following deductions are allowed: subdivision e amounts, current-year losses from an office and employment, business or property, as well as investment business losses.

3. Compute taxable income under subsection 2(2) by deducting additional amounts specified in Division C from section 3 net income.

4. Finally, compute tax payable by multiplying applicable rates to taxable income and subtracting tax credits.

The following chart summarizes the computation of net income, taxable income, and tax for individuals:

---

tions" ("CCPCs") are taxed at the general corporate rate of 15 per cent: these corporations benefit from a rate reduction of 13 per cent from the general corporate tax rate of 38 per cent (which is generally reduced by 10 per cent to "make room" for provincial income taxation through the "provincial abatement"). In the case of CCPCs, there are two other possible rates for business income: a lower "small business rate" for active business income earned in Canada and a higher rate on incorporated employment income. There are also refundable taxes on investment income, which are intended to discourage tax rate advantages from accruing to individuals who earn investment income in their private corporations: refundable Part IV tax applies to dividends received by all private corporations, but the higher refundable Part I rate applies only to CCPCs.

[59] For a further discussion, see Chapter 14.

Exhibit 1-1 **OVERVIEW OF COMPUTATION OF NET INCOME, TAXABLE INCOME, AND TAX FOR INDIVIDUALS**
Subdivision a: Income from an office or employment
+ Subdivision b: Income from a business or property
+ Subdivision c: Net taxable capital gains
+ Subdivision d: Other sources of income
- Subdivision e: Other deductions
Division B Net Income
- Division C Deductions
Taxable Income
× Applicable Progressive Rates (15%, 22%, 26%, 29%, 33%)
Tax
- Tax Credits
Part I Federal Tax
+ Provincial Income Tax
Total Income Tax

For example, consider Margo Barreto, a single taxpayer, who earned the following amounts in 2017: $50,000 of income from employment, $500 of interest income (income from property) and $500 in net taxable capital gains from a mutual fund investment. She also has $12,000 in other deductions ($8,000 for child care expenses for two children, ages 8 and 10, and $4,000 for her RRSP contribution) and a $200 net capital loss carryforward (from a bad investment she sold in 2010).

Based on these facts, Margo's tax liability is computed as follows:

- Net income under Division B is $39,000 ($50,000 + $500 + $500 minus $12,000).

- Taxable income under Division C is $38,800 ($39,000 minus $200 of the net capital loss carryforward).

- Federal tax payable is $5,820: $38,800 × 15% (because her taxable income is less than $45,916).

- Assuming she is eligible for $4,000 of federal tax credits, her net federal tax is $1,820 ($5,820 minus $4,000).

- Assuming Margo is a resident of Ontario and is eligible for $1,200 in Ontario tax credits, her net provincial income tax is $759, which is $1,959 ($38,800 × 5.05%, because her taxable income is $42,401 or less) minus $1,200.

- Total income tax is, therefore, $3,349 (i.e., $1,820 of federal income tax and $759 of Ontario income tax).[60]

(iv) — Alternative minimum tax

The alternative minimum tax ("AMT") is "alternative" because taxpayers must calculate both the amount of their AMT and their "ordinary tax", and then pay whichever figure is greater. As many of the tax preferences are available only to wealthy individuals, higher-income taxpayers are sometimes able to avail themselves of sufficient tax preferences to reduce their tax liability to an extremely low figure. Indeed, it became apparent in the mid-1980s that tax preferences enabled a few wealthy individuals to escape the bite of tax altogether. The ensuing public protest caused the enactment in 1986 of the alternative minimum tax under section 127.5 of the *ITA*. In light of the purpose of this tax, individuals whose main source of income is employment are not the targets of the AMT.

(e) — Tax administration

(i) — Canada Revenue Agency

The CRA[61] is responsible for the collection of income tax, and issues the forms and guides that are necessary to prepare an income tax return. The agency was established "to achieve three objectives: provide better service to Canadians; become a more efficient and effective organization; and establish a closer partnership with the provinces and territories".[62] The federal government oversees the CRA through a management board composed of private sector representatives nominated by the provinces and territories, but the Minister of National Revenue is still accountable to Parliament for the delivery of tax, customs and trade programs.

The administration of the *ITA* involves the collection of tax through the system of tax returns, assessments, source deductions, refunds, audits and enforcement. The Act itself always describes its administrator as "the Minister", which is defined in subsection 248(1) as the Minister of National Revenue, but, in practice, of course, nearly all of the Minister's functions are performed by officials in the CRA.

The CRA also has the authority to enter into new partnerships with the provinces, territories and other government bodies to administer taxes and provide other ser-

---

[60] This calculation ignores the Ontario tax reduction and the Ontario Health Premium.

[61] The CRA was formerly known as "Revenue Canada" and "Canada Customs and Revenue Agency". Before 1999, Revenue Canada (or the Department of National Revenue) administered the *ITA*. In 1999, the functions of Revenue Canada were taken over by the Canada Customs and Revenue Agency ("CCRA"). In 2003, the Canada Border Service Agency was created and customs administration was moved to this new agency. Without "Customs", the CCRA became the CRA. The CRA is accountable to the Minister of National Revenue. In tax cases, the CRA is represented by the Minister of National Revenue.

[62] Canada Revenue Agency, The Canada Revenue Agency: The First Five Years, online: <http://publications.gc.ca/Collection/Rv4-3-2005E.pdf> at 7.

vices. The CRA has its headquarters in Ottawa. The headquarters develops policies for the CRA in all its areas of activity; it issues forms, publications and advance tax rulings; and it deals with some individual files that are in the appeal process. The CRA has several taxation centres, which are controlled by six regional offices. Taxpayers send their returns to the nearest taxation centre. The taxation centres process the returns and issue notices of assessment; when the process is complete, the taxation centres store the files.

(ii) — The self-assessment system

The income tax system is based on voluntary compliance or self-assessment. As discussed in more detail in Chapter 15, the *ITA* requires all taxpayers to file an annual tax return reporting their income and expenses accurately, together with a calculation of the amount of tax owing. The primary rationale for self-assessment is cost-effectiveness.

The self-assessment system is supported by:

1. an extensive information reporting system under which payers of interest, dividends, and income from partnerships or trusts must report the recipient of the income to the CRA;

2. source withholding of taxes by employers and residents making payments to non-residents;

3. the CRA's audit processes and enforcement powers; and

4. penalties for non-compliance.

When all of these mechanisms are considered, compliance with the tax law is not exactly voluntary. Tax procedures and penalties are discussed in more detail in Chapter 15.

(iii) — Resolution of tax disputes

A tax dispute between a taxpayer and the CRA is resolved through administrative appeals and/or judicial appeals. The process begins with a notice of objection filed by a taxpayer who disagrees with the CRA's assessment. The notice of objection is considered by the Appeals Branch of the CRA, which may confirm, vary or vacate the assessment. If the assessment is confirmed or varied in a manner that is unsatisfactory to the taxpayer, the taxpayer may appeal to the courts.

All income tax appeals are heard in the first instance by the Tax Court of Canada. The judgment of the Tax Court may be appealed to the Federal Court of Appeal,[63] and from there (with leave) to the Supreme Court of Canada. In all appeals, the taxpayer bears the burden to disprove any factual assumptions on which the CRA's assessment was based.

---

[63] If the case is tried under the informal procedure at the Tax Court, there is no further right of appeal, although the Court's decision is subject to judicial review by the Federal Court of Appeal. The appeal process is discussed in greater detail in Chapter 15.

Litigation in the Tax Court, Federal Court and Supreme Court of Canada on behalf of the Minister of National Revenue is conducted by counsel in the tax law section of the Department of Justice, which is located in the head office and each of the regional offices of the Department of Justice. Prosecutions of tax evaders in the provincial courts are conducted by criminal prosecutions counsel in the head or regional offices of the Department of Justice or by private lawyers employed as agents by the Department of Justice.

Taxpayers are aided by tax practitioners. Tax law has grown to the point where no one can possibly know all of the rules and approaches to various business and personal planning problems. Tax practitioners (lawyers and accountants) thus play an important role in advising clients. Although the judicial attitude towards tax avoidance and the plain meaning approach to statutory interpretation have provided ample room for creative and innovative tax strategies, there remains a line between ethical and unethical tax planning. Tax lawyers are subject to ethical standards, which are discussed in more detail in Chapter 15 of this book.

1.6 — Income tax terminology and concepts

(a) — Terminology

This book uses some basic income tax terminology and concepts. It is important for students to be familiar with them. Some of these have already been mentioned in the previous section, such as "tax base", "income", "capital gains" and "capital losses", "taxable income", "person", "corporation", "source of income", "deductions", and "credits." This section reviews some other terms and concepts.

(i) — Realization and recognition

Realization and recognition are important terms of art in income tax law. The *ITA* does not generally recognize a gain or loss until it is "realized". In computing a gain or loss, a revenue receipt is generally recognized when it is "earned", which generally means when the taxpayer has acquired the legal right to be paid, or when it is "received". A cost or expense is generally recognized when it becomes "payable" or is "paid". These concepts are further discussed in Chapters 5 to 8. A discussed in Chapter 10, capital gains or losses are recognized when a capital property is "disposed of" (mostly by way of a sale).

(ii) — Cost and expense

Cost of property and expenses are generally recognized in tax law by way of a deduction in computing income or loss. However, whether the cost is immediately deductible in full depends on the purpose of incurring the cost (or the use of the property) and the characterization of the cost as "capital" or "current". As further discussed in Chapters 8, 9 and 10, if a car dealer buys a car for sale, the car is "inventory" and its cost is fully deductible when the car is sold. If a taxi driver buys a car for his business, the car is a "capital property" and the cost can only be "depreciated" (deducted) over a period of several years. If a law professor buys a car for commuting between her home and the law school, the cost of the car is not recognized at all (unless in the rare event that the value of the car increases and a gain is realized when she sells the car. In such case, the cost is deductible in computing the gain).

(iii) — Business entities

Business entities, such as corporations, partnerships and trusts, are legal devices for carrying on business and investment activities. As discussed in more detail in Chapter 14, each of these entities is taxed differently.

A corporation is treated as a separate taxpaying entity. Corporations compute the amount of their income, for the most part, according to the same rules as those applicable to the business activities of individuals. Unlike individuals, however, corporations pay income tax at a flat rate.[64] In order to minimize double taxation of income earned through corporations, the *ITA* provides some "integration" of corporate tax and personal income tax payable by shareholders.

A trust is a legal device by which one person, the trustee, holds and invests property for the benefit of another person, the beneficiary. The *ITA* treats a trust as a "flow-through" entity or "conduit" in certain circumstances and a separate taxpaying entity in other circumstances. When a trust pays tax, it generally pays tax at the top personal marginal rate.

A partnership is a legal arrangement through which two or more people carry on a business for profit in common (or as co-owners). The *ITA* does not treat a partnership as a separate taxpaying entity. Instead, the income or loss of a partnership must be allocated to its partners (individuals or corporations) for tax purposes.

A sole proprietor, on the other hand, is a human being who owns a business solely and directly, that is, without having any partners or other co-owners and using any entity as a legal device. Any income or loss of the business is treated for tax purposes as the income or loss of the individual sole proprietor.

(b) — Characterization

Character may or may not determine fate,[65] but character determines tax consequences. You have seen from the treatment of entities that the legal character of an entity is important in tax law. The tax character of an amount or transaction is also very important. For example, a receipt or gain is taxable only if it has the character of income for the purposes of income tax law. As discussed further in Chapter 4, an amount that is a windfall, personal gift, personal injury or punitive damage award or is strike pay does not have the character of income and is, thus, tax-free. The *ITA* does not tax all income the same. Subsequent chapters of this book will explain how employment income is taxed differently from business income and investment

---

[64] *Supra* note 58.

[65] Thomas Hardy, *The Mayor of Casterbridge: A Story of a Man of Character* (London: Sampson Low, Marston, Searle & Rivington, 1887) at 156: "Character is Fate, said Novalis . . .".

income, and how "regular" income is taxed differently from dividends and capital gains. The flip side of "income" or "gain" is "loss" and loss must be characterized as well. While "regular" losses are fully deductible against other income, "capital losses" are partially deductible and only against capital gains.

The character of income is important, and the *ITA* has recently been amended to deter so-called "character transformation transactions" in response to instances of tax avoidance.[66] Character transformations of particular concern were certain highly structured financial transactions designed to transform ordinary income into capital gains or income of a particular qualitative character, such as a dividend.[67]

Costs and expenses must be characterized for tax purposes in determining their recognition in tax law. For example, if an expense has the character of a "current expense", it is fully deductible when it is paid or payable, whereas a "capital expense" can only be "amortized" (or deducted) over a period of time. Similarly, a "personal expense" is not deductible in computing income, whereas a "business expense" or "income-earning expense" is.

Drawing the line between the different characters for tax law purposes is sometimes difficult and arbitrary. The *ITA* rarely provides a "bright-line" test, so the issue is left to the courts. Canadian case law heavily relies on the legal arrangement by the taxpayer in determining the character. Chapter 16 discusses the statutory interpretation approach that places value on "legal form" over the "substance" of a transaction.

Where a different character of an amount results in different tax consequences, it is natural for taxpayers to "structure" their transactions to benefit from the tax-favoured characterization. For example, if a non-compete payment is not taxable, taxpayers will structure the sale of a business to include a portion of the sale price

---

[66] These recent changes were influenced by judicial decisions in Canada and elsewhere, as well as a better understanding of such transactions by the CRA and the Department of Finance, and the sharing of tax policy and administration experiences and best practices at various international forums.

[67] The *ITA* includes a variety of provisions intended to preserve the underlying character and treatment of an amount as income or capital gain and to deter the use of forms of transactions to transform an amount of one character into an amount of the other. Examples are rules such as s. 55(2) and its related provisions, and ss. 212.1, 212.2 and 212.3, to prevent, respectively, what are referred to descriptively as "capital gains strips" via the deduction enjoyed by corporations for inter-corporate dividend deductions, and "dividend strips" that would seek to avoid or have the effect of avoiding non-resident withholding tax on actual or constructive distributions of underlying corporate income. The *ITA* continues to be amended to deal with "character transformation", particularly as it may occur by way of complex and often highly structured financial transactions; reference is made to "derivative forward agreements", "synthetic disposition arrangements" and "synthetic equity arrangements", all as defined in subsection 248(1), with effects in the Act contemplated in, respectively, ss. 20(1)(z.7) and 20(1)(xx), 80.6, and modifications to the rules applicable to "dividend rental arrangements", which restrict access by corporations to the inter-corporate dividend deduction when they are considered not to own a share in an economically meaningful way.

as a "non-compete payment". Similarly, if an income trust is treated as a "flow-through" entity and pays no entity-level income tax, taxpayers will carry on business activities through an income trust as opposed to a corporation to avoid corporate tax. In cases where taxpayers' ability to avoid tax through structuring threatens the integrity of the income tax system or violates fundamental policies, Parliament introduces specific and general anti-avoidance rules. Many specific anti-avoidance rules strive to align the "legal form" with the "economic substance" of the transaction.

(c) — Timing

Timing is everything. This is definitely true in tax law. By controlling the timing of the recognition of revenue and expenses in computing income, the income (and, therefore, the tax on such income) can be deferred. Tax deferred is tax saved (for the year in question). In order to achieve a tax deferral, taxpayers must be able to accelerate the deduction of expenses or delay the inclusion of revenues.

There are two general timing methods for tax accounting: the "cash method" and "accrual method". Under the cash method, an item of revenue is included in income when received and an expense is deducted when paid. As explained in Chapters 5 and 6, this method is used to compute income from employment, office, property, and income from the business of farming. Under the accrual method, an item of revenue is included in computing income when it is receivable (i.e., the taxpayer has the legal right to be paid), and an expense is deductible when it is payable (i.e., the taxpayer has the legal obligation to pay the amount). The accrual method is the standard method for computing income from a business. Capital gains and capital losses are also generally recognized when a capital property is disposed of and the proceeds are receivable.

The *ITA* also contains many exceptions to the general rules listed above. These exceptions include specific rules designed to:

1.   promote certain socially and economically desirable activities (e.g., saving for retirement, the transfer of property between spouses, employee participation in employer stock option plans, charitable giving and environmental protection);

2.   conform with commercial accounting principles (e.g., the rules for doubtful debt reserves and prepaid expenses); or

3.   to control undesirable tax deferral (e.g., the recognition of interest income on long-term investments). Overall, there are many opportunities for tax planning to achieve tax deferral.

(d) — Time value of money

Timing is important because of the time value of money. This reflects the idea that a sum of money that is due to be received in the future is worth less than the same sum of money that is due to be received immediately. The assumption underlying the time value of money is that a sum of money on hand today could be invested at compound interest, which over a period of time would cause it to grow. The longer the period of compounding, and the higher the rate of interest, the more the sum will grow. A useful guide is the rule of 72: money invested at compound interest will double in the number of years obtained by dividing 72 by the after-tax rate of interest. Thus, a sum invested inside a registered retirement savings plan (where income is untaxed) at a rate of 7.2 per cent compound interest will double in 10 years; a sum invested at 10 per cent compound interest will double in 7.2 years.

Another way of expressing the idea of the time value of money is by reference to the "present value" of a sum of money to be received in the future. Determining the present value of a future obligation is known as "discounting", and it is simply the reverse of compounding. The present value of a future obligation decreases as 1) the payment date extends further into the future, and 2) the discount rate increases. For example (recalling our rule of 72), the present value of $1,000 to be received in 10 years' time is $500, using an after-tax discount rate of 7.2 per cent. If a discount rate of 15 per cent were used, instead of 7.2 per cent, the present value of the $1,000 to be received in 10 years' time would shrink to $247. This is the same as saying that $247 invested at 15 per cent compound interest would grow to $1,000 in 10 years. The practical consequence of the present value concept is that, when the applicable rate of return stands at 15 per cent, a rational person ought to be indifferent as between 1) paying (or receiving) $247 now, and 2) paying (or receiving) $1,000 in 10 years' time.

From the standpoint of the taxpayer, the longer that an obligation to pay tax can legally be put off, the more the present value of the obligation shrinks. A very simple concrete example will illustrate the point. Suppose that T, who pays tax at a rate of 50 per cent, has received a sum of $1,000 that he or she can either a) recognize as taxable income in the current year, or b) not recognize until a future year. Assume that he or she invests the $1,000 income at 7.2 per cent. Consider alternatives a) and b) after 10 years:

a) If he or she pays tax immediately:

Income		$ 1,000
Less: tax on $1,000 in Year 1		(500)
Total available for investment		500
Add: Interest over 10 years	500	
Less: tax on interest	(250)	250
Net result of investment		$ 750

b) If he or she postpones payment of tax for 10 years:

	$ 1,000
Income	
Less: tax on $1,000 in Year 1	Nil
Total available for investment	1,000
Add: Interest over 10 years	1,000
Total before tax	2,000

Less: tax on $2,000 in Year 10	(1,000)
Net result of investment	$ 1,000

The net result of the investment in alternative b) (postponement) is $250 more than in alternative a), a difference of one-third. This substantial gain is entirely the result of the postponement of tax. Notice that, in alternative b), the postponement case, there is no actual saving of tax. On the contrary, the taxpayer pays one-third more tax, $1,000 instead of $750. But the net result is still more favourable to the taxpayer because the total taxable income is also one-third more. What has happened in alternative b) is that the money that would otherwise have been paid in tax ($500) has also been earning income ($500 in all), and only half of that extra income ($250) is paid in tax by T (who pays tax at a rate of 50 per cent).

(e) — Tax deferral

Understanding timing and tax deferral is key to understanding the determination of the tax base (especially the timing of recognition of income and expenses), the concept of annual taxation, and tax planning. Tax deferral is one of the most important objectives in tax planning. The *ITA* provides many opportunities for deferral,[68] but at the same time contains rules to curb deferral.[69]

The primary advantage to the taxpayer is that the taxpayer retains the use of money that would otherwise have to be paid to the government in tax. This is an obvious benefit to the taxpayer who needs extra cash (for working capital in a business, for example), and who would otherwise have to borrow the money at current interest rates. But even a taxpayer who has no special need of the money will benefit by having extra funds available for investment. Tax postponed is like an interest-free loan from the government to the taxpayer. In other words, the taxpayers take advantage of the time value of money. The above example demonstrates that the advantages of tax postponement are so substantial that even if the taxpayer has moved into a higher tax bracket during the period of postponed liability (10 years in our example) he or she would still make more money by postponing tax. But a taxpayer with the means of deferring taxable income may be able to recognize that income in a year, or over a period of years, when his or her other income has fallen and taken the taxpayer down into a lower tax bracket. This is a great feature of the registered pension plans and registered retirement savings plans that are permitted by the *ITA*. Contributions to these plans are deductible from income (subject to certain limits) so that the contributor is in effect investing not only the money he or she would have been able to save after the payment of tax, but also the money he or she would have paid in tax. This means that the fund invested will grow very much

---

[68] Some examples were discussed earlier in this chapter. Other examples of tax postponement will be encountered as we move through this book. For example, in Chapter 9, we shall see that the advantage of the deduction of capital cost allowances (the term in the *ITA* for depreciation charges) that are higher than the actual decline in value of capital assets is that it causes a postponement of tax.

[69] See Chapters 7 and 8.

larger than would a fund built up solely of the money saved from after-tax dollars. Moreover, the income of the fund is not taxed as it is earned. The money in the fund is taxed when it is paid to the taxpayer in his or her years of retirement. In retirement, other income has normally fallen off, and the pension receipts, swollen by their years of tax-sheltered growth, are accordingly taxed at lower rates than would have been applicable in the years when the contributions were actually earned.[70]

Sometimes there are other advantages of tax postponement. Occasionally, something "turns up" that unexpectedly diminishes the taxpayer's liability. One way in which this may occur is that the law may change in the taxpayer's favour. Another way in which postponed tax liabilities may be reduced is where a taxpayer's personal circumstances change to his or her advantage. For example, the taxpayer may incur a business loss in a particular year, which would make it advantageous to recognize some of the deferred income. Or a taxpayer may become a non-resident of Canada, and be able to recognize the deferred income at a low 15 per cent rate of withholding tax (where there is a tax treaty) that is applicable to much of the income of a non-resident. In other words, the old adage that one should not put off until tomorrow what one can do today is one that only the CRA can be expected to endorse. For the taxpayer, there are bound to be economic gains in tax postponement. And, occasionally, the predictable economic gains are further sweetened by an unpredictable windfall.

(f) — Tax minimization

Taxpayers regularly organize their transactions so that they can minimize the tax they pay. Sometimes the generous tax treatment results from the way the transaction is characterized for the purposes of the *ITA*, and sometimes the generous tax treatment results from the way in which a particular statutory provision is interpreted. In all cases, however, the starting point for a tax analysis is the nature of the transaction as the general, or private, law sees it. We have mentioned earlier that tax law is accessory in nature, which means that it is dependent on other common law principles and statutes except to the extent that it has its own deeming rules. One of the organizational forms that Canadian general law recognizes, and indeed in important respects creates, is a "corporation",[71] which is imbued with features of

---

[70] These retirement savings plans are discussed in Chapter 11 at heading 11.3 — Tax-assisted private pension plans.

[71] Much of Canadian income taxation, from its beginnings, has concerned the relationship between "corporations" — the "doers" of income-earning activities that could equally be undertaken without the corporate form — and their owners, who are "shareholders". See Campbell & Raizenne, *supra* note 6; Wilson, *supra* note 6; Wilkie, *supra* note 6. Even from the earliest stages of Canadian tax jurisprudence, respect for the formality of the corporation has been controversial; see two early cases reaching contrasting results, interestingly during the relatively early stages of income taxation in Canada: *Palmolive Manufacturing Co. (Ontario) Ltd. v. R.*, [1933] S.C.R. 131, 1 D.T.C. 238 (S.C.C.) (also cited as *Colgate-Palmolive-Peet Co. Ltd. v. The King*) and *Pioneer Laundry & Dry Cleaners Ltd. v. M.N.R.*, 1

a natural person. The nature of transactions and other arrangements in which taxpayers participate to earn income are also, for the most part, creations of the general law, not the tax law. In some cases, the tax law may modify the consequences or implications of these private law "forms", but the starting point is the legal forms themselves.

It is natural that taxpayers will structure their transactions to take advantage of any inconsistency, ambiguity, loophole or tax incentive in order to minimize their tax burden. A taxpayer's right to tax planning and tax avoidance has been well-recognized in the Canadian income tax system, and Lord Tomlin's famous statement from the *Duke of Westminster* (1936) is considered to be "deeply entrenched in our tax law":

> Every man is entitled if he can to order his affairs so as that the tax attaching under the appropriate Acts is less than it otherwise would be.[72]

The "Duke of Westminster" principle is attenuated only in cases where tax avoidance is considered to be abusive within the meaning of the GAAR.[73] But even before considering the effect of the GAAR and various more specific anti-avoidance rules, it is important to remember that, although the tax system is commonly described as form-driven, it is not formalistic in the sense of being blind to an informed textual, contextual and purposive evaluation of what tax law is trying to achieve.

While some describe the judicial analysis required in a tax avoidance setting with reference to the "economic substance" of a transaction, it is true that this is a short-sighted, inaccurate and, indeed, not very incisive or rigorous portrayal of what statutory interpretation and application entails. It is not uncommon for economically equivalent transactions to have quite dramatically different tax outcomes. This is not because one or another way of arranging an economic event is "bad". It is because we operate in a legal system where the nature of rights and obligations that the law creates is different for different legal arrangements.

Tax is not levied on the basis of the "economic substance" of transactions.[74] An evidence-based legal inquiry into a taxpayer's transactions and arrangements searches to identify and confirm the "legal substance" of transactions. Taxpayer behavior or conduct aligned with the particular legal forms or arrangements

---

D.T.C. 499-69, [1938-39] C.T.C. 911, [1939] 4 D.L.R. 481, [1940] A.C. 127, [1939] 4 All E.R. 254 (P.C.).

[72] *Inland Revenue Commissioners v. Duke of Westminster*, [1936] A.C. 1 (U.K. H.L.) at 19 per Lord Tomlin. As Justice Wilson stated in *Stubart*, *supra* note 45 at para. 72: "I think Lord Tomlin's principle is far too deeply entrenched in our tax law for the courts to reject it in the absence of clear statutory authority."

[73] *Canada Trustco*, *supra* note 46; and *Mathew v. Canada*, [2005] 5 C.T.C. 244, 2005 D.T.C. 5538 (S.C.C.).

[74] See *Shell*, *supra* note 44.

adopted by them is important to this evidence-based inquiry.[75] But equally important to thoughtful legal inquiry and analysis is the parallel discipline of interpreting
the *ITA*'s provisions not only according to their text, but in their statutory contexts
with due regard to their purposes — according to "text, context and purpose".

---

[75] See the reasons of Bowman J. in *Continental Bank of Canada v. R.* (1994), [1995] 1
C.T.C. 2135, 94 D.T.C 1858 (T.C.C.); additional reasons 1994 CarswellNat 2669 (T.C.C.);
affirmed [1996] 3 C.T.C. 14, 96 D.T.C. 6355 at 6368 (Fed. C.A.); affirmed [1998] 4 C.T.C.
77, 98 D.T.C. 6501 (S.C.C.); reversed [1997] 1 C.T.C. 13, 96 D.T.C. 6355 (Fed. C.A.);
reversed [1998] 4 C.T.C. 119, 98 D.T.C. 6505 (S.C.C.) at 1869–1871 [D.T.C. (T.C.C.)],
appealed to and ultimately upheld by the Supreme Court of Canada but cited here for its
commons on a legal substance analysis. For the importance of inquiring into the "legal substance" of taxpayers' arrangements, see also *The Queen v. GlaxoSmithKline Inc.* (2012),
[2012] 3 S.C.R. 3, [2013] 1 C.T.C. 99, 2012 D.T.C. 5147 (Eng.), 2012 D.T.C. 5148 (Fr.)
(S.C.C.) at paras. 52–58, in which the Supreme Court of Canada effectively anticipates the
possibility that the formal written contracts in a transfer pricing case might not fully reflect
all the contractual relations that matter for the application of the *ITA*. These cases and *Shell*,
supra note 44, are discussed briefly in Chapter 16.

2
HISTORY AND POLICY

2.1 — Introduction

Chapter 1 provides an overview of the role and structure of the income tax. This chapter briefly discusses the history of the *Income Tax Act* (the *"ITA"*)[1] and fundamental tax policy issues. Subsequent chapters will further discuss the policy issues related to specific aspects of income tax law.

A basic familiarity with history and tax policy is helpful to understanding the *ITA*. The Act is laden with legislative judgments about social and economic policy. Tax policy debates often make the front page of newspapers and feature prominently in election campaigns. At the centre of the debate is the fundamental conflict between society's demand for government provision of goods and services (such as health care and education) and each individual's desire to minimize his or her own tax burden. The outcome of the debate finds its way into the provisions of the *ITA*, which inevitably reflects political compromises and the balancing of competing interests.

2.2 — History

(a) — Pre-1917

The *Income War Tax Act, 1917* was enacted on September 20, 1917.[2] It was a "new departure in Canadian methods of raising money for federal purposes".[3] Prior to that, income tax was only imposed by some provinces.

At the time of Confederation in 1867, the most important sources of governmental revenue were the "indirect" taxes of customs and excise, which accounted for 80 per cent of the revenues of the uniting provinces. By section 122 of the *British North America Act*, "the customs and excise laws of each province" were transferred to the new federal government.[4] By subsection 91(3), the new federal government was given the power to raise money "by any mode or system of taxation", which authorized the imposition of any new taxes, direct or indirect. The provinces,

---

[1] R.S.C. 1985 (5th Supp.), c. 1 [*ITA*].

[2] S.C. 1917, c. 28.

[3] R. Easton Burns, *The Income War Tax Act 1917: A Digest* (Toronto: Canadian Chartered Accountant, 1917) at 2. The Digest provides a clause-by-clause commentary of the Act.

[4] *British North America Act, 1867* (U.K.), 30 & 31 Vict., c. 3, S.C. 1867–69, c. 3.

by subsection 92(2), were confined to "direct" taxation and, by subsection 92(9), licence fees.

The courts have adopted, as their definition of direct and indirect taxes, the language of John Stuart Mill in 1848 as follows:

> A direct tax is one which is demanded from the very person who it is intended or desired should pay it. Indirect taxes are those which are demanded from one person in the expectation and intention that he shall indemnify himself at the expense of another.[5]

An income tax is an example of a direct tax, because the taxpayer is normally unable to pass on the burden of the tax to anyone else. A customs or excise tax, on the other hand, is indirect, because, although it is paid by the importer or manufacturer, the tax will normally be passed on as part of the price that the importer or manufacturer charges for the taxed goods.[6]

Excluded from the historically lucrative indirect taxes,[7] the provinces gradually developed various forms of direct taxation. Property taxes, corporation taxes (on the basis of place of business, paid-up capital, etc.), and inheritance taxes began to be levied by the turn of the century. Income taxes (being direct) were available, but the provinces initially shied away from income taxes because of their unpopularity. British Columbia and Prince Edward Island were the only provinces to levy income taxes in the half century after Confederation.[8] Between 1923 and 1939, five more provinces followed their example;[9] the remaining three provinces waited until 1962.[10]

---

[5] *Bank of Toronto v. Lambe* (1887), 12 App. Cas. 575, [1917–1927] C.T.C. 82 (P.C.) at 87 [C.T.C.].

[6] On the distinction between direct and indirect taxes, and the constitutional position generally, see P.W. Hogg, *Constitutional Law of Canada*, 5th ed. (Toronto: Carswell, 2007) at ch. 6, 30. The most detailed account is G.V. La Forest, *The Allocation of Taxing Powers under the Canadian Constitution*, 2nd ed. (Toronto: Canadian Tax Foundation, 1981).

[7] Customs and excise duties are indirect taxes. An indirect tax is levied on producers, importers or sellers in the expectation that they will pass it on to their customers in the form of higher prices for their products. An indirect tax cannot take account of the individual circumstances of the widely dispersed and unascertained class of people who will ultimately bear the tax, and so customs and excise duties tend to take the form of flat-rate charges on the value of each article or transaction that is taxed.

[8] C. Campbell & R. Raizenne, "The 1917 Income War Tax Act: Origins and Enactment" in J. Li, J.S. Wilkie & L. Chapman, eds., *Income Tax at 100 Years: Essays and Reflections on the Centennial of the Income War Tax Act* (Toronto: Canadian Tax Foundation) [forthcoming in 2017] at 2:1.

[9] These provinces are Alberta, Saskatchewan, Manitoba, Ontario and Quebec. For further details, see J. H. Harvey Perry, *Taxes, Tariffs and Subsidies: A History of Canadian Fiscal Development*, vol. 1 (Toronto: University of Toronto Press, 1955).

[10] For more historical background on income taxation, see Campbell & Raizenne, *supra* note 8; and L.D. Matteo, *A Federal Fiscal History: Canada, 1867-2017* (Fraser Institute, 2017).

(b) — 1917 to 1971

The *Income War Tax Act, 1917* was supposed to be a temporary wartime measure because it was accepted that the field of direct taxation should be left to the provinces. This temporary tax became permanent after the war and, in 1948, the word "War" was dropped and the Act was renamed the *"Income Tax Act"*.[11]

(c) — Tax reform of 1971 and the Carter Report

(i) — The Carter Report

Since its genesis in 1917, the *ITA* has been frequently amended, and it was substantially revised in 1945 and 1952, but in 1962, there was widespread agreement that a further revision was necessary. In that year, the federal government established a Royal Commission on Taxation under the chairmanship of Kenneth Carter, a chartered accountant who practised in Toronto. The Commission reported in 1966 with a six-volume document that constitutes perhaps the most thorough, lucid and brilliant analysis of income tax policy that has ever been produced. The *Carter Report* provided a comprehensive study of Canada's income tax system and a design for a radically different system of tax.[12]

The *Carter Report* was acclaimed by tax experts all over the world, and will continue for a long time to be a major contribution to the literature of taxation. The general philosophy of the report was that all gains in wealth should be taxed — "a buck is a buck is a buck" — and this led the Commission to recommend the inclusion in income of capital gains, gifts, inheritances and windfalls. These and other proposals attracted strong opposition, not only from those who would have had to pay more tax, but also from those who would have benefited from the general lowering of tax rates that would have been a consequence of the broadening of the tax base.

The federal government moved slowly in implementing the recommendations of the Commission. A government White Paper was issued in 1969, which accepted some of the Commission's recommendations, including the full taxation of capital gains.[13] A Senate Committee reported on the White Paper,[14] and so did a House of Commons Committee.[15] Both committees thought that even the White Paper had

---

[11] S.C. 1948, c. 52.

[12] Canada, *Report of the Royal Commission on Taxation* (Ottawa: Queen's Printer, 1966) (Chairman: Kenneth Le M. Carter) [*Carter Report*]. The Report is admirably summarized in vol. 1 at 1–49. The Commission also published 30 studies on aspects of tax policy, which are listed in vol. 1 at 131.

[13] E.J. Benson, *Proposals for Tax Reform* (Ottawa: Queen's Printer, 1969).

[14] Canada, Standing Senate Committee on Banking, Trade and Commerce, *Report on the White Paper Proposals for Tax Reform presented to the Senate of Canada* (Ottawa: Queen's Printer, 1970).

[15] Canada, *Eighteenth Report of the Standing Committee on Finance, Trade and Economic Affairs respecting the White Paper on Tax Reform* (Ottawa: Queen's Printer, 1970).

reformed too much of the old system. In June 1971, the government introduced its final proposals for tax reform. These became the *ITA* that was enacted in 1971 to take effect (for the most part) in 1972.[16] That Act, revised by frequent amendments since 1972, continues in force today.[17]

(ii) — Major changes

The end result of the process of tax reform was a far cry from the recommendations of the *Carter Report*. However, the 1971 legislation made three basic changes in the Act: 1) it broadened the tax base; 2) it restructured the rates of tax; and 3) it altered the taxation of corporations and shareholders so as to partially "integrate" the corporate and personal income taxes.

So far as the tax base was concerned, the principal reform was the inclusion of one-half of capital gains in income. Some other items that had previously not been taxable were also added to income; these included adult training allowances, research grants and scholarships and, most importantly in terms of revenue, employment insurance benefits.[18] At the same time there was an increase in deductions. Deductions from employment income were made more generous, including a general expense allowance of 3 per cent of employment income up to a maximum of $150.[19] The limits of deductibility of pension plan and savings plan contributions and of charitable donations were increased. New deductions were established for capital losses, unemployment insurance premiums (now employment insurance (or "EI") premiums), child care expenses, and moving expenses.

The rate structure was altered by an increase in the personal and married exemptions and a reduction in tax rates at the top end of the scale. In other respects, tax rates rose slightly after reform. The increase in rates was required because the increases in exemptions and deductions more than offset the inclusion of one-half of capital gains and other increases in assessed income and had the effect of reducing the total amount of taxable income. Some increase in rates was, therefore, necessary to keep revenue constant. Only in the highest income bracket did taxable income rise after reform: in that bracket, the inclusion of one-half of capital gains was the dominating factor.

In the corporate area, the 1971 *ITA* allowed a low rate of tax (approximately 25 per cent)[20] on the investment income of private corporations and, within limits, on the active business income of Canadian-controlled private corporations. Dividends

---

[16] S.C. 1970-71-72, c. 63.

[17] *ITA, supra* note 1.

[18] The rules for scholarships have changed over the years. At the present time, most scholarships are tax-exempt. See Chapter 11.

[19] This deduction was repealed in 1988, but its purpose is similar to the employment tax credit introduced in 2006.

[20] In 1988, the rate was lowered to approximately 20 per cent. It has since been lowered to the present 15 per cent. See Chapter 14.

were to be taxed in the hands of shareholders by a gross-up-and-credit procedure, which had the effect of giving the shareholder credit for at least some of the tax paid by the corporation.

(d) — Introduction of indexing and the MacEachen budget

The years between the major tax reforms of 1971 and 1988 saw many alterations in the income tax structure. Perhaps the most important was the "indexing" of the system, which became effective in 1974. The effect of indexing is that the fixed-dollar deductions, credits, and tax brackets expand automatically by the rate of inflation, so that increases in a taxpayer's income that match the rate of inflation are taxed at the same average rate as the previous year's income. In the years of high inflation that followed, indexing caused a major expansion of the exemptions, credits and brackets.[21]

In 1981, the budget introduced by Finance Minister MacEachen proposed major revisions to the tax system. One of the most notable features of this budget was to close the loopholes and broaden the tax base. This budget also contained a parallel proposal to reduce personal tax rates, so that the top marginal rate was to be reduced from approximately 62 per cent (including provincial tax) to approximately 50 per cent. This budget proved to be extremely controversial: the elimination of preferences was vigorously attacked by various business groups. These attacks were so successful that many of the preferences were restored by the government. The lowering of rates, to which no one objected, but which made sense only as a complement to the elimination of the tax preferences, was not altered. The result was that the federal government endured much controversy, looked weak by backing down on many of its budget proposals, and, because of the lowering of rates, ended up with a system that raised less revenue. After this experience, the federal Liberal government lost interest in the removal of tax preferences. Later budgets did not touch any tax preferences and introduced a few new ones. The government even stopped publishing tax expenditure accounts: the publications of 1979 and 1980 were not repeated from 1981 to 1984. Nevertheless, the 1981 proposals were the beginning of a general movement in Canada to improve fairness by removing loopholes and unjustified incentives.[22]

---

[21] From 1986 to 2000, the system was partially de-indexed. As a result of this change, only inflation above 3 per cent was taken into account by the indexing provisions, thus permitting an upward creep in government revenues without the need to enact an increase in rates. Full indexing was restored in 2000.

[22] See R.D. Brown & J. Mintz, "The Big Picture" in H. Kerr, K. McKenzie & J. Mintz, eds., *Tax Policy in Canada* (Toronto: Canadian Tax Foundation, 2012) ch. 1 at 1:18.

(e) — Tax reform of 1988

In 1987, the Conservative government introduced a White Paper into Parliament, which proposed many amendments to the *ITA*.[23] Most of these amendments were enacted in 1988. The major changes included: 1) the lowering of personal tax rates; 2) the broadening of the tax base; 3) converting personal tax deductions into tax credits, and 4) introducing the general anti-avoidance rule ("GAAR"). A second phase of tax reform, also contemplated by the 1987 White Paper, resulted in more equitable and generous tax subsidies for retirement saving and the introduction of the Goods and Services Tax ("GST") in 1991.

The number of tax brackets for individuals was reduced from 10 to 3, and the marginal rates were reduced. After the reform, the rate structure was 17 per cent on taxable income not exceeding $27,500; 26 per cent on taxable income between $27,500 and $55,000; and 29 per cent on taxable income exceeding $55,000.[24] According to the White Paper, the lower rates were designed to increase the incentives to work and save, and to bring Canada's rates of income tax into closer conformity with those of the United States.[25]

Broadening the tax base was achieved through increasing the taxable portion of capital gains from one-half to two-thirds for 1988 and 1989, and to three-quarters for 1990 and subsequent years to 2000 (when it was moved back to one-half). Increasing the inclusion rate during this period saw the Canadian tax system move closer to Carter's recommendation of full inclusion and improved its equity. Other base-broadening measures included restrictions on the deductibility of business expenses relating to car expenses, meals and entertainment.

Converting tax deductions to tax credits was significant in improving fairness of the tax system.[26] Before 1988, taxpayers were entitled to a number of personal deductions, for example, a basic personal exemption (to which everyone was entitled) and deductions for a dependent spouse and other dependants. There were also deductions for contributions to the Canada Pension Plan and Unemployment Insurance (now Employment Insurance), and for charitable contributions, tuition fees, and a number of other expenses not directly related to the earning of income. The

---

[23] M.H. Wilson, *Tax Reform 1987* (Ottawa: Canada Department of Finance, 1987) at 3. The amendments were adopted in 1988. A second phase of tax reform, also contemplated by the 1987 White Paper, resulted in the introduction of the Goods and Services Tax ("GST"), which is a value-added sales tax. The GST was enacted in 1990, and came into force at the beginning of 1991.

[24] The rates for 1987 were: 6% ($1,320 or less), 16%, 17%, 18%, 19%, 20%, 23%, 25%, 30%, and 34% ($63,347 or more).

[25] Wilson, *supra* note 23 at 69-70. As discussed below, the three-bracket rate structure of 1988 continued in force until 2001, when the rates were reduced and a fourth bracket was added. Historically, the top marginal federal tax rate was reduced from 80 per cent in 1960 to 43 per cent in 1980.

[26] This conversion, and the policy basis for tax credits generally, is more fully explained in Chapter 12 at heading 12.1(b)(ii) — Technical design of tax expenditure measures.

trouble with these provisions was that they all took the form of deductions from income, and under progressive rates of tax a deduction from income is more valuable to a high-income taxpayer (whose income is being taxed at higher rates) than it is to a low-income taxpayer (whose income is being taxed at lower rates). The 1988 amendments converted these deductions into credits against tax. The new credits yield the same reduction in tax to all taxpayers regardless of their level of income.

The GAAR was one of the more controversial reforms of 1988. It seeks to deny taxpayers the tax benefits arising from any avoidance transactions that may result in a misuse or abuse of specific provisions of the *ITA* or the Act read as a whole. The GAAR was introduced to prevent avoidance transactions that escaped the many specific anti-avoidance provisions of the *ITA*. It was (and remains) controversial, because of the difficulty in applying it. The GAAR is discussed in greater detail in Chapter 17.

The 1988 reform took place in Canada right after the major overhaul of the U.S. income tax system by the Reagan administration in 1986. As a sign of internationalization of tax policy, all major developed countries undertook similar reforms.[27]

(f) — Post-1988 reforms

Frequent changes have been made since 1988. Many of the changes were designed to deal with: 1) lowering taxation on capital gains and savings; 2) lowering tax rates; 3) social and environmental issues; 4) international competitiveness; and 5) tax avoidance.

The taxable portion of capital gains was reduced from three-quarters to one-half in general,[28] and to zero for gains realized from donating certain publicly listed securities and ecological properties.[29] Also, a new deferral rule was introduced in respect of gains from disposition of small business corporation shares, and the limit for lifetime capital gains exemption for such shares was increased from $500,000 to $800,000 in 2014, and indexed after 2014.[30] Measures relating to savings include an increase in tax-deduction rooms for registered retirement savings plans ("RRSPs") and the introduction of the tax-free savings account ("TFSA").

The trend of tax cuts continued. The 5 per cent surtax on individuals was eliminated in 2001. Personal tax cuts included staged reductions in the lowest tax bracket from 17 per cent in 1988 to the present 15 per cent. The general corporate tax rate dropped from 22.12 per cent in 2006 to 18 per cent in 2010, and to 15 per

---

[27] K. Messere, F. de Kam & C. Heady, *Tax Policy: Theory and Practice in OECD Countries* (Oxford: Oxford University Press, 2003); Organisation for Economic Co-operation and Development, *Recent Tax Policy Trends and Reforms in OECD Countries* (Paris: OECD Publishing, 2004).

[28] The fraction was first reduced from three-quarters to two-thirds (in the February 28, 2000 budget) for the period from February 28, 2000 to October 17, 2000, and then reduced to one-half (in the October 18, 2000 economic statement) for the period after October 17, 2000.

[29] See *ITA*, *supra* note 1, ss. 38(a.1), (a.2).

[30] The indexed lifetime limit is $835,716 in 2017.

cent in 2012. The annual limit for the low small business rate of tax (after claiming the small business deduction) was raised from $200,000 to $300,000 in 2006, and to $500,000 in 2012.

Some changes were aimed at meeting certain social policy objectives. These include equal tax treatment of same-sex couples and heterosexual couples; introduction of a tax-free income-tested child tax benefit to assist low-income families with children (increased in 2016 and renamed Canada child benefit); increased tax assistance for the cost of post-secondary education; new tax relief for taxpayers who adopt a child and taxpayers with disabilities; increased tax relief for charitable donations; introduction of a first-time home buyers' tax credit; a temporary home renovation tax credit; an income splitting rule for income eligible for the pension credit; more tax relief for families (some of which was repealed: the family tax cut, the children's fitness and arts credit and the child credit are examples); and tax relief for low-income earners and employees in general.[31] Environmental issues have also featured prominently. The government introduced measures to allow higher tax depreciation rates for environmentally-friendly energy generation and other equipment. A new credit for taking public transit was introduced (now repealed). International measures were introduced to improve tax compliance, protect the Canadian tax base, and keep Canadian rates competitive.[32]

A number of measures were also introduced to prevent tax avoidance: restrictions on the use of tax shelters; the deduction of interest expense on "weak currency loans"; the tax on split income "kiddie tax" (introduced to attack certain income-splitting arrangements with minor children); new transfer pricing rules to prevent cross-border tax avoidance; an increase in the collection period for unpaid taxes (from 6 to 10 years); measures to counter abuses in connection with charitable giving; and new anti-avoidance measures to address the issue of tax havens. To encourage tax compliance, new penalty and reporting rules were introduced. These included increases in penalties for failure to file tax returns and information slips and to remit source deductions; higher interest rates for unpaid taxes; and third-party penalty rules. New reporting rules included requirements for foreign investments, partnership income, real estate sales, construction contractors and aggressive tax avoidance transactions, and were also accompanied by penalties for non-compliance. The federal government chose to subsidize a number of areas that are under provincial domain through the tax system rather than make additional transfers of funds to the provinces. These areas include public transit and fitness credits (now repealed), child care (an increased deduction) and post-secondary education (more generous registered education savings plan rules, and an increased tax exemption for scholarships).

---

[31] For further discussion of tax credits, see Chapter 12 at heading 12.5 — Tax credits.

[32] For further discussion, see Canada, *Report of the Technical Committee on Business Taxation* (Ottawa: Department of Finance, 1997); and Canada, Advisory Panel on Canada's System of International Taxation, *Final Report: Enhancing Canada's Tax Advantage* (Ottawa: Department of Finance, 2008).

(g) — Federal-provincial relations

At the beginning of World War II, the federal government and seven of the provinces were each levying their own income taxes. In 1941, the provinces agreed to abandon their income taxes and leave the federal government alone in the field. The provinces were compensated for the lost revenue by grants from the federal government. This arrangement was intended to last only for the duration of the war, but after the war (in 1947) the federal government persuaded all provinces except Ontario and Quebec to enter into "tax rental agreements", under which the agreeing provinces would continue to refrain from introducing their own income taxes in return for grants ("rent") from the federal government. In 1952, on the renewal of the five-year agreements, Ontario joined the system, so that only Quebec was levying a provincial income tax.

The tax rental agreements ended in 1962 and were replaced by the "tax collection agreements". Under these agreements, the provinces imposed their own income taxes at their own rates. However, it was agreed that, if a province levied its tax as a percentage of the federal tax (so that the federal *ITA* became the basis of the provincial tax), the federal government would collect the provincial tax free of charge. In this way, taxpayers would only have to satisfy a single set of federally-enacted rules for the computation of their taxable income, and would only have to file a single return. In 1962, all provinces except Ontario and Quebec signed collection agreements covering both personal and corporate income taxes; Ontario signed a collection agreement for its personal income tax, but collected its own corporate income tax until 2009; Quebec still collects its own personal and corporate income taxes. Alberta has since opted out of the corporate tax collection system, but remains within the personal tax collection system. The tax collection agreements have been renewed every five years. A province that has not entered into a tax collection agreement needs to provide for the collection of the provincial tax by the provincial government. The effect of the tax collection agreements is to make the federal *ITA* extremely important, because it defines the tax base of not only the federal income taxes but most of the provincial income taxes as well.

In 1997, the federal government agreed to enter into tax collection agreements allowing the provinces to compute personal income tax directly on provincial taxable income rather than as a percentage of federal tax (which had been the previous system). All provinces now use this "tax on income" ("TONI") approach, which allows them to make adjustments in computing provincial taxable income and to choose their own tax rates and credits. Provincial taxes are still collected by the Canada Revenue Agency (except in the case of Quebec).

2.3 — Why does tax policy matter?

Why do we rely on the *ITA* as the main source of tax revenue? Why is income of individuals taxed at progressive rates? Why do we tax capital gains differently from ordinary income? Why was the GAAR enacted? Another way of asking these questions is: what is the "object, spirit, and purpose" of the *ITA*, or section 117, paragraph 3(b) and section 245 of the Act?

A basic familiarity with tax policy is helpful to the understanding of the income tax law. We explore this in greater depth in Chapters 16 and 17. Under the textual, contextual, and purposive approach to statutory interpretation, it is imperative that a provision of the *ITA* is interpreted to give effect to the legislative purpose and rationale. This is particularly important in applying the GAAR. The Supreme Court of Canada stated in *Copthorne Holdings Ltd. v. Canada* (2012):

> In a GAAR analysis the textual, contextual and purposive analysis is employed to determine the object, spirit or purpose of a provision. Here the meaning of the words of the statute may be clear enough. The search is for the rationale that underlies the words that may not be captured by the bare meaning of the words themselves.[33]

At a broader level, tax policy matters because it determines how the government allocates the burden of taxes, influences private decisions, allocates resources, and shapes the economic and social well-being of Canadians. We have already spoken about this in Chapter 1 and will return to it elsewhere in this text, in particular in Chapter 16. In short, tax policy captures taxation and fiscal influences that both reflect and propel how we define what kind of society we have or want. As the American jurist Oliver Wendell Holmes observed, "taxes are the price we pay for civilization".[34] On a much more mundane level, taxes are the price we pay for collective consumption — to "buy" the "things" we have decided to consume, as if we were shopping for goods and other things that sustain us in our private consumption decisions.

2.4 — Policy objectives

(a) — Traditional approach

As mentioned in Chapter 1, the three main purposes of the *ITA* are to raise revenue, redistribute social income, and regulate private activities. Such multiple purposes require different policy criteria for evaluation.

The provisions of the *ITA* designed to raise revenue and redistribute income can be generally evaluated according to the traditional approach. The traditional approach states that revenue should be secured in an equitable, efficient and sustained manner and uses three main criteria to evaluate tax policy: equity, neutrality and simplicity. Some definitions of these three criteria are set out below. However, while there is widespread agreement that the criteria are equity, neutrality and simplicity, there is less agreement as to the precise meaning of these criteria, the relative priorities that they should be given, and how they can be implemented. This is illustrated in the debates about progressivity discussed below.

---

[33] *Copthorne Holdings Ltd. v. Canada (2012)*, [2011] 3 S.C.R. 721, [2012] 2 C.T.C. 29, 2012 D.T.C. 5006 (Fr.), 2012 D.T.C. 5007 (Eng.) (S.C.C.) at para. 70.

[34] R.W. McGee, ed., *The Ethics of Tax Evasion: Perspectives in Theory and Practice* (New York: Springer Science+Business Media, 2012) at 50. For more discussion on Canadian tax policy, see *Tax Policy in Canada, supra* note 22. See also J. Li & S. Wilkie, "Celebrating the Centennial of the *Income War Tax Act, 1917*: The Future by the Light of 100 Candles" in Li, Wilkie & Chapman, *supra* note 8 at 1:1.

But the traditional approach (using the three criteria of equity, neutrality and simplicity) is not the most appropriate method of evaluating the growing number of regulatory and tax expenditure provisions. Tax expenditures are better assessed like other government spending programs. They "cost" money and are intended to benefit some taxpayers or to be "distortive" by effecting behavioural change.

The increasing globalization of the Canadian economy has meant that Canada's tax policy can no longer be confined to Canadian borders. Taxpayers and their income have become more borderless; Canadian tax policy is now affected by what goes on in other countries and the administration of the *ITA* requires more international coordination and cooperation. The internationalization of Canadian tax policy requires some rethinking about the existing approaches and parameters of tax policy.

(b) — Equity

Fairness is sometimes considered the glue of a democratic society.[35] It is a key issue in designing a tax regime. Once a certain level of government spending and taxation is accepted, the tax policy question is how the tax burden is shared among the taxpayers. The benefit principle and the "ability to pay" principle provide some insights into thinking about the fairness question.

(i) — Benefit principle

The benefit principle suggests that taxpayers contribute in proportion to the benefit they derive from the government. It assumes that taxes are really the purchase by taxpayers of governmental services. In Canada, a person's ability to earn income to a substantial extent depends on a number of factors, such as the existence of a civil society; good legal, health care, educational and public safety systems; and opportunities produced by a dynamic economy, which, in turn, depends on a sound legal system that defines and protects property rights and regulates the function of the markets.

The implications of the benefit principle are usually unclear. There is no agreement on the distribution of the benefit of public goods to each individual. Since the most expensive governmental services, such as defence, criminal justice, education, medical care and highways are provided to all citizens, regardless of income, in roughly similar quantities, it can be argued that it is not fair to require high-income individuals to pay tax at a higher rate than low-income individuals. On the other hand, the benefit principle can be understood to imply that the government is a partner in each income-earning activity undertaken by the taxpayer and, therefore, is entitled to share in the income. As such, the level of benefit enjoyed by an individual rises with his or her income.[36]

---

[35] R.M. Bird & J.S. Wilkie "Tax Policy Objectives" in *Tax Policy in Canada, supra* note 22, ch. 2 at 2:3.

[36] In fact, it can be argued that part of the success of high-income earners can be attributed to social factors, such as publicly supported education in developing human capital, or past scientific and technological breakthroughs that properly belong to society as a whole rather

In spite of the difficulty in using pre-tax income to measure the benefit of each individual, the benefit principle remains relevant to the design of tax policy in certain areas, such as the jurisdictional provisions in the *ITA* and enforcement efforts in respect of Canadians who earn offshore income.

(ii) — Ability to pay principle

The Carter Commission[37] took the view, which is still widely shared,[38] that equity (or fairness) should be the major objective of the income tax system and equity should be based on the ability to pay principle. The Commission distinguished between "horizontal equity", which requires that persons in similar circumstances bear the same taxes, and "vertical equity", which requires that persons in different circumstances bear "appropriately different" taxes.[39]

Phrases such as horizontal equity and vertical equity do not help us decide the policy questions of what circumstances should be recognized by the tax system as relevant, and what differences in taxation should flow from differences in the circumstances. Carter held, and again his view is widely shared, that both dimensions of equity required that tax be levied in accordance with "ability to pay". How does one measure ability to pay? John Stuart Mill, the nineteenth-century philosopher and economist, said that the idea of ability to pay was to achieve "equality of sacrifice".[40] By this he meant that contributions to the expenses of government should be so apportioned that each person "shall feel neither more nor less inconvenience from his share of the payment than any other person experiences from his".[41] Mill acknowledged that this standard could not be completely realized, but he averred that "the first object in every political discussion should be to know what perfection is".[42]

In practice, of course, it is very difficult to secure agreement on what counts as equality of sacrifice. The problem is not just that people differ greatly in wealth, but also that many other features of social and economic life arguably affect the

---

than to individuals who reap the benefits of such breakthroughs. A part of the success of business people results from government policies that enhance markets for their products and services by enforcing property rights and by giving them degrees of monopoly power (e.g., through patent legislation on pharmaceuticals and computer software, and copyright laws). For some illustrations of society's role in making some individuals into billionaires, see N. Brooks & L. McQuaig, *The Trouble with Billionaires: How the Super-Rich Hijacked the World and How We Can Take It Back* (Toronto: Viking Canada, 2010).

[37] *Carter Report*, *supra* note 12 and accompanying text.

[38] *Fair Taxation in a Changing World: Report of the Ontario Fair Tax Commission* (Toronto: University of Toronto Press, 1993) at 44–68.

[39] *Carter Report*, *supra* note 12, vol. 1 at 4–5.

[40] J.S. Mill, *Principles of Political Economy* (New York: Appleton, 1923), bk. 5, ch. 2, sec. 2.

[41] *Ibid.*

[42] *Ibid.*

amount of sacrifice that taxpayers must make. There is room for considerable difference of opinion as to how to design a tax system around the concept of equality of sacrifice (or ability to pay). The Carter Commission took the view that the criterion of ability to pay required that:

- tax be levied at progressive rates;

- tax be levied on a "comprehensive tax base" as opposed to the relatively narrow concept of "income";

- tax be levied on families as opposed to individuals;

- tax concessions to particular industries or activities be avoided; and

- corporate and personal income tax on corporate profits be integrated to avoid double taxation.[43]

Each of these recommendations is examined in the appropriate place later in this book.

While the criterion of ability to pay is widely accepted as the measure of equity in a tax system, the opposition to Carter's recommendations showed that many people could not accept all the implications that Carter drew from that criterion. As explained above, the *ITA* of 1971 accepted some of Carter's recommendations and rejected others, but the net effect of the reform was an improvement in the equity of the system. This pattern has continued with subsequent reforms seeking to improve the equity or fairness of the system. On the whole, however, recent changes indicate a major retreat from Carter's idea that equity should be the predominant objective in the design of a tax system. If this trend continues, there may be more emphasis in the future on international competitiveness and lower taxes and, consequently, less emphasis on equity.

The notion of vertical equity demands that persons with greater ability to pay tax do so at a higher rate. A person with a low income needs all or most of the income simply to survive. A person with a high income can provide for necessities and have a substantial amount left over. The taxpayer's ability to pay taxes is determined by the amount of income available for discretionary use. In general, the greater the total income, the higher is the fraction of that income that is available for discretionary use. The ability to pay principle dictates not merely that upper-income taxpayers should pay more dollars in tax than lower-income taxpayers, but that upper-income taxpayers should pay a greater proportion of their income in tax than lower-income taxpayers. This conclusion necessitates a progressive rate schedule.

The personal income tax is particularly adaptable to the graduated rates that make it progressive. That is because the taxpayer typically cannot shift the tax to others. It can be designed to take account of the personal circumstances of each taxpayer,

---

[43] *Carter Report, supra* note 12.

and, in particular, the total amount of the taxpayer's income, his or her family circumstances, and other factors that bear on the taxpayer's ability to pay.[44]

The notion of horizontal equity states that people with the same incomes should pay the same amount of tax. It is not distinct from vertical equity, but rather a logical implication of vertical equity: if the tax rate is set for each level of income, it follows that people with the same level of income should be taxed at the same rate. Horizontal equity underlies the movement towards a comprehensive tax base. Capital gains became taxable in 1972, albeit not fully. Many types of fringe benefits are taxable as they enhance the recipient's ability to pay, just like wages and salaries. The introduction of many anti-avoidance rules is justified on the ground of horizontal equity. However, the *ITA* falls short on horizontal equity in many respects. For example, the "source" theory of income excludes amounts that clearly add to a taxpayer's ability to pay from the tax base. Many tax expenditure provisions violate the principle of horizontal equity, although other policy objectives provide legitimate justifications for them.

While the criterion of ability to pay is widely accepted as the measure of equity in a tax system, equity is not the only tax policy concern of government. Neutrality and simplicity sometimes require the sacrifice of tax equity.

(c) — Neutrality

Tax neutrality means that a tax system and its rules should be "designed to bring about a minimum change in the allocation of resources within the private sector of the economy".[45] The reason is that, "at least in the present state of knowledge, the allocation of resources in response to free market forces will in general give in the short run the best utilization of resources, and in the long run the most satisfactory rate of increase in the output of the economy".[46] The market is presumed to be efficient. Economic efficiency is a desirable goal of tax policy: it grows the tax base.

In a neutral tax system, people's work practices and business and investment decisions would be no different than they would have been in a world without taxes. To the extent that behaviour is influenced by the tax system, there is a tax-induced change in the allocation of society's resources and the tax system is not neutral. Tax neutrality calls for a comprehensive definition of income and elimination of tax preferences and leakages.

But the market is not always efficient: the recent global financial crisis is but one example. It also may fail to produce socially desired outcomes. In such cases, there is a role for tax policy to intervene. The *ITA* contains many provisions designed to correct market failures and provide incentives for certain activities. Even the Carter Commission did not always remain true to its goal of neutrality. For example, the

---

[44] *Ibid.*, vol. 3 at 243.

[45] *Ibid.*, vol. 2 at 8.

[46] *Ibid.*

Commission favoured a tax deduction for persons who saved for their retirement[47] and a fast write-off of capital costs for new small businesses.[48] These deliberate "non-neutral" provisions are analyzed as "tax expenditures" below.

Neutrality is not synonymous with equity. A poll tax levied in the same amount on every individual would be the most neutral tax; nothing could be done to avoid it, and, therefore, it would not change anyone's behaviour. But such a tax would not be an equitable tax because it would not be related to ability to pay. On the other hand, a tax that violates neutrality also violates horizontal equity. The concept of vertical equity is criticized for violating neutrality because of its potential disincentive effect on taxpayers.

(d) — Simplicity

The policy objective of simplicity and administrative efficiency demands that compliance costs for taxpayers and administrative costs for the tax authorities be minimized as much as possible. If a tax is difficult to administer or if compliance burdens are excessive, no matter how perfect it may appear in theory or design, the tax will fail to serve its intended function as a reliable source of revenue. Therefore, this policy objective often requires some sacrifice of equity and neutrality concerns.

Simplicity has influenced the design of the rules in many key areas of income tax law. Examples are the taxation of employment income (which has very few deductions) and the timing of recognition of capital gains or losses (which are taxed on a realization rather than accrual basis). Simplicity is the reason for federal-provincial tax collection agreements that require taxpayers to only file one personal or corporate tax return based on federal and provincial rules that are fairly similar.[49]

In reality, however, simplicity seems like an unreachable goal. The *ITA* is probably the most complex statute in Canada, an antithesis of simplicity. It is indeed a daunting task to draft a statute that performs multiple functions in a manner that potentially affects every taxpayer.[50] As far as individuals are concerned, especially wage earners, much of the complexity is irrelevant. The driving forces of complexity are complex transactions, anti-avoidance concerns, and the special treatment of certain taxpayers or activities.

---

[47] *Ibid.*, vol. 3 at ch. 15.

[48] *Ibid.*, vol. 4 at 276–282. These recommendations were considered compromises between the goal of neutrality and other considerations deemed of equal value in the circumstances. Concessions to help particular industries or activities were not, in Carter's system, to be a normal, recurring use of the income tax.

[49] Simplicity is also the reason that a taxpayer no longer computes his or her entitlement to certain income-tested refundable credits and benefits, such as the GST/HST credit, the Canada child benefit and the guaranteed income supplement; he or she simply files a tax return.

[50] Organisation for Economic Co-operation and Development, *Tax Expenditures: Recent Experiences* (Paris: OECD Publishing, 1996) [*OECD Recent Experiences*].

2.5 — Tax unit

(a) — "Person" as tax unit

The Act treats each "person" as a tax unit. Every individual or corporation is a separate taxpayer, regardless of familial or corporate relationships.

The choice of taxing individuals (as opposed to families) has significant policy implications in terms of tax equity between families with one income-earning spouse and families with two income-earning spouses, as well as tax equity between families and unattached individuals. The differences in how different manifestations of families are treated by taxation can also have an impact on how families configure their households as economic and social units by influencing a variety of household decisions including the division of labour between spouses, the purpose and nature of caregiving (child and elder care), and the participation of women in the paid workforce.

While the individual continues to be the basic taxation unit in Canada, the *ITA* does recognize the interdependence of family members in various ways. One example of this is the set of rules that governs a taxpayer's eligibility for tax exemptions, credits and special deductions. For example, the ability to designate a home as a principal residence to obtain an exemption from capital gains is lost if the homeowner's spouse or child under 18 has made a rival designation.[51] The *ITA* also provides for tax credits[52] for a dependent spouse or common-law partner and his or her medical expenses, and allows the transfer from one spouse or common-law partner to another of the benefit of certain unused tax credits, and the transfer from a child to a parent of the disability and tuition credits. In addition, the *ITA* allows a deduction for a contribution to an RRSP for the spouse of the taxpayer.[53] There are other ways, too, in which the *ITA* seeks to "consolidate" the family, for example, by providing instances in which spouses and children may "split" income (and when they may not), and by facilitating the transfer of wealth without taxation.[54]

The income-tested benefits programs administered by the *ITA* also use family income, rather than individual income, to determine benefit eligibility. A taxpayer's entitlement to receive the child tax benefit or the goods and services tax ("GST") credit and the working income tax benefit ("WITB") are each dependent on the combined income of the taxpayer and his or her spouse or common-law partner,[55] and many provinces also have refundable income-tested provincial credits based on this measure of family income. The use of family income as the test of eligibility for these credits is consistent with federal and provincial social security programs,

---

[51] See Chapter 10 at heading 10.4(d) — Principal residence exemption.

[52] See Chapter 12 at heading 12.5 — Tax credits.

[53] *ITA*, *supra* note 1, s. 146(5.1), discussed in Chapter 12 at heading 11.3(d) — Registered retirement savings plans (RRSPs).

[54] The main example is the spousal rollover for capital property at cost during lifetime (s. 73) and on death (s. 70(6)).

[55] See Chapter 12 at heading 12.5(h) — Refundable credits.

which tend to use the same approach, denying benefits to the spouse of the million-aire even if he or she has no personal income. And yet, it is not easy to see why we should pool the shared consumption of poor families because that will reduce their entitlement to income support, but we should not pool the shared consumption of more affluent families because that would increase their liability to pay tax.[56]

(b) — Equity between families

The discrepancy in tax liability between one large income and two smaller incomes is the inevitable result of a progressive tax system. The higher-income earner has the ability to pay a higher proportion of his or her income in tax than the lower-income earner. Therefore, if ability to pay is the criterion of tax equity, the higher marginal and average rates of tax that the higher-income earner bears are fair. This rationale only holds true as long as the comparisons are between financially independent taxpayers.

The fairness of the result may be questioned when families, rather than individuals, are used as the basis of comparison. Assume that family A has one income earner with an income of $100,000, and family B has two income earners each with an income of $50,000. Each family has a total income of $100,000, and (assuming that each family is otherwise similarly situated) would seem to have an equal ability to pay tax. Yet family A (with one income of $100,000) pays far more tax than family B (with two incomes of $50,000). The credit for the dependent spouse,[57] which is available to the income earner in family A, but not available to either income earner in family B, is worth about $2,000 (in 2017) to family A.[58] As a result, the credit only slightly offsets the great advantage of family B's income split. Under a flat-rate income tax system, of course, there would be no difference between the tax liability of family A and family B.

The Carter Commission argued that it was inequitable that a family with one in-come earner should pay more tax than a family with two (or more) income earners and the same total income. In the Commission's view, the proper measure of ability to pay was the income of a family (spouses and children under 18) rather than the

---

[56] Moreover, it is arguable that income support and income tax should, as a matter of policy, be treated as two sides of the same coin. The refundable credits provide a limited model for a negative income tax, under which any tax filer reporting income below a stipulated "poverty line" would receive a payment from the government. A negative income tax is probably the simplest way of implementing a guaranteed annual income, which would replace all existing welfare or income support programs. If a negative income tax were implemented, the poverty line would probably be defined by reference to family income rather than individual income. But if family income becomes the basis for entitlement to tax refunds to the poor, it is going to be difficult to explain why it should not also be the basis for tax liability for everyone else.

[57] *ITA*, *supra* note 1, s. 118(1)(a). See Chapter 12 at heading 12.5 — Tax credits.

[58] In 2017, the federal spousal credit is $1,745 (15% × $11,635). The provincial spousal credit varies by province: in Ontario in 2017, it is $515 (5.05% × $10,171).

income of individuals within a family.[59] If the family were the taxpaying unit, then two families with the same total income would pay the same amount of tax regardless of how the income was split among individual members of each family. The Commission accordingly recommended that the family become the taxpaying unit. For adult individuals who were not living within a family, the individual would, of course, remain as the taxpaying unit.

The White Paper that was issued by the federal government after the *Carter Report* agreed that there was "logic in the argument that the family, or at least the husband and wife together, is the basic spending unit".[60] However, the White Paper went on to say that "the Commission's proposed family unit tax would have imposed a 'tax on marriage' — that is, a husband and wife each having an income would together pay more tax than two people with the same income who were not married".[61] The government took the view that such a "tax on marriage" would be "unfair and undesirable", and decided against any change.[62] The *ITA* that was enacted in 1971, therefore, continued to recognize the individual, and not the family, as the basic taxation unit in Canada.[63]

The argument that an individual's marital status and familial relationships are relevant to the determination of his or her ability to pay is based on certain assumptions about families, each of which is controversial. The first assumption is that the family is the basic economic and social unit in society. This assumption is undermined by high divorce rates and the prevalence of a variety of cohabitation arrangements. At the very least, difficult questions of definition would have to be resolved, and it would be hard to avoid investigations into the living arrangements of people who might be cohabiting in lieu of marriage or for other reasons.

The second assumption is that taxation should be based on the benefit derived from income, rather than on legal title to income.[64] Under a legal title test, even if the

---

[59] *Carter Report, supra* note 12, vol. 3 at ch. 10.

[60] Benson, *supra* note 13 at 15.

[61] *Ibid.*

[62] *Ibid.* at 14.

[63] In 1999, a House of Commons Finance Sub-committee revisited this issue briefly when it found that most of the difference in the way that single-earner and two-earner families are treated by Canada's tax system is due to the system's progressive rate structure and its recognition of the individual as the basic unit of taxation. The Sub-committee ". . . concluded that the tax system treats families in an equitable manner because they are taxed as individuals. Any changes to the basic nature of the tax system would constitute broad tax reform, which is well beyond the mandate of this Committee". See Canada, House of Commons Standing Committee on Finance, Nick Discepda & Maurizio Bevilacqua, *For the Benefit of the Children: Improving Tax Fairness*, Nineteenth Report of the Standing Committee on Finance, Sub-Committee on Tax Equity for Canadian Families with Dependent Children (Ottawa: House of Commons, 1999).

[64] Academics analyze the question of whether the individual or the family is the most appropriate taxation unit with reference to two principles: 1) the legal control principle, which

sole income earner in a family did typically share the income with the other members of the family, the income earner's legal title to the income gives him or her a degree of control over expenditure decisions which, it could be argued, makes it reasonable to treat him or her as the sole taxpayer in respect of the income. Under a benefit test, if sharing is typical, then it may be appropriate to share the tax burden by treating the family as the taxation unit. Oddly enough, this particular issue does not arise in other taxation contexts, and it is difficult to derive a principled answer to the question whether it is legal title or benefit that counts.

If the first two assumptions are accepted, the third assumption has to be considered, namely that the benefit of family income is usually shared among the members of the family regardless of who actually earns the income. Intuitively, it seems obvious that sharing is prevalent and substantial in a family that shares the run of the house or apartment, eats the same food, is clothed to the same standard, and goes on vacations together. For most families, these consumption expenditures would absorb most of the income. On the other hand, there do not seem to be comprehensive empirical studies of the patterns of family expenditures, and those studies that do exist cast doubt on the prevalence of sharing.[65] As Brooks states, however:

> . . . as a conceptual matter, the debate is not really over whether the family or the individual is the correct unit of account. Few people claim that the household is that natural unit to which utility — or anything else that matters for tax purposes — accrues. Instead, the individual is the proper focus of fairness in any social institution; therefore, the proper question is, in determining an individual's tax liability, should that individual's marital status, or other personal relationships, be relevant?[66]

(c) — Impact on household labour and employment

Whether or not families are taxed as units may have significant impact on household labour and women's participation in the workforce. A possible difference be-

---

holds that individuals should pay tax on the income they control; and 2) the economic benefit principle, which holds that individuals should be taxed on income from which they benefit. Those who favour the legal control principle support the individual as the unit of taxation. Those who favour the economic benefit principle, and assume that families share the income that they earn, support the family as the unit of taxation. But the evidence is that many families do not share. Because of this, many argue that income that a taxpayer legally controls is a better measure of ability to pay, and that the individual is the better unit of taxation than family in terms of equity, neutrality and gender equality. See, e.g., N. Brooks, "The Irrelevance of Conjugal Relationships in Assessing Tax Liability" in J.G. Head & R. Krever, eds., *Tax Units and the Tax Rate Scale* (Melbourne: Australian Tax Research Foundation, 1996).

[65] See, e.g., J. Pahl, "Patterns of Money Management within Marriage" (1980) 9 J. of Social Policy 313 at 328; L. Dulude, "Taxation of the Spouses" (1985) 23 Osgoode Hall L. J. 67 at 94; F. Woolley, "Women and Taxation: A Survey" (1991) Ontario Fair Tax Commission Working Paper at 13; Ontario Fair Tax Commission, *Women and Taxation Working Group Report* (Toronto: Ontario Fair Tax Commission, 1992) [*OFTC Report*]; and *Fair Taxation*, *supra* note 38 at 269-270.

[66] Brooks, *supra* note 64 at 47.

tween the one-job family and the two-job family (each with the same total cash income), lies in the amount of "imputed income" derived by each family.[67] Imputed income is the value of the benefit derived by a person from his or her own personal services (such as caregiving, cooking, cleaning, maintenance, repairs, or whatever else people do for themselves) or from the use of his or her own property (such as a house, a cottage, or an automobile).

It is arguable that the family with only one spouse working has greater taxable capacity because of the imputed income of the non-earning spouse (or common-law partner), who usually increases the taxable capacity of the family by performing caregiving and other unpaid household services that the two-job family would have to purchase (or forego). The value of this work, like other forms of imputed income, is not directly recognized for tax purposes. The present higher tax on the one-job family could be defended as an indirect recognition of that family's higher imputed income from unpaid household services. However, since the present law is not based on any measurement of this amount, it is, therefore, a very arbitrary recognition of this imputed income. Should some attempt be made to measure the imputed income from unpaid household services and incorporate it into the tax base? The Carter Commission rejected this approach on the ground that it was unfair to single out and tax one form of imputed income while ignoring other forms of imputed income.[68] Of course, like other forms of imputed income, household labour is difficult to value, and it does not bring in any of the cash that would be needed to pay the tax.[69]

Using the family as the tax unit would probably operate as a disincentive to a non-earning spouse (or common-law partner) entering the paid labour force. (It is, of course, hard to know to what extent people take into account tax considerations in making occupational choices, but it seems reasonable to assume that tax considerations have some influence.) Under the present system, when a non-earning spouse (or common-law partner) starts earning income, the new income is taxed as if it were the income of a single individual. The advantage of that income split would be lost if the family became the unit of taxation: the new income would have to be added to the existing income and would not be taxed at the lower rates appropriate to a separate individual. The possible discouragement of the non-earning spouse (or

---

[67] See Chapter 4 at heading 4.5 — Imputed income.

[68] *Carter Report, supra* note 12, vol. 3 at 118.

[69] Another problem with the taxation of imputed income from household services is that most home-centred work is performed by women, so that the taxation of imputed income would indirectly place a disproportionate burden on women. This has led to other proposals to reduce the bias in the tax system in favour of unpaid household work, as well as proposals to use the tax system to compensate for the economic disparities between men and women. For a discussion of a variety of proposals, see K. Lahey, "The Tax Unit in Income Tax Theory" in E.D. Pask, C.A. Brown & K.E. Mahoney, eds., *Women, the Law and the Economy* (Toronto: Butterworths, 1985) 273 at 299–302; M. Maloney, "Women and the *Income Tax Act:* Marriage, Motherhood and Divorce" (1989) 3 C.J.W.L. 182 at 194–203; *OFTC Report, supra* note 65 at 24–25; and *Fair Taxation, supra* note 38.

common-law partner) from entering the paid work force has formed the basis for some opposition to the idea of the family as a unit of taxation.[70]

(d) — Equity between families and unattached individuals

The adoption of the family as the taxation unit implies a decision that families with equal incomes should be treated alike, but it does not decide the question of how tax burdens should be allocated as between families and single individuals. The question remains whether the aggregated family income should be taxed at the same rates as are applicable to the income of a single individual, or at lower rates. There are two polar positions. At one pole (represented in some European systems), the aggregated income of the two spouses is taxed under a rate schedule that is applicable to single taxpayers as well; under this system, a married couple in which H earns $50,000 and W earns $40,000 would pay the same tax as a single individual earning $90,000. At the other pole (represented in the United States from 1948 until 1969), the aggregated income of the two spouses is taxed as if each spouse had earned exactly one-half of it; under this system, a married couple in which H earned $50,000 and W earned $40,000 would pay the same tax as two single individuals each earning $45,000; in other words, the married couple is given the benefit of a perfect income split. The Carter Commission recommended a middle ground.[71] The Commission recommended that tax should be levied on the family under a rate schedule that would differ from the rate schedule applicable to a single individual; the two rate schedules should be so designed such that a family would pay less tax than one single individual with the same income as the family, but more than two single individuals with the same total income as the family.

(e) — Corporations and trusts as taxpayers

So far in this section and in the balance of this chapter we have concentrated on the taxation of individuals. We did allude to and will return throughout this text to the two other "persons" the *ITA* treats as taxpayers: corporations and trusts.

The *ITA* is more concerned with how corporations are taxed than with how trusts are taxed, since most businesses are carried on in corporations, and having internationally "competitive" corporate tax rates is important for the Canadian economy. Corporations are generally imbued under the corporate law with perpetual personality and the *ITA* treats them as "persons" separate from their owners (the shareholders) despite having a common or shared "economic interest". The tax policy implications of taxing owners separately from the legal formulations of the means by which that income is earned is particularly acute for "private corporations", which typically are created to serve the interests of their ultimately human shareholders — individuals. However, the *ITA* is equally concerned about this kind of separation for larger public corporations and their shareholders, especially when the shareholders are non-residents of Canada.

---

[70] See Dulude, *supra* note 65; Lahey, *supra* note 69.

[71] *Carter Report*, *supra* note 12, vol. 3 at ch. 10.

The *ITA* also assimilates a trust, which is a particular kind of obligation governed by the private law of trusts, to the status of a "person" and makes this constructive person a taxpayer. As a result, the *ITA* has allowed those with the economic means and know-how to establish trusts to create additional "persons" in the "family" for various reasons (including the care of seniors and disabled taxpayers) and use the family unit as the *de facto* basis of taxation. The reasons for this have as much to do with the administration of the tax law (without unwarranted tax "leakage") as with fundamental decisions about tax policy.

As we examine the way in which the *ITA* applies to persons other than human beings, we will continually consider how the statute effectively integrates the taxation of individuals with intermediaries between them (corporations, partnerships and trusts) and the earning of income that they "own" indirectly. The tax policy underlying the *ITA* seeks to achieve a variety of objectives, including supporting small business and the economy in general (by allowing lower corporate rates and a deferral of taxation) as well as avoiding the unwarranted double taxation of the same income.

2.6 — Tax rates for individuals

(a) — Graduated rates

(i) — Rates and brackets

Section 117 of the *ITA* applies graduated rates to incomes earned by individuals. Progressive rates are an important means to achieve the end goal of fairness and redistribution of social income.[72] However, progressive taxation has costs to taxpayers and society. While enabling redistribution from the richer to the poorer, progressive taxation may also depress work effort and risk-taking, and, thus, reduce overall welfare. There are, therefore, two kinds of progressivity questions: 1) how to design the tax rates and credits for people with low or negative income; and 2) how high should the top marginal rate be? There is little disagreement about the first question, but a great deal of debate about the second one. In 1971, the combined federal-provincial top marginal rate was in excess of 80 per cent and this was reached when taxable income exceeded $400,000. In 1972, tax reform effectively reduced the combined top rate to just above 60 per cent when the top federal rate was set at 47 per cent of taxable income exceeding $60,000; at the same time, the number of brackets was also reduced from 18 to 13. As the table below shows, brackets began to be indexed in 1974 and the federal top rate fell further to 34 per

---

[72] Income taxation is generally considered the most appropriate for progressive taxation as the tax burden cannot be shifted. A subsidiary advantage of a progressive rate structure is that it has a stabilizing effect on the economy. In a time of economic decline, tax receipts are reduced disproportionately to the decline in taxable incomes, thereby helping to sustain disposable income and bolster consumer expenditures. In a time of economic expansion, tax receipts increase more than proportionately to the increase in taxable incomes, thereby acting as a brake on consumer expenditures. In this way, the tax system tends to restrain contractions or expansions of economic activity. See the *Carter Report, supra* note 12, vol. 3 at 243.

cent by 1987. The 1988 tax reform substantially altered the rate structure, reducing the total number of tax brackets from 10 to 3 and reducing the top rate to 29 per cent. The current 33 per cent top bracket was introduced in 2016, along with the 20.5 per cent rate for the second bracket. Before 2016, only four brackets existed (15 per cent, 22 per cent, 26 per cent and 29 per cent) and, except for the lowest bracket, the rates had been the same since 2000 (the current 15 per cent dates from 2006).

The upper limit for the lowest bracket has increased over time from $1,500[73] in 1917 to $27,500 in 1988, and $45,916 for 2017. Because of the basic personal credit (which was an "exemption" or deduction before 1988), there is a basic amount of income exempt from tax. This amount rose from $6,000 for 1988 to $11,635 for 2017.

The *ITA* also provides for a "negative" tax in the form of refundable tax credits: the goods and services tax credit, the Canada child benefit, the refundable medical expense credit, and the working income tax benefit. Individuals eligible for these amounts receive refunds from the government that are in the nature of social support. So, for these persons, the tax rate is negative.

Table 2-1: History of Graduated Rates					
Year	**Lowest Bracket**		**Top Bracket**		**Number of Brackets**
	$	**%**	**$**	**%**	
1917	Up to 1,500	4	>100,000	25	7
1972	Up to 500	17	> 60,000	47	13
1974	Up to 533	12	> 63,960	47	13
1987	Up to 1,320	6	> 63,347	34	10
1988	Up to 27,500	17	> 55,001	29	3
2001	Up to 30,754	16	> 100,000	29	4
2017	Up to 45,916	15	> 202,800	33	5

(ii) — Effect on incentives and tax avoidance

A number of factors may influence the design of graduated rates, including: 1) the disincentive to work; and 2) the potential for tax avoidance and income shifting.

There has been considerable debate on the question of whether a progressive rate structure provides a disincentive to work. On the one hand, it is reasonable to expect that the incentive to work would decline as the after-tax return from work declines, creating a preference for leisure. On the other hand, it is also reasonable to expect that the reduction in disposable income that is caused by the income tax creates an incentive to work longer and harder to make up some of the lost income.

---

[73] $3,000 for married persons with children.

It is hard to know what the net effect of these competing pulls will be on any given individual. Of course, most individuals have little choice as to their hours of work and cannot give effect to their preferences anyway. For those who do control their hours of work, many influences other than after-tax monetary returns affect their decisions to work, for example, job satisfaction, power, and prestige. Empirical studies suggest that the income tax has little effect on the total supply of labour in the economy.[74]

There is also room for debate about whether a progressive rate structure provides a disincentive to entrepreneurial activity and risk-taking. On the one hand, it is reasonable to expect that the incentive to take risks would decline when any profits have to be shared with the government. On the other hand, since the tax system allows losses to be deducted, it is also reasonable to expect that the sharing of losses with the government would increase the incentive to take risks. As is the case with the propensity to work, the propensity to take risks seems to be pulled in the opposite direction by a progressive tax structure. The nominal tax rate is only one factor that may affect risk-taking. The generosity and effectiveness of tax expenditures designed to stimulate economic growth need to be taken into account.

Even if it can be said that a progressive income tax has little effect on the aggregate amount of work or risk-taking in the economy, it should not be assumed that it is entirely neutral. Individual taxpayers may well have reduced or increased their efforts as the result of the rising rates of tax. Even if the reductions are roughly balanced by the increases, so that the aggregate of effort is unchanged, there is still some distortion in the allocation of resources.

A progressive income tax may divert effort into attempts to avoid paying the higher rates of tax. Income splitting is the most obvious direct consequence of progressive rates. Efforts to receive tax-free forms of income (e.g., fringe benefits), or less heavily taxed forms of income (e.g., capital gains), are also stimulated by high marginal rates. It is probably fair to conclude that many forms of tax avoidance would be abandoned if all income were taxed at a single, relatively low, flat rate. However, this consideration is not sufficient, in the view of most tax theorists, to outweigh the case for equity and progressive rates.[75]

(iii) — Effect on redistribution

As discussed at the beginning of Chapter 1, redistribution of social income is a key function of the *ITA*. One way of assessing the effect of redistribution is to see the extent to which it can reduce inequality in pre-tax incomes. This can be done by

---

[74] See, generally, H.S. Rosen et al., *Public Finance in Canada*, (Toronto: McGraw-Hill Ryerson, 1999) at ch. 21; V. Salyzyn, *Canadian Income Tax Policy: An Economic Evaluation*, 4th ed. (Toronto: CCH Canadian, 1990) at 221–224; R.B. Goode, *The Individual Income Tax* (Washington, D.C.: Brookings Institution,1976) at ch. 4; and M. Babey et al., "Effects of the Personal Income Tax on Work Effort: A Sample Survey" (1978) 26 Can. Tax J. 582.

[75] L. Murphy and T. Nagel, *The Myth of Ownership: Taxes and Justice* (Oxford: Oxford. University Press, 2002) at 130–41.

comparing the income inequality before tax and after tax plus transfer payments (e.g., elderly benefits, children's benefits and unemployment insurance benefits). Studies generally do not single out the effect of the *ITA*, but the comparison is illustrative as the Act is the only, or the most important, tax instrument for income redistribution.

The Gini coefficient is usually used to measure income inequality. It is measured on a scale of zero to one. Named after the Italian statistician Corrado Gini, the Gini coefficient calculates the extent to which the distribution of income among individuals within a country deviates from an exactly equal distribution. A Gini coefficient of zero means that income distribution is perfectly equal, while a coefficient of one means that it is absolutely unequal — that is, one person has all the income and the rest of the society has none.

Studies have found that Canada's after-tax income Gini coefficient, which measures inequality after taxes and transfers, was 0.395 in 2010, 0.123 points or 23.7 per cent lower than the pre-tax income Gini coefficient (i.e., inequality before taxes and transfers) of 0.518. Of the total 23.7 per cent reduction in the Gini coefficient, 70.7 per cent was due to transfers and 29.3 per cent was due to taxes. During the last three decades, pre-tax income inequality in Canada has increased by 0.084 points, or 19.4 per cent and only 44 per cent of this increase was offset by changes in the transfer and tax system.[76] Overall, the *ITA* has played some direct role in reducing income inequality.

In terms of bearing the burden of income taxation, the top 0.7 per cent of taxpayers who reported taxable income of over $250,000 paid 19.7 per cent of total taxes in 2008. The top 2.1 per cent of taxpayers who reported income of over $150,000 paid 29.9 per cent of total taxes. 73.8 per cent of taxpayers reported income of less than $50,000 and paid 18.5 per cent of total taxes.[77]

(b) — Flat rate

Under a flat tax system, other than a basic exemption, one constant rate applies to the entire tax base. The advantages of a flat rate are mainly simplicity, economic efficiency and fewer incentives for income shifting. As for equity, the proponents of a flat tax system would acknowledge the need for exemption of the lowest-income individuals, which, of course, makes the flat-rate system mildly progressive.

Aside from this low-income exemption, proponents of flat tax argue that considerations based on ability to pay do not outweigh the advantages of a flat rate. They

---

[76] A Sharpe & E. Capeluck, *The Impact of Redistribution on Income Inequality in Canada and the Provinces, 1981–2010* (Ottawa: Centre for the Study of Living Standards Research Report, 2012); Organisation for Economic Co-operation and Development, *Divided We Stand: Why Inequality Keeps Rising* (Paris: OECD Publishing, 2011). Canada is not alone in seeing the gap between the rich and poor widened during the last 30 years. This has occurred in the more traditionally egalitarian Nordic countries.

[77] See L. Chapman & J. Mintz, "Personal Income Taxation" in *Tax Policy in Canada, supra* note 22, ch. 4 at 4:27.

also defend flat tax in terms of fiscal accountability. According to this argument, the public (most of whom are not rich) accedes to increased governmental spending on the assumption that someone else (the rich) will pay for it. If taxes were levied at a single flat rate, it would be obvious to everyone (so the argument goes) that increases in spending would cause increases in everyone's taxes. Therefore, there would be a greater sense of shared responsibility for the expenses of government, and politicians would be required to be more prudent in their spending decisions.[78] Another argument for a flat rate proceeds from an assumption that taxes are really the purchase by taxpayers of governmental services. Since everyone roughly receives the same amount of benefit, it follows that high-income individuals should not have to pay at a higher rate than low-income individuals.

(c) — Dual rates

A dual tax system has two rate structures: progressive rates for income from labour and a flat rate for income from capital. It has been introduced in Northern European countries, including Norway, Sweden and the Netherlands. For example, in Norway, a flat rate applies to net income, which includes wages, pension and capital income less tax deductions. (The same rate is used for corporate income.) Progressive taxation applies to wage and pension income in addition to the flat rate, by means of a surtax on gross income from wages and pensions above a certain threshold level. In order to ensure an equal tax treatment of wage earners and the self-employed, self-employment income is divided into two components: a labour income component as a reward for work effort and a capital income component as the return to the savings invested in the proprietorship. The labour income component is taxed at the progressive rate schedule, while the capital income component is taxed at the flat rate.

The dual tax system was intended to preserve vertical equity through progressive taxation of income from labour, which is less internationally mobile, and to protect the tax base and international tax competition through proportional taxation of income from capital, which is more mobile. One of the problems with the dual income tax system is its complexity and the incentives it provides for tax planning. The large difference in top marginal tax rates on labour and capital income has provided taxpayers with a tax-induced incentive to have their income characterized as capital income rather than as labour income, for instance by incorporating themselves. The fact that social security contributions are often levied only on labour income strengthens the motivation for income shifting.

In practice, Canada and the majority of Organisation for Economic Co-operation and Development ("OECD") countries may be characterized as having "semi-dual" income tax systems. For example, because only one-half of a capital gain is subject to tax, the effective tax rates for capital gains are half of the standard rates. For this

---

[78] For further discussion, see S. Forbes, *Flat Tax Revolution: Using a Postcard to Abolish the IRS* (Washington, D.C.: Regnery Publishing, Inc., 2005); and R.E. Hall & A. Rabushka, *The Flat Tax*, 2nd ed. (Stanford: Hoover Institution Press, 1995).

and other reasons, the effective Canadian tax rates on savings are much lower than those on labour income.

2.7 — Tax expenditures

(a) — Concept

The idea of tax expenditures appears straightforward: all concessions and preferences in the tax system that deviate from the normal, benchmark system are similar to direct spending programs. They achieve policy objectives at the cost of lower tax revenue. For government, a tax expenditure is a loss in revenue; for a taxpayer, it is a reduction in tax liability.

The term "tax expenditure" is attributed to Professor Stanley S. Surrey of Harvard Law School. While serving as assistant secretary of the U.S. Treasury (working on tax policy) in 1967, he had a list of preferences compiled and used it to build political support for broadening the tax base, to rationalize government spending programs and to improve the budget process. The concept rests on the assumption that it clarifies thinking about tax provisions if they are divided into two broad categories: technical tax provisions (or fiscal provisions), which should be analyzed using traditional tax policy criteria; and tax expenditures, which should be analyzed using budgetary criteria.[79]

Drawing a line between fiscal provisions and tax expenditure provisions is not straightforward. It is difficult to define the benchmark against which tax expenditures should be measured. Reasonable differences of opinion exist about what should be considered part of the benchmark tax system and, hence, about what should be considered a tax expenditure. Surrey argued that the benchmark should be the broad Haig-Simons definition of comprehensive income (discussed in Chapter 4). The OECD defines tax expenditures as reductions in tax liabilities in comparison with a benchmark tax system.[80] The Department of Finance Report on Federal Tax Expenditures, 2017 takes a broad approach and includes the revenue loss associated with all but the most fundamental structural elements of the tax system, such as the progressive personal income tax rate structure.[81]

---

[79] S.S. Surrey, *Pathways to Tax Reform: The Concept of Tax Expenditures* (Cambridge, Mass.: Harvard University Press, 1973) and S.S. Surrey & P.R. McDaniel, *Tax Expenditures* (Cambridge, Mass.: Harvard University Press, 1985) are the seminal works on the topic. There is a vast body of literature on tax expenditures. Two recent additions are L. Philipps, N. Brooks & J. Li, eds., *Tax Expenditures: State of the Art* (Toronto: Canadian Tax Foundation, 2011); and Y. Brauner and M.J. McMahon, Jr., *The Proper Tax Base: Structural Fairness from an International and Comparative Perspective — Essays in Honor of Paul McDaniel* (The Netherlands: Kluwer Law International, 2012).

[80] *OECD Recent Experiences*, *supra* note 50.

[81] Canada, Department of Finance, *Report on Federal Tax Expenditures: Concepts, Estimates and Evaluations 2017* (Ottawa: 2017) [*2017 Tax Expenditures Report*], available online at <https://www.fin.gc.ca/taxexp-depfisc/2017/taxexp17-eng.asp.>.

Tax expenditures can be found in all of the basic elements of our tax system: exclusions and exemptions from income; deductions in computing income from a source and subdivision e deductions; tax credits or reduced tax rates; and tax deferrals.

For analytical purposes, tax expenditures in the *ITA* can be categorized as:

- technical tax expenditures that are required for the efficient administration of the tax system, such as the taxation of capital gains when they are realized;
- social tax expenditures that serve the same purpose as analogous social benefit programs, such as the Canada child benefit and the working income tax benefit;
- economic tax expenditures that serve the same purpose as analogous grants or bailout programs; and
- behaviour-inducing tax expenditures that are designed to modify taxpayer behaviour to advance social objectives (e.g., charitable gifts) or economic objectives (research and development, investment in Canadian-owned small businesses).

Except for the technical tax expenditure category, all tax expenditures can be removed from the *ITA* without affecting its basic function. There are advantages and disadvantages of using the tax system to deliver social and economic-oriented government programs.

(b) — Evaluative criteria

Tax expenditure analysis differs from the traditional evaluative criteria discussed earlier. It treats tax expenditures as if they were direct expenditures. Looking at provisions of the *ITA* in this way, it is not appropriate to criticize them as violating tax equity or tax neutrality or eroding the tax base. The traditional tax-policy criteria would not be used to criticize a direct expenditure, and, therefore, should not be used to criticize a tax expenditure. Tax expenditure analysis assumes a benchmark tax structure that is equitable, neutral and comprehensive. The tax expenditure is then analyzed on its merits as if it were a separate assistance program.

Under a tax expenditure analysis, the pertinent policy questions are 1) Why is a tax expenditure necessary? 2) How much does it cost? 3) Is it effective in meeting its objectives? 4) What are the allocative and distributional consequences (i.e., who benefits from it)? [82]

(i) — Justifications

The use of a tax expenditure may be justified for socio-economic, political or institutional reasons.

---

[82] The objectives of tax expenditures (taken from budget documents, speeches and other sources) were listed for the first time in Canada, Department of Finance, *Government of Canada Tax Expenditures* (Ottawa: 1998).

Many tax expenditures are intended to advance both social and economic goals. For example, the non-taxation of capital gains from the sale of a family home (the principal residence exemption) is one of the most costly tax expenditures. It was introduced when capital gains became taxable in 1972. Unlike its analogous poor cousin, social housing, however, the principal residence exemption benefits homeowners who are generally not low-income individuals. Subsidizing middle- and higher-income taxpayers to purchase houses is clearly not intended to provide social support.[83] But, as explained further in Chapter 10, it can be justified as a measure of promoting social stability, economic stimulation and savings.[84]

Behaviour-modifying tax expenditures assume that certain private behaviours benefit not only the taxpayers but also the society as a whole. Examples are the (now repealed) tax credits for taking public transit and for children's fitness and arts activities, as well as the preferential treatment of registered retirement savings plans ("RRSPs") and tax-free savings accounts ("TFSAs"). The logic behind the introduction of the children's fitness credit in 2006 was something like this: the physical fitness of children leads to healthy children, better students, happier parents, lower public health care costs and, eventually, productive members of society and it was hoped that by providing the $75 per child non-refundable credit, parents would be encouraged to enroll their children in physical fitness programs. Then some design flaws were corrected: the maximum credit was doubled (to $150) and made refundable (so low-income families could benefit) but the credit was still ineffective and in 2016 it was eliminated by a new government.[85]

The tax subsidies provided to RRSPs and TFSAs are to correct the problem of myopia. Myopia about savings is a problem — many people just do not save enough. Individuals without adequate retirement savings will depend more on public pensions and social income support programs in their old age.[86] The tax subsidies entice people to save when they are younger and earning income.

The hidden nature of tax expenditures makes them a handy instrument for achieving political purposes. The process of making tax policy is inherently political. As the history of the tax system illustrates, the tax provisions in force today reflect yesterday's political compromises. According to the public choice theory, voters, politicians and political parties are primarily motivated out of self-interest and will

---

[83] For more, see M. Fallis, "Tax Expenditures and Housing" in Philipps, Brooks & Li, *supra* note 79 at 10:1–10:26.

[84] See Chapter 10 at heading 10.4(d) — Principal residence exemption.

[85] See "Evaluation of the Children's Fitness Tax Credit and the Children's Arts Tax Credit" in *2017 Tax Expenditures Report, supra* note 81 at Part 4. For an earlier evaluation, see T. Larre, "The Children's Fitness Tax Credit: Right Message, Wrong Policy Instrument" in Philipps, Brooks & Li, *supra* note 79 at 12:1–12:24.

[86] For more, see J. Li, "Tax Treatment of Retirement Savings Plans: Past, Present, and Future" in Philipps, Brooks & Li, *supra* note 79 at 14:1–14:29.

select taxes and other policies that maximize their utility.[87] Political parties favour policies that get them re-elected. Voters favour policies that maximize the benefits they get from government expenditures and minimize the taxes they have to pay. Overall, however, general voters are "rationally ignorant", as it takes time and effort to understand issues (especially if they are complex) and the probability of an individual's vote actually affecting the election's outcome is negligible. But voters who are organized can advocate for a tax expenditure with effective lobbying. Many tax reform proposals are made by political parties in connection with election campaigns. For example, the federal government's introduction of pension income splitting in 2007 to provide tax breaks to seniors was largely politically motivated. Targeting tax measures to voters who are relatively well-informed and organized (like senior citizens) is politically efficient.

Political motivations explain why all political parties like to provide tax subsidies and expenditures through the tax system. Even though the economic effect of the myriad of tax breaks is probably the same as lowering taxes in general, the government and voters much prefer tax breaks. For example, instead of keeping college and university tuition fees low by increasing the direct funding to universities, the federal and provincial governments have chosen to direct the funding to students through student loan and low-income grant programs and through the tax system (through Registered Education Savings Plans, by not taxing scholarships and bursaries, and by providing tuition and student loan interest credits). Voters prefer this: some may think that colleges and universities waste funds that are given to them, others may think that not everyone should go to college or university and that only the very best students and low-income students should be supported and that parents who save for this should be supported.

There are also some institutional characteristics of the income tax that may explain why it is used as a spending instrument by the federal and provincial governments. These characteristics include the following: it affects only persons who file a tax return and claim the benefit; the form of benefit is monetary and can be capped and offset against taxes owing; the benefit is delivered once a year (with the exception of refundable tax credits that are paid several times a year); the amount of the benefit is based on verifiable numbers; and it captures most of the adult population.

The *ITA* has some institutional advantages over direct spending. Direct spending programs are often not easy to control effectively and require a costly bureaucracy to administer them. In many cases, direct expenditures are discretionary, in the sense that officials must pass judgment on the qualifications of applicants or even

---

[87] See, e.g., I. Gillespie, *Tax, Borrow and Spend: Financing Federal Spending in Canada, 1867–1900* (Ottawa: Carleton University Press, 1991) and D.G. Hartle, "Some Analytical, Political and Normative Lessons from Carter" in W.N. Brooks, ed., *The Quest for Tax Reform* (Toronto: Carswell, 1988) This is not to say that voters, politicians and political parties do not have altruistic, ethical or ideological motivations. It just means that their primary motivation is self-interest. See also N. Brooks & T. Hwong, "Personal Tax Expenditures in Canada's Income Tax Act: The First 100 Years" in Li, Wilkie & Chapman, *supra* note 8 at 16:1.

choose between qualified applicants. Discretion has its merit, since in principle it enables assistance to be directed to where it is most needed. But discretion carries with it the danger that the administrators will succumb to pressures from members of Parliament and lobbyists of various kinds so that the administration will not be as fair as it ought to be. The provisions of the *ITA* typically involve little discretion on the part of officials: the rules are set down in black and white and are administered with total indifference to political pressures. Under the self-assessment system, taxpayers determine their own entitlement to the tax benefit and receive immediate benefit by reducing the amount of tax payable. There is no need for a separate transfer from the government. The administration of social assistance programs through the tax system might actually be cost-effective compared to the direct expenditure alternative, especially if separate bureaucracies were set up to administer each program.

As mentioned already, a tax expenditure can be located anywhere in the tax structure. The choice of an exemption, deduction, tax credit, tax deferral or rate reduction has equity implications. A tax credit computed at the same rate is more equitable than other forms, as it provides the same amount of tax saving to all taxpayers while other forms generally benefit higher-income earners more.[88] For both technical and political reasons, the *ITA* is better suited for tax expenditures that are designed to benefit well-informed taxpayers in higher-income brackets. That is perhaps why the "big items", such as the principal residence exemption and the preferential treatment of retirement savings, have not been converted into tax credits. Converting these tax expenditures into direct government spending programs would be politically unwise. On the other hand, the *ITA* is arguably a poor vehicle for more narrowly targeted tax expenditures, such as the children's fitness credit (which was available from 2007 to 2016). Other than the signaling effect, the actual effect of this credit was highly questionable.[89]

Because provincial income taxes in all provinces but Quebec largely rely on the tax base defined in the *ITA*, the federal government can support various activities that generally fall within provincial jurisdiction through exemptions and deductions. This may be another reason that some tax expenditures relating to health and education have not been converted into tax credits.

(ii) — Estimating the cost

When Surrey introduced the concept of tax expenditures, he wanted to subject them to public scrutiny. In 1969, the United States Treasury prepared a "tax expenditure budget", which listed and estimated the cost of various tax concessions in the U.S. tax system. This became an annual practice, which, under the *Congressional Budget Act of 1974*, is now required by law. Some American states have also begun to develop tax expenditure budgets.

---

[88] See heading 2.2(e) — Tax reform of 1988, above.

[89] See Larre, *supra* note 85.

In Canada, until 1979, tax expenditures were immune from the annual scrutiny that is applied to direct expenditures.[90] In 1979, the Department of Finance issued a document entitled "Government of Canada Tax Expenditure Account" (1979), in which an attempt was made to identify all of the tax concessions in the Canadian income tax system, and to estimate the cost in foregone revenue of each concession.[91] The budget introduced by Finance Minister MacEachen on November 12, 1981 was influenced by the tax expenditure accounts of 1979 and 1980. The defeat of the budget led to the suspension of the publication of tax expenditure accounts from 1981 to 1984. In 1984, the Liberal government was defeated and a Progressive Conservative government took office. In 1985, the Department of Finance issued a document entitled "Account of the Cost of Selected Tax Measures", which

---

[90] The cost of a tax expenditure did not appear in any budget, and once established it did not need to win annual approval from the Treasury Board, Cabinet or Parliament. Indeed, the cost of a particular tax concession was only estimated officially upon its first introduction, and then only for the first year of its operation. If this estimate was wrong, or if the cost increased dramatically, there was no regular procedure for discovering the new facts, let alone debating them: no further figures were ever provided. And, despite the Carter Commission's widely-accepted warning of the inefficiency of tax concessions, there was rarely any examination of the degree to which a tax concession was accomplishing its stated objectives, or of who was benefiting from it. This situation attracted criticism, and various unofficial analyses of tax expenditures began to appear and to receive publicity. Canada, *The Hidden Welfare System: A Report by the National Council of Welfare on the Personal Income Tax System in Canada* (Ottawa: National Council of Welfare, 1976); Canada, *The Hidden Welfare System Revisited: A Report by the National Council of Welfare on the Growth in Tax Expenditures* (Ottawa: National Council of Welfare, 1979); D. Perry, "Fiscal Figures" (1976) 24 Can. Tax J. 528; J.R. Kesselman, "Non-Business Deductions and Tax Expenditures in Canada: Aggregates and Distributions" (1977) 25 Can. Tax J. 160; and R.S. Smith, *Tax Expenditures* (Toronto: Canadian Tax Foundation, 1979).

[91] Department of Finance, *Government of Canada Tax Expenditure Account* (Ottawa: 1979) at 30. The tax expenditure account was divided into the same categories as are used for direct expenditures in the public accounts of Canada. The figures were preceded by an analysis of the concept of a tax expenditure and the criteria for identifying it and estimating its cost. The document did not provide estimates for some of the concessions, no attempt was made to estimate the total cost, and no attempt was made to show the distribution of benefits by income classes. However, the document did show that there was a very large number of concessions, that many were very costly, and that they had been growing in both numbers and cost. The document, true to its scholarly approach, even speculated that the existence of budgetary restraint policies in the 1970s had led to an increase in tax expenditures as a means of avoiding the restraint policies. The message implicit in this last comment was picked up by the federal government, which instituted a new budgetary management system (known as the "envelope" system) under which tax expenditures as well as direct expenditures are taken into account in allocating spending limits ("expenditure envelopes") to each area of policy. In 1980, a second "Tax Expenditure Account" reported on this new system: Department of Finance, *Government of Canada Tax Expenditure Account: A Conceptual Analysis and Account of Tax Preferences in the Federal Income Tax and Commodity Tax Systems* (Ottawa: 1980).

was essentially an update of the accounts published in 1979 and 1980. Once again, tax expenditures, now described as "selective tax measures", were catalogued and costed. In 1988, in a different political climate, the Progressive Conservative government was able to do what had caused the Liberal government so much grief. The tax reform of 1988 eliminated a number of tax preferences and lowered rates. However, the government did not resume issuing tax expenditure accounts until 1992. Since then, accounts have appeared annually, for the most part,[92] and budgets with tax measures have included the related tax expenditures.

Estimating the amount of revenue loss from a tax expenditure is not straightforward. It first involves identifying each tax expenditure in the *ITA* by drawing the line between the benchmark system and deviations from the system. Then, a number of assumptions need to be made in estimating the amount of each tax expenditure. In principle, the amount consists of the revenue foregone by the tax expenditure, or, in other words, the extra revenue that would be raised if the tax expenditure were removed. The tax expenditure accounts estimate the cost "by estimating the revenues that the federal government forgoes as a result of the measure. This involves comparing the amount of revenues actually collected with the amount of revenues that would be collected in the absence of the measure, accounting for any changes in income-tested entitlements and assuming all else is unchanged",[93] so that the revenue impact is measured by reference to the existing rather than the benchmark tax structure. As well, if a tax concession were removed, people would alter their behavior and economic activity, causing a series of changes with various effects on tax revenues. But the estimates do not take the potential impact on economic activity into account.[94] In some cases, there is apparently insufficient information about a tax expenditure to enable any estimate to be calculated and this point is noted.

---

[92] E.g., *2017 Tax Expenditures Report, supra* note 81 provides tax expenditure estimates for the years 2011 to 2018.

[93] *Ibid.* at 16.

[94] This point is regularly acknowledged in the Department of Finance's tax expenditure accounts. See, e.g., *2017 Tax Expenditures Report, supra* note 81 at 19.

Table 2-2, below, contains projected figures from the Department of Finance's most recently published list of revenue losses in millions of dollars for selected major personal income tax expenditures:[95]

Table 2-2: Estimated Cost of Major Personal Income Tax Expenditures ($ millions)

	2016	2017	2018
Charitable donation credit	$ 2,850	$ 2,980	$ 3,080
Employment credit	2,260	2,325	2,380
Employee stock option deduction	695	725	755
Basic credit	34,690	35,745	36,705
Spousal credit	1,540	1,585	1,620
Spousal equivalent credit	925	940	960
Non-taxation of business-paid health benefits	2,605	2,740	2,865
Age credit	3,330	3,465	3,620
Non-taxation of gains on principal residences[96]	7,490	6,770	6,615

The 2017 Report also contains estimates of corporate income tax expenditures and goods and services tax ("GST") expenditures. The magnitude of tax expenditures in the *ITA* is staggering. In effect, the Act is one of the federal government's biggest spending instruments. The projected value of personal and corporate tax expenditures for 2017 is between $27 and $30 billion.[97]

(iii) — Effectiveness

Among the different categories of tax expenditures, the technical tax expenditures and social benefit tax expenditures are arguably effective. In contrast, behaviour-modifying tax expenditures, like several of the recently repealed tax credits (e.g., the children's fitness credits) are often ineffective. It is hard to argue that taxpayers who purchase personal residences are not influenced by the principal residence exemption and there is no denying the popularity of TFSAs and RRSPs. But the effectiveness of tax preferences for retirement savings is unclear because people who take advantage of the tax preferences may save in any event. In some cases, the tax

---

[95] This table shows estimates and projections of tax expenditures by some of the major items. For a complete list of tax expenditures, see *2017 Tax Expenditures Report, supra* note 81. The spouse equivalent credit is also called the eligible dependant credit.

[96] Note the year-over-year predicted decrease in this tax expenditure. The report is silent on whether this reflects the changes made to the principal residence exemption rules in 2016 or a prediction about the residential real estate market (or both). The rules and the changes are discussed under in Chapter 10 at heading 10.4(d) — Principal residence exemption.

[97] See J. Lester, "Reviewing Federal Tax Expenditures" in Li, Wilkie & Chapman, *supra* note 8 at ch. 17-2.

expenditures may have unintended effects. For example, the preferential taxation of capital gains has led taxpayers to order their affairs so as to receive capital gains rather than ordinary income. Tax credits in respect of charitable donations have, in the past, inspired extremely aggressive tax schemes designed to get the credits without contributing to deserving charities.[98] Public confidence in the fairness of the tax system may be eroded when it is known that so many groups are allowed concessions or loopholes, such as the ones for employee stock options.

(iv) — Distributional effect

Tax expenditures are generally assumed to favour higher-income taxpayers. Other than tax credits, the value of these tax expenditures depends on the recipient's marginal tax rate. Higher-income taxpayers are generally better positioned to take advantage of the tax expenditures.

This general result is confirmed by a recent study of 64 personal income tax expenditures, including pension income splitting, charitable donation tax credit, tax-free savings account, medical expense tax credit, employee stock option deduction, RRSPs, and principal residence exemption.[99] According to the study, of those 64 tax expenditures, only five, including non-taxation of social assistance and disability tax credit, can be described as relatively progressive, and the remaining 59 regressive tax expenditures cost the federal government $100.5 billion in 2011.

2.8 — Tax policy in a globalizing economy

The new world economy makes national boundaries less important in business and investment so that national economies are increasingly integrated. At the same time, political boundaries and national sovereignty remain important in non-economic areas. Canadian tax policy is inevitably influenced by international factors because tax policy is a key instrument of economic policy. The traditional policy criteria of equity, neutrality and simplicity remain relevant, but need to be reimagined in the context of economic globalization.

Canadians' view of equity and fairness may require high and steeply progressive rates on capital income, but Canada's ability to implement such a policy is thwarted when citizens shift wealth into foreign corporations and trusts located in low-tax jurisdictions. That is why the *ITA* contains measures intended to limit this shifting and encourage voluntary disclosure. However, gathering reliable tax information from foreign countries is still difficult (and impossible if the foreign country has bank secrecy laws or has no tax information exchange agreement with Canada). Canada relies on tax treaties and tax information exchange agreements to obtain information from other governments. As part of the recent international collabora-

---

[98] For an example, see Chapter 15 at heading 15.9 — Duty to other parties.

[99] D. Macdonald, "Out of the Shadows: Shining a light on Canada's unequal distribution of federal tax expenditures" (December 2016), available online: <https://www.policyalternatives.ca/loopholes>.

tion in the base erosion and profit shifting ("BEPS") project, Canada has strengthened information-gathering powers through information exchange mechanisms established at the international level.

The fact that the Canadian economy is highly integrated with the world economy, especially that of the United States, also means that Canadian tax policy decisions cannot be made in isolation. This is particularly true in the taxation of business income and corporate income.

Neutrality in the international context refers to capital import neutrality (taxing non-residents and residents similarly) and capital export neutrality (taxing foreign-source income and domestic income of residents similarly). Since 1987, one of the main impetuses for changes in the Canadian system has been international competitiveness, especially in the area of corporate income tax and taxation of investment income. For example, the corporate income tax rate is generally in line with that in other developed countries. In the past, some personal and corporate tax reform measures were enacted specifically to compete with the United States and this may happen again.

The growing globalization of the Canadian economy and the associated increasing mobility of capital inevitably impose some limits on Canadian sovereignty in determining its tax policy, especially in areas affecting cross-border trade and investment. The increasing mobility of capital is likely to help shift Canadian tax policy more towards economic efficiency and tax competitiveness and shift the tax burden towards less mobile factors, such as labour and consumption.

3
RESIDENCE

3.1 — Section 2

(a) — Technical design

Subsection 2(1) of the *Income Tax Act* (the "*ITA*")[1] provides that an income tax is payable on the taxable income of every person resident in Canada at any time in the year. The definition of taxable income in subsection 2(2) then points the reader to the computation of income under section 3 and the deductions permitted by Division C.

Subsection 2(3) speaks to persons who are non-residents of Canada. Such persons are taxable in Canada under Part I of the *ITA* only on income derived from three

---

[1] R.S.C. 1985 (5th Supp.), c. 1 [*ITA*].

Canadian sources, namely income from employment in Canada, carrying on business in Canada, or the disposition of taxable Canadian property.

As a result, the *ITA* imposes tax liability on the basis of "residence" under subsection 2(1) and on the basis of "source of income" under subsection 2(3). Residence emphasizes the taxpayer's connection to Canada, whereas "source of income" emphasizes the fact that the income-earning activity is in Canada. A person falling outside these two jurisdictional rules is not taxable under Part I of the *ITA*.[2] The *ITA* contains several provisions that deem a person to be a resident or non-resident in certain circumstances, but leaves the ordinary meaning of "residence" to be determined by the courts.

(i) — Legislative scheme for taxing residents

A person resident in Canada is liable for tax on the person's taxable income. According to subsection 2(2), the "taxable income" of a resident taxpayer is essentially the taxpayer's section 3 income minus deductions specified in Division C of the Act. As explained further in Chapter 4, section 3 income includes income "from a source inside or outside Canada". Accordingly, Canadian residents are taxable on their worldwide income. If a taxpayer is resident in Canada for only part of the year, section 114 permits the taxpayer to be taxable on his or her worldwide income earned during that part of the year.

One important corollary of the worldwide tax principle is the potential double taxation of foreign income earned by Canadian residents. Foreign income is generally subject to tax in the foreign-source country pursuant to that country's tax rules. The *ITA* provides measures for preventing double taxation, the most important of which is the foreign tax credit under section 126. Because a Canadian resident can use a foreign corporation to earn foreign income to avoid Canadian tax until the foreign income is repatriated to Canada, the *ITA* contains complex rules to deny the tax benefits of using foreign corporations. It is beyond the scope of this book to discuss these rules.[3]

(ii) — Legislative scheme for taxing non-residents

Non-resident persons are taxable under Part I of the *ITA* on three types of Canadian-source income: employment income, business income and capital gains. The amount of "taxable income" of such persons is determined under more or less the same rules as those for resident persons, but limited to those Canadian sources.

---

[2] Such person may be subject to tax under Part XIII of the *ITA* in respect of investment income received from Canada.

[3] For further discussion of Canadian international taxation, see Brian J. Arnold, *Reforming Canada's International Tax System towards Coherence and Simplicity* (Toronto: Canadian Tax Foundation, 2009); J. Li, *International Taxation in the Age of Electronic Commerce: A Comparative Study* (Toronto: Canadian Tax Foundation, 2003) ch. 3; and J. Li, A. Cockfield & J.S. Wilkie, *International Taxation in Canada: Principles and Practices*, 3rd ed. (Markham, Ont.: LexisNexis Canada, 2014) ch. 4.

In addition, Part XIII (e.g., section 212) and Part IV (e.g., section 219) of the *ITA* impose withholding taxes on non-residents receiving "passive" investment income from Canada, such as dividends, interest, rents, royalties, and pension income or branch profits. These taxes are known as "withholding taxes" because the Canadian resident payer is legally responsible for withholding the tax from payments to the non-resident. This book does not discuss this scheme in any detail.

(b) — Purpose and rationale

The purpose of section 2 is to articulate the basis and scope of Canadian tax jurisdiction. A country may wish to tax everyone in the world but it generally confines its taxes to people who have some connection with the country. It would be impossible for Canada to enforce a tax against people lacking any connection with Canada. Even if it were possible, there is no moral justification for forcing such people to help finance Canada's government. Canada, like every other country, has to employ some factor or factors to identify the class of people liable to pay Canadian income tax.

(i) — Theoretical rationale

There are several justifications for the taxation of international income on the basis of residence and the source of income. They include economic allegiance theory, benefit theory, the "ability to pay" principle, neutrality, and enforceability of tax collection.

The doctrine of economic allegiance was considered a starting point for modern international tax theory and administration.[4] The doctrine suggests that countries should be entitled to tax cross-border transactions if a taxpayer has a sufficient economic connection with the taxing country. To determine whether this connection exists, tax theorists have asked questions such as 1) where is the value-added economic activity taking place? 2) where are the suppliers of capital located? and 3) where are consumers of goods and services located? The answer to the first question is relevant to source-based taxation, and the answers to the other two questions point to residence-based taxation.

The benefit theory is perhaps one of the most obvious arguments for exercising tax jurisdiction. Under this theory, those who benefit from the public services provided by a country should be charged for such services. In the context of corporate income tax, such benefits may be seen in the way of reducing the cost of production, or enhancing profitability. Income taxes could be viewed as "the prior claim of the state upon the private profits which public expenditures or the business environment maintained by the state have in part produced".[5] This theory justifies the taxa-

---

[4] This doctrine was advocated in a groundbreaking report of the League of Nations, *Report on Double Taxation Submitted to the Financial Committee by Professors Bruins, Einaudi, Seligman and Stamp* (Geneva, 1923).

[5] Thomas S. Adams, "The Taxation of Business," in *Proceedings of the Eleventh Annual Conference on Taxation* (New Haven, CT: National Tax Association, 1918) 185 at 192.

tion of residents as well as the taxation of domestic-source income earned by non-residents.

The ability to pay principle is the foundation of progressive personal income taxation in Canada and other countries. Adam Smith has been credited with the earliest rendering of this theory. The first of his four famous canons regarding taxes is that "[t]he subjects of every state ought to contribute towards the support of the government, as nearly as possible, in proportion to their respective abilities".[6] As explained further in Chapters 2 and 4 of this volume, the ability to pay is measured by net income. This definition is the foundation of the "comprehensive income tax base" recommended by the 1966 *Carter Report*.[7] The concept of ability to pay is inherently global — the income of a resident must include income earned from both domestic and foreign sources.[8] The taxation of Canadian residents on their worldwide income is consistent with this principle.

Both residence and source of income can also be justified on grounds of enforceability, although source-based taxes are generally easier to collect. For example, Canadian tax on investment income (dividend, interest, rent or royalties) earned by non-residents is typically withheld by resident payers; Canadian tax on business income or employment income earned by non-residents can be collected because the taxpayer is, or the taxpayer's business assets are, often in Canada. The collection of a residence-based tax is possible because the taxpayer has significant social and economic ties with Canada. However, it is more difficult to enforce than source-based taxation. Taxpayers may not accurately report their foreign income on their tax returns and it is very difficult for the tax administration to obtain and verify tax information in respect of offshore activities.

(ii) — Social and economic ties with Canada

Residence is the principal connecting factor used for Canadian income tax purposes. It emphasizes the social and economic connections between a person and the taxing jurisdiction. The factor of residence, it could be argued, produces the largest class of taxpayers with strong social and economic ties with Canada. Canadian residents benefit from the public expenditures financed with tax revenues and, thus, have a moral obligation to finance the government, and they are all people against whom enforcement is practicable. It is probably the best of all the alternatives, although the taxation of a resident alien (who cannot vote) can be criticized as "taxation without representation", and the concept of residence (as we shall see) is far from precise.

---

[6] Adam Smith, *An Inquiry into the Nature and Causes of the Wealth of Nations*, 4th ed. by Edwin Cannan. (London: Methuen & Co., 1925) at 310. Smith's first edition was published in 1776.

[7] Canada, *Report of the Royal Commission on Taxation* (Ottawa: Queen's Printer, 1966) (Chairman: Kenneth Le M. Carter) at vol. 3, ch. 8.

[8] *Ibid.* at 503.

The *ITA* does not adopt the tests of citizenship or domicile that are used by other countries in determining tax jurisdiction. Citizenship (or nationality) is used by the United States (but not by Canada and most other countries). The factor of citizenship emphasizes the political connection between a person and the taxing jurisdiction. The argument for using this factor is that even citizens living outside the United States are entitled to protection by the U.S. government. Moreover, citizenship enables the taxing country to tax its citizens who have moved to tax havens such as the Bahamas or Bermuda (although such people could change their citizenship, and, even if they did not, enforcement would be difficult). The disadvantage of citizenship is that it would sweep in many people whose economic and social links with the taxing country have become very tenuous, and it would exclude many people living permanently in the taxing country. That is why the United States also taxes aliens who are residents of the United States.

Domicile is used as a connecting factor in the U.K. The concept of "domicile" is encrusted with archaic and often artificial rules. A person's "domicile of origin" (which is determined at birth, usually by the father's domicile) and a person's "domicile of dependence" (under which a married woman assumes the domicile of her husband) may bear little relationship to a person's actual permanent home. Even a person's "domicile of choice", which involves residing in a country with the intention of remaining there permanently, is not an entirely satisfactory criterion for taxation: the element of intention raises difficult questions of proof and excludes people who may be long-standing residents of the taxing country if they lack the intention to stay permanently.

3.2 — Residence of individuals

(a) — Common law residence

Given the importance of the concept of residence, one might expect to find an exhaustive definition of this term in the *ITA*. Such a definition does not exist. The Act simply deems certain individuals to be residents in certain circumstances, leaving the meaning of residence to be defined in the common law. As Rand J. of the Supreme Court of Canada stated in *Thomson v. M.N.R.* (1946):

> It is quite impossible to give it a precise and inclusive definition. It is highly flexible, and its many shades of meaning vary not only in the contexts of different matters, but also in different aspects of the same matter.[9]

However, there is a plethora of cases defining the meaning of residence. The courts have held "residence" to be "a matter of the degree to which a person in mind and fact settles into or maintains or centralizes his ordinary mode of living with its accessories in social relations, interests and conveniences at or in the place in ques-

---

[9] *Thomson v. M.N.R.* (1946), [1946] C.T.C. 51, 2 D.T.C. 812 (S.C.C.) [*Thomson*] at para. 47.

tion".[10] Ultimately, the common law test is based on the facts and circumstances of the case.

The leading case on the residence of an individual is *Thomson*.[11] In this case, the taxpayer, a wealthy Canadian citizen who had gone to a lot of trouble to give up his Canadian residence, was held nonetheless to be a resident of Canada. In 1923, he sold his home in New Brunswick, announced that Bermuda was now his residence, and went to Bermuda. In the following years, he actually spent very little time in Bermuda, mainly living in the United States, where he built a house that was kept permanently ready for occupancy and where he spent most of his time. Starting in 1932, he began to regularly return to New Brunswick for four or five of the warmer months every year, and he eventually built a house there that was kept available all year long. Every year, however, he kept his stay in New Brunswick to less than 183 days (to avoid the sojourning rule).[12] The taxpayer's wife and child accompanied him in these regular migrations. The Supreme Court of Canada, by a majority, held that the taxpayer was resident in Canada. Rand J., who wrote the principal opinion, said that the taxpayer's time in Canada was not a temporary "stay" or "visit":

> His living in Canada is substantially as deep rooted and settled as in the United States. In terms of time [the United States] may take precedence but at best it is a case of *primus inter pares*. He is [in Canada] as at his "home"; and the mere limitation of time does not qualify that fact . . . That brings him within the most exacting of any reasonable interpretation of "resides" or "ordinarily resident.[13]

Taschereau J., who dissented, held that the taxpayer was "a resident of the United States, making occasional visits to Canada".[14]

Several points emerge from the *Thomson* case. First, the intention of the taxpayer, while obviously relevant in determining the "settled routine" of a taxpayer's life, is not determinative. In *Thomson* (as in many other cases), it was the external facts as to his customary mode of life that persuaded the Court that his home was in Canada, notwithstanding his intention not to be resident in Canada. Second, a person can be resident in more than one country at the same time. In *Thomson*, it was clear that the Court thought that the taxpayer was resident in the United States as well as in Canada (he was, in fact, being taxed in the United States as a resident).[15]

---

[10] Canada Revenue Agency, Folio S5-F1-C1, "Determining an Individual's Residence Status" at para. 1.5.

[11] *Thomson, supra* note 9.

[12] See heading 3.2(c) — Sojourner, below.

[13] *Thomson, supra* note 9 at para. 56.

[14] *Ibid.* at 60.

[15] There was no tax treaty between Canada and the United States during the years in issue in this case. At present, Article IV of the Canada-United States Convention with Respect to Taxes on Income and on Capital, 26 September 1980 (entered into force 16 August 1984) [Canada-U.S. Tax Convention] provides a tie-breaker.

Third, every person is presumed to be resident somewhere:

> For the purposes of income tax legislation, it must be assumed that every person has at all times a residence. It is not necessary to this that he should have a home or a particular place of abode or even a shelter. He may sleep in the open. It is important only to ascertain the spatial bounds within which he spends his life or to which his ordered or customary living is related.[16]

Although Rand J. points out in the above statement that a taxpayer may not have a home, the homeless rarely raise issues of income tax. It is "the peripatetic lifestyle of the leisurely wealthy"[17] that raises residence questions. Such people usually have at least one home. The country in which the taxpayer makes his or her home will be "the place where he, in the settled routine of his life, regularly, normally or customarily lives".[18] The availability of a place where the taxpayer has the right to stay is usually the critical element in determining the country of residence, although the courts will look at other factors as well, such as the frequency and duration of visits, and the presence of social and business connections. The object of the exercise, though, is to identify the country in which the taxpayer is resident. If more than one country is indicated, the courts will not hesitate to find a person to be resident in more than one country. Nor is there anything surprising in the proposition that a person may be resident in more than one country, although it is rarely desirable from a tax standpoint.

As indicated in the discussion of *Thomson*, above, the common law has established that several factors are important in determining whether an individual is resident in Canada, but none are conclusive.

The maintenance of a *dwelling in Canada* available for occupation by the taxpayer is a key factor in the *Thomson* case. It is regarded by the Canada Revenue Agency (the "CRA") as a significant factor in determining whether a taxpayer has ceased to be a resident of Canada.[19]

Another factor is whether the taxpayer's spouse and children are residents of Canada. The relevance of having a spouse and children resident in Canada varies, depending on the other facts of the taxpayer's situation. In *Allchin v. R* (2003),[20] for example, the taxpayer worked in the United States from 1992 to 1997. During this period, she stayed with relatives and friends while her husband and two children lived in Canada. She also set up a U.S. bank account, arranged for her credit card bills to be sent to a U.S. address and attempted to move her family to the U.S. by retaining the services of an immigration lawyer. The Tax Court concluded that the taxpayer remained a Canadian resident during the years 1993 to 1995 because of

---

[16] *Thomson, supra* note 9 at para. 49, per Rand. J.

[17] *R. v. Reeder*, [1975] C.T.C. 256, 75 D.T.C. 5160 (Fed. T.D.) at 260 [C.T.C.].

[18] *Thomson, supra* note 9 at para. 71.

[19] Folio S5-F1-C1, *supra* note 10 at para. 1.12.

[20] *Allchin v. R.* (2003), [2003] 4 C.T.C. 2702, 2003 D.T.C. 935 (T.C.C.); reversed [2004] 4 C.T.C. 1, 2004 D.T.C. 6468 (Fed. C.A.).

the temporary nature of her accommodation and due to her continuing ties to Canada: her husband and children, her Ontario driver's licence, her OHIP (Ontario Health Insurance Plan) coverage, a club membership, and the fact that her husband swore in an affidavit when he purchased a house that his wife was a resident of Canada. Subsequently, however, the taxpayer was successful in arguing that she was a resident in the United States under the tie-breaker rules in the Canada-United States Tax Convention.[21]

In contrast to *Allchin*, in *Shih v. R.* (2000)[22] and *Schujahn v. M.N.R.* (1962),[23] the fact that the spouse and children stayed in Canada did not make the taxpayer who was living and working outside Canada a Canadian resident. In *Shih*, the primary reason for the spouse and children to stay in Canada was to enable the children to receive a Canadian education, and in *Schujahn*, the primary reason for the spouse and child to remain in Canada after the taxpayer had left Canada was to facilitate the sale of their house in Canada. One possible explanation is that, in these two cases, the taxpayers were originally non-Canadian residents and came to Canada temporarily, whereas the taxpayer in *Allchin* was trying to abandon Canadian residency.

For individuals attempting to abandon Canadian residency, the following factors are often relevant. First, the length of time during that the taxpayer is physically present in Canada.[24] Second, the taxpayer's ties to another country. This may be a relevant factor because the assumption is that an individual must be resident somewhere at all times. If the taxpayer cannot establish to the satisfaction of the court that he or she is resident in a foreign country, the taxpayer may be considered a Canadian resident if he or she has ties to Canada.[25] However, the opposite is not true: the fact that an individual is a resident of another country does not mean that

---

[21] See *Allchin v. R.*, [2005] 2 C.T.C. 2701, 2005 D.T.C. 603 (T.C.C.); Canada-U.S. Tax Convention, *supra* note 15.

[22] *Shih v. R.* (2000), [2000] 2 C.T.C. 2921, 2000 D.T.C. 2072 (T.C.C.). In *Shih*, the taxpayer immigrated to Canada with his wife and three sons, purchased a home in Canada and returned to Taiwan to work in the same year. He visited Canada annually to see his family but his stays did not exceed 59 days in any given year. He had several residential ties to Taiwan: other family members; a job that he had held for 25 years; a house that he owned; various memberships; a driver's licence and bank accounts. Based on these facts, the Court concluded that the taxpayer was a resident in Taiwan. The Court went on to inquire whether the taxpayer had a dual residence. The Court held that the taxpayer's connections with Canada (his house and wife and sons) were not strong enough to make him a resident of Canada. The taxpayer's primary reason for having a connection to Canada was to educate his children.

[23] *Schujahn v. M.N.R.* (1962), [1962] C.T.C. 364, 62 D.T.C. 1225 (Can. Ex. Ct.) [*Schujahn*]. This case is discussed in more detail at heading 3.5(b) — Deemed dispositions, below.

[24] *Thomson*, *supra* note 9, is an example.

[25] In *Ferguson v. Minister of National Revenue*, [1989] 2 C.T.C. 2387, 89 D.T.C. 634 (T.C.C.), the taxpayer was held to be a Canadian resident because the Court was not satisfied that he had established residence in Saudi Arabia.

he or she cannot also be considered a resident of Canada (a dual resident).[26] Third, the taxpayer's social and economic ties with Canada. These ties include ownership of property (e.g., furniture, clothing, automobile, bank accounts, credit cards, etc.), club memberships, family, medical insurance coverage, and professional or other memberships in Canada (on a resident basis). Finally, the taxpayer's intention to return to Canada[27] and the failure to pay tax or file tax returns in a foreign country[28] could be relevant as well.

In cases where taxpayers are motivated to abandon their Canadian residence by moving to countries with lower taxes and warmer temperatures, the judge must determine if the taxpayer has sufficiently cut his or her ties with Canada to become a non-resident. In *Hauser v. R.* (2005),[29] for example, an Air Canada pilot did not sufficiently "divorce" himself from Canada when moving to the Bahamas. The Tax Court remarked:

> Canada was a magnet that attracted the Hausers. After they set up residence in the Bahamas both of Mr. and Mrs. Hauser, and particularly Mr. Hauser, continued to have a presence in Canada. Mr. Hauser spent over a third of a year in Canada each year. Air Canada required Mr. Hauser to be in Canada to fly airplanes; he reported to work at Pearson Airport and other airports in Canada. Most of his flights left from and returned to Pearson; much of his training was at Pearson. Pearson Airport was part of the routine of life. Mr. Hauser's presence in Canada during the years in appeal was not occasional, casual, deviatory, intermittent or transitory. He was in Canada in great part because he had to be, to earn a living.[30]

(b) — Ordinarily resident

Subsection 250(3) provides that "a person resident in Canada includes a person who was at the relevant time ordinarily resident in Canada".[31] This provision is often alluded to in the cases, but it is doubtful whether it adds anything to the com-

---

[26] Folio S5-F1-C1, *supra* note 10 at para. 1.21.

[27] See, e.g., *Glow v. M.N.R.*, [1992] 2 C.T.C. 245, 92 D.T.C. 6467 (Fed. T.D.). The *Beament* decision (*Beament v. M.N.R.*, [1952] CTC 327, 52 DTC 1183 (S.C.C.)) emphasizes that intention is not the crucial factor in determining residence. In this case, the taxpayer always regarded his absence from Canada as temporary and intended to return. Nevertheless, he was held not to be a resident until his actual return. See also *Allchin, supra* notes 20, 21, in which the taxpayer was held to be a dual resident and the tie-breaker rules assigned her residency to the United States: the facts were similar and, in each case, the taxpayer did not intend to return to Canada.

[28] *R. v. Sherwood*, [1978] C.T.C. 713, 78 D.T.C. 6470 (Fed. T.D.).

[29] *Hauser v. R.* (2005), [2005] 4 C.T.C. 2260, 2005 D.T.C. 1151 (T.C.C.); affirmed [2006] 4 C.T.C. 193, 2006 D.T.C. 6447 (Fed. C.A.).

[30] *Ibid.* at para. 58.

[31] *ITA, supra* note 1, s. 250(3).

mon law. As Rand J. said in *Thomson*, if the common law concept of residence is given its full significance, "ordinarily resident" becomes "superfluous".[32]

However, subsection 250(3) can be relied upon together with the common law test to determine whether a person who has been absent from Canada for a significant period of time retains his or her Canadian residence. It reinforces the proposition that a temporary absence from Canada (even one lasting more than one or two years) does not necessarily involve a loss of Canadian residence.

Many people planning a temporary but lengthy period of absence from Canada (e.g., on a transfer outside Canada, an exchange of jobs, a sabbatical leave or even an extended holiday) would like to establish non-resident status for Canadian tax purposes. However, unless an individual severs all significant residential ties with Canada (i.e., dwelling place, spouse or common-law partner, and dependants) upon leaving the country, the CRA will generally consider the individual to remain a Canadian resident.[33] The CRA's position is supported by a number of cases, including a series of "sabbatical" cases decided by the Tax Review Board in 1980.[34]

In each case, a university professor who had left Canada for up to one year on sabbatical leave was held to have retained his resident status. In each case, the professor had leased his home in Canada but had not severed all residential ties during his leave, and he had resumed teaching duties on returning to Canada.

Similar decisions were reached in some recent cases where the taxpayer left Canada for work in other countries. In *McFadyen v. R.* (2000),[35] the taxpayer moved to Japan with his wife, who accepted a position at the Canadian embassy there. The taxpayer lived in Japan for three years and was employed there at various times. While in Japan, he obtained a certificate of residency of Japan. The Tax Court of Canada came to the conclusion that the taxpayer maintained ties with Canada that were largely economic but partly personal (family ties, real property, furniture and appliances, bank accounts, a safety deposit box, a registered retirement savings plan, credit cards, and a provincial driver's licence), and, thus, considered him to be ordinarily resident in Canada during the period he was in Japan.

In contrast, the taxpayer in *Nicholson v. R.* (2003)[36] was found to have severed his residential ties with Canada. The taxpayer was assigned by his employer to work in

---

[32] *Thomson, supra* note 9 at para. 52.

[33] Folio S5-F1-C1, *supra* note 10 at paras. 1.10–1.21.

[34] *Saunders v. M.N.R.*, [1980] C.T.C. 2436, 80 D.T.C. 1392 (T.R.B.); *Mash v. M.N.R.*, [1980] C.T.C. 2443, 80 D.T.C. 1396 (T.R.B.); *Brinkerhoff v. M.N.R.*, [1980] C.T.C. 2441, 80 D.T.C. 1398 (T.R.B.); *Breskey v. M.N.R.*, [1980] C.T.C. 2445, 80 D.T.C. 1400 (T.R.B.); and *Magee v. M.N.R.*, [1980] C.T.C. 2450, 80 D.T.C. 1403 (T.R.B.).

[35] *McFadyen v. R.* (2000), [2000] 4 C.T.C. 2573, 2000 D.T.C. 2473 (T.C.C.); reversed in part [2003] 2 C.T.C. 28, 2003 D.T.C. 5015 (Fed. C.A.); leave to appeal refused 2003 CarswellNat 999, 2003 CarswellNat 1000 (S.C.C.). A similar decision was reached in *Gaudreau v. R.*, [2005] 1 C.T.C. 2701, 2005 D.T.C. 66 (T.C.C.); affirmed [2006] 1 C.T.C. 137, 2005 D.T.C. 5702 (Fed. C.A.).

[36] *Nicholson v. R.* (2003), [2004] 2 C.T.C. 2310, 2004 D.T.C. 2013 (T.C.C.).

the U.K. for a year and a half but maintained a matrimonial home in Canada and his provincial health program during that period. He was held not be a resident in Canada based on several factors, including: he had no intention to return to Canada when he accepted the position in the U.K.; he and his first wife were separated and divorced; and he lived with his new wife in the U.K., where her child attended school.

(c) — Sojourner

Paragraph 250(1)(a) of the *ITA* provides that a person shall "be deemed to have been resident in Canada throughout a taxation year if the person (a) sojourned in Canada in the year for a period of, or periods the total of which is, 183 days or more".[37] This deeming rule is only important when an individual is a non-resident throughout the year under common law. It is obviously not important when an individual is a resident in Canada throughout the year at common law and it does not apply to a part-year resident (an individual who becomes or ceases to be a resident of Canada during the year).[38]

The term "sojourn" means something less than residence. A sojourner is a person who is physically present in Canada, but on a more transient basis than a resident. A sojourner lacks the settled home in Canada that would make him or her a resident. A person who is a resident of another country and who comes to Canada on a vacation or business trip would be an example of a sojourner. In most cases, of course, a sojourner would stay in Canada for only a short period of time, but if the sojourner stays for a period of 183 days, or for several periods totalling 183 days, then the effect of paragraph 250(1)(a) is to tax the sojourner as if he or she were a resident for the whole year. The rationale is that a person spending so much time in Canada has a stake in the country that is not markedly different from that of a resident, and that entails a contribution to the financing of the government. There is also the administrative convenience that paragraph 250(1)(a) will eliminate some of the arguments over whether a person is a resident or not.

In the *Thomson* case, the taxpayer contended that he was a mere sojourner in Canada, and that, since he had never remained in Canada for 183 days in any year, he could not be deemed a resident. The Court held, however, that his visits to Canada did not have the transient character of sojourning: they were not unusual, casual, or intermittent. On the contrary, they were part of the permanent, settled routine of his life. The taxpayer was, therefore, held to be resident in Canada for the year, although he had spent less than 183 days in the country. As we noticed earlier, the length of time spent physically present in Canada is not crucial in determining

---

[37] *ITA, supra* note 1, s. 259(1)(a). Paragraph 250(1)(b) also deems members of the armed forces and federal and provincial civil servants who are stationed outside Canada to have been resident in Canada. The most important and interesting provision is para. (a), under which a person who "sojourned" in Canada for 183 days in a taxation year is deemed to have been resident for the entire year.

[38] This is explained at heading 3.5(a) — Part-year residents, below.

whether or not a person is a resident at common law. It is, however, crucial in applying the 183-day sojourning rule, because physical presence is essential to sojourning and sojourning has no taxation relevance unless it continues for 183 days.

3.3 — Residence of corporations

(a) — Common law residence

The primary taxing provisions of sections 2 and 3 apply to "persons" and "taxpayers", and both these terms include corporations. It is, therefore, as necessary for a corporation as it is for an individual to determine the place of residence in order to decide whether the corporation is liable to Canadian tax on its world income. In the absence of any exhaustive definition of residence in the *ITA*, the courts have developed a test of residence for corporations just as they have for individuals. The test was first enunciated in *De Beers Consolidated Mines v. Howe* (1906): "[The] real business [of a corporation] is carried on where the central management and control actually abides."[39]

Corporate law confers on the board of directors of a corporation the legal power to manage the affairs of the corporation. In the ordinary case, therefore, the place where a corporation's board of directors meets will be the place where the central management and control actually abides. In *De Beers*, the corporation whose residence was in issue was incorporated in South Africa, had its head office in South Africa, and carried on its business of mining in South Africa.' Because a majority of the board of directors lived in England, and the board always met in England and made all major policy decisions there, the House of Lords held that the corporation was resident in England.

Corporate law does not confer upon the shareholders of a corporation the power to manage its affairs. That is the task of the directors, who are not the servants or agents of the shareholders, and who are under no legal obligation to follow the wishes of the shareholders. Therefore, the residence of the shareholders is not normally relevant in determining the location of the central management and control of a corporation. However, the shareholders do own the corporation, and they do possess some important powers, in particular, the power to elect (or remove) the directors. In a closely held corporation (or sometimes even in a widely held corporation), in which one shareholder or a group of shareholders wields effective voting power, the major shareholder will be able to influence the decisions of the directors, if he or she chooses to do so, and in some corporations the major shareholder will dictate the decisions of the directors.

In *Unit Construction Co. v. Bullock* (1959),[40] three corporations that were incorporated in Kenya, that carried on business in Kenya, and whose directors resided and met in Kenya, were held to be resident not in Kenya but in England. The three corporations were subsidiaries of an English corporation, and they were effectively

---

[39] *De Beers Consolidated Mines v. Howe*, [1906] A.C. 455 (U.K. H.L.) at 458.

[40] *Unit Construction Co. v. Bullock* (1959), [1960] A.C. 351 (Eng. C.A.).

controlled in fact from England by the directors of the parent corporation. The House of Lords held that the location of central management and control was a question of fact, and that, in this case, it actually resided in England.

It is usually difficult to determine whether the board of directors of a corporation is exercising an independent discretion, albeit influenced by a shareholder or other outsider, or whether the board has actually surrendered its discretion to the outsider. Even if the facts are known, the question is one of degree, which is not easy to determine. In addition, there are often evidentiary problems in establishing that a board of directors actually acts under the dictation of an outsider. It is significant that in *Unit Construction* it was to the advantage of the three Kenyan corporations and their parent for the corporations to be held resident in England, and the evidence of *de facto* control from England was, therefore, readily available.

There have been a number of Canadian cases in which the evidence appeared to establish *de facto* control by the major shareholder, and yet the courts refused to conclude that central management and control was exercised from outside the board of directors.[41] These cases reverted to a *de jure* control test, which was rejected by the House of Lords in *Unit Construction*. The results of these cases are admittedly hard to explain on any other basis. In general, however, there seems to be no reason to doubt that *Unit Construction* represents the law of Canada as well as the U.K. Where it can be established that the board of directors of a corporation does not, in fact, exercise independent management and control, then the place of residence of the person who dictates the board's decisions is the place of residence of the corporation.

In a recent U.K. case, *Wood v. Holden*,[42] a holding company was incorporated in the Netherlands as part of a scheme designed to facilitate the sale of shares in a U.K. operating company owned by U.K. resident shareholders. Under U.K. tax law at the time, the capital gain from the sale of the shares was tax-free if the Dutch company was a non-resident. The Dutch company had one corporate director who signed all the documents in the Netherlands. The Dutch company was held by the Court of Appeal to be a resident in the Netherlands because its central management and control was located there. In reaching the decision, the Court stated that:

> [I]t is essential to recognize the distinction between cases where management and control of the company was exercised through its own constitutional organs (the board of directors or the general meeting) and cases where the functions of those constitutional organs were "usurped" — in the sense that management and control was exercised independently of, or without regard to, those constitutional organs.[43]

---

[41] *Sifneos v. M.N.R.*, [1968] Tax A.B.C. 652, 68 D.T.C. 522; *Zehnder & Co. v. M.N.R.*, [1970] C.T.C. 85, 70 D.T.C. 6064 (Can. Ex. Ct.); and *Bedford Overseas Freighters v. M.N.R.*, [1970] C.T.C. 69, 70 D.T.C. 6072 (Can. Ex. Ct.).

[42] *Wood v. Holden*, [2004] S.T.C. 416 (S.C.D.); reversed [2005] EWHC 547 (Ch. D.); affirmed [2006] S.T.C. 443, EWCA Civ. 26, [2006] 2 B.C.L.C. 210 (Eng. C.A.).

[43] *Ibid.* at para. 27 [(C.A.)].

Unlike the facts and circumstances test for residence of individuals, the common law test for corporate residence is more formalistic. A corporation can reside virtually anywhere it chooses. As such, even though a corporation may be indifferent as to its residence for business reasons, the *ITA* relies on the residence test in defining Canadian tax jurisdiction over the corporate income. As discussed earlier, because a Canadian resident can use a foreign corporation to earn foreign income to avoid Canadian tax until the foreign income is repatriated to Canada, the *ITA* contains complex anti-avoidance rules to deny the tax benefits of using foreign corporations in order to protect the tax base. It is beyond the scope of this book to discuss these rules.

(b) — Statutory definition

Paragraph 250(4)(a) deems all corporations incorporated in Canada after April 26, 1965 to be resident in Canada. Corporations that were incorporated in Canada before April 27, 1965 are deemed to be resident in Canada if, at any time after April 26, 1965 they were resident in Canada under the common law test or carried on business in Canada (paragraph 250(4)(c)). This deeming rule is essentially a "citizenship" test for corporations and it reduces the importance of the central management and control test for corporations incorporated in Canada.

3.4 — Residence of trusts

Subsection 104(2) of the *ITA* provides that a trust shall be deemed to be "an individual". An individual is defined in subsection 248(1) as "a person other than a corporation".[44] It follows that a trust is a "person" and a "taxpayer" so that sections 2 and 3 are applicable, and the question whether the trust is resident in Canada is as crucial as it is for genuine individuals and for corporations: if resident in Canada, a trust will be liable to Canadian tax on its world income, and if not resident in Canada, a trust will be liable to Canadian tax only on the Canadian-source income. A trust resident in a foreign country is eligible for exemptions of Canadian tax provided by any tax treaty between Canada and that country.

The *ITA* does not supply any rules for determining the residence of a trust. As both an anti-avoidance rule and an important framework for income "owned" by Canadians but earned in international circumstances, section 94 deems an offshore trust to be a resident in certain circumstances. There is also a dearth of case law on the issue of factual residence, and the CRA has adopted the position that the residence of a trust is a question of fact depending on the circumstances of each particular case, although where the trustee or trustees reside when they manage the trust's property is, as we discuss shortly, an important determinant, applying tests that are more closely associated with the common law test of corporate residence ("central management and control").[45]

---

[44] *ITA, supra* note 1, s. 248(1) "individual".

[45] Canada Revenue Agency, Folio S6-F1-C1, "Residence of a Trust or Estate" at para. 1.1.

Until the decision in *Garron Family Trust (Trustee of) v. R.*,[46] the generally accepted legal principle was that a trust resides where the managing or controlling trustee resides. This view found implicit support in subsection 104(1) of the *ITA*, which provides that a reference to a trust shall be read as a reference to "the trustee . . . having ownership or control of the trust property".[47] It was also consistent with the *Thibodeau Family Trust v. R.* (1978) decision,[48] which held that a trust was resident in Bermuda when two of the three trustees were resident of Bermuda even though the third trustee was a Canadian resident who was a member of the family for whom the trust had been established and the chief executive officer of a corporation owned by the trust. This test of determining a trust's residence on the basis of the residence of its trustee(s) was, for many years, used by Canadians to avoid Canadian tax on trust income.

The decision in *Garron* clarified that the relevant legal principle is that "a trust resides . . . where its real business is carried on . . . which is where the central management and control of the trust actually takes place" and that the residence of the trustee does not always determine the residence of the trust.[49] In *Garron*, two trusts were created in Barbados for the purpose of avoiding Canadian tax on Canadian-source capital gains derived from the sale of shares of private Canadian companies. The pertinent facts were as follows:

- St. Michael Trust Corp. (St. Michael) was the trustee of two trusts: one for Mr. Garron and his family and another for his business partner, Mr. Dunin. The trusts were settled by an individual resident in St. Vincent in the Caribbean. The beneficiaries were residents of Canada. St. Michael was a corporation resident in Barbados.

- Under the terms of the trust indentures, Mr. Garron and Mr. Dunin and their spouses alone could replace the protector, who in turn could replace the trustee, if the trustee acted against their wishes.

- The limited role of the trustee was understood by all parties at the outset. It was made very clear that the trustee would have no decision-making role in relation to the sale of the trusts' interests in the Canadian companies, the investment of the cash proceeds received on the sale, and the making of distributions to the beneficiaries. Such decisions would be implemented by the trust upon Mr. Garron's direction.

- There was no documentary evidence that the trustee took an active role in managing the trusts. The trustee had no involvement in the affairs of the trust

---

[46] *Garron Family Trust (Trustee of) v. R.*, [2012] 3 C.T.C. 265, 2012 D.T.C. 5063 (Eng.), 2012 D.T.C. 5064 (Fr.) (S.C.C.) [*Garron*]. (The *Garron* case is also reported as *Fundy Settlement v. Canada*.)

[47] *ITA, supra* note 1, s. 104(1).

[48] *Thibodeau Family Trust v. R.* (1978), [1978] C.T.C. 539, 78 D.T.C. 6376 (Fed. T.D.).

[49] *Garron, supra* note 46 at para. 15. This is also the view of the CRA: see Folio S6-F1-C1, *supra* note 45 at paras. 1.2, 1.3.

except the execution of documents and in administrative, accounting and tax matters.

- St. Michael was an arm of an accounting firm and had no expertise in the management of trust assets.

The trusts claimed exemption from Canadian tax on the capital gains on the ground that they were residents of Barbados and eligible for a treaty exemption of such gains by virtue of Article XIV of the Canada-Barbados Treaty.[50] The Minister rejected the claims for exemption and took the position that the trusts were Canadian resident and not eligible for treaty exemption.

Justice Woods of the Tax Court decided that the test for determining residence for corporations should be applied to trusts so that a trust is resident in the country where its central management and control is exercised. In relation to the trusts, the essential responsibility for decision-making was intended from the outset to be exercised, and was in fact exercised, by Mr. Garron and Mr. Dunin, not the trustee. Therefore, she found the central management and control of the trusts was located in Canada, and the trusts were resident in Canada. The Tax Court's decision was upheld by the Federal Court of Appeal and the Supreme Court of Canada.

Justice Rothstein, who wrote for the unanimous Supreme Court, stated the following about the test for residency for a trust:

> [T]here are many similarities between a trust and corporation that would, in our view, justify application of the central management and control test in determining the residence of a trust, just as it is used in determining the residence of a corporation. Some of these similarities include
>
> (1) Both hold assets that are required to be managed;
>
> (2) Both involve the acquisition and disposition of assets;
>
> (3) Both may require the management of a business;
>
> (4) Both require banking and financial arrangements;
>
> ((5) Both may require the instruction or advice of lawyers, accountants and other advisors; and
>
> 6) Both may distribute income, corporations by way of dividends and trusts by distributions.
>
> As Woods J. noted: "The function of each is, at a basic level, the management of property" (para. 159).
>
> As with corporations, residence of a trust should be determined by the principle that a trust resides for the purposes of the Act where "its real business is carried on" (*De Beers*, p. 458), which is where the central management and control of the trust actually takes place. As indicated, the Tax Court judge found as a fact that the main beneficiaries exercised the central management and control of the trusts in Canada.

---

[50] Agreement Between Canada and Barbados for the Avoidance of Double Taxation and the Prevention of Fiscal Evasion with Respect to Taxes on Income and on Capital, 22 January 1980, E102234 — CTS 1980 No. 29 [Canada-Barbados Income Tax Agreement] at Article XIV.

She found that St. Michael had only a limited role — to provide administrative services — and little or no responsibility beyond that (paras. 189-90). Therefore, on this test, the trusts must be found to be resident in Canada. This is not to say that the residence of a trust can never be the residence of the trustee. The residence of the trustee will also be the residence of the trust where the trustee carries out the central management and control of the trust, and these duties are performed where the trustee is resident. These, however, were not the facts in this case.[51]

When making a determination as to where the central management and control of a trust actually takes place, the CRA will "look to any evidentiary support that demonstrates the exercise of decision-making powers and responsibilities over the trust".[52] Relevant factors include those mentioned in *Garron*:

- the factual role of a trustee and other persons with respect to the trust property, including any decision-making limitations imposed thereon, either directly or indirectly, by any beneficiary, settlor or other relevant person; and

- the ability of a trustee and other persons to select and instruct trust advisors with respect to the overall management of the trust.[53]

It is to be noted that the *Garron* case involved potentially serious implications for the effectiveness of the statutory residence determination in section 94 of the *ITA*. As mentioned earlier, section 94 deems certain "foreign trusts" to be Canadian residents. This is to ensure that income that is regarded as belonging to Canadian residents is not directed away from the Canadian tax jurisdiction. However, when more than one country may assert a tax claim, conflicts of residence, among other issues, are resolved by tax treaties — by resident "tie-breaker" rules that may involve the intervention of the two countries' tax authorities to decide which country has the primary taxing right. The *Garron* case also involved a conflict between the deemed Canadian residence rule in section 94 and the possible conclusion under the relevant tax treaty that the trust would not be a Canadian resident if it was managed and controlled outside Canada. As a result, section 4.3 was added to the *Income Tax Conventions Interpretation Act*[54] to provide that, in the event of such a conflict, the residence determination in section 94 will apply.

3.5 — Change in residence status

When a taxpayer changes residence during the year by either giving up or acquiring Canadian residence, there are two important tax consequences. One consequence is the part-year residence treatment under section 114 for individuals. Another consequence is the deemed disposition and reacquisition of property under section 128.1 for individuals and corporations.

---

[51] *Garron, supra* note 46 at paras. 14, 15.

[52] Folio S6-F1-C1, *supra* note 45 at para. 1.6.

[53] *Ibid.*

[54] R.S.C. 1985, c. I-4.

(a) — Part-year residents

When an individual becomes a Canadian resident or ceases to be a Canadian resident, he or she is a resident for only part of a taxation year. Because subsection 2(1) of the *ITA* taxes "every person resident in Canada at *any time* in the year" (emphasis added),[55] part-year residents are taxable on their worldwide income earned during the entire year. Such a result is obviously very harsh and potentially discourages cross-border mobility of workers. Section 114 provides relief by allowing a part-year resident to exclude from taxable income all foreign income earned during the part of the year when the taxpayer was not resident in Canada.

The sojourning rule of paragraph 250(1)(a) does not interact very happily with section 114 because paragraph 250(1)(a) deems a sojourner to have been resident in Canada "throughout" the taxation year and section 114 applies only where a person was a resident for "part" of a taxation year. The word "sojourn" implies transient or short-term residence, so paragraph 250(1)(a) does not apply to a person who becomes or ceases to be resident in Canada during the year. Therefore, a sojourner can never be a part-year resident for the purposes of section 114 and will be deemed to be a resident of Canada for the entire year.[56]

(b) — Deemed dispositions

Section 128.1 has the effect of imposing a "departure tax" on persons giving up Canadian residence. The policy is to prevent Canadian residents from leaving the country without reporting capital gains that had accrued (but not been realized) while they were residents of Canada.[57] The technique employed by section 128.1 is to deem a taxpayer who has ceased to be a resident of Canada to have disposed of most property at fair market value immediately before ceasing to be a resident and to have reacquired the same property at a cost equal to the deemed proceeds of disposition. This ensures that any accrued capital gains (or losses) are recognized for Canadian tax purposes. If adequate security is provided to the CRA, no tax is actually due until later, when the property is actually sold (and no interest is charged until then).

For people leaving Canada permanently, there is usually little doubt that residence has been lost. A difficulty can arise, however, in determining the date at which Canadian residence ceased. The date will usually be important as marking the end of the period when Canada taxes world income.[58] It is also important as marking the time at which the "departure tax" becomes applicable. In *Schujahn*, for exam-

---

[55] *ITA*, *supra* note 1, s. 2(1).

[56] As discussed at heading 3.6 — Dual residency, below, there are treaty tie-breaker rules for dual residents, which override the sojourner rule. See, e.g., *Elliott v. R.*, 2013 TCC 57, [2013] 3 C.T.C. 2021, 2013 D.T.C. 1070 (Eng.) (T.C.C. [General Procedure]).

[57] As explained in Chapter 10, the general rule is that capital gains are taxed only when realized; Chapter 10 also discusses in more detail the "deemed dispositions" of which the so-called departure tax is an example.

[58] See heading 3.5(a) — Part-year residents, above.

ple, the taxpayer was transferred by his employer to the United States on August 2, 1957. He departed Canada on that date and put his house up for sale. His wife and child remained in Canada in the house until it was sold, which was not until February 1958, and then they joined the taxpayer in the United States. Was he a resident of Canada for the whole of 1957 or only until August 2? The Exchequer Court held that he had given up residence on August 2. The continued occupation of the Canadian house by his family would normally indicate continued residence, but in this case "was explained in a satisfactory manner" as being solely for the purpose of facilitating the sale.[59]

The deemed disposition and reacquisition rules also apply to taxpayers who become Canadian residents (i.e., immigrants) during the year. These rules ensure that capital gains accrued prior to becoming a Canadian resident are tax-free in Canada, but gains accrued after the date of immigration are taxable.

3.6 — Dual residency

Dual residency refers to the situation where a person is resident in Canada and another country under the domestic laws of both countries. Typical dual residence scenarios include those of: an individual who is resident in a foreign country but who is deemed (under paragraph 250(1)(a)) to be a resident of Canada because he or she has sojourned 183 days or more in Canada; a person, such as Mr. Thomson,[60] who maintains strong residential ties with Canada and another country; and a corporation that is incorporated in Canada after April 26, 1965 but has its place of central management and control in a foreign country (or *vice versa*). In such cases, the person may be subject to worldwide taxation in both countries.

This dual residency problem is dealt with under tax treaties. Canada has concluded over 90 bilateral tax treaties with other countries in order to, primarily, prevent double taxation or international fiscal evasion. Each treaty has the force of law in Canada and overrides provisions of the *ITA* in the case of any inconsistency between the treaty and the Act. Article IV of the treaties typically provides for a tie-breaker if a taxpayer is found to be resident in both Canada and another country. The tie-breaker rule identifies only one country as the resident country by considering a number of factors: the place of permanent home, habitual abode, and nationality are taken into account; where these factors do not supply an answer, the treaties allow "the competent authorities" of the two countries to determine the question "by mutual agreement". In the case of a corporation, the tie-breaker rules generally determine the corporation's residence on the basis of the place of management and control, the place of incorporation, or by mutual agreement. Once a person is deemed to be a non-resident of Canada under the treaty tie-breaker rules, that person is also deemed under subsection 250(5) of the *ITA* to be a non-resident of Canada for the purposes of the Act.

---

[59] *Schujahn, supra* note 23.

[60] *Thomson, supra* note 9.

3.7 — Provincial residence

The foregoing discussion has addressed the question of whether a particular tax-payer is resident in Canada. However, for resident taxpayers, it is also necessary to determine in which province the taxpayer is resident. This determines liability for provincial income tax, and since rates of provincial income tax vary considerably, it is a question of some importance.

For individuals, Regulation 2601 of the *Income Tax Regulations* (the "Regulations")[61] provides that the province in which the individual resided on the last day of the taxation year is entitled to tax the individual on his or her entire income for the year. It is immaterial that the individual may have resided in another province or provinces for most of the year, and (with one exception to be noted) it is immaterial that the individual's income may have been derived from sources outside the province.[62] Regulation 2601 makes an exception for an individual who has income from a business with a permanent establishment outside the province of last-day residence. In that case, the income attributable to the business is deemed to have been earned in the province or country where the permanent establishment is located.[63]

Where an individual has permanent establishments in more than one province or country, Regulation 2603 supplies the rule for apportioning the income between jurisdictions.

For corporations, Regulation 402 allocates the income to the province in which the corporation had a permanent establishment in the taxation year. Where a corporation has permanent establishments in more than one province or country, rules similar to those for the business income of individuals enable the income to be apportioned between the jurisdictions.[64]

The Regulations are silent on trusts, but since a trust is deemed by subsection 104(2) to be an individual, the rules for individuals would be applicable.

---

[61] C.R.C., c. 945.

[62] The constitutionality of a province taxing its residents in respect of income earned outside the province was upheld in *Kerr v. Supt. of Income Tax*, [1942] S.C.R. 435 (S.C.C.); and *Canadian Pacific Railway v. Manitoba (Treasurer)*, [1953] 4 D.L.R. 233 (Man. Q.B.).

[63] Subsection 120(1) of the *ITA* provides that income of an individual that escapes provincial tax (e.g., income from a business with a permanent establishment outside Canada) is subject to a federal surtax of 48 per cent of the appropriate portion of the federal tax payable by the individual. In other words, the federal government takes up the tax room left open by the absence of provincial tax.

[64] Various special kinds of corporations are subjected to special rules by regs. 403–414.

4
INCOME

4.1 — Section 3

(a) — Defining the tax base

What is income? For the purpose of the *Income Tax Act* (the "*ITA*"),[1] the short answer is: whatever section 3 is interpreted to say that it is. Section 3 reads:

3. The income of a taxpayer for a taxation year for the purposes of this Part is the taxpayer's income for the year determined by the following rules:

(a) determine the total of all amounts each of which is the taxpayer's income for the year (other than a taxable capital gain from the disposition of a property) from a source inside or outside Canada, including, without restricting the generality of the foregoing, the taxpayer's income for the year from each office, employment, business and property,

(b) determine the amount, if any, by which

(i) the total of

(A) all of the taxpayer's taxable capital gains for the year from dispositions of property other than listed personal property, and

(B) the taxpayer's taxable net gain for the year from dispositions of listed personal property,

exceeds

(ii) the amount, if any, by which the taxpayer's allowable capital losses for the year from dispositions of property other than listed personal property exceed the taxpayer's allowable business investment losses for the year,

(c) determine the amount, if any, by which the total determined under paragraph (a) plus the amount determined under paragraph (b) exceeds the total of the deductions permitted by subdivision e in computing the taxpayer's income for the year (except to the extent that those deductions, if any, have been taken into account in determining the total referred to in paragraph (a)), and

---

[1] R.S.C. 1985 (5th Supp.), c. 1 [*ITA*].

(d) determine the amount, if any, by which the amount determined under paragraph (c) exceeds the total of all amounts each of which is the taxpayer's loss for the year from an office, employment, business or property or the taxpayer's allowable business investment loss for the year,

and for the purposes of this part,

(e) where an amount is determined under paragraph (d) for the year in respect of the taxpayer, the taxpayer's income for the year is the amount so determined, and

(f) in any other case, the taxpayer shall be deemed to have income for the year in an amount equal to zero.

Section 3 does not actually define the meaning of income.[2] By leaving the term "income" undefined, the *ITA* defers to the ordinary meaning of this term and case law principles. The ordinary meaning of "income" may emerge from a simple syllabic examination of the word. "In" and "come" suggest that it is "something" arising from or flowing out of a "place" that remains intact. As something separate from that "place" it becomes independently at the disposal of the "recipient" who "receives" it. Conceptually, this is fine. But a system for sustaining the fiscal needs of a country needs to be systematic. The *ITA* does not, and cannot, leave the foundational tax base question to "hang" in the uncertainty of ordinary meaning and case law. Section 3 and the entire Division B of Part I provide rules to anchor the determination of income for purposes of the Act.

Paragraph 3(a) picks up most or all of the common types of income sources (i.e., office, employment, business and property). These sources produce income known as salaries, wages, business profits and income from investments, such as dividends, interest, rent and royalties. Paragraph 3(a) also uses the all-embracing language that income is the "total" income and "source" is not limited to those enumerated, nor to Canadian sources. Paragraph 3(b) includes taxable capital gains (net of allowable capital losses) in income. Paragraphs 3(c) and (d) permit deductions for amounts permitted by the *ITA* on a social policy basis and for current-year losses from office, employment, business and property.

Section 3 requires income from all sources to be aggregated each year. Income from each source must be determined separately pursuant to section 4. Common expenses incurred in respect of several sources must be allocated to each source on a reasonable basis. Other provisions in Division B provide more details for the computation of income from each source mentioned in paragraph 3(a), capital gains or losses, as well as other income and subdivision e deductions.

---

[2] See, e.g., *Global Equity Fund Ltd. v. R.* (2012), [2013] 1 C.T.C. 135, 2013 D.T.C. 5007 (Eng.) (F.C.A.); leave to appeal refused 2013 CarswellNat 932, 2013 CarswellNat 933 (S.C.C.) at para. 59 [(C.A.)].

(b) — Purpose and rationale

(i) — Comprehensive income and ability to pay

The purpose of section 3 is grounded in the words of this provision and can be gleaned from its context. The inherent notions expressed in legislative words, underlying the construction of the "system", do not necessarily have self-evident meanings. Like the use of words generally, their meanings are influenced by the context in which they arise, to be used as threads in the legislative fabric in which they are woven to achieve their fiscal and legislative purpose.

The main purpose is to determine the scope of "income". The use of the word "is" rather than "includes" in section 3 suggests an intention to make the definition exclusive of any other meaning that the term "income" might bear. The comprehensive nature of the provision would seem to indicate that "it was designed to embrace all receipts that can ordinarily be regarded as of the nature of revenue and income".[3] The use of the phrase "without restricting the generality of the foregoing" indicates the plain and unmistakable intent of Parliament that the numerated sources are not designed to be exhaustive. The forms that commercial dealings and other income-earning activities can take in the changing world, and the "labels" that can be assigned to income from different sources, are simply too various for any listing to fully comprehend! Paragraph 3(a) uses the phrase to supplement the enumeration by including any unenumerated items that can properly be understood as "income".

Paragraph 3(a) originates from subsection 3(1) of the *Income War Tax Act, 1917*,[4] which states:

> 3. (1) For the purposes of the Act, "income" means the annual net profit or gain or gratuity, whether . . . as being wages, salary . . . or as being profits from a trade or commercial or financial or other business or calling . . . and shall include the interest, dividends or profits from . . . investment, and . . . also the annual profit or gain from any other source . . .[5]

The above provision was influenced by the United States *Revenue Act of 1913*, which defines "gross income" to mean "all income from whatever source derived".[6] The notion of "source" was not used to exclude income from tax. Like the

---

[3] H.A.W. Plaxton, *The Law Relating to Income Tax and Excess Profits Tax of the Dominion of Canada*, 2nd ed. (Toronto: Carswell, 1947) at 29, commenting on the predecessor of paragraph 3(a).

[4] S.C. 1917, c. 28 [*IWTA 1917*].

[5] *Ibid.*, s. 3(1).

[6] The United States *Revenue Act of 1913* (ch. 16, 38 Stat. 114, October 3, 1913), provided in Section II.B. that:

> . . . subject only to such exemptions and deductions as are hereinafter allowed, the net income of a taxable person shall include gains, profits, and income derived from salaries, wages, or compensation for personal service of whatever kind and in whatever form paid, or from professions, vocations, businesses, trade, commerce, or

United States, the Canadian definition of income is the aggregate total of amounts from all sources. It is the "total" income that forms the tax base, taxable at the stipulated rates. This is different from the U.K. tax law which treats income on a "schedular" basis by assigning different rates to different sources of income.[7]

In light of the reasons for introducing income tax in Canada in 1917, it made sense to measure income comprehensively in order to ascertain the taxpayer's ability for sharing the burden of financing the nation and the war efforts. Subsequent reforms, especially those that resulted from the *Carter Report*,[8] continued the comprehensive nature of section 3 and expanded it to include capital gains.

Paragraph 3(b) was added when the Act was amended in 1971.[9] It broadens the scope of income by including taxable capital gains (net of allowable capital losses). As explained in more detail below and in Chapter 10, capital gains are not considered to be "income from a source", but as gains realized on the disposition of a source of income (e.g., a capital property, such as real property or shares).

Ultimately, section 3 provides the legislative basis for determining income, which is a proxy for measuring a taxpayer's "ability to pay". Section 3 income also serves as a baseline for determining "means-tested" tax credits for individuals, including refundable tax credits, such as the Canada child benefit, which are better characterized as tax-free fiscal transfer payments.[10]

(ii) — Net income

Section 3 does not explicitly say that income is net income. The notion that income is net of deductions is borne out by the history of the provision.[11] Section 3 of the *Income War Tax Act, 1917* stated that income "means the annual net profit or gain".[12] The word "net" stands out as affirming the ordinary meaning of profit and

---

sales, or dealings in property, whether real or personal, growing out of the ownership or use of or interest in real or personal property, also from interest, rent, dividends, securities, or the transaction of any lawful business carried on for gain or profit, or gains or profits and income derived from any source whatever . . .

[7] See C. Campbell & R. Raizenne, "The 1917 Income War Tax Act: Origins and Enactment" in J. Li, J.S. Wilkie & L. Chapman, eds., *Income Tax at 100 Years: Essays and Reflections on the Centennial of the Income War Tax Act* (Toronto: Canadian Tax Foundation) [forthcoming in 2017] at 2:1.

[8] Canada, *Report of the Royal Commission on Taxation* (Ottawa: Queen's Printer, 1966) (Chairman: Kenneth Le M. *Carter) [Carter Report]*. See Chapter 2 at heading 2.2(c) — Tax reform of 1971 and the Carter Report, and heading 4.2(c) — Carter Commission's 'comprehensive tax base', below.

[9] S.C. 1970-71-72, c. 63 (Bill C-259, which came into force on January 1, 1972).

[10] *ITA, supra* note 1, ss. 122.6–122.63, discussed in Chapter 12 at heading 12.5(h)(iv) — Canada child benefit.

[11] *Ludco Enterprises Ltd. v. Canada* (2001), [2002] 1 C.T.C. 95, 2001 D.T.C. 5505 (Eng.), 2001 D.T.C. 5518 (Fr.) (S.C.C.) at para. 57.

[12] *IWTA 1917, supra* note 4, s. 3(1).

gain established by the English and Canadian courts.[13] The words "net profit and gain" were replaced with "income" in section 3 of the *Income Tax Act* of 1948.[14] This change in wording was not intended to overrule the common law principle that income means net income,[15] as other sections of the *ITA* (such as section 9) affirm that income is a net concept.

To recognize the fact that a taxpayer may have multiple sources of income and that some sources may result in a loss, the *ITA* allows losses to offset income. So, the total income under section 3 is net of current-year losses. Allowable capital losses offset taxable capital gains; current-year losses from the enumerated sources offset income from a source as well as taxable capital gains.

The aggregate total of these amounts reflects the increase in a taxpayer's economic income realized in a year. But, it is not the tax base. It is reduced by special deductions permitted in subdivision e of Division B.[16] These deductions are policy-based, and include the deductions for RRSP contributions under section 60, moving expenses under section 62, and child care expenses under section 63.

(iii) — Realization and attribution of income

Section 3 refers to "the taxpayer's income for the year", requiring income be computed annually in respect of each taxpayer. However, section 3 does not *per se* shed any light on the annual accounting requirement or income attribution requirement. It creates gateways to specific rules in the rest of Division B, where more clarity is provided.

The annual accounting and timing question is a recurrent and fundamental aspect of income taxation. It is about "when" income is required to be reported. On the basis of pertinent provisions in the *ITA* and case law principles, it can be said that the Act requires income to be "realized" to be taxable. The notion of realization is expressed by using concepts such as "received" or "receivable". For example, wages and salary are taxable when they are received (subsection 5(1))[17] and business revenues and their resulting net profit are recognized when the revenues are "receiva-

---

[13] Francis E. LaBrie, *The Meaning of Income in the Law of Income Tax* (Toronto: University of Toronto Press, 1953) at 27.

[14] S.C. 1948, c. 52.

[15] This principle is well-entrenched in Canadian jurisprudence. See, e.g., *Shaw v. Minister of National Revenue* (1939), [1938-39] C.T.C. 346 (S.C.C.) at 348; *Lumbers v. Minister of National Revenue*, [1944] C.T.C. 67 (S.C.C.) at 70; *Irwin v. Minister of National Revenue*, [1964] S.C.R. 662, [1964] C.T.C. 362, 64 D.T.C. 5227 (S.C.C.); *Associated Investors of Canada Ltd. v. Minister of National Revenue*, [1967] C.T.C. 138, 67 D.T.C. 5096 (Can. Ex. Ct.); *Symes v. R.* (1993), [1994] 1 C.T.C. 40, 94 D.T.C. 6001 (S.C.C.); and *Canderel Ltd. v. R.*, [1998] 2 C.T.C. 35, 98 D.T.C. 6100 (S.C.C.).

[16] Because s. 4(2) specifically denies the deduction of items in subdivision e in determining income from a particular source, these items can only be claimed as subdivision e "other deductions".

[17] See Chapter 5.

ble", which is generally when the taxpayer has the legal right to receive payments (section 9).[18] The realization requirement was more explicit in subsection 3(1) of the *Income War Tax Act, 1917*, which uses words such as annual net profit or gain "whether ascertained and capable of computation" and "directly or indirectly received by a person".[19] If an amount is not ascertainable in law, it does not have the quality of income for tax purposes. The realization principle is more clearly expressed by the *ITA* in respect of capital gains. Appreciation in value of property is not taxable until it is realized by way of sales or other forms of disposition.[20]

Attributing income and loss to a specific taxpayer is critical because the *ITA* treats each person as a tax unit and generally applies graduated tax rates to the income of a human being and flat tax rates to the income of corporations and trusts. The question of "whose income is it", though, is not answered by section 3 or the Act in general. The *ITA* contains some anti-income shifting rules,[21] but generally leaves the question to be settled under private law.

4.2 — Concept of income

(a) — General meaning

(i) — "Income"

Students of tax law may be surprised to find that there is no universally accepted definition of "income" for income tax purposes. Laypersons may find it hard to believe that there are major problems in defining income. They tend to think in terms of cash wages and salaries, and other types of money that "come in". Other items like interest and dividends are also easily identified as income. These are all clearly income for tax purposes. However, there is a grey area, which is relatively small but has been the focus of judicial attention since the beginning of the income tax system.[22] The elusive nature of income makes it extremely difficult to formulate a definition that catches "the many shapes which income may assume and the illimitable variety of circumstances in which it may be derived".[23]

The concept of "income" is, as noted already, fundamental to the scheme of the *ITA*. Technically, it determines the tax base. Whether an item or receipt constitutes income determines whether it is subject to tax. If a receipt does not have the attributes of income, it is not taxable. In addition, since the *ITA* is used as a policy instru-

---

[18] See Chapters 6 and 8.

[19] *IWTA 1917, supra* note 4, s. 3(1).

[20] See Chapter 10.

[21] See Chapter 13.

[22] There is a vast body of case law distinguishing between capital and income, capital gains and business income, and windfall gains and income gains. See Chapter 7 at heading 7.2 — Characterization of incoming amounts and Chapter 10 at heading 10.2 — Capital gain.

[23] J.P. Hannan & A. Farnsworth, *The Principles of Income Taxation* (London: Stevens & Sons, 1952) at 3.

ment in the redistribution of income, the concept of income has significant policy implications. The manner in which income is defined makes a difference in designing tax expenditure provisions aimed at income redistribution. For example, all refundable tax credits that are designed to deliver (tax-free) social assistance through the tax system to low-income earners are based on the income of the taxpayer and (if one exists) the taxpayer's spouse. Even several non-refundable credits are tested on the basis of the income of a taxpayer or the taxpayer's dependants.

Ideally, income should reflect a taxpayer's "ability to pay". Given that tax equity is one of the most important objectives of income taxation, the definition of income is inherently linked to tax equity. Therefore, the inquiry into the meaning of income goes well beyond technical issues and involves fundamental value judgments about tax equity. Because section 3 refers to "income from a source", the case law has predominantly focused on the "source" notion. Because the economic concept of income is more helpful in understanding the nature of income, it has been more influential when changes are made to the *ITA*. Both concepts are discussed below.

(ii) — Legal meaning

Canadian courts recognize that "the notion of what receipts constitute income for purposes of taxation is central to the workings of the Act".[24] The word "income" "had to be given its ordinary meaning, bearing in mind the distinction between capital and income, and the ordinary concepts and usages of mankind".[25] Robertson J. states in *Bellingham v. R.* (1996):

> Standing alone the term income is susceptible to widely diverging interpretations. Narrowly construed, income may be defined to include only those amounts received by taxpayers on a recurring basis. Broadly construed, income may be defined so as to capture all accretions to wealth. Canadian taxpayers are more likely to embrace the former definition. The latter approach reflects the economist's concern for achieving horizontal and vertical equity in a taxation system. Such a concern translates into a broad understanding of what receipt items should be included in income. This perspective is reflected in the *Report of the Carter Commission.*[26]

The courts have typically adopted the narrower construction. Generally speaking, an economic gain is not income for tax purposes if it is on capital account or is a capital receipt, is not realized, or is not coming from a "source".

(iii) — Income versus capital

A receipt of money by a taxpayer for his or her own benefit is generally considered either as a receipt of a capital nature or of an income nature. The distinction be-

---

[24] *Bellingham v. R.* (1995), [1996] 1 C.T.C. 187, 96 D.T.C. 6075 (Fed. C.A.) [*Bellingham* cited to C.T.C.] at para. 24.

[25] *Curran v. Minister of National Revenue*, [1959] C.T.C. 416, 59 D.T.C. 1247 (S.C.C.) [*Curran*].

[26] *Bellingham, supra* note 24 at para. 24.

tween income and capital can be analogized as the fruit and the tree. Income is fruit only and never the tree.[27]

The notion of "capital" is akin to a fund of "after-tax dollars". A taxpayer's savings out of after-tax salary, business profits, etc. are capital. So are his or her windfall gains, inheritances, or other amounts received tax-free. Capital may be in the form of cash, personal assets, real property or investments. There is a rich body of case law on the distinction between capital and income.[28] In making the distinction, the courts have held that payments for the surrender of a potential source of profit are capital receipts.[29]

(b) — Economic concept

(i) — Haig-Simons theory

When economists put their minds to the definition of income for tax purposes, they found the source theory underlying section 3 to be "narrow", "artificial", "eccentric", and "little less than absurd",[30] as it does not fully measure a taxpayer's ability to pay tax. Robert Murray Haig, an American economist writing in 1921, proposed a more comprehensive definition of income. Haig stated that, for tax purposes, the definition of income should be "the money value of the net accretion to one's economic power between two points of time".[31] Under this definition, any accretion to economic power in the course of a taxation year, regardless of its source, would count as income for the year.

In 1938, Henry C. Simons, another American economist, proposed a more elaborate version of Haig's definition. Simons stated: "Personal income may be defined as the algebraic sum of (1) the market value of rights exercised in consumption and (2) the change in the value of the store of property rights between the beginning and the end of the period in question".[32] This definition was fundamentally the same as Haig's, but Simons' definition explicitly took account of consumption,

---

[27] *Stratton's Independence v. Howbert*, 231 U.S. 399 (1913); and *Ryall v. Hoare*, [1923] 2 K.B. 447, 8 T.C. 521 (K.B.). These cases have been accepted by Canadian courts. Another Canadian case on this issue is *R. v. Fortino* (1999), [2000] 1 C.T.C. 349, 2000 D.T.C. 6060 (Fed. C.A.) [*Fortino*], in which payments made under non-competition agreements were held to constitute capital receipts not taxable under s. 3. As discussed in notes 63–65 and accompanying text, *infra*, the *ITA* now taxes such payments under s. 56.4.

[28] See Chapter 7 at heading 7.2 — Characterization of incoming amounts and Chapter 10 at heading 10.2 — Capital gain.

[29] *Fortino, supra* note 27.

[30] Robert M. Haig, "The Concept of Income — Economic and Legal Aspects" in Robert M. Haig, ed., *The Federal Income Tax* (New York: Columbia University Press, 1921) at 1.

[31] *Ibid.* at 7.

[32] Henry C. Simons, *Personal Income Taxation* (Chicago: University of Chicago Press, 1938) at 50.

treating the value of the goods and services consumed by the taxpayer during the year as part of the taxpayer's accretion to wealth for that year.

According to the Haig-Simons theory, income equals consumption plus gain in net worth over a taxation year. It does not matter whether the gain in net worth consists of periodic payments from a source (such as salary, wages, business income or property income), profits from the sale of property (capital gains), transfers from other people (such as gifts, inheritances or gambling winnings), the direct products of one's own labour (such as homegrown fruit and vegetables or home renovation), or the direct benefits of one's own property (such as the right to occupy one's own home). Nor does it matter whether the gain in net worth is expected or unexpected, regular or irregular, deliberate or accidental, realized or accrued, in cash or in kind. All gains should be taken into account in measuring a taxpayer's income for tax purposes.

(ii) — Implications for tax law

The Haig-Simons definition of income has been used by analysts as a basis for testing the equity of the income tax. However, this definition has not been enacted into law in any country in the world. In defining income for tax purposes, the rules must not only provide a measure of an individual's ability to pay, they must also be sufficiently practical to be administered by the government. The Haig-Simons definition is difficult to implement. It assumes that the accretion in wealth can be quantified in terms of market prices or at least objectively valued. In the case of unrealized gains and non-monetary benefits, this presents a huge valuation task, not to mention the problem of detection. It is more convenient to tax gains on realization than on accrual. In addition, there is the liquidity issue. Taxpayers might have to sell the assets producing their income in order to pay their taxes, notwithstanding their increase in wealth. Finally, there may be overriding social and political reasons for not taxing certain economic benefits, such as gifts, damages for pain and suffering, or the value of unpaid housework, even if they constitute gains.

Even though section 3 of the *ITA* does not codify the economic concept of income, this does not mean that the concept has no influence on the Act. To the contrary, the tax base has been broadened over the past decades towards the economic notion of income. For example, section 6 (employment benefits), section 12 (inclusions in computing business and property income) and section 56 (other income) have "grown" to specifically list amounts as taxable because they bring about economic advantages or material acquisitions in the nature of income. Paragraph 3(b) was added in 1917 to include taxable capital gains. Moreover, the *ITA* has added rules that limit the deduction of certain business expenses that have elements of personal pleasure or discretion, such as entertainment expenses (section 67.1) and home office expenses (subsection 18(12)).[33]

---

[33] See Chapter 8 at heading 8.5 — Business expenses subject to statutory limitations.

(c) — Carter Commission's "comprehensive tax base"

(i) — Comprehensive tax base

The Carter Commission, which was much influenced by Haig and Simons, restated the Haig-Simons theory in these terms:

> The comprehensive tax base has been defined as the sum of the market value of goods and services consumed or given away in the taxation year by the tax unit [the taxpayer], plus the annual change in the market value of the assets held by the unit.[34]

The Carter Commission argued that the definition of income should be suited to the purpose for which the definition was to be used. If the definition was to be the basis of an equitable tax system, then it should be a reasonably comprehensive measure of the annual increase in a taxpayer's ability to pay tax. The traditional, source-based concept of income, however apt to other purposes (such as trust accounting), was not a satisfactory measure of the annual increase in a taxpayer's ability to pay tax, because it excluded from income so many accretions to wealth. In principle, income should include every accretion to wealth, regardless of its source, because every accretion to wealth increases the recipient's ability to pay tax. This theory, which became the Commission's guiding principle, was aptly described as "a buck is a buck is a buck".

The Carter Commission proposed that the traditional definition of income be replaced by a "comprehensive tax base", a concept that drew heavily on the Haig-Simons theory but was not quite as comprehensive as the pure Haig-Simons definition. The Carter Commission recognized that many of the annual valuations required by the Haig-Simons theory were impractical. Accordingly, the Commission modified the definition so that, for the most part, the additions to the tax base were confined to items that could readily be measured in dollars, such as realized capital gains, gifts, inheritances and windfalls.

(ii) — Taxation of capital gains

The most important (and perhaps the least radical) new element of the Carter Commission's comprehensive tax base, which was excluded from income under the previous regimes, was capital gains. The argument for the inclusion of capital gains as income is, of course, that they increase the wealth of the recipient, and hence the ability to pay, just as surely as income from employment, business or property does.

Moreover, the exclusion of capital gains seriously undermined the progressivity of the system. In both the United States, where capital gains have been taxed for a long time, and Canada, where capital gains have been taxed since 1972, capital gains comprise a very small proportion of the income reported by low-income individuals, and a very large proportion of the income reported by high-income individuals. The *Carter Report* displayed figures that showed that, in the United States in

---

[34] *Carter Report, supra* note 8, vol. 3 at 39.

1963, when the percentage of capital gains to all other income reported by all individuals was 4 per cent, for individuals earning between $100,000 and $200,000 the relevant percentage was 48 per cent, and for individuals earning in excess of $200,000 the relevant percentage was 128 per cent.[35] The Carter Commission concluded that, in Canada, taxes were "probably a decreasing proportion of comprehensive income for upper income individuals and families", despite the fact that marginal rates at the time rose to 80 per cent.[36] The Commission concluded that the adoption of the comprehensive tax base (which, of course, would include gifts, inheritances and windfalls as well as capital gains) would allow a lowering of tax rates at all levels and a drastic lowering of rates at the upper levels. Its recommendation was to lower the top marginal rate from its level of 80 per cent all the way down to 50 per cent. It argued that, after this drastic lowering of rates, the tax system would not only yield the same revenue as before, but would be more progressive than before.

The Carter Commission departed from the pure Haig-Simons theory in recommending against the inclusion of unrealized (or accrued) capital gains. The Commission recognized "that income arises where there is an increase in economic power, and that economic power increases when the market value of property increases".[37] The Commission also recognized that it was inequitable to tax gains only when realized "in that taxpayers who retain investments which have appreciated in value are, in effect, allowed a tax-free investment of the accumulated gains that are built up free of tax, while others, who turn over their investments, are denied this privilege".[38] Nevertheless, with some hesitation, the Commission concluded that the administrative problems involved in taxing accrued gains were too difficult, and accordingly recommended that capital gains be taxed only when realized. However, in order to limit the period for which recognition of gains could be postponed, the Commission recommended that there should be a "deemed disposition" of capital property on death, on the making of a gift and on giving up Canadian residence, even though no gain would actually be realized on those occasions.

The government was initially receptive to the Carter Commission's proposal that realized capital gains be included in full in income. The government's White Paper that followed the *Carter Report* mainly accepted the proposal,[39] but the government altered its position during the period of debate on its White Paper. The final decision, embodied in the 1971 Act, was to tax gains only on a realization basis (except for the Carter Commission's deemed dispositions, which were accepted), and to include only one-half of realized gains in income. Thus, the Carter Commis-

---

[35] *Ibid.* at 332.

[36] *Ibid.*, vol. 2 at 261.

[37] *Ibid.*, vol. 3 at 378.

[38] *Ibid.* at 379.

[39] E.J. Benson, *Proposals for Tax Reform* (Ottawa: Queen's Printer, 1969) at 40. (An exception was to be made for publicly-traded Canadian corporate securities, the gains from which were to be only one-half included.)

sion did succeed in adding capital gains to the tax base, albeit on a preferential basis.

4.3 — Income from a "source"

(a) — Source theory

The source theory has been influential in Canadian income tax law. The theory is that income is a yield from a productive source. Section 3 of the *ITA* codifies this theory by stating that only income from a source is included in computing a taxpayer's income under paragraph 3(a), and that only a loss from a source is deductible under paragraph 3(d).

It has been suggested that the source theory of income arose in the U.K. at a time when the economy was primarily agricultural and it was natural to think of income in terms of the fruit and tree.[40] Another factor was probably the distinction between capital and income that the courts had developed for the law of trusts, where it was necessary to distinguish between the rights of a life tenant (or income beneficiary) and those of a remainderman (or capital beneficiary).[41] The idea that income was the yield from a productive source, and that the source itself was capital, became part of the Anglo-Canadian way of thinking about income. Accordingly, the Income Tax statutes of the U.K. and Canada, while taxing income from employment, business or property, did not at first attempt to tax capital gains, gifts, inheritances or windfalls, and many other miscellaneous receipts that were not considered to have a source.

As noted earlier, however, section 3 of the *ITA* was originally created to be different from the U.K.'s schedular system of income taxation, under which the source of income was critical. The drafters of the *Income War Tax Act, 1917* deliberately adopted the American approach to aggregating income from all sources, and using the enumerated sources as illustrations. They adopted the word "source" without borrowing the U.K. schedular system of taxation. As such, the meaning of "source" should be consistent with the legislative context in Canada. "Unthinking reliance on U.K. case law" is a "potential detriment to the proper articulation of Canadian tax principles.[42]

(b) — Characteristics of source

In the case law, adjectives, such as "real", "productive", or "profitable" have all been used to describe or qualify the word "source". In *Nathan v. Federal Commissioner of Taxation (N.S. Wales)* (1918), Isaacs J. stated that "source" means "something which a practical man would regard as a real source of income".[43] In *R.*

---

[40] *Carter Report, supra* note 8, vol. 3 at 64–65.

[41] *Ibid.* at 65.

[42] Campbell & Raizenne, *supra* note 7.

[43] *Nathan v. Federal Commissioner of Taxation (N.S. Wales)* (1918), 25 C.L.R. 183 (Aust. H.C.) at 189. These words were quoted in *Robertson v. M.N.R.*, [1954] C.T.C. 110, 54

v. Cranswick (1982), LeDain J. stated that "income from a source will be that which is typically earned by it or which typically flows from it as the expected return".[44] In *Bellingham*, Robertson J. held that income from a source refers to a productive source (i.e., a source that is capable of producing income).[45] In *Stewart v. R.* (2002), Iacobucci and Bastarache JJ. held that "whether a taxpayer has a source of income from a particular activity is determined by considering whether the taxpayer intends to carry on the activity for profit, and whether there is evidence to support that intention".[46]

Based on the case law, an income source seems to have one or more of the following characteristics:

- It recurs on a periodic basis;[47]

- It involves organized effort, activity, or pursuit on the part of the taxpayer;

- It involves a marketplace exchange;

- It gives rise to an enforceable claim to the payment by the taxpayer; and

- In the case of a business or property source, there is a pursuit of profit.

Ultimately, the source of income is capital (represented by property), labour (efforts and services of employees), or a combination of both (business). Investment income, wages and salaries, and business income are, thus, typical categories of income. Personal goodwill, pain and suffering, good fortune, a hobby, or a windfall do not generally constitute sources of income.[48] Drawing the line between these two categories is difficult in many cases.

(c) — Enumerated sources

Paragraph 3(a) identifies four traditional sources of income: office, employment, business and property. The characterization of each of these sources is discussed in subsequent chapters of this book. It is worthwhile to note at this stage that these four sources are not exhaustive, leaving much room for judicial interpretation.

D.T.C. 1062 (Can. Ex. Ct.) at 120–22 [C.T.C.]; *James v. M.N.R.*, [1973] C.T.C. 457, 73 D.T.C. 5333 (Fed. T.D.) at 461–63 [C.T.C.].

[44] *R. v. Cranswick* (1982), [1982] C.T.C. 69, 82 D.T.C. 6073 (Fed. C.A.); leave to appeal refused (1982), 42 N.R. 355 (S.C.C.) at para. 15 [(Fed. C.A.)].

[45] *Bellingham, supra* note 24 at 198.

[46] *Stewart v. R.* (2002), [2002] 3 C.T.C. 439, 2002 D.T.C. 6969 (Eng.), 2002 D.T.C. 6983 (S.C.C.) at para. 61.

[47] This has been considered an important factor in holding that personal gifts and windfalls are not income from a source.

[48] See headings 4.4(c) — Windfalls and 4.4(d) — Damages and settlements, below, for a detailed discussion of these two topics.

In determining whether a receipt has a source, the courts tend to first fit the receipt into one of the enumerated sources before deciding that the receipt is a non-taxable gift or a windfall gain. Some examples include the following:

- The source of gains from gambling activities is the business of gambling in some cases.[49]

- The source of gifts received by a taxpayer in respect of employment is employment.[50]

- The source of payments in consideration of the loss of pension rights, chances for advancement, and opportunities for re-employment is employment.[51]

- The source of money stolen by a lawyer from his clients' trust accounts is business.[52]

- The source of fraudulently acquired funds from a company in which the tax-payer was an officer or employee is employment.[53]

- The source of damages and settlements may have a source from an enumer-ated source under the "surrogatum" principle.[54]

- The source of payments from a fraudulent Ponzi scheme is property (invest-ments) even though the promoter used other people's money to pay the taxpayer.[55]

(d) — Unenumerated sources

Because "income from a source" is undefined in the *ITA*, the concept must be given its ordinary meaning. Judicial interpretation of this concept has been very restric-tive. The courts have been reluctant in finding that receipts with the characteristics of income are taxable where the source of the payment is not enumerated. For ex-ample, in *Canada v. Fries* (1990), the Supreme Court of Canada held that it was not satisfied that strike pay was "income . . . from a source" within the meaning of

---

[49] See *Graham v. Green (Inspector of Taxes)*, [1925] 2 K.B. 37, 9 T.C. 309 (Eng. K.B.); and *M.N.R. v. Walker*, [1951] C.T.C. 334, 52 D.T.C. 1001 (Can. Ex. Ct.).

[50] See Chapter 5 at heading 5.5 — Benefits.

[51] *Curran, supra* note 25.

[52] *Buckman v. M.N.R.*, [1991] 2 C.T.C. 2608, 91 D.T.C. 1249 (T.C.C.) [*Buckman*].

[53] *R. v. Poynton*, [1972] C.T.C. 411, 72 D.T.C. 6329 (Ont. C.A.) [*Poynton*].

[54] Under the "surrogatum" principle, the tax consequences of a damage or settlement pay-ment depend on the tax treatment of the item for which the payment is intended to substitute. The surrogatum principle is discussed in detail at heading 4.4(d)(i) — The "surrogatum" principle, below.

[55] *Johnson v. R.*, 2012 FCA 253, [2013] 1 C.T.C. 10, 2013 D.T.C. 5004 (Eng.) (F.C.A.); leave to appeal refused 2013 CarswellNat 633 (S.C.C.).

section 3; and "the benefit of the doubt" should go to the taxpayers.[56] In a surprisingly brief judgment on an issue of fundamental importance, the Court did not analyze whether strike pay had the character of income and the fact that a union had an obligation to make payments to its members on strike.

In *Schwartz v. Canada* (1996),[57] the Supreme Court of Canada held that a payment of damages for breach of contract was not taxable. The contract was a contract of employment, which the prospective employer had rescinded before the prospective employee had actually started work. The prospective employer paid the prospective employee $360,000 as damages for the breach of contract. The Court found that the sum was not a "retiring allowance" within the meaning of subsection 56(1) because the statutory definition of a "retiring allowance" calls for a "loss" of employment and, since the employment had never commenced, it had not been lost. More importantly, the Court also held that the payment was not income from the enumerated source of employment, because it was not possible to determine what portion of the damages related to foregone income under the contract of employment and what portion related to other factors. Following the line of cases that held that payments for wrongful dismissal were tax-free,[58] the Court refused to treat paragraph 3(a) as a general provision of the *ITA* that captured the amount as income from an unenumerated source.

Although the payment in *Schwartz* was held to be a non-taxable windfall, La Forest J. for the majority affirmed the conventional view that the sources specifically mentioned in paragraph 3(a), namely office, employment, business and property, were not the only sources of income. He also referred with approval to the proposition that all accretions to wealth "regardless of source" should be included in the tax base in order to measure a taxpayer's ability to pay.[59] However, Major J., in a separate concurring opinion, took issue with this conventional view, stating that "a literal adoption of this position would arguably constitute a dramatic departure from established tax jurisprudence"[60] and should be limited to issues of "fundamental importance".[61] He even doubted whether there were any unenumerated sources of income, stating: "In 1966, the Carter Commission recommended the extension of taxation to all sources of income and all accretions to purchasing power, but its recommendations were not implemented by Parliament and it is hardly the role of the judiciary to do so."[62]

---

[56] *Canada v. Fries* (1990), [1990] 2 C.T.C. 439, 90 D.T.C. 6662 (S.C.C.).

[57] *Schwartz v. Canada*, [1996] 1 C.T.C. 303, 96 D.T.C. 6103 (S.C.C.); reversing [1994] 2 C.T.C. 99, 94 D.T.C. 6249 (Fed. C.A.) [*Schwartz*].

[58] Ironically these were the cases that caused the *ITA* to be amended to include payments for wrongful dismissal in income as "retiring allowances" under s. 56(1). *Schwartz, ibid.*, is also discussed in Chapter 11 at heading 11.5(a) — Retiring allowance.

[59] *Schwartz, supra* note 57 at 327–328 [C.T.C. (S.C.C.)].

[60] *Ibid.* at 334.

[61] *Ibid.* at 336.

[62] *Ibid.* at 334–336.

With respect, Major J.'s view is wrong as a matter of interpretation of section 3, which clearly leaves open the possibility of non-specified sources of income. It is also questionable in terms of the policy objectives of income tax. His approach permits some individuals to receive substantial additions to their economic power, repeatedly or occasionally, without paying tax as they would if the additions came from an enumerated source. Accordingly, the redistributive power of the income tax is perhaps reduced, and questions of its equity and neutrality are raised, and substantial revenue may be foregone. However, Major J. may be right as a matter of practical reality; based on past jurisprudence, the courts are very reluctant indeed to impose tax on receipts that are not specifically covered by the *ITA*.

In reaction to the court's narrow interpretation of the source concept, Parliament often amends the *ITA* by adding a specific rule. For example, *Fortino v. R.* (1999)[63] and *Manrell v. R.* (2003)[64] involve taxpayers who sold shares of a corporation that carried on active business and included a portion of the sale proceeds in the form of non-compete payments under a restrictive covenant. The Court held in *Fortino* that non-compete payments did not constitute income from a source. The *Manrell* case followed *Fortino* and further addressed whether such payments were proceeds of dispositions of property resulting in a capital gain. The Court held in this case that the payments were not proceeds of disposition because the right to compete was not "property". To overrule these decisions, section 56.4 was proposed in 2003 and enacted in 2013 (retroactive to October 7, 2003) to specifically tax non-compete payments as either income or capital gains.[65]

(e) — Illegal source

The source concept of income is not limited to income from lawful sources. The case law has clearly established the principle that earnings from illegal operations or illicit businesses, such as stealing from clients,[66] embezzlement[67] or prostitution,[68] are clearly taxable.

Should the government seek to live on the avails of prostitution or other illegal activities? Is the state coming forward to take a share of unlawful gains? Rowlatt J. in *Mann v. Nash* (1932) answered as follows:

> It is mere rhetoric. The State is doing nothing of the kind; they are taxing the individual with reference to certain facts. They are not partners; they are not principals in

---

[63] *Fortino, supra* note 27.

[64] *Manrell v. R.* (2003), [2003] 3 C.T.C. 50, 2003 D.T.C. 5225 (Fed. C.A.).

[65] See Chapter 11 at heading 11.6(b) — Non-compete payments.

[66] *Buckman, supra* note 52.

[67] *Poynton, supra* note 53; and *Taylor v. R.*, [1995] 2 C.T.C. 2133, 95 D.T.C. 591 (T.C.C.); affirmed [1997] 2 C.T.C. 201, 97 D.T.C. 5120 (Fed. C.A.); leave to appeal refused (1997), 223 N.R. 399 (note) (S.C.C.).

[68] *Minister of National Revenue v. Eldridge*, [1964] C.T.C. 545, 64 D.T.C. 5338 (Can. Ex. Ct.) [*Eldridge*].

the illegality, or sharers in the illegality; they are merely taxing a man in respect of those resources. I think it is only rhetoric to say that they are sharing in his profits, and a piece of rhetoric which is perfectly useless for the solution of the question which I have to decide.[69]

The taxation of illegal income removes the anomaly of having the income of an honest taxpayer taxed while the similar gains of a criminal are not. This overrides any concern about the double penalty of having a taxpayer prosecuted for the crime that resulted in his or her obtaining ill-gotten income and subsequently being required to pay taxes on the illegal income.[70]

4.4 — Characterization of selected receipts

(a) — Overview

Some items of receipt have given rise to a body of case law. Ostensibly, a receipt of an amount of money or property increases the recipient's consumption power and savings, which constitute income in an economic sense. For tax purposes, as discussed above, the receipt may be on account of capital (such as recovery of cost of capital investment) or a windfall (having no source). This section discusses briefly the characterization of gifts, windfalls, damages and settlements.

(b) — Gifts

The traditional concept of income did not include gifts and inheritances. Gifts are a "voluntary and gratuitous transfer of property"[71] with no strings attached (i.e., there is no valuable consideration). Gifts can be made in cash or in kind. Gifts can be *inter vivos* (between living persons) or testamentary (inheritances). In addition to personal gifts, there are gifts in the commercial or employment context. Gifts give rise to characterization and tax policy issues.

(i) — Personal gifts and inheritances

An individual who works is taxed, but one who lives off the generosity of others is not. Does that make sense? The Carter Commission recommended gifts and inheritances to be included in the comprehensive tax base. The argument was essentially the same as the argument for the inclusion of capital gains. Like capital gains, gifts and inheritances increase the economic power of those who receive them, and should, therefore, be included in a tax base that purports to measure ability to pay. As well, like capital gains, gifts and inheritances are received disproportionately by high-income individuals, so that their inclusion would steepen the progressivity of the income tax system.

---

[69] *Mann v. Nash* (1932), 16 T.C. 523 (Eng. K.B.) at 530. This passage was quoted by Cattanach J. in *Eldridge, supra* note 68 at para. 25.

[70] Expenses incurred by an illegal business are generally deductible. See Chapter 8 at heading 8.5(d)(i) — Illegal payments and illegal businesses.

[71] *Bellingham, supra* note 24 at para. 34.

However, the inclusion of gifts and inheritances in the income of the recipient, where they would be taxed at the graduated rates that applied to all of the recipient's ordinary income, would undoubtedly have increased the total burden of tax on gifts and inheritances. The severity of including a large gift or inheritance in the income of a single year (the problem is the same with capital gains and other non-recurring receipts) was mitigated by recommendations for generous provisions for "forward averaging", which would have enabled taxpayers to smooth out their income by spreading the recognition (and enjoyment) of unusual income receipts over a period of years.[72] The problem of keeping track of numerous small gifts was addressed by a recommendation for the exemption of gifts up to an annual limit, so that only large gifts would need to be recorded and reported.

In 1966, when the Carter Commission reported, gifts and inheritances were subject to federal estate and gift taxes as well as provincial succession duties and gift taxes in Ontario, Quebec and British Columbia. However, these taxes were entirely independent of the income tax, and the rates and exemptions did not take account of the recipient's income. The Carter Commission recommended the repeal of these other taxes on gifts and inheritances.

The Carter Commission's proposal to tax gifts and inheritances as income was never accepted by the government and was not part of the 1971 Act. However, the federal government repealed its estate and gift taxes in 1971, giving as its reason the introduction of capital gains taxation with deemed dispositions on death and on gifts.[73] Over the next 14 years, all of the provinces withdrew from (or never entered) the field of death and gift taxation. Ironically, the indirect effect of the 1971 tax reform has been to substantially reduce the taxes exigible on gifts and inheritances. This is unfortunate, because the taxation of wealth at the time of gift or inheritance has a place in a mix of taxes that seek to reflect the ability to pay.

However, there are policy reasons for excluding gifts from income: they are transfers of "capital" or they are not from a productive source. As Robertson J. stated in *Bellingham*,

> There is no need to cite authorities for the proposition that gifts and inheritances are immune from taxation. It is well accepted that these items represent non-recurring amounts and the transfer of old wealth. Underlying the source doctrine is the understanding that income involves the creation of new wealth. Gifts do not flow from a productive source of income.[74]

From a policy perspective, there are perhaps three reasons for not taxing gifts and inheritances. First, the tax-free treatment of gifts may encourage, or at least not discourage, the redistribution of wealth that gifts often entail, as it is usually the richer taxpayers that give to the poorer ones. Second, it may make sense to keep tax

---

[72] Averaging is briefly discussed in Chapter 1 at heading 1.5(c)(ii) — Income fluctuation. Since 1988, the *ITA* has contained no averaging provisions.

[73] Capital gains arising on these deemed dispositions are discussed in Chapter 10 at heading 10.3(d) — Deemed dispositions.

[74] *Bellingham, supra* note 24 at para. 34

auditors away from the Christmas tree and birthday cake — to relieve familial gifts from any tax cost or tax compliance requirements.[75] It may also be difficult for a recipient to pay an income tax on a gift, especially when the gift is in kind, not in cash. Third, the donor is taxed on any capital gains (as well as recaptured capital cost allowance) realized when making the gift.[76]

(ii) — Commercial gifts

The tax-free treatment of gifts is limited to personal gifts. Gifts received in a business or employment context are treated differently. If an amount is given because of some relationship to an office or employment or a business, it is likely treated as income from an office, employment or a business. For example, subsection 5(1) of the *ITA* specifically includes "gratuities" in computing income from an office or employment. The value of a gold ring received by an employee for his long service to the company was a taxable benefit under section 6.[77] A sum of cash received by a professional swimmer from a newspaper was held to be a payment for services, despite the fact that the newspaper was not contractually liable to pay unless the taxpayer successfully swam Lake Ontario and the taxpayer in fact failed by one-half mile (thus the payment was gratuitous).[78]

The same is generally true for gifts received in the course of a business if services are provided. For example, corporate gifts received by a self-employed unordained minister who conducted teaching sessions were held to be payment for services because the wife of one of the principal shareholders of the corporation regularly attended the sessions.[79] In comparison, a sum paid to the secretary of a corporation who had acted as liquidator in the corporation's voluntary winding-up without remuneration was not taxable, because the amount in question was paid by the shareholders after the winding-up as a tribute or testimonial and not as payment for services.[80] The distinction between a payment for services and a gift is easy to grasp but not always easy to apply.

---

[75] John K. McNulty, *Federal Income Taxation of Individuals in a Nutshell*, 6th ed. (St. Paul, MN: West Group, 1999) at 62.

[76] *ITA, supra* note 1, ss. 69(1)(b), 70(5). There is no capital gain in the case of a spousal gift unless an election is made out of the spousal rollover rules in ss. 73(1) and 70(6).

[77] *Wisla v. R.* (1999), [2000] 1 C.T.C. 2823, 2000 D.T.C. 3563 (T.C.C. [Informal Procedure]).

[78] *Campbell v. R.* (1958), 59 D.T.C. 8, 21 Tax A.B.C. 145 (Can. Tax App. Bd.).

[79] *Campbell v. R.*, [1992] 2 C.T.C. 2256, 92 D.T.C. 1855 (T.C.C.).

[80] *Cowan v. Seymour*, [1920] 1 K.B. 500, 7 T.C. 372 (Eng. C.A.). In a Canadian case, *McMillan v. Minister of National Revenue*, [1982] C.T.C. 2345, 82 D.T.C. 1287 (T.R.B.), the taxpayer, who was an insurance broker, received gratuity payments on a tax-free basis from another broker when his major client switched to that broker.

(iii) — Gift of property

While the value of gifts is tax-free to the donee, the donor may be liable to income tax on any capital gain realized at the time of gifting. As discussed further in Chapter 10 of this book, subsection 69(1) of the *ITA* deems the donor to have sold the property for fair market value and the donor is forced to recognize any gain or loss for tax purposes. Gifting of property by one spouse to another or by a shareholder to his or her company can take place on a "rollover" basis, resulting in no immediate gain or loss to the donor.

(c) — Windfalls

Windfalls, such as a lottery prize or a valuable find, were not taxed when the Carter Commission reported. No doubt this reflected the "source" concept of income. Gambling activities are generally of a personal nature. Even for compulsive gamblers who continually try their luck at a game of chance, winning is a matter of luck. "The 'odds' of one ticket winning a game of chance such as Lotto 6/49 are said to be one in 13.5 million."[81] However, since windfalls increase taxable capacity no differently than dollars received in other ways, the Carter Commission recommended their inclusion in income.[82] Taxing gambling winnings raised the question of whether gambling losses should be deductible, to which the Carter Commission answered no (except against gambling winnings).[83]

The government did not accept the Commission's recommendations with respect to windfalls. When the House of Commons Standing Committee on Finance revisited this issue in 1994 and recommended that lottery and casino winnings over $500 be taxed, with losses deductible against winnings, these recommendations were also never implemented.[84] Windfalls accordingly remain untaxed.[85]

With the introduction of capital gains tax in Canada in 1972, it became necessary to deal with the possibility that lottery winnings that were not income might nonetheless attract tax as capital gains. To maintain the tax-free treatment, paragraph 40(2)(f) deems any gain or loss from the disposition of lottery tickets to be nil. As Bowman J. succinctly stated in *Leblanc v. R.* (2006), "the general perception that lottery winnings are not taxable is deeply embedded in the Canadian fiscal psyche".[86] Whenever the idea is revisited (as it is from time to time), the issue is always whether to allow taxpayers a deduction for the cost of all their losing tickets (as the tax system does for one-half of capital losses).

---

[81] *Leblanc v. R.*, [2007] 2 C.T.C. 2248, 2007 D.T.C. 307 (T.C.C.) [*Leblanc*] at para. 23.

[82] *Carter Report, supra* note 8, vol. 3 at 70.

[83] *Ibid.* at 526–527.

[84] See Canada, House of Commons, *Confronting Canada's Deficit Crisis — Tenth Report of the Standing Committee on Finance* (Ottawa: 1994) at 32.

[85] In the United States, windfall gains are taxable under §61(a) of the *Internal Revenue Code*.

[86] *Leblanc, supra* note 81 at para. 38.

Gambling winnings are taxable as income from a business if gambling activities were organized and carried out systematically.[87] For example, gambling gains have been held to be taxable where the gambling was an adjunct or incident of a business carried on, for example, by a casino owner who gambles in his own casino or an owner of horses who trains and races horses and who bets on the races.[88] Similarly, gambling gains have been held taxable where a taxpayer uses his own expertise and skill to earn a livelihood in a gambling game in which skill is a significant component (for example the pool player who, in cold sobriety, challenges inebriated pool players to a game of pool).[89]

(d) — Damages and settlements

(i) — The "surrogatum" principle

A person who suffers harm caused by another may seek compensation for loss of income, expenses incurred, property destroyed, or personal injury, as well as punitive damages. For tax purposes, damages or compensation received pursuant to a court judgment or an out-of-court settlement may be considered as on account of income, capital or windfall to the recipient. The nature of the injury or harm for which compensation is made generally determines the tax consequences of damages.

Under the surrogatum principle, the tax consequences of a damage or settlement payment depend on the tax treatment of the item for which the payment is intended to substitute:

> Where, pursuant to a legal right, a trader receives from another person, compensation for the trader's failure to receive a sum of money which, if it had been received, would have been credited to the amount of profits (if any) arising in any year from the trade carried on by him at the time when the compensation is so received, the compensation is to be treated for income tax purposes in the same way as that sum of money would have been treated if it had been received instead of the compensation.[90]

Generally, compensation for a loss of income is taxed as income. For example, compensation for a finder's fee,[91] loss of profits,[92] or disability insurance benefits

---

[87] See Chapter 6 at heading 6.2(c)(iii) — Personal endeavors, where *Leblanc, supra* note 81, and other relevant cases are discussed.

[88] *Badame v. Minister of National Revenue* (1951), 51 D.T.C. 29 (Can. Tax App. Bd.).

[89] *Luprypa v. R.*, [1997] 3 C.T.C. 2363, 97 D.T.C. 1416 (T.C.C.).

[90] This principle was articulated by Diplock J. in *London & Thames Haven Oil Wharves Ltd. v. Attwooll*, [1966] 3 All E.R. 145 (Ch. D.); reversed [1967] 2 All E.R. 124 (Eng. C.A.) at 134 [(C.A.)]. It has been adopted and applied by the Federal Court of Appeal in *Manley v. R.*, [1985] 1 C.T.C. 186, 85 D.T.C. 5150 (Fed. C.A.); leave to appeal refused (1986), 67 N.R. 400 (note) (S.C.C.) and *Schwartz, supra* note 57 at para. 17 [(C.A.)].

[91] *Manley, supra* note 90.

[92] For example, in *Charles R. Bell Ltd. v. R.*, [1992] 2 C.T.C. 260, 92 D.T.C. 6472 (Fed. C.A.); leave to appeal refused (1993), 156 N.R. 239n (S.C.C.), the amount of the settlement

in arrears[93] have all been held to be taxable as income. The recovery of an expense is not income, unless the expense was deducted. A payment for damaged or destroyed property is treated as an amount received in a sale or exchange of the property.[94] A payment for the loss of capital is treated on account of capital. A capital receipt is generally not income. However, compensation on account of capital may be taxable if it is considered an "eligible capital amount",[95] or if there is a disposition of property where the payment is made in exchange for the discharge of a legal right.[96] Damages for personal injuries and punitive damages are generally excluded from income.

(ii) — Damages for personal injury

Damages for personal injuries are not income for tax purposes because they are not from a productive source. Justice Maloney stated in *Schwartz*: "In the case of the personal injury victim, the source of the right to damages is that person's right not to be injured by the tort of another. That is not a source of income within the contemplation of paragraph 3(a) of the *Income Tax Act*."[97]

---

received on termination of a distributorship agreement was held to be income since the payment was intended to replace the taxpayer's loss of profits. Similarly, in *Zygocki v. R*, [1984] C.T.C. 280, 84 D.T.C. 6283 (Fed. T.D.), the amount received by the taxpayer, a trader in real estate, for termination of a contract was found to be income. In *Schofield Oil Ltd. v. Canada*, [1992] 1 C.T.C. 8, 92 D.T.C. 6022 (Fed. C.A.), a payment to release the taxpayer from the remaining 20 months of contractual obligations was held to be compensation for future profits.

[93] *Tsiaprailis v. R.*, [2005] 2 C.T.C. 1, 2005 D.T.C. 5119 (S.C.C.).

[94] Compensation for damages to depreciable property is included in the taxpayer's income (s. 12(1)(f)), but only to the extent that the compensation is not expended on repairing the damaged property. Repair costs are deducted in computing income. Compensation for the destruction or loss of a capital property is "proceeds of disposition" (s. 54), giving rise to either a capital gain or loss from the disposition of the property.

[95] Eligible capital amounts are proceeds received on the disposition of a business' intangible assets (e.g., goodwill). This topic is discussed in detail in Chapter 9 at heading 9.4 — Expenditure on intangible assets. In *Pepsi Cola Canada Ltd. v. R.*, [1979] C.T.C. 454, 79 D.T.C. 5387 (Fed. C.A.), an amount received upon the termination of a bottling franchise was held to be payment for goodwill. A compensation for the loss of profits resulting from destruction or materially crippling of the whole structure of the taxpayer's profit-making apparatus was held not to be an eligible capital amount but proceeds of disposition resulting in a capital gain: see *Pe Ben Industries Co. v. M.N.R.*, [1988] 2 C.T.C. 120, 88 D.T.C. 6347 (Fed. T.D.).

[96] According to *Mohawk Oil v M.N.R.*, [1992] 1 C.T.C. 195, 92 D.T.C. 6135 (Fed. C.A.); leave to appeal refused (1992), 141 N.R. 393 (note) (S.C.C.), moneys paid in exchange for the discharge of even a questionable legal claim may constitute income in the hands of the taxpayer.

[97] *Schwartz, supra* note 57 at para. 17 [(C.A.)]. Although the Federal Court of Appeal decision was reversed by the Supreme Court of Canada, this statement was not overruled.

Personal injuries include both physical injuries (the loss of a limb) and non-physical injuries (loss of dignity or reputation as a result of libel or defamation). Damages for personal injuries or death generally include amounts paid on account of compensation for pain and suffering, the loss of amenities of life, the loss of earning capacity, the shortened expectation of life, the loss of financial support caused by the death of the supporting individual, reimbursement of out-of-pocket expenses (such as medical and hospital expenses), or compensation for accrued or future loss of earnings.[98] Damages for personal injury may also include compensation for lost wages.

Several considerations may justify the exclusion of personal injury damages from taxation. It is offensive to tax a payment for pain and suffering, as the victim should be assisted rather than taxed. A recovery for out-of-pocket expenses should not be taxed, as there is no net accretion to wealth. A recovery of human capital (loss of income-earning capacity) should be tax-free. Similarly, a recovery for non-taxable items, such as personal reputation, good health, privacy, and the freedom from harassment, should not be taxable. Furthermore, the legal theory of personal injury damages (*restitutio in integrum*) is that the amount received is intended to put the plaintiff (the injured party) in the position that he or she would have been in if the tort had not been committed.[99] It follows that, if the damage payments received were subject to tax, the after-tax amount received would be less than the actual damages incurred and the injured party would not be as whole as before the injury.

(iii) — Punitive damages

Punitive damages are amounts the person who caused the harm must pay to the victim as punishment for outrageous conduct. Because punitive damages are intended to punish the wrongdoer and not to compensate the victim, the victim may be considered an incidental beneficiary. Although a punitive award may actually put the victim in a better economic position than before the harm was experienced, it is not considered to be income from a source under section 3. Such an award may be analogized with a gift in *Bellingham*, at least from the perspective of the recipient.[100] The absence of a market transaction or *quid pro quo* in relation to punitive damages also led them to be characterized as windfalls.[101] Since both gifts and windfalls are excluded from income, punitive damages are similarly excluded.

---

[98] Canada Revenue Agency, Interpretation Bulletin IT-365R2, "Damages, Settlements and Similar Receipts" (1987).

[99] *Andrews v. Grand & Toy Alberta Ltd.*, [1978] 2 S.C.R. 229, 83 D.L.R. (3d) 452 (S.C.C.).

[100] *Bellingham, supra* note 24.

[101] *Ibid.* at para. 41, where Robertson J. stated: "The critical factor is that the punitive damage award does not flow from either the performance or breach of a market transaction."

4.5 — Imputed income

(a) — Concept

Imputed income consists of the flow of benefits derived from labour on one's own behalf as well as the benefits from the ownership or use of property. Economists generally consider imputed income as income that should be taxed because consumption is part of income under the Haig-Simons concept. The relevance of consumption to the measurement of income is that not all things that are used or consumed are purchased in ordinary market transactions. When a person uses (or consumes) his or her own personal services or his or her own property, this type of consumption increases the person's economic power and ability to pay. A completely comprehensive definition of income must include the benefit of the personal services and personal property consumed by the taxpayer in the year. This benefit must be valued and "imputed" to the consumer as income.[102]

The *ITA* does not recognize imputed income as income. Even if human effort or services or property are "sources", there is no "taxable event" from the standpoint of the Act. The value may be hard to ascertain. The non-recognition of imputed income in the tax base poses some interesting policy questions, especially in regard to owner-occupied homes.

(b) — Policy implications

(i) — Owner-occupied home

The use of one's own property is a major source of imputed income. The imputed rent of an owner-occupied home provides the clearest example. A tenant has to pay rent out of his or her after-tax earnings in order to obtain the benefit of accommodation. However, a homeowner receives no taxable income from his or her investment in a home, which provides the homeowner with a tax-free benefit of accommodation. If you doubt the great advantage enjoyed by the homeowner, consider the following example.

A taxpayer (the Homeowner in the chart below) with a marginal tax rate of 50 per cent owns a house, free and clear, which could be rented for $12,000 per year, and he lives in the house. Assume that he moves to another city and becomes a renter (the Renter in the chart below). He leases his house in the old city for $12,000 per year and rents an equivalent house in the new city for $12,000 per year. See how this move leaves him worse off to the tune of $6,000 per year.

---

[102] The Carter Commission recommended that imputed income continue to be exempt from tax. See the *Carter Report, supra* note 8 at 118.

	Homeowner	Renter
Salary	$ 100,000	$ 100,000
Rental income (old city)	0	12,000
Taxable income	$ 100,000	$ 112,000
Tax (at 50 per cent)	(50,000)	(56,000)
Cost of rent (old city)	0	(12,000)
Discretionary income	$ 50,000	$ 44,000

Why does this happen? As a Homeowner, he paid no rent and received no rental income. But when he becomes a Renter, he pays rent of $12,000 and receives rental income of $12,000. If we disregard tax liability, his rental payment and his rental income cancel each other out perfectly. But the $12,000 the Renter pays is not deductible from taxable income, while the $12,000 he receives is subject to tax at 50 per cent. Therefore, the Renter becomes liable to pay an extra $6,000 in tax and the net result is that he is worse off by $6,000 each year. How would the position be changed if the imputed rent value of his home were brought into income for tax purposes each year? When the taxpayer was a Homeowner, he would have had to include in his income a notional rent of $12,000 each year (just like the Renter), and this would increase his tax by $6,000. He would still pay no rent, and receive no rental income, but he would pay an additional amount of tax, namely $6,000.

The tax advantage that the homeowner enjoys by virtue of the non-taxation of imputed rent[103] could be corrected in one of two ways. The most obvious way is to bring imputed rent into income, and to allow the deduction for mortgage interest as an expense incurred to earn income. However, as noted by the Carter Commission, this raises the administrative problems of assessing the rental value of all owner-occupied dwellings in Canada, and it raises the policy problem of whether it is fair to tax imputed rent without also taxing other forms of imputed income. A second way of roughly equalizing the positions of owners and renters would be to allow renters to deduct for tax purposes some portion of the rent on their homes. This second approach was suggested by the Carter Commission as an alternative to taxing imputed income.[104] Rent is one of the most important types of personal consumption expenditures that are not deductible in computing net income.

(ii) — Unpaid housework

The consumption of personal services is one element of imputed income. Most people buy clothes out of after-tax earnings. A person who makes his or her own clothes receives the same benefit tax-free (apart from the cost of materials). Home

---

[103] A complete analysis of the effect of the tax system on the relative costs of owning and renting a home would also have to take account of the fact that the homeowner's principal residence exemption could eliminate his or her capital gain on the sale of the home. This is another concession to the homeowner relative to the renter.

[104] *Carter Report, supra* note 8, vol. 3 at 48.

repairs and improvements, homegrown food, and automobile maintenance by the owner are similarly tax-free imputed benefits.

In a family where one spouse earns income and the other remains at home to care for children and keep house, the homemaker's duties are unpaid and consequently untaxed. Yet the unpaid household work confers a considerable benefit on the family, because the family is spared the cost of paying for child care and housework, which the two-earner family would have to purchase.

The non-taxation of the value of unpaid household labour could be perceived as a tax benefit to the one-earner family[105] and a disincentive to seeking work outside the home. The reason for this perception is that the value of work performed in the home is not taxed whereas the value of work performed outside the home is taxed. The non-taxation of housework also has implications in other areas involving the income tax treatment of families. For example, the child care expense deduction is generally only available to the lower-income parent and is generally only available for expenses incurred to earn income from employment or a business.[106] This means that a one-income family will not be able to claim a child care deduction because the stay-at-home parent (the lower-income parent) has no such qualifying income. Similarly, as discussed in Chapter 11, the contribution limits for government-provided and tax-assisted retirement savings vehicles, such as the Canada Pension Plan ("CPP") and registered retirement savings plans ("RRSPs"), are based on qualifying amounts of income for tax purposes.[107]

4.6 — Statutory inclusions and exclusions

(a) — Partial inclusion of capital gains

Paragraph 3(b) of the *ITA* specifies that taxable capital gains are included in computing income. Until 1972, capital gains were excluded from income. Paragraph 3(b) was a legislative reaction to the Carter Commission's comprehensive tax base.

Although included in income under section 3, capital gains are not income from a source in a traditional sense — rather, capital gains are income from the disposition

---

[105] Although self-performed services are technically a form of tax avoidance, people do not resent this form of avoidance as it is achieved through personal initiative and effort rather than class privilege or expensive tax advice. Indeed, the largest amounts of imputed income from services would probably be concentrated in the lower-income groups, who cannot afford to pay for services such as house-cleaning, gardening or home repair.

[106] See the definition of child care expenses in s. 63(3). There are some exceptions. For example, if the lower-income spouse is attending a designated education institution or is infirm, child care expenses can be claimed by the higher-income spouse (s. 63(2)). See Chapter 8 at heading 8.4(a)(iii) — Expenses enabling taxpayers to work, and Chapter 11 at heading 11.10 — Child care expenses.

[107] On the other hand, the *ITA* allows the income-earning spouse to claim a credit for a dependent spouse who has very little income (s. 118(1)(a)). It also allows an income-earning spouse to use his or her own contribution limit to contribute to a spousal RRSP (s. 146(5.1)) and to split his or her CPP retirement benefits with a spouse.

of a source. Subsection 9(3) also makes it clear that income from property does not include capital gains. The *ITA* also "quarantines" capital losses from the traditional sources of income: capital losses generally can only be used to offset capital gains. On the other hand, capital gains are only partially taxed (currently 50 per cent).

(b) — Other income

In addition to the enumerated sources, section 3 contemplates income from other sources. Subdivision d (sections 56 to 59.1) specifies items to be included in computing income. Amounts that are required to be included in income by subdivision d are clearly "income" in the sense that they increase the ability to pay, but it is not clear whether the source is a "productive source". The inclusions are necessary to achieve certain policy objectives. For example, the inclusion in income of pension benefits and scholarships reflects the fundamental objective of equity based on the ability to pay principle. The inclusion in income of spousal support (in combination with the deduction of the amounts to the payer under section 60) reflects a policy objective of providing tax subsidies to broken marriages.

As indicated earlier, in using the wording "without restricting the generality of section 3, there shall be included in computing the income of a taxpayer for a taxation year . . ." at the beginning of subsection 56(1), Parliament made it clear that the enumeration in section 56 was not to be interpreted as restricting the generality of section 3.[108] Therefore, it is possible that a receipt falling outside section 56 constitutes income from a source under section 3.

(c) — Exclusions

(i) — Indigenous income

The *ITA* provides, in paragraph 81(1)(a), that an amount "that is declared to be exempt from income tax by any other enactment of Parliament" is excluded from income. The *Indian Act* is one of such other enactment of Parliament and provides in section 87 the following:

> (1) Notwithstanding any other Act of Parliament or any Act of the legislature of a province, . . . the following property is exempt from taxation:
>
>> (a) the interest of an Indian or a band in reserve lands or surrendered lands; and
>>
>> (b) the personal property of an Indian or a band situated on a reserve.
>
> (2) No Indian or band is subject to taxation in respect of the ownership, occupation, possession or use of any property mentioned in paragraph (1)(a) or (b) or is otherwise subject to taxation in respect of any such property.[109]

---

[108] In *Schwartz, supra* note 57 at 328 [C.T.C. (S.C.C.)], La Forest J. stated: "The phrasing adopted by Parliament, in s. 3(a) and in the introductory part of s. 56(1) is probably the strongest that could have been used to express the idea that income from *all* sources, enumerated or not, expressly provided for in subdivision d or not, was taxable under the Act."

[109] *Indian Act*, R.S.C. 1985, c. I-5, s. 87.

The meaning of "personal property . . . situated on a reserve" has been interpreted by a body of case law. "Income" has been held to be "personal property" in *Nowegijick v. R.* (1983).[110]

Whether "income" is "situated on a reserve" must be established on the basis of "sufficient connecting factors" or the "situs" of income. In general, whether the income is integral to the life of the reserve or preservation of the Indian way of life is irrelevant.[111] In *Williams v. R.* (1992)[112] the Supreme Court of Canada emphasized the importance of considering the scheme and purposes of the *Indian Act* and the *Income Tax Act* in order to determine whether taxing the receipt in issue (unemployment insurance benefits) would amount to eroding the entitlement of an Indian *qua* Indian on a reserve. Connecting factors must be assessed in reference to the type of property and the nature of the taxation levied. In respect of unemployment insurance benefits, the Court articulated the following factors: the residence of the debtor; the residence of the person receiving the benefits; the place the benefits are paid, and the location of the employment income giving rise to the benefits. Among these factors, the Court found that the strongest factor was the location of the qualifying employment on which the benefits were based.

The situs of employment income is generally determined based on whether the employer was located on the reserve, the work was performed on the reserve, the taxpayer resided on the reserve, and the taxpayer was paid on the reserve.[113] Employment income of a status Indian who lives on a reserve and works on the reserve or is paid by an employer resident on the reserve is "situated on the reserve" and, thus, exempt from tax under the *ITA*.

The situs of business income is generally based on where the business activities are conducted. For example, in *Dickie v. Canada* (2014),[114] the taxpayer's business included clearing off-reserve trees for oil companies and had the business administration, sales, contract signing and equipment storage on-reserve. His income was found to be situated on a reserve. In *Murray v. R.* (2013),[115] the taxpayer earned management fees from his off-reserve companies for work done mostly off-reserve and the income was found not to be situated on a reserve. The fact that the income

---

[110] *Nowegijick v. R.*, [1983] C.T.C. 20, 83 D.T.C. 5041 (S.C.C.).

[111] *Dube v. R.*, [2011] 5 C.T.C. 149, 2011 D.T.C. 5119 (Fr.), 2011 D.T.C. 5120 (Eng.) (S.C.C.).

[112] *Williams v. R.*, [1992] 1 C.T.C. 225, 92 D.T.C. 6320 (S.C.C.).

[113] *Monias v. R.*, [2001] 3 C.T.C. 244, 2001 D.T.C. 5450 (Fed. C.A.); leave to appeal refused 2002 CarswellNat 504, 2002 CarswellNat 505 (S.C.C.); *Akiwenzie v. R.* (2003), [2004] 2 C.T.C. 18, 2004 D.T.C. 6007 (F.C.A.); leave to appeal refused 2004 CarswellNat 1727, 2004 CarswellNat 1728 (S.C.C.).

[114] *Dickie v. Canada* (2014), 2014 FCA 40, 2014 D.T.C. 5038 (Eng.) (F.C.A.).

[115] *Murray v. R.* (2013), 2013 TCC 253, 2013 D.T.C. 1211 (Fr.), 2014 D.T.C. 1085 (Eng.) (T.C.C. [General Procedure]).

is earned by a corporation owned by an Indian band does not render the income exempt.[116]

The situs of interest and other investment income is based primarily on the location of the financial institution, the place where payment is required to be made, the location of the term deposits, the conclusion of contract on the reserve, and the source of the capital giving rise to the interest.[117]

(ii) — Miscellaneous items

The *ITA* specifically excludes a number of items from income. Examples include income from property or capital gains from the disposition of property received as compensation for physical or mental injury (paragraphs 81(1)(g.1), (g.2) and (5)); expense allowances paid to an elected member of assembly or elected officer (subsections 81(2) and (3)); and income from the office of the Governor General of Canada other than salary (paragraph 81(1)(n)).

The *ITA* also excludes certain amounts in computing income from a specific source (rather than from income in general). Examples are the benefit of an employer's contribution to a private health plan (paragraph 6(1)(a)) and one-half of all capital gains (paragraph 38(a)). In a few instances, the exclusion is accomplished by deducting an amount (which may or may not be 100 per cent, depending on the circumstances) that would otherwise be included in income (typically called an "exemption"): examples are the principal residence exemption (paragraph 40(2)(b)) and the scholarship exemption (subsection 56(3)).

When the *ITA* wants to include an amount in net income (which is used as a "means test" for some tax credits and other rules) but not to tax it, it achieves the same outcome as an exemption by including the amount in income under section 3, and then allowing a deduction in computing taxable income under Division C. One example is the taxable income deduction for taxable capital gains from the sale of qualified small business corporation shares (section 110.6), which effectively excludes these taxable capital gains from being taxed in the hands of an individual. Another example is the deduction (paragraph 110(1)(f)) for social assistance payments and workers' compensation payments that are initially included in the income of an individual (subsection 56(1)).

(iii) — Income of tax-exempt organizations

The income earned by certain taxpayers is exempt from tax under section 149. These taxpayers include charities, non-profit organizations (hospitals and universities), pension plans and crown corporations. All these exclusions are primarily tax expenditures, designed to fulfill social policy objectives.

---

[116] *Tron Power v. Saskatchewan*, 2013 CarswellSask 322 (Sask. Q.B.).

[117] *Bastien v. R.*, [2011] 5 C.T.C. 111, 2011 D.T.C. 5117 (Fr.), 2011 D.T.C. 5118 (Eng.) (S.C.C.).

5
EMPLOYMENT INCOME

5.1 — Legislative scheme

(a) — Technical design

Most individuals in Canada make a living from employment. Employment and office are listed in paragraph 3(a) of the *Income Tax Act* (the *"ITA"*)[1] as two specific sources of income and generate the lion's share of personal income in Canada.[2] Taxation of employment income makes the income tax a "democratic" tax or a "mass" tax in terms of the number of taxpayers involved. The sheer magnitude of tax on employment income makes it imperative for the *ITA* to strive for fairness and administrative efficiency. It also enables the Act to function as a key instrument for achieving social and economic objectives.

Sections 5 to 8 provide for rules on the computation of employment income (or loss). The same rules apply to income from office. Sections 5, 6 and 7 specify what and when amounts must be included in the computation, and section 8 specifies what and when amounts are deductible. Tax incentive measures are scattered in these provisions. Sections 5 to 8 are drafted, by and large, in general language. This is particularly true with the key inclusion rules, such as subsection 5(1), paragraphs 6(1)(a) and (b), and the general deduction rule in subsection 8(2). The effect of all-embracing inclusion rules and highly restrictive deduction rules is that employment income is taxable more or less on a gross basis for most taxpayers.[3]

---

[1] R.S.C. 1985 (5th Supp.), c. 1 [*ITA*].

[2] According to Statistics Canada, about 64 per cent of the Canadian population had some wages and salary income in 2010, accounting for 69 per cent of total income. See Table 1: Income Composition in Canada, 2010 at <http://www12.statcan.gc.ca/nhs-enm/2011/as-sa/99-014-x/2011001/tbl/tbl01-eng.cfm>.

[3] The regime for taxing employment income differs from that for business income in terms of the scope of deductions. In computing business income, all expenses incurred for the purpose of earning income are deductible unless the deduction is specifically prohibited by the *ITA*. In contrast, in computing income from employment, no expenses are deductible unless section 8 specifically permits the deduction.

To simplify tax compliance and ensure tax collection, section 153 requires employers to withhold and remit tax from employment income.[4] The amount of tax withheld during the year is credited against an employee's tax payable after filing a tax return.[5] Unless the employee has significant non-employment income, he or she will receive a tax refund for the excessive tax withheld.

The scheme for employment income is distinct from those for business or property income (sections 9 to 37) and capital gains (sections 3 to 55). It is legislatively simpler, encompassing only four provisions, and has minimal intersection with the rest of Part I of the *ITA*. The employment scheme intersects with the capital gains scheme only in respect of employee stock options.[6] It intersects with the business income and taxation of corporate income in respect of characterization of services[7] and incorporated employees.

(b) — Purpose and rationale

The distinct regime for taxing employment income is justifiable on the policy grounds of tax base protection, equity, and simplicity (or administrative efficiency). As discussed below, however, these policy objectives are sometimes conflicting.

(i) — Tax revenue and base protection

The legislative scheme for employment income aims at capturing income from employment and office as broadly as possible. Since much of the income earned by Canadians is employment income, this scheme defines a tax base that is capable of producing a reliable source of revenue for the Canadian government. The provisions are drafted in a manner to minimize leakage in the tax base, as even a tiny leakage may cause a huge loss of tax revenue.[8]

---

[4] *ITA, supra* note 1. Employers must also remit payroll taxes, including the employer's share of Canada Pension Plan and Employment Insurance premiums as well as Worker's Safety Insurance Board ("WSIB") premiums and provincial payroll taxes, such as the Ontario Employer Health Tax. Regulations 200 and 205 of the *Income Tax Regulations*, C.R.C., c. 945 [Regulations], require employers to make an information return in prescribed form (T4 — Statement of Remuneration Paid). Under this system, the payer of income (i.e., the employer) is legally required to withhold income tax (as well as Canada Pension Plan contributions and Employment Insurance premiums) from the employee's pay and submit the tax payment to the Minister of National Revenue.

[5] The excessive taxes are not automatically refunded in the absence of a tax return. For further discussion on the tax collection system, see Chapter 15.

[6] See heading 5.7 — Employee stock options, below.

[7] See heading 5.2 — Characterization of "employment", below, and Chapter 6 at heading 6.2(c)(v) — Employment distinguished.

[8] The shrinkage in the income tax base could also lead to the erosion of the base for payroll taxes. Employment income is also the base for payroll taxes, which finance important parts of our social security system.

The *ITA* defines the notion of "employment" broadly and provides for anti-avoidance rules to prevent individuals from minimizing taxation through incorporating their employment services. In order to minimize tax base erosion, the *ITA* attempts to tax not only wages or salaries but also non-cash "fringe benefits" and other amounts that are in the nature of employee compensation. Non-taxation of fringe benefits would pose a threat to the tax base. The concern about tax base protection also helps explain the limited deductions available to employees.

(ii) — Equity

Equity is a key policy objective of the income tax. Vertical equity or progressive taxation is a hallmark of the personal income tax. Given the pivotal role of employment income in the tax base, the taxation of this type of income has serious equity implications.

To achieve equity between employees receiving different forms of compensation, subsection 5(1) includes the typical forms of wages and salaries as well as gratuities, and sections 6 and 7 include various types of fringe benefits, economic benefits received from employers, and employee stock options. If the *ITA* taxed only an employee's salary or wages, employers and employees would become very fond of fringe benefits. Assuming that a fringe benefit is deductible by the employer as an expense of doing business, it is immaterial to the employer whether he or she pays an employee a full salary of $80,000 or a salary of $70,000 plus fringe benefits worth $10,000. But if the fringe benefits were not taxed as part of the employee's income, then (assuming that the employee's marginal rate is about 50 per cent) the fringe benefits would be worth nearly twice as much to the employee as they cost the employer, and the latter alternative would be equivalent to a fully-taxed salary of nearly $90,000. In effect, the government would be contributing to the employee's pay by foregoing tax on part of the pay.

Broad-based inclusion rules in sections 6 and 7 reduce inequities among employees in different types of industries. In some industries, employees may receive (either free or purchased at a discount) goods and services that the employer sells to the general public. In other industries, non-cash compensation is rarely used. It would be unfair for the *ITA* to treat cash and non-cash compensation differently, thereby shifting a disproportionate tax burden to those individuals whose compensation is in the form of cash.

Considering the fact that non-cash compensation is used predominantly for employees in high-income brackets, such as executives and high-level managers, the broad inclusion rules reflect vertical equity in the system. "A disparity in the tax treatment of an employee who receives all his compensation as salary and wages and one who receives the same amount of compensation but partly in the form of fringe benefits is not defensible."[9]

---

[9] *McNeill v. Minister of National Revenue*, [1986] 2 C.T.C. 352, 86 D.T.C. 6477 (Fed. T.D.) at para. 44.

The fact that there are fewer deductions also allows for equity between employees: it means that higher-income employees who can afford to purchase additional items to assist them in their work (such as those listed above) cannot reduce their taxes by claiming the deductions for these items. If each employee were allowed to deduct employment-related expenses, it would be difficult to verify the deduction, as most employees do not keep the kinds of detailed records that would be entailed. The administrative task of processing the claims would be too great.[10]

(iii) — Administrative efficiency

The near gross-basis taxation and source withholding requirement are motivated by administrative concerns. Given the sheer number of taxpayers affected, if millions of taxpayers had to spend time and resources figuring out their tax liability every year, the Spring tax filing season would be a worse nightmare than it already is. Many individuals do not keep proper accounting records for their income and expenses and would prefer not to engage the assistance of accountants in filing their tax returns. Saving enough cash to pay taxes every year could be another challenge for many taxpayers. Auditing and verifying the millions of individual tax returns would be costly to the government. If taxpayers perceived differential treatment by the tax administration, it would erode the public confidence in the integrity of the income tax system.

The *ITA* limits deductions on the assumption that employment-related expenses are paid by the employer, not the employee. In addition, the Act relies heavily on employers to verify the types of deductions that can be claimed by employees (such as travel expenses and home office expenses).[11] The *ITA* requires employers to assist the government in collecting taxes and assist employees by providing accurate information at the end of the year.[12] To provide certainty to employees and employers, the *ITA* stipulates ways of computing the amount of taxable benefits in respect of automobiles, loans and relocation-related housing expenses.

---

[10] See E.J. Benson, *Proposals for Tax Reform* (Ottawa: Queen's Printer, 1969) at 10, 16. The 1971 *Income Tax Act*, S.C. 1970-71-72, c. 63, implemented the Benson 1969 White Paper proposal, allowing all employees a deduction of 3 per cent of their income up to a ceiling of $150. The deduction was later raised to 20 per cent with a ceiling of $500 before it was eliminated in 1988. The value of the basic personal tax credit available to all taxpayers was increased to recognize the fact that most taxpayers were employees. See Michael H. Wilson, *Tax Reform 1987: Income Tax Reform* (Ottawa: Department of Finance, 1987) at 88. In 2006, a separate employment credit was introduced in s. 118(10) of the *ITA*, *supra* note 1.

[11] E.g., subsection 8(10) requires an employer to sign a prescribed form T2200 to confirm that the requirements for the deductions claimed have been met.

[12] Employers must provide employees with an information return (T4 slip), reporting the amount of employment income earned by each employee during the year.

(iv) — Social policy

The *ITA* provides subsidies to employees or employers in certain circumstances on grounds of social policy. For example, to encourage employers to provide group plans to promote the health and well-being of employees, paragraph 6(1)(a) excludes benefits associated with employer contributions to registered pension plans and pooled pension plans, group sickness or accident insurance plans (e.g., group disability insurance plans), private health care services plans (e.g., drug or dental plans), supplementary unemployment insurance plans, and deferred profit sharing plans; counselling services relating to mental health, re-employment, or retirement; and education benefits. Subsection 6(16) excludes from income disability-related employment benefits. In respect of employee stock options, subsection 7(1.1) provides favourable timing rules for options of Canadian-controlled private corporations and paragraphs 110(1)(d) and 110(1)(d.1) provide a deduction equal to one-half of the benefit from exercising employee stock options.

Some of the deductions under section 8 are allowed for social or cultural policy reasons. For example, a taxpayer who is a member of the clergy or a religious order can deduct expenses related to a residence (paragraph 8(1)(c)); musicians can deduct costs related to their instruments (paragraph 8(1)(p)); and artists can also deduct additional employment costs (paragraph 8(1)(q)).

5.2 — Characterization of "employment"

(a) — Statutory guidance

Subsection 248(1) defines "employment" to mean "the position of an individual in the service of some other person (including Her Majesty or a foreign state or sovereign) and 'servant' or 'employee' means a person holding such a position".[13]

This definition expressly states only individuals can be employees. To avoid being an employee, an individual can create a corporation and have the corporation hire him or her to provide services to another person who would otherwise be an employer. This is the so-called "incorporated employee" situation. The *ITA* contains "personal service business" rules that tax incorporated employees similarly to ordinary employees in terms of effective tax rate and the scope of available deductions.[14]

---

[13] *ITA, supra* note 1, s. 248(1) "employment". "Office" is also defined in s. 248(1). The key to the difference is a phrase in the definition of employment that is absent from the definition of office, namely "in the service of some other person". This requires a contract of service (or employment) between the taxpayer and an employer. Where there is a fixed or ascertainable remuneration but no contract of service, the taxpayer will be an "officer" and his or her remuneration will be income from an office. The examples of offices (which are given in the definition of office) are judges, ministers of the Crown, members of legislative bodies, and directors of corporations.

[14] The *ITA* uses the term "personal services business" to describe incorporated employment income. *ITA, supra* note 1, ss. 125(7), 248(1). As discussed in Chapter 14, corporations are taxable on their income and Canadian-controlled corporations enjoy low rates of tax on their

The nature of the relationship between a worker (or service provider) and the hirer (or service recipient) is one of "subordination"; the reference to "servant" makes this point clearly. The most challenging phrase in the definition is "in the service of some other person". The meaning of this phrase distinguishes services rendered by an employee and services rendered by an independent contractor who is carrying on a business. For tax purposes, a taxpayer would prefer the "business" characterization because of the broader range of deductions.

In law, if the relationship between a worker and the hirer is governed by a contract of service, the worker is an employee, and "in the service of" the hirer. On the other hand, if the relationship is governed by a "contract for services", the worker is not in the service of the hirer and provides the services on his or her own account as an independent contractor. The distinction is left to the courts. In most cases, the distinction is perfectly clear. For example, a partner in a law firm provides services to clients as an independent contractor, but the partner's assistant works for the partner as an employee and "is in the service of" the partner. In cases where the distinction is unclear, the courts have identified some factors for making the distinction.

(b) — Common law

The courts have defined the meaning of "employment" for tax purposes by reference to general law. The general law of all the provinces, including Quebec, draws a distinction between a "contract of service", which creates an employment relationship between the employer and the employee (or the master and the servant), and a "contract for services", which creates an independent contract relationship between the employer and the "independent contractor". The distinction arose first (and is still important) in the context of employment law and the law of torts: an employer (master) is vicariously liable for torts committed in the course of employment by an employee (servant) but an employer is not vicariously liable for torts committed by an independent contractor.

The leading cases on this issue are *Wiebe Door Services Ltd. v. Minister of National Revenue* (1986)[15] and *671122 Ontario Ltd. v. Sagaz Industries Canada Inc.* (2001).[16] In *Wiebe Door*, the Court cited the following statement as "perhaps the best synthesis found in the authorities" of the common law to date:

> . . . the fundamental test to be applied is this: "Is the person who has engaged himself to perform these services performing them as a person in business on his own account?" If the answer to that question is "yes," then the contract is a contract for services. If the answer is "no" then the contract is a contract of service. *No exhaus-*

---

business income. These reduced rates do not apply to income from a personal services business, which is taxed at a higher rate closer to the top personal tax rate.

[15] *Wiebe Door Services Ltd. v. Minister of National Revenue* (1986), [1986] 2 C.T.C. 200, 87 D.T.C. 5025 (Fed. C.A.) [*Wiebe Door*].

[16] *671122 Ontario Ltd. v. Sagaz Industries Canada Inc.*, [2001] 4 C.T.C. 139, 204 D.L.R. (4th) 542 (S.C.C.); reconsideration / rehearing refused 2001 CarswellOnt 4155, 2001 CarswellOnt 4156 (S.C.C.) [*Sagaz*]. This case dealt with matters of tort law, not tax law.

tive list has been compiled and perhaps no exhaustive list can be compiled of considerations which are relevant in determining that question, nor can strict rules be laid down as to the relative weight which the various considerations should carry in particular cases [emphasis added] . . . The application of the general test may be easier in a case where the person who engages himself to perform the services does so in the course of an already established business of his own; but this factor is not decisive, and a person who engages himself to perform services for another may well be an independent contractor even though he has not entered into the contract in the course of an existing business carried on by him.[17]

In *Sagaz*, which followed *Wiebe Door*, Major J. of the Supreme Court summarized *Wiebe Door's* non-exhaustive list of "considerations" as "factors":

The central question is whether the person who has been engaged to perform the services is performing them as a person in business on his own account. In making this determination, the level of control the employer has over the worker's activities will always be a factor. However, other factors to consider include whether the worker provides his or her own equipment, whether the worker hires his or her own helpers, the degree of financial risk taken by the worker, the degree of responsibility for investment and management held by the worker, and the worker's opportunity for profit in the performance of his or her tasks.

It bears repeating that the above factors constitute a non-exhaustive list, and there is no set formula as to their application. The relative weight of each will depend on the particular facts and circumstances of the case [emphasis added].[18]

(c) — Control

The statutory definition of "employment" is based on the position of the worker "in the service of some other person" and a "servant" is given as an example of a person holding such a position. The element of "control" is clearly implied. In the example of a law partner and his or her associate, the partner's relationship with his or her clients is independent and the partner is not "controlled" by his or her client in any way in respect of the legal services provided. In contrast, the partner's associate is under the partner's control and direction.

The control test was originally the only test at case law. Now, it is one of several tests. The question is: control over what? Is it control over where and how the work is done? Naturally, the degree of control varies depending on the nature of the work involved. In *Wiebe Door*, the "control" by the appellant and the door installers was limited:

The workers worked mostly on their own. They were free to accept or refuse a call. They were not required to work or attend at the Appellant's place of business, except to pick up a door or parts. The Appellant did exercise some measure of control

---

[17] *Market Investigations v. Minister of Social Security*, [1968] 3 All E.R. 732 (Eng. Q.B.) [*Market Investigations*] at 738-39, as cited in *Wiebe Door, supra* note 15 at para. 16. The missing portion of text in the middle of the paragraph (after the italics) is very similar to the statement in *Sagaz*: see note 18 and accompanying text.

[18] *Segaz, supra* note 16 at paras. 47, 48.

over the workers. Firstly, the Appellant assigned the jobs to the installer. The job was guaranteed for one year. Within that time the Appellant would require the installer to correct any faulty or defective installation or repair.[19]

In *Royal Winnipeg Ballet v. R.* (2006), the Court found control over the work of dancers to be less clear. On the one hand, a dancer "is not free to dance his or her assigned role in a manner that departs from the choreography or the artistic vision of the artistic director", while, on the other hand, "each dancer's artistic expression is necessarily unique, even while performing choreographed dance movements."[20]

The shortcomings of control have been acknowledged by the courts. For example, the Court in *W.B. Pletch Co. v. R.* (2006) remarked:

> I am faced with the frequently encountered problem of determining whether the independence in the performance of a role of a worker is attributable to the freedom that derives from the nature of the relationship, from the party in a position to control choosing not to exercise control or whether it is attributable to the nature of the tasks assigned and the worker's particular skills to perform such tasks without direction. In the case at bar the freedom of the worker derives primarily from the nature of the relationship which the worker imposed and from the worker's skills to perform the work.[21]

As a result, the control test is no longer found to be decisive on its own.

(d) — Worker's own account

The distinction between employees and independent contractors is made based on a combination of factors, including control, ownership of tools, chance of profit, and risk of loss.[22] Whether the worker buys his or her own tools or hires helpers, enjoys the financial reward or bears the risk of loss, are hallmarks of independent contractors who work on their own account. As previously noted:

> the fundamental test to be applied is this: "Is the person who has engaged himself to perform these services performing them as a person in business on his own account?" If the answer to that question is "yes," then the contract is a contract for services. If the answer is "no" then the contract is a contract of service.[23]

Independent contractors generally have more than one client.[24] However, having only one client for several years does not mean the worker is not an independent

---

[19] *Wiebe Door, supra* note 15 at para.3.

[20] *Royal Winnipeg Ballet v. R.* (2006), [2008] 1 C.T.C. 220, 2006 D.T.C. 6323 (Eng.) (F.C.A.) [*Winnipeg Ballet*] at para. 9.

[21] *W.B. Pletch Co. v. R.* (2005), [2006] 1 C.T.C. 2582, 2006 D.T.C. 2065 (Eng.) (T.C.C. [General Procedure]) at para. 9.

[22] See *Wiebe Door, supra* note 15; *Wolf v. R.*, [2002] 3 C.T.C. 3, 2002 D.T.C. 6853 (Fed. C.A.) [*Wolf*].

[23] *Market Investigations, supra* note 17 at 738-739, as cited in *Wiebe Door, supra* note 15 at para. 16.

[24] In *Pletch, supra* note 21, the Court, after exhaustively listing the relevant factors, cited as particularly significant the fact that neither the corporation nor the incorporated employee

contractor. In *Wolf v. R.* (2002),[25] for example, a taxpayer with specialized skills who worked exclusively under a five-year contract with one Canadian company was found to be an independent contractor because he had "financial risk". The taxpayer had no job security or benefits, and the agreement entered into by the parties indicated their intent to have an independent contractor relationship.[26]

(e) — Contract

The intention of parties in a contractual relationship is considered relevant, but not determinative, in characterizing the nature of the relationship for tax purposes when other factors are not decisive. This is the case in *Wolf* and *Winnipeg Ballet*.[27] In *Wolf*, Noël, J. remarked:

> This is not a case where the parties labelled their relationship in a certain way with a view of achieving a tax benefit. No sham or window dressing of any sort is suggested. It follows that the manner in which the parties viewed their agreement must prevail unless they can be shown to have been mistaken as to the true nature of their relationship. In this respect, the evidence when assessed in the light of the relevant legal tests is at best neutral. As the parties considered that they were engaged in an independent contractor relationship and as they acted in a manner that was consistent with this relationship, I do not believe that it was open to the Tax Court Judge to disregard their understanding . . .[28]

Although tax law is generally accessory to private law, including contracts, the private law characterization must make sense in light of the context and purpose of the provisions in the *ITA*. When parties to a private contract have the common intention to characterize the relationship as one of "contract for services" in order to obtain tax benefits, great care must be exercised in giving weight to such intention to protect the integrity of the tax system.

> When a dispute arises over the proper legal character of a contract, there are good reasons to attach little if any weight to the parties' understanding of it, or to their objective in entering into the contract. First, it is difficult to understand on what basis the parties' view of their contract's legal characterization is relevant, or how it should be weighed with the objective *Wiebe Door/Sagaz* factors. It is one thing to draw an inference about the legal nature of a contract based on, for example, the factors of control, and risk of loss and opportunity for profit. It is quite another to

---

had other clients. But, in considering the number of clients a taxpayer has, the consideration should not be limited to the specific taxation year in issue. The number of clients in the years before and/or after should be considered as well. See *Dynamic Industries Ltd. v. R.*, [2005] 3 C.T.C. 225, 2005 D.T.C. 5293 (Fed. C.A.).

[25] See *Wolf, supra* note 22.

[26] As a U.S. resident working in Canada as an independent contractor, Mr. Wolf was exempt from Canadian tax under Article XIV of the Canada-United States Convention with Respect to Taxes on Income and on Capital, 26 September 1980 (entered into force 16 August 1984). He would have been taxable in Canada if he was an employee.

[27] *Wolf, supra* note 22; *Winnipeg Ballet, supra* note 20.

[28] *Wolf, supra* note 22 at paras. 123–124.

draw an inference from the parties' view of the legal nature of their contract, which is the ultimate question that the court must decide.[29]

In *Connor Homes* (2013), the Federal Court of Appeal described this as a two-step process of inquiry:

> Under the first step, the subjective intent of each party to the relationship must be ascertained. This can be determined either by the written contractual relationship the parties have entered into or by the actual behaviour of each party, such as invoices for services rendered, registration for GST purposes and income tax filings as an independent contractor. The second step is to ascertain whether an objective reality sustains the subjective intent of the parties.[30]

5.3 — Timing

(a) — Cash Method

Subsection 5(1) stipulates that a taxpayer's income from an office or employment for a taxation year must be "received by the taxpayer in the year". Similarly, a taxable benefit is generally included in income under section 6 or 7 when it is "received" or "enjoyed". Deductions are allowed under section 8 when they are paid. The effect of the word "received" and "paid" is to require employment income be reported for tax purposes on a "cash basis".[31] This method provides certainty for both employees and employers.

Usually, there is not much doubt about the time for inclusion or deduction under the cash method, and the timing is not critical as long as it is within the same taxation year. Issues arise when taxpayers have control over when to receive or pay an amount and the time is close to the year-end.

(b) — Meaning of "receipt"

Generally, when a taxpayer actually receives cash, property and a bank transfer, there is no question about timing. Special issues arise when a taxpayer receives something other than cash, such as a cheque. A cheque is a mechanism for making payment and is generally treated as cash. When the payments of salary or wages are mailed to an employee, subsection 248(7) deems the payments to have been received on the day that they are mailed. Thus, a paycheque mailed by the employer on December 31, 2017 and actually received by the employee in January 2018 would be deemed to have been received by the employee in 2017. The amount of the cheque would, thus, form part of the employee's income for 2017.

The time of receipt of a wage or salary can be different from the year in which the work is done. This commonly occurs when an employee receives a late (retroac-

---

[29] *Winnipeg Ballet, supra* note 20 at para. 98, per Evans J. (dissenting).

[30] *1392644 Ontario Inc. o/a Connor Homes et al. v. M.N.R.*, 2013 FCA 85, 2013 CarswellNat 663, 444 N.R. 163 (F.C.A.) at paras. 38–40.

[31] For further discussion of the cash method of accounting, see Chapter 6 at heading 6.5(c)(i) — Cash method.

tive) pay raise or the last month's salary is paid in January of the following year. The payment will be included in the year of receipt, not the year in which it was earned.[32] Conversely, when an employee is paid in advance — in December 2017 for work to be done in January 2018 — the payment is included in computing employment income in 2017.[33]

In order to constitute a "receipt" of money for tax law purposes, is it necessary for the taxpayer to "actually touch or feel it, or have it in his bank account?"[34] The Court answered this question in *Jean-Paul Morin v. The Queen* (1975):

> We regret to say that this proposition seems to us absolutely inadmissible, because the word "receive" obviously means to get or to derive benefit from something, to enjoy its advantages without necessarily having it in one's hands.[35]

When money is paid by an employer to a third party for the benefit of the taxpayer, the payment constitutes constructive receipt in the hands of the taxpayer.[36] An amount of money is deemed received by an employee when it is available to the employee. For example, in *Blenkarn v. Minister of National Revenue* (1963),[37] where the money to pay the taxpayer's salary in 1960 was available but he voluntarily chose not to be paid until 1961, he was considered to have actually received the money. The payment was held to be "received" as soon as he had an unconditional right to be paid, which was in 1960.

---

[32] Because an employer will usually be reporting (business) income on an accrual basis, the employer will usually deduct an item of employee's salary in the year in which it was earned, even if it was not paid until a later year. The employee, on the other hand, will report the salary on a cash basis and will, therefore, not recognize an item of salary for tax purposes until it is received. The early deduction of the salary expense and late inclusion of the salary in income results in a postponement of tax. If payment of the salary could be delayed for a long time, the postponement of tax would become exceedingly valuable for owner-managers of private corporations. Subsection 78(4) of the *ITA*, *supra* note 1, accordingly limits the deferral by requiring that any remuneration deducted by the employer that remains unpaid 180 days after the year-end must be added back into the employer's income.

[33] In *Randall v. M.N.R.*, [1987] 2 C.T.C. 2265, 87 D.T.C. 553 (T.C.C.), an advance on account of future earnings is distinguished from a loan from the employer to the employee. A loan bearing market rate of interest does not give rise to income to the employee. If it is a disguised form of compensation, it is taxable. See also *Park v. M.N.R.* (1950), 1 Tax A.B.C. 391 (T.A.B.) (advance against future employment income held to be income) and *Ferszt v. M.N.R.*, [1978] C.T.C. 2860, 78 D.T.C. 1648 (T.R.B.) (advance against future commissions held to be income).

[34] *Jean-Paul Morin v. The Queen*, [1975] C.T.C. 106, 75 D.T.C. 5061 (Fed. T.D.).

[35] *Ibid.* at 110 [C.T.C.].

[36] *Markman v. Minister of National Revenue*, [1989] 1 C.T.C. 2381, 89 D.T.C. 253 (T.C.C.).

[37] *Blenkarn v. Minister of National Revenue* (1963), 63 D.T.C. 581, 32 Tax A.B.C. 321 (T.A.B.).

5.4 — Salary, wages and other remuneration

(a) — Salary and wages

Subsection 5(1) of the *ITA* brings into income from an office or employment "the salary, wages and other remuneration, including gratuities, received by the taxpayer in the year".[38] The terms "salary" and "wages" are not defined for the purpose of section 5.[39] There is no distinction in principle, or in tax treatment, between salary and wages. In common parlance, however, salary is usually computed by reference to a relatively long period, often a year, while wages are usually computed by reference to a relatively short period, often an hour or a week. Both salary and wages represent remuneration paid to employees for work performed or services provided.

(b) — Other remuneration

Other remuneration must be included in computing employment income under subsection 5(1) of the *ITA*. This includes tips, commissions, and other amounts that are similar in nature to wages or salaries.[40] "Gratuities" in the hospitality industry are often part of the remuneration package and are explicitly mentioned as taxable. To provide certainty, subsection 6(3) specifies that signing bonuses and non-compete payments paid by an employer to an employee before or after the employment are taxable as employment income.

Upon termination of employment, the departing employee may receive from the employer a lump-sum payment as compensation for the loss of employment.[41] The amount of the severance payment is normally calculated by reference to the salary that the departing employee would have received during a legally-required period of notice. The period of notice may be stipulated by the contract of employment (or collective agreement) or by employment standards legislation or by a common law standard of reasonableness. Such payments are usually characterized as income from employment.[42] In some cases, the payments may fall within the definition of "retiring allowance" and be taxed as "other income".[43] Where an employee is dis-

---

[38] *ITA, supra* note 1, s. 5(1).

[39] Subsection 248(1) of the *ITA, supra* note 1, defines "salary or wages" for purposes other than section 5 and section 63 to mean income from an office or employment.

[40] Other remuneration also includes directors fees: *ITA, supra* note 1, s. 6(1)(c).

[41] Sometimes the payment takes the form of a continuation of salary payments for an agreed period of time after the termination of employment.

[42] Canada Revenue Agency, Folio S2-F1-C2, "Retiring Allowances" at para. 2.21. Section 5 of the *ITA*, which taxes "remuneration", is extended by s. 6(3) to include payments made under agreements entered into before or after the period of employment. A signing bonus, paid under an agreement made before employment starts, is caught, for example. A severance payment, even if made under an agreement entered into after employment ends, is also caught.

[43] Folio S2-F1-C2, *supra* note 42. Subsection. 248(1) of the *ITA, supra* note 1, defines "retiring allowance".

missed and receives damages for breach of a "pre-employment contract"[44] or for defamation,[45] the damages are generally considered income for purposes of the *ITA*. However, damages for breach of a contract of employment before the employment has actually commenced are not considered to be income.[46]

5.5 — Benefits

(a) — Paragraph 6(1)(a)

Paragraph 6(1)(a) of the *ITA* includes in a taxpayer's income from an office or employment: "[T]he value of board, lodging and other benefits of any kind whatever received or enjoyed by the taxpayer in the year in respect of, in the course of, or by virtue of an office or employment."[47]

By using the phrase "any kind whatever", paragraph 6(1)(a) clearly intends to capture not only the listed types of benefits (board and lodging), but many other types of benefits that are associated with employment. Indeed, this phrase "casts a wide net"; "the scope contemplated by this phrase is plain and unambiguous: all types of benefits imaginable are to be included".[48] The phrase "in respect of" in paragraph 6(1)(a) indicates that it was intended to emphasize "that only the smallest connection to employment is required to trigger the operation of the section".[49] Any ancillary or fringe benefits associated with employment are taxable under this provision.

---

[44] *Richardson v. M.N.R.*, [1988] 1 C.T.C. 2219, 88 D.T.C. 1134 (T.C.C.).

[45] *Bedard v. M.N.R.* (1990), [1991] 1 C.T.C. 2323, 91 D.T.C. 567, 91 D.T.C. 573 (T.C.C.).

[46] *Schwartz v. Canada*, [1996] 1 S.C.R. 254, [1996] 1 C.T.C. 303, 96 D.T.C. 6103 (S.C.C.), discussed in Chapter 4 at headings 4.3(d) — Unenumerated sources and 4.4(d) — Damages and settlements, and in Chapter 11 at heading 11.5(a) — Retiring allowances.

[47] *ITA, supra* note 1, s. 6(1)(a).

[48] *Blanchard v. R.*, [1995] 2 C.T.C. 262, 95 D.T.C. 5479 (Fed. C.A.); leave to appeal refused (1996), 203 N.R. 320 (note) (S.C.C.) at para. 4. In this case, the taxpayer was employed by a mining company that required him to work in Fort McMurray, Alberta. In order to make the move to Fort McMurray more attractive, the employer had a housing policy under which the employer agreed to buy back the homes of employees if they were relocated or if they left the company. The employer later terminated this housing policy, and paid $7,240 to the taxpayer as compensation for the rescission of the buy-back right. The taxpayer argued that the payment had nothing to do with his past or future services to the employer; the payment was to compensate him for relinquishing a contractual right. The Federal Court of Appeal held that the payment was a benefit of employment. Following *R. v. Savage*, [1983] C.T.C. 393, 83 D.T.C. 5409 (S.C.C.) [*Savage* cited to C.T.C.] (see also note 50 and accompanying text), the Court concluded that "the smallest connection to employment" was required to trigger paragraph 6(1)(a) of the *ITA*. Since the taxpayer was eligible for the payment only by virtue of his employment, the payment should be treated as being "in respect of" the employment within the meaning of paragraph 6(1)(a). The facts of the *Savage* case are discussed at heading 5.5(c) — Relationship to employment, below.

[49] *Blanchard, supra* note 48 at para. 6.

Technically, paragraph 6(1)(a) apples where there is a "benefit" "in respect of" employment, and includes the value of such benefit in computing income.

(b) — "Benefit" as any economic advantage or material acquisition

The word "benefit" in paragraph 6(1)(a) was interpreted by the Supreme Court of Canada in *R. v. Savage* (1983)[50] to mean an economic advantage or material acquisition. Dickson J. stated:

> I do not believe the language to be restricted to benefits that are related to the office or employment in the sense that they represent a form of remuneration for services rendered. If it is a material acquisition which confers an economic benefit on the taxpayer and does not constitute an exemption, e.g., loan or gift, then it is within the all-embracing definition of s. 3.[51]

An economic advantage or benefit may be conferred upon an employee by an employer in various forms. Typical forms include the reimbursement of personal expenses, free use of employer's property (cars or buildings), receipt of employer-provided parking or education without charge, employer-provided interest-free loans, cash allowances, and employee stock options.

In general, whether a benefit exists under paragraph 6(1)(a) depends on the underlying nature of the expense covered by the benefit. If the expense is personal, such as daycare expenses or rent, an economic advantage is conferred on the employee when it is paid by the employer through reimbursement or allowances. The employee is in the same economic position if his or her salary is increased and he or she spends the increased salary to pay for the expense. On the other hand, if the expense is employment-related and part of the business expenses of the employer (such as office supplies), when the expense is reimbursed to the employee, there is no economic advantage to the employee. Therefore, a benefit is conferred on the employee in the case of the reimbursement of the cost of purchasing a laptop computer for personal use, legal fees incurred by an employee in defending criminal charges laid against him or her personally,[52] and the cost of personal travel,[53] but not the cost of clothing required by the job, such as a lawyer's robe or a plain-clothes police officer's suits.

---

[50] *Savage, supra* note 48. The facts of this case are discussed at heading 5.5(c) — Relationship to employment, below.

[51] *Savage, supra* note 48 at 399, approving the judgement of Evans, J. in *R. v. Poynton*, [1972] C.T.C. 411, 72 D.T.C. 6329 (Ont. C.A.).

[52] *Clemiss v. M.N.R.*, [1992] 2 C.T.C. 232, 92 D.T.C. 6509 (Fed. T.D.). See also *Pellizzari v. M.N.R.*, [1987] 1 C.T.C. 2106, 87 D.T.C. 56 (T.C.C.).

[53] *O'Brien v. M.N.R.*, [1967] Tax A.B.C. 250 (T.A.B.) (the cost of periodic trips home made by the employee's wife and children while the employee was posted abroad was held to be a taxable benefit).

In *Huffman v. R.* (1989),[54] a plainclothes police officer was reimbursed by his employer for clothing expenses. The taxpayer could not wear the clothes off duty because they were loose-fitting in order to accommodate the equipment that he had to carry and because of rapid wear-and-tear. Although clothes are generally a personal consumption expense, the Court was persuaded that the taxpayer received no benefit because the clothes were purchased for employment use. Had it been a uniform with a logo, arguably there would have been no tax issue in the first place.

Another approach to determining if a benefit is conferred on the employee is to look at whether the primary purpose of the expense is to benefit the employer. "Where something is provided to an employee primarily for the benefit of the employer, it will not be a taxable benefit if any personal enjoyment is merely incidental to the business purpose."[55] This approach has been applied by the courts to such benefits as free meals at the workplace (generally taxable except for overtime meals),[56] golf club memberships,[57] business trips and conventions,[58] and free parking.[59]

---

[54] *Huffman v. R.* (1989), [1989] 1 C.T.C. 32, 89 D.T.C. 5006 (Fed. T.D.); affirmed [1990] 2 C.T.C. 132, 90 D.T.C. 6405 (Fed. C.A.).

[55] *McGoldrick v. R.*, [2004] 3 C.T.C. 264, 2004 D.T.C. 6407 (F.C.A.) [*McGoldrick*] at para. 9, citing *Lowe v. R*, [1996] 2 C.T.C. 33, 96 D.T.C. 6226 (Fed. C.A.) [*Lowe*] at 6230 [D.T.C.]. This statement is cited in Canada Revenue Agency, Folio S2-F3-C2, "Benefits and Allowances Received from Employment" at para. 2.23. The Canada Revenue Agency (the "CRA") uses this approach in its assessing policy with respect to a large range of employee benefits. For example, regarding employer-provided cellphones, the CRA does not consider an employee's personal use be a taxable benefit if the cost of the plan is reasonable, the plan is a basic plan with a fixed cost, and the personal use does not result in charges that are more than the basic plan cost. See Government of Canada, "Cellular phones and Internet services" (8 December 2016), online: <http://www.cra-arc.gc.ca/tx/bsnss/tpcs/pyrll/bnfts/prvdd/cll-eng.html>.

[56] In *McGoldrick, supra* note 55, an employee was found to have received a taxable benefit for free meals and seasonal gifts provided by his employer. In *Deputy Minister of Revenue for Quebec v. Confederation des Caisses Populaires et d'economie Desjardins du Quebec* (2001), 2002 D.T.C. 7404 (Que. C.A.), it was held that overtime meals were not a taxable benefit because the personal enjoyment was merely incidental to the business purpose (cited with approval in the T.C.C decision in *McGoldrick, (ibid.)* at paras. 17–18). The CRA assessing practice is that no taxable benefit will generally be assessed as long as the allowance or cost of the meal is reasonable, the employee has worked at least two hours overtime, and the overtime is not frequent and is occasional in nature (usually less than three times a week). See Government of Canada, "Overtime meals or allowances": (8 December 2016), online: <http://www.cra-arc.gc.ca/tx/bsnss/tpcs/pyrll/bnfts/mls/llwnc-eng.html>.

[57] In *Rachfalowski v R.*, [2009] 1 C.T.C. 2073, 2008 D.T.C. 3626 (T.C.C.) [*Rachfalowski*], the taxpayer was found not to have received a taxable benefit for a golf club membership. This case is discussed at heading 5.5(e) — "Received" or "enjoyed", below.

[58] See *Lowe, supra* note 55.

[59] See, e.g., *Anthony et al. v. R.*, 2011 FCA 336, 2012 D.T.C. 5019 (F.C.A.) [*Anthony*].

For example, in *Lowe v. R.* (1996),[60] the taxpayer was sent by his employer to New Orleans to accompany the employer's successful brokers and their wives, who were expected to enjoy what was described as "four sun-filled days and fun-filled nights". The taxpayer was found to receive no personal benefit from the trip. While the taxpayer derived some personal pleasure from the trip, the Court found that he had little time left over for his own pleasure after looking after his employer's business, and any pleasure derived by the taxpayer was merely incidental to the trip's business purpose. The Court also found the taxpayer's wife's trip was for the purpose of the employer's business, as she attended the same meetings as her spouse.[61]

By including the phrase "board, lodging and other benefits of any kind whatever", paragraph 6(1)(a) clearly contemplates the taxation of benefits that are not convertible into money. It overrules the traditional doctrine that an in-kind benefit must be "convertible into money" to be taxable.[62] In *Waffle v. M.N.R.* (1968),[63] for example, the taxpayer was offered a free Caribbean cruise with his wife. He could not have assigned or otherwise converted his right to go on the cruise into cash; he either went on the cruise or received nothing. The Court held that factor not relevant under paragraph 6(1)(a).

(c) — Relationship to employment

Paragraph 6(1)(a) applies only to benefits received or enjoyed by the employee "in respect of, in the course of, or by virtue of an office or employment". The early jurisprudence interpreted this language to mean benefits received by a person in his

---

[60] *Lowe, supra* note 55. A similar conclusion was reached in *Arsens v. M.N.R.* (1968), 69 D.T.C. 81 (Can. Tax App. Bd.) (cost of a trip to Disneyland in California, which was undertaken primarily as a publicity promotion for the benefit of the employer's company) and *Romeril v. R.* (1998), [1999] 1 C.T.C. 2535, 99 D.T.C. 221 (T.C.C.) (taxpayer attended a convention at request of the employer). These cases may be compared with *Philp v. M.N.R.*, [1970] C.T.C. 330, 70 D.T.C. 6237 (Can. Ex. Ct.) [*Philp*], where the taxable benefit relating to a convention in the Bahamas was determined to be one-half of the employer's cost because of the considerable time available for leisure activities.

[61] *Lowe, supra* note 55.

[62] *Tennant v. Smith*, [1892] A.C. 150 (U.K. H.L.). In this case, it was held that a bank employee, who was required to live in part of the bank premises, did not have to report the value of the accommodation as a benefit of his employment. Since the employee could not assign or sublet his right to occupy the premises, he had received no benefit that could be converted into money. Lord Macnaghten conceded that the employee had received a benefit in the sense of having been relieved of the expense of providing his own accommodation, but he asserted that a person is chargeable for income tax "not on what saves his pocket, but on what goes into his pocket".

[63] *Waffle v. M.N.R.* (1968), [1968] C.T.C. 572, 69 D.T.C. 5007 (Can. Ex. Ct.) [*Waffle*].

or her capacity as an employee as remuneration for services.[64] The *Savage* case rejected this narrow interpretation.[65]

In *Savage*, the taxpayer, who was employed by a life insurance company, had received a payment of $300 from her employer. The employer had offered its employees $100 per course as a "prize" for passing courses in life insurance, and the taxpayer had passed three courses. The employer did not require its employees to take the courses; they were taken voluntarily. Obviously, the $300 was a benefit, and the benefit had been provided by the taxpayer's employer; but was it received "in respect of, in the course of, or by virtue of" the taxpayer's employment? The Supreme Court of Canada answered yes. To be sure, the payment was not made for services rendered to the employer; it was made for passing courses. The courses were taken by the taxpayer to improve her employment skills, not for any recreational motive; and this was enough to decide that the employer's payment to the taxpayer was "in respect of" her employment. The $300 was, therefore, held to be a taxable benefit under paragraph 6(1)(a). The Court held that benefits received in a person's capacity as an employee were covered by paragraph 6(1)(a), and indicated that the words "in respect of" are words of the "widest possible scope . . . intended to convey some connection between two related subject matters".[66]

In effect, the *Savage* case creates a presumption that any benefit received by an employee from his or her employer is derived from the employment relationship. For example, the value of free travel rewards received out of a frequent flyer program was considered a benefit received or enjoyed in respect of employment when the rewards were earned by the frequent travels of the employee in the course of his employment.[67] This presumption can be rebutted, but only if the employee can establish that the benefit is received in his or her personal capacity.[68] For example, a person might receive a wedding or birthday present from a friend who is also the recipient's employer; such a present would not be a benefit in respect of employment.[69]

---

[64] See, e.g., *Estate of Phaneuf v. R.*, [1978] C.T.C. 21, 78 D.T.C. 6001 (Fed. T.D.); and *Ransom v. M.N.R.*, [1967] C.T.C. 346, 67 D.T.C. 5235 (Can. Ex. Ct.) [*Ransom*].

[65] *Savage*, *supra* note 48.

[66] *Ibid.* at 399.

[67] *Giffen v. R.*, [1995] 2 C.T.C. 2767, 96 D.T.C. 1011 (T.C.C.) [*Giffen* cited to C.T.C.]. In practice, the CRA may not assess the employee if a personal credit card is used. See Government of Canada, "Loyalty and other points programs" (30 January 2017), online: <http://www.cra-arc.gc.ca/tx/bsnss/tpcs/pyrll/bnfts/gfts/wrds/menu-eng.html#lyltyprgms>.

[68] In *Phillips v. M.N.R.*, [1994] 1 C.T.C. 383, 94 D.T.C. 6177 (Fed. C.A.); leave to appeal refused (1994), 5 C.C.P.B. 41 (note) (S.C.C.) [*Phillips*], although the Court did not reject outright the notion that an employee can receive a payment from an employer in his or her personal capacity, it indicated that such situations would be rare.

[69] In *Busby v. R.*, [1986] 1 C.T.C. 147, 86 D.T.C. 6018 (Fed. T.D.), the Court held that benefits received from stock options were not taxable as employment income because they were received by reason of the taxpayer's personal relationship with her employer.

To fall within paragraph 6(1)(a), the benefit does not need to be conferred by the employer. In the *Waffle* case,[70] the free cruise trip was not provided by the employer (a car dealership), but by Ford Motor Company. There are other cases where a manufacturer or wholesaler has rewarded an effort by an employee of a retailer with the result that the employee must report the reward as a taxable benefit from employment.[71]

(d) — Valuation

The value of a benefit is included in computing employment income. The *ITA* provides guidance on determining the value of some specific types of benefits, such as relocation housing benefits, interest-free loans and car expenses. In general cases, the value may be determined by reference to the employee's cost saved by the benefit, the realization value of in-kind benefits, or reasonable apportionment.

Where an employee's personal or living expenses are reduced because of the employer's reimbursement of expenses or the free use of the employer's property or services, the value of the benefit should be the amount of the expense that would otherwise be paid by the employee. This method has been used to value the benefit derived from the free education of an employee's child if the employer is a school,[72] free parking at an employer's premises,[73] and the benefit derived from an employee's frequent flyer points accumulated on business travel.[74]

With respect to in-kind benefits, the value of the benefit can be established by the fair market value of the property.[75] If the employee sells the property for fair mar-

---

[70] *Waffle, supra* note 63.

[71] *Philp, supra* note 60; and *Ferguson v. M.N.R.*, [1972] C.T.C. 2105, 72 D.T.C. 1097 (T.A.B.).

[72] See *R. v. Spence et al.*, [2011] 5 C.T.C. 188, 2011 D.T.C. 5111 (Fed. C.A.) [*Spence*], which followed *Schroter v. R.*, 2010 4 C.T.C. 143, 2010 D.T.C. 5062 (Fed. C.A.) [*Schroter*]. In both cases, the value of the education benefit was determined to be the tuition fee (the cost that the employee would have otherwise paid). The result of these cases is now overruled by statute because of an exemption for education benefits in paragraph 6(1)(a)(vi) of the *ITA*, which applies to benefits received or enjoyed on or after October 31, 2011 where the employer deals at arm's length with the employee and it is reasonable to conclude that the benefits are not a substitute for salary. The reasons for this statutory exemption appear to be social policy and simplicity.

[73] The cases on free parking at the employer's premises follow the same valuation approach as the tuition cases. See, e.g., *Anthony, supra* note 59.

[74] In *Giffen, supra* note 67 at 2777-8, Bonner J. stated that "the value of a reward ticket in either business or first class was equal to that proportion of an unrestricted business or first class fare which the price of the most heavily discounted economy class fare on that flight is of the price of a full fare economy class ticket".

[75] In *Spence, supra* note 72 and *Schroter, supra* note 72, the taxpayer argued that the value of the benefit should have been the employer's actual cost rather than the benefit's fair market value (which was the tuition fee). The Court rejected this argument in both cases stating:

ket value, that value is the amount of the benefit. For example, the value of a gold ring given by an employer for long service was its scrap value because the ring was stamped with the employer's logo and the employer could not sell it as a piece of jewelry.[76] In another case, the value of a new suit given as a Christmas bonus was the value of a second-hand suit (the value that could be realized if the employee sold the suit).[77]

Sometimes a payment by an employer to or for the benefit of an employee has a dual character: it covers expenses incurred partly for the employer and partly for the personal benefit of the employee. In such situations, the value of the benefit for the employee should be a reasonable portion of the expense based on the facts of the case. For example, in the case of a trip to the Bahamas with a mixture of business and pleasure, supplied by a wholesaler to grocery store employees and their spouses, the taxable benefit was found to be one-half of the cost.[78] Apportionment is used where the employer's payment to or for the employee is for business purposes, but involves the provision of facilities that are unreasonably luxurious (and, therefore, expensive). The luxurious portion may be considered to benefit the employee personally, thereby giving rise to a taxable benefit. For example, in *Zakoor v. M.N.R.* (1964),[79] the employer supplied the taxpayer (president of the corporation taxpayer) with a Cadillac. Although the proportion of personal use of the car was only one-fifth, it was held that the personal benefit from the provision of the car was enhanced by its luxurious character and should be assessed at one-third of the operating expenses.[80]

(e) — "Received" or "enjoyed"

In order for there to have been an economic benefit or advantage conferred upon an employee, the employee must, in fact, have received or enjoyed a benefit or advantage. Thus, the determination of whether a benefit or advantage is actually received or enjoyed has sometimes been the issue in taxable benefit cases. *In Rachfalowski v. R.* (2008),[81] the taxpayer was found not to have received a taxable benefit for a golf club membership provided by the employer. The Court accepted the taxpayer's evidence that he hated golf and could not golf. He had asked for an alternate club membership but did not receive one. He rarely used the facilities and when he did it

---

"The equal treatment of taxpayers is facilitated by valuing their benefits at their fair market value." See *Spence* (*ibid.*) at para. 13, citing *Schroter* (*ibid.*) at para. 47.

[76] *Wisla v. R.*, [2000] 1 C.T.C. 2823, 2000 D.T.C. 3563 (T.C.C.).

[77] *Wilkins v. Rogerson*, [1960] Ch. 437 (Ch. D).

[78] *Philp, supra* note 60.

[79] *Zakoor v. M.N.R.* (1964), 35 Tax A.B.C. 338 (T.A.B.)

[80] This principle still stands, although the result of this case for cars is now overruled by statutory rules (the "standby charge") discussed at heading 5.6(c) "Automobiles", below.

[81] *Rachfalowski, supra* note 57.

was to attend staff functions or to develop business contacts for the employer. The Court stated:

> From the appellant's point of view the membership was clearly not an advantage to him. He did not even want it. It is a fair inference that the employer wanted its senior executives to belong to a golf club. It enhanced the company's image and prestige and provided a place for its executives to entertain clients of the company. Objectively, I think the membership in the golf club was primarily for the benefit of the employer.[82]

Similarly, a taxpayer was found not to have received any benefit for getting a free parking pass from the employer because he did not drive to work.[83] However, where a taxpayer was provided with free meals by the employer, prohibited from bringing his own food and had limited time for eating off the premises, the argument that no benefit was received or enjoyed did not persuade the court.[84]

5.6 — Specific fringe benefits

(a) — Overview

In addition to the all-embracing rule under paragraph 6(1)(a), the *ITA* provides for specific rules governing the treatment of some common types of employee benefits in order to provide certainty for computation or overrule inconsistent case law on the issue (e.g., housing benefits). These specific rules backstop the general rule under paragraph 6(1)(a). Allowances, automobiles, employee loans and housing benefits are discussed in this section. Employee stock options are discussed separately at heading 5.7, below, owing to their special treatment under the *ITA*.

(b) — Allowances

Paragraph 6(1)(b) provides that "all amounts received by the taxpayer in the year as an allowance for personal or living expenses or as an allowance for any other purpose" must be included in computing income from employment or office.[85] Literally, it applies to all allowances, regardless of the purpose. Even employees receiving an allowance for business travel or a car allowance for work-related driving must include the allowance in their income unless a specific paragraph exclusion is met. The purpose of the exclusions is to ensure that the expenses purportedly covered by the allowances are, in fact, reasonable and related to employment activities.[86] In other words, all allowances are taxable unless an allowance fits in one of the exclusions. The *ITA* clearly dislikes employers giving allowances to employees.

---

[82] *Ibid.* at para. 23.

[83] *Adler et al. v. R.*, [2007] 4 C.T.C. 2205, 2007 D.T.C. 783 (Eng.) (T.C.C. [General Procedure]) at para. 105.

[84] *McGoldrick, supra* note 55.

[85] *ITA, supra* note 1, s. 6(1)(b).

[86] The most commonly encountered tax-free allowances are reasonable allowances for travel expenses and motor vehicle (or car) expenses (ss. 6(1)(b)(v)–(xi)). If an allowance is in-

What makes an allowance so "unwelcoming" from tax policy perspective? The term "allowance" is not defined in the *ITA*. The ordinary meaning accepted by the Canada Revenue Agency is the following:

> [T]he word "allowance" means any periodic or other payment that an employee receives from an employer without having to account for its use. An allowance or advance is:
>
> • usually an arbitrary amount that is predetermined without using the actual cost;
>
> • usually for a specific purpose; and
>
> • used as the employee chooses, since the employee does not provide receipts.[87]

Two key notions in the above definition are that the amounts are usually arbitrary and the recipient has no duty to account for the use of the money. Because an allowance is different from a reimbursement (which is a repayment of the actual amount of expenses incurred) allowances can function as "disguised" remuneration. This is why the *ITA* treats most allowances as taxable benefits and there are very few exclusions.

The main exclusions include: allowances fixed by an Act of Parliament or by the Treasury Board; travel and separation allowances received by members of the Canadian Forces; allowances for travel expenses paid to an employee who is employed to sell property or negotiate contracts for the employer; allowances for travel expenses paid to an employee where the employee is required to travel away from the municipality where his or her employer's establishment is located; and allowances for the use of automobiles for travelling in the performance of the duties of an office or employment. In addition, most allowances must be reasonable and automobile allowances must be based solely on kilometres driven for employment purposes.

(c) — Automobiles

Automobiles are commonly used by employees who have to work in different places. Because of the personal benefit component of employer-provided cars and the luxury element of expensive cars, it is often difficult to determine the amount of taxable benefit. That is why the *ITA* contains detailed rules for computing taxable benefits in respect of employer-provided cars (the "standby charge")[88] and al-

---

cluded in income under paragraph 6(1)(b), the employee may sometimes be able to claim offsetting deductions discussed at heading 5.8, below. A number of allowances are exempted from the general rule of taxability by paragraph 6(1)(b) itself and by other provisions of the Act (e.g., ss. 6(6), 81(2), 81(3), 81(3.1)).

[87] Folio S2-F3-C2, *supra* note 55 at para. 256

[88] *ITA*, *supra* note 1, ss. 6(1)(e), (2). The term "automobile", which is used in the employee taxable benefit rules in s. 6, is defined in s. 248(1) to exclude emergency response vehicles and taxis, as well as vehicles that carry more than eight passengers, and vans and pickup trucks that carry not more than two passengers.

lowances and reimbursements in respect of car expenses incurred by the employee.[89]

The "standby charge" is the taxable benefit related to having the automobile available for use by, or on "standby" for, the employee.[90] The amount of taxable benefit is a "reasonable standby charge", which is determined under a rather complex formula. Simply stated, a maximum annual benefit is 24 per cent (2 per cent per month) of the original cost of a car owned by the employer and two-thirds of the lease cost if the car is leased by the employer. The amount of the taxable benefit is reduced if the employee's use of the car is primarily (more than 50 per cent) for employment purposes — that is, if the employee's personal use (including trips from home to the office and back) is less than 50 per cent or less of the total mileage of the car.[91]

If an employer reimburses an employee for the cost of car expenses such as gasoline, there will be a taxable benefit called the "operating cost" or "operating expense" benefit. In principle, the amount of this taxable benefit reflects the portion of the reimbursement covering the employee's personal use. But the *ITA* deals with the taxable benefit calculation differently, depending on who is providing the car (the employer or the employee). If the car is provided by the employee, the taxable benefit is generally computed by multiplying the total expenses reimbursed by the percentage of the kilometres driven for personal purposes.[92] However, if the car is provided by the employer, the benefit is based on a prescribed per kilometre amount (25 cents per kilometre in 2017) multiplied by the number of kilometres driven for personal purposes. In the case of an employee receiving a car allowance (rather than a reimbursement), the same rule applies to both situations: the amount of allowance is taxable unless one of the exclusion rules applies.[93]

---

[89] The *ITA* also restricts an employer's deduction in respect of tax-free car allowances (s. 18(1)(r)) and car expenses (ss. 67.2, 67.3; reg. 7307 and Class 10.1, Sch. II of the Regulations, *supra* note 4). The same restrictions on car expenses apply when an employee provides his or her own car for use in his or her employment.

[90] *ITA*, *supra* note 1, ss. 6(1)(e), (2), (2.1).

[91] In these situations, s. 6(1)(e) provides that the benefit is multiplied by a fraction equal to total personal kilometres driven divided by 20,004 (but only if that fraction is less than 100%). If the car is available for less than 12 months, the denominator is 1,667 per month or part month. Although the statute says the standby charge is "reasonable", the rationale for dividing personal kilometres by 20,004 (1,667 per month) rather than total kilometres driven is unclear. It can't be administrative simplicity or verifiability, since, in order to qualify for the reduction, an employee must keep some sort of log of his or her employment-related driving and compute personal kilometres as the difference between total kilometres driven (as per their car's odometer) and the log.

[92] *ITA*, *supra* note 1, ss. 6(1)(k), (l).

[93] *Ibid.*, ss. 6(1)(b)(v), (vii.1), (x), (xi).

(d) — Loans

Where an employee borrows money from his or her employer (as opposed to a bank), he or she will have a taxable benefit if the loan is interest-free or forgiven. Since the interest rate is set by the market or prescribed in the *Income Tax Regulations*,[94] this computation of the benefit is generally straightforward. The amount of taxable benefit is the amount of interest payment waived (computed by using the prescribed rate)[95] or the principal of the loan forgiven[96] by the employer.

Special rules apply to home purchase loans (where the employee uses the loan to buy a home)[97] and home relocation loans (where the employee has also moved at least 40 kilometres closer to a new work location).[98] The prescribed interest is the lesser of the prescribed rate at the time the loan is made and the prescribed rate during the relevant period.[99] This rule attempts to mirror commercial practice (i.e., five-year fixed rate residential home mortgages) in taxing employee loans.[100]

(e) — Relocation housing benefits

In addition to providing interest-free or low-interest loans to employees, employers may provide assistance to employees in connection with relocation to defray the related housing costs. Housing costs typically include a loss from the sale of a house in the former location, an increase in the cost of purchasing a comparable house in the new location, and increased mortgage expenses. The case law is incon-

---

[94] Regulations, *supra* note 4. The "prescribed rate of interest" is set each quarter based on the average yield of 90-day treasury bills in the first month of the previous quarter: reg. 4301.

[95] *ITA*, *supra* note 1, ss. 6(9), 80.4(1).

[96] *Ibid.*, ss. 6(1)(a), 6(15), 6(15.1).

[97] *Ibid.*, s. 80.4(7).

[98] *Ibid.*, s. 248(1). The 40-kilometre test is borrowed from rules that allow a deduction for moving expenses in s. 62: see Chapter 11 at heading 11.9 — Moving expenses. The home relocation loan deduction is described in s. 110(i)(j) and is available for the first five years of the loan. The 2017 budget proposes to eliminate the deduction for 2018 and subsequent taxation years.

[99] *ITA*, *supra* note 1, s. 80.4(4). These loans are also deemed to be new loans every five years, which means that the "prescribed rate at the time that the loan is made" changes every five years.

[100] *Ibid.*, s. 80.4(b)

sistent on whether there is a taxable benefit for the employee.[101] The *ITA* was amended in 1998 to provide certainty.[102]

(i) — Housing loss

Reimbursement of losses suffered by an employee from the sale of a house was held not to be a taxable benefit under paragraph 6(1)(a) because the relocation was primarily for the benefit of the employer. In *Ransom v. M.N.R.* (1967),[103] the taxpayer was transferred by his employer from Sarnia to Montreal, and sold his house in Sarnia at a loss. He received a reimbursement from the employer for the loss. The Exchequer Court held that the reimbursement was not taxable as a benefit because the loss had been incurred "by reason of" his employment. This decision is questionable, because owning a home is a personal decision and the loss was created by the housing market. Reimbursement of personal expenses is generally a taxable benefit. On the other hand, the loss was realized because of the "forced" sale due to employment relocation.

The legislative response to *Ransom* was the introduction of subsections 6(19) to (22). These provisions deal with payments made to employees who suffer losses on the sale of their homes as a result of work-related relocation. They apply where a taxpayer moves to a new residence that is at least 40 kilometres closer to a new work location. The first $15,000 of any payment received from his or her employer for an eligible housing loss is received tax-free, and one-half of anything received above that amount is a taxable benefit to be included in income.[104] For example, if

---

[101] Even with these statutory rules, the *Ransom* (*supra* note 64) line of cases will likely remain important for distinguishing between reimbursements and taxable benefits in other contexts. See, e.g., *Guay v. R.*, [1997] 3 C.T.C. 276, 97 D.T.C. 5267 (Fed. C.A.), where the taxpayer was an employee whose job required periodic relocations outside Canada. He enrolled his children in a private French-language school that was compatible with an international system of French-language schooling, and was reimbursed for the schooling costs by his employer. The Federal Court of Appeal held that the decision to incur the schooling costs was imposed on the taxpayer by the nature of his employment. Therefore, the reimbursement did not fall within the scope of paragraph 6(1)(a). Applying *Canada v. Hoefele* (1995), [1996] 1 C.T.C. 131, 95 D.T.C. 5602 (Fed. C.A.); leave to appeal refused (1996), 204 N.R. 398 (note) (S.C.C.) [*Hoefele*] (see also note 107 and accompanying text), the Court further stated that the reimbursement was not a benefit under paragraph 6(1)(a) because it only put the taxpayer in the same economic position he would have been in if he have not been forced by the nature of his employment to incur the schooling costs. Compare to other cases in which arguments based on *Hoefele* were rejected and the benefit was held to be taxable: e.g., *Dionne v. R.* (1996), 97 D.T.C. 265 (Fr.), 97 D.T.C. 265 (T.C.C.); affirmed (1998), [1999] 2 C.T.C. 158, 98 D.T.C. 6677 (Fr.), 99 D.T.C. 5282 (Eng.) (Fed. C.A.) (re: the reimbursement of extra cost of food in a remote area); and *McGoldrick, supra* note 55.

[102] See headings 5.6(e)(i) and (ii) immediately below.

[103] *Ransom, supra* note 64.

[104] The total taxable benefit will be the same whether there is one payment to the taxpayer or several payments are made over a number of years.

a relocating taxpayer lost $40,000 on the sale of his or her home, and was compensated for $30,000 of the loss by his or her employer, the taxpayer would have a taxable benefit of $7,500 (1/2 × ($30,000 - $15,000)).

(ii) — Housing subsidies

Where a taxpayer is relocated and has to pay more for a similar home in the new (more expensive) location, he or she may receive subsidies from the employer in respect of the purchasing cost or mortgage expenses. A payment received from the employer to offset the extra cost of the new home was held to be a taxable benefit in *Phillips v. M.N.R.* (1994).[105] The Court distinguished this case from *Ransom*[106] on the basis that the taxpayer in *Ransom* had been reimbursed for an actual loss on the sale of his home, whereas the taxpayer in this case purchased a more valuable home and his net wealth had been increased by the employer's payment.

In contrast, a subsidiary towards a higher mortgage cost was held not to be a taxable benefit in *Canada v. Hoefele* (1995).[107] In this case, the taxpayers were relocated from Calgary to Toronto and needed larger mortgages to buy more expensive houses that were comparable to the ones in Calgary. The majority of the Federal Court of Appeal held that the subsidy was not a taxable benefit, because the net worth of the employees had not been increased by the subsidy: they had comparable homes and no additional equity in those homes.[108] As the dissenting opinion of Robertson J. pointed out, the majority's reasoning ignored the fact that the mortgage-interest subsidy, like the lump-sum payment in *Phillips*,[109] helped the employees to purchase more valuable homes.[110] It is true that the lump-sum payment in *Phillips* had the effect of immediately increasing the net worth of the employee, whereas the interest subsidy in *Hoefele* had no immediate effect on the employees' net worth. But, in identifying an economic benefit, it is hard to see why the distinc-

---

[105] *Phillips, supra* note 68.

[106] *Ransom, supra* note 64.

[107] *Hoefele, supra* note 101 (also reported as *Krull v. Canada*). The majority opinion was written by Linden J. with MacGuigan J. concurring; the dissenting opinion was written by Robertson J.

[108] The majority also rejected the application of subsection 80.4(1) on the basis that the loans taken out by the employees were incurred in order to own a home, not "because of or as a consequence of" their employment.

[109] *Phillips, supra* note 68.

[110] Compare *R. v. Splane*, [1990] 2 C.T.C. 199, 90 D.T.C. 6442 (Fed. T.D.); additional reasons [1991] 1 C.T.C. 406, 91 D.T.C. 5130 (Fed. T.D.); affirmed (1991), 92 D.T.C. 6021 (Fed. C.A.); affirmed [1991] 2 C.T.C. 224, 91 D.T.C. 5549 (Fed. C.A.) (no taxable benefit where a mortgage-interest subsidy on relocation compensated only for a rise in interest rates, covering the difference in interest payments between the old and the new mortgage on the same principal amount). See also *Siwik v. R.*, [1996] 2 C.T.C. 2417, 96 D.T.C. 1678 (T.C.C.) (no taxable benefit where an interest-free loan was given to compensate for increased mortgage principal after a transfer to a higher-cost city).

tion between principal and interest should make any difference. The economic benefit to the employee of the interest subsidy does not disappear simply because the employer's payments are made over a period of time rather than once and for all. Indeed, a present value[111] can be placed on the future stream of payments made by the employer — and that is the value of the benefit to the employee.

Because of *Hoefele* and similar decisions, subsection 6(23) requires an employee to include in employment income the amount paid or the value of assistance provided by an employer to the employee in respect of the cost of, the financing of, the use of, or the right to use a residence.

5.7 — Employee stock options

(a) — Nature and purpose of section 7

Section 7 deals with a specific type of fringe benefit that arises only if the employer is a corporation or mutual fund trust that has agreed to sell or issue securities of its own or those of a corporation or trust with which it does not deal at arm's length (such as a parent or subsidiary corporation). This type of agreement is known as an employee stock option ("ESO") agreement. Not all corporations have such agreements. Even when a corporation has ESO arrangements, they often cover only some employees, typically executives or key employees.

An employee stock option is a right conferred upon an employee to purchase a specified number of shares of the corporation at a fixed price during a certain period of time. The shares are typically issued from the treasury by the employer. The option price is often the fair market value of the stock at the time that the option is granted, but it can be more or less than this amount. The right under the agreement is a property *per se* and can be disposed of by the employee. In most cases, however, the employee exercises the option right by purchasing shares at the option price when the market price is higher (that is, at a discount). The employee may hold the shares as investments or sell them immediately to realize cash.

In an economic sense, when the employer issues shares to the employee under the ESO agreement, there is a capitalization transaction. The employee is subscribing for the shares with cash plus the option (or discount). The option (or discount) represents the value of his or her employment effort that earned him or her the option right in the first place. The arrangement is tantamount to paying the employee for that effort, and the employee returning the amount to the employer *qua* subscription for shares, which is a capital transaction. When the employee exchanges rights under the ESO agreement for shares or a buyout, there is a disposition of property, namely the ESO rights. The *ITA* transforms the resulting capital

---

[111] The present value of a future payment is explained in Chapter 1 at heading 1.6(d) — Time value of money.

gain into employment income because there is a sufficient nexus to employment compensation.[112]

Technically, section 7 sets out the rules for the taxation of benefits specifically derived from the exercise or disposition of stock options in the course of employment. The basic rules include: the main charging rules in subsection 7(1); a special timing rule for Canadian-controlled private corporations in subsection 7(1.1); special rules to prevent double taxation and deduction by employers (subsection 7(3)) and to confirm that a benefit not received in respect of the employment is not within this rule (subsection 7(5)); and definitions: a "qualifying person" means a corporation or a mutual fund trust, and a "security" means a share or unit of the trust (subsection 7(7)).

Section 7 is viewed as a "complete code" on ESO by the courts in cases such as *Rogers Estate v. R.* (2014)[113] and *Mathieu v. R.* (2014).[114] If a taxable event falls within section 7 but none of the charging rules in section 7 apply, it is not subject to any other provisions of the *ITA*, including section 6. On the other hand, if a taxable event falls outside the scope of section 7, it is subject to the general rules in section 6. In other words, the "code" only applies to transactions within the coded environment. To have a benefit excluded from elsewhere, it has to be in the code in the first place. In the *Rogers Estate* case, the taxpayer surrendered the rights to the employer for a "Surrender Payment". The ESO arrangement was within the scope of the opening words of subsection 7(1), so the "code" was invoked, but the transaction was excluded by paragraph 7(1)(b)[115] (in force during the relevant taxation years) because the taxpayer and the employer were not at arm's length. The Tax Court held that the Surrender Payment was not taxable because paragraph 7(3)(a) provides that section 7 is a complete code for ESO. If the Surrender Payment was free from tax under section 7, it was free from tax under sections 5 or 6. The Surrender Payment was treated as proceeds of disposition, resulting in a capital gain.[116]

The main purpose of section 7 is to provide clarity about the character and timing of recognition of benefits received by employees under ESO programs. It recognizes the dual character of the taxable event: income for the employee, but capital for the employer. Paragraph 7(3)(b) ensures that the employer cannot deduct the cost of the shares even though it was treated as employment income for the employee. The asymmetrical treatment is "reduced" by giving employees a one-half

---

[112] This is the case even where the *ITA* taxes only one-half of the benefit because of the s. 110(1)(d) or (d.1) deduction; see below.

[113] *Rogers Estate v. R.* (2014), [2015] 3 C.T.C. 2137, 2015 D.T.C. 1029 (Eng.) (T.C.C. [General Procedure]) [*Rogers Estate*] at para. 38.

[114] *Mathieu v. R.*, 2014 TCC 207, 2015 D.T.C. 1073 (Eng.), 2014 D.T.C. 1165 (Fr.) (T.C.C. [General Procedure]) [*Mathieu*] at para. 85.

[115] Paragraph 7(1)(b.1) has since been added to include this type of transaction, effective March 4, 2010. The *Rogers Estate* case concerned the taxpayer's 2007 taxation year.

[116] A similar conclusion was reached in *Mathieu, supra* note 114.

deduction under paragraph 110(1)(d) under specified conditions, but the character of the benefit remains employment income.

From a tax policy perspective, the special code for stock options is part of the legislative scheme that "assists businesses in their efforts to attract and retain highly skilled employees and encourages employee participation in the ownership of the employer's business to promote increased productivity".[117] This measure is considered particularly important for businesses in the high-tech sector or start-up companies. There is also the "brain-drain" argument: that is, in the absence of favourable taxation of stock options, highly skilled Canadian workers would move to the United States. As well, the one-half treatment is now only available when the employer does not get a deduction. The tax assistance is delivered through special timing rules and the deductions under paragraphs 110(1)(d) and (d.1). Section 7 grants the employee a deferral of taxation until the employee actually subscribes for the shares. Under the general timing rules for employment income, one could argue that the employee should be taxable at this point to the extent that he or she received employment compensation (the option value of the shares), but section 7 allows the employee to include the benefit only when the employee has actually "cashed in" on the option value and subscribed for shares.

(b) — Scope of section 7

Subsection 7(1) applies where a "particular qualifying person has agreed to sell or issue securities . . . to an employee".[118] A "qualifying person" is defined under subsection 7(7) as a corporation or mutual fund trust. "Securities" means shares of a corporation or units of a mutual fund trust. The discussions below focus on corporations and shares. In addition to shares of the employer corporation, subsection 7(1) explicitly covers shares of another corporation that deals at non-arm's length with the employer.

For the purposes of section 7, the term "employee" is defined in subsection 248(1) to include an officer. However, subsection 7(5) provides that section 7 does not apply "if the benefit conferred by the agreement was not received in respect of, in the course of, or by virtue of, the employment".[119] This raises an interesting question — if a director (officer) of a corporation is granted the option to acquire shares of the corporation, does section 7 apply to tax the benefit arising from the option? The courts answered "yes" in *Taylor v. M.N.R.* (1988).[120] Rip J. of the Tax Court of Canada (as he then was) stated:

> The evidence leads me to infer the options were granted in consideration of the services Mr. Taylor was to perform as a director and he received the option *qua* director, an employee of each of the corporations. The benefits he received by the exer-

---

[117] Canada, Department of Finance, *Report on Federal Tax Expenditures: Concepts, Estimates and Evaluations 2016* (Ottawa: 2016) at 128.

[118] *ITA, supra* note 1, s. 7(1).

[119] *Ibid.*, s. 7(5).

[120] *Taylor v. M.N.R.* (1988), [1988] 2 C.T.C. 2227, 88 D.T.C. 1571 (T.C.C.).

cise of his rights under the option agreements are taxable pursuant to section 7(1) since he received the benefits by virtue of his employment with the corporations.[121]

In *Scott v. R.* (1994),[122] the Federal Court of Appeal confirmed the reasoning in *Taylor*. These decisions make sense in terms of tax policy, as the *ITA* generally treats income from an office and income from employment in the same manner. ESO agreements typically cover both directors and senior executives.

If a stock option is granted to an individual not in the capacity of employee, section 7 does not apply. Similarly, in the absence of a legal "agreement" between the employer and the employee, section 7 does not apply. In such cases, the general rules in section 6 or 5 are applicable.[123]

(c) — Acquisition of securities

(i) — Amount of taxable benefit

A benefit arising from exercising an option and acquiring shares is subject to paragraph 7(1)(a). The amount of the benefit is the difference between the fair market value of the shares and the option price (which is the amount paid by the employee for subscribing for the shares). If the employee had to pay the employer to receive the option right, the cost of the option is deductible in computing the taxable benefit. In essence, the benefit is the "cost" of the share "saved" by the ESO agreement or the discounted acquisition price for the shares.

Assume that in 2016, an employer agrees to issue shares to an employee at $20,000 per share. In 2017, when the share price is $25,000 the employee exercises the option and acquires a share (with $20,000 of savings). The employee sells the share in 2018 for $29,000. Under paragraph 7(1)(a), the employee's benefit will be $5,000 ($25,000 value of the share minus $20,000 option price) and the employee's capital gain is $4,000. The $5,000 is in the nature of employment income. This treatment is similar to the situation in which an employee receives a bonus of $5,000 (obviously taxable under section 5) and buys the share with $20,000 of savings and the $5,000 bonus.

(ii) — Timing of recognition

There are generally three possible timing points in the case of stock options: the time when the option right is acquired by the employee; the time when the option is

---

[121] *Ibid.* at 2234 [C.T.C.].

[122] *Scott v. R.* (1994), [1994] 1 C.T.C. 330, 94 D.T.C. 6193 (Fed. C.A.) at para. 16: "Pursuant to section 248(1) of the Act, an officer of a corporation is an employee of that corporation and necessarily has an employment relationship with the corporation."

[123] E.g., s. 7 did not apply in *Henley v. Canada*, 2007 FCA 370, [2008] 1 C.T.C. 295, 2008 D.T.C. 6017 (Eng.) (F.C.A.), because the employee received warrants for shares of a company that was not related to the employer. Section 7 also did not apply where the employer was an individual: *Robertson v. Canada*, [1990] 2 F.C. 717, [1990] 1 C.T.C. 114, 90 D.T.C. 6070 (Fed. C.A.); leave to appeal refused (1990), 113 N.R. 319 (note) (S.C.C.).

exercised by acquiring the shares or the option is disposed of by the employee; and the time when the shares are sold by the employee. As shown in the above example, when these points are in different taxation years, the timing of recognition becomes critical.

The timing rule under paragraph 7(1)(a) refers to when the option is exercised and the share is acquired. In the above example, there is no taxable benefit in 2016 when the employee acquires the option right. The taxable benefit is received only in 2017 when the employee buys the share.[124] In fact, if the employer is a Canadian-controlled private corporation ("CCPC"), the benefit is recognized when the share is sold in 2018 because of subsection 7(1.1).

The timing rule for stock option benefits is, thus, different from the general rule for recognizing employment income discussed above. The stock option right is property for tax purposes and has intrinsic value. It is, in effect, in-kind remuneration for the employee. Outside section 7, an in-kind benefit is taxable when it is received by the employee. Section 7 defers the recognition of this benefit until its amount is "finalized".

In the case of CCPCs, the benefit is recognized when the employee sells the shares. In the case of other corporations, the benefit is taxable when the employee acquires the shares. The assumption is that the shares of a private corporation may not be able to be sold and, if they can, there is limited market for them. As a result, the employee has to find cash to pay tax on the benefit, which may discourage the use of ESO agreements. And that would reduce the intended tax assistance to such corporations.

In contrast, shares of publically traded corporations can easily be sold for cash. A public company employee can, therefore, sell some of the shares acquired with the options in order to pay the tax. As well (and perhaps more importantly), the employee's decision to continue to hold all the shares (or not) will not change the section 7 tax consequences. In other words, the employee who is not a sophisticated investor will be able to make his or her investment (or divestment) decision on its merits and will not be persuaded to continue to hold the shares in order to defer tax.

(iii) — Adjusting the cost of shares

Section 7 does not address the "capital" aspect of the transaction when an employee acquires shares under the stock option agreement. Paragraph 7(3)(b) addresses the employer's aspect of the transaction by denying a deduction for the cost of the option. As mentioned earlier, the *ITA* provides for asymmetrical treatment of the employee and employer with respect to the stock option: the value of the option is taxable as employment income, but as cost of capital for issuing shares for the employer. A symmetrical treatment would allow the employer to deduct the cost of the benefit like other types of remuneration to employees. The *ITA* opted for the asymmetrical treatment.

---

[124] Detailed rules in ss. 7(1)(b)–(e) cover the tax consequences when options are disposed of prior to exercise.

As for the employee, the *ITA* recognizes that the shares acquired under the stock option agreement are capital property to the employee. Because the ordinary meaning of cost is the purchase price[125] (e.g., $20,000 in the above example), paragraph 53(1)(j) allows the amount of taxable benefit under section 7 to be added to the cost (in the example, the adjusted cost of the share will be $25,000). This is to prevent the amount of benefit to be taxed again as capital gains when the shares are disposed of. In the above example, if the employee sells the shares in 2018 for $29,000, the employee will have a capital gain of $4,000 ($29,000 - $25,000).[126]

(d) — Transfer or disposition of option rights

The stock option rights acquired by employees can be "transferred or otherwise disposed of", giving rise to a taxable benefit for the employee.[127] The amount of benefit is the value of the consideration for the disposal or transfer less the amount, if any, paid by the employee for the option rights. In the above example, if the employee sells the option right to an arm's-length purchaser for $4,000 in 2017,[128] the employee's benefit will be $4,000 under paragraph 7(1)(b). The same rule applies where the employee surrenders the option right to the employer for cancellation and receives consideration, such as the Surrender Payment in the *Rogers Estate* case discussed above.[129] The time of recognition of the income is the year of the disposition or transfer.

(e) — Capital gains-like treatment

A stock option benefit is characterized as income from employment, but receives capital gains treatment if the employee is eligible for the special one-half deduction under paragraphs 110(1)(d) or (d.1). Only one-half of the benefit under section 7 is included in the employee's taxable income, which is the same inclusion rate as for capital gains.[130]

---

[125] See Chapter 10 at heading 10.4(a)(ii) — "Adjusted cost base".

[126] If the value of the shares decreases to $22,000, the employee will realize a capital loss of $3,000. Capital gains and losses are discussed in Chapter 10.

[127] *ITA, supra* note 2, ss. 7(1) (b), (b.1), (c), (d), (d.1), (e).

[128] The purchaser can use the option right to acquire shares at the option price of $20,000.

[129] *Rogers, supra* note 113 and accompanying text.

[130] From March 31, 1977 to December 31, 1984, CCPC employee stock option benefits were taxed as capital gains. When the capital gains exemption under s. 110.6 was introduced in 1985, this tax treatment was changed in two ways: first, to extend the one-half inclusion to the options in public companies and, second, to ensure a stock option benefit was not eligible for the capital gains exemption by characterizing it as employment income. The result of this change is still with us today: the net amount included in income is the same as for a capital gain (i.e., one-half) but is not characterized as a capital gain (and, therefore, cannot be eligible for the capital gains exemption or offset by a capital loss). This net amount consists of two parts: an employee benefit for the full amount and a Division C deduction equal to one-half of the benefit.

The deduction is available under certain conditions. These conditions are necessary to ensure that the tax subsidy benefits the targeted businesses and is not used by avoid tax on employment income. One condition is that the employee must deal at arm's length with the employer. This is to limit the deduction to "genuine" employees as opposed to employees who are controlling shareholders of the corporation that granted the option.[131] The policy objective of the deduction is to assist businesses to retain or attract a talented labour force, not to be a direct financial aid to the owners of the businesses. In the absence of this condition, a shareholder/manager of a corporation can convert otherwise fully taxable employment income into stock option benefits and qualify for the deduction under paragraph 110(1)(d).

Another condition for the deduction is that the employee must generally receive shares (and not cash) on the exercise of the options and the shares must be "prescribed shares" (generally common shares).[132] If cash is received, the deduction may be claimed only if the employer elects not to take the deduction for the payment.[133] This is to be consistent with the asymmetrical treatment of issuance of shares under a stock option agreement.

The third condition for the deduction is that the stock option price must be greater or equal to the fair market value of the shares on the date that the options are granted.[134] In the case of employee stock options in a company that was a CCPC at the time that the options were granted, this special deduction is also available if the shares are held for at least 24 months.[135]

5.8 — Deductions

(a) — Deductions denied

The deductions that are allowed against employment income are confined to the specific expenses enumerated in section 8 of the *ITA* and must be reasonable in the circumstances.[136] As noted earlier, this limitation is made explicit in subsection 8(2). There is no general deduction for expenses laid out to earn employment income. It has already been pointed out that this violation of equity and neutrality can be justified on the grounds of tax base protection, equity and administrative simplicity.[137]

---

[131] An individual who controls a corporation is deemed to be a related person and, thus, they are not arm's length to one another. See *ITA, supra* note 1, ss. 251(1), (2).

[132] *ITA, supra* note 1, ss. 7(1.1), 110(1)(d), (d.1); Regulations, *supra* note 4, reg. 6204.

[133] *ITA, supra* note 1, s. 110(1)(d)(i)(B).

[134] *Ibid.*, s. 110(1)(d).

[135] *Ibid.*, s. 110(1)(d.1). For the definition of CCPC, see Chapter 14 at heading 14.3(b) — Canadian-controlled private corporations (CCPCs).

[136] *ITA, supra* note 1, s. 67.

[137] See heading 5.1(b) — Purpose and rationale, above.

(b) — Deductions permitted

Section 8 permits the deduction for travel expenses (paragraphs 8(1)(h), (h.1)), legal expenses incurred to collect salary or wages (paragraph 8(1)(b)), union dues, professional membership dues, contributions to a registered pension plan (paragraph 8(1)(m)), supplies (when required by contract), the salaries of assistants, rent, and other specified amounts (paragraph 8(1)(i) and subsection 8(5)). Sales personnel who receive commissions (or a bonus based on sales) are entitled to some extra deductions akin to those available against business income (such as meals and entertainment and promotion) but the total amount of these deductions (including the deduction for travel expenses) is limited by the commissions received.[138] As well, employees are only allowed to deduct interest expense and capital cost allowance (tax depreciation) in respect of automobiles and planes.[139] There are, however, no deductions for interest expense and capital cost allowance in respect of assets such as furniture and equipment, computers, or an office.

Travel expenses (including motor vehicle and meal expenses) are only allowed in closely defined circumstances. An employee who "was ordinarily required to carry on the duties of the office or employment away from the employer's place of business or in different places" may deduct his or her travel expenses under paragraphs 8(1)(h) and (h.1). However, the employee must be required to travel, must be required to pay the travel expenses incurred, must not have received an allowance for travel expenses that was exempted from taxation under paragraph 6(1)(b), and must have a T2200 form signed by his or her employer attesting to those requirements (subsection 8(10)).

Meal expenses are subject to additional restrictions under subsection 8(4) and are only one-half deductible by virtue of section 67.1. Unless these conditions are met, the expenses are not deductible.

Travel expenses incurred in the course of employment, whether deductible or not, must be distinguished from the expenses of travel to or from the place of employment. Such commuting expenses are regarded as personal or living expenses. The journey from home to work is outside the scope of employment. It is true, of course, that the journey is made by reason of employment, but it is not made in the course of employment. This is well-established in case law,[140] and also makes sense as a matter of tax policy. A line has to be drawn somewhere, and arrival at the place of work is a better point than departure from home. The nature of the

---

[138] *ITA, supra* note 1, s. 8(1)(f). Only 50 per cent of meals and entertainment costs are generally deductible (s. 67.1).

[139] *Ibid.*, s. 8(1)(j). See *Gifford v. R.*, [2004] 2 C.T.C. 1, 2004 D.T.C. 6120 (Eng.), 2004 D.T.C. 6128 (Fr.) (S.C.C.).

[140] *Ricketts v. Colquhoun* (1925), [1926] A.C. 1 (U.K. H.L.); and *R. v. Diemert*, [1976] C.T.C. 301, 76 D.T.C. 6187 (Fed. T.D.).

journey from home to work is, after all, dictated primarily by a consumption decision as to the location of the home.[141]

In cases where an employee is required by the contract of employment to pay office rent, or to hire an assistant, or to purchase supplies, those expenses are deductible under paragraph 8(1)(i). The deduction for home office expenses is similar to that available to self-employed taxpayers but, as mentioned above, cannot include any claims for interest expense or capital cost allowance.[142] The deduction for supplies is confined to consumable supplies such as stationery. Items with longer lives, such as books, tools, equipment, special clothing and uniforms, are not deductible. Nor is there any provision for the deduction of entertainment expenses from employment income (except, as noted above, for sales personnel remunerated by commission or a bonus based on sales).

(c) — Loss from employment

Technically, a loss from employment occurs when section 8 deductions exceed the inclusions required by sections 5 to 7. This might happen if, for example, a taxpayer lost his or her job and paid $20,000 of legal fees to collect unpaid salary or wages. If he or she had no inclusions under sections 5 to 7, the deduction of the legal fees would result in a loss.

It is not common to see a loss from employment because of the limited deductions under section 8 and the two-stop loss rules applicable to two of the potentially larger deductions. Paragraph 8(1)(f) applies to salespersons' expenses, the deduction of which is limited to the commissions received by the taxpayer under paragraph 8(1)(f)). Subsection 8(13) limits the deduction of home office expenses to the amount of income from employment (net of other section 8 deductions).[143]

---

[141] The classification of commuting expenses as personal expenses means, of course, that they are not only not deductible from employment income, but they are not deductible from business income either. See Chapter 8 at heading 8.4(a) — Personal or business.

[142] The expense of a home office could be deductible under s. 8(1)(i) (as office rent and supplies), or under s. 8(1)(f) (for sales personnel remunerated by commission), or under s. 8(1)(q) (for artists' expenses not exceeding $1,000). The home office deduction under ss. 8(1)(i) and (f) is strictly regulated by s. 8(13), which imposes conditions virtually identical to those imposed by s. 18(12) on the home office deduction from business income: see Chapter 8 at heading 8.5(c) — Home office expenses.

[143] An excess s. 8(1)(f) deduction for home office expenses will be lost because of the commission limitation. An excess home office expense deduction under s. 8(1)(i) can be carried forward according to the rules in s. 8(13).

6

BUSINESS AND PROPERTY INCOME: PROFIT

6.1 — Section 9

(a) — Pivotal provision

Section 9 of the *Income Tax Act* (the *"ITA"*)[1] is pivotal, bridging section 3 and the specific provisions related to the determination of income or loss from a business or property. In computing a taxpayer's income for the year, the *ITA* requires that the taxpayer's income from a business and property be included under paragraph 3(a) and loss from a business and property be deducted under paragraph 3(d). Section 9 and its supporting provisions provide guidance on the determination of these two important sources of income. The main supporting provisions include sections 10 to 37 in subdivision b (regarding computation of profit); sections 248 and 249 (defining some key terms such as "business" and "taxation year"); section 67 and other provisions in subdivision f (governing general computation of income); and some anti-avoidance rules, such as section 247 (the transfer pricing rule) and section 245 (the general anti-avoidance rule, or "GAAR").

Subsection 9(1) states that "a taxpayer's income for a taxation year from a business or property is the taxpayer's profit from that business or property for the year". The heart of the provision is "profit". Profit is determined annually and separately for a business and property. Subsection 9(2) deals with losses. In addition to mirroring the language about computation of profit, subsection 9(2) subjects the computation of a loss to more specific limitations imposed by section 31 (farm losses) and other provisions of the *ITA* (not just those in Part I as in subsection 9(1)). It emphasizes the importance of source-by-source computation by stating that a taxpayer's loss for a taxation year from a business or property is the amount of the taxpayer's loss from that source. Subsection 9(3) clarifies that income or loss from property must be distinguished from any capital gain or loss from the disposition of the property. The income stream and capital are thus kept separate: the former is relevant to paragraph 3(a) or paragraph 3(d) and the latter is relevant to paragraph 3(b).

The *ITA* delegates the task of defining "profit" to the courts by leaving this concept undefined. This "reflects the reality that no single definition [of profit] can adequately apply to the millions of different taxpayers bound by the Act . . . [because] each taxpayer must be able to compute his or her income in such a way as to constitute an accurate picture of his or her income situation, subject, of course, to express provisions in the Act which require specific treatment of certain types of expenses or receipts".[2] The courts have obliged. Section 9 is one of the most litigated provisions of the *ITA*.

---

[1] R.S.C. 1985 (5th Supp.), c. 1 [*ITA*].

[2] *Canderel Ltd. v. R.*, [1998] 2 C.T.C. 35, 98 D.T.C. 6100 (S.C.C.) [*Canderel*] at para. 29, per Iacobucci J.

Accounting principles have a significant influence on the computation of profit for tax purposes. Accounting predates the federal income tax. When the *Income War Tax Act* was introduced in 1917,[3] it seems to have been decided that tax accounting would begin with, although not be bound by, the accounting of profit or loss for business purposes. The Act's "deference" to accounting presumably reduces compliance costs and unpredictability. In the case of corporate taxpayers, the *Canada Business Corporations Act*[4] and provincial corporations and securities legislation require companies to prepare financial statements in accordance with the generally accepted accounting principles ("GAAP") as set out in the *CPA Handbook*.[5] The *CPA Handbook* says that publicly accountable enterprises must use the International Financial Reporting Standards ("IFRS") and private enterprises may elect to use the IFRS or the Accounting Standards for Private Enterprises ("ASPE"). The IFRS and ASPE are generally acceptable for tax purposes unless the *ITA* or common law principles require otherwise.

(b) — Purpose and rationale

A textual and contextual interpretation of section 9 reveals a clear intent and purpose. First, the intent is to tax net income from a business or property, which is indicated by using the term "profit". As such, relevant costs and expenses are generally deductible. In fact, section 9 is often cited by courts as permitting a deduction of expenses.

Second, the *ITA* defers to accounting for the computation of profit by leaving "profit" undefined. In the absence of specific provisions or common law principles, accounting principles are generally applicable. This has been confirmed in cases such as *Canderel v. R.* (1988).[6] However, accounting principles are not "law", and the *ITA* rejects or modifies accounting principles in order to achieve its policy objectives.

Third, section 9 reiterates that it is "a taxpayer's income" or "loss" for a taxation year that must be determined. Parliament clearly intends to tax profit annually. Each taxpayer's annual income or loss must be determined, requiring the tracking of the income or loss to the taxpayer who owns the business or property. Implicitly, section 9 disallows shifting of one taxpayer's income or loss to another taxpayer, to a different source, or to a different taxation year. The choice of words in subsection 9(2) highlights this legislative intent. Further, when an individual carries on business through a corporation, the individual and the corporation are separate taxpay-

---

[3] S.C. 1917, c. 28 [*IWTA 1917*].

[4] R.S.C. 1985, c. C-44 [*CBCA*]. See, e.g., s. 261(1)(f) and Part 8 of the *Canada Business Corporations Regulations, 2001*, SOR/2001-512.

[5] *CPA Canada Handbook — Accounting* (Toronto: Chartered Professional Accountants of Canada, 2014-) [*CPA Handbook*]. For a further discussion, see heading 6.4(c) — Relevance of accounting principles, below.

[6] *Canderel, supra* note 2. See also *Symes v. Canada* (1993), [1994] 1 C.T.C. 40, 94 D.T.C. 6001 (S.C.C.).

ers. Income from the business is section 9 profit to the corporation and is the shareholder's income only if the corporation pays a dividend.[7]

Fourth, the terms "profit", "business" and "property" indicate the presence of business or economic substance. Profit must reflect a taxpayer's "true financial position" for a given year. Ordinarily, taxpayers undertake business or investment activities for the purpose of making a profit. As explained by the Supreme Court of Canada in *Stewart v. R.* (2002)[8] and *Walls v. R.* (2002),[9] whether an activity is undertaken in pursuit of profit determines whether it qualifies as a business or property source of income for tax purposes. When section 9 is read together with sections 3, 4 and 111, the underlying rationale is to deny the deduction of paper losses or losses created through vacuous and artificial transactions that lack any air of economic or business reality.[10]

Finally, there is a distinction between "income or loss" and "capital gain or loss". Subsection 9(3) explicitly says that "income from a property" excludes capital gains and "loss from a property" excludes capital losses. In combination with subsection 39(1), subsections 9(1) and (2) ensure that a gain or loss from a sale of property is taxed as business income or loss to the extent that the property is inventory or held in an adventure or concern in the nature of trade. The *ITA* quarantines the deduction of expenses, such as interest, to earning income, not capital gains.

The rest of this chapter discusses the characterization of "business", "property" and "profit", the computation of "profit for the year" and recognition of "loss for the year" from a business or property. Chapters 7 to 9 discuss general principles and rules governing the computation of profit in terms of revenue inclusions and deductions in respect of current expenses and capital expenditures.

6.2 — "Business"

(a) — Statutory guidance

"Business" is one of the most important concepts in the *ITA*. It determines a key source of income under section 3. In the context of corporate tax and international tax rules, business income is treated differently than non-business income.[11] In the case of individuals, business income is computed differently from other types of income. Business is also a term that enjoys an ordinary meaning and has no particular legal meaning.

---

[7] See Chapter 14.

[8] *Stewart v. R.* (2002), [2002] 3 C.T.C. 439, 2002 D.T.C. 6969 (S.C.C.); reversing [2000] 2 C.T.C. 244, 2000 54 D.T.C. 6163 (Fed. C.A.) [*Stewart*].

[9] *Walls v. R.* (2002), [2002] 3 C.T.C. 421, 2002 D.T.C. 6960 (S.C.C.) [*Walls*].

[10] *Global Equity Fund Ltd. v. R.*, [2013] 1 C.T.C. 135, 2013 D.T.C. 5007 (Fed. C.A.); leave to appeal refused 2013 CarswellNat 932, 2013 CarswellNat 933 (S.C.C.) at paras. 67, 68 [Fed. C.A.)].

[11] See heading 6.3(b)(i) — Relevance of the distinction, below.

The *ITA* chose not to give a comprehensive definition. Instead, subsection 248(1) defines "business" by giving illustrative examples:

"business" includes a profession, calling, trade, manufacture or undertaking of any kind whatever and . . . an adventure or concern in the nature of trade but does not include an office or employment;

The above definition is clear about what is not a business — an office or employment is not a business. It is also clear about what is a business — "profession", "calling", "trade", "manufacture", "undertaking" or "adventure or concern in the nature of trade" is a business. However, the *ITA* provides no further guidance on the meaning of business. Like any statutorily undefined term, the *ITA* relies on the ordinary meaning, and/or the meaning under private law, of these concepts. For any unlisted activity, the common nature of the listed items should inform the characterization exercise. The listed activities are, in general, profit-motivated, organized, continuous, or systematic operations.

(b) — Organized activity

One common thread among the listed examples is organized activity. "Profession", "calling" and "trade" involve human skill, knowledge and experience. "Trade" also means the commercial activity of buying and selling goods for profit. "Manufacture" is an example of industrial, productive activity that often involves both labour and assets (financial, tangible, intangible or real estate). The level of organization often separates a personal hobby, such as compulsive gambling, from a commercial activity, such as a betting shop or casino. It also helps determine if irregular or isolated sales of property constitute trade or disposition of investment assets.

More specifically, professions involve "special skill or ability or experience" possessed by persons carrying them on.[12] Many professions, such as law, accounting, medicine and engineering, require organized learning prior to obtaining the licence to practice, and the practice of these professions requires regulatory compliance. "Calling" has a broader meaning than profession and includes "occupation", "vocation" or "trade". "Trade" refers to the practice of some occupation, business or profession habitually to make a living, and has a similar meaning to "calling".

The noun "manufacture" is defined in the Oxford dictionary as "[t]he making of articles on a large scale using machinery".[13] The making is done directly or indirectly by a "human being" through the manipulation of machinery or equipment. The articles that are made are physical objects, such as shoes or tires. The making of intangible or intellectual property is not "manufacturing".

"Undertaking of any kind whatever" also has a broad meaning. The Oxford dictionary defines "undertaking" as "the action of undertaking to do something" or an

---

12 *Bower v. M.N.R.*, [1949] C.T.C. 77, 49 D.T.C. 554 (Can. Ex. Ct.), per Thorson P.

13 Oxford Dictionaries, "manufacture", online: <https://en.oxforddictionaries.com/definition/manufacture>.

"enterprise".[14] The meaning of "any kind whatever" is influenced by the context, and should mean the "business" kind of undertaking, as opposed to the "personal" kind.

(c) — "Pursuit of profit"

(i) — Raison d'être of business

The pursuit of profit is a common thread among the listed activities. Trade is the "action of buying and selling goods and services" and a calling is a "profession or occupation";[15] both are habitually carried on for profit as a means of livelihood or gain. "Business" and "profit" are often used together. The often-quoted common law definition of a "business" is "anything which occupies the time, attention and labour of a man for the purpose of profit".[16] This "pursuit of profit" test was adopted by the Supreme Court in *Stewart* and *Walls*.[17]

The pursuit of profit test is relevant in cases where activities are undertaken for non-commercial or "personal" reasons, such as helping a family member or pursuing personal pleasure or enjoyment, or for the purpose of "making a loss" for tax purposes. Taxpayers are motivated to characterize their activities as "business" in order to offset the losses against other income. If the activities were actually profitable, taxpayers often argue the opposite — there is no "business" and the profits are not taxable as it is just "a pleasurable pursuit".[18]

(ii) — "Reasonable expectation of profit" not required

The pursuit of profit test originally had a higher threshold — "reasonable expectation of profit" ("REOP") — until *Stewart* and *Walls*. Where there is a personal or hobby element to the activity, it was said that the taxpayer must "establish that his or her predominant intention is to make a profit from the activity and that the activity has been carried out in accordance with objective standards of businesslike behaviour".[19] Objective factors included those listed by Dickson J. in *Moldowan* (1977),[20] such as the profit and loss experience in past years, the taxpayer's train-

---

[14] *Ibid.*, "undertaking", online: <https://en.oxforddictionaries.com/definition/undertaking>.

[15] *Ibid.*, "trade", online: <https://en.oxforddictionaries.com/definition/trade> and "calling", online: <https://en.oxforddictionaries.com/definition/calling>.

[16] *Smith v. Anderson* (1880), 15 Ch. D. 247 (Eng. C.A.), cited by the Supreme Court in *Stewart, supra* note 8 at paras. 38, 51 [(S.C.C.)]. See also *Terminal Dock and Warehouse Co. Ltd. v. M.N.R.*, [1968] C.T.C. 78, 68 D.T.C. 5060 (Can. Ex. Ct.); affirmed 68 D.T.C. 5316 (S.C.C.).

[17] *Stewart, supra* note 8; *Walls, supra* note 9.

[18] *Leblanc v. R.* (2006), [2007] 2 C.T.C. 2248, 2007 D.T.C. 307 (Eng.) (T.C.C. [General Procedure]) [*Leblanc*] at para. 37.

[19] *Stewart, supra* note 8 at para. 54 [S.C.C.)].

[20] *Moldowan v. The Queen* (1977), [1977] C.T.C. 310, 77 D.T.C. 5213 (S.C.C.) [*Moldowan*] at para. 12, cited in *Stewart, supra* note 8 at para. 55 [(S.C.C.)]. *Moldowan* was reversed in

ing, the taxpayer's intended course of action to convert present losses into future
profits, and the capability of the venture (as capitalized) to show a profit after capital cost allowance. The amount of time the taxpayer spends on the activity in question was also relevant.[21] The taxpayer's expectation of profit had to be reasonable.

In *Stewart* (2002),[22] the Supreme Court of Canada replaced the REOP test with the
pursuit of profit test. In this case, the taxpayer was engaged in property rental activities. He bought four condominium units from the same developer. The units were
all rented to arm's-length parties and there was no evidence that the taxpayer intended to make use of any of the properties for his personal benefit. The taxpayer
incurred losses from the outset. The losses arose primarily from interest on money
borrowed to acquire the units. The Minister denied the losses. Both the Tax Court
and the Federal Court of Appeal found that there was no reasonable expectation of
profit from property because the scheme "held out no expectation of profit from the
rental income".[23] The scheme was promoted by the vendor/developer as a tax shelter to "use rental losses to offset other income and realize a gain at the end of the
day from the expected appreciation in the value of the property."[24] The Supreme
Court reversed the lower courts' decisions and found that there was a source of
property income because the investment was in pursuit of profit. The Court framed
the characterization question as a two-stage test that asks the following questions:

(i) Is the activity of the taxpayer undertaken in pursuit of profit, or is it a personal
endeavour?

(ii) If it is not a personal endeavour, is the source of the income a business or
property?

The first stage of the test assesses the general question of whether or not a source of
income exists; the second stage categorizes the source as either business or property.

. . . it is logical to conclude that an activity undertaken in pursuit of profit, regardless
of the level of taxpayer activity, will be either a business or property source of income . . .[25]

---

part in *Canada v. Craig*, [2012] 5 C.T.C. 205, 2012 D.T.C. 5115 (Eng.), 2012 D.T.C. 5116
(Fr.) (S.C.C.) [*Craig*], in regard to the application of section 31 as it then read. See heading
6.6(d) — Farm losses, below.

[21] *Sipley v. R.* (1994), [1995] 2 C.T.C. 2073 (T.C.C.) at 2075.

[22] *Stewart, supra* note 8.

[23] *Ibid.* at paras. 16, 19 [(S.C.C.)].

[24] *Stewart, supra* note 8 at para. 10 [(Fed. C.A.)], citing the Tax Court Judge's finding.

[25] *Ibid.* at paras. 50, 51 [(S.C.C.)]. This approach was also applied in *Walls, supra* note 9,
where the taxpayer incurred losses from a mini warehouse operated by a limited partnership,
which was structured as a tax shelter. The losses were denied by the Tax Court for lack of a
reasonable expectation of profit, but allowed by the Federal Court of Appeal because it was a
commercial venture devoid of any personal elements. The Supreme Court applied the pursuit
of profit test and held that the investment constituted an income source. According to the
Court, at para. 20, "it is self-evident that such an activity is commercial in nature, and there
was no evidence of any element of personal use or benefit in the operation".

Further, "the motivation of capital gains accords with the ordinary business person's understanding of 'pursuit of profit', and may be taken into account [as one of several factors] in determining whether the taxpayer's activity is commercial in nature".[26] However, the motivation of capital gains cannot be the sole determinative factor, as the mere acquisition of property in anticipation of an eventual gain does not provide a source of income for the purposes of section 9, because subsection 9(3) stipulates that income from property excludes capital gains.

(iii) — Personal endeavours

The Court in *Stewart* stated:

> We emphasize that this "pursuit of profit" source test will only require analysis in situations where there is some personal or hobby element to the activity in question . . . Where the nature of an activity is clearly commercial, there is no need to analyze the taxpayer's business decisions. Such endeavours necessarily involve the pursuit of profit . . .[27]

The test is, therefore, relevant only in cases that involve the pursuit of pleasure or other goals. When an individual devotes a great deal of time and effort to gambling, it is often difficult to determine whether the activity falls into the hobby category or the business category. In *M.N.R. v. Morden* (1961),[28] the taxpayer, a hotel proprietor, was an "inveterate gambler", who "was prepared to place a bet on the outcome of baseball, hockey and football matches, and on card games, whether he was a player or merely placed side bets".[29] Despite the evidence of extensive gambling, the Court held that it did not establish that the taxpayer "in relation to his betting activities conducted an enterprise of a commercial character or had so organized these activities as to make them a business calling or vocation".[30] Similarly in *Cohen v. R.* (2011),[31] a lawyer who quit a law practice to take up poker-playing on a full-time basis was found not to be engaged in a business of poker-playing on the grounds that there was inadequate evidence of training as a professional poker player (he had attended one seminar in Las Vegas and read books and articles, which he claimed as office expenses); lack of a reasonable business plan or any serious systematic method of winning; and lack of a budget.

---

[26] *Stewart, supra* note 8 at para. 68 [(S.C.C.)]. The Federal Court of Appeal decision in *Tonn v. R.* (1995), [1996] 1 C.T.C. 205, 96 D.T.C. 6001 (Fed. C.A.) at para. 77 also seemed to indicate that capital gains could be considered in determining whether the expectation of profit is reasonable.

[27] *Stewart, supra* note 8 at para. 53 [(S.C.C.)].

[28] *M.N.R. v. Morden* (1961), [1961] C.T.C. 484, 61 D.T.C. 1266 (Can. Ex. Ct.).

[29] *Ibid.* at para. 15.

[30] *Ibid.*

[31] *Cohen v. R.* (2011), [2011] 5 C.T.C. 2199, 2011 D.T.C. 1195 (Eng.) (T.C.C. [General Procedure]).

On the other hand, in *Walker v. M.N.R.* (1951),[32] the taxpayer, a farmer, was held to be engaged in the business of gambling and to be taxable on his winnings. In this case, the taxpayer regularly attended horse races in four cities and bet substantially and successfully at them; he was a part-owner of several horses and moved in a racing milieu, which gave him access to inside information. The Court held that the gambling activity was not a mere amusement or hobby, but was sufficiently extensive and systematic to constitute a business. The facts in *Luprypa v. R.* (1997),[33] which followed *Walker*, were similar and the taxpayer was also held to carry on a business: he was a skilled gambler who gambled five days a week; gambling was his primary source of income; he had a system of minimizing the risk; and he won most of the games he played.

The volume of gambling and the size of winnings are relevant but not decisive factors. In *Leblanc v. R.* (2007),[34] the taxpayers were brothers. From 1996 to 1999, they played sport lotteries four to five times per week, purchasing thousands of tickets each week, paying friends to pick up tickets from stores, and developing a computer program to help pick the games. During this period, it cost them $50 million to produce $55.5 million in gross winnings. The Minister included the net winnings in the taxpayers' income from a business but the Court found that the taxpayers' activities were personal in nature. Based on the evidence, the taxpayers had won in spite of having no system, they bet massively and recklessly, and their chances of losing were far greater than their chances of winning. The large number of bets in itself was not indicative of anything other than a tendency to bet heavily. As Bowman J. remarked:

> The appellants are not professional gamblers who assess their risks, minimize them and rely on inside information and knowledge and skill. They are not like the racehorse-owner, who has access to the trainers, the horses, the track conditions and other such insider information on which to base his wagers. Nor are they like seasoned card players or pool players who prey on unsuspecting, inexperienced opponents. Rather, they are more accurately described as compulsive gamblers, who are continually trying their luck at a game of chance.[35]

(iv) — Risk of loss

The pursuit of profit test is not an outcome-based test, as the nature of business involves an element of risk. Loss-producing activities are no less "business" than profitable ones. The element of risk is a common feature of the listed activities in subsection 248(1), although the level of risk may be lower for professional busi-

---

[32] *Walker v. M.N.R.* (1951), [1951] C.T.C. 334, 52 D.T.C. 1001 (Can. Ex. Ct.).

[33] *Luprypa v. R.* (1997), [1997] 3 C.T.C. 2363, 97 D.T.C. 1416 (T.C.C.). *Luprypa* was cited with approval in *Epel v. R.*, 2003 D.T.C. 1361 (T.C.C. [General Procedure]). The Court in *Epel* concluded that the taxpayer was not engaged in a business because most of the facts present in *Luprypa* were not present in that case.

[34] *Leblanc, supra* note 18.

[35] *Ibid.* at para. 48.

nesses than for trading or manufacturing businesses. It is helpful in determining if personal services are rendered as a "business" activity or "employment" activity and if there is a genuine pursuit of profit when the losses generate "personal" enjoyment.

The fact that a commercial venture incurs losses year after year (as in *Stewart* and *Walls*)[36] does not necessarily mean that no business exists. However, "where a taxpayer does not organize his or her activities in a business-like manner" and "a reasonable expectation of profit has turned into an impossible dream",[37] the court may deny the existence of a business if there are personal elements involved.[38] The "hobby farmer" has given rise to many cases regarding denial of loss deductions due to a finding of hobby rather than business.[39] Losses have been disallowed in other kinds of cases where a taxpayer could not show a reasonable expectation of profit. Examples are an author who had published six books;[40] a professional race-car driver who occasionally won prize money;[41] a restaurateur whose restaurant regularly attracted customers;[42] a producer of machine tools intended for sale;[43] a boat charter business where the owner was employed full-time in other occupations and could not afford the 48-foot cruiser for his own use exclusively;[44] a horse-breeding and racing operator who spent the bulk of her time and energy on the operation;[45] a hobby dog breeder known as the best in the country;[46] and a lawyer

---

[36] *Stewart, supra* note 8; *Walls, supra* note 9.

[37] *Landry v. R.* (1994), [1995] 2 C.T.C. 3, 94 D.T.C. 6499 (Fr.), 94 D.T.C. 6624 (Eng.) (Fed. C.A.); leave to appeal refused (1995), 187 N.R. 237 (note) (S.C.C.); reconsideration / rehearing refused (February 8, 1996), Doc. 24370 (S.C.C.) [*Landry*] at para. 6 [(Fed. C.A.)].

[38] For example, in *Landry, ibid.*, the taxpayer was a 71-year-old lawyer who recommenced the practice of law after a hiatus of 23 years. The case concerned the losses he claimed in respect of his legal practice. The Federal Court of Appeal found that the taxpayer had no reasonable expectation of profit, and, thus, no business income source: he had continued losses over 15 years, did not keep good records, did not have a budget, did not advertise other than through a listing in the telephone directory, did not always bill clients for services rendered, had not taken any professional development courses to update his skills, and had not changed his practices over the years in the face of these losses. In *Stewart, supra* note 8 at para. 53, the Supreme Court stated that the Federal Court of Appeal in *Landry* erred because there was no personal element to the activity. With respect, it is arguable that Mr. Landry's law practice had personal elements (i.e., the deductions relating to his home office, as well as his personal satisfaction and standing in the community).

[39] See heading 6.6(d) — Farm losses, below.

[40] *Payette v. M.N.R.* (1977), [1978] C.T.C. 2223, 78 D.T.C. 1181 (T.R.B.).

[41] *Cree v. M.N.R.*, [1978] C.T.C. 2472, 78 D.T.C. 1352 (T.R.B.).

[42] *Sirois v. M.N.R.* (1987), [1988] 1 C.T.C. 2147, 88 D.T.C. 1114 (T.C.C.).

[43] *Knight v. M.N.R.*, [1993] 2 C.T.C. 2975, 93 D.T.C. 1255 (T.C.C.).

[44] *Chequer v. R.*, [1988] 1 C.T.C. 257, 88 D.T.C. 6169 (Fed. T.D.).

[45] *Urquhart v. R.* (1996), [1997] 1 C.T.C. 2611 (T.C.C.).

[46] *Escudero v. M.N.R.*, [1981] C.T.C. 2340, 81 D.T.C. 301 (T.R.B.).

with only two clients.[47] Under the pursuit of profit test established in *Stewart*, the restaurant and law practice would be characterized as commercial ventures, constituting a business income source.[48]

(v) — Employment distinguished

As discussed in Chapter 5, personal services rendered by an individual give rise to employment income if the individual has no chance of profit and bears no risk of loss. The loss is borne by the "employer". If the individual pays for the necessary expenses and bears the risk of not being paid, he or she is likely engaged in an independent business.

(d) — "Adventure or concern in the nature of trade"

"An adventure or concern in the nature of trade" is included in the definition of "business" under subsection 248(1) of the *ITA*. The word "adventure" indicates that the dealing is isolated (or involves very few transactions) and speculative in nature. The essence of "trade" is systematic buying and selling with a view to profit. An adventure or concern *in the nature of trade* is an isolated transaction (that lacks the frequency or system of a trade) in which the taxpayer buys property with the intention of selling it at a profit, and then sells it (normally at a profit, but sometimes at a loss). Accordingly, when a taxpayer enters into an isolated transaction (or only a few transactions), he or she is not a trader. But, if the transaction was a speculative one, intended to yield a profit, it is in the nature of a business.[49]

The courts have used a number of factors to determine whether a taxpayer was engaged in an adventure in the nature of trade or in a capital transaction, resulting in a capital gain or loss. The case law principles governing the distinction are discussed further in Chapter 10.

6.3 — "Property"

(a) — Broad meaning

Property is another basic concept in tax law. Property is a source of income for section 3 purposes. Property is often used in businesses or is the object of trading. The disposition of property gives rise to capital gains or losses. In the context of corporate tax and international tax rules, property income is treated differently from

---

[47] *Landry, supra* note 37.

[48] *Stewart, supra* note 8 at para. 53 [(S.C.C.)].

[49] See *M.N.R. v. Taylor*, [1956] C.T.C. 189, 56 D.T.C. 1125 (Can. Ex. Ct.), and *Regal Heights v. M.N.R.*, [1960] C.T.C. 384, 60 D.T.C. 1270 (S.C.C.), discussed in Chapter 10 at heading 10.2(c) — Adventure or concern in the nature of trade. Property that is the subject of an adventure in the nature of trade is inventory: *Friesen v. R.*, [1995] 2 C.T.C. 369, 95 D.T.C. 5551 (S.C.C.) [*Friesen*]. The inventory of an adventure in the nature of trade must be valued at cost (*ITA, supra* note 1, s. 10(1.01)) rather than at the lower of cost or fair market value. See Chapter 8 at heading 8.8 — Inventory.

business income. Subsection 248(1) defines "property" to mean "property of any kind whatever whether real or personal, immovable or movable, tangible or intangible, or corporeal or incorporeal and, without restricting the generality of the foregoing, includes (a) a right of any kind whatever, a share or a chose in action, (b) . . . money . . ."[50] This definition is extremely broad, indicating the intent that the tax law meaning of "property" goes beyond the ordinary meaning of property in private law.

Because the statutory definition is tied to the ordinary meaning of "property" and "right", it is important to refer to private law and case law for such meanings. For example, in *Manrell v. R.* (2003),[51] the Federal Court of Appeal quoted the following:

> Property is sometimes referred to as a bundle of rights. This simple metaphor provides one helpful way to explore the core concept. *It reveals that property is not a thing, but a right, or better, a collection of rights (over things) enforceable against others.* Explained another way, the term property signifies a set of relationships among people that concern *claims to tangible and intangible items.* (emphasis original)[52]

The Court stated that a "property" must have or entail some exclusive right to make a claim against someone else. It held that the legal right to receive a non-competition payment is not a "right of any kind whatever", and thus not "property" as defined under the *ITA*. According to the Court, "property" has consistently been interpreted as entailing an exclusive and legally enforceable claim and a shared right to carry on business did not meet this definition.[53]

(b) — Property income distinguished from business income

(i) — Relevance of the distinction

Section 9 and its related provisions generally apply to both business income and property income. However, the *ITA* treats the two sources differently in some cases in order to achieve the desired policy objectives. For example, the timing rule is generally accrual (receivable) for business income but cash (received) for income from property. The attribution rules of sections 74.1 and 74.2 generally apply only to income from property, which is often the object of income shifting.[54] The *ITA* taxes active business income of Canadian-controlled private corporations ("CCPCs") at an effective lower rate as a means of incentivizing job creation and

---

[50] *ITA, supra* note 1, s. 248(1) "property".

[51] *Manrell v. R.* (2003), [2003] 3 C.T.C. 50, 2003 D.T.C. 5225 (Fed. C.A.) [*Manrell*], discussed in Chapter 4 at heading 4.3(d) — Unenumerated sources.

[52] *Manrell, supra* note 51 at para. 24, quoting Bruce H. Ziff, *Principles of Property Law*, 3rd ed. (Scarborough: Carswell, 2000) at 2 (emphasis added).

[53] *Manrell, supra* note 51.

[54] See Chapter 13.

economic growth and subjecting passive property income to anti-deferral rules.[55] Similarly, in an international context, the *ITA* treats foreign business income more favourably than foreign property income.[56] In the case of non-residents, the *ITA* imposes withholding taxes on common types of property income, but not on business income.[57]

(ii) — Level of activity test

To constitute a source of income, both business and property must satisfy the pursuit of profit test. The difference between these two sources lies in the level of activity.[58] A business activity entails a certain level of "busyness". A commercial activity that falls short of being a business may constitute a source of property income. In other words, where the income is derived primarily from the ownership of property, it is income from property; where the income is derived primarily from the activity of the owner or the owner's employees, it is income from a business. For example, interest earned from a savings account of a law professor is typically income from property, but interest earned from mortgage loans by a bank is business income.

The distinction has proved most difficult to draw in respect of the rental of real estate and the holding of passive investments, such as bonds, shares and other financial assets. *Prima facie*, interest, dividends, rent or royalties are income from property. However, the form of the income is not determinative, and income from a business clearly may be derived from property. Therefore, even though rent, royalties, or interest may usually be thought of as being derived from property, the activity associated with earning these amounts may push the income into the realm of income from a business.

---

[55] See Chapter 14.

[56] For example, active business income earned by a foreign affiliate in a treaty country is "exempt" from Canadian tax, whereas income from property is subject to anti-deferral rules under sections 91 to 95 of the *ITA*. As discussed in Chapters 2 and 3, these rules reflect the policy objective of capital import neutrality by allowing active business income earned by Canadian corporations through their foreign affiliates to be taxed primarily in the foreign-source country, as well as capital export neutrality by taxing foreign passive income on an accrual basis in Canada. As with sections 129 and 186, sections 91 to 95 are necessary to protect the integrity of the "ability to pay" principle that underlies the design of the *ITA*. See J. Li, A. Cockfield & J.S. Wilkie, *International Taxation in Canada: Principles and Practices*, 3rd ed. (Markham, Ont.: LexisNexis Canada, 2014) ch.14.

[57] For further discussion, see Li, Cockfield & Wilkie, *supra* note 56, ch. 8, 10.

[58] In *Stewart, supra* note 8 at para. 51, the Supreme Court noted that the difference between business and property sources was one of the level of activity: "Business income is generally distinguished from property income on the basis that a business requires an additional level of taxpayer activity . . . As such, it is logical to conclude that an activity undertaken in pursuit of profit, regardless of taxpayer activity, will be either a business or property source of income."

The level of activity required naturally depends on the nature of the activity. In the case of real estate, a landlord may provide services beyond those that are customarily included with rented premises, such as cooking and cleaning. In the case of holding investments, activities may include seeking investment opportunities and arranging financing. At one end of the spectrum, where no or little activity is involved on the part of a taxpayer, such as the mere rental of an apartment or ownership of a government bond, the source of rent or interest is obviously the property. At the other end of the spectrum, where a taxpayer is engaged in extensive activities to manage the property and provide services to customers, such as a hotel or a bank, then the source of income is the activity. Characterization becomes difficult in cases falling between the two ends of the spectrum.[59]

In the case of corporate taxpayers, there is a rebuttable presumption that a corporation carries on a business. In *Canadian Marconi Company v. The Queen* (1986), Wilson J. remarked:

> The case law thus provides ample support for the existence of the presumption and, in my view, rightly so. An inference that income is from a business seems to be an eminently logical one to draw when a company derives income from a business activity in which it is expressly empowered to engage.[60]

The taxpayer bears the burden of refuting the presumption if it wishes to characterize its income as income from property. In *Canadian Marconi* and many other cases, however, it was the Minister who sought to characterize the taxpayer's income as non-business income because non-business income is subject to either anti-deferral rules (as in the case of private corporations) or Part XIII withholding taxes in the case of non-residents.

6.4 — "Profit"

(a) — Net concept

Section 9 has its roots directly in subsection 3(1) of the *Income War Tax Act, 1917*, which defines income to include "the annual net profit or gain" of a trade or business.[61] This expression has been understood "to have no technical meaning and the words are used as indicating the sum left after setting against the receipts of the

---

[59] For examples, see *Malenfant v. M.N.R.*, [1992] 2 C.T.C. 2431, 92 D.T.C. 2097 (T.C.C.); *Etoile Immobiliere S.A. v. M.N.R.*, [1992] 2 C.T.C. 2367, 92 D.T.C. 1984, 92 D.T.C. 1978 (T.C.C.); and *Burri v. R.*, [1985] 2 C.T.C. 42, 85 D.T.C. 5287 (Fed. T.D.).

[60] *Canadian Marconi Company v. The Queen* (1986), [1986] 2 C.T.C. 465, 86 D.T.C. 6526 (S.C.C.) at para. 10. The issue was whether income of the appellant from short-term securities was income from an active business for the purpose of computing its Canadian manufacturing and processing profits under subsection 125.1(1) of the *ITA*.

[61] *IWTA 1917*, *supra* note 3, s. 3(1).

trade or business the expenses necessary to earn them".[62] Profit "is inherently a *net* concept".[63] In *Canderel* (1998), the Supreme Court stated:

> In the simplest cases, it will not even be necessary to resort formally to the various well-accepted business principles, as the simple formula by which revenues are set against expenditures incurred in earning them is always the basic determinant.[64]

(b) — Question of law

The meaning of "profit" is ultimately a question of law. Subsection 9(1) makes it clear that the determination of profit is subject to the specific provisions of the *ITA*. By not defining "profit", however, the Act invites the use of the ordinary meaning and accounting meaning of profit. The amount of profit determined by taxpayers in accordance with well-accepted business principles is acceptable for tax purposes unless adjustments are required by the provisions of the *ITA*, by case law principles, or by "rules of law".[65]

There are important reasons that profit remains a legal concept and tax profit diverges from accounting profit. First, the fundamental purpose of determining profit is different. The purpose of determining accounting profit is "to provide accurate and reliable information about the financial performance of an entity for potential users of that information".[66] The needs of different users (e.g., shareholders versus debt holders or mangers) may be different. Accounting principles provide considerable flexibility for enterprises to adopt different accounting policies and treat particular items of revenues and expenses differently, thereby resulting in different amounts of profit. For income tax purposes, the purpose of determining profit is to determine the amount of taxable income and tax. The government is the sole user of that information. As such, while flexibility may be important in accounting, it can undermine the tax policy objectives of horizontal equity or neutrality, and certainty and predictability. While some users of financial accounting may prefer to maximize profit for a year, taxpayers rarely prefer to maximize profit for tax purposes.

More broadly speaking, as a key concept of tax law, the meaning of profit should be determined by Parliament or the courts. If profit were left to be defined by taxpayers or their accountants, it would undermine the democratic process and intro-

---

[62] Herbert A.W. Plaxton, *The Law Relating to Income Tax of the Dominion of Canada* (Toronto: Carswell, 1939) at 49.

[63] *Symes, supra* note 6. The courts have stated that it is the reference to "profit" in s. 9(1) that provides the primary rule governing the deduction of expenses in the computation of income from business or property. See also *Daley v. M.N.R.*, [1950] C.T.C. 254, 4 D.T.C. 877 (Can. Ex. Ct.); and *Royal Trust Co. v. M.N.R.*, [1957] C.T.C. 32, 57 D.T.C. 1055 (Can. Ex. Ct.).

[64] See *Canderel, supra* note 2 at para. 50.

[65] *Friesen, supra* note 49 at para. 41; *Canderel, supra* note 2 at para. 34.

[66] Brian J. Arnold et al., *Timing and Income Taxation: The Principles of Income Measurement for Tax Purposes*, 2nd ed. (Toronto: Canadian Tax Foundation, 2015) at 26.

duce tremendous uncertainty. For example, if accounting profit were determinative for tax purposes, when GAAP changed (as it did in Canada in 2011), profit determination would be changed for tax purposes. The courts have, therefore, been correct "to avoid delegating the criteria for the *legal* test of profit to the accounting profession".[67]

(c) — Relevance of accounting principles

Generally accepted accounting principles ("GAAP") are not rules of law. As the foundation of well-established business principles, they function as interpretive aids in interpreting provisions of the *ITA*. Financial statements prepared in accordance with accounting principles are often the starting point for determining profit for tax purposes. Indeed, "it would be unwise for the law to eschew the valuable guidance offered by well-established business principles".[68]

GAAP may be defined as the rules that are used by accountants in the preparation of financial statements, and that are accepted by the accounting profession as producing useful information about the financial condition of the person or enterprise that is the subject of the statements. These "principles" become "generally accepted", not by legislation or other formal *imprimatur*, but simply by their acceptance and use by accountants. Canadian GAAP changed in 2011. Prior to 2011, one set of GAAP applied to all businesses in Canada. After the change, publicly accountable enterprises are required to use the IFRS,[69] and private enterprises may elect to use the IFRS or the ASPE.[70] The *CPA Handbook* sets forth the IFRS and ASPE.[71] The IFRS objectives are to provide information with respect to the financial position, performance, and changes in financial position of an entity, that is useful to a wide range of users in making economic decisions. The ASPE are simpler and less onerous, especially with respect to disclosure requirements, and are similar to pre-2011 Canadian GAAP. But the objectives of financial statements have remained largely as before the 2011 change: to provide useful and accurate information for decision-making by the users.[72]

---

[67] *Canderel, supra* note 2 at para. 3.

[68] *Ibid.* at para. 35.

[69] The IFRS are established by the International Accounting Standards Board ("IASB"), which is the standard-setting body of the International Accounting Standards Committee Foundation, and are set out in Part I of the *CPA Handbook, supra* note 5. The IFRS were adopted in Canada because they are a common international standard. Most Organisation for Economic Co-operation and Development ("OECD") countries, with the exception of the United States, use the IFRS.

[70] The ASPE are established by the Accounting Standards Board and are set out in Part II of the *CPA Handbook, supra* note 5.

[71] *CPA Handbook, supra* note 5.

[72] A major change is to put more focus on an entity's financial position or balance sheet (assets, liabilities and equity) and changes in its financial position. As a result, the balance

As discussed in more detail in the following three chapters, accounting principles are generally relevant to the determination of profit in respect of the timing of recognition of revenues and expenses. To a lesser extent, they may also affect the deductibility of certain outlays. In *Symes* (1993),[73] for example, the Court considered accounting practices as a relevant factor in deciding that child care expenses are not deductible business expenses. Accounting principles are generally not relevant to the characterization question, such as whether a receipt is as on account of income or capital or a windfall. Characterization for the purposes of the *ITA* is a legal determination.

6.5 — Computation of profit for the year

(a) — Annual accounting requirement

Section 9 of the *ITA* requires profit or loss to be computed for each taxation year. By virtue of section 249, individuals carrying on a business as sole proprietors or owning investment property must use the calendar year to account for income or loss from the business or property. Corporations can use a fiscal period, which can be any period not exceeding 53 weeks.[74] Profit or loss from each business or property must be computed separately.

The annual accounting requirement makes the issue of timing very important. Taxpayers would be motivated to defer taxes by delaying the inclusion of revenues and advancing the deduction of expenses. Taxes deferred means taxes saved because of time value of money. The *ITA* defers to accounting practices in general, but stipulates timing rules for many types of revenues and expenses; the significant ones are discussed in the following chapters.

The real world of business and investment is volatile in terms of producing profit or loss. In the absence of relief for losses, the annual accounting requirement would mean that taxpayers would pay tax in profitable years even though a longer business cycle ends up in a loss or less profit for the taxpayer. The *ITA* recognizes this reality: paragraph 3(d) allows losses from business or property sustained in a year to offset income from other sources and taxable capital gains; and subsection 111(1) allows losses to be carried over to other taxation years in computing taxable income.

---

sheet, which shows an entity's economic resources and financial structure, is now more important than it was earlier.

[73] *Symes, supra* note 6.

[74] A partnership in which an individual is a partner must have its fiscal period end in the calendar year in which it began (i.e., using a calendar year), unless an election is made to use an off-calendar fiscal period. Income from business earned through a partnership is included in a partner's income in the taxation year in which the fiscal period ends. See *ITA, supra* note 1, s. 96(1)(f); see also Chapter 14.

(b) — Financing accounting as starting point

The computation of profit for a taxation year can be very simple for some taxpayers. If they already have financial statements (e.g., a balance sheet and an income statement), the profit or loss shown on the income statement is the starting point for the preparation of their tax return.[75] In order to provide useful and accurate information, GAAP focuses on the elements on which the computation of profit is made, namely "income"[76] or revenues,[77] and expenses.[78] A basic overview of an income statement is provided below.

The income statement (or statement of profit and loss or statement of earnings) of a business sets out the income of the business over a period of time, such as three months, six months, or (usually) one year. It shows the gross revenue from the business for the period and all the expenses incurred to produce that revenue. As shown in the sample, the "net income" or "profit" is the revenue after deduction of the expenses.

---

[75] Corporate taxpayers use the same financial statement numbers for tax purposes, disclosed in a prescribed format using standardized coding and accompanied by a form making only those adjustments that are specifically required by the *ITA* or case law. Individuals use a different prescribed form.

[76] "Income" for accounting purposes is different from income for purposes of section 3 of the *ITA*. Under the IFRS, income is defined to mean "increases in economic benefits during the accounting period in the form of inflows or enhancements of assets or decreases of liabilities that result in increases in equity": *CPA Handbook, supra* note 5, Part I IFRS, Conceptual Framework at QC12.

[77] Under the ASPE, "revenues" are defined to mean "increases in economic resources, either by way of inflows or enhancements of assets or reductions of liabilities, resulting from the ordinary activities of an entity": *CPA Handbook, supra* note 5, Part II ASPE at s. 1000.32.

[78] "Expenses" are defined under the IFRS as "decreases in economic benefits during the accounting period in the form of outflows or depletions of assets or incurrences of liabilities that result in decreases in equity": *CPA Handbook, supra* note 5, Part I IFRS, Conceptual Framework at para. 4.25. "Expenses" are defined under the ASPE to mean "decreases in economic resources, either by way of outflows or reductions of assets or incurrences of liabilities, resulting from an entity's ordinary revenue generating or service delivery activities." Losses arising from an entity's ordinary activities are also regarded as "expenses": *CPA Handbook, supra* note 5, Part II ASPE at ss. 1100.33, 1100.35.

MASSIVE MERCHANDISING COMPANY LTD.
INCOME STATEMENT (in thousands)
for the year ended June 30, 2017

REVENUES:

Sales		$	111,222

EXPENSES:

Cost of goods sold	$	83,645		
Salaries		13,637		
Rent		6,110		
Administrative		3,890		
Depreciation		1,007		
Municipal taxes		777		
Interest on long-term debt		228		
Interest on short-term debt		24		
Loss on investment		4	$	109,322
INCOME BEFORE INCOME TAXES:			$	1,900
Income taxes				285
NET INCOME FOR YEAR:			$	1,615

For the income statement, the question is how to ensure that the statement presents an accurate picture of the income of the business for the year (or other accounting period) that it covers. In accounting terms, the issue is: which receipts and expenditures should be "recognized" (included in the income statement) for the year or other accounting period?

(c) — Methods of accounting

There are two main accounting methods for recording various financial transactions: cash and accrual. These methods determine when revenues or expenses are recognized for accounting purposes. For example, in the case of the sale of goods, these methods determine when the seller recognizes revenue and the buyer recognizes the expense. In the absence of specific provision in the *ITA* or common law principle, these accounting methods determine profit or loss for tax purposes.

(i) — Cash method

Under the cash method, all items of income actually received in the accounting period are recognized for that period, and all expenses actually paid in the accounting period are recognized for that period. The income statement does not take account of amounts receivable or amounts payable. The cash method of accounting has the advantage of simplicity, but has little else going for it. As a result, it is rarely used for business income and only farmers and fishermen[79] are allowed to use it for tax purposes.

The cash method will often fail to provide a realistic statement of the result of business operations for a particular period. For example, if revenue earned over two years was received in a lump sum in the second year, the cash method would make the first year (without the cash receipt, and hence without the income) look unjustifiably bad, and the second year (with the full amount of cash received) look unjustifiably good. Similarly, if a two-year supply of inventory was acquired in a single purchase, the cash method would make the first year (with its large inventory expense) look unjustifiably bad and the second year (with no inventory expense) look unjustifiably good. Under the cash method, even the cost of a capital asset, such as a building, machinery or vehicle, which would be useful to the business for many years, would be recognized as an expense in the year in which it was paid for. It should be noted that this method of accounting for capital assets has never been permitted for tax purposes, even for cash-method taxpayers, because of the prohibition under paragraph 18(1)(b) on the deduction of "capital" outlays.

Generally speaking, income from property (such as rental income) can be computed by either the cash method or the accrual method, provided that 1) either method would produce an appropriate statement of income, and 2) the method chosen is used consistently. As a result, while many corporations will use the accrual method for rental income, many individuals will use the cash method. In the case of interest income, subsections 12(3), (4) and (9) and regulation 7000 limit the use of the cash method to postpone recognition of the income.[80] In the case of royalties and dividends from corporate shares, paragraphs 12(1)(g) and (j) require the use of the cash method.

Capital gains, which can be reported in a business' financial statements, are taxed under a special code of rules in subdivision c.[81] It is not appropriate to describe those rules as either the cash method or the accrual method, but they are closer to the cash method, because they generally tax only realized gains.

(ii) — Accrual method

For most businesses, the "accrual method" of accounting is the only one that is acceptable under GAAP. Under the accrual method, revenue items are recognized as income when they are earned (regardless of whether or not the corresponding payment from the customer has been received). Expenditure items are recognized as charges against income when they are incurred (even if they have not yet been

---

[79] *ITA, supra* note 1, s. 28 expressly permits income from a "farming or fishing business" to be computed by the cash method. Paragraph 12(1)(b) and s. 28 require amounts to be included in income when they become receivable in the case of the sale of goods and services that are sold in the course of a business other than farming or fishing.

[80] See Chapter 7 at heading 7.8 — Interest.

[81] See Chapter 10.

paid), with the exception of inventory and capital asset expenditures. Inventory expenditures are charged against income when the corresponding revenue is recognized; capital asset expenditures are charged against income over the life of the asset, as its productive capacity is consumed. The general idea is that revenues should be matched to the period to which they relate and expenses should also be so matched. This is often described as the "matching" concept or principle.[82]

Recognizing an item of revenue before payment has been received or recognizing an expense before it has been paid is known as making an "accrual", which leads to the description of the accrual method of accounting. The opposite process to accrual, namely deferral, is, as we shall see, an equally important part of the so-called accrual method of accounting. Revenue[83] is normally treated as "earned" for financial accounting purposes in the period in which the recipient substantially completes performance of everything he or she is required to do as long as the amount due is ascertainable and there is no uncertainty about its collection. Thus, a lawyer or other supplier of services will normally recognize a fee as revenue when he or she completes a client's work and is ready to render a bill. A seller of goods will normally recognize a sale as revenue when the goods are delivered. An expense[84] is "incurred" when a cost is used up in the business. Costs that relate to the current period must be recognized in that period, even if they have not yet been paid, and even if there is no immediate liability to pay them. For example, a telephone bill may not be received until several weeks after the calls have been made. However, under the accrual method of accounting, the bill must be recognized as an expense of the period in which the calls were made. This is also normally the case for tax purposes, unless the *ITA* provides otherwise.[85]

Accrual is the process of recognizing a revenue or expense item before the corresponding cash receipt/payment has been received/paid. The reverse situation, called deferral, occurs when the cash receipt/payment has been received/paid in advance of the item being recognized as a revenue/expense item respectively. For example, if a business received a fee or payment in the year before it had substantially completed performance of its side of the agreement, it would normally defer the item of income. The fee or payment would be recognized on the balance sheet as an increase in cash, but it would not appear in the income statement for the year of receipt. Instead, it would be carried on the balance sheet as a liability. It is a liability in the loose accounting sense that, if performance was not ultimately completed, the business would have to repay the amount. The liability would eventually be

---

[82] Under the IFRS, an expense is only allowed to be deferred if it results in an asset (economic benefit). Conversely, a revenue can only be deferred if it results in a liability. The matching principle is discussed further at heading 6.5(d)(i) — Matching principle, below.

[83] See *CPA Handbook, supra* note 5, Part I IFRS, IAS 18, Revenue.

[84] *Ibid.*, Part I IFRS, IAS Framework for the Preparation and Presentation of Financial Statements.

[85] E.g., s. 20(1)(aa) of the *ITA, supra* note 1, allows a deduction for landscaping expenses only if they have been paid in the year.

removed from the balance sheet and recognized as a revenue item in the income statement in the year performance was completed. This is normally the case for tax purposes as well.[86]

(d) — Timing principles

(i) — Matching principle

The matching principle says that expenses are recognized in the period the related income is earned, and income is recognized in the period the related expenses are incurred. In essence, income is matched with expenses and *vice versa*. This is reflected in the accrual method of accounting. The cash method of accounting violates this principle, as expenses are charged to the income statement in the accounting period in which they are paid irrespective of whether they relate to the revenue earned during that period.

However, the matching principle is not a principle of law. This was made clear in the *Canderel* (1998)[87] and *Toronto College Park* (1998)[88] decisions. The taxpayers were landlords that had paid tenant inducement payments ("TIPs") to tenants in order to induce them to enter into long-term lease contracts. The issue in these cases was not the deductibility of the TIPs, but the timing of deduction, that is, whether the TIPs should be deducted in full in the year of payment (current deduction) or deducted over the life of the leases to which they related (the so-called "amortization" method). GAAP allows TIPs to be recognized as either an operating expense, which is fully deductible in the year it was paid, or a capital expenditure amortized over the life of the relevant lease, depending on the circumstances.[89] In both cases, the taxpayers' accountants had decided that the amortization method was the most appropriate financial statement method in the circumstances.[90] For tax purposes, the taxpayers claimed a full deduction in the year of payment, which reduced the taxpayers' profit and resulted in a deferral of tax. The Minister reassessed the taxpayers, arguing that the TIPs should be amortized over the term of the lease in order for the deduction to be matched to the income from the lease contracts.

As will be explained in Chapters 8 and 9, the distinction between current expenses and capital expenses involves the issue of the timing of deductions. The general principle is to determine whether an expense brings value to the business for the

---

[86] For tax purposes, the deferral of an income receipt is regulated by ss. 12(1)(a) and 20(1)(m), discussed in Chapter 8 at heading 8.7(d)(iv) — Unearned amounts.

[87] *Canderel, supra* note 2.

[88] *Toronto College Park v. R.*, [1998] 2 C.T.C. 78, 98 D.T.C. 6088 (S.C.C.) [*College Park*], which the Supreme Court heard immediately after *Canderel, ibid.*

[89] The *CBCA, supra* note 4, and most provincial corporations and securities legislation, require companies to prepare financial statements for their shareholders in accordance with generally accepted accounting principles ("GAAP") as defined in the *CPA Handbook*.

[90] Amortization is the preferred GAAP method for tenant inducement payments ("TIPs").

current year only, or to the current year as well as future years. If an expense has an "enduring benefit", it is a capital expense and should be amortized; if the value of an expense is totally used up in the current year, it is a current expense. The Court found that the TIPs gave rise to significant immediate benefits to the general business of the taxpayer. Because the TIPs were not referable to any particular items of income (i.e., they could not be correlated directly, or at least not principally, with the rents generated by the leases that they induced), they, therefore, qualified as running expenses to which the matching principle did not apply. The Court also emphasized that the matching principle was not a rule of law.[91] Since there was no accurate way of apportioning the benefits generated by TIPs, the Court allowed the taxpayers to deduct the TIPs in the year of payment to obtain an "accurate picture of profit". According to the Court, the Minister had not proved that the amortization method was more accurate.[92]

While the courts have said that the matching principle is not law, it is important to note that the *ITA* has adopted the matching principle in the design of several statutory rules for deductions. Among them are the deferral of prepaid expenses[93] and the paragraph 20(1)(a) deduction for capital cost allowance (tax depreciation).[94]

(ii) — Realization principle

The realization principle is discussed in more detail in Chapters 7 and 10. It determines when a receipt has the quality of time and must be recognized for tax purposes. In *Kruger Inc. v. R.* (2016),[95] the Federal Court of Appeal held that the realization principle is not an overarching principle and the timing methods for revenue inclusions are governed by the "accurate picture of profit" rule established in *Canderel*.[96]

In *Kruger*, the taxpayer used the "mark-to-market" valuation method to value foreign currency option contracts for the purposes of computing its losses under subsection 9(2) of the *ITA*. The Court found that the taxpayer's method of accounting provided an accurate picture of income, that there was nothing in the statute or

---

[91] *Canderel, supra* note 2 at para. 47.

[92] *Ibid.* at para. 64; and *College Park, supra* note 88 at para. 19. Presumably, if the taxpayers had wanted to amortize the payments over the term of the lease, they would have been able to do that as well, since this method was just as accurate. However, if this had been the situation, the case would never have come to court.

[93] *ITA, supra* note 1, s. 18(9), discussed in Chapter 8 at heading 8.7(e) — Prepaid expenses.

[94] The capital cost allowance deduction is explained in Chapter 9.

[95] *Kruger Inc. v. R.* (2016), 2016 FCA 186, [2016] 6 C.T.C. 161, 2016 D.T.C. 5079 (F.C.A.) [*Kruger*].

[96] *Canderel, supra* note 2.

common law that excluded this method, and that the Minister had not proved that an alternative method was more accurate.[97]

6.6 — "Loss for the year"

(a) — Policy concerns about losses

A business activity involves a degree of financial risk. Indeed, the taxation of business income softens the financial risk by allowing the deduction of business losses (and carryovers to other years if necessary). If a taxpayer engages in a business-like activity that consistently incurs losses, can the losses be deducted by the taxpayer (who may have other income, perhaps professional income, that would be sheltered by the losses)? Until the *Stewart* case,[98] the courts had answered no to this question: for an activity to be a business, there had to be a "reasonable expectation of profit" ("REOP").[99] The Canada Revenue Agency (the "CRA") had used the REOP test to deny the recognition of losses from tax shelters (as well as personal hobbies) on the grounds that these losses were not from a business or property source, and were, thus, not deductible under paragraph 3(d) of the *ITA*.

Many tax shelters involve investments in real estate or stocks. These investments offer the possibility of earning rent or dividends (income from property) as well as obtaining capital gains in the future. Because of the current deduction of interest expense and capital cost allowance in the case of rental property, the income stream produces a loss, while the capital stream produces a profit. In the past, the CRA has challenged the deduction of losses on the grounds that 1) interest was not deductible under paragraph 20(1)(c), as in *Ludco Enterprises Ltd. v. Canada* (2001),[100] and 2) there was no source of income for the purposes of paragraph 3(d), as in *Stewart*[101] and *Walls*.[102] The CRA did not prevail in these cases.

The *Stewart* and *Walls* cases terminated the use of the REOP test as a judicial stop-loss rule. In *Ludco*, the taxpayer deducted about $6 million in interest expenses during the period in which only $600,000 in dividends was received. The dividend stream was intended to generate losses as a result of the interest expense deduction. The investment was "profitable" to the taxpayer because of the favourable treatment of capital gains from the disposition of the shares. The Supreme Court al-

---

[97] In response to *Kruger, supra* note 95, the 2017 federal budget proposed to allow taxpayers who hold any derivatives on income account to elect to be taxed on those derivatives on a mark-to-market basis, provided that such derivatives are valued at fair market value under accounting principles. This election is to be available in respect of taxation years beginning after March 22, 2017 and can be revoked with the consent of the Minister.

[98] *Stewart, supra* note 8.

[99] See heading 6.2(c)(ii) — "Reasonable expectation of profit" not required, above.

[100] *Ludco Enterprises Ltd. v. Canada* (2001), [2002] 1 C.T.C. 95, 2001 D.T.C. 5505 (Eng.), 2001 D.T.C. 5518 (Fr.) (S.C.C.), discussed in Chapter 8 at heading 8.9(c) — Purpose test.

[101] *Stewart, supra* note 8.

[102] *Walls, supra* note 9.

lowed the interest deduction under paragraph 20(1)(c) without addressing the issue of whether there is a source of income from property. The Court was in an unenviable position in these cases and in *Ludco*. If an investment activity was held not to constitute a business, then the taxpayer would be denied the losses on the income stream, while paying tax on the capital gains. In computing capital gains, no deduction is allowed for interest expenses incurred in respect of the investment property, as there is no mechanism under the *ITA* that allows the taxpayer to capitalize or defer interest expenses or the losses. This is contrary to the fundamental principle that income is a net concept (net of losses), but it is the unfortunate outcome that results from having two distinct legislative schemes for taxing income from a source and capital gains.

As the Supreme Court of Canada has repeatedly stated: "[I]n matters of tax law, a court should always be reluctant to engage in judicial innovation and rule-making."[103] It is clear that the solution to the tax shelter loss problem must come from Parliament. In October 2003, the Department of Finance released, for public consultation, draft legislation to restrict the deductibility of losses (draft section 3.1 of the *ITA*). This draft legislation attracted a great deal of controversy because of concerns about the potential effects on normal business and capital market activities. Accordingly, although other more modest proposals were considered and introduced, section 3.1 was withdrawn in 2014.[104]

In terms of the legislative purpose and rationale of sections 9 and 3, it is clearly problematic to treat an investment in a tax shelter as a "source of income" when it is designed to produce a loss from the property while generating potential capital gains. Many tax shelter investments *per se* would not produce any economic profit for the investor were it not for the immediate deductibility of losses on the income stream and the one-half taxation of the eventual capital gain. Allowing tax shelter losses to reduce or even eliminate the investor's tax base would frustrate the legislative purpose. As discussed further in Chapter 17, that is why the GAAR may be invoked to deny the losses.

(b) — Section 9(2)

It will be recalled that paragraph 3(d) of the *ITA* allows a taxpayer to deduct a loss from a business or property in computing his or her income for the year, and if the taxpayer's positive income for the year is not sufficient to absorb the loss, paragraph 111(1)(a) allows the excess amount to be deductible in computing taxable income for the 3 prior years and the 20 subsequent years as a non-capital loss.[105]

---

[103] See, e.g., *Stewart, supra* note 8 at para. 42.

[104] See the government's first report under s. 162(2) of the *Financial Administration Act*, R.S.C. 1985, c. F-11, which did not include draft s. 3.1 of the *ITA*. This report was tabled in the House of Commons on November 6, 2014 and listed all outstanding tax legislative proposals announced before April 1, 2013 that had not previously been withdrawn or enacted.

[105] See Chapter 12 at heading 12.3(b)(ii) — Non-capital losses.

What is a loss from a business or property? Subsection 9(2) provides that, subject to section 31 (for farm losses), a taxpayer's loss from a business or property is the amount of the taxpayer's loss from "that source" computed by applying the provisions of the *ITA* respecting the computation of income from "that source" with such modifications as the circumstances require. Subsection 9(3) also clarifies that a loss from property excludes any capital loss from the disposition of that property.[106]

If an activity has no personal element and is clearly commercial, it will be a "source" (of income) for the purposes of section 9, and the loss from the activity will be a loss from "that source". The rules for personal or hobby losses and the section 31 restrictions for farm losses are discussed below.

(c) — Personal or hobby losses

As discussed earlier, if a taxpayer has a loss from an activity that has a personal element or is a hobby, the common law pursuit of profit test must be met in order to determine whether there is a "source" (of income) from a business or property.[107] If this test is not met, there is no "source" (of income) and, therefore, no loss from a business or property. Personal or hobby losses that do not meet the pursuit of profit test are losses resulting from personal consumption, and allowing their deduction would violate the "ability to pay" principle.

(d) — Farm losses

Losses from the business of farming are treated differently than losses from other businesses. Subsection 31(1), as amended by a 2013 federal budget proposal, reads as follows:

> If a taxpayer's chief source of income for a taxation year is neither farming nor a combination of farming and some other source of income *that is a subordinate source of income for the taxpayer (italics added)*, then for the purposes of sections 3 and 111 the taxpayer's loss, if any, for the year from all farming businesses carried on by the taxpayer is deemed to be the total of
>
> (a)   the lesser of
>
>   (i)   the amount by which the total of the taxpayer's losses for the year, determined without reference to this section . . . from all farming businesses carried on by the taxpayer exceeds the total of the taxpayer's incomes for the year, so determined from all such businesses, and
>
>   (ii) $2,500 plus the lesser of
>
>   (A)   1/2 of the amount by which the amount determined under subparagraph (i) exceeds $2,500, and
>
>   (B) $15,000[108]

---

[106] See heading 6.1 — Section 9, above.

[107] See heading 6.2(c) — "Pursuit of profit", above.

[108] *ITA, supra* note 1, s. 31(1).

The words in italics (i.e., "that is a subordinate source of income for the taxpayer") were added to the so-called "combination test" and are applicable to taxation years ending after March 21, 2013.

The phrase "chief source of income" is not defined in the *ITA*. In *Moldowan v. R.* (1977),[109] the Supreme Court of Canada held that a taxpayer's "chief source of income" was not to be determined solely by comparing the amount of income earned from farming with the amount earned from other sources. It depended as well on the taxpayer's lifestyle. Thus, a taxpayer for whom farming was the main occupation in terms of time and effort would be held to have farming as his or her "chief source of income", even if other sources of income tended to be more profitable.[110] Such a taxpayer would be free of the restrictions of section 31.

In *Moldowan*, the combination test, which at that time referred to a taxpayer whose chief source of income is "a combination of farming and some other source of income", was interpreted as requiring that the "other source of income" be ancillary or subordinate to farming. In *Canada v. Craig* (2012),[111] the Supreme Court of Canada overruled the *Moldowan* interpretation of the "combination test", holding that there was no requirement that farming be the predominant source of income. The current rule is the 2013 federal budget's response to the decision in *Craig*, which was to amend section 31 and effectively makes the *Moldowan* interpretation a statutory requirement.

In the end, section 31 applies to the taxpayer who operates a farm as a sideline business and does not meet the "chief source" or "combination test". A typical case might be a taxpayer in a high tax bracket whose chief source of income is not farming (for example, a lawyer like the taxpayer in *Craig*), but who also owns a farm as a recreational property and farms it (at least partly as a hobby). If that person could deduct all farming losses, the deduction would enable him or her to shelter from tax some professional income. Of course, even if the losses only cost the taxpayer 50 cents on the dollar, that is still a cost. However, the farm is only a source of recreation for the taxpayer and it may be appreciating in value (an appreciation that may eventually be half-taxed as a capital gain, or perhaps less than that, if the principal residence exemption applies). Section 31 accordingly restricts the deductibility of a part-time farmer's farming losses.

Under the current rules, section 31 permits the recognition of the first $2,500 of losses and one-half of the next $25,000 of losses from farming.[112] The result is that a farmer subject to the section 31 restriction on losses cannot deduct more than $15,000 of farming losses from his or her non-farming income in any taxation year,

---

[109] *Moldowan, supra* note 20.

[110] The objective factors to be considered were set out in *Moldowan, ibid.*, and are discussed briefly at heading 6.2(c)(ii) — "Reasonable expectation of profit" not required, above.

[111] *Craig, supra* note 20.

[112] These limits apply to taxation years ending after March 21, 2013. The limits for earlier years were the first $2,500 and half of the next $12,500 of losses (i.e., a maximum of $8,750 in a given taxation year).

and can deduct that much only if the farm suffered a loss of $27,500 or more. For example, a taxpayer who incurs a loss from farming of $22,500 would be entitled to recognize a loss for the current year of $12,500 ($2,500 plus one-half of $20,000). The balance of the loss, namely $10,000, would be disallowed. The portion of the loss from farming that is disallowed by section 31 (in our example, $10,000) is described by subsection 31(1.1) as the taxpayer's "restricted farm loss" for the year, and can be carried over to other years, but only against farming income.[113]

Section 31 applies only where the part-time farming operation is conducted with the pursuit of profit. As discussed earlier, if there is no pursuit of profit, there is no "source" and losses are completely disallowed as "hobby" losses. It is certainly arguable that, where a farm is operated with the pursuit of profit, any losses should be fully recognized. However, in the case of the part-time farmer, the farm, although operated with the pursuit of profit, often serves as a place of recreation as well. If the farm incurs a loss, it is often realistic to attribute part of the loss to the recreational benefit: to that extent, the loss is a consumption expense (personal or living expense) that should not be deductible. Yet it is very difficult to determine on a case-by-case basis what portion of a farming loss is to be treated as a deductible business loss and what portion is to be treated as a non-deductible personal loss. It is this difficulty that led Parliament to create an arbitrary halfway house between the full-time farmer whose losses are recognized in full and the hobby farmer whose losses are not recognized at all, and convinced the government to override the decision in *Craig* with a statutory amendment. Section 31, by restricting the recognition of the losses of the part-time farmer whose chief source of income is not farming or a "a combination of farming and some other source of income that is a subordinate source of income for the taxpayer", attempts to prevent the use of the tax system to finance what may be partly a hobby.

---

[113] Paragraph 111(1)(c) allows restricted farm losses to be carried back 3 years and forward 20 years, but only against farming income. Like non-capital losses, which are deductible under paragraph 111(1)(a), paragraph 111(1)(d) allows farm losses that are not restricted farm losses to be carried back 3 years and forward 20 years without any restriction.

7

BUSINESS AND PROPERTY INCOME: INCLUSIONS

7.1 — Legislative scheme

(a) — Technical design

Section 9 of the *Income Tax Act* (the *"ITA"*)[1] says that a taxpayer's income from a business or property for a taxation year is the taxpayer's profit from that business or property. As discussed in the previous chapter, by leaving "profit" undefined, the *ITA* generally defers to generally accepted accounting principles ("GAAP") and other well-accepted business principles for the computation of profit. As a net concept, profit is the result of deducting costs and expenses from revenues. In the absence of specific provisions in the *ITA* or case law principles, inclusions in computing profit under GAAP are generally accepted for tax purposes.

Sections 12 to 17 provide specific "inclusion" rules. Section 12 deals with revenues arising from common business activities or investment property. Section 13 is a technical provision to "recapture" the excessive depreciation (capital cost allowance, or "CCA") deducted in previous years.[2] Sections 15 to 17 are, in essence, rules to capture the economic substance of the transactions. Subsection 15(1) includes in income of a shareholder the value of various benefits received by virtue of a shareholding, including shareholder loans received by individuals. Subsection 16(1) includes in income any "disguised" or "imputed" interest in blended payments, debt obligations issued at a discount, or indexed debt obligations. Section 17 imputes interest to a Canadian corporation in respect of any amount owed to the corporation by a related foreign corporation (typically a parent or sister corporation) in certain circumstances. These statutory inclusion rules speak to characterization and timing issues. This chapter discusses the basic rules in section 12 and the blended payment rules in section 16.

(b) — Purpose and rationale

As part of the ecosystem for computing profit, the inclusion rules support section 9 in several ways. First, they express a broad scope of what is included in computing income from a business or property. Examples include:

- "any amount receivable by the taxpayer in respect of property sold or services rendered in the course of a business in the year ..." (paragraph 12(1)(b));

---

[1] R.S.C. 1985 (5th Supp.), c. 1 [*ITA*].

[2] See Chapter 9 at heading 9.3 — Capital cost of depreciable property.

- "any amount received or receivable by the taxpayer in the year . . . as, on account of, in lieu of payment of or in satisfaction of, interest" (paragraph 12(1)(c));

- "any amount received by the taxpayer in the year that was dependent on the use of or production from property whether or not that amount was an instalment of the sale price of the property . . ." (paragraph 12(1)(g)); and

- "any particular amount . . . received . . . in the course of earning income from a business or property" from a person, partnership or government "where the particular amount can reasonably be considered to have been received as an inducement . . . refund, reimbursement . . ." (paragraph 12(1)(x)).[3]

These provisions indicate that, as long as the origin or source of an amount is a business or property, it is included in computing profit. The *ITA* uses such terms as "in the course of a business", "in the course of earning income from a business or property", "as interest" and "dependent on the use of or production from property" to indicate the link between an amount of revenue and business or property. In other words, for an amount to be treated as non-taxable capital receipt or windfall, it needs to be "divorced" from the business or property.

These provisions recognize three timing methods: received, receivable and accrual.[4] As discussed in more detail below, the received or cash method applies to taxpayers (mostly individuals) in respect of interest, rent, royalties, and dividend, as well as farming or fishing business. The receivable method applies to businesses involving the sale of property or the rendering of services. The annual accrual method applies to interest arising from investment contracts. These specific rules are not exhaustive. Financial businesses are allowed to compute their profit by using a "mark-to-market" method in respect of financial property held on revenue account.

In conjunction with their companion deduction rules, some inclusion rules are intended to reflect the matching principle in accounting. For example, in recognition of the fact that paragraphs 12(1)(a) and (b) mandate the inclusion of an amount that is not economically earned or is to be used to pay for a future liability, paragraphs 20(1)(m) and (n) allow a "reserve" to be deducted in the year, as a timing relief measure. At the same time, paragraphs 12(1)(d) and (e) include the reserve deduction in a previous year in computing income for the current year.

The fundamental purpose of these rules is to provide greater certainty while deferring to financial accounting as a starting point in computing profit. Subsection 12(2) states that the inclusions under "[p]aragraphs 12(1)(a) and (b) are enacted for greater certainty and shall not be construed as implying that any amount not referred to in those paragraphs is not to be included in computing income from a

---

[3] *ITA, supra* note 1, s. 12(1).

[4] As we shall see, sometimes the notions of accrual and receivable are much less clear than might be expected, although specific provisions frequently overcome the significance of such distinctions.

business for a taxation year whether it is received or receivable in the year or not". Section 9 and well-accepted business principles may require other amounts to be included.

7.2 — Characterization of incoming amounts

(a) — Revenue versus capital receipts

(i) — Legal question

In the course of carrying on a business or earning income from property, a taxpayer may receive or be legally entitled to receive amounts that fall into three categories: "revenue" (or "income")[5] receipts, capital receipts or windfalls. Depending on the characterization, the receipt is taxed differently. Capital receipts do not give rise to income, although they may give rise to capital gains if they constitute proceeds of disposition of a capital property. Windfalls are not income for tax purposes. Only amounts on revenue account are included in computing profit.

Each receipt needs to be considered individually in order to ascertain its true character.[6] Characterization is a pure legal question. "The legal distinction between receipts or expenditures that are on capital account and receipts or expenditures that are on revenue account is both meaningful and important in the context of the *Income Tax Act*. It is not meaningful in the preparation of financial statements."[7] "Capital" or "revenue" receipts are not accounting concepts, and accounting principles offer no assistance on the characterization question.[8]

The *ITA* provides some "clues" for distinguishing between capital and revenue receipts. For example, paragraph 12(1)(x) and section 56.4 indicate that inducements or payments received under restrictive covenants are on account of revenue unless they give rise to capital gains from disposition of property, such as shares of a corporation. (It should be noted that section 56.4 is not confined to "non-compete" agreements or any other contractual formulation, as the *ITA* seeks to detect collateral payments that might not otherwise be included in computing income.) In other words, the *ITA* recognizes such receipts as either proceeds of disposition or income,

---

[5] In the context of characterizing a receipt, the term "income" does not necessarily mean income for the purpose of section 3 of the *ITA*, but the accounting notion of "revenue". "Revenue" and "income" are used interchangeably in cases, such as *Ikea v. Canada*, [1998] 1 S.C.R. 196, [1998] 2 C.T.C. 61, 98 D.T.C. 6092 (S.C.C.); affirming [1996] 3 C.T.C. 307, 96 D.T.C. 6526 (Fed. C.A.); affirming (1993), [1994] 1 C.T.C. 2140, 94 D.T.C. 1112 (T.C.C.) [*Ikea*] at paras. 21–27 [(S.C.C.)].

[6] *Ibid.* at para. 27 [(S.C.C.)].

[7] *Ibid.* at para. 11 [(T.C.C.)].

[8] Accounting principles are relevant to the timing of recognition of revenue and expenditures.

not windfalls.[9] Subsection 39(1) indicates that any gain from a disposition of property is a capital gain only if it is not otherwise recognized as income under section 9. Paragraph 12(1)(g) incorporates the "substance over form" doctrine in characterizing receipts from the sale of property when the true nature of the receipts is rent or royalty income.

There is a large body of case law on the characterization issue. Typical receipts that require characterization are non-recurring or unusual receipts. Ordinary receipts in respect of the sale of property or the rendering of services are clearly on revenue account. Unusual receipts include subsidies or grants from government, inducements, compensation for cancellation of contract, loss of business or property, damages and gifts.

(ii) — Principles of characterization

Several principles emerge from the pertinent case law and a contextual and purposive interpretation of relevant provisions of the *ITA*. To begin with, to constitute a revenue receipt, the receipt cannot be a windfall or fortuitous. For example, the tenant inducement payment in *Nesbitt Thomson* (1991)[10] and *Ikea* (1998)[11] was neither fortuitous nor a windfall, given that "it was expected, requested, and arose out of active negotiation".[12] The receipt needs to be linked to a "source" of income that is either a business or property. This linkage is expressed in the wording of paragraph 12(1)(x): an inducement, reimbursement or assistance received "in the course of earning income from a business or property."[13] Under paragraph 12(1)(u), a federal home insulation grant or energy conversion grant received in respect of a property used by the taxpayer principally for the purpose of earning income from a business or property must be included in computing the taxpayer's income from that business or property.[14] Under case law, payments arising from the ordinary incident of an ongoing business are generally on revenue account.

The "surrogatum" principle helps characterize receipts such as damages, inducements, refunds and compensation.[15] The characterization of the receipt is deter-

---

[9] See Chapter 4 at heading 4.3(d) — Unenumerated sources, and Chapter 11 at heading 11.6(b) — Non-compete payments, for further discussion of s. 56.4 and the reason it was introduced.

[10] *Nesbitt Thomson Inc. v. Minister of National Revenue*, [1991] 2 C.T.C. 2352, 91 D.T.C. 1113 (T.C.C.) at 1115 [D.T.C.].

[11] *Ikea, supra* note 5.

[12] *Ibid.* at para. 28 [(S.C.C.)].

[13] The situation was the same for reimbursements under common law until paragraph 12(1)(x) was introduced in 1985.

[14] Such a grant received in respect of a property not used to earn income is required to be included in computing the taxpayer's income (or that of the taxpayer's spouse or "common-law partner" under the more general provision in paragraph 56(1)(s)).

[15] The Part XIII non-resident withholding tax rules use the phrase "in lieu of", and, thus, do not have to rely of the surrogatum principle: see *Transocean Offshore Limited v. R.*, [2005] 2

mined by the character of the item for which the receipt is intended to substitute.[16] For example, compensation received for loss of profit from non-performance of business contracts is on account of revenue — if there were no breach of the contract, the receipt would be on revenue account.[17] Compensation for loss of capital property, goodwill, or a source of business is generally on account of capital.

In the case of reimbursements, the crucial question is "what is the nature of the expense that the receipt is designed to reimburse?"[18] If the expense is a capital expenditure (such as the cost of goodwill or pipelines for transporting gas), the receipt is on capital account.[19] If the expense is a current expense, such as rent, the receipt is on revenue account. Paragraph 12(1)(x) confirms this principle by stipulating that the reimbursements be treated as revenue if they are "in respect of an amount included in or deducted as the cost of property" (i.e., inventory) or "any outlay or expense".

In the case of compensation for the loss or destruction of property, the above principle also applies. If the property is inventory, the compensation is clearly on revenue account. If the property is a capital asset, the compensation is a capital receipt.[20] The key question is "whether the payment is made for the termination, disposition or sterilization of a capital asset or is one of the ordinary incidents of an ongoing business so that the receipt properly forms part of the normal receipts of the trade".[21]

Finally, the characterization of a receipt as revenue or capital should be analyzed from the perspective of the recipient and not the payer.[22] The payer's motivations

---

C.T.C. 183, 2005 D.T.C. 5201 (Eng.) (F.C.A.); leave to appeal refused 2005 CarswellNat 3125, 2005 CarswellNat 3126 (S.C.C.) [*Transocean*] at para. 51 [(Fed. C.A.)]. In *Transocean*, damages paid for breach of contract to rent a drilling rig were found to be paid "in lieu of" rent and subject to Canadian withholding tax.

[16] See Chapter 4 at heading 4.4(d) — Damages and settlements.

[17] "Where, pursuant to a legal right, a trader receives from another person compensation for the trader's failure to receive a sum of money which, if it had been received, would have been credited to the amount of profits (if any) arising in any year from the trade carried on by him at the time when the compensation is so received, the compensation is to be treated for income tax purposes in the same way as that sum of money would have been treated if it had been received instead of the compensation. The rule is applicable whatever the source of the legal right of the trader to recover the compensation.": *London & Thames Haven Oil Wharves Ltd. v. Attwooll* (1966), [1967] 2 All E.R. 124 (C.A.) at 134-135, per Diplock J.

[18] *Ikea, supra* note 5 at para. 43 [(T.C.C.)].

[19] See *Consumers' Gas Co. v. The Queen* (1986), [1987] 1 C.T.C. 79, 87 D.T.C. 5008 (Fed. C.A.).

[20] See *T. Eaton Co. v. R.*, [1999] 2 C.T.C. 380, 99 D.T.C. 5178 (Fed. C.A.) at paras. 17, 18.

[21] *BP Canada Energy Resources Co. v. R.* (2002), [2003] 1 C.T.C. 2497, 2002 D.T.C. 2110 (T.C.C. [General Procedure]) at para. 54.

[22] *RCI Environnement Inc. v. R*, 2008 FCA 419, 2009 D.T.C. 5037 (Fr.), 2009 D.T.C. 5105 (Eng.) (F.C.A.); leave to appeal refused 2009 CarswellNat 1832, 2009 CarswellNat 1833

or the circumstances in which the payment is made should generally not affect the characterization of the payment in the hands of the recipient. For this reason, the decision in *Henco Industries* (2014)[23] is questionable, as the court put much emphasis on the "extraordinary surrounding circumstances"[24] in characterizing the taxpayer's receipt of $15.8 million from the Government of Ontario "to dispose of all its right and interest in the DCE property".[25] The Court held the receipt to be on capital account, but not as consideration for any specific property, because the circumstances rendered the land worthless and destroyed the business (hence, no goodwill). The Court reached that conclusion despite the evidence showing that the DCE property was transferred to Ontario, and the $15.8 million amount received was based on the fair market value of the DCE property, before the circumstances occurred.

(b) — Different types of revenue

The issue of characterization is important even when a receipt is on an income account. This is because the *ITA* further differentiates the types of receipts for various policy reasons. For example, the timing rule is different for revenue from the sale of property, revenue from rendering services, and dividends or interest.

The *ITA* provides no general characterization rules. As such, private law, case law principles and even dictionaries are relevant. Under the "form over substance" principle, in the absence of a sham, the legal form of a transaction adopted by the taxpayer is generally binding for the purposes of the Act.[26] However, in some cases, the *ITA* requires a "substance over form" approach and characterizes the revenue on this basis. Examples are paragraph 12(1)(g) and subsection 16(1).

7.3 — Timing of recognition of revenue

(a) — Overview

The annual accounting requirement under section 9 of the *ITA* makes it important to determine whether a revenue amount is included in computing profit for a spe-

---

(S.C.C.) at para. 51 [(F.C.A.)]. This case is about the characterization of capital receipt for the purposes of section 14 (eligible capital expenditure), which is now repealed (S.C. 2016, c. 12, s. 4). There is no reason that this principle should not apply for the characterization of other types of capital receipts.

[23] *Henco Industries Ltd. v. R.*, 2014 TCC 192, 2014 D.T.C. 1161 (Eng.) (T.C.C. [General Procedure]).

[24] The circumstances included blockades by protesters from Six Nations to prevent Henco Industries from developing the DCE property, in spite of court injunctions and government intervention. The Court found that the Government of Ontario was "to defuse a volatile situation and perhaps do the right thing by Henco": *Henco Industries, ibid.* at para. 163.

[25] *Ibid.* at para. 1.

[26] The sham doctrine is discussed further in Chapter 16 at heading 16.4(e) — Sham.

cific taxation year. Deferring the inclusion means deferring the taxation of the profit to a future year, resulting in time value of money for the taxpayer.

Since 1917, the *ITA* and its predecessors have codified timing rules in a manner that allows the continuous influence of accounting rules. For example, subsection 3(1) of the *Income War Tax Act, 1917*, said that income "means the annual net profit or gain . . . received by a person . . .",[27] but it did not indicate the method by which the annual net profit or gain of a business was to be computed. Financial accounting was the starting point for computing profit for tax purposes, and it used the accrual method. As such, the term "received" in the *ITA* was to "be understood as meaning "accrued" or "earned" so that profits earned, but not actually received or paid, should be recorded as received for the purpose of assessment".[28] When the term "received" was given a restricted interpretation, in cases such as *Trapp* (1946),[29] to exclude the accrual method of accounting, the *ITA* was amended in 1948 to drop "received" from the definition of income. The rationale was as follows: "If the decision in the *Trapp* case is accepted as good law, it will force all taxpayers who file income tax returns on an 'accrual' basis to change their book-keeping system for income tax purposes to a 'cash' basis. Many of the provisions of the Act will not be capable of sensible interpretation and the purposes of the Act, itself, in many respects, will fail of accomplishment."[30]

The current *ITA* addresses timing in provisions such as subsection 12(1) and sections 142.2 to 142.5. These rules differentiate the type of business (such as trading, manufacturing, financial, farming or services) and the type of property (such as debt, equity, leasing or licensing rights). They tend to codify specific financial accounting methods to provide certainty. For example, when financial accounting rules changed to allow the use of mark-to-market method for financial products, sections 142.2 to 142.5 were added to allow this method to be used by financial institutions.[31]

---

[27] S.C. 1917, c. 28, s. 3(1).

[28] Herbert A.W. Plaxton, *The Law Relating to Income Tax of the Dominion of Canada* (Toronto: Carswell, 1939) at 51.

[29] *Trapp v. Minister of National Revenue*, [1946] Ex. C.R. 245, [1946] C.T.C. 30, 2 D.T.C. 784 (Can. Ex. Ct.).

[30] H.A.W. Plaxton, *The Law Relating to Income Tax and Excess Profits Tax of the Dominion of Canada*, 2nd ed. (Toronto: Carswell, 1947) at 36–37.

[31] See heading 7.9 — Mark-to-market rule for financial institutions, below. In practice, the Canada Revenue Agency (the "CRA") also allowed mark-to-market accounting to be used beyond the scope of these rules. In *Kruger Inc. v. R.*, 2016 FCA 186, [2016] 6 C.T.C. 161, 2016 D.T.C. 5079 (F.C.A.) [*Kruger*], the Court agreed with the CRA's practices and allowed the use of the mark-to-market method with respect to foreign exchange option contracts by a non-financial institution. The 2017 federal budget proposes to allow taxpayers who hold any derivatives on income account to elect to be taxed on those derivatives on a mark-to-market basis, provided that such derivatives are valued at fair market value under accounting principles. This election is to be available in respect of taxation years beginning after March 22, 2017 and can be revoked with the consent of the Minister.

(b) — The realization principle

It is well-accepted that income or loss is recognized for tax purposes when it is "realized".[32] According to the realization principle established in case law, an amount is not realized until it obtains the "quality of income".[33] The courts have enunciated the following test as to whether an amount received has this quality: "Is his right to it absolute and under no restrictions, contractual or otherwise, as to its disposition, use or enjoyment?"[34] "[A]n amount may have the quality of income even though it is not actually received by the taxpayer, but only 'realized' in accordance with the accrual method of accounting."[35] The ultimate effect of the realization principle is that "amounts received or realized by a taxpayer, free of conditions or restrictions upon their use, are taxable in the year received, subject to any contrary provision of the Act or other rule of law".[36]

The above notion of realization is broader than the dictionary meaning of this term. For example, the Oxford dictionary defines "realization" to mean the "conversion of an asset into cash", such as "a sale of goods".[37] It is close to the notion of "recognition" in accounting.[38] For example, the timing of recognition of revenue and gains under the International Financial Reporting Standards ("IFRS") is when: 1) it is probable that future economic benefits associated with the revenue or gain will flow to the entity, and 2) the amount of the revenue or gain can be measured reliably (i.e., when there is complete, neutral and error-free information on which the measurement is based).[39] In the case of sale of goods, revenue is recognized under the IFRS when the beneficial ownership of the goods passes from the seller to the buyer and there is probability of collection and reliable measurement.

The realization principle is considered by the courts to be important, but not overarching. This point is particularly significant in cases where a taxpayer seeks to "realize" a loss inherent in property, such as foreign exchange option contracts

---

[32] E.g., *Friesen v. R.*, [1995] 3 S.C.R. 103, [1995] 2 C.T.C. 369, 95 D.T.C. 5551 (S.C.C.) [*Friesen*] at para. 45; *Ikea, supra* note 5 at para. 37 [(S.C.C.)].

[33] *Ikea, supra* note 5 at para. 37 [(S.C.C.)], citing *Robertson v. M.N.R.*, [1944] C.T.C. 75, 2 D.T.C. 655 (Can. Ex. Ct.) [*Robertson* cited to C.T.C.].

[34] *Robertson, supra* note 33 at 91. Section 28 of the *ITA* provides an exception for income from a farming and fishing business: such income can be reported using the "cash method" if the taxpayer so elects. The discussion in this chapter ignores this exception.

[35] *Ikea, supra* note 5 at para. 37.

[36] *Ibid.*

[37] Oxford Dictionaries, "realization", online: <https://en.oxforddictionaries.com/definition/realization>.

[38] Brian J. Arnold, et al., *Timing and Income Taxation: The Principles of Income Measurement for Tax Purposes*, 2nd ed. (Toronto: Canadian Tax Foundation, 2015) [Arnold 2015] at 217.

[39] *Ibid.* at 218.

(*Kruger*),[40] gold future contracts (*Friedberg*),[41] or property held in an adventure in the nature of trade (*Friesen*),[42] Other than inventory, the *ITA* does not explicitly allow the "write down" in value (or "paper loss"), triggering a loss for tax purposes.[43] Under case law, taxpayers have the freedom to choose either the realization principle or another principle, such as mark-to-market or matching, to report its profit or loss, as long as the chosen method provides an "accurate picture"[44] of its income for the year.

(c) — "Received" or cash basis

(i) — Relevance

Section 12 of the *ITA* provides that certain amounts "received" by a taxpayer in the year are to be included in computing income from a business or property. Examples are paragraphs 12(1)(c) (interest), 12(1)(g) (rent or royalty), 12(1)(j) (dividend from Canadian corporations), and 12(1)(x) (inducement). This is the cash method of accounting. Because corporations generally follow the receivable or accrual method of accounting under GAAP, the cash method applies primarily to individuals. Taxpayers in a farming or fishing business may elect to use the cash method under paragraph 12(1)(b).

Paragraph 12(1)(a) requires an inclusion in income of any amount received in the year in the course of a business "that is on account of services not rendered or goods not delivered before the end of the year or that, for any other reason, may be regarded as not having been earned in the year or a previous year". Typical amounts contemplated by subparagraph 12(1)(a)(i) include prepayments for work to be done under contract not yet begun or goods not yet delivered, and amounts received from the sales of transportation tickets, seasonal tickets, payments for the warranty of merchandise, and container deposits.

Standing alone, paragraph 12(1)(a) represents a departure from the realization principle. In general, an amount that has actually been received has the quality of income at the time of receipt, if the recipient has done what is required to earn it and, thus, has an immediate and unrestricted right to dispose of it.[45] By contrast, an amount received as a deposit against the fulfillment of a future obligation does not have the quality of income until the obligation is fulfilled.[46] The severity of para-

---

[40] *Kruger, supra* note 31.

[41] *Friedberg v. R.*, [1993] 4 S.C.R. 285, [1993] 2 C.T.C. 306, 93 D.T.C. 5507 (S.C.C.) [*Friedberg*].

[42] *Friesen, supra* note 32.

[43] See Chapter 8 at heading 8.8 — Inventory.

[44] See Chapter 6.

[45] *Robertson, supra* note 33; *Ikea, supra* note 5.

[46] This is explained by Thorson J. in *Robertson, supra* note 33 at 92: "Where an amount is paid as a deposit by way of security for the performance of a contract and held as such, it cannot be regarded as profit or gain to the holder until circumstances under which it may be

graph 12(1)(a) is reduced by a deduction under paragraph 20(1)(m) for a reasonable reserve of unearned amounts.[47] Paragraphs 12(1)(a) and (20(1)(m) produce a net result that is effectively the same as under the receivable method and consistent with the realization principle.

(ii) — "Amount received"

The term "amount" is defined in subsection 248(1) to mean "money, rights or things expressed in terms of the amount of money or the value in terms of money of the right or thing . . ." The term "received" is not defined in the *ITA*. The dictionary meaning of "received" is to "be given, presented with, or paid (something)".[48] The legal meaning of this term can be interpreted narrowly, requiring "being put in possession of something" or a "physical operation involving a transfer of funds".[49] Under this approach, an offset of debt would not be considered received by the creditor. A contextual and purposive interpretation of subsection 12(1) dictates a broader meaning. An amount received can be manifested in cash or cash equivalent, and a transfer of funds can be physical, such as handing over cash, or financially equivalent, such as a deposit into the taxpayer's bank account or an offset. In computing a taxpayer's profit from a business or property, the manner of receiving the amount of revenue earned is the means, not the end. If the taxpayer has the use of and control over the amount, it will be considered to have been received.[50]

For example, a farmer who sells wheat to a buyer for $10,000 can be paid with $10,000 cash (say, one hundred $100 bank notes), a deposit of $10,000 into his or her bank account, a cheque payable to him or her for $10,000, a promissory note of $10,000, or a charge of $10,000 to the buyer's credit card. The farmer can agree to receive $10,000 worth of property, such as a used pick-up truck, a share of the

---

retained by him to his own use have arisen and, until such time, it is not taxable income in his hands, for it lacks the essential quality of income, namely, that the recipient should have an absolute right to it and be under no restriction, contractual or otherwise, as to its disposition, use or enjoyment."

[47] *ITA*, *supra* note 1, ss. 20(1)(m), (m.2), which are discussed further in Chapter 8 at heading 8.7(d)(iv) — Unearned amounts.

[48] Oxford Dictionaries, "receive", online: <https://en.oxforddictionaries.com/definition/receive>.

[49] In *Blais et al., v. M.N.R.* (1989), [1990] 2 C.T.C. 2005 (Eng.), 92 D.T.C. 1497, 90 D.T.C. 1494 (T.C.C.), the Court considered whether the taxpayer "received" alimony when her debt to her estranged husband was offset by his obligation to pay alimony to her under former paragraphs 56(1)(b) and 60(d). The Tax Court of Canada adopted the ordinary meaning and held that the taxpayer did not receive alimony. It stated at para. 21: "In fact, the expression 'received' involves the idea of being put in possession of something. Whether the amount is 'paid' or 'received', both expressions involve the idea of a physical operation involving a transfer of funds." In contrast, a debt setoff was considered "received" in *Armstrong v. M.N.R.* (1987), [1988] 1 C.T.C. 2019, 88 D.T.C. 1015 (T.C.C.).

[50] Arnold 2015, *supra* note 38 at 185.

buyer corporation, or even a "bitcoin". The farmer can also agree to offset the $10,000 against his or her debt to the buyer for the same amount or ask the buyer to pay $10,000 directly to his or her third-party creditor. For purposes of the *ITA*, the farmer has earned $10,000 by selling the produce and the timing for including the $10,000 is when he or she gets paid one way or the other.

Similarly, a taxpayer who has an investment account holding shares of a Canadian corporation "receives" $5,000 dividends when $5,000 is credited to his or her account. The taxpayer can also "receive" the $5,000 by getting a cheque, a promissory note, or another property.

The cash method of accounting gives the taxpayer more flexibility about timing. Since profit is computed on an annual, as opposed to a transactional, basis, a taxpayer would generally prefer to defer the receipt of cash for transactions that have occurred before the end of the year to after the year-end. In the above example of the farmer, he or she can agree to be paid in the beginning of the next year for wheat sold in November of the current year.

In modern payment systems, the moment of payment or transfer is recorded electronically. In more traditional ways of payments, such as by cheque or by mail, there may be some uncertainties. For example, a cheque payable upon receipt is mailed on December 27 of Year 1 and received on January 3 of Year 2. Is the amount received in Year 1 or Year 2? It depends. If it is sent by "first class mail or its equivalent", paragraph 248(7)(a) deems a person to whom it was sent to receive the amount on the day it was mailed. In other cases, the amount is presumably received on the day of actual receipt. However, if the recipient chooses not to open the mail or cash the cheque in order to defer the inclusion of the amount in computing income, it would be reasonable to deem the person to have received the amount when the cheque was received. This kind of deemed or constructive receipt principle is necessary to prevent "undue" delay in actually receiving the amount.

(d) — "Receivable" basis

(i) — Paragraph 12(1)(b)

Paragraph 12(1)(b) includes in income "any amount receivable by the taxpayer in respect of property sold or services rendered in the course of a business in the year, notwithstanding that the amount or any part thereof is not due until a subsequent year, unless the method adopted by the taxpayer for computing income from the business and accepted for the purpose of this Part does not require the taxpayer to include any amount receivable in computing the taxpayer's income for a taxation year unless it has been received in the year . . ."

Paragraph 12(1)(b) codifies the accrual method of accounting in respect of businesses involving the sale of property or the rendering of services. It carves out taxpayers who are statutorily allowed to use the cash method of accounting for tax purposes (e.g., section 28 gives taxpayers earning income from farming or fishing the option to use the cash method). It is not conclusive on the issue of timing. To the extent that a revenue amount is not covered by paragraph 12(1)(b), section 9 applies so that the accounting method becomes relevant.[51] As discussed below, the meaning of "receivable" for tax law purposes is close to the idea on when revenue is earned in accounting.[52]

(ii) — "Receivable"

There is no statutory definition of "receivable" in the *ITA*. The dictionary meaning is "able to be received"[53], which is too wide to be helpful for tax purposes. Case law adopts a narrower meaning by introducing more certainty as to the right and the quantum of an amount. The long-accepted definition of "receivable" comes from *J. Colford Contracting Co.* (1960),[54] in which Kearney J. stated:

> In the absence of a statutory definition to the contrary, I think it is not enough that the so-called recipient has a precarious right to receive an amount in question, but he must have a clearly legal, though not necessarily immediate, right to receive it.[55]

The issue in *Colford* was the recognition of "holdbacks" under the predecessor of paragraph 12(1)(b).[56] The taxpayer engaged in furnishing and installing heating, air conditioning and ventilation equipment as a subcontractor or in contracts directly with the owner. In either case, the usual industry practice is for the client to make interim payments to the contractor from time to time based on formal progress reports. These progress payments are normally subject to a percentage "holdback" in order to ensure the satisfactory completion of the job. The holdbacks are normally not paid to the contractor until the client receives professional assurance that the work is acceptable (such as by a certificate issued by the architect or engineer appointed by the client). In computing its taxable income for the taxation year ended March 31, 1953, the taxpayer excluded the holdbacks. The Exchequer Court in *Colford* held that holdbacks were not receivable because, at private law, the contractor had no legal right to the holdback until the certificates in question were issued by the architect or engineer.

In *Colford*, the amount of holdbacks was not an issue. In cases where the amount is uncertain (such as compensation for expropriated property, an arbitration award, or a court award), an additional test must be met. In addition to obtaining a right to receive compensation, there must be a binding agreement between the parties or a

---

[51] See Chapter 6 at heading 6.5(c)(ii) — Accrual method.

[52] Arnold 2015, *supra* note 38 at 216: "The issue of when an amount should be taken into account in the computation of profit is essentially the same for accounting purposes as it is for tax purposes."

[53] Oxford Dictionaries, "receivable", online: <https://en.oxforddictionaries.com/definition/receivable>.

[54] *M.N.R. v. J. Colford Contracting Co.* (1960), [1960] C.T.C. 178, 60 D.T.C. 1131 (Can. Ex. Ct.); affirmed [1962] C.T.C. 546, 62 D.T.C. 1338 (S.C.C.) [*Colford*].

[55] *Ibid.* at 187 [C.T.C. (Can. Ex. Ct.)]. This test was adopted without question in *Maple Leaf Mills Ltd. v. M.N.R.* (1976), [1977] 1 S.C.R. 558, [1976] C.T.C. 324, 76 D.T.C. 6182 (S.C.C.).

[56] *Income Tax Act*, R.S.C. 1952, c. 148, s. 85B(1)(b).

judgment fixing the amount.[57] In other words, the amount must be reasonably ascertainable for it to be receivable for tax purposes.[58]

The basic principle is that a revenue amount is receivable when the taxpayer has acquired an absolute and unconditional right to receive payment. This usually occurs when all the events have occurred that fix the right to receive a future amount, provided that the amount is reasonably ascertainable.[59] Whether an amount is due is not relevant. It is a question of law whether the taxpayer acquires a clear and absolute right to receive the amount: in *Colford*, the Court said that a holdback became receivable at the time the certificate was issued. The quantum of the amount does not need to be absolutely certain, just reasonably ascertainable: *West Kootenay Power* (1991)[60] held that a reasonable estimate of the amount earned at a year-end is sufficiently ascertainable to be an amount receivable.

(e) — "Accrual" basis

The accrual method of revenue recognition is used in subsections 12(3) and (4) in respect of interest, and in subsections 142.2 to 142.5 in respect of the mark-to-market rules. As discussed later in this chapter, these specific rules require taxpayers to include in revenue amounts that are not legally receivable but are reasonably ascertainable.[61]

---

[57] For example, in *M.N.R. v. Benaby Realties Ltd.*, [1967] C.T.C. 418, 67 D.T.C. 5275 (S.C.C.), the Court held that compensation for expropriated property became receivable when the amount was fixed by arbitration or agreement, notwithstanding that the right to receive compensation was acquired earlier, at the moment of expropriation.

[58] *Colford, supra* note 54. *Colford* was followed in *Vaughan Construction Co. Ltd. v. M.N.R.*, [1970] C.T.C. 350, 70 D.T.C. 6268 (S.C.C.). Other cases have held that the possibility of a successful appeal did not derogate from the "quality of income" of the payments in issue at the time they were received. When paid to the taxpayer, the amounts were not subject to any specific or unfulfilled conditions, and the necessity of returning the moneys, in whole or in part, if the appeal was successful, was viewed as a condition subsequent that did not affect the unrestricted right of the taxpayer to use the funds when received. See *Cementation Co. (Canada) Ltd. v. M.N.R.*, [1977] C.T.C. 2360, 77 D.T.C. 249 (T.R.B.); *Commonwealth Construction Co. Ltd. v. R.*, [1982] C.T.C. 167, 82 D.T.C. 6152 (Fed. T.D.); affirmed [1984] C.T.C. 338, 84 D.T.C. 6420 (Fed. C.A.); and *R. v. Foothills Pipe Lines (Yukon) Ltd.*, [1990] 2 C.T.C. 448, 90 D.T.C. 6607 (Fed. C.A.); leave to appeal refused (1991), 134 N.R. 320 (note) (S.C.C.).

[59] As discussed in Chapter 8, an expense is payable and deductible when all events have occurred that fix the obligation to make the payment, provided that the amount of future payment is reasonably ascertainable.

[60] *West Kootenay Power and Light Company Limited v. The Queen* (1991), [1992] 1 C.T.C. 15, 92 D.T.C. 6023 (Fed. C.A.) [*West Kootenay*].

[61] In general, the accrual method of accounting is consistent with the receivable basis under the *ITA*. For discussion, see Chapter 6 at heading 6.5(c)(ii) — Accrual method.

The term "accrual" or "accrued" is used in some cases, such as *Canadian General Electric Co.* (1961),[62] *Friedberg*[63] and *Kruger*,[64] but not defined in any case. The Oxford dictionary meaning of the verb "accrue" is: "(of a benefit or sum of money) be received by someone in regular or increasing amounts over time" as in "financial benefits will accrued from restructuring"; "Accumulate or receive (payments or benefits) over time" as in "they accrue entitlements to holiday pay" and "Make provision for (a charge) at the end of a financial period for work that has been done but not yet invoiced" as in "at 31 December the amount due for the final quarter is accrued".[65]

7.4 — Sale of property

(a) — "Property sold in the course of a business"

Where a property is sold in the course of a business, the amount receivable by the taxpayer must be included in computing profit under paragraph 12(1)(b). The concept of "sale" is undefined in the *ITA*. The ordinary meaning of this term is the transfer of the ownership of property for money. Ownership is a bundle of rights, entailing elements of risk, reward and control. When risk, reward and control are transferred, there is a sale.

The property sold in the course of a business is in the nature of "inventory". An inventory property can be any type of property, including tangible goods, electricity, intangible property, real or immovable property, or financial products. The sale of capital property, which gives rise to capital gains or losses, falls outside paragraph 12(1)(b).[66]

As a timing rule, the purpose of paragraph 12(1)(b) "is to ensure that income from a business is computed on the accrual basis, not a cash basis, with certain specific

---

[62] *Canadian General Electric Co. v. Minister of National Revenue* (1961), [1962] S.C.R. 3, [1961] C.T.C. 512, 61 D.T.C. 1300 (S.C.C.). The issue in this case was whether foreign exchange profits inherent in the taxpayer's U.S.-dollar liabilities, as evidenced by outstanding promissory notes, could be brought into income on an accrued basis according to the relative value of the Canadian dollar at year-end (taxpayer's position), or whether they could only be recognized in the year in which the notes were actually retired (the Minister's position). The Majority of the Supreme Court upheld the taxpayer's position.

[63] *Friedberg, supra* note 41, held that the taxpayer was entitled to use the realization method for reporting his trading losses involving gold futures, even though marking to market (recognizing income accrued over the years during which the gold futures were held) was allowed by GAAP.

[64] *Kruger, supra* note 31.

[65] Oxford Dictionaries, "accrue", online: <https://en.oxforddictionaries.com/definition/accrue>.

[66] See Chapter 10.

exceptions".[67] It does not operate to exclude amounts that are otherwise includible in computing profit under section 9. As part of subsection 12(1), it operates, in fact, to "expand s. 9(1)'s ambit of inclusion".[68] It has been applied in cases involving, among others, the supply of electricity (*West Kootenay* (1991)[69] and the sale of real property (*Huang and Danczkay* (2000)[70] and *West Hill Redevelopment Co.* (1991)).[71]

(b) — "Amount receivable"

Under the *Colford* definition of "receivable", an amount for the sale of property becomes receivable when the vendor acquires a clear and absolute right to receive the payment. It does not require an immediate right to receive payment.

When does the sale price become receivable to the vendor? Is it the time when: 1) a purchase and sale contract is concluded; 2) title to the property passes to the purchaser; 3) the property is delivered; 4) the purchaser is billed; or 5) payment is received by the vendor?[72] In a sale of goods, delivery of the property and passing of legal title to the property often occur simultaneously. In such a case, the sale price becomes receivable at the time of delivery.[73] For example, when you buy a book in a bookstore, all of the above-mentioned events take place simultaneously. The timing of the recognition of the sale to the store is easily determined. However, if the book is to be delivered in a week, when does the sale price become receivable? According to the administrative policy of the CRA, the sale price becomes receivable on the date of exchange stipulated by the parties in the contract.[74] Where the date of exchange is not expressly stipulated, the time when attributes of ownership (primarily possession, use and risk) pass to the purchaser is presumed to be the date when the sale price is receivable.[75]

---

[67] *Maritime Telegraph and Telephone Company, Limited. v. R.*, [1992] 1 C.T.C. 264, 92 D.T.C. 6191 (Fed. C.A.) [*Maritime Telegraph*] at para. 23.

[68] *Ibid.* at para. 18.

[69] *West Kootenay, supra* note 60.

[70] *R. v. Huang and Danczkay Ltd.*, [2000] 4 C.T.C. 219, 2000 D.T.C. 6549 (Fed. C.A.) [*Huang and Danczkay*].

[71] *West Hill Redevelopment Co. v. M.N.R.* (1991), [1991] 2 C.T.C. 83, 91 D.T.C. 5430 (Fed. T.D.); affirming [1986] 2 C.T.C. 2235, 86 D.T.C. 1685 (T.C.C.) [*West Hill*].

[72] For an excellent discussion of the timing of recognition of the sale price, see Brian J. Arnold, *Timing and Income Taxation: The Principles of Income Measurement for Tax Purposes* (Toronto: Canadian Tax Foundation, 1983) [Arnold 1983] at 133–150.

[73] *Ibid.* at 136.

[74] Canada Revenue Agency, Interpretation Bulletin IT-170R, "Sale of Property — When Included in Income Computation" (1980) at para. 7.

[75] *Ibid.* at para. 8: "Factors that are strong indicators of the passing of ownership include: (a) physical or constructive possession, (b) entitlement to income from the property, (c) assumption of responsibility for insurance coverage, and (d) commencement of liability for interest on purchaser's debt that forms a part of the sale price."

In the case of the sale of real property, many agreements provide a "closing date" for the completion of the sale. This is normally the date that beneficial ownership is intended to pass from the vendor to the purchaser and the time that the vendor is entitled to the sale price. Advance payments received by the vendor are not required to be included by paragraph 12(1)(a), which is applicable only to the sale of goods (not real estate).

Where property is sold or delivered, the rendering of an account (or invoice) is not a precondition to the right to payment. For example, in *West Kootenay Power* (1991),[76] revenues for unbilled payments for the supply of electricity by the taxpayer were considered to be receivable because the amounts were quantifiable and the property was delivered. Amounts can be receivable even if there is no immediate right to payment. In other words, "receivable" does not mean "payable" or "due". The important event is the one that creates the purchaser's legal obligation to pay and the vendor's legal right to be paid. This is typically when title to the property passes to the purchaser. "How" and "when" the amount is paid is not important.

Whether the right is enforceable is not important.[77] Generally, taxpayers cannot manipulate their income by "choosing" when their receipts have the quality of income and are recognized as such for tax purposes. In *Huang & Danczkay* (2000)[78] the taxpayer was a real estate developer that developed and sold multiple-unit residential buildings ("MURBs") and received purchase money in promissory notes secured by mortgages. These promissory notes and mortgages were stated to be subject to some future financial obligations that the taxpayer was to fulfil (such as cash flow guarantees). The fulfilment by the taxpayer of these obligations would affect the remedy it might obtain in the event that the purchaser refused to make a payment under the promissory notes or mortgages, because a right of setoff might be applicable. The taxpayer took the view that it had no enforceable right to payment and, hence, no amount was receivable for the sale of MURBs because of the right of setoff. The Federal Court of Appeal disagreed and held that the right of setoff did not preclude the notes and mortgages from coming into existence at the outset. The notes were enforceable from the outset according to their terms, even though payment under the notes by instalments was delayed. Another way of looking at this case is that the taxpayer had sold MURBs and legally earned the right to be paid. The taxpayer's choice of the method of payment or its agreement to a setoff should not affect its right to be paid for the MURBs. The proceeds for the MURBs became legally receivable when the MURBs were sold.

---

[76] *West Kootenay*, *supra* note 60 at para. 40.

[77] To recognize the circumstances in which income is earned but there is a delay of payment, the *ITA* offers a reserve in some cases. See Chapter 8 at heading 8.7(d)(iii) — Deferred payments.

[78] *Huang and Danczkay*, *supra* note 70.

The amount receivable is generally determined by the taxpayer's sale price. In *West Hill* (1991),[79] the taxpayer built and sold condominiums in a competitive market at a stated price and took back mortgages from purchaser at interest rates well below prevailing rates. In computing its income, the taxpayer sought to reduce the sale price by the difference between the face value of the mortgage and its fair market value based on prevailing rates at the date of sale. The Minister treated the sale price as the full value expressed in the sale, and the Court agreed with the Minister that the sale price was the amount receivable under paragraph 12(1)(b).

In *Daishowa-Marubeni International* (2003),[80] the Supreme Court of Canada addressed whether the taxpayer's sale price should include the estimated cost of a reforestation obligation assumed by purchasers on the sale of forest tenures. The Court held that a reforestation obligation was not a separate existing debt of the vendor that was assumed by the purchaser, but was, instead, a future expense that was embedded in the property and served to "depress the value" of the property. As such, it was not part of the sale price.

7.5 — Services

(a) — "Services rendered in the course of business"

The *ITA* does not define "service". The dictionary meaning of this term includes "the action of helping or doing work for someone".[81] Paragraph 12(1)(b) applies to services rendered in the course of business (i.e., as a business activity, not employment). There is a broad range of services, including personal services, professional services, hospitality, construction, transportation, education, entertainment and telecommunications provided by individuals and corporations. Some services are provided on a project-by-project or client-by-client basis (such as hair-cutting and construction) and others are continuous (such as electricity and telecommunications).

(b) — "Amount receivable"

Payments for services generally become receivable when the performance of the services is completed. At such time, the taxpayer acquires the absolute and unconditional, although not necessarily immediate, legal right to receive payment. Whether or not the taxpayer has billed for the amount is not relevant, as long as the amount is reasonably ascertainable.[82] Ascertaining the amount of service fees can

---

[79] *West Hill, supra* note 71.

[80] *Daishowa-Marubeni International Ltd. v. R.* (2003), [2013] 2 S.C.R. 336, [2013] 4 C.T.C. 97, 2013 D.T.C. 5085 (Eng.), 2013 D.T.C. 5086 (Fr.) (S.C.C.). This case is about the meaning of "proceeds of disposition" under subsection 13(21), but the rationale applies to sale proceeds for the purpose of paragraph 12(1)(b).

[81] Oxford Dictionaries, "service", online: <https://en.oxforddictionaries.com/definition/us/service>.

[82] See *West Kootenay, supra* note 60, and *Maritime Telegraph, supra* note 67.

be straightforward if it is based on an hourly or daily rate.[83] Depending on industry practices, the service provider may bill the client on the basis of passage of time (say monthly), usage of something (such as data), percentage of completion of a project, total completion or completion with a favourable result (i.e., the contingency basis).

Paragraph 12(1)(b) modifies the general rule by deeming an amount as having become receivable for services performed on the day the account would have been rendered had there been no undue delay in rendering the account.[84] In other words, the amount for services becomes receivable when it is billed, not when the services are rendered.

Interpreted literally, paragraph 12(1)(b) applies to all types of services, as it does not qualify the word "services" by any adjective such as continuous, discrete, project-by-project, etc. As illustrated in the *Maritime Telegraph* (1992)[85] case, the courts have distinguished between continuous and discrete service providers. The issue in *Maritime Telegraph* was whether revenues for unbilled telephone services rendered in the last month of a year were receivables in law in that year. The Court found that the taxpayer's records indicated the exact times at which its services were rendered, making the amounts readily quantifiable at year-end and sufficiently ascertainable to be considered receivable. As such, the same timing rule applied to the supply of telephone services in this case and the supply of electricity in *West Kootenay* (1991):[86] paragraph 12(1)(b), when read together with subsection 12(2), does not apply to exclude unbilled services revenue from profit under section 9, and this method is "particularly applicable to businesses who deal in . . . the sale of services when those services are performed at a discrete time or times".[87] This interpretation makes sense, as it treats taxpayers supplying continuous services in the same way.

Taxpayers who render professional services as accountants, dentists, lawyers, doctors and chiropractors can report revenues on a billed basis. In addition, under section 34 (proposed for elimination in the 2017 budget), they are eligible for an election that allows them to deduct the cost of work in progress inventory (e.g., salaries) from income while excluding "any amount in respect of work in progress

---

[83] This is the case even if the performance of services under the contract will not be completed until a subsequent year: see Arnold 1983, *supra* note 72 at 175.

[84] This deeming rule was introduced in 1982 to extend to all services a similar rule that previously applied only to services rendered in the course of a professional business under section 34 of the *ITA*. See the technical notes accompanying the introduction of paragraph 12(1)(b).

[85] *Maritime Telegraph*, *supra* note 67.

[86] *West Kootenay*, *supra* note 60.

[87] *Maritime Telegraph*, *supra* note 67 at para. 10 [(Fed. T.D.)], per Reed J (affirmed by the Federal Court of Appeal (*ibid.*)).

at the end of the year" from business income.[88] The section 34 election essentially provides capital indirectly to these professional practices by not taxing the work that may not be at a stage where accounts could be billed so as to create a receivable, while permitting related expenses to be deductible. The resulting loss (from the deduction of expenses) can shelter otherwise taxable amounts. For some professional practices, especially small practices where the risk of non-collection is higher, there are situations where it is simply not possible to bill work that is in progress, and not feasible to impose rigid billing and collection protocols. Since having professionals serve the broad public is likely thought to be a social "good", the *ITA* recognizes these realities. However, this rationale cannot be extended to professional practices in general, and large professional firms in particular.

7.6 — Dividends

The *ITA* does not define the term "dividend". Under common law, dividend generally refers to a *pro rata* distribution from a corporation to its shareholders, unless the distribution is made on the liquidation of the corporation or on an authorized reduction of corporate capital.[89] Subsection 248(1) specifically includes a "stock dividend" as a dividend: a stock dividend is a dividend paid in shares of the corporation rather than cash.[90] Several provisions of the *ITA*, such as sections 84 and 84.1, deem certain transfers of value from a corporation to a shareholder to be a dividend.

Paragraphs 12(1)(j) and (k) require dividends to be included in the income of a shareholder when dividends are received.[91] Under corporate law, a corporation can declare and pay dividends as long as the corporation remains solvent after the pay-

---

[88] Work in progress ("WIP") of a profession is "inventory" under s. 10(5) of the *ITA*. Under s. 10(4), the fair market value of WIP is what it is reasonable to expect would be receivable if it were billed. Absent s. 34, s. 10(1) applies to determine the inclusion: lower of cost or fair market value or, as permitted by reg. 1801 of the *Income Tax Regulations*, C.R.C., c. 945 [Regulations], fair market value. Many professional firms use internal accounting systems that value WIP based on billing rates (fair market value).

[89] See, e.g., *Hill v. Permanent Trustee Co. of New South Wales*, [1930] A.C. 720 (New South Wales P.C.); and *Commissioners of Inland Revenue v. Burrell*, [1924] 2 K.B. 52 (Eng. C.A.). This broad definition has been accepted by the CRA and Canadian courts. See, e.g., *Cangro Resources Ltd. (in Liquidation) v. Minister of National Revenue*, [1967] Tax A.B.C. 852, 67 D.T.C. 582 (T.A.B.).

[90] Subsection 248(1) deems the "amount" of a stock dividend to be the amount by which the paid-up capital of the corporation paying the dividend is increased because of the payment of the dividend.

[91] Corporate shareholders may include dividends on a receivable basis (when dividends have been declared but not yet paid) in accordance with s. 9, since s. 12(1) is for greater certainty, not an exclusive rule. For further discussion, see Arnold 2015, *supra* note 38 at 317–318.

ment, and a corporation may pay a dividend by issuing fully paid shares of the corporation (i.e., a stock dividend) or pay a dividend in money or property.[92] As discussed in more detail in Chapter 14, the *ITA* contains detailed rules regarding the taxation of dividends, which take into account the residence of the corporation, the nature of the underlying corporate income, and whether the shareholder is an individual or corporation. The main policy concern is the minimization of double taxation of income earned through corporations and the tax deferral of passive investment income through the use of private holding corporations.

7.7 — Rent and royalties

(a) — "Payments based on production or use"

(i) — Nature of rent or royalty

Paragraph 12(1)(g) requires a taxpayer to include in computing income any amount received that is dependent on the use of or production from property. Although this provision does not use the term "rent" or "royalties", rents and royalties are typical types of payments that are based on the use of or production from property.

The term "rent" or "royalty" is undefined in the *ITA*. The courts have interpreted this term as an amount paid as compensation for the use or occupation of property, or for the right to use or occupy property.[93] A rent is generally a fixed payment (usually periodic) for the use of property for a given period of time, after which the right to use the property expires.[94] In private law, the owner of property grants the tenant or lessee the right to use the property for a price while retaining ownership of the property. The amount of the rent typically depends on the amount of time of the use.

The ordinary meaning of "royalties" includes "a sum of money paid to a patentee for the use of a patent or to an author or composer for each copy of a book sold or for each public performance of a work".[95] It is similar to rent, but is used more in respect of intellectual property (such as patent, copyright or trade-mark) and other intangibles (such as trade secrets, information, or goodwill). Like rent, there is an element of contingency in the amount of payment, but not in the legal right of the owner to receive the payment.[96] A royalty or similar payment is, therefore, "one

---

[92] E.g., *Canada Business Associations Act*, R.S.C. 1985, c. C-44, ss. 42, 43.

[93] See *Transocean*, *supra* note 15 at para. 54. This case is about the meaning of "rent" and payment in lieu of rent for the purposes of s. 212(1)(d). There is no indication in the *ITA* that the meaning of "rent" is different under s. 12(1)(g).

[94] See *R. v. Saint John Shipbuilding & Dry Dock Co.*, [1980] C.T.C. 352, 80 D.T.C. 6272 (Fed. C.A.); leave to appeal refused (1980), 34 N.R. 348n (S.C.C.).

[95] Oxford Dictionaries, "royalty", online: <https://en.oxforddictionaries.com/definition/royalty>.

[96] *M.N.R. v. Wain-Town Gas and Oil Co. Ltd.*, [1952] C.T.C. 147, 52 D.T.C. 1138 (S.C.C.) [*Wain-Town*] at 151 [C.T.C.], per Kerwin J. The courts have held, that "the term 'royalties'

made for the use of property, rights or information whereby the payments for such use are contingent upon the extent or duration of use, profits or sales by the user".[97]

(ii) — Sales distinguished

The phrase "based on the production or use" was added in 1934 to the predecessor of paragraph 12(1)(g), to overrule the decision in *Spooner v. M.N.R.* (1933).[98] In that case, the taxpayer sold 20 acres of a ranch in Alberta to Vulcan Oils Ltd. for $5,000 cash, 25,000 fully paid shares of Vulcan and a royalty of "ten per cent of all the petroleum, natural gas and oil produced and saved from the said lands free of costs". The taxpayer received a $95,000 royalty and treated it as part of proceeds for the sale of the land. The Minister sought, without success, to tax it as income.

Whether an amount is "based on the production or use" of property is sometimes difficult to establish as a matter of fact. Typical cases involve a "sale" of property with the sale price being paid in instalments and the amount being contingent on some kind of output, production or use of the property, such as the quantity of gravel taken from the land or gross sales from the use of a patent. In *Lackie v. R.* (1978), the Court stated:

> [I]f what is sold relates to the use of land, including excavation for gravel, that is a profit à prendre, thus taxable income . . . Profit à prendre implies a continuing licence, or continuous right to use land; a single final transaction transferring all the property (i.e., gravel) would not be a profit à prendre.[99]

In other cases, the proceeds of sale of gold, sand, shale and topsoil were considered to be payments falling within paragraph 12(1)(g) when the price was based on the amount of gold, sand, shale or topsoil removed.[100] On the other hand, payments for the cutting of timber on farmland have been held to fall outside the scope of paragraph 12(1)(g) if the sale of timber is a one-time sale of all the timber on the pro-

---

normally refers to a share in the profits or a share or percentage of a profit based on use or on the number of units, copies or articles sold, rented or used. When referring to a right, the amount of the royalty is related in some way to the degree of use of that right . . . Royalties, which are akin to rental payments . . . are either based on the degree of use of the right or on the duration of use to be made of it . . .": *Vauban Productions v. R.*, [1975] C.T.C. 511, 75 D.T.C. 5371 (Fed. T.D.); affirmed [1979] C.T.C. 262, 79 D.T.C. 5186 (Fed. C.A.).

[97] *Syspro Software Ltd. v. The Queen*, [2003] 4 C.T.C. 3001, 2003 D.T.C. 931 (T.C.C. [General Procedure]) at para. 22. This case is about the meaning of "royalties" or similar payments within the meaning of s. 212(1)(d). The basic meaning of "royalty" is relevant to s. 12(1)(g).

[98] *Spooner v. M.N.R.* (1933), [1928–34] C.T.C. 184, 33 D.T.C. 258 (Jud. Com. of Privy Coun.).

[99] *Lackie v. R.* (1978), [1978] C.T.C. 157, 78 D.T.C. 6128 (Fed. T.D.), para. 23; affirmed [1979] C.T.C. 389, 79 D.T.C. 5309 (Fed. C.A.) at para. 23 [(T.D.)].

[100] *Pallett v. M.N.R.* (1959), 59 D.T.C. 230 (T.A.B.); *Irwin v. M.N.R.* (1963), 63 D.T.C. 251 (T.A.B.); *Flewelling v. M.N.R.* (1963), 63 D.T.C. 489 (T.A.B.); *Mouat v. M.N.R.* (1963), 63 D.T.C. 548 (Can. Tax App. Bd.); *Huffman v. M.N.R.* (1954), 11 Tax A.B.C. 167 (Can. Tax App. Bd.); and *Lamon v. M.N.R.*, [1963] C.T.C. 68, 63 D.T.C. 1039 (Can. Ex. Ct.).

perty.[101] The sale of agricultural land is excluded from the wording of paragraph 12(1)(g). Whether the price amount is established by reference to the production or use of the property sold, and, thus, caught by paragraph 12(1)(g), is a question of fact.

In cases involving "intangibles", the price may be based on production or use in the future because the parties may not know the true value of the property at the time of the contract. Paragraph 12(1)(g) would apply to the sale of a copyrighted sales manual for a fixed price where payments were based on a percentage of the products sold by the purchaser,[102] and to the sale of a franchise to supply natural gas, in return for an amount based on gross receipts from all the sales of natural gas under the franchise.[103] In *Smith v. R.* (2011),[104] the taxpayer sold a client list for a fixed price of $351,000 payable in instalments. According to the agreement, this price was adjusted each year based on actual commissions received by the purchaser. This amount was held to fall within paragraph 12(1)(g) because "[t]he source of the commissions received was indeed the client list, all amounts received by the appellant, although expressed as instalments of the sale price of the client list, were dependent entirely on the use of or production from that property and were taxable under paragraph 12(1)(g)".[105]

(b) — Timing of inclusion

Paragraph 12(1)(g) adopts the "received" method. Taxpayers that use the accrual method of accounting in computing profit may include rent or royalties on a receivable basis pursuant to section 9. Rent or royalty becomes receivable when the lessor or licensor has acquired a clear and absolute right to receive payment, which is generally when the property has been made available for the use of the lessee or licensee and the day for payment has arrived. The due date for payment, such as the first day of the month for rent, is often the time when the amount is receivable. Unlike interest (see heading 7.8, below), the *ITA* does not require rent to be included in income on an accrual basis, even though, in economic terms, rent and interest both accrue on a daily basis and share a common nature — compensation for the use of property.

---

[101] See *Wright v. R.* (2002), [2003] 1 C.T.C. 2726, 2003 D.T.C. 763 (T.C.C. [General Procedure]).

[102] *Gingras v. M.N.R.*, [1963] C.T.C. 194, 63 D.T.C. 1142 (Can. Ex. Ct.).

[103] See *Wain-Town, supra* note 96.

[104] *Smith v. R.* (2011), [2012] 1 C.T.C. 2282, 2011 D.T.C. 1332 (T.C.C. [General Procedure]) at paras. 13, 14. The parties fixed the $351,000 purchase price based on annual generated commissions of $156,000 times an acquisition factor of 2.25, and agreed to adjust the purchase price each year for the period based on actual commissions received. The Court found that the initial price of $351,000 was only an estimate: the price was not fixed and could fluctuate depending upon the annualized commissions received on any anniversary payment date.

[105] *Ibid.* at para. 15.

7.8 — Interest

(a) — Nature of interest

Paragraph 12(1)(c) applies to interest as well as "any amount ... as, on account of in lieu of payment of or in satisfaction of, interest".[106] It clearly intends to capture not only payments in the form of interest, but also payments that are in the nature of interest, regardless of the form or label used in the contract or arrangement. Interest is included in income when it is received or receivable, depending on the method regularly followed by the taxpayer.

Interest is perhaps one of the most common types of income from property for individuals. Anyone who has a bank account earns some interest. As explained in more detail below, like rent, interest is charged on a period basis, such as year, month or day. The time factor is critical in determining the amount (i.e., the time value of money). The other factor is the interest rate, which is often set by the market and affected by the borrower's creditworthiness, currency risks, inflation and other factors. Further, the interest earned at the end of the period, if not paid to the lender, operates as a further loan to the borrower, which itself will earn interest, and so on. This is the notion of compound interest. In economic terms, a borrower is expected to pay rent (interest) for the use of money borrowed from the lender, whether or not interest is explicitly stated. Further, interest accrues on a day-by-day basis.

"Interest" is not defined in the *ITA*. The Oxford dictionary defines it to mean "money paid regularly at a particular rate for the use of money lent, or for delaying the repayment of a debt".[107] The Supreme Court of Canada provided a classic definition of interest in *Saskatchewan (Attorney General) v. Canada (Attorney General)* to include "the return or consideration or compensation for the use or retention by one person of a sum of money, belonging to, in a colloquial sense, or owed to another".[108] Such a broad definition is consistent with the purpose of paragraph 12(1)(c). The fundamental nature of interest is that it is the compensation for the use of money, it accrues on a daily basis, and it is generally computed by reference to the principal outstanding at any time. However, there is no need for interest to be expressed on a daily basis. An amount of compensation for the use of money for a stipulated period can be said to accrue day-by-day.[109]

---

[106] Similar wording is used in s. 20(1)(c) (deductibility of interest) and s. 212(1)(b) (withholding tax on interest paid to non-residents).

[107] Oxford Dictionaries, "interest", online: <https://en.oxforddictionaries.com/definition/interest>.

[108] *Saskatchewan (Attorney General) v. Canada (Attorney General)*, [1947] S.C.R. 394 (S.C.C.); affirmed (1948), [1949] A.C. 110 (Jud. Com. of Privy Coun.) at 411 [S.C.R. (S.C.C.)].

[109] *Sherway Centre Ltd. v. Canada*, [1998] 2 C.T.C. 343, 98 D.T.C. 6121 (Fed. C.A.) at para. 11 (considering whether participating interest is interest for the purpose of s. 20(1)(c)). The legal definition of interest was developed in non-tax cases. It is considered to have three requirements: "1) an amount must be compensation for the use of money; 2) the amount

The characterization of an amount as interest is determined under private law and is generally straightforward. It is the return on debt instruments or obligations. A loan is a common form of debt obligation. Other types of debt obligations include a promissory note, a bank account, a term deposit, a guaranteed investment certificate, a mortgage, a treasury bill, a bond, a debenture, or a note. The nomenclature varies according to the personality of the borrower (issuer of security), the nature of the security, the term of the loan, and other characteristics of the obligation.[110]

(b) — Payments in lieu of interest

Paragraph 12(1)(c) uses language to broadly capture amounts that are in the nature of interest even if the "label" for the amounts is different. Canadian courts have adopted a "substance over form" approach to characterizing interest. For example, in *Wenger's Ltd. et al. v. M.N.R.* (1992), Rip J. said: "I must review all the circumstances to determine whether in substance — not merely in form — the amounts in issue are interest payments or represent surcharges."[111]

Late payment charges are in the nature of interest, as they are generally calculated as a percentage of the amount outstanding in respect of the sale price of the goods or services for the period from the due date to the time of payment.[112] The amount of sale price that is overdue is, in effect, a loan. For example, imagine Taxpayer X sells goods to a Client for $10,000 payable on a stipulated due date. When X does not receive payment on the due date, he or she is, in effect, providing a loan of $10,000 to the Client. X can stipulate that late payments are subject to a penalty or charge computed by reference to an interest rate.

In an economic sense, all deferred payments include an element of interest. In the absence of the *ITA* (which taxes capital gain preferentially to interest), a taxpayer who sells an asset for $1,000 payable immediately will be indifferent to this transaction and one in which he or she sells the asset for $1,100 payable a year later if he or she can invest the cash received today at a market interest rate of 10 per cent per year. The time value of $1,000 for one year is $100. No rational business person would accept less than $1,100 a year later because of the time value of money. The *ITA* does not, however, deem every deferred payment arrangement to contain

---

must be referable to a principal sum; and 3) the amount must be calculated by reference to the time during which the principal is outstanding — that is, it must accrue on a daily basis or be apportionable in time on such a basis.": see Tim Edgar, "The Concept of Interest under the *Income Tax Act*" (1996) 44 Can. Tax J. 277 at 284.

[110] For specific purposes, such as non-resident withholding tax, the *ITA* treats interest on participating debts more like a dividend (s. 212(1)(b)). The meaning of interest for deduction under s. 20(1)(c) is discussed in Chapter 8 at heading 8.9 — Interest expense.

[111] *Wenger's Ltd. et al. v. M.N.R.* (1992), [1992] 2 C.T.C. 2479, 92 D.T.C. 2132 (T.C.C.) [*Wenger's*] at 2491 [C.T.C.].

[112] See *M.N.R. v. Thyssen Canada Ltd.* (1986), [1987] 1 C.T.C. 112, 87 D.T.C. 5038 (Fed. C.A.); leave to appeal refused (1987), 79 N.R. 400 (note) (S.C.C.); *Taran Furs (Montreal) Inc. v. M.N.R.* (1995), [1996] 1 C.T.C. 2819 (T.C.C.); *Wenger's, ibid.*

an implicit loan. Subsection 16(1) deals with blended payments of capital and income to "unbundle" the payments and single out the interest element for tax purposes in certain circumstances.

(c) — Blended payments

Under paragraph 16(1)(a), "where, under a contract or other arrangement, an amount can reasonably be regarded as being in part interest . . . and in part an amount of a capital nature . . . the part of the amount that can reasonably be regarded as interest shall, irrespective of when the contract or arrangement was made or the form or legal effect thereof, be deemed to be interest on a debt obligation held by the person to whom the amount is paid or payable". This provision adopts a "reasonableness" test to overrule the characterization under the contract or arrangement. It looks through the legal form of the transaction to recharacterize the blended payments as including an interest element.[113]

Examples of blended payments are:

1. mortgage payments, because each payment is partly interest and partly repayment of the principal sum, the amount of which is steadily reduced over the life of the loan;

2. debt issued at a discount — a treasury bill or commercial paper that pays no nominal interest is sold at a discount and the redemption payment on maturity is a blended payment that combines interest (the discount) and the return of capital;

3. a debt obligation embedded in a deferred sale price of property.

What is the test for determining whether part of a blended payment can be reasonably considered as interest? In the case of deferred sale price, it is the fair market value of the property at the time of the sale. In *M.N.R. v. Groulx* (1967),[114] for example, the taxpayer sold a farm for $395,000, of which $85,000 was payable immediately and $310,000 was payable in instalments over a period of six years; no interest was payable by the purchaser on the outstanding balance of the purchase price. The Supreme Court of Canada held that the payment of $310,000, which was received in instalments by the vendor-taxpayer, could reasonably be regarded as being, in part, a payment of interest by the purchaser on the basis that the purchaser had agreed to pay a price above the market value of the farm in return for the vendor's agreement to forego interest on the unpaid balance of the purchase price.[115]

Consistent with the principle underlying paragraph 16(1)(a), subsection 20(14) says that the sale proceeds of a debt obligation with accrued interest must be treated as

---

[113] The imputed interest under s. 16(1)(a) is treated as interest for purposes of other provisions of the *ITA*, such as ss. 12(1)(c) and 20(1)(c).

[114] *M.N.R. v. Groulx* (1967), [1967] C.T.C. 422, 67 D.T.C. 5284 (S.C.C.).

[115] See also *Club de Courses v. M.N.R.*, [1979] C.T.C. 3022, 79 D.T.C. 579 (T.R.B.), where the purchase price exceeded fair market value by $100,000.

having an interest component and be taxed as interest, as opposed to proceeds of disposition of the debt, which would give rise to a capital gain. For example, imagine Taxpayer Z owns a debt property with a principal amount of $2,000, earning a 5 per cent interest per annum ($100 per year) payable on maturity in one year. Assume that halfway through the year (when the accrued interest is $50), Z sells the property. If interest rates don't change, Z will receive $2,050 for the debt property: the $2,000 face value plus $50 of accrued interest. Since the accrued interest is $50, subsection 20(14) treats $50 as interest: the proceeds of disposition are, therefore, reduced to $2,000 and Z will have no capital gain.[116]

(d) — Discounts, bonuses and premiums

Owners of capital can lend their money to another person for compensation expressed as stated interest payable at a stipulated rate on stipulated dates or the economical equivalents of stated interest, such as discounts, bonuses and premiums of debt obligations. The term "discount" refers to the amount by which the issue or selling price of a debt obligation is less than its face value.[117] A bonus or premium is the opposite of a discount, referring to an amount payable to the holder of a debt obligation in excess of the face amount of the obligation, usually on the maturity or repayment of the obligation.

Discounts, bonuses or premiums affect the timing for paying compensation for the use of the debtholder's money (generally discount upfront and premium on maturity), not the nature of the amounts. The concept of time value of money renders the timing factor irrelevant. For example, an investor would be indifferent to the following arrangements: 1) a one-year bond with a face value of $1,100 and no nominal interest rate was issued for $1,000 (i.e., a bond issued at a discount of $100); and 2) a one-year bond with a face value of $1,000 and no nominal interest rate was issued for $1,000 and redeemable for $1,100. The $1,000 earns $100 interest when the annual interest rate is 10 per cent. The investor can also put his or her $1,000 in a savings account that pays 10 per cent annual interest.

The *ITA* recognizes the nature of interest through the blended payments rule discussed above, and the mandatory annual interest accrual rules under subsections 12(3) and (4), and Regulation 7000 of the *Income Tax Regulations*.[118] For example, where a discount arises on an original issue of an obligation, the discount is generally treated as interest when the debt obligation is redeemed on maturity,

---

[116] If, instead, interest rates go down (compared to 5 per cent), the debt property earning 5 per cent will be more valuable and Taxpayer Z will receive more than $2,050. Imagine, for example, he or she receives $400 more (i.e., $2,450). Since the accrued interest is $50, subsection 20(14) still treats $50 as interest: the proceeds of disposition are, therefore, reduced to $2,400 and the capital gain (which is half-taxable) is the additional $400 he or she received: $2,400 minus $2,000.

[117] Canada Revenue Agency, Folio S3-F6-C1, "Interest Deductibility" at para. 1.94. There is no definition of "discount", "bonus" or "premium" in the *ITA*.

[118] Regulations, *supra* note 88, s. 7000.

under paragraph 16(1)(a) and case law.[119] Subsection 12(9) and Regulation 7000 deem the full amount of the discount on an interest-free debt obligation to accrue to the holder in annual instalments during the term of the bond.[120]

(e) — Timing methods

(i) — "Received" or "receivable"

Paragraph 12(1)(c) permits taxpayers to include interest in income when it is "received" or "receivable", depending on the method regularly followed by the taxpayer in computing profit. For example, a corporation must use the "receivable" method, whereas a law professor can use the cash method. Even though the nature of interest is that it accrues daily, paragraph 12(1)(c) treats it similarly to other types of income from property.

---

[119] In *Satinder v. R.*, 95 D.T.C. 5340 (Fed. C.A.), for example, the Federal Court of Appeal held that an original issue discount ("OID") was indeed interest income.

[120] *ITA, supra* note 1, s. 12(9) applies to a "prescribed debt obligation", which is defined in reg. 7000(1) of the Regulations, *supra* note 88, to include several types of obligations that do not pay interest or have deferred interest payment terms. Regulation 7000(2) stipulates the rules for computing the prescribed amount of accrued interest to be included in income annually by holders of such obligations. "Zero coupon bonds" represent one type of interest-free debt obligation. They are created by a stockbroker who will strip the interest coupons off a conventional bond (a "stripped bond"). The principal (residue) of the bond and the interest coupons are then sold separately as non-interest-bearing obligations. Zero coupon bonds and stripped bonds are issued or sold at a sufficient discount to make up for the lack of interest payments; the return to the investor consists solely of the original issue discount ("OID"); nothing will be received until the maturity of the bond. When interest rates are high, zero coupon bonds and stripped bonds are attractive to investors who want to lock in a long-term rate of return and do not need or want periodic payments. As mentioned earlier, s. 12(9) and reg. 7000 apply to deem the full amount of the OID to accrue to the holder in annual instalments during the term of the bond. If the *ITA* made no specific provision for these and other interest-free obligations, the OID would not be taxed under subsection 16(1) until later (when it was "paid or payable" on the maturity of the bond); in some cases, the discount might even be taxed as a capital gain.

Interest-bearing bonds may also be issued at a discount (or premium), depending on a variety of factors, including the anticipated rate of inflation and interest rate. If a debt obligation is issued with an interest rate lower than the rate currently available for that class of obligations, the market value of the obligation will be "discounted" to a figure below its face value — a figure that will make the effective yield to the purchaser closer to the current interest rate. If a debt obligation is issued with an interest rate higher than the rate currently available for that class of obligations, the obligation will issue at a premium. A premium is a figure higher than its face value that will make the effective yield to the purchaser closer to the current interest rate. This is the reason for a phenomenon that some investors find puzzling: when interest rates rise, bond prices fall, and when interest rates fall, bond prices rise. Paragraph 16(1)(a) will apply to the OID, but the profit or loss that occurs when bond prices rise and fall is on account of capital.

Like other types of revenue, the time when interest is receivable is when the taxpayer has an absolute and unconditional right to receive the amount under private law. It is generally the time when the interest payment is due and the lender has fulfilled its obligation to provide money for the use of the borrower for a specified period of time.[121] For example, where interest on a three-year term loan is payable on January 5 of each year, interest accrued from January 6 of Year 1 to January 5 of Year 2 is receivable in income in Year 2, even though most of the interest accrued in Year 1.

The difference between receivable and received matters for taxpayers when they fall in different taxation years. For example, where the interest payment is due on December 31, Year 1, and, thus, receivable in Year 1, but not received until January 3, Year 2, the interest is included in Year 2 for a cash-basis taxpayer.

These methods of reporting interest make it possible for taxpayers to "control" the timing of interest inclusion, especially in the case of long-term investment.[122] Taxpayers reporting bond interest by the cash method used to be able to postpone recognition of the interest by not cashing the coupons as they fell due. The advantage of deferring the recognition is more attractive if the interest compounds. As another example, Canada Savings Bonds are available on a compound basis, under which no interest is payable during the term of the bond, and on the maturity date all of the interest, compounded, is paid to the bondholder (along with the principal sum). This is why the *ITA* contains specific rules to require accrual.

(ii) — Annual accrual

Subsections 12(3) and (4)[123] require interest accrued to the end of the taxation year to be included in income to the extent that it is not receivable or received in the year. Subsection 12(3) applies to corporations, partnerships and unit trusts or any trust of which a corporation or a partnership is a beneficiary.[124] Subsection 12(4) applies to individuals in respect of an "investment contract" with a term of more than one year.

---

[121] Arnold 2015, note 38 at 298.

[122] For the benefit of tax deferral, see Chapter 1 at heading 1.6(e) — Tax deferral.

[123] Paragraph 12(1)(c) and ss. 12(3) and (4) are subject to s. 12(4.1) for taxation years ending after September 1997. A financial institution or taxpayer in the business of lending money does not have to include interest in income under ss. 12(1)(c), 12(3) or 12(4) if the collection of the principal or interest of the underlying loan is uncertain. Other taxpayers must include the interest for doubtful debts in income and then can deduct a reserve under s. 20(1)(l)(i).

[124] This requirement is consistent with the timing rule for accounting purposes. For example, under the IFRS, interest is recognized in accordance with the "effective interest" method, which calculates the exact rate of interest that is necessary to discount the expected future cash receipts (principal and interest) over the expected life of a financial instrument. This effective rate is then applied each year to calculate the interest income (for assets) or interest expense (for liabilities) for the period. In this way, interest income or expense is recognized on a consistent basis each year.

For example, where on January 3, Year 1, an individual acquires a two-year bond with a face value of $1,000 and a stated interest rate of 5 per cent per annum, and principal and interest are payable on January 2, Year 3, the interest accrued to January 2, Year 2 (i.e., $50) must be included in computing the individual's income in Year 2. When the bond is redeemed on January 2, Year 3, the interest accrued from January 3, Year 2 to January 2, Year 3 ($50) will be included in Year 3.[125]

7.9 — Mark-to-market rule for financial institutions

In the case of property sold in the course of business, the gain or loss in the property is "realized" only when the property is sold and the sale proceeds are "receivable". In the case of certain financial products ("mark-to-market property") of financial institutions, the *ITA* allows the taxpayer to include any inherent or accrued gain or loss in the financial products without a sale. Technically, subsection 142.5(2) deems the taxpayer to have disposed of the mark-to-market properties for fair market value at the end of the year and include the proceeds in computing profit.[126] For the purpose of computing the gain or loss, the taxpayer's cost amount is deemed to be the fair market value of the property at the end of the preceding year. As a result, only the changes in value during the year are recognized. For example, if the fair market value of a taxpayer's mark-to-market property is $100,000 at the year-end of 2017 and $150,000 at the year-end of 2018, the taxpayer must include $50,000 in computing profit for 2018.

The term "mark-to-market property" is defined in subsection 142.2(1) to mean shares, specified debt obligations held by an investment dealer, specified debt obligations that are fair value properties, and "tracking properties" that are fair value properties. It is beyond the scope of this book to fully explain these properties.[127] A basic requirement is that the fair value of the property is "readily available". Financial institutions use mark-to-market rules in their financial statements under GAAP. As discussed earlier,[128] the 2017 federal budget proposes to allow taxpayers who hold derivatives on income account to elect to be taxed on those derivatives on a mark-to-market basis.

---

[125] The subsection 12(4) accrual method is sometimes called the "anniversary date" method, as it is a simple arbitrary method that requires 365 days of interest to be reported at a time. The normal accrual method is the one that subsection 12(3) requires for other taxpayers: it requires 363 days of interest to be reported in Year 1 ($44.50), 365 days in Year 2 ($50) and 2 days in Year 3 ($5.50).

[126] The taxpayer is also deemed to reacquire the property at the same time at a cost equal to the fair market value. This is the same as in other deeming rules, some of which are discussed in Chapter 10.

[127] For further discussion, see Arnold 2015, *supra* note 38 at 331–342.

[128] See *supra* note 31.

8
BUSINESS AND PROPERTY INCOME: DEDUCTIONS

8.1 — Legislative scheme

(a) — Technical design

Section 9 of the *Income Tax Act* (the "*ITA*")[1] is the most important provision in the Act that deals with the deduction of costs and expenses in computing income from a business or property. As discussed in Chapter 6, profit is a net concept and is generally computed by following the well-accepted business principles and practices (including generally accepted accounting principles, or "GAAP"). Sections 18 to 37 in subdivision b provide specific deduction rules, and sections 67 to 67.6 in subdivision f contain additional rules relating to deductibility of certain types of expenses. These rules form part of the ecosystem for computing profit by reducing gross revenues to net profit.

Unlike the all-embracing inclusion rules discussed in Chapter 7, the deduction rules limit what can be excluded in computing profit. Presumably, the statutory rules were drafted to counter the natural tendencies of taxpayers to "understate" revenues and "overstate" expenses. In reality, taxpayers who operate a business or hold investments often incur expenses that may relate to the business or investment as well as personal consumption, such as the cost of entertaining potential clients. In the

[1] R.S.C. 1985 (5th Supp.), c. 1 [*ITA*].

absence of clear rules, different taxpayers may treat the same expense differently, resulting in unfairness and inconsistency.

The deduction rules are organized from the more general provisions to the specific ones.[2] Sections 18 and 19 are restrictive. Section 18 denies a deduction for amounts that are not incurred for the purpose of earning income from business or property, and prohibits deductions for specific types of items for various policy reasons. Sections 19 and 19.1 limit the deduction of advertising expenses. Section 20 is "permissive", allowing the deduction for specified costs and expenses, such as the cost of depreciable property and interest expenses.

Technically speaking, the deduction rules address the fundamental questions of deductibility (whether the amount is deductible) and timing (when is the amount deductible). After a brief overview of the characterization of expenses, this chapter discusses expenses that are not deductible under either the general income-earning purpose requirement under sections 9, 18(1)(a) and 18(1)(h), or specific statutory limitations. It then discusses the general timing rules under sections 18 and 20, as well as the treatment of inventory and interest expenses.

(b) — Purpose and rationale

(i) — Providing certainty and predictability

One of the goals of the *ITA* is "to provide sufficient certainty and predictability to permit taxpayers to intelligently order their affairs".[3] In filing their tax returns, taxpayers must make various determinations as to the deductibility and timing of deductions of many types of expenses. Accounting principles and practices allow flexibility and choices in computing profit for accounting purposes.[4] It thus makes sense for tax law to provide as much certainty and predictability as possible. The detailed and sometimes highly technical rules under sections 18 to 21 certainly spell out the treatment of a large number of expenses, ranging from cost of capital property (s. 20(1)(a)) to interest expense (s. 20(1)(c)). The *ITA* also defers to accounting principles in regard to issues that it does not specifically address. As such, taxpayers' profit computed for financial accounting purposes remains a starting point for computing profit for tax purposes.

---

[2] E.g., s. 21 gives the taxpayer an election to either deduct the interest expense or capitalize it when the borrowed money is used to acquire depreciable property or for exploration or development. Sections 22 to 25 address the consequences of ceasing to carry on business. Sections 26 to 37 deal with special cases, such as banks (s. 26), crown corporations (s. 27), farming and fishing (s. 28), professional practices (s. 34), and scientific research and experimental development (s. 37).

[3] *Canada Trustco Mortgage Co. v. Canada*, [2005] 5 C.T.C. 215, 2005 D.T.C. 5523 (Eng.), 2005 D.T.C. 5547 (Fr.) (S.C.C.) at para. 75. The Supreme Court of Canada has reiterated this point in a number of its recent decisions, including *65302 British Columbia Ltd. v. R.* (1999), [2000] 1 C.T.C. 57, 99 D.T.C. 5799 (Eng.), 99 D.T.C. 5814 (Fr.) (S.C.C.) [*65302 B.C.*].

[4] See Brian J. Arnold et al., *Timing and Income Taxation: The Principles of Income Measurement for Tax Purposes*, 2nd ed. (Toronto: Canadian Tax Foundation, 2015).

As discussed in more detail below, the *ITA*'s treatment of fines, penalties and illegal payments was introduced for public policy reasons to override the case law. As well, without restrictions, there could be a wide range of discretion and room for manipulation in respect of deductions of entertainment expenses, home office expenses and other amounts. The *ITA* contains rules to limit the deduction of certain expenses, such as the reasonable requirement (section 67), entertainment expenses (section 67.1), fines and penalties (section 67.6), illegal payments (section 67.5), and home office expenses (subsection 18(12)) to reflect public policy and provide certainty.

(ii) — Measuring profit accurately

Profit is "the difference between the receipts from the trade or business *during such year* . . . and the expenditure laid out to earn those receipts".[5] In determining profit, "the goal is to obtain an accurate picture of the taxpayer's profit".[6] The deduction rules contribute to that goal by denying deductions for costs and expenses that do not contribute to earning revenues in the year.

Section 9 and paragraphs 18(1)(a) and (h) prohibit the deduction of expenses that are not incurred for income-earning purposes, such as personal consumption expenses. Expenses incurred for personal purposes result in personal enjoyment, not additional business revenues. They should not be deductible. More importantly, personal consumption is an important indicator of the taxpayer's income in an economic sense and with regard to ability to pay. Allowing the deduction of a personal expense would result in inequity between taxpayers who have the same ability to pay. Allowing a taxpayer a $10,000 deduction is the same as allowing a taxpayer to receive $10,000 of his or her income on a tax-free basis.

With respect to the timing of deductions, paragraphs 18(1)(b) and 20(1)(a), regarding depreciable property, and subsection 18(9), regarding prepaid expenses, aim to recognize costs or expenses in a year to the extent that they contribute to the income-earning process of that year. The reserve deduction rules under paragraphs 20(1)(l), (m) and (n) seek to recognize profit that is earned or realized in a given year.

8.2 — Characterization of outlays and expenses

(a) — Current versus capital expenditures

Business owners need to spend money to make profit. For example, a lawyer who receives $100,000 in fees from his or her client this year may not have any profit left if he or she spent more money on employee's wages, Internet access, office rent, interest, advertising, licensing fees, or purchasing equipment or goodwill. The

---

[5] *Irwin v. Minister of National Revenue*, [1964] S.C.R. 662, [1964] C.T.C. 362, 64 D.T.C. 5227 (S.C.C.) at 664 [S.C.R.], quoted in *Canderel Ltd. v. R.*, [1998] 2 C.T.C. 35, 98 D.T.C. 6100 (S.C.C.) [*Canderel*] at para. 30.

[6] *Canderel, supra* note 5 at para. 53.

ITA refers to these outgoing payments as "expense", "outlay" and "cost". Although these terms are used interchangeably in business practices, the *ITA* tends to use "cost" in respect of the money spent on acquiring a property.[7]

An outlay or expense incurred for the purpose of earning income from a business or property is deductible, unless it is on account of capital, or is a capital expenditure. Paragraph 18(1)(b) prohibits the deduction of an expenditure "on account of capital" unless another provision of the *ITA* specifically allows a deduction. The distinction between capital and other expenditures is, as the Carter Commission commented, "one of timing and not of any inherent quality".[8] Paragraph 20(1)(a) allows the deduction of capital cost in respect of most business assets whose value decreases over time. Generally speaking, the amount of deduction each year depends on the estimated useful life of the assets. In effect, the deduction each year is limited to the portion of the cost that was "wasted away" during the year.

For purposes of the *ITA*, expenses are generally current expenses unless they are capital expenditures. The general meaning of "capital expenditure" is found in case law: any expense that brings to the business an enduring value or benefit that is not consumed or realized in the year in which the expense is incurred is a capital expenditure.[9] The meaning and recognition of capital expenditures are discussed in Chapter 9. The rest of this chapter focuses on current expenses.

(b) — Running expenses

Running expenses are expenses that are neither clearly current expenses nor clearly capital expenditures. The courts use "running expenses" to refer to expenses that are not "related to any particular item of revenue",[10] but relate to "the running of the business as a whole".[11] The benefits of running expenses generally extend beyond the current year. An example of "running expenses" were the tenant induce-

---

[7] The term "capital cost" is used in the capital cost allowance ("CCA") scheme (see Chapter 9) and "adjusted cost base" is used in the capital gains scheme (see Chapter 10).

[8] Canada, *Report of the Royal Commission on Taxation* (Ottawa: Queen's Printer, 1966) (Chairman: Kenneth Le M. Carter) vol. 4 at 249.

[9] There is, however, no statutory definition of what constitutes an expense on "capital account". Rather than using GAAP, the courts have relied on other sources, particularly trust law notions, to determine what is a capital expense and what is a current expense. Trust law notions were developed for very different purposes, namely to decide which of two competing classes of beneficiaries of a trust — the life or income beneficiaries, or the remainder or capital beneficiaries — should bear the cost of expenses incurred by a trust, and the use of trust law doctrines to characterize expenses for tax purposes has led to many problems.

[10] In *Oxford Shopping Centres v. R.* (1979), [1980] C.T.C. 7, 79 D.T.C. 5458 (Fed. T.D.); affirmed [1981] C.T.C. 128, 81 D.T.C. 5065 (Fed. C.A.), at 18 [C.T.C.], Thurlow J. referred to a running expense as an "expense that is not referable or related to any particular item of revenue".

[11] *Naval Colliery Co. v. Commissioners of Inland Revenue* (1928), 12 T.C. 1017 (H.L.) at 1027, per Rowlatt J.

ment payments in the *Canderel* (1998)[12] case. In that case, the taxpayer was in the business of managing and developing commercial real estate properties and, in 1986, paid tenants to induce them to enter into leases. The taxpayer deducted the full amount of the inducements in computing its income for tax purposes for 1986, but amortized the payments over the initial term of the related leases for accounting purposes. The Supreme Court of Canada held that the inducement payments were running expenses because they "were not referable to any particular items of income, i.e., they cannot be correlated directly, or at least not principally, with the rents generated by the leases which they induced".[13] Running expenses can be deducted like current expenses, even though the payments are amortized for accounting purposes.

8.3 — General purpose test

(a) — Income-earning purpose

The principle that only expenses incurred for the purpose of earning income from a business or property are deductible is reflected in subsection 9(1) and paragraphs 18(1)(a) and (h) of the *ITA*. As discussed in Chapter 6, section 9 recognizes the relevance of well-accepted principles of commercial accounting and business practices, including GAAP in determining profit. Expenditures that are not incurred for the purpose of earning income, or are incurred as personal or living expenses, are not deductible in computing profit for accounting purposes. As such, they are not deductible under section 9. To further clarify, paragraph 18(1)(a) prohibits the deduction of "an outlay or expense except to the extent that it was made or incurred by the taxpayer for the purposes of gaining or producing income from the business or property". Paragraph 18(1)(h) prohibits the deduction of "personal or living expenses of the taxpayer, other than travel expenses incurred by the taxpayer while away from home in the course of carrying on the taxpayer's business".[14]

There is a body of case law on the "income-earning purpose" test. For example, in *Imperial Oil* (1947),[15] the taxpayer paid a damages settlement as the result of a collision between one of its ships and another ship. The Minister denied the deduction on the ground that the damages were made not for "the purpose of gaining or producing income" but to discharge a legal liability. Thorson P. of the Exchequer

---

[12] *Canderel, supra* note 5 at para. 53: "[I]n seeking to ascertain profit, the goal is to obtain an accurate picture of the taxpayer's profit for the given year." This case is discussed in Chapter 6 at heading 6.5(d) — Timing principles.

[13] *Canderel, supra* note 5 at para. 65.

[14] These provisions may be viewed as redundant in the sense of merely confirming what would be the result under section 9. With the exception of charitable donations, there are no examples of expenses that would be allowed for accounting principles but disallowed by paragraph 18(1)(a) or (h). However, in some cases, the courts have found the statutory provisions as useful additional hooks on which a decision can be hung.

[15] *Imperial Oil Ltd. v. M.N.R.*, [1947] C.T.C. 353, 3 D.T.C. 1090 (Can. Ex. Ct.) [*Imperial Oil*].

Court pointed out that that was true of every expense. The language of paragraph 18(1)(a) could not be taken literally, because an expense by itself could never directly accomplish the purpose of gaining or producing income. The issue, his lordship said, was whether the liability that made the expense necessary arose "as part of the operations, transactions or services by which the taxpayer earned the income".[16] If so, then it was part of the income-earning process, and it was deductible. Since the transportation of petroleum products was one of Imperial Oil's business operations, and the risk of collision at sea (even when caused by the negligence of an employee) was a normal hazard of those operations, any resulting liability for damages was one of the costs of Imperial Oil's operations and was, therefore, deductible.

(b) — Mixed purposes

An expense may be incurred for both income-earning and other purposes. On its face, paragraph 18(1)(a) looks to be almost wholly otiose — clearly, expenses not incurred for the purposes of gaining or producing income from business or property are not relevant for determining a taxpayer's profit from business. However, the apportionment language — an expense is deductible *to the extent* that it was incurred for the purpose of gaining or producing income — suggests that taxpayers could have dual-purpose expenses that are only partially deductible; in fact, that is how the courts have sometimes interpreted it. For example, if a taxpayer made a trip to another city intending to spend half of the time in the other city for business and half for tourist and vacation purposes, under paragraph 18(1)(a) only half of the expenses would be deductible.

8.4 — Personal and living expenses

(a) — Personal or business

(i) — Distinguishing factors

The distinction between personal expenses and income-earning expenses presents what may be one of the hardest characterization problems in tax law. The reason for the difficulty, presumably, is that people tend to combine work with pleasure to some degree; no one is able to separate and quantify the two elements at every point, nor to identify which objective is predominant. In other words, separating a business owner's personal life from his or her business life can be difficult in real life. And yet, the *ITA* cares only about the business life and expects the distinction be made. In a self-assessment tax system, taxpayers can be genuine and "generous" in characterizing their expenses as business expenses.

The *ITA* defines the term "personal or living expenses" in subsection 248(1) to include

> the expenses of properties maintained by any person for the use or benefit of the taxpayer or any person connected with the taxpayer by blood relationship, marriage

---

[16] *Ibid.* at para. 15.

or common-law partnership or adoption, and not maintained in connection with a business carried on for profit or with a reasonable expectation of profit.

The usefulness of this statutory definition is limited, since it is an inclusive definition that deals only with expenses related to properties maintained for the use or benefit of the taxpayer or a related person. Examples are houses or cars bought for personal use. The definition does not deal with other types of expenses. It does indicate, though, that the notion of "person" is broad, including not only the taxpayer, but also persons connected with the taxpayer, such as children, spouse and parents.

Case law identifies some factors as relevant to determining if an expense is a personal or living expense, but no factor is conclusive on its own. These factors include:

1. Whether the expense is deductible according to accounting principles or practices, such as GAAP. This factor generally concludes the inquiry in many cases.

2. Whether the expense is normally incurred by other taxpayers carrying on similar businesses. If it is, there may be an increased likelihood that the expense is a business expense.

3. Whether a particular expense would have been incurred if the taxpayer were not engaged in the pursuit of business or property income, or whether, in absence of the business activity, the need to incur an expense (such as food, clothing and shelter) would still be there.

4. Whether the taxpayer could have avoided the expense without affecting gross income.

5. Whether the expense is an expense "of the trader" or "of the trade". If the expense was an incident of the trade (i.e., part of the business operation itself), it is an income-earning expense.

6. Whether a particular expense was incurred in order to approach the income-producing circle or was incurred within the circle itself.[17]

On the basis of the general income-earning purpose test and the above factors, expenses incurred by business persons can perhaps be classified as those that: 1) meet the basic needs of every human being (subsistence expenses); 2) are additional expenses incurred in order to enable the taxpayer to carry on business activities (enabling expenses); and 3) are incurred in the process of earning income or to meet a need originating from the business.

---

[17] These factors were summarized in Neil Brooks, "The Principles Underlying the Deduction of Business Expenses" in Brian G. Hansen, Vern Krishna, & James A. Rendall, eds., *Canadian Taxation* (Don Mills, Ont.: De Boo, 1981) at 198–201, and were cited by Iacobucci J. in *Symes v. Canada* (1993), [1994] 1 C.T.C. 40, 94 D.T.C. 6001 (S.C.C.) [*Symes*] at para. 52.

(ii) — Everyday living expenses

Everyday living expenses are not business expenses, as they are the expense of the business person, not the person's business. These include all consumption expenditures — food, shelter, clothing, recreation — that enable taxpayers to carry on the day's activities. They are clearly personal or living expenses, the deductibility of which is expressly denied by paragraph 18(1)(h).

Other expenses arising from personal needs or circumstances also fall into this category. An example is legal fees paid by a person to defend criminal charges in respect of personal conduct that has nothing to do with the person's business activities. In some cases, however, a link to business may be alleged by taxpayers. For example, in *Leduc v. The Queen* (2006),[18] the taxpayer, a lawyer, sought to deduct legal fees paid to defend himself against several sexual offence charges. He argued that he would have lost his licence to practise law if convicted. He alleged that the charges arose out of some form of conspiracy due to his law practice. The Tax Court held that the legal fees were not deductible because the charges did not arise in the course of the taxpayer's business.

(iii) — Expenses enabling taxpayers to work

In order to be able to carry on business activities, taxpayers may need to incur additional expenses. These additional expenses of earning a living differ from the basic expenses of just living, because the reason for incurring the additional expenses is work. Examples are business clothing, child care, housekeeping, or commuting. In the case of child care, for example, a parent who stays home can save the expense, but a parent who has to operate a business outside the home cannot. Canadian courts have rejected the argument that the taxpayer cannot do his or her business "but for" the services of a babysitter, a housekeeper, etc. and, therefore, the latter's fee should be a business expense

In *Symes v. Canada* (1993).[19] the taxpayer was a self-employed lawyer with two small children. She paid a nanny to look after the children, as she needed to work long and irregular hours in her litigation practice. She and her husband (who was employed) made a "family decision" that she would pay for the nanny. A majority

---

[18] *Leduc v. The Queen* (2006), [2005] 1 C.T.C. 2858, 2005 D.T.C. 250 (Eng.) (T.C.C. [General Procedure]).

[19] *Symes, supra* note 17. *Symes* is the leading case not only on the deductibility of child care expenses, but also on the application of s. 15 of the *Canadian Charter of Rights and Freedoms*, Part I of the *Constitution Act, 1982*, being Schedule B to the *Canada Act 1982* (U.K.), 1982, c 11 [*Charter*] to the *ITA*. The taxpayer argued that her section 15 *Charter* right was infringed by the *ITA*. The Court split along gender lines on this issue. The majority (consisting of male judges) rejected an equality-based *Charter* challenge to the restrictions under s. 63 of the *ITA* on the deductibility of child care expenses. The majority rejected the argument that the restrictions had a disproportionate impact on women: although women were more likely to bear the social costs of child care, there was no evidence that women were more likely to bear the financial costs of child care; and the restrictions affected only the financial costs of child care.

of the Supreme Court of Canada held that the child care expenses were not business expenses according to traditional tests of deductibility. Although child care expenses had to be borne in order to allow the taxpayer to go to the office, they were not incurred in the income-earning process, but merely to make the taxpayer available to the business. The deductibility of an expense was traditionally governed by the commercial needs of the business rather than by the personal circumstances of the proprietor. The Court acknowledged that this rule respecting deductibility had developed at a time when businesspersons were mostly males with spouses who were at home during the day and looked after the family's children. In this situation, child care was a private matter, quite separate from a taxpayer's business activity. Now that businesspeople include women as well as men, and the care of their children is an inescapable part of their business arrangements, it might be appropriate for the courts to "reconceptualize" the nature of a business expense, and, in particular, to re-examine the rule that disallows expenses that are incurred to make the taxpayer available to the business. However, the Court did not pursue this interesting suggestion, because section 63 allows a deduction for child care expenses for all taxpayers.[20]

Housekeeping expenses were considered in *Benton v. M.N.R.* (1952).[21] The taxpayer was a 62-year-old farmer, single and in poor health. He hired a housekeeper. The portion of the housekeeper's salary was found to be personal or living expenses because the "housekeeper engaged in the usual domestic duties performable on a farm and . . . her contribution to the income-earning work of the farm was necessarily of a secondary nature, however helpful it may have been to the [taxpayer]."[22]

The *Symes* and *Benton* cases show that expenses incurred in order to enable the taxpayer to work are not deductible, as they are personal expenses. Salary paid to a person helping the farmer on the farm (not at home) would be a business expense. In *Benton*, a portion of the wages paid to the housekeeper were held to be deductible, reflecting time she spent doing farm work.

(iv) — Expenses of business

Expenses incurred by a taxpayer while carrying on business activities are business expenses. These expenses can be otherwise personal or living expenses, such as food, beverages, entertainment, legal expenses or commuting. Taking a client for lunch or a hockey game is considered to be an expense for income-earning purposes. Commuting expenses are personal expenses, as the journey to the place of business is a precondition of earning business income, and the nature of the journey to work is dictated by personal consumption decisions such as where to locate one's home and what mode of transportation to take. However, travelling between

---

[20] Section 63 of the *ITA*, *supra* note 1, is discussed in Chapter 12.

[21] *Benton v. M.N.R.* (1952), 6 Tax A.B.C. 230 (Can. Tax App. Bd.).

[22] *Ibid.*

different places of business, such as a lawyer travelling from office to courthouse or the client's premises, is for income-earning purposes.

In *Scott v. R.* (1998),[23] the taxpayer was a self-employed courier. He travelled approximately 150 kilometres per day on foot and the subway. His commission was based on the distance of the delivery and the weight of the package. Each day, he consumed an extra meal at the cost of $11 ($8 for food and $3 for bottled water and juice). He sought to deduct the $11 as business expenses. The deduction was allowed. The Court distinguished between the cost of regular food and beverages and the cost of extra food and beverages that Scott needed as a result of his business. The Court analogized Scott's need for extra food and beverages to a courier who needed more gasoline for his or her car because of its business use.

In *Cumming v. M.N.R.* (1967),[24] the taxpayer was a doctor, an anaesthetist, who rendered all his professional services at a hospital near his home. He had no office at the hospital in which he could do the bookkeeping and paperwork of the practice, or read medical journals. He established an office at his home that was used exclusively for those purposes. The Exchequer Court held that the home office was the base from which the practice was operated. Therefore, the journeys to and from the hospital were not commutes, but journeys made in the course of the practice. The cost of these journeys was accordingly business expenses.

(b) — Travel expenses

Paragraph 18(1)(h) does not deny the deduction of "travel expenses incurred by the taxpayer while away from home in the course of carrying on the taxpayer's business". The term "travel expenses" refers to transportation costs and the ordinary living expenses (meals and lodging) that are incurred by a taxpayer in connection with a business trip. To distinguish between ordinary living expenses and travel expenses, paragraph 18(1)(h) uses the phrase "away from home". "Home" presumably refers to the location of the taxpayer's family residence and/or the taxpayer's regular place of business. The phrase "in the course of business" emphasizes the business nature of the trip. Mixing pleasure with business activities while away on business is not uncommon. In such cases, either the dominant purpose of the trip is determinative, or a reasonable apportionment can be made.

8.5 — Business expenses subject to statutory limitations

(a) — Policy concerns

The *ITA* denies the deduction of otherwise deductible business expenses on the ground of tax policy or public policy. Section 67.1 and subsection 18(12) limit the deduction of entertainment expenses and home office expenses, respectively, on the ground of fairness and equity and administrative efficiency. Both expenses are commonly claimed as business expenses, but have elements of personal pleasure or

---

[23] *Scott v. R.* (1998), [1998] 4 C.T.C. 103, 98 D.T.C. 6530 (Fed. C.A.).

[24] *Cumming v. M.N.R.* (1967), [1967] C.T.C. 462, 67 D.T.C. 5312 (Can. Ex. Ct.).

discretion. Sections 67.5 and 67.6 deny the deduction of specified illegal payments, fines and penalties. In addition, other expenses of "egregious or repulsive" nature may be denied deduction based on the common law for moral reasons.

(b) — Entertainment expenses

Entertainment expenses are amounts spent on entertaining customers and clients, including expenses for meals, parties, sporting events, theatres, and membership in social and recreational clubs. These expenses present problems in terms of tax policy, as they have an element of personal pleasure, the extent of which may be difficult to ascertain. Under case law, they can be deducted in full. For example, in *Royal Trust Co. v. M.N.R.* (1957),[25] the taxpayer paid fees to enable some of its officers to belong to social and recreational clubs. The Court found that such payments were a normal business practice of trust companies, and produced business contacts and opportunities, and were, thus, deductible. Paragraph 18(1)(l) was enacted to overrule the result in *Royal Trust*. It denies the deduction of membership fees in social and recreational clubs.

Other types of entertainment expenses also provide personal pleasure to the individuals involved in the entertainment (as in the case of a taxpayer taking his or her client to a professional baseball game). Full deduction of such expenses could be open to abuse by the incurring of excessively high expenses that have only a tenuous relationship to business income but that the Canada Revenue Agency (the "CRA") could not in practice effectively police. Taxpayers who benefit from the full deductibility rule are often business owners or business executives. If the top marginal rate is 50 per cent and the taxpayer can deduct a $100 entertainment expense, his or her after-tax cost is only $50. While denying the full deduction (like paragraph 18(1)(l) does for club dues) is too heavy-handed, the difficulty of isolating and valuing the element of personal enjoyment on a case-by-case basis is significant. In order to overcome this problem, section 67.1 was introduced into the *ITA* in 1988.

Section 67.1 limits the deductibility of expenses for "food or beverages or the enjoyment of entertainment" to 50 per cent of the amount actually paid, or 50 per cent of the "amount in respect thereof that would be reasonable in the circumstances". There are some exemptions, but the section applies even when a taxpayer can prove that he or she did not participate in the consumption or enjoyment.[26] In a rough-and-ready way, this 50 per cent disallowance rule purports to approximate and filter out the personal consumption benefit that inheres in any entertainment activity. Ob-

---

[25] *Royal Trust Co. v. Minister of National Revenue* (1957), [1957] C.T.C. 32, 57 D.T.C. 1055 (Can. Ex. Ct.).

[26] *Stapley v. R.*, [2006] 3 C.T.C. 188, 2006 D.T.C. 6075 (F.C.A.). In this case, a real estate broker gave vouchers for meals, drinks and entertainment to his clients, and was denied the deduction for 50 per cent of the cost of the gifts. Had he given other types of gifts (flowers or art work), he would have been able to deduct the full cost.

BUSINESS EXPENSES SUBJECT TO STATUTORY LIMITATIONS   8.5(c)

viously, a 50/50 rule is no more or less defensible as a matter of theory than any other ratio, but it draws a clear line.

(c) — Home office expenses

The expenses of maintaining a home typically include utilities (heat, electricity and water), maintenance, property taxes and mortgage interest (or rent if the home is rented). If a businessperson does some business-related work at home, then these expenses have a dual character. Case law is inconsistent in dealing with these home office expenses. In *Logan v. M.N.R.* (1967),[27] for example, a doctor was permitted to deduct the portion of home office expenses that were attributable to a room in his home that was used as an office. The taxpayer was able to establish that the office was used exclusively for work-related activities, such as medical writing, bookkeeping, and meeting with other doctors. In *Mallouh v. M.N.R.* (1985),[28] by contrast, a doctor was denied a deduction for expenses related to a home office that occupied half of the basement in the doctor's home. In that case, the office was more of a general study or den in which business-related work was not the exclusive activity.

Subsection 18(12) was added to the *ITA* in 1988 to establish more precise and restrictive rules.[29] To be deductible, home office expenses must satisfy one of the two tests in paragraph 18(12)(a): either the office must be the individual's "principal place of business",[30] or, if the office is not the principal place of business, it must be "used on a regular and continuous basis for meeting clients, customers or patients" or used exclusively for the purpose of earning business income. Where a home office fails to satisfy one of these two tests, no deduction will be allowed.

In addition to the above deductibility tests, subsection 18(12) is, in effect, a "stop-loss" rule that prevents taxpayers from generating a loss by deducting the home office expenses and then using the loss to "shelter" other income from tax. Technically, paragraph 18(12)(b) provides that the deduction for home office expenses is allowed only to the extent that the taxpayer has positive income from the business before that deduction. In other words, the home office deduction can reduce business profit to nil, but not negative. Paragraph 18(12)(c) provides that expenses that are disallowed by paragraph (b) can be carried forward indefinitely so long as the home office continues to qualify for the deduction. Therefore, the portion of the home office expenses that cannot be deducted in a particular year will be deductible in a future year if the income from the business is sufficient in that year.

---

[27] *Logan v. M.N.R.* (1967), 67 D.T.C. 189, [1967] Tax A.B.C. 276 (Can. Tax App. Bd.).

[28] *Mallouh v. M.N.R.* (1985), [1985] 1 C.T.C. 2297, 85 D.T.C. 250 (T.C.C.).

[29] The rule permitting the deduction of home office expenses by employees (s. 8(13)), which is discussed in Chapter 5 at heading 5.8(b) — Deductions permitted, note 142, contains the same restrictive language.

[30] The word "principal" is not defined. It is considered by the CRA to have a meaning similar to "chief" or "main": Canada Revenue Agency, Folio S4-F2-C2, "Business Use of Home Expenses" at para. 2.11.

For example, X operates a home-based business. In Year 1, he has revenue of $10,000, home office expenses of $3,000, and other expenses of $9,000. In Year 1, he can deduct only $1,000 of home office expense (i.e., profit otherwise computed without the home office expense deduction). His income for Year 1 will be nil. In Year 2, if revenue rises to $15,000 and expenses remain the same, his home office expense is deemed to be $5,000 ($3,000 in Year 2 plus the $2,000 disallowed amount in Year 1). Since his profit otherwise computed is $6,000 (i.e., $15,000 of revenue - $9,000 other expenses), he can deduct the full $5,000 home office expense and realize of profit of $1,000.

(d) — Cost of illegal or unethical activities

(i) — Illegal payments and illegal businesses

Section 67.5 prohibits the deduction of expenditures made in order to commit certain offences under the *Criminal Code*[31] or the *Corruption of Foreign Public Officials Act*,[32] including bribes to judges, public officials, and law enforcement officers; payments made for the purpose of influencing municipal officers and payments made to buy an official appointment; kickbacks and frauds on the government; and bribes to foreign officials.[33] Prior to the enactment of this provision, these payments made or incurred by taxpayers for the purpose of earning or producing income were held deductible by the courts. For example, in *United Color & Chemicals Ltd.* (1992),[34] the taxpayer paid "secret commissions" (kickbacks) to the purchasing agents of its customers in order to secure contracts. The Court allowed the deduction because the purpose of the payment was for the gaining or producing of income and "such arrangements were standard in the industry".[35] Section 67.5 was introduced because the deduction of illegal payments was considered to frustrate public policy.

Section 67.5 does not distinguish illegal payments made by legal or illegal businesses. Since income from an illegal business, such as bootlegging, bookmaking or prostitution, is subject to tax,[36] there is no plausible argument for disallowing the expenses of such businesses. In *M.N.R. v. Eldridge* (1964),[37] the Exchequer Court held that the taxpayer, who carried on an illegal call girl business, could deduct

---

[31] R.S.C. 1985, c. C-46.

[32] S.C. 1998, c. 34.

[33] Until 1999, section 67.5 of the *ITA* applied only to bribes to Canadian officials. Bribes to foreign officials are now included.

[34] *United Color & Chemicals Ltd. v. Minister of National Revenue* (1992), [1992] 1 C.T.C. 2321, 92 D.T.C. 1259 (T.C.C.).

[35] *Ibid.* at para. 10.

[36] *Minister of Finance v. Smith* (1926), [1917–27] C.T.C. 251, 1 D.T.C. 92 (Jud. Com. of Privy Coun.) (bootlegging); *cf. R. v. Poynton*, [1972] C.T.C. 411, 72 D.T.C. 6329 (Ont. C.A.) (proceeds of embezzlement taxable income, although not business income).

[37] *M.N.R. v. Eldridge* (1964), [1964] C.T.C. 545, 64 D.T.C. 5338 (Can. Ex. Ct.).

business expenses such as rent, legal expenses, assistance for call girls, cost of bail bonds, and casual wages. To disallow expenses would mean taxing illegal business on gross income as opposed to net profit as required by section 9. The courts have no mandate to use the tax system as a vehicle to impose extra penalties on illegal activity that is already penalized by other statutes. Most of the expenses of an illegal business will, in any case, be perfectly legitimate in themselves (e.g., rent, utilities, supplies and equipment). Those expenses that are illegitimate (e.g., fines, penalties, bribes or kickbacks) surely do not raise any different issue than attempts by a legal business to deduct such expenses.

(ii) — Fines and penalties

There are competing policy concerns with respect to the deductibility of fines and penalties. Allowing the deduction would reduce the sting of fines and penalties and frustrate the policy of the statute that imposed the fine or penalties. On the other hand, disallowing the deduction would violate the principle of taxing net income. So, the question is whether the policy of giving full effect to the statutes under which the fines and penalties are imposed is sufficiently strong to outweigh the basic principle of income tax.

In the absence of statutory rules, the courts must balance these competing policies. In the past, the courts looked at whether the expense was avoidable or whether the unlawful act was incidental to the business being carried on.[38] In *Day and Ross v. R.* (1976),[39] for example, while allowing the deduction of the fines, the Court stressed that the unlawful acts (the violation of weight restrictions in the trucking industry) were not intentional or avoidable, and were not "outrageous transgressions of public policy". Similarly, in *Rolland Paper Co. v. M.N.R.* (1960),[40] the Court, in allowing the deduction of the legal expenses of defending the anti-trust prosecution, was careful to repeat a statement made by the sentencing court that the directors of the company had not been "guilty of moral turpitude or wicked intention". The implication of these *dicta* was, of course, that a deliberate, outrageous or morally culpable illegality would require a tax court to deny the deductibility of a fine or associated legal expenses. This was confirmed in *65302 British Columbia Ltd.*[41]

---

[38] See *Imperial Oil, supra* note 15 and accompanying text.

[39] *Day and Ross v. R.* (1976), [1976] C.T.C. 707, 76 D.T.C. 6433 (Fed. T.D.) [*Day and Ross*].

[40] *Rolland Paper Co. v. M.N.R.* (1960), [1960] C.T.C. 158, 60 D.T.C. 1095 (Can. Ex. Ct.) [*Rolland Paper*] at para. 15. In this case, the issue did not involve a fine. A paper company was permitted to deduct the legal expenses of defending an anti-trust prosecution. The company was convicted and fined, but apparently did not attempt to deduct the fine. The Exchequer Court held that the company's illegal trade practices were "followed for the purpose of earning income from the business", and the legal expenses of defending the practices from prosecution were deductible.

[41] *65302 B.C., supra* note 3.

In *65302 British Columbia Ltd.*, the taxpayer intentionally exceeded the production quota allotted to it by the British Columbia Egg Marketing Board, rather than purchasing additional quota. When the overproduction was discovered, the taxpayer was subjected to a fine.[42] The taxpayer deducted the fine and the Minister disagreed. The Supreme Court of Canada allowed the deduction, but was split (5 to 2) on the general question of the deductibility of fines and penalties. The majority held that all fines and penalties should be deductible if they were incurred for the purpose of earning income, irrespective of public policy considerations. The minority reasoned that fines and penalties should be deductible only if the deduction did not frustrate or undermine the statutory scheme under which the fine or penalty was levied. The minority classified fines and penalties into two groups: those intended to have a deterrent effect and those intended to be compensatory. Public policy doctrine would deny the deduction of the former, but not the latter. The over-quota levy fell within the latter category and was, thus, deductible. The Court concluded that "such public policy determinations are better left to Parliament".[43]

Parliament introduced section 67.6 of the *ITA* to deny the deduction of most government fines and penalties imposed after March 22, 2004. Fines and penalties imposed by the *ITA* itself are disallowed under paragraph 18(1)(t).

(iii) — Damages

To the extent that damages, fines and penalties fall outside the scope of sections 67.5 and 67.6, their deductibility remains governed by case law principles. At case law, in determining whether such payments are incurred for the purpose of earning income, the courts have considered the nature of the breach that gives rise to the payment. Payments arising from actions that amount to "outrageous transgressions of public policy" (*Day and Ross*)[44] or are committed by persons "guilty of moral turpitude or wicked intention" (*Rolland Paper*)[45] would not be deductible. In *65302 British Columbia Ltd.*, the Supreme Court contemplated that "[i]t is conceivable that a breach could be so egregious or repulsive that the fine subsequently imposed could not be justified as being incurred for the purpose of producing income".[46] However, damages for breach of contract are unlikely to be deemed to fall into this category. For example, in *McNeill v. R.* (2000),[47] an accountant who deliberately breached a non-competition agreement on the sale of his practice was

---

[42] *Ibid.* The taxpayer was also ordered to dispose of the excess birds. Under the relevant legislation, an egg producer that failed to comply with the rules and orders of the Marketing Board could also be subject to more serious monetary fines and penalties, as well as imprisonment.

[43] *65302 B.C., supra* note 3 at para. 62.

[44] *Day and Ross, supra* note 39.

[45] *Rolland Paper, supra* note 40 at para. 14.

[46] *65302 B.C., supra* note 3 at para. 69.

[47] *McNeill v. R.* (2000), [2000] 2 C.T.C. 304, 2000 D.T.C. 6211 (Fed. C.A.) [*McNeil*] at para. 15.

ordered to pay damages for the breach. The breach was found not be "egregious or repulsive".

8.6 — "Reasonable" requirement

(a) — Quantitative limitation

Section 67 prohibits the deduction of an otherwise deductible expense except to the extent that the expense was "reasonable in the circumstances".[48] It deals with the quantity, not the purpose or nature, of an expense. If an expense is not otherwise deductible, there is no need to consider section 67. The purpose of this provision is to limit "artificial" reduction of profit through deducting inordinate amount of expenses that are wholly under the control of the taxpayer, such as payments to family members and lavish business travels or meals. It is not intended to empower the Minister or the courts to second-guess business decisions of taxpayers in general circumstances. The Court in *Gabco Ltd. v. Minister of National Revenue* (1968)[49] described section 67 as a "reasonable business person" test:

> It is not a question of the Minister or this Court substituting its judgment for what is a reasonable amount to pay, but rather a case of the Minister or the Court coming to the conclusion that no reasonable business man would have contracted to pay such an amount having only the business consideration of the appellant in mind.[50]

Whether an amount is "reasonable in the circumstances" is a question of fact. As discussed below, reasonableness can be tested by comparison with amounts paid in similar circumstances in other businesses of the same kind, or amounts that would be paid in the absence of special relationships or personal elements.

(b) — Unreasonable amount attributable to personal elements

There are a number of cases in which expenses have been wholly or partially disallowed on the ground that the taxpayers purchased facilities or assets that were excessively luxurious for the purpose sought to be achieved. The purchase of an ex-

---

[48] In the pre-1972 Act, the predecessor of s. 67 was s. 12(2), which limited deductions in computing business and property income to a reasonable amount. When the Act was amended, the "reasonable" requirement was placed in s. 67 in subdivision f of Division B (which has a collection of rules relating to the computation of income), rather than subdivision b. As a result, s. 67 is applicable to deductions from income from any source. However, its main application is to deductions from business and property income, because deductions from employment income are more closely regulated and less susceptible to abuse.

[49] *Gabco Ltd. v. Minister of National Revenue* (1968), [1968] C.T.C. 313, 68 D.T.C. 5210 (Can. Ex. Ct.).

[50] *Ibid.* at 5216 [D.T.C.]. This "reasonable business person" test was referred to by the Federal Court of Appeal in *GlaxoSmithKline v. R.*, 2010 FCA 201, [2010] 6 C.T.C. 220, 2010 D.T.C. 5124 (Eng.) (F.C.A.); affirmed (2012), [2013] 1 C.T.C. 99, 2012 D.T.C. 5147 (Eng.), 2012 D.T.C. 5148 (Fr.) (S.C.C.) at para. 69 [(F.C.A.)], per Nadon J. (*GlaxoSmithKline* dealt with the meaning of "reasonable in the circumstances" under the former s. 69(2) of Act).

pensive car,[51] and extravagant entertainment expenses[52] and travelling expenses,[53] are examples.

An unusual case is *No. 511 v. M.N.R.* (1958),[54] in which the taxpayer, a lumber company, sought to deduct $22,500 to sponsor a baseball team. The Tax Appeal Board agreed that this was a legitimate and deductible form of advertising, but held the amount was too high because it was more than half of the company's profits. The Board held that $5,000 would be reasonable using newspaper and radio advertisements. Underlying this decision is probably an unexpressed factual judgment that the sponsorship of the baseball team was essentially a hobby for the principal shareholder of the taxpayer-corporation, so that the expense was only partially laid out for a business purpose.[55]

(c) — Unreasonable amount in non-arm's-length payments

When taxpayers make payments to family members and other non-arm's-length persons, the amount is often not the result of hard bargaining or influenced by market prices, but motivated by tax reasons. Section 67 has been applied to management fees, rents, or salaries paid to non-arm's-length parties.[56] In *Mulder Bros. v. M.N.R.* (1967),[57] for example, the taxpayer was a corporation controlled by two brothers, A and B. The taxpayer paid salaries as follows: Brother A, $20,000; Brother B, $13,000; Brother B's wife, $13,000. All three persons genuinely worked as employees of the corporation, but the Minister took the view that the wife's services were only worth $6,000. In his opinion, the total salary of $26,000 paid to the B family had been divided between B and B's wife to produce the most favourable income split, rather than to reward their actual contributions of work. The Minister used section 67 to reduce the company's deduction for the wife's salary to $6,000. The Board raised the reasonable figure to $8,500, disallowing the balance.

While corporate salaries or director fees paid to the taxpayer's spouse or children are challenged under section 67, this provision has been invoked in other non-

---

[51] E.g., *Kent and Co. v. M.N.R.*, [1971] Tax A.B.C. 1158 (Can. Tax App. Bd.).

[52] E.g., *Chabot v. M.N.R.* (1961), 61 D.T.C. 193, 26 Tax A.B.C. 204 (Can. Tax App. Bd.).

[53] E.g., *No. 589 v. M.N.R.* (1958), 59 D.T.C. 41, 21 Tax A.B.C. 153 (Can. Tax App. Bd.).

[54] *No. 511 v. M.N.R.* (1958), 19 Tax A.B.C. 248 (Can. Tax App. Bd.).

[55] *Ibid.* In this case, s. 67 is a vehicle by which an element of personal consumption is disallowed or stripped from an otherwise legitimate business expense. This could be done without recourse to s. 67, since ss. 9, 18(1)(a) and 18(1)(h) all prohibit the deduction of non-business expenditures, but s. 67 is a convenient tool for the CRA and the court.

[56] Related persons are deemed by s. 251(1) not to deal with each other at arm's length, and, thus, are non-arm's-length persons to each other. Individuals are related to each other by reason of blood, marriage or adoption (s. 251(2)). When a related party is a non-resident corporation, s. 247 of the *ITA* applies the arm's-length standard to require that the amount paid, or received, by the resident taxpayer reflects the arm's-length price.

[57] *Mulder Bros. v. M.N.R.* (1967), 67 D.T.C. 475, [1967] Tax A.B.C. 761 (Can. Tax App. Bd.) [*Mulder Bros.*].

arm's-length payments. Examples are: $12,000 of rent paid by a dentist for premises owned by his wife was limited to $5,000;[58] management fees of $1,000 paid by a lawyer to a corporation owned by himself and his wife was found to be reasonable;[59] and fees paid by a dentist to his family trust to do his bookkeeping were found to be too high and reduced to a lower amount based on a 15 per cent markup on the cost of the services.[60] In *Aessie v. R.* (2004),[61] on the other hand, an accountant with gross revenue of $55,000 was allowed to deduct management fees of $34,500 paid to his wife's management company for administrative services (including reception, typing, record keeping, and other administrative activities). The Court found that the arrangement was "a common and reasonable business deal".[62]

8.7 — Timing of deductions

(a) — Importance of timing

Timing of deductions is extremely important both to tax policy and tax planning. Indeed, the acceleration of a deduction may be equivalent to a full or partial exclusion of the income generated by the deductible expense. An important tax planning objective is to achieve a tax deferral through the acceleration of a deduction or the mismatch of a deduction and income.

Section 9 of the *ITA* defers to accounting principles and business practice for the determination of profit. Sections 18 and 20 contain specific rules governing the timing of deductions, some of which are discussed below. The accounting principle of matching underlies some of the statutory rules, such as prepaid expenses under subsection 18(9) and the reserves rules under paragraph 20(1). Under the interpretive framework established in *Canderel*,[63] taxpayers may choose any method of determining profit that is in accordance with well-accepted commercial accounting and business principles, subject to any overriding provision of the *ITA* or established case law.

---

[58] *Cohen v. M.N.R.* (1963), 63 D.T.C. 237, 31 Tax A.B.C. 216 (Can. Tax App. Bd.).

[59] *Shulman v. M.N.R.*, [1961] C.T.C. 385, 61 D.T.C. 1213 (Can. Ex. Ct.); affirmed (1962), 62 D.T.C. 1166 (S.C.C.).

[60] *Costigane v. R.*, [2003] 3 C.T.C. 2087, 2003 D.T.C. 254 (T.C.C. [General Procedure]).

[61] *Aessie v. R.* (2004), [2004] 4 C.T.C. 2159 (T.C.C. [Informal Procedure]).

[62] In essence, section 67 disallows the deduction of an expense to the extent that it is unreasonable. This has the effect of increasing the income of the payer. Section 67 does not correspondingly adjust the amount for the recipient. The payee must recognize the full amount of the payment received for tax purposes. In *Mulder Bros., supra* note 57, the wife would have to report as income her full $13,000 salary, even though $4,500 of it had been denied to the employer as a deduction. The unreasonable portion of the salary would, therefore, be taxed twice.

[63] *Canderel, supra* note 5.

What follows is a brief discussion of the basic approach to recognizing current expenses, limitations on the deduction of contingent liabilities and prepaid expenses, and deduction of reserves.

(b) — Basic rule: when an expense is incurred (payable)

Paragraph 18(1)(a) precludes a deduction if the amount cannot properly be described as an "expense incurred". Section 20 uses terms such as amount "paid", "payable" or "incurred" and payments "made by the taxpayer in the year". Generally speaking, an expense is recognized as a deduction in the year in which it was incurred. When an expense is incurred is determined by case law.

The term "expense" has been interpreted by the courts to be an obligation to pay a sum of money. For example, Pratte J. defined the term in *R. v. Burnco Industries Ltd.* (1984) as follows:

> . . . an expense, within the meaning of paragraph 18(1)(a) of the *Income Tax Act*, is an obligation to pay a sum of money. An expense cannot be said to be incurred by a taxpayer who is under no obligation to pay money to anyone . . . [A]n obligation to do something which may in the future entail the necessity of paying money is not an expense.[64]

For a deduction to be possible, there must be an expense. A notional expense does not meet the test of deductibility. For example, a notional (but unpaid) rent during a rent-free period provided in a lease was held not to be deductible, even though an amortized monthly amount might be deductible under generally accepted accounting principles.[65]

The leading case on when an amount is incurred or payable is *J.L. Guay Ltée v. M.N.R.* (1971).[66] It established the principle that an expense is deductible in the year in which the taxpayer has a legal and unconditional, though not necessarily immediate, obligation to pay an amount. The facts in this case are the opposite of those in *Colford*,[67] discussed in Chapter 7. In *Guay Ltée*, the taxpayer was a gen-

---

[64] *R. v. Burnco Industries Ltd. et al.* (1984), [1984] C.T.C. 337, 84 D.T.C. 6348 (Fed. C.A.). In this case, the taxpayer operated a gravel pit and was required to backfill areas excavated in the course of the year. In computing its income for its 1974 taxation year, the taxpayer sought to deduct an amount as the estimated future cost of backfilling the gravel pit. The deduction was disallowed.

[65] *Buck Consultants Limited v. The Queen* (1999), [2000] 1 C.T.C. 93, 2000 D.T.C. 6015 (Fed. C.A.); leave to appeal refused 2000 CarswellNat 2401, 2000 CarswellNat 2402 (S.C.C.).

[66] *J.L. Guay Ltée v. M.N.R.* (1971), [1971] C.T.C. 686, 71 D.T.C. 5423 (Fed. T.D.); affirmed (1972), [1973] C.T.C. 506, 73 D.T.C. 5373 (Fed. C.A.); affirmed [1975] C.T.C. 97, 75 D.T.C. 5094 (S.C.C.) [*Guay Ltée*]. The decision was affirmed without reasons by both the Federal Court of Appeal and the Supreme Court of Canada. until the architect's certificate was issued

[67] The result in *Guay Ltée, ibid.*, is the converse of the *M.N.R. v. Colford Contracting Co. Ltd.*, [1960] C.T.C. 178, 60 D.T.C. 1131 (Can. Ex. Ct.); affirmed [1962] C.T.C. 546, 62

eral contractor seeking a deduction of holdbacks to the subcontractors. Under the contractual arrangement, the holdback became payable after a certificate of acceptance was issued by the architects and engineers to the effect that the work was completed in accordance with the contract. The Court held that the taxpayer was not entitled to deduct the holdback, even though all of the construction had been completed by the subcontractors, because the payment of the holdback was conditional on the issuance of the certificate. There was an element of contingency in both the liability and the quantum: until the issuance of the certification, it was possible that the holdback would be used to pay damages incurred by the owner or the general contractor resulting from the subcontractors' failure to perform the work. If the damages corresponded to, or exceeded, the holdback, the general contractor could keep the entire amount of holdback.

The time when a payment becomes payable is generally the same as when the payment becomes receivable to the payee. The cost of services becomes payable when the services are rendered, and the cost of property becomes payable when the property is delivered. Thus, the time when the payment is actually made is largely irrelevant. For example, the salary for the month of December of Year 1 is payable to the employee at the end of the month, even if the salary is not paid until January of Year 2. Similarly, employee benefits relating to salaries earned but not paid in the year are incurred in the year, and, thus, deductible.[68] However, as indicated in *Guay Ltée*, a contingent liability is not deductible.

Similarly, if the taxpayer's liability for items of indebtedness is contested in the courts or tribunals, the liability is not unconditional. The taxpayer must await litigation or settlement and claim a deduction when the liability is finally adjudicated or settled. This issue often arises in cases determining whether damages are deductible in the year in which the event occurred or in the year in which the damages payment is finally determined. The courts have held that it is the latter because the taxpayer's liability to pay damages becomes absolute and unconditional only when the liability and the quantum of damages are finally ascertained by the court or a binding settlement between the parties.[69]

D.T.C. 1338 (S.C.C.). For a discussion of the latter case, see Chapter 7 at heading 7.3(d)(ii) — "Receivable".

[68] In *Federation des caisses populaires Desjardins de Montreal et de l'Ouest du Quebec v. R.* (2001), [2002] 2 C.T.C. 1, 2002 D.T.C. 7413 (Eng.), 2001 D.T.C. 5173 (Fr.) (Fed. C.A.), the Court held an amount accrued for payroll taxes and benefits relating to vacation pay earned in the year was deductible in the year under s. 18(1)(a), since the legal obligation to pay the amount was incurred in the year. See also *Provigo Distributions Inc. v. R.* (2000), 33 C.C.L.I. (3d) 133, 2000 D.T.C. 2112 (Fr.) (T.C.C. [General Procedure]); and *Wawang Forest Products Ltd. v. R.*, [2001] 2 C.T.C. 233, 2001 D.T.C. 5212 (Fed. C.A.).

[69] *McNeill, supra* note 47 at para. 19.

(c) — Contingent liability or amount

Paragraph 18(1)(e) denies deduction of "a contingent liability or amount".[70] It backstops the general rule mentioned above. As indicated in *Guay Ltée*, if the legal liability to pay or the amount of payment is contingent, the payment is not deductible.[71] Whether a liability or amount is contingent is a legal question.

The often-quoted definition of "contingent liability" was articulated by Lord Guest in *Winter et al. v. IRC* (1961)[72] and adopted by the Supreme Court of Canada in *Canada v. McLarty* (2008):

> I should define a contingency as an event which may or may not occur and a contingent liability as a liability which depends for its existence upon an event which may or may not happen.[73]

In other words, to determine if a legal obligation is contingent at a particular point in time, one needs to ask "whether the legal obligation has come into existence at that time, or whether no obligation will come into existence until the occurrence of an event that may not occur".[74] "The simple fact that its exact quantum will be determined later does not impact the prior existence of the obligation."[75] Examples of contingent liabilities include: an obligation to pay an amount equal to a percentage of earned revenues is a contingent obligation unless the revenues are earned;[76] and an obligation to pay a management bonus if the money is available is a contingent obligation unless the money is available.[77] In contrast, in *McLarty*, the court held that the obligation of a taxpayer was not contingent despite the fact that it was unlikely that the full amount of the obligation would ever be paid due to the creditor's limited recourse.[78]

---

[70] As well, section 143.4 applies to deem an amount to be a contingent liability where a taxpayer has a right to reduce or eliminate the amount that is required to be paid. See discussion in Canada Revenue Agency, Folio S3-F6-C1, "Interest Deductibility" [Folio S3-F6-C1] at paras 1.16–1.18.

[71] *Guay Ltée, supra* note 66.

[72] *Winter et al. v. IRC* (1961), [1963] A.C. 235 (H.L.).

[73] *Canada v. McLarty* (2008), [2008] 4 C.T.C. 221, 2008 D.T.C. 6366 (Fr.), 2008 D.T.C. 6354 (Eng.) (S.C.C.) [*McLarty*] at para. 17, per Rothstein J.: "The focus is therefore on two particular types of uncertainty: 1) whether an event may or may not occur; and 2) whether a liability depends for its existence upon whether that event may or may not happen."

[74] *Wawang, supra* note 68.

[75] *Imperial Oil Resources Limited v. AGC* (2014), [2015] 1 C.T.C. 1, 2014 D.T.C. 5113 (Eng.) (F.C.); affirmed [2016] 6 C.T.C. 135, 2016 D.T.C. 5057 (F.C.A.) at para. 28 [(F.C.)].

[76] *Mandel v. R.*, [1978] C.T.C. 780, 78 D.T.C. 6518 (Fed. C.A.); affirmed [1980] C.T.C. 130, 80 D.T.C. 6148 (S.C.C.).

[77] *R. v. Ken and Ray's Collins Bay Supermarket*, [1975] C.T.C. 504, 75 D.T.C. 5346 (Fed. T.D.); affirmed (1977), [1978] C.T.C. xvi (Fed. C.A.); leave to appeal refused [1978] 1 S.C.R. ix (S.C.C.).

[78] *McLarty, supra* note 73. This issue is now addressed by s. 143.4, *supra* note 70, which is applicable for taxation years ending after March 16, 2011.

In *General Motors of Canada Ltd. v. R.* (2004),[79] the Federal Court of Appeal found that the obligation to accrue the amounts contributed to a special fund established under an agreement with the union was contingent. According to the agreement, as the overtime worked by certain of its employees reached a specified level, General Motors was obliged to contribute to the fund that was to be used to pay the benefit of the employees when specified contingencies were met. In the year in question, General Motors "accrued" an amount as the overtime levels were reached but did not actually set aside monies in trust or put monies into a separate bank account to fulfill its obligations. The monies were still available for the general use of General Motors until there was a need to draw down on the funds to finance the payments under the agreement. The accruals were held to be contingent because they depended on the occurrence of an event (the use of funds for specific programs) that might not occur.

(d) — Reserves

(i) — Timing relief

Paragraph 18(1)(e) of the *ITA* prohibits the deduction of contingent liabilities and "reserves". The ordinary meaning of "reserve" is to "set aside" an amount for the future. For example, in financial accounting, corporations commonly have a reserve for deferred taxes by setting aside an additional amount of income tax "expense" when accounting income is greater than taxable income. The purpose of the reserve is to better match the tax "expense" to the accounting income. Because a reserve is a not a legal liability, an increase in a reserve is not an "expense incurred" for tax purposes. Subsection 20(1) of the *ITA* allows a number of reserves to conform to accounting practices and to provide relief from the general timing requirements. We will discuss three such reserves below to illustrate their application:

- reserve for doubtful debts (paragraph 20(1)(l));

- reserve for unearned amounts (paragraph 20(1)(m));

- reserve for deferred payments (paragraph 20(1)(n)).

Unlike actual expenses, a reserve that is deducted in one year must be brought back as a revenue inclusion in the following year. The general purpose of these reserve rules is to better match the profit realized by the taxpayer.

(ii) — Doubtful debts and bad debts

Paragraph 20(1)(l) permits a deduction in computing income from a business or property of "a reasonable amount as a reserve for . . . doubtful debts" that have

---

[79] *General Motors of Canada Ltd. v. R.* (2004), [2005] 1 C.T.C. 56, 2004 D.T.C. 6716 (F.C.A.); leave to appeal refused 2005 CarswellNat 1376, 2005 CarswellNat 1377 (S.C.C.). After this decision, the documentation was amended specifically to create an absolute liability to contribute to the contingency fund. Despite the amendment, the unexpended portion of the fund remained a contingent liability, and not deductible; see *The Queen v. General Motors of Canada Limited*, [2008] 4 C.T.C. 79, 2008 D.T.C. 6381 (Eng.) (F.C.A.).

been previously included in computing income or that have arisen from loans made in the ordinary course of a money-lending business. The reserve for doubtful debts attempts to reduce the value of an account receivable to the amount likely to be realized.

The term "doubtful debt" is undefined in the *ITA*. It "can mean only what it says — the debt is owing and possible of collection, but that possibility is not sufficiently certain in the mind of the taxpayer that he wishes to be placed in the disadvantageous position of having to pay income tax thereon before that possibility has become more of a certainty".[80] If there is a reasonable doubt that an account receivable is not collectible, it is a doubtful debt. The case law with respect to the doubtful debt reserve seems to leave the taxpayer with a great degree of flexibility in using business judgment with regard to the inclusion amounts in such a reserve. However, there are some objective factors that the courts have considered in determining whether a debt is reasonably doubtful: the age of the overdue account, although delay in payment alone is not a sufficient factor; the history of the account; the financial position of the debtor; any increase or decrease in the debtor's total sales; the taxpayer's past bad debt experience; and the general business condition in the country and the business condition in the particular locality.[81]

Only a "reasonable amount" of the doubtful debt is deductible under paragraph 20(1)(l).[82] The reserve under paragraph 20(1)(l) must be added back to income under paragraph 12(1)(d) in the following year. If the debt remains doubtful, another reserve can be deducted.

For example, Taxpayer L, a lawyer, renders services in Year 1 and sends a bill to the client on May 1 for $10,000, payable on May 30, Year 1. She incurred expenses in rendering the services of $6,000. The bill is not paid by the end of the year. L has sufficient grounds to doubt her client's capability to pay the bill. In computing her

---

[80] *Highfield Corporation Ltd. v. M.N.R.*, [1982] C.T.C. 2812, 82 D.T.C. 1835 (T.R.B.) at 2828 [C.T.C.]. See also *Copley Noyes & Randall Ltd. v. R.*, [1991] 1 C.T.C. 541, 91 D.T.C. 5291 (Fed. T.D.); varied (1992), 93 D.T.C. 5508 (Fed. C.A.) at para. 30 [(Fed. T.D.)].

[81] See *No. 81 v. M.N.R.* (1953), 53 D.T.C. 98, 8 Tax A.B.C. 82 (Can. Tax App. Bd.) at 104 [D.T.C.].

[82] Canada Revenue Agency, Interpretation Bulletin IT-442R, "Bad Debts and Reserve for Doubtful Debts" (1991) at para. 24 states:

> This calculation should preferably be based on the taxpayer's past history of bad debts, the experience in the industry if that information is available, general and local economic conditions, costs of collection, etc. This procedure may result in a reserve being calculated as a percentage of the total amount of the doubtful debts or a series of percentages relating to an age-analysis of those debts. However, a reserve that is merely based on a percentage of all debts, whether doubtful or not, a percentage of gross sales or some similar calculation is not considered to be a reserve determined on a reasonable basis as required by s. 20(1)(l)(i). However, a reserve for doubtful debts that is less than the amount that could have been claimed in accordance with a determination such as that described above will be viewed as a reasonable amount.

profit for Year 1, L includes the $10,000 under paragraph 12(1)(b). In addition to deducting the ordinary business expense of $6,000, she can deduct a reserve for doubtful debt of $10,000 (assuming the whole amount of the debt is doubtful by the end of Year 1). She would end up with a loss of $6,000 (from the expenses). For Year 2, she must include the $10,000 reserve deducted in Year 1 in income pursuant to paragraph 12(1)(d), recognizing a profit of $10,000 (assuming the debt is paid in Year 2). After deducting the loss carryover from Year 1, she ends up with a taxable income of $4,000. If the debt remains doubtful in Year 2, she can claim a reserve under paragraph 20(1)(l) to offset the inclusion under paragraph 12(1)(d), ending up with nil profit.

Eventually, when the debt becomes "bad", a deduction is permitted by paragraph 20(1)(p) (rather than paragraph 20(1)(l)). There is no requirement that a s. 20(1)(p) amount be added back in the following year. However, if the "bad" debt is actually collected, the amount is included in income under s. 12(1)(i).

(iii) — Deferred payments

Paragraph 20(1)(n) effectively postpones the realization of income when the payment of the purchase price for a property sold is deferred to a future year. It provides

> If an amount included in computing a taxpayer's income from the business for the year or for a preceding taxation year in respect of property sold in the course of the business is payable to the taxpayer after the end of the year and, except where the property is real or immovable property, all or part of the amount was, at the time of the sale, not due until at least 2 years after that time, [a taxpayer may deduct] a reasonable amount as a reserve in respect of any part of the amount that can reasonably be regarded as a portion of the profit from the sale.[83]

Technically, three conditions must be met for a deferred payment reserve deduction: 1) the amount from the sale of the property must be included in income; 2) the property must be an inventory property; and 3) except where the property is real property, all or part of the purchase price must not be due until at least two years after the time of the sale.[84] The amount of the reserve is the amount that "can reasonably be regarded as a portion of the profit from the sale".[85] This requires the computation of the "profit" from the sale, and then a reasonable apportionment of such profit. The apportionment is considered reasonable if it is based on the ratio of the amount not due until after the end of the year to the total sale price.[86] Expressed as a formula, the amount of reserve is determined as follows:

---

[83] *ITA, supra* note 1, s. 20(1)(n).

[84] Paragraph 20(8)(b) prohibits a deduction under s. 20(1)(n) if the sale occurred more than 36 months before the end of the year. Therefore, the deferred payment reserve is available only for a maximum of four years.

[85] *ITA, supra* note 1, s. 20(1)(n).

[86] Canada Revenue Agency, Interpretation Bulletin IT-154R, "Special Reserves" (1995) [IT-154R] and Canada Revenue Agency, Interpretation Bulletin IT-152R3, "Special reserves —

$$\text{Profit} \times \frac{\text{Amount not due until after the end of the year}}{\text{Total sale price}} = \text{reserve}$$

The amount of reserve deduction in Year 1 under paragraph 20(1)(n) must be included in computing income in Year 2 under subparagraph 12(1)(e)(ii). If the conditions for the reserve are met in Year 2, the taxpayer may deduct a reserve in that year, in which case this amount must be included in income in Year 3.

For example, in Year 1, Taxpayer X sells inventory property with a cost of $60,000 for a price of $100,000, of which $50,000 is payable immediately and $25,000 in each of Years 2 and 3. X's profit from the sale is $40,000 (the $100,000 sale price *less* the $60,000 cost of the property sold), but X will receive only half of the sale price, and, thus, half of the profit in the year of sale. By virtue of paragraph 20(1)(n), X may deduct a reserve of $20,000 in Year 1, computed as follows:

Year 1

$$\$40,000 \times \frac{\text{Amount not due until after the end of Year 1 (\$50,000)}}{\text{Total sale price (\$100,000)}} = \$20,000$$

Consequently, X's profit from the sale for Year 1 will be $20,000 ($40,000 total profit from the sale less the reserve of $20,000). For each of Years 2 and 3, X's net income from the sale will be $10,000, computed as follows:

Year 2

Income inclusion (s. 12(1)(e) re: reserve in Year 1)	$ 20,000
Less:	
Reserve = $40,000 × 25,000 / $100,000	($ 10,000)
Net income	$ 10,000

Year 3

Income inclusion (s. 12(1)(e) re: reserve in Year 2)	$ 10,000
Less:	
Reserve	
= $40,000 × 0 (no amount due after Year 3) / $100,000	0
Net income	$ 10,000

The $40,000 profit from the sale is, thus, recognized over the period of three years in which the sale price is received.

(iv) — Unearned amounts

Taxpayers may receive payments for services to be provided in a future year or goods to be delivered in a future year. Examples are retainers received by lawyers and deposits or advance payments received by landlords. These amounts must be

---

Sale of land" (1985). As discussed in Chapter 10 at heading 10.4(b) — Reserve for deferred payments, the formula in respect of capital property and capital gains is different (para. 40(1)(a)).

included in computing profit in the year of receipt under paragraph 12(1)(a). And yet, they are not legally earned because the recipient has no clear and absolute right to receive the amount until services are rendered or goods are sold. Paragraph 20(1)(m) allows the taxpayer to deduct a reasonable amount in respect of goods that will be delivered, or services that will be rendered, in a subsequent year.[87] In effect, paragraph 20(1)(m) allows a better "matching" of the cost and revenue. In the absence of this reserve, a taxpayer would include an amount in income that is received but not earned in one year, and recognize the cost of earning that income in a future year, resulting in an inaccurate picture of income in both relevant years.

Like the two other reserves discussed above, the amount of reserve under paragraph 20(1)(m) must be "reasonable". What is "reasonable" is a question of fact depending upon the circumstances. The CRA's administrative policy is to allow the full amount included under paragraph 12(1)(a) as a reasonable amount for the reserve "in respect of those goods or services which past experience or other things indicate will have to be delivered or provided after the end of the year".[88] Therefore, the reserve completely offsets the inclusion under paragraph 12(1)(a), and no profit will be taxable until the future year in which the income is earned. The reserve under paragraph 20(1)(m) must be included in income in the subsequent year under s. 12(1)(a). If goods are not delivered in that year, or services are not rendered in that year, another reserve is available, in which case the reserve in Year 2 must be included in income in Year 3, and so on.

(e) — Prepaid expenses

A "prepaid expense" is generally an expense paid in respect of services or goods to be received in a future year (the expense of the payer of the unearned revenue amounts discussed above). Examples are rent and municipal taxes paid in advance of the period to which they relate, insurance premiums on multi-year policies, and expenditures on promotional material (catalogues, brochures, etc.) to be used in a future year. The combination of paragraphs 12(1)(a) and 20(1)(m) results in non-recognition of the amounts for the recipient, and subsection 18(9) limits the deduction for the payer.

Subsection 18(9) provides that certain categories of prepaid expenses must not be deducted in full in the year of payment, and must be deducted in the years to which they relate. The stipulated categories of prepaid expenses are payments for future services, interest, taxes, rent, royalties and insurance. It is not clear why subsection 18(9) is limited to those categories of prepayments. The CRA takes the view that

---

[87] The reserve is not available for an obligation to deliver land (which is not a "good") in the future, or an obligation in respect of warranty, indemnity or guarantee (paragraph 20(7)(a)). By virtue of subsection 20(6), reserves in respect of articles of food and drink or transportation that must be provided after the end of the taxation year are, in effect, limited to one year. Revenue from unredeemed food or drink coupons or transportation tickets must be recognized in the year following the sale of the coupons or tickets.

[88] IT-154R, *supra* note 86 at para. 4.

this provision was enacted for greater certainty, and, although it does not cover all categories of prepaid expenses, there is a general requirement that "... the accounting for these expenses for income tax purposes should be in accordance with generally accepted accounting principles which would, in most cases, require that the expenses be matched to the year in which the benefit is to be derived ..."[89]

8.8 — Inventory

(a) — Notion of "inventory"

In a merchandising or manufacturing business, there will be assets that have been purchased either for immediate resale or for resale after they have been assembled or used in the manufacture of some product. Such assets are called "inventory" or "stock-in-trade". Subsection 248(1) contains a broad definition of "inventory":

> "inventory" means a description of property the cost or value of which is relevant in computing a taxpayer's income from a business for a taxation year or would have been so relevant if the income from the business had not been computed in accordance with the cash method and, with respect to a farming business, includes all of the livestock held in the course of carrying on the business.[90]

Typically, what assets constitute inventory depends upon the nature of the business and the use of the assets. Motor vehicles, which would be capital assets for most businesses, will be inventory for an automobile dealer. Stocks and bonds, which would normally be investments, will be inventory for a securities dealer. Subsection 10(5) deems inventory to include, among others, advertising or packaging materials, supplies, and work in progress of a business that is a profession (e.g., doctors, lawyers, etc.). Work in progress generally refers to those tasks upon which work has been done but that have not yet been completed and billed. Property held in an adventure or concern in the nature of trade is inventory.[91]

(b) — Timing of deduction

The cost of inventory is clearly deductible in computing profit under subsection 9(1) because it is incurred for the purpose of earning income. The only major issue is the timing of the deduction. Should the cost of inventory be deducted at the time when the cost was incurred (i.e., purchased) like other expenses, or when the goods were sold?

Assume Taxpayer Z has a computer store and opens for business in 2017. During 2017, Z buys computers for a total cost of $100,000. On December 1, 2017, the computers that remain unsold (known as "closing inventory") have a cost of $30,000 and a fair market value of $50,000. Z's total proceeds of sales in 2017 are $110,000. What is the cost of inventory that Z can deduct in 2017? What if no

---

[89] Canada Revenue Agency, Interpretation Bulletin IT-417R2, "Prepaid expenses and deferred charges" (1997).

[90] *ITA, supra* note 1, s. 248(1) "inventory".

[91] *Friesen v. R.*, [1995] 2 C.T.C. 369, 95 D.T.C. 5551 (S.C.C.) [*Friesen*].

computers were sold in 2017 and the market value of the computers dropped to $70,000?

In the absence of any statutory provisions, this issue is governed by accounting principles. For taxpayers using the cash method of accounting, the cost of all inventory purchased in one year is deductible in that year regardless if any inventory is sold in that year. In the above example, Z would deduct $100,000. As explained in Chapter 6, the cash method of accounting results in mismatching of revenue and expenses if the goods are sold in a future year. If Z sold nothing in 2017, he can still deduct the cost, and realize a loss of $100,000 (which is, in effect, a "paper loss" because he still owns the computers).

As discussed in Chapter 6, taxpayers (other than those in the business or farming or fishing) cannot use the cash method of accounting and must use the accrual method of accounting. This method recognizes as an expense for an accounting period only the cost of those goods sold during the period, and carries the goods still on hand at the end of the period as an asset on the balance sheet. In principle, the cost of inventory is treated in the same way as other costs incurred by a business. To the extent that inventory has been sold (goods sold), its cost has been used up in the current period and is recognized as an expense. To the extent that inventory has not been sold (closing inventory), its cost has a continuing value to the business and is carried on the balance sheet as an asset of the business. Accordingly, inventory accounting is aimed at accurately reflecting income by matching inventory cost against related revenues. It also prevents inventory manipulation to defer the recognition of profit. If inventory costs were deductible at the time when they were incurred, a taxpayer could expense and deduct the costs of buying or producing *all* property during the year. By building up the supply of property in inventory over the years, the taxpayer could indefinitely postpone recognition of any profit, or the taxpayer could manipulate the recognition to suit his or her purposes, apart from the real gains from the business activities. Inventory accounting prevents this opportunity by limiting the deduction for the cost of goods sold to the cost of those goods that were *actually* sold during the taxation year in question.

(c) — Cost of goods sold

The most obvious way of calculating the cost of goods sold is to keep a record of the actual cost of each item in stock, and to keep a record of the sale of each item sold. At the end of the year, all of the costs of the items sold can be totalled and recognized as an expense (cost of goods sold), and all of the costs of the items unsold can be totalled and included as an asset in the closing inventory. This method of determining inventory cost is called "specific identification", and it is acceptable for accounting purposes. It is, however, normally used only by businesses with a relatively small volume of high-cost, heterogeneous inventory and a relatively low turnover, such as dealers in automobiles, antiques or arts.

For businesses that manufacture or sell a high volume of homogeneous goods, such as bread or shoes or nuts and bolts, it is not feasible to keep the kinds of records entailed by the method of specific identification. For most businesses, the cost of goods sold (CGS) is determined by the following formula:[92]

opening inventory + cost of goods purchased during the year - closing inventory

Opening inventory is the inventory on hand at the beginning of the accounting year, which is the inventory on hand (unsold) at the end of the previous year. The closing inventory plus purchases made during the year constitute the inventory available for sale during the year. Closing inventory is inventory on hand at the end of the year, which is generally ascertained by a physical inventory count at year-end. The total available inventory for sale *minus* the closing inventory results in the cost of goods sold in the year.

In the above example, Taxpayer Z's cost of goods sold in 2017 will be $70,000, which is: 0 (opening inventory) + $100,000 (purchases in 2017) - $30,000 (assuming lower of cost and fair market value).

The formula for determining cost of goods sold involves two steps. The first is valuation: to choose a method by which an overall cost (or value) is assigned to the goods in inventory at the beginning and end of the year. Because subsection 10(2) of the *ITA* requires that the value attributed to the opening inventory be the same as that attributed to the closing inventory of the previous year, the key is to value the closing inventory. The second step is tracing: to choose a way by which to determine the goods in the closing inventory and how much they cost. This is necessary because the cost of those goods unsold at the year-end must not be treated as part of the cost of goods sold (since they are still on hand) and those goods might be purchased at different costs at different times.

(i) — Valuation methods

By a process of counting or measuring or weighing, it is ordinarily fairly easy to determine the number of units in the inventory at any given time. But tax computations must be made in dollars, and to put the inventory into dollars requires assigning a value in dollars or cents to each unit in the inventory. What value should be used: cost or fair market value?

The main method for valuing inventory in the *ITA* is the "lower of cost or fair market value" method under subsection 10(1). It is clear from the "Subject to this Part" wording in subsection 9(1) that subsection 10(1) overrides the common law rules for computing profit under section 9. Taxpayers can use the method under subsection 10(1) even when a different method of valuation under the accounting rules produces a more accurate picture of profit.[93]

---

[92] This formula has been accepted for tax purposes. See, e.g., *Friesen, ibid.*

[93] *CDSL Canada Ltd. v. Canada* (2008), 2008 F.C.A. 400, 2009 D.T.C. 5030 (Fr.), 2010 D.T.C. 5055 (Eng.) (F.C.A.). The taxpayers in CDSL were a group of companies carrying on a computer technology consulting business. For accounting purposes, the taxpayers valued

The terms "cost" and "fair market value" are not defined in the *ITA*. Generally speaking, cost is the actual laid-down cost.[94] Pursuant to GAAP, the fair market value of an inventory item may be based on one of the following three prices: 1) the prevailing purchase price (useful for raw materials); 2) the selling price (useful for finished goods); or 3) the cost of replacement (useful for semi-finished goods where it is usually not possible to obtain a purchase price and it is not possible to sell the article). Paragraph 10(4)(b) requires the use of the third method in respect of an inventory item that is advertising or packaging material, parts, supplies, or other property of this nature. Paragraph 10(4)(a) provides that the fair market value of work in progress of a professional business is the amount that can reasonably be expected to become receivable after the end of the year.

If the fair market value of a closing inventory item is lower than its cost, GAAP requires the inventory item to be written down to its market value. This results in the fair market value of the item being reported on the balance sheet and the amount of the writedown being recognized as an expense of the period. As a result, the writedown will reduce the income of the year by the unrealized loss in market value of the goods still on hand. On the other hand, if the market price has been going up, an inventory item valued at market price would include in income the unrealized increase in market value of the goods still on hand.

In the above example of the computer store, if Taxpayer Z sold nothing in 2017 and the fair market value of the computers is $70,000 (while the cost is $100,000), the writedown would be $30,000. This $30,000 is deductible in 2017, producing a loss of $30,000 because the revenue is nil. Applying the above formula, Z's opening inventory is nil (because this is the first year of business), cost of goods purchased during the year is $100,000 and closing inventory is $70,000 (using fair market value), and cost of goods sold is $30,000 (0 + $100,000 - $70,000).

---

their work in progress at fair market value (using billing rates), which resulted in the profit related to unbilled work in progress being included 1) in inventory and 2) in accounting income. However, for tax purposes, they valued the work in progress at the lower of cost or market in accordance with subsection 10(1), which resulted in a lower income for tax purposes. The Court held that the "Subject to this Part" wording in s. 9(1) allowed the taxpayers to do this even though this practice did not produce an accurate picture of the income.

[94] In the case of inventories of merchandise purchased for resale or of raw materials, the cost is the laid-down cost, which includes the invoice cost plus customs and excise duties, freight and insurance charges. In the case of goods in process or finished goods in the inventory of a manufacturer, the cost includes the cost of direct labour and, in some cases, the applicable share of overhead expenses (such as heat, light and power, and maintenance, property taxes and insurance). In the case of professional services, "work in progress" is inventory (s. 10(5)(a)) but accountants, dentists, lawyers, doctors and chiropractors can make a s. 34 election to effectively value it at nil. In the case of other professionals providing services (e.g., engineers, architects, consultants, etc.), the cost is the salary of staff members plus disbursements.

There are two exceptions to the main "lower of cost or fair market value" method. The first exception is the "fair market value" method under Regulation 1801.[95] Under this method, fair market value is used to determine the closing inventory. The accrued gain (writeup) or loss (writedown) is recognized for the period. For financial institutions, however, this method is mandatory in respect of mark-to-market property under section 142.5 and specified debt obligations under section 142.3.

The second exception is the cost method under subsection 10(1.01), which is mandatory for inventories of a business that is an adventure in the nature of trade.[96] This rule was introduced to override the result in *Friesen*,[97] in which the taxpayer owned only one asset in inventory (as a single parcel of land inventory) and was allowed to deduct the "paper loss" by using the lower of cost and fair market value method.

Taxpayers are allowed to choose between the lower of cost or fair market value method and the fair market value method. Once a method is chosen, the taxpayer is generally required to use it consistently. A change from the first to the second method, or *vice versa*, cannot be made without the Minister's permission.[98]

(ii) — Tracing methods

The identification of the cost of a closing inventory presents difficulty when (as is usual) inventory has been purchased at different prices. Where this is the case, there are a number of methods of placing a value on the cost of goods sold. One is the "average cost" method, which assumes that the cost of each unit of closing inventory and of goods sold was the average of the cost of all units held at the beginning of the year (opening inventory) and purchased during the year (purchases). A second method is FIFO (first in, first out), which assumes that the goods sold were the first goods purchased, and allocates the most recent costs to closing inventory and the oldest costs to the goods sold. The LIFO method (last in, first out) makes the opposite assumption, allocating the oldest costs to closing inventory and the most recent costs to the goods sold.

While previous Canadian GAAP allowed the LIFO method, current Canadian accounting rules under both the IFRS and ASPE disallow LIFO. LIFO was rarely used by Canadian companies even before the change. In *M.N.R. v. Anaconda American Brass* (1955),[99] the Privy Council held that the LIFO method was not acceptable for tax purposes.

---

[95] *Income Tax Regulations*, C.R.C., c. 945.

[96] The definition of an adventure in the nature of trade is discussed in Chapter 10 at heading 10.2(c) — Adventure or concern in the nature of trade.

[97] *Friesen, supra* note 91.

[98] *ITA, supra* note 1, s. 10(2.1).

[99] *M.N.R. v. Anaconda American Brass* (1955), [1955] C.T.C. 311, [1956] A.C. 85, 55 D.T.C. 1220 (Jud. Com. of Privy Coun.).

8.9 — Interest expense

(a) — Paragraph 20(1)(c)

Paragraph 20(1)(c) is a mini code on interest deduction. It contains the three essential elements of a deduction rule: 1) deductibility based on an income-earning purpose test; 2) timing of deduction based on "paid" or "payable", depending on the method regularly followed by the taxpayer; and 3) reasonable requirement. Generally speaking, the timing methods and reasonable requirements are less controversial than the income-earning purpose test. Interest expense is generally deductible when it is paid or payable. It can also be deductible on an accrual basis pursuant to accounting practices that are accepted by the CRA. The timing for deduction by the debtor is generally the same for inclusion by the creditor.[100] The amount of interest is reasonable where the interest rate is established in a market of lenders and borrowers acting at arm's length from each other.[101]

What is the purpose of paragraph 20(1)(c)? According to the Supreme Court of Canada, paragraph 20(1)(c) is an incentive provision designed to encourage the accumulation of capital that produces taxable income.[102] Why does the *ITA* treat interest "specially"? Or does it actually? The Court is of the view that, in the absence of this statutory allowance, an interest expense would not be deductible because it is an outlay "on account of capital" under paragraph 18(1)(b).[103] The only possible exception appears to be interest expense incurred by money lenders: it is considered to be a current expense.[104] It is unclear why interest is treated differently from the cost of using other property, such as rent, which is a current expense. Ordinary interest is paid in arrears as the price for the use of borrowed funds in the period prior to payment. The minute interest is paid, the borrower starts accruing a new liability to pay more interest for the continued use of borrowed funds.[105]

---

[100] See Arnold, *supra* note 4 at 457; see also Chapter 7 at heading 7.8(e) — Timing methods.

[101] *Mohammad v. R.*, [1997] 3 C.T.C. 321, 97 D.T.C. 5503 (Fed. C.A.) at 5509 [D.T.C.]; *Irving Oil Ltd. v. R.*, [1991] 1 C.T.C. 350, 91 D.T.C. 5106 (Fed. C.A.); leave to appeal refused (1991), 136 N.R. 320 (note) (S.C.C.) at 359 [C.T.C. (Fed. C.A.)]; *Shell Canada Ltd. v. R.* (1999), [1999] 4 C.T.C. 313, 99 D.T.C. 5669 (Eng.), 99 D.T.C. 5682 (Fr.) (S.C.C.) [*Shell*] at para. 34.

[102] E.g., *Shell*, *supra* note 101 at para. 28; *Ludco Enterprises Ltd. v. Canada* (2001), [2002] 1 C.T.C. 95, 2001 D.T.C. 5505 (Eng.), 2001 D.T.C. 5518 (Fr.) (S.C.C.) [*Ludco*] at para. 63.

[103] *Canada Safeway v. M.N.R.*, [1957] C.T.C. 335, 57 D.T.C. 1239 (S.C.C.) at paras. 42, 51; *Bronfman Trust v. R.*, [1987] 1 C.T.C. 117, 87 D.T.C. 5059 (S.C.C.) [*Bronfman Trust*] at para. 27; *Ludco*, *supra* note 102.

[104] *Gifford v. R.*, [2004] 2 C.T.C. 1, 2004 D.T.C. 6120 (Eng.), 2004 D.T.C. 6128 (Fr.) (S.C.C.).

[105] GAAP treats interest as an ordinary and necessary expense of earning income that is deductible, just like other business expenses, to arrive at a taxpayer's net income.

251

Perhaps due to the "special" status of interest expense, the courts have adopted a different purpose test and have required tracing to establish the deductibility of interest. We will turn to these issues after a brief overview of the meaning of interest for the purpose of paragraph 20(1)(c).

(b) — "Interest"

The concept of "interest" is not defined under the *ITA*. As discussed in the previous chapter, the courts have interpreted "interest" to refer to "the return or consideration or compensation for the use or retention by one person of a sum of money, belonging to, in a colloquial sense, or owed to, another".[106] From the borrower's perspective, it is the cost of using another person's money or the cost of borrowed money. Interest is generally computed by reference to a principal amount at a specified rate.[107] Economically, interest accrues on a daily basis.

For the purposes of paragraph 20(1)(c), interest is characterized according to the contract between the lender and the borrower. In the absence of a sham, there is no need to examine the economic realities of the borrowing transactions.[108] For example, in *Shell Canada Ltd. v. R.* (1999),[109] a "weak-currency hedge loan" was used to create the financial equivalent of a 9.1 per cent US dollar loan. Rather than borrowing in US dollars and paying interest of 9.1 per cent, Shell borrowed 150 million in NZ dollars and paid and deducted interest of 15.4 per cent. Upon receiving the loan in NZ dollars, Shell immediately converted the funds into US dollars and entered into a forward contract with a bank to convert US dollars into NZ dollars at predetermined exchange rates on the interest payment dates and the principal repayment due date. When the loan was due, the taxpayer repaid about US$21 million less than it originally received when it had converted the loan proceeds from NZ dollars into US dollars in the first place. This foreign currency exchange gain was reported by Shell as a capital gain, which was, accordingly, only partially taxable (and Shell used it to offset capital loss carryovers).

The Minister allowed Shell to deduct only the interest payable at the rate it would have paid had it borrowed US dollars (i.e., 9.1 per cent). Based on the economic realities of the transactions, the excess interest payment was converted into ex-

---

[106] *References as to the Validity of Section 6 of the Farm Security Act, 1944 of Saskatchewan*, [1947] S.C.R. 394 (S.C.C.); affirmed (1948), [1949] A.C. 110 (Jud. Com. of Privy Coun.). This definition was quoted by McLachlin, J. in *Shell, supra* 101 at para. 30.

[107] Interest rates are fixed by market forces. Some factors that bear on the interest rate are particular to each loan, namely the creditworthiness of the borrower, the value of any security provided by the borrower, and the term of the loan. Other factors are of general application, and the most important one is the expected rate of inflation over the term of the loan. For purpose of the *ITA*, interest is the nominal interest, including the portion that merely compensates for inflation or currency or other financial risk.

[108] The form and substance doctrine is discussed in more detail in Chapter 16 at heading 16.4 — Characterization of facts.

[109] *Shell, supra* note 101.

change gains on capital account, which should not be deductible under paragraph 20(1)(c). The Supreme Court of Canada rejected this argument and permitted the taxpayer to deduct the full amount of interest paid. McLachlin J. (as she then was) found that, as between Shell and the foreign lenders, there was no indication that the payments made by Shell were "anything but consideration for the use . . . of the NZ $150 million that Shell had borrowed".[110] She further stated:

> This Court has repeatedly held that courts must be sensitive to the economic realities of a particular transaction, rather than being bound to what first appears to be its legal form . . . But there are at least two caveats to this rule. First, this Court has never held that the economic realities of a situation can be used to recharacterize a taxpayer's bona fide legal relationships. To the contrary, we have held that, absent a specific provision of the Act to the contrary or a finding that they are a sham, the taxpayer's legal relationships must be respected in tax cases.[111]

Consequently, the legal form of a transaction governs its characterization. Where a *bona fide* lending agreement refers to a payment as interest, that payment is interest for tax purposes. Although the specific result of *Shell Canada* has been reversed by section 20.3,[112] the approach to characterization of transactions remains the law.

(c) — Purpose test

To be deductible under paragraph 20(1)(c), an interest expense must be paid or payable on the borrowed money used for the purpose of earning income from a business or property. If money is borrowed to pay for personal expenses, such as buying a home or paying for a vacation, the interest is not deductible. Similarly, if the borrowed funds are used to earn exempt income, the interest is not deductible. The same is true for interest paid on money borrowed to earn capital gains, because subsection 9(3) explicitly provides that a capital gain is not income from property. Questions arise when borrowed funds are used to acquire property that has the potential to produce both income (such as rent or dividend) and a capital gain. Ideally, the amount of the interest should be apportioned and only the portion relating to the earning of income should be deductible. In practice however, apportionment is difficult at the time when interest expense is incurred, and the market value of the property may frequently change. Therefore, assuming all the other tests are met, the entire expense is considered deductible by the courts and by the Minister.[113]

In a case of tax-motivated investment arrangements designed to enable a taxpayer to take advantage of interest deduction while the primary purpose is to earn capital gains, the Minister sought to deny the deduction on the ground that the primary

---

[110] *Ibid.* at para. 30.

[111] *Ibid.* at para. 39.

[112] *ITA, supra* note 1, s. 20.3 limits the deduction for interest expense in respect of a weak-currency debt, for taxation years ending after February 27, 2000, to the amount that would have been deductible if the taxpayer had instead incurred or assumed an equivalent amount of debt in the final currency.

[113] Folio S3-F6-C1, *supra* note 70 at paras. 1.69–1.70.

purpose of borrowing was to earn capital gains. As mentioned earlier in this chapter, the primary purpose test has been applied to other mixed expenses. The Supreme Court of Canada rejected this argument in a unanimous decision in *Ludco Enterprises Ltd. v. Canada* (2001).[114]

The taxpayers in *Ludco* borrowed money to acquire shares in companies incorporated in Panama with headquarters in the Bahamas. These companies invested in Canadian and U.S. government bonds, which paid significantly less interest than the interest expense incurred on the borrowing. During the taxation years in issue, the taxpayers received $600,000 of dividends and paid about $6 million in interest expenses. They disposed of the shares of the companies at a capital gain of $9.2 million.

The above arrangements generate two types of tax benefit for the taxpayers. The first is timing. While interest expenses are currently deductible in computing income, dividends are taxable only when received and capital gains are taxable only when realized through a disposition of the shares. The annual deduction of interest results in a loss from property and the loss is used to offset the taxpayers' income from other sources. The second is preferential treatment of capital gains. While interest expense is deducted in full, capital gains are taxable in half.

The issue in *Ludco* was whether the $6 million interest expenses was deductible by the taxpayers. The Supreme Court rejected the Minister's argument that the text of paragraph 20(1)(c) requires a primary, dominant, or *bona fide* income-earning purpose. It held that "it is perfectly consistent with the language of section 20(1)(c)(i) that a taxpayer who uses borrowed money to make an investment for more than one purpose may be entitled to deduct interest charged, provided that one of those purposes is to earn income".[115] Further, to stratify the purpose test, income is not necessarily net income. As long as the taxpayer has a reasonable expectation of gross income, the purpose test is met. Whether the expectation of earning gross income is reasonable is an objective inquiry. However, there is no "sufficiency of income" requirement in applying the test, short of "sham, window dressing or other vitiating circumstance".[116] The threshold for finding "window dressing" is unclear, but gross income amounting to one-tenth the interest expense was found not be window dressing in this case.

(d) — Tracing the use of borrowed money

(i) — Importance of tracing

Because money is fungible, there is no "correct" way to determine, with any degree of certainty, the purpose for which funds were borrowed. For purposes of paragraph 20(1)(c), the courts have held that the proper test is whether "a direct link can

---

[114] *Ludco, supra* note 102.

[115] *Ibid.* at para. 50.

[116] *Ibid.* at para. 59.

be drawn between the borrowed money and an eligible use".[117] This requires that the use of the borrowed funds be determined by factually tracing the use of the funds. It is the current use of the borrowed funds that governs.

Under the tracing approach, the ordering of a taxpayer's transactions is crucial, especially where borrowed funds are commingled with other funds (e.g., by being deposited to a bank account that contains other funds of the taxpayer). Assume that a taxpayer has $1,000 cash in a bank and borrows $1,000. If the taxpayer uses the borrowed funds to buy shares, the interest on the loan is deductible. The fact that the taxpayer may subsequently use the $1,000 cash as a down payment for a car (for personal use) will not affect the interest deductibility. However, if the taxpayer had used the cash to buy the shares and then borrowed the loan to buy his car, the interest would not be deductible. The taxpayer has the burden of ordering the use of the funds. Because income-earning interest expense is deductible and personal interest is not, a taxpayer generally would arrange his or her affairs so as to use the borrowed funds to finance income-earning expenditures and to use savings to finance personal expenditures.

Needless to say, the tracing approach presents tax savings opportunities for those who plan their transactions carefully and creates "traps" for the unknowing or unwary. The former is illustrated by the *Singleton v. R.* (2001)[118] case. Mr. Singleton was a partner in a small law firm. On October 27, 1988, he had at least $300,000 in his capital account with the firm. On that day, he withdrew the $300,000 from his capital account and used the money to buy a personal residence. Later that day, he borrowed approximately $300,000 from a bank and deposited it into his capital account in the law firm. There was some disagreement as to the exact sequence of the transactions that occurred on that day, but all relevant cheques were deposited and honoured. The taxpayer paid interest on the loan and deducted interest under paragraph 20(1)(c) in computing his income from the partnership. The Minister denied the deduction. The Tax Court of Canada took a realistic and practical view of the transactions (i.e., the "shuffle of cheques" as described by Bowman J.) and held that the taxpayer borrowed $300,000 for the purpose of buying a house, and the interest was, thus, not deductible. The Federal Court of Appeal disagreed on the basis that each of the transactions must be considered separately and independently. Under this approach, it was clear that the taxpayer used the borrowed funds to refinance his capital account, and the interest was thus deductible. This approach was upheld by the Supreme Court of Canada. In a 5 to 2 decision, the majority of the Court held that the interest was deductible. The Court reiterated the standard re-

---

[117] *Shell, supra* note 101; *Singleton v. R.* (2001), [2002] 1 C.T.C. 121, 2001 D.T.C. 5533 (Eng.), 2001 D.T.C. 5545 (Fr.) (S.C.C.) [*Singleton*].

[118] *Singleton, supra* note 117.

frains that economic realities are irrelevant and that taxpayers are entitled to structure their affairs to reduce tax.[119]

(ii) — Current use

The general rule is that it is "the current use rather than the original use of borrowed funds" that determines eligibility for a deduction.[120] If funds were originally borrowed for an ineligible use (to buy a cottage, for example), and the ineligible use was changed to an eligible use (by the sale of the cottage and the use of the proceeds to purchase income-earning investments, for example), then the interest expense on the loan, which had been non-deductible, would become deductible as from the commencement of the eligible use. Conversely, if funds were originally borrowed for an eligible use (to buy a rental property, for example), and the eligible use was changed to an ineligible one (by the taxpayer occupying the property as a personal residence, for example), then the interest expense on the loan, which had been deductible, would cease to be deductible as from the commencement of the ineligible use.

In *Tennant v. M.N.R.* (1996),[121] for example, the taxpayer borrowed $1 million to purchase shares. These shares were subsequently exchanged for some other shares with a declared fair market value of $1,000. The Supreme Court held that the taxpayer was allowed to continue to deduct the interest on the full amount of the loan because the new shares (an eligible use) could be traced to the entire amount of the loan.

In *Tennant*, the taxpayer still owned the property, and, therefore, remained eligible for the interest deduction even though the value of the property had declined below the amount of borrowed money. But what if the taxpayer had instead sold the shares for $1,000 and used the $1,000 to reduce the outstanding balance of the loan to $999,000? To provide relief, the so-called "disappearing source rules" in section 20.1 deem the $999,000 unpaid balance of the loan to continue to be used for the purpose of earning income from a business or property, which enables the interest on the remaining $999,000 loan balance to continue to be deductible under paragraph 20(1)(c).[122] Section 20.1 would also provide relief when a property purchased with borrowed money ceases to earn income (or a business purchased with borrowed money ceases to be carried on), and there is still a portion of the loan outstanding.

---

[119] *Ibid.* LeBel J., in dissent, was of the view that the economic realities of a situation are relevant in determining whether the legal relations are *bona fide*. The majority of the Supreme Court did not agree: see Chapter 16 at heading 16.4(d)(ii) — Step transactions.

[120] *Bronfman Trust, supra* note 103.

[121] *Tennant v. M.N.R.* (1996), [1996] 1 C.T.C. 290, 96 D.T.C. 6121 (S.C.C.).

[122] Folio S3-F6-C1, *supra* note 70 at para 1.41.

(iii) — Direct use

In classifying the use to which borrowed funds have been put, it is the direct use that is determinative. For example, a taxpayer who borrows money for the purpose of purchasing a personal residence is denied a deduction for the interest payments on the loan even if the loan enabled the taxpayer to retain income-earning investments.

The "direct use" rule was confirmed in *Bronfman Trust v. R.* (1987),[123] where a trust made a payment of capital to a beneficiary. Judging that the time was not right to sell any of the trust's investments, the trustees borrowed the money to make the capital payment. Three years later, the trustees did sell off some of the trust's investments and repaid the loan. The trust (which is deemed to be an individual for tax purposes) sought to deduct the interest payments in each of the three years that the loan was outstanding. In this case, the direct use of the borrowed funds was ineligible for the deduction, because the payment to the beneficiary yielded no income from business or property. The trust argued, however, that the indirect use of the borrowed funds had yielded income from property, because the trust had retained investments that, without the loan, would have been sold, and those investments had produced income. The Supreme Court of Canada held that it was the direct use that was determinative, and denied the deduction. Dickson J., who wrote for the Court, pointed out that, if the preservation of income-producing assets counted as an eligible use, then any loan for any purpose (a vacation, for example) would give rise to deductible interest, provided the borrower owned income-producing assets. This would be unfair as between rich and poor (the rich would always qualify for the deduction), and "would make a mockery of the statutory requirement that, for interest payments to be deductible, borrowed money must be used for circumscribed income-earning purposes".[124]

---

[123] *Bronfman Trust, supra* note 103.

[124] *Ibid.* at 126 [C.T.C.].

9
BUSINESS AND PROPERTY INCOME: CAPITAL EXPENDITURES

9.1 — Legislative Scheme

Paragraph 18(1)(b) of the *Income Tax Act* (the *"ITA"*)[1] prohibits the deduction of "an outlay . . ., a payment on account of capital or an allowance in respect of depreciation . . . except as expressly permitted by this Part". In effect, it disallows deductions for the cost of acquiring property whose useful life extends substantially beyond the close of the taxation year. Buildings, machinery and equipment, and patents and trade-marks are major types of assets that continue in use for more or less extended periods of time. Since the cost of such properties represents a present payment by the taxpayer for economic benefits that will accrue to the business in the future, the *ITA* requires that the expenditures be "capitalized" rather than deducted as a current expense. However, this does not mean that the taxpayer will never be allowed to deduct such expenditures. Paragraph 20(1)(a) permits a taxpayer to deduct "such part of the capital cost to the taxpayer of property, or such amount in respect of the capital cost to the taxpayer of property, if any, as is allowed by regulation". Part XI of the *Income Tax Regulations*[2] provides detailed rules for determining the amount of the deduction, known as "capital cost allowance" ("CCA"). In effect, the *ITA* authorizes an annual allowance for the wear and tear of capital assets, so that the cost will be recovered on a year-by-year basis during the useful lives of the assets. The CCA is the equivalent of the accounting notion of depreciation or amortization.

If a capital expenditure does not qualify for the CCA rules, its deduction is prohibited by paragraph 18(1)(b) unless another statutory exception is met.[3] There are only a few such prohibited expenditures. Because the CCA deductions are allowed for an asset whose value is presumed to be wasted away in the process of earning income, land does not have a determinable useful life and its cost is outside the CCA system. The same is true with the cost of investment assets, such as shares and bonds. The cost of land and investment assets is "deductible" only in computing capital gains or losses when the asset is disposed of. Some expenditures may end up being "nothings", in that they are never deductible in computing income or capital gains. Examples are expenditures that did not result in acquisition of any depreciable property as well as expenditures that cannot be deducted because of statutory prohibitions.[4]

---

[1] R.S.C. 1985 (5th Supp.), c. 1 [*ITA*].

[2] *Income Tax Regulations*, C.R.C., c. 945 [Regulations].

[3] Such exceptions include investment counsel fees (s. 20(1)(bb)), expenses of representation to government bodies (s. 20(1)(cc)) and the costs of issuing shares, debt or partnership units (over five years under s. 20(1)(e)).

[4] Examples of the latter include expenses of recreational facilities or clubs (s. 18(1)(l)) and the non-deductible portion of meals and entertainment (s. 67.1).

(a) — Technical design

The CCA rules are technical and detailed. They apply to all types of "depreciable property", including tangible and intangible assets. The CCA regime does not attempt to measure the economic loss in value or depreciation directly. Such measurement would be impossible as a practical matter because of the need to measure annually the changes in value of an untold number of business and investment assets. For administrative reasons, the statutory rules governing the deduction of capital expenditures merely "estimate" the amount of decline in value and arbitrarily determine the amount of deduction each year.

Conceptually, the structure of the CCA regime is simple. It applies to depreciable properties on a class-by-class basis. Properties are assigned to certain classes, largely based on their estimated average useful lives. A rate of depreciation is specified for each class. Classes for assets with longer useful lives have a lower CCA rate and classes for assets with shorter useful lives (e.g., because of technological obsolescence) have a higher rate. For example, 4 per cent is the general rate for Class 1 (most buildings and other structures), but the rate is 30 per cent for Class 10 (automotive equipment), 50 per cent for Class 53 (manufacturing equipment), 55 per cent for Class 50 (computer equipment) and 100 per cent for Class 12 (computer application software and films).

The amount of deductible CCA for each class is determined as the specified percentage of the undepreciated capital cost ("UCC") of the class as of the end of the taxation year.[5] Expressed as a formula,

$$CCA = CCA \text{ rate} \times UCC \text{ at end of year}$$

The *ITA* defines the key notions related to the determination of UCC in section 54 and subsections 13(21) and 248(1). Conceptually, the UCC account for each class at the end of a specific taxation year reflects the cost of all properties in that class minus the CCA deducted in previous years and the proceeds of disposition of properties (up to the original cost). There are timing rules to govern when the cost of a property is added to the UCC and when the proceeds of disposition are deducted. Because the CCA is merely an estimated amount, when properties in a class are disposed of, the taxpayer recovers the cost by receiving proceeds of disposition. By then, the actual amount of economic depreciation is known. The *ITA* requires a kind of "reconciliation" of the actual economic depreciation with the CCA that has been claimed: if the CCA claimed is greater than the economic depreciation, there is a "recapture" under subsection 13(1); in the opposite situation, there is a "terminal loss" deduction under subsection 20(16) if there are no assets left in the class. As discussed in more detail below, however, these rules are complicated, technically speaking.

Whether a given outlay is treated as a current expense or capital expenditure is normally clear. However, there are inevitably instances in which the proper treatment is in doubt. The *ITA* leaves the characterization question to case law.

---

[5] Regulations, *supra* note 2, reg. 1100(1).

(b) — Policy and rationale

The CCA system is entirely statute-based. The deduction of capital cost is a major area of divergence between tax accounting and financial accounting. In addition to providing certainty and predictability, the CCA system delivers tax incentives to taxpayers with respect to investment in certain assets. This is done by assigning assets to a specific class with a higher CCA rate. For example, to encourage the construction of new buildings for commercial activities, the CCA rate is 6 per cent (rather than 4 per cent) for new buildings acquired for commercial activities (10 per cent if used in manufacturing). To encourage investment in films, a "certified feature film or certified production" is in Class 12 with a 100 per cent rate of depreciation. Another example is the incentive for "green energy industry". While most electricity generating and distributing equipment is Class 1 property (4 per cent CCA rate), renewable energy and energy conservation systems fall within Class 43.1, qualifying for a 30 per cent CCA rate.

CCA deductions may give rise to a loss from a business or property. Such losses are "valuable" to taxpayers if they can offset income from other sources with the loss, or "shift" the loss to another taxpayer by "leasing" the assets (as opposed to "purchasing" the assets). Through some "tax shelter" arrangements, taxpayers may attempt to "create" paper losses through CCA deductions at the same time as the property's economic value has actually increased. The *ITA* contains rules to prevent the use of CCA as a tax shelter in some circumstances, such as in the case of investment in rental property or leasing property.

9.2 — "Capital expenditure"

(a) — Enduring benefit test

The *ITA* does not define the terms "capital expenditure" or "amount on account of capital". The meaning of these terms is, thus, determined on the basis of case law principles. There are many cases in which the courts have had to determine whether or not a particular expenditure is on account of capital. As Sir Wilfred Greene noted in 1938:

> . . . there have been . . . many cases where this matter of capital or income has been debated. There have been many cases which fall upon the borderline: indeed, in many cases it is almost true to say that the spin of a coin would decide the matter almost as satisfactorily as an attempt to find reasons.[6]

While a variety of definitions of "capital expenditures" have been offered, most of the cases have used the "enduring benefit" test. The test was formulated by Viscount Cave L.C. in *British Insulated and Helsby Cables v. Atherton* (1926):

> But, when an expenditure is made, not only once and for all, but with a view to bringing into existence an asset or an advantage for the enduring benefit of a trade, I think there is very good reason (in the absence of special circumstances leading to

---

[6] *British Salmson Aero Engines Ltd. v. CIR* (1938), 22 T.C. 29 (Eng. C.A.) at 43.

an opposite conclusion) for treating such an expenditure as properly attributable not to revenue but to capital.[7]

The expenditure in issue in *British Insulated* was a large lump sum paid by a company to provide the initial funding to establish a new pension scheme for its employees. The House of Lords held that this payment could not be deducted in full from current revenue as the company claimed. The benefit of the payment would last for many years beyond the current year, because it would "obtain for the company the substantial and lasting advantage of being in a position throughout its business life to secure and retain the services of a contented and efficient staff".[8] It followed that the expenditure had brought into existence "an asset or an advantage for the enduring benefit of a trade". The expenditure was therefore a capital one.

The leading Canadian case is *Johns-Manville Canada Inc. v. R.* (1985).[9] In this case, the taxpayer operated an open-pit asbestos mine and purchased land on a regular basis in order to extend the perimeter of the mine to maintain a gradual slope and prevent landslides. The taxpayer deducted the cost of land as a current business expense. The Minister disagreed and treated the cost as a capital expenditure. The Supreme Court of Canada held that the expenditures were not on account of capital on the ground of tax policy and common sense. The Court stated:

> [T]hese expenditures by the taxpayer were incurred *bona fide* in the course of its regular day-to-day business operations. Common sense dictated that these expenditures be made, otherwise the taxpayer's operations would, of necessity, be closed down. These expenditures were not part of a plan for the assembly of assets. Nor did they have any semblance of a once and for all acquisition. These expenditures were in no way connected with the assembly of an ore body or a mining property which could itself be developed independently of any ore body, hence the inability to find entitlement for depletion or capital cost allowance for this expenditure under the statute.[10]

The somewhat unusual facts in the *Johns-Manville* case show that the lands had no enduring value to the business as new land had to be acquired as the operations progressed. The previous lands were turned into holes on the ground and had no intrinsic value.

The enduring benefit test asks the right question. If an expenditure is made to produce a benefit to the business that will last beyond the current taxation year, then it should not be deducted in full in the current year. That would understate the income for the current year. However, if one really takes seriously the concept of capital expenditure as anything that benefits the business beyond the current period in which the expenditure is made, it would require capitalizing every salesperson's

---

[7] *British Insulated and Helsby Cables v. Atherton* (1926), [1926] A.C. 205 (U.K. H.L.) at 213-214.

[8] *Ibid.* at 214.

[9] *Johns-Manville Canada Inc. v. R.* (1985), [1985] 2 C.T.C. 111, 85 D.T.C. 5373 (S.C.C.) [*Johns-Manville*].

[10] *Ibid.* at para. 44.

salary, since his or her selling activities create goodwill for the company and goodwill is an asset yielding income beyond the year in which the salary expense is incurred. This is a result that naturally makes little sense. Overall, though, the enduring benefit test is helpful.

The enduring benefit test can be applied in different circumstances. For example, payments for the establishment or expansion of the business structure of a taxpayer tend to have an enduring benefit and are, thus, capital expenditures, whereas payments made as "part of the money-earning process" are current expenses.[11] In *B.P. Australia Ltd. v. Commissioner of Taxation of Commonwealth of Australia* (1966),[12] for example, an inducement payment to a service station operator that entered into an exclusive agency agreement to distribute the taxpayer's products was characterized as a current expense on the basis that the expenditure was made as part of the money-earning process in the continuous and recurrent struggle to get orders and sell petrol. Applying a similar test, the Court in *Sun Newspapers* (1938)[13] reached an opposite conclusion: a lump-sum non-competition payment made to a competitor was characterized as a capital expenditure on the ground that the expenditure was a large non-recurrent unusual expenditure made for the purpose of obtaining an advantage for the enduring benefit of the taxpayer's trade, namely, the exclusion of what might have been serious competition.

Costs incurred by an acquirer or a target in a corporate takeover may also be capital or current in nature, depending on the facts. In the case of the target, the courts seem to consider costs incurred in the course of fighting hostile takeover bids to be capital expenditures, whereas expenses incurred to facilitate friendly takeovers are characterized as current expenses under section 9.[14] In the past, expenses incurred

---

[11] As Lord Radcliffe stated in *Commissioner of Taxes v. Nchanga Consolidated Copper Mines Ltd.*, [1964] A.C. 948 (Rhodesia P.C.) at 960:

> [The] courts have stressed the importance of observing a demarcation between the cost of creating, acquiring or enlarging the permanent (which does not mean perpetual) structure of which the income is to be the produce or fruit and the cost of earning that income itself or performing the income-earning operations.

The above statement was cited in *B.P. Australia Ltd. v. Commissioner of Taxation of Commonwealth of Australia* (1966), [1966] A.C. 224 (Australia P.C.) [*B.P. Australia*] at 262 and in *Rona Inc. v. R.*, [2003] 4 C.T.C. 2974, 2003 D.T.C. 264, 2003 D.T.C. 979 (T.C.C. [General Procedure]) [*Rona*] at 987 [D.T.C.]. In *Rona*, recurring costs relating to an expansion plan were held to be capital expenditures: costs relating to some 50 abandoned projects, including an unsuccessful takeover bid, were held to be eligible capital expenditures (now CCA Class 14.1).

[12] *B.P. Australia*, *supra* note 11.

[13] *Sun Newspapers Ltd. v. Federal Commissioner of Taxation* (1938), 61 C.L.R. 337 (Australia H.C.) at 363, cited with approval by the Federal Court of Appeal in *Gifford v. Canada*, [2002] 4 C.T.C. 64, 2002 D.T.C. 7197 (Fed. C.A.); affirmed [2004] 2 C.T.C. 1, 2004 D.T.C. 6120 (S.C.C.) at para. 19 [(Fed. C.A.)].

[14] In *Boulangerie St-Augustin Inc. c. R.* (1994), [1995] 2 C.T.C. 2149, 95 D.T.C. 56 (Fr.), 95 D.T.C. 164 (Eng.) (T.C.C.); affirmed (1996), 2002 D.T.C. 6957, 97 D.T.C. 5012 (Fed. C.A.),

by the acquirer have generally been characterized as capital expenses. In *Neonex International Ltd. v. M.N.R.* (1978),[15] for example, the Court stated that "legal expenses . . . incurred in an effort to complete the takeover . . . were outlays associated with an investment transaction and thus were made on capital account."[16] More recently, in *Rio Tinto Alcan Inc. v. R.* (2016),[17] the Tax Court differentiated between "oversight expenses" incurred during the decision-making or oversight process (which were current expenses under section 9) and "execution costs" associated with the actual implementation of an approved capital transaction (which created an enduring benefit and were capitalized).[18]

In the case of doubt, the benefit often goes to the taxpayer. In *Johns-Manville*, if the expenditures on acquiring the lands were capitalized, they would not be deductible because land is not "depreciable property" for CCA purposes.[19] The Court ruled in favour of the taxpayer:

> [If] the interpretation of a taxation statute is unclear, and one reasonable interpretation leads to a deduction to the credit of a taxpayer and the other leaves the taxpayer with no relief from clearly *bona fide* expenditures in the course of his business activ-

---

the taxpayer incurred the cost of preparing information circulars in connection with three friendly takeover bids. The expenses were held to be current expenses. The Tax Court of Canada noted, however, that if the corporation had incurred expenses to fight the takeover bids, "in particular by hiring a business appraiser to show that those bids were not reasonable or other advisors to assist it in putting defence mechanisms into place, the expenses would have been characterized as payments on account of capital within the meaning of s. 18(1)(b) of the Act" (para. 55).

[15] *Neonex International Ltd. v. M.N.R.* (1978), [1978] C.T.C. 485, 78 D.T.C. 6339 (Fed. C.A.).

[16] *Ibid.* at 496-497 [C.T.C.]. See also *Graham Construction and Engineering Ltd. v. R.* (1997), 97 D.T.C. 342 (T.C.C.) [*Graham Construction*] and *Rona, supra* note 11.

[17] *Rio Tinto Alcan Inc. v. R.*, 2016 TCC 172, [2017] 1 C.T.C. 2103, 2016 D.T.C. 1142, 2016 D.T.C. 1144 (T.C.C. [General Procedure]); additional reasons 2016 CarswellNat 9892 (T.C.C. [General Procedure]). This case involved fees incurred for professional advice (investment banking and legal and accounting advice) in connection with a takeover transaction (the acquisition of a large competitor) followed by a spinoff transaction (to satisfy European competition rules). Noting that one of the taxpayer's "business priorities was the maximization of shareholder value" and that it "had a long history of major acquisitions and transactions it had entered into for this purpose" (para. 9), and looking at the purpose of the work done by the taxpayer's advisors, the Court found that the pre-commitment advisory expenses (incurred prior to formally entering into the two transactions) were oversight expenses because they served an income-earning purpose and did not create an enduring benefit. This case is on appeal at the time of writing.

[18] Some execution costs were deductible because of a statutory exception, such as s. 20(1)(cc) regarding expenses of presentation to government bodies.

[19] See heading 9.3(b) — Depreciable property, below.

ities, the general rules of interpretation of taxing statutes would direct the tribunal to the former interpretation.[20]

(b) — Repair of tangible assets

Every business has to expend money regularly to repair or maintain damaged or worn out equipment and other tangible assets. Often the repair or maintenance will involve the purchase and installation of new parts (e.g., a new window for a building or a new muffler for an automobile), and those parts have a life that is expected to last long beyond the current accounting period. However, the cost of the window or the muffler is generally treated as a currently deductible expense. The cost is small in relation to the asset being repaired, the cost is of a kind that will regularly recur, and its purpose is simply to restore the original asset to its normal operating capacity. However, where the cost is large in relation to the asset being repaired (or improved), where it is not of a kind that will regularly recur, and where the purpose is to improve the quality of the asset substantially beyond its original condition, then the cost will be treated as a capital expenditure. There are situations that lie in between such clear cases. In instances of relatively large-scale outlays, the aim of which is not merely to correct a malfunction or replace a worn-out part, the characterization becomes difficult and the decisions are very fact-based. The following cases demonstrate the difficulty in dealing with the cost of replacing a roof or floor.

In *Earl v. M.N.R.* (1993),[21] the taxpayer spent $33,039 on the purchase of a new roof for a commercial rental property. In reporting her income for tax purposes for the year, the taxpayer claimed the entire amount as a current expense. The Minister disagreed, arguing that the amount was a capital expenditure. The Tax Court of Canada agreed with the Minister's assessment, and found that "the new pitched roof created an improvement to the building of an enduring nature and was different in kind from the old flat roof".[22] In contrast, in *Janota v. R.* (2010),[23] the taxpayer's $37,000 repair cost was held to be on current account. The taxpayer and his son bought a century-old duplex for $419,000. He renovated the lower half of the building as a rental property while the son lived in the upper half. The repair was made to cupboards, plumbing, doors, counter tops, ceiling, stairs, drainage, painting, floors, damaged plaster, and patching the foundation. The Court found the expenses to be relatively minor compared to the cost of the property, and that the repair was required to restore the property to its original condition, not to improve it.

---

[20] *Johns-Manville, supra* note 9 at para. 27.

[21] *Earl v. M.N.R.* (1993), [1993] 1 C.T.C. 2081, 93 D.T.C. 65 (T.C.C.).

[22] *Ibid.* at para. 11.

[23] *Janota v. R.*, 2010 D.T.C. 1268 (T.C.C.) [*Janota*].

The cost of replacing a floor was treated differently in *Canada Steamship Lines v. M.N.R.* (1966)[24] and *Shabro Investments v. R.* (1979).[25] In the *Canada Steamship* case, the taxpayer replaced the floors and walls of the cargo carrying holds in its ships. The expenditures involved were substantial in relation to the value of the ships and the repair experience of previous years. On the other hand, the work was necessitated by normal wear and tear (so that it was recurrent in one sense), and the new floors and walls did no more than restore the holds of the ships to full operating capacity (so that there was no substantial improvement or addition to the ships). The Exchequer Court held that the expenditures were current expenses.[26] In the *Shabro Investments* case, the issue concerned the replacement of a concrete floor in a commercial building. The original floor had consisted of concrete slabs reinforced by wire mesh laid directly on land fill; the floor broke when the underlying ground subsided. The taxpayer spent $95,000 in 1973 in removing the broken floor, in driving new piles to properly support the new floor, and in pouring a new reinforced concrete floor supported by the new piles. The result of all this effort was simply to provide a ground floor that was suitable for its intended use, and to restore the building to normal operating condition. On the other hand, the expense was substantial and unlikely to recur, and the new floor was an improvement in quality over its inadequate predecessor. The Federal Court of Appeal held that the expenditure was capital.

(c) — Protection of intangible assets

The issue of characterization arises with respect to expenses incurred in the defence or protection of title to property, especially intellectual property and other types of intangible property. One type of such expenses is legal cost. This issue has been considered by Canadian courts, but not addressed consistently.

In *M.N.R. v. Dominion Natural Gas Co.* (1940),[27] the legal costs of defending a challenge to Dominion Natural Gas' licence to supply gas to a particular locality were held to confer an enduring benefit and, therefore, to be capital expenditures. The Supreme Court found that there was no distinction between the expenses incurred to obtain the right to carry on a business and those incurred for the purpose of preserving that right. There was an enduring benefit in the sense that, after the litigation, the taxpayer had a less vulnerable and more valuable licence than it had ever had before.

---

[24] *Canada Steamship Lines v. M.N.R.* (1966), [1966] C.T.C. 255, 66 D.T.C. 5205 (Can. Ex. Ct.).

[25] *Shabro Investments v. R.* (1979), [1979] C.T.C. 125, 79 D.T.C. 5104 (Fed. C.A.).

[26] However, on the issue of the cost of replacing boilers on one of the steamships, the Court treated the expenditure as capital: the new boilers were of a different and superior kind than those they were purchased to replace.

[27] *M.N.R. v. Dominion Natural Gas Co.* (1940), [1940–41] C.T.C. 155, [1920–1940] 1 D.T.C. 499–133 (S.C.C.).

In contrast, the *Canada Starch Co. v. M.N.R.* (1968)[28] case involved a payment made by the taxpayer to a competitor to settle a dispute about Canada Starch's right to use a particular trade-mark. The Court held that the settlement payment was a current expense because it related to the "process" of earning income rather than the "business entity, structure, or organization".[29] The Court also applied the enduring benefit test to reinforce its conclusion. A similar decision was reached in *Kellogg Co. of Canada v. M.N.R.* (1943),[30] where the cost of litigating a dispute about Kellogg's right to use the name "Shredded Wheat" was held not to be a capital expenditure.

The decisions in *Canada Starch* and *Kellogg* are hard to reconcile with *Dominion Natural Gas*. These two cases have been rationalized on the basis that "expenses made to preserve capital assets" should be deductible as current expenses".[31] There is an implicit analogy to the repair of a tangible asset. While the litigation in *Canada Starch* and *Kellogg* did have the effect of protecting an asset (an intangible asset), it did not simply restore the situation as it existed before the litigation. Arguably, the effect of the litigation was to remove a cloud on the taxpayer's title to use a particular business mark or name. The removal of that cloud improved the quality of the taxpayer's title, thereby conferring an enduring benefit on the business. On the other hand, however, the title might be challenged by other parties and Canada Starch or Kellogg would need to defend the title whenever that happened. In this sense, the expenditures in *Canada Starch* and *Kellogg* were like the repair of tangible assets and were likely to recur.

The effect of the decisions in *Canada Starch* and *Kellogg* was to permit the expenditures in question to be wholly deducted in the year in which they were incurred. It is possible that the Courts' reluctance to hold that these expenditures were capital in nature was related to the fact that, if the expenditures were capital, they could not be deducted at all. This was the position before 1972. The harshness of non-deduction may have influenced the Courts to rule in favour of treating expenditures for intangibles as current expenses.[32]

---

[28] *Canada Starch Co. v. M.N.R.* (1968), [1968] C.T.C. 466, 68 D.T.C. 5320 (Can. Ex. Ct.) [*Canada Starch*].

[29] The business structure versus earning process test, which is derived from the enduring benefit test and is sometimes considered to be a separate test on its own, is also discussed briefly at heading 9.2(a) — Enduring benefit test, above.

[30] *Kellogg Co. of Canada v. M.N.R.* (1943), [1943] C.T.C. 1, 2 D.T.C. 601 (S.C.C.) [*Kellogg*].

[31] Neil Brooks, "The Principles Underlying the Deduction of Business Expenses" in Brian G. Hansen, Vern Krishna, & James A. Rendall, eds., *Canadian Taxation* (Don Mills, Ont.: De Boo, 1981) 206 at 221.

[32] See also *Algoma Central Railway v. M.N.R.*, [1967] C.T.C. 130, 67 D.T.C. 5091 (Can. Ex. Ct.); affirmed [1968] C.T.C. 161, 68 D.T.C. 5096 (S.C.C.) [*Algoma*], where the cost of a survey designed to encourage the future development of the area served by the Algoma Central Railway was held to be currently deductible.

Since 1972, the cost of patents, franchises, concessions or licences for a limited period in respect of property has been added to CCA Class 14.[33] Until recently, the cost of capital expenditures for other intangibles (i.e., those with no limited legal life, such as goodwill) could be amortized and deducted under former paragraph 20(1)(b), which was similar to (but different than) the CCA deduction under paragraph 20(1)(a).[34] As of 2017, the cost of intangibles such as goodwill falls in the newly created Class 14.1 for CCA purposes.[35]

(d) — Goodwill

Goodwill consists of all the intangible advantages possessed by an established business: its name and reputation, its location, the nature of its competition, its connections with suppliers, the expertise of its employees, the loyalty of its customers, and other hard-to-define characteristics that spell the difference between business success and business failure. It is essentially "the capitalized value of the earning power of a going concern business over and above a reasonable return on the value of its other assets".[36]

Goodwill can be created by the taxpayer through advertising and other promotional efforts, or be purchased together with a going concern business. The case law clearly establishes that "advertising expenses paid out while a business is operating, and directed to attract customers to a business, are current expenses",[37] and that "expenses of other measures taken by a businessman with a view to introducing particular products to the market — such as market surveys and industrial design studies — are also current expenses".[38] These expenses are incurred in the process

---

[33] Property in Class 14 is eligible for amortization on a straight-line basis over the property's legal life (in days). Straight-line-basis amortization in days means the cost is apportioned over the life of the property so that the amount of allowance each year is the same (if the property has been owned for 365 days).

[34] Before January 1, 2017, paragraph 20(1)(b) permitted an annual allowance deduction in respect of "cumulative eligible capital" ("CEC") balances in respect of the cost of acquiring intangible assets such as goodwill. A taxation year ending on or before December 31, 2016 was the last year for such a deduction. A taxpayer's CEC balance at December 31, 2016 was transferred to a new CCA class (Class 14.1) on January 1, 2017. For further discussion, see heading 9.4 — Expenditure on intangible assets, below.

[35] The expenditures in *Canada Starch*, *supra* note 28, and *Kellogg*, *supra* note 30, if classified as capital expenditures and incurred in 2017, would be deductible as Class 14.1 assets.

[36] Edwin C. Harris, *Canadian Income Taxation*, 4th ed. (Toronto: Butterworths, 1986) at 171.

[37] *Algoma*, *supra* note 32 at 136-137 [C.T.C. (Ex. Ct.)]. Justice Mogan also stated this succinctly in *Graham Construction*, *supra* note 16 at 345: "There is no doubt that certain costs (e.g., advertising) incurred for the purpose of expanding an existing business are deductible as current expenses in computing income. Similarly, certain other costs incurred to expand a business (e.g., the purchase of shares to acquire a new subsidiary carrying on a similar business) are an outlay of capital and not deductible."

[38] *Canada Starch*, *supra* note 28 at para. 11.

of carrying on a business. The cost of purchasing goodwill is, however, a capital expenditure and is now included in Class 14.1.

9.3 — Capital cost of depreciable property

(a) — Capital cost allowance system

Capital cost allowance ("CCA") is deductible under paragraph 20(1)(a) of the *ITA* in respect of depreciable property. The technical details for determining the annual amount of CCA are found in the Regulations. Regulation 1100(1) stipulates that the amount of deduction is a percentage of the undepreciated capital cost ("UCC") of property in a specific class.[39] The purpose of the CCA provisions is "to provide for the recognition of money spent to acquire qualifying assets to the extent that they are consumed in the income-earning process".[40]

The CCA system is designed to make a set of uniform and necessarily arbitrary rules as acceptable as possible. Without uniform rules for all taxpayers, the system would be difficult to administer, and it would give rise to the possibility of taxpayers in similar situations paying different amounts of tax.[41] On the whole, the rates of CCA are fairly generous so that quite often the CCA deduction is more favourable to the taxpayer than the depreciation expense that the taxpayer deducts for accounting purposes. The "declining balance" method[42] produces high CCA deductions in the early years of an asset's life and, thereby, reduces profit and the tax thereon in those years.

(b) — Depreciable property

The CCA system covers the cost of depreciable property. Technically, subsection 13(21) of the *ITA* defines "depreciable property" to mean any property of the tax-

---

[39] Regulations, *supra* note 2, reg. 1100(1).

[40] *Duncan v. R.*, 2002 FCA 291, [2003] 2 F.C. 25, [2002] 4 C.T.C. 1, 2002 D.T.C. 7172 (Fed. C.A.); leave to appeal refused 2003 CarswellNat 707, 2003 CarswellNat 708 (S.C.C.) at para. 44 [(Fed. C.A.)].

[41] This was the situation before 1948 when the Act gave the Minister discretion as to whether to allow a taxpayer's depreciation charges and the Minister normally accepted the taxpayer's book depreciation. Since various different methods and rates were acceptable under generally accepted accounting principles ("GAAP"), the same variety was accepted by the tax system. Uniform rules for income tax purposes were introduced into the Act in 1948, but with the restriction that taxpayers could not claim a CCA deduction for tax purposes that was greater than their accounting depreciation. In 1954, the restriction was lifted, so that tax rules operated independently of a taxpayer's accounting practices.

[42] The declining balance method involves applying a uniform rate of depreciation to the unrecovered cost of the asset. Because the amount of unrecovered cost decreases each year, the amount of depreciation decreases accordingly; hence the name "declining balance method". Under the declining balance method, the book value of an asset never reaches zero, reflecting perhaps the reality that there is usually some salvage value at the end of the asset's useful life.

payer in respect of which a paragraph 20(1)(a) deduction is allowed. Because Regulation 1100(1) permits such deduction in respect of properties included in any of the prescribed classes listed in Schedule II,[43] one can say that any property listed in Schedule II is a depreciable property.[44]

Depreciable properties include tangible properties[45] that tend to wear and tear, such as buildings (Class 1: 4 per cent), manufacturing and processing equipment (Class 43: 30 per cent), and automotive equipment (including automobiles costing $20,000 or less) (Class 10: 30 per cent). Depreciable properties also include intangible assets, such as a leasehold interest (Class 13), property that is a patent, franchise, concession or licence for a limited period (Class 14) and goodwill (Class 14.1).

To be consistent with the general deductibility test, Regulation 1102(1) effectively excludes from the CCA system any property that was not acquired for the purpose of gaining or producing income. For example, a building acquired for business or rental use qualifies as a depreciable property, but a house acquired for personal use does not. If the cost of property is otherwise deductible in computing profit, it is also excluded from being a depreciable property; inventory is an example.[46]

(c) — Capital cost

The terms "cost" and "capital cost" are undefined in the *ITA*. The Supreme Court of Canada stated in *Canada Trustco Mortgage Co. v. R* (2005)[47] that "the CCA provisions use 'cost' in the well-established sense of the amount paid to acquire the assets". The Court also stated that:

> "Cost" in the context of CCA is a well-understood legal concept. . . . [W]e see nothing in the GAAR or the object of the CCA provisions that permits us to rewrite them to interpret "cost" to mean "amount economically at risk" in the applicable provisions. To do so would be to invite inconsistent results. The result would vary with the degree of risk in each case. This would offend the goal of the Act to provide

---

[43] Regulations, *supra* note 2, reg. 1100(1).

[44] *Ibid.*, Schedule II. An inventory property or a property the cost of which is deductible as a current expense is not a depreciable property: reg. 1102(1)(b).

[45] Class 8 (20 per cent) is a catch-all category that includes "a tangible capital property that is not included in another class".

[46] See note 44.

[47] *Canada Trustco Mortgage Co. v. R* (2005), [2005] 5 C.T.C. 215, 2005 D.T.C. 5523 (Eng.), 2005 D.T.C. 5547 (Fr.) (S.C.C.) [*Canada Trustco*] at para. 74. In this case, the taxpayer purchased a fleet of trailers from an American company and immediately leased back the same fleet to that company. The trailers never physically left the American company, although a complex set of legal agreements was entered into and offshore companies were used to arrange the transactions. The primary motivation for the transactions was to generate CCA deductions. The Court found that the taxpayer was entitled to claim CCA in respect of the trailers and that the general anti-avoidance rules did not apply. This case is discussed in more detail in Chapter 17 at heading 17.3(a)(iii) — Canada Trustco.

sufficient certainty and predictability to permit taxpayers to intelligently order their affairs.[48]

The "amount paid to acquire the assets" generally means the laid-down cost. It is "the actual, factual, or historical cost to the [taxpayer] of the depreciable property when acquired".[49] It generally includes "legal, accounting, engineering or other fees incurred to acquire the property; site preparation, delivery, installation, testing or other costs incurred to put the property into service; and in the case of a property a taxpayer manufactures for [its] own use, material, labour and overhead costs reasonably attributable to the property, but not any profit which might have been earned had the asset been sold".[50]

The *ITA* contains a number of special rules for determining the cost of acquisition of property. For example, with respect to buildings, subsection 18(3.1) requires the capitalization of certain soft costs that are attributable to the period of, and relating to, the construction, renovation, or alteration of the building so that such costs are added to the cost of the building.[51] Where a taxpayer acquires a property by way of a gift, the cost of the property is deemed to be its fair market value at the time of the gift.[52] In certain cases, the *ITA* allows a property to "roll over" from one taxpayer (the transferor) to another taxpayer (the transferee) on a cost basis; that is, the cost to the transferee is deemed to be the original cost to the transferor, irrespective of the fair market value at the time of the transfer. Such rollovers are available to inter-spouse transfers of property,[53] transfers of property to a corporation or corporate reorganizations.[54]

---

[48] *Ibid.* at para. 75.

[49] *Cockshutt Farm Equipment of Canada Ltd. v. M.N.R.* (1966), 66 D.T.C. 544 (Can. Tax App. Bd.) at para. 28. In this case, an unexpected increase in the taxpayer's outlay for depreciable property purchased abroad, caused by an adverse fluctuation in the rate of foreign exchange, was held not to form part of the capital cost of the property acquired.

[50] Canada Revenue Agency, Folio S3-F4-C1, "General Discussion of Capital Cost Allowance" [Folio S3-F4-C1] at para. 1.45.

[51] *ITA*, *supra* note 1, ss. 18(3.1)–(8.7). As noted in *Janota*, *supra* note 23 at paras. 16–22, although the term "soft costs" is not used in the *ITA*, it is used in the Department of Finance's Technical Notes in 1982 and 1994 explaining amendments to s. 18(3.1), and has been defined by the courts. It is well-established that soft costs do not include repairs and maintenance incurred during a period of construction, renovation or alteration. Soft costs do include amounts such as interest and other financing expenses, property taxes, mortgage insurance fees, legal and accounting expenses, and site investigation fees, which would otherwise be deductible as current expenses.

[52] *ITA*, *supra* note 1, s. 69(1)(c).

[53] See Chapter 10 at heading 10.4(c)(iv)(A) — Rollovers for transfers to a spouse or common-law partner. In cases where a depreciable property is acquired from a non-arm's-length person and the transferor has claimed CCA in respect of the property, there are special rules for determining the cost of the property (e.g., ss. 13(7)(e), 73(3), 70(6)).

[54] It is beyond the scope of this book to discuss the rollover rules under ss. 51, 85, 85.1, 86, 87 and 88. These rules are briefly discussed in Chapter 10 at heading 10.4(c)(iv)(C) — Roll-

Where a taxpayer acquires a property from a non-arm's-length person,[55] and the purchase price is higher than the fair market value, the cost of the property is deemed under paragraph 69(1)(a) to be the fair market value.[56] The capital cost of luxury passenger vehicles is deemed under paragraph 13(7)(g) to be $30,000 for CCA purposes, even if the actual cost exceeds that amount. This reflects the policy concern that the use of luxury cars has an element of personal consumption that should not be deductible in computing profit.[57]

(d) — Undepreciated capital cost (UCC)

The concept of "undepreciated capital cost" ("UCC") is the basis for computing the amount of CCA. It is essentially the unrecovered cost of the assets in a prescribed class. It is a cumulative tax account: capital cost of each property in the class is added, the proceeds of disposition of each property (capped by the capital cost) are subtracted, and the CCA deductions previously claimed are subtracted.

Subsection 13(21) defines "undepreciated capital cost" to a taxpayer of depreciable property of a prescribed class as of any time by way of a formula, the essential elements of which are:

$$(A + B) - (E + F)$$

where

A   is the total of all amounts each of which is the capital cost to the taxpayer of a depreciable property of the class acquired before that time,

B   is the total of all amounts included in the taxpayer's income under this section for a taxation year ending before that time, to the extent that those amounts relate to depreciable property of the class . . .

E   is the total depreciation allowed to the taxpayer for property of the class before that time,

F   is the total of all amounts each of which is an amount in respect of a disposition before that time of property . . . of the taxpayer of the class, and is the lesser of

(a)   the proceeds of disposition of the property minus any outlays and expenses to the extent that they were made or incurred by the taxpayer for the purpose of making the disposition, and

(b)   the capital cost to the taxpayer of the property.

---

overs regarding corporate transactions, but for further discussion of these rules, see K.A. Siobhan Monaghan et al. *Taxation of Corporate Reorganizations*, 2nd ed. (Toronto: Carswell, 2012).

[55] *ITA, supra* note 1, s. 251.

[56] For further discussion of s. 69(1), see Chapter 10 at heading 10.4(c)(iii) — Transfers with non-arm's-length persons.

[57] The amount was originally $20,000 but has been increased over time to $30,000.

At any specific point in time, the UCC balance of a taxpayer can be determined. Item A presents the total of capital cost of each property acquired before that time. Item B is a mechanical adjustment: it becomes relevant only when the balance becomes negative and is recaptured under subsection 13(1) as income. The recaptured amount is added back to the UCC to bring it to zero.[58]

Items E and item F reduce the UCC amount. E represents the "total depreciation"[59] previously allowed to the taxpayer. "Total depreciation" is primarily the CCA deductions under paragraph 20(1)(a). It also includes a mechanical adjustment to account for the situation where a taxpayer has claimed terminal loss deductions under subsection 20(16).[60] Item F represents the capital cost recovered by the taxpayer through dispositions. Technically, when a depreciable property is disposed of, the proceeds of disposition up to the capital cost of the property are subtracted from the UCC. If the property is disposed of for more than its capital cost, which should be unusual for most depreciable properties as they are supposed to decline in value, only the capital cost is subtracted.[61] Conceptually, when a taxpayer did not lose any value of the property in producing income, there is no economic cost to be deducted.

The determination of UCC can be illustrated by the following example (ignoring the half-year rule for now).

> Taxpayer X operates a business. In Year 1, X acquires Asset A for $20,000 and Asset B for $10,000, and both assets are Class 10 with a CCA rate of 30 per cent. The UCC at the end of Year 1 will be $30,000, which is the total of the cost of both assets under item A. None of the other elements in the UCC computation are relevant. The CCA for Year 1 will be $9,000, which is $30,000 × 30%.
>
> In Year 2, X continues to use the assets in the business. At the end of Year 2, the UCC will determined by A–E because item B and F are not relevant. A will be $30,000, and E will be $9,000 (CCA deducted in Year 1), resulting in the UCC being $21,000 (i.e., $30,000 - $9,000). $21,000 is the total capital cost that remains unrecognized as a deduction under the *ITA*. X claims a CCA deduction of 30 per cent of the $21,000, that is $6,300.
>
> In Year 3, X sells Asset B for $4,000 and purchases Asset C for $15,000. As explained below, the sale of Asset B will not result in any recapture or terminal loss. At the end of Year 3, the UCC is computed as follows:
>
> A = $20,000 (Asset A) + $10,000 (Asset B) + $15,000 (Asset C) = $45,000
>
> E = $9,000 (Year 1 CCA) + $6,300 (Year 2 CCA) = $15,300.
>
> F = $4,000 (lesser of proceeds of disposition and capital cost of Asset B).
>
> UCC = $45,000 - [$15,300 + $4,000] = $25,700
>
> CCA = $25,700 × 30% = $7,710

---

[58] This will be clearer after the recapture rule, explained below, has been understood.

[59] This term is defined under s. 13(21) of the *ITA*, *supra* note 1.

[60] See heading 9.3(f)(ii) — Terminal loss, below.

[61] The gain over capital cost is a capital gain and is, thus, left out of the UCC account.

If X had not replaced Asset B with Asset C in Year 3, the UCC would have been $30,000 (total cost of Asset A and Asset B) - $15,300 (total CCA in Year 1 and Year 2) = $14,700. X's CCA will be $4,410 (30% × $14,700).

You can see from the above example that the UCC is computed for each class of property. Assets are grouped in a class on the basis of their estimated useful life. One advantage of the class method is its simplicity. Another advantage is that some assets may last longer than their estimated life while others may have to be retired prematurely. In a group of related assets, any under-depreciation on some assets will probably be balanced by over-depreciation on others. The UCC account is cumulative and ongoing, accounting for new acquisitions and dispositions of assets in the class. For CCA computation purposes, it is the year-end balance that is relevant pursuant to Regulation 1100(1)(a).

In certain circumstances, similar properties may be placed in separate classes. For example, each rental building that costs $50,000 or more is required to be put in a separate class.[62] The rationale for this rule is to prevent taxpayers from avoiding the recapture of CCA upon the disposition of a rental property by acquiring another similar property of the same class. Similar properties used for earning income from different sources must be placed in separate classes as well, because profit for each source must be computed separately and the CCA in respect of each source must be determined.[63] For example, where a taxpayer owns a building for business use and another similar building to earn rental income, each of the buildings must be placed into a separate class.

(e) — Proceeds of disposition

The term "disposition" is defined in subsection 248(1) to include "any transaction or event entitling a taxpayer to proceeds of disposition of the property". For the purposes of CCA rules, "proceeds of disposition" is defined in subsection 13(21) to include the sale price of property and compensation for property unlawfully taken, damaged, destroyed or appropriated.

Because these two statutory definitions are merely inclusive, one still needs to determine the ordinary meaning of these terms to interpret the *ITA*. In *R. v. Compagnie Immobiliere BCN Ltée* (1979),[64] the Supreme Court of Canada stated that the term "disposition of property" should be given the broadest possible meaning, including the destruction of tangible property or the extinction of an item of intangible property. Therefore, a property is "disposed of" for tax purposes when it is sold or abandoned by the owner (for example, when a building is demolished or a car is given away for free), or when it is destroyed or stolen without any insurance coverage. In the case of a gift, the disposition is deemed to have been made at

---

[62] Regulations, *supra* note 2, reg. 1101(1ac).

[63] For an earlier discussion of the concept of source, see Chapter 4 at heading 4.3 — Income from a "source".

[64] *R. v. Compagnie Immobiliere BCN Ltée* (1979), [1979] C.T.C. 71, 79 D.T.C. 5068 (S.C.C.).

fair market value.[65] The proceeds of disposition are zero when a property is destroyed or stolen without insurance coverage.

(f) — Recapture or terminal loss

The CCA regime estimates the extent of depreciation each year on a class-by-class basis. On the sale or retirement of an existing asset, the proceeds of its disposition (or the original cost, if that is less than the proceeds, which is often the case) are subtracted from the UCC of the class. Such subtractions may lead to a positive, negative or nil UCC balance at the end of the year. The recapture rule under subsection 13(1) and the terminal loss rule under subsection 20(16) deal with these situations.

(i) — Recapture

Subsection 13(1) of the *ITA* provides that when the negative elements (e.g., item E and item F) of the UCC computation exceed the positive elements (e.g., item A and item B), the negative balance of the UCC at the end of a taxation year must be included in income. The negative balance represents, in essence, the overestimated depreciation under the CCA system. The previously deducted excessive amount of CCA is recaptured and added to the UCC computation in the following year, so that the UCC is restored to nil. The following example illustrates the recapture rule.

Assume a prescribed class has only one asset. The capital cost of the asset is $100, CCA previously deducted is $60, and the UCC immediately before the disposition is $40. The asset is disposed of for $55. After the disposition, the UCC of the class becomes a negative $15: [$60 (item E) + $55 (item F)] - $100 (item A). The *ITA* estimates a depreciation of $60 when the actual decline in value is only $45 ($100 - $55). The excessive $15 CCA is recaptured and added to income.

Because the recapture occurs when the UCC of the class becomes negative, taxpayers can avoid the recapture by acquiring assets in the class.[66]

---

[65] *ITA, supra* note 1, s. 69(1)(b). If the donee is the spouse of the donor, the gift may take place at the taxpayer's cost for tax purposes: the proceeds of disposition of depreciable property are deemed to be equal to the UCC of the asset (s. 73(1)).

[66] Because a recapture is included in income, it is fully taxable. If the taxpayer has to replace the former property with new property in order to carry on the business, it would be beneficial to the taxpayer to defer the recognition of the recapture and use the total proceeds of disposition to acquire the replacement property. Subsection 13(4) provides the taxpayer with an election to defer all or part of the recapture if the disposition of property is involuntary (stolen or lost) or the property disposed of is a "former business property" and the taxpayer acquires a replacement property by the deadline specified in the *ITA*. The mechanism for the deferral is to effectively transfer part of the proceeds of disposition of the former property from the year of the disposition to the year in which the replacement property is acquired so that there is no negative balance in the UCC account. Section 44 provides a similar rule for capital gains purposes: see Chapter 10 at heading 10.3(c) — Timing of disposition, note 56.

In some unusual cases (e.g., buildings, intangible assets), a depreciable property may actually appreciate in value. For example, if the asset in the above example is sold for $105, the full amount of CCA deducted ($60) will be recaptured in the year of the disposition (unless a replacement property is acquired in the same class). The gain of $5 over the original cost (i.e., the excess of the proceeds of disposition over the original capital cost) is taxed as a capital gain (see Chapter 10).

(ii) — Terminal loss

A "terminal loss" is the converse of recapture of CCA. Under subsection 20(16) of the *ITA*, a terminal loss arises only if the taxpayer no longer owns any property in the class and the balance in the UCC of the class is positive at the end of the year. In other words, when properties in the class have been disposed of, the total proceeds of disposition fail to recover the undepreciated capital cost of the properties in the class. This means that the CCA taken in previous years is less than the amount of actual depreciation. The remaining undepreciated capital cost is deductible in full as terminal loss. The loss is terminal in the sense that the class has no more property and is terminated. But because the class must be kept open for the future, the terminal loss is added to the item E amount to restore the UCC opening balance (for the next year) to nil.

For example, the capital cost of the sole property in a class is $100, $60 CCA has been deducted in previous years, the property is sold for $30 this year. Between the cost recovered through the CCA deductions ($60) and the sale proceeds ($30), $90 is recovered by the taxpayer. The remaining $10 is a terminal loss deduction.

(iii) — Example

The following example provides an overview of four depreciable properties, each acquired in Year 1 for $100, each depreciated at different rates for tax purposes (because each was in a different class with no other assets in the class), and each disposed of in Year 6 for various proceeds of disposition.

	Asset 1	Asset 2	Asset 3	Asset 4
1. Cost	100	100	100	100
2. UCC before sale	40	50	60	70
3. Proceeds of disposition	40	70	110	30
4. Recapture	Nil	20	40	Nil
5. *Capital gain*	*Nil*	*Nil*	*10*	*Nil*
6. Terminal loss	Nil	Nil	Nil	40

Asset 1: The proceeds of disposition are equal to its UCC. The CCA matched the actual depreciation. There is a full cost recovery through the CCA and the disposition.

Asset 2: The proceeds of disposition exceed its UCC by $20 and the excess is recaptured in Year 6. There is an overestimation of CCA by $20.

Asset 3: The proceeds of disposition exceed the original capital cost by $10. There is no depreciation at all. In addition to recapturing the entire CCA deducted previously, there is a $10 capital gain in Year 6.

Asset 4: The proceeds of disposition are $40 less than its UCC. The actual depreciation exceeds the CCA claimed. The excess is a terminal loss.

(g) — Timing rules

(i) — Time of acquisition and available for use

When should the cost of acquiring a depreciable property be added to the UCC calculation? The wording of item A in the UCC definition suggests that the cost of a depreciable property may be added only when the property is "acquired" by the taxpayer. According to the jurisprudence, a "purchaser has acquired assets of a class . . . when title has passed, assuming that the assets exist at that time, or when the purchaser has all the incidents of title, such as possession, use and risk, although legal title may remain in the vendor as security for the purchase price as is the commercial practice under conditional sales agreement".[67]

For CCA purposes, a depreciable property is acquired by a taxpayer when the taxpayer has "a current ownership right in the asset itself and not merely rights under a contract to acquire the asset in the future".[68] In determining whether or not ownership is acquired by the taxpayer, the legal relationship between the taxpayer and the vendor must be reviewed, and general laws on contract, property, as well as the provincial *Sale of Goods Act*, need to be considered.

In addition, subsection 13(26) provides that the cost of property purchased by a taxpayer may not be added to the UCC of a class until the property purchased becomes "available for use" or until 24 months after the actual acquisition of the property. Subsection 13(27) provides that property becomes available for use when it is "first used by the taxpayer for the purpose of earning income". The available for use rule prevents taxpayers from claiming CCA on depreciable property that is not being used in the business (e.g., machinery that had been bought but was still sitting in its packing case at the end of the taxation year or a newly constructed building not yet occupied by the taxpayer). This deeming rule ensures that a depreciable asset is actually used in the income-earning process so that its depreciation is matched with the income that it helps to generate.

(ii) — Recognition of proceeds of disposition

The time to account for proceeds of disposition is when the proceeds become receivable. Under the general principles of realization, proceeds of disposition become receivable when the taxpayer has acquired the legal, not necessarily immediate, right to payment.[69] In the case of a sale of property, a disposition generally

---

[67] *M.N.R. v. Wardean Drilling Ltd.*, [1969] C.T.C. 265, 69 D.T.C. 5194 (Ex. Ct.).

[68] Folio S3-F4-C1, *supra* note 50 at para. 1.28.

[69] See Chapter 7 at heading 7.4(b) — "Amount receivable".

occurs when title to the property has passed to the purchaser. However, the normal incidence of title, namely possession, use and risk, must be examined in order to determine whether ownership has transferred and the taxpayer is legally entitled to be compensated.[70] The provincial legislation governing the sale of goods is also important in determining when property is disposed of for tax purposes, because the disposition of property takes place when ownership is passed under provincial law.[71]

In the case of involuntary dispositions (i.e., expropriation, loss, theft or destruction), subsection 44(2) deems a property to be disposed of at the earliest of the following times: 1) the date of an agreement fixing the full amount of compensation; 2) the date on which a board, tribunal, or court finally determines the amount of compensation; and 3) if the taxpayer does not commence some kind of legal proceeding within two years of the loss, destruction or expropriation, the date that is two years after the loss, destruction or expropriation.

(iii) — Half-year rule

The CCA for each year is calculated as a percentage of the UCC "as of the end of the taxation year". Before 1981, when a depreciable property was acquired during the year — even close to the end of the year — the taxpayer was able to add the full cost of the newly acquired property to the UCC, and thereby claim the full amount of CCA in respect of the property, even though it had not been owned or used for the full year. In that case, of course, the taxpayer had not, in fact, suffered a full year of depreciation. In 1981, Regulation 1100(2) introduced the "half-year rule", the effect of which is to deny to the taxpayer 50 per cent of the CCA that would otherwise be available in respect of a depreciable property acquired during the taxation year.

The half-year rule still provides some tax advantage for the taxpayer who acquires a depreciable property after the halfway point of the year. The more accurate method would be to prorate the CCA according to the number of days in the year that the property was owned (and available for use). This would present no special difficulty if each depreciable property were depreciated individually. As we have noticed, however, the *ITA* and Regulations require that CCA be calculated by the class method, and it would be quite complicated to arrange a system of prorating for the portion of the CCA attributable to those assets in the class that were acquired during the last taxation year. The half-year rule is easier to apply than a more refined rule would be.

---

[70] According to *Browning Harvey Ltd. v. M.N.R.*, [1990] 1 C.T.C. 161, 90 D.T.C. 6105 (Fed. T.D.), the normal incidence of title — namely possession, use and risk — must be examined: there is no disposition of property when only the right to use the property is transferred while other attributes of ownership, such as the right to dispose of it or to use it as security, remain with the transferor.

[71] This was confirmed in a unanimous decision in *Hewlett Packard (Canada) Ltd. v. R.*, [2004] 4 C.T.C. 230, 2004 D.T.C. 6498 (Fed. C.A.).

Regulation 1100(2) applies only when a taxpayer acquired a depreciable property in the taxation year. Technically, the mechanism for the half-year rule is complicated,[72] but the application of the half-year rule is shown in the example below.

Suppose in Year 1 the taxpayer purchases four Class 8 assets at a unit cost of $100. There is no disposition of any assets during the year. The actual UCC (without taking into account of the half-year rule) is $400, which is the amount in "A" in the UCC definition. The notional UCC under the half-year rule is $200, which is $400 (actual UCC) - 50% of [$400 (cost of newly acquired assets) - 0 (proceeds of disposition)]. Thus, the amount of CCA is $40, which is $200 (UCC) × 20% (Class 8 rate).[73]

Suppose in Year 2 the taxpayer purchases another Class 8 asset at a cost of $100, and sells a Class 8 asset for proceeds of disposition of $80. The elements of the UCC are as follows:

A is $500, which is the total capital cost of Class 8 assets ($400 + $100);

E is $40, which is depreciation allowed for Year 1;

F is $80, which is the lesser of the proceeds of disposition ($80) and the capital cost of the property ($100)

$$UCC = A - (E + F) = \$500 - (\$40 + \$80) = \$380$$

The actual UCC at the end of Year 2 is, thus, $380. Under the half-year rule, the notional UCC is $370, that is $380 (actual UCC) - 50% of [$100 (cost of newly acquired property) - $80 (proceeds of disposition of asset purchased in Year 1)]. The amount of CCA is, thus, $74 ($370 × 20%).

---

[72] Regulations, *supra* note 2, reg. 1100(2) requires the CCA for the year of acquisition to be calculated on the basis of a notional UCC defined by reg. 1100(2), rather than the actual UCC. The notional UCC is derived by first calculating the actual UCC as of the end of the year (including the full capital cost of acquisitions), and then subtracting 50 per cent of the capital cost of acquisitions during the year. If depreciable property of the same class was disposed of in the year, then 50 per cent of the net figure (cost of acquisitions minus proceeds of dispositions up to capital cost) is subtracted from the UCC. The notional UCC is used only to calculate CCA for the year of acquisition. Note that if the proceeds of dispositions exceeded the cost of acquisitions, then reg. 1100(2) does not apply; there must be a net increase in the UCC account for reg. 1100(2) to apply.

[73] In a scenario where a taxpayer starts a new business and the first taxation year is less than 365 days (e.g., a business is started in March, 2017 and has a December 31, 2017 year-end), the taxpayer is affected by two rules: the 50 per cent rule described above, and reg. 1100(3), which requires the taxpayer to prorate the $40 CCA by the number of days in the taxation year over 365 (i.e., by 334/365).

In Year 3, there are no new acquisitions or dispositions. The elements of the UCC are as follows:

A   is $500

E   is $114 ($40 + $74)

F   is $80

$$UCC = A - (E + F) = \$500 - (\$114 + \$80) = \$306$$

CCA for Year 3 is $61.20.

(h) — Limitations on CCA deductions

(i) — Rental property

Taxpayers invest in buildings and other rental properties for dual purposes: to earn income from rent, which is typically characterized as income from property, as well as to realize capital gains from the increase in value of the properties. It is not uncommon that the rental income is modest, while the potential of a capital gain is significant. Some investment vehicles are structured to generate losses from the income stream while the property appreciates in value, and to generate a capital gain when sold.

For the purposes of the CCA regime, the total capital cost of the rental property is added to the UCC and subject to the CCA deduction. As explained earlier, the declining balance method of depreciation that underlies the design of the CCA system results in greater deductions in early years. For example, the CCA on an apartment building or office building, in particular, will provide substantial annual deductions to the owner, especially in the early years of the life of the building, although the building may not be declining in value at all. If the CCA exceeded the net rental income from the property (before CCA), then a loss would be generated for tax purposes. Not only would the owner report no income from that property, the loss would be available to offset the owner's income from other sources as well. The losses from rental properties are "artificial" in that no economic loss has really been suffered.

Regulation 1100(11) was adopted in 1972 to restrict the CCA that may be claimed on a "rental property".[74] A rental property is defined in Regulation 1100(14) as a building used "principally for the purpose of gaining or producing gross revenue that is rent".[75] The effect of Regulation 1100(11) is to limit the CCA that may be claimed on a rental property to a maximum of the rental income less all deductions

---

[74] There is also a requirement that each rental property acquired for more than $50,000 be placed in a separate class (reg. 1101(1ac)). This prevents the sheltering of recapture of capital cost allowance on the disposition of the property: see discussion at heading 9.3(f)(i) — Recapture, above.

[75] The word "principally" is considered to mean more than 50 per cent, generally based on floor space: *Mother's Pizza Parlour v. R.*, [1988] 2 C.T.C. 197, 88 D.T.C. 6397 (Fed. C.A.).

other than CCA. This provision means that CCA on a rental property can be deducted only to the point where the income from the property for tax purposes is reduced to zero. CCA deductions may not be used to create or increase losses that would shelter the owner's income from other sources.

(ii) — Leasing property

Similar restrictions under Regulation 1100(15) apply to "leasing property", which is moveable depreciable property used "principally for the purpose of gaining or producing gross revenue that is rent, royalty or leasing revenue".[76] Examples would be construction equipment, boats or aircraft, which are rented out to users.

A subset of leasing property is "specified leasing property", which is leasing property worth more than $25,000 and is subject to additional restrictions.[77] These restrictions were introduced in 1989 in response to a proliferation of sale leaseback transactions by non-taxable entities, such as government agencies, municipal bodies, charities, and corporations with large losses or loss carryforwards. For example, a transit authority might own a fleet of buses upon which it would not be able to claim CCA, because the authority was tax-exempt. The transit authority would sell the buses to a taxable entity (the lessor), which could claim CCA on the buses, and which would lease the buses back to the transit authority. The transit authority would receive not only the purchase price of the buses, but also favourable rental rates, as the lessor would pass on part of the tax savings generated by the lessor's CCA deduction on the buses. Both the lessor and the lessee (the transit authority) would be better off, at the expense of the tax system. This practice has now been blocked by deeming the sale leaseback of "specified leasing property" to be a loan of the purchase price by the lessor to the lessee at the government's prescribed interest rate,[78] so that the rent received by the lessor is deemed to be a blended payment of interest and principal on the loan. The lessor's claim to CCA[79] is restricted to the amount of principal notionally repaid on the loan each year.[80]

If the "principally" test is met, the entire building is classified as a rental property: *Canada Trust Co. v. M.N.R.*, [1985] 1 C.T.C. 2367, 85 D.T.C. 322 (T.C.C.).

[76] Regulations, *supra* note 2, reg. 1100(17). Corporations are exempt from the rental and leasing property restrictions if their "principal business" (accounting for 90 per cent of gross revenues) is the leasing, rental, development or sale of real property (reg. 1100(12), in the case of the rental property restriction) or the renting or leasing of leasing property (reg. 1100(16), in the case of the leasing property restriction).

[77] Regulations, *supra* note 2, regs. 1100(1.1)–(1.3).

[78] Adjusted quarterly under reg. 4302.

[79] There is also a requirement that each specified leasing property be placed in a separate class (reg. 1100(1.1)), as is the requirement for rental properties acquired for more than $50,000.

[80] The rules discussed above apply to the lessor. Section 16.1 of the *ITA* gives a lessee the opportunity to elect to be under similar rules in certain circumstances.

These statutory rules are necessary in order to ensure that CCA deductions are not used as tax shelters. A similar effect would be achieved by deeming a financing lease to be a sale or a loan. This is the approach taken under generally accepted accounting principles ("GAAP"), which deem a lease to be a sale or a loan for accounting purposes on the basis of the economic substance of the situation.[81] Such an approach has not been adopted for tax law purposes: as long as the legal relationship created by the terms of the agreement is a lease and there is no sham, a lease is a lease for tax purposes.[82]

Moreover, a number of properties are exempted under Regulation 1100(1.3) from the "specified lease property" definition. Trailers, office furniture, etc. are among such exempt properties. It is because of these exemptions that purchase and lease-back transactions, such as those in *Canada Trustco*,[83] continue to provide significant tax savings.

9.4 — Expenditure on intangible assets

Intangibles typically include purchased goodwill, trade-marks, quotas, franchises and licences for an unlimited period, customer lists, "know-how", stock exchange seats, and organization costs.[84] Before 2017, most intangibles, and, notably, goodwill, were not listed in Schedule II and were therefore not "depreciable property".[85]

Before 1972, when a taxpayer purchased a business, the portion of the purchase price allocated to goodwill was not deductible. Goodwill and some other expenditures came to be called "nothings". The Carter Commission proposed that the cost of purchased goodwill (and other intangible assets of more or less permanent life) should continue to be non-deductible for tax purposes, on the basis that goodwill, like land, generally does not depreciate.[86] Other classes of expenditures for intangibles that have a long run-but not permanent value to the business were to be listed and pooled in a new capital cost allowance class with a rate of 20 per cent. Any other costs of intangibles were to be deductible in full when incurred.

---

[81] These types of leases are called "capital leases" for accounting purposes.

[82] Until *Shell Canada Ltd. v. R.*, [1999] 4 C.T.C. 313, 99 D.T.C. 5669 (S.C.C.), the CRA took the position was there was a "capital lease" rule for tax purposes based on the economic substance of the transaction: see Canada Revenue Agency, Interpretation Bulletin IT-233R, "Lease option agreements; Sale leaseback agreements" (1983), withdrawn on June 14, 2001.

[83] *Canada Trustco, supra* note 47.

[84] E.g., legal fees for incorporation of a company. Costs of financing are specifically deductible under s. 20(1)(e) over a five-year period.

[85] Class 14 and Class 44 list intangible properties for CCA purposes before 2017. Class 14.1 was added effective January 1, 2017.

[86] Canada, *Report of the Royal Commission on Taxation* (Ottawa: Queen's Printer, 1966) (Chairman: Kenneth Le M. Carter), vol. 4 at 245.

The government did not accept Carter's recommendations in detail, but it did ameliorate the treatment of "nothings". The 1971 Act[87] provided for the amortization of most of the former nothings (including purchased goodwill) by the creation of a category of capital expenditures called "eligible capital expenditures". One-half of eligible capital expenditures were to be placed in a pool called "cumulative eligible capital" ("CEC") and amortized (by way of a CECA deduction) at a maximum rate of 10 per cent per annum by the declining balance method. In 1988, the Act was amended to increase the portion of an eligible capital expenditure that is added to the pool of cumulative eligible capital from one-half to three-quarters because the inclusion rate (fraction) for capital gains was also being increased from one-half to three-quarters. At the same time, the rate at which the cumulative eligible capital could be written off each year was reduced from 10 per cent to 7 per cent, still on a declining balance basis.[88]

As of January 1, 2017, the CEC system no longer exists. Goodwill and other capital expenditures that were subject to the eligible capital expenditure treatment are in newly created CCA Class 14.1 with a CCA rate of 5 per cent. CEC balances at Dec. 31, 2016 were transferred to new Class 14.1 on January 1, 2017. The CCA rate for new purchases is 5 per cent (2.5 per cent with the one-half rule). However, the CCA rate for the transferred CEC balance is 7 per cent for the first 10 years until January 1, 2027 (because only three-quarters of the cost of being amortized and 3/4 × 7 per cent is about 5 per cent).[89]

---

[87] *Income Tax Act*, S.C. 1970-71-72, c. 63.

[88] Because 1/2 × 10 per cent is 5 per cent, which is approximately equal to 3/4 × 7.

[89] See *ITA, supra* note 1, ss. 13(34)–(40), and Regulations, *supra* note 2, regs. 5 1100(1)(a)(xii.1), 1100(1)(c.1)(i). The rules for the pre-2017 CEC system are in s. 14 and s. 20(1)(b) of the *ITA*.

10
CAPITAL GAINS

10.1 — Legislative scheme

(a) — Distinct scheme

Subdivision c is the mini code within the *Income Tax Act* (the "*ITA*")[1] that governs the taxation of capital gains or losses from the disposition of property. Section 38 starts by defining "taxable capital gain", "allowable capital loss" and "allowable business investment loss", and prescribes the "taxable" or "allowable" portion to be 50 per cent. Sections 39 to 55 provide details to support the determination of capital gains or losses in a myriad of situations, involving different types of properties.

As discussed in Chapter 4, capital gains were initially excluded from the tax base by virtue of the "source theory", which dominated the Anglo-Canadian conception of income. Under the influence of the Haig-Simons conception of income, the Carter Commission proposed to include capital gains in determining the compre-

---

[1] R.S.C. 1985 (5th Supp.), c. 1 [*ITA*].

hensive tax base.[2] The Commission acknowledged that it was impracticable to assess capital gains that had accrued but not realized, and recommended taxation of only realized capital gains (with some exceptions). This recommendation generated a great deal of debate and was "watered down" in the final legislation: only one-half of realized capital gains become taxable as income, and one-half of capital losses were allowed to be deducted against those gains. In this way, capital gains became taxable for the first time in 1972,[3] but on a basis more favourable than other types of income. The tax reform of 1988 increased the inclusion rate from one-half to three-quarters, thereby reducing, but not eliminating, the tax preference for capital gains. In 2000, the inclusion rate was changed back to 50 per cent.

(b) — Technical design

Subsection 39(1) of the *ITA* stipulates that a capital gain is a gain from the disposition of a property if that gain would not be included in income under section 3 but for paragraph 3(b), and a capital loss is a loss from the disposition of property if that loss would not be otherwise deductible as a loss under section 3. It, thus, makes it clear that the capital gains scheme is secondary to the income schemes discussed in previous chapters. It captures gains and losses from disposition of property to the extent that they would escape from these other schemes.

Subsections 40(1) and (2) contain the basic rules for the computation of a gain or loss and limitations on the recognition of certain losses or gains. A gain or loss from the disposition of property is measured by calculating the difference between the "proceeds of disposition" and the "adjusted cost base" of the property. If the amount of proceeds of disposition exceeds the adjusted cost base, the excess is a gain. Otherwise, it is a loss. For various policy reasons that are discussed below, a gain or loss may be deemed to be nil in certain circumstances. For example, a gain from the disposition of a principal residence is effectively deemed to be nil under paragraph 40(2)(b) (the "principal residence exemption"), and a "superficial loss" is deemed to be nil under paragraph 40(2)(g).

Sections 41 to 52 provide specific rules for different types of property and transactions. Section 41 limits the losses from dispositions of listed personal property by allowing the offset of such losses against gains from dispositions of the same kind of property. Section 46 provides a $1,000 *de minimus* rule for personal-use property. Sections 42 to 45 address issues arising from dispositions subject to warranty, involuntary dispositions, the relocation of a business, part dispositions, and the change of use of a property. Sections 47 to 51 deal with identical properties, "eligible small business corporation shares", options, bad debts and shares of bankrupt corporations, and convertible properties.

---

[2] Canada, *Report of the Royal Commission on Taxation* (Ottawa: Queen's Printer, 1966) (Chairman: Kenneth Le M. Carter) [*Carter Report*]. See Chapter 4 at heading 4.2(c) — Carter Commission's "comprehensive tax base".

[3] The transitional provisions are briefly discussed under note 75, *infra*.

Sections 52 and 53 provide rules for determining the cost and adjusted cost base of properties. Section 54 provides definitions of the key concepts, including "capital property", "proceeds of disposition", "disposition", and "adjusted cost base". Section 55 is an anti-avoidance rule applicable to corporate surplus distributions.

And yet, the above rules in subdivision c are not totally independent of the rest of the *ITA*. To the contrary, subdivision c rules are closely linked to the determination of a taxpayer's income under section 3 and taxable income under subsection 2(2) and Division C. At a more micro level, they interact with the scheme for depreciable capital property, the scheme for employee stock options, and the gifting of property to charitable purposes. Whether an amount is characterized as on account of capital or revenue is relevant throughout the *ITA* and is a precondition for applying the capital gains rules. Many provisions of the *ITA* deal with dispositions of property, including section 69 (gifting and other transfers of property for inadequate consideration), section 70 (transfer of property in the event of death), section 73 (*inter vivos* transfers of property by individuals), and section 128.1 (property owned by immigrants and emigrants). They are inherently related to subdivision c. In addition, the general anti-avoidance rule ("GAAR") in section 245 applies to abusive transactions involving the disposition of property.

A distinguishing feature of the capital gains regime is its technicality, even though the idea of a capital gain is simple. Expressed in a formula, Gain = proceeds of disposition - (adjusted cost base + selling expenses). Most of the provisions in subdivision c stipulate the amount or timing of one or more elements of the formula to achieve a specific policy outcome. For example, section 46 deems the proceeds of disposition and adjusted cost base of a personal-use property to be the greater of $1,000 and actual amount, so that the capital gain is mathematically guaranteed to be zero for most household items.

Another feature of the capital gains regime is the use of formulary drafting. For example, the principal residence exemption under paragraph 40(2)(b) eliminates all or part of the capital gain on a principal residence by permitting a deduction determined by a formula.[4] A reserve deduction in respect of deferred payments is similarly defined in order to ensure a mathematical certainty about the amount and timing of the deferral that is to be allowed for a capital gain.[5]

Finally, the capital gains regime relies on numerous deeming rules to trigger a "realization" of the gain or loss accrued in a property or to deliver desired policy goals. For example, sections 44 (exchange of property) and 44.1 (exchange of eligible small business corporation shares) provide for a deferral by deeming the proceeds of disposition of the former property to be equal to its adjusted cost base and reducing the adjusted cost base of the replacement property by the deferred gain on the former property. To allow taxpayers who own worthless assets (such as bad debts and shares of bankrupt companies) to recognize the loss without selling the

---

[4] See heading 10.4(d) — Principal residence exemption, below.

[5] See heading 10.4(b) — Reserve for deferred payments, below.

assets (who would buy them?), subsection 50(1) deems the proceeds of disposition to be nil.

It is also worth noting that, more recently, the *ITA* is concerned with various kinds of transactions, particularly financial transactions, that would have the effect, if sustained, of transforming ordinary income into capital gains, deferring the realization and recognition of capital gains well beyond the limits of any reserve that might otherwise apply, and accessing the benefit of tax relief through the inter-corporate dividend deduction for dividends received by corporations in circumstances where the recipient is not "at risk" in respect of the share on which the dividends are paid and the person who bears the risk is considered to be "indifferent" to Canadian taxation (including persons exempt from tax under the *ITA* and certain non-residents). Examples of these kinds of additions to the *ITA* in the last few years are the "derivative forward agreement" rules (to address "character conversion") defined in subsection 248(1) and effected mainly via paragraphs 12(1)(z.1) and 20(1)(xx); the "synthetic disposition arrangement" rules (to address schemes that realize the economic value of property with its actual disposition) defined in subsection 248(1) and effected mainly via section 80.6; and the "synthetic equity arrangement" rules (to deal with the tax effects associated with monetizing (arbitraging) the value of an inter-corporate dividend deduction in computing taxable income where the recipient of the dividend is not "at risk") defined in subsection 248(1) ("specified synthetic equity arrangement", "synthetic equity arrangement" and "tax-indifferent investor") and effected mainly via subsections 112(2.3) to (2.34).

(c) — Purpose and rationale

(i) — Equity

As is mentioned above, the main purpose of including taxable capital gains in computing income under section 3 is to define "income" comprehensively in order to measure a taxpayer's ability to pay. Since a capital gain represents an increase in the taxpayer's ability to pay tax, the capital gain should be included in income (and a capital loss should be deducted from income). This argument is, of course, grounded in the idea of tax equity: in comparing the taxable capacity of different taxpayers, "a buck is a buck is a buck".[6] The taxpayer who makes a dollar in the form of a capital gain should be treated no differently than the taxpayer who makes a dollar in the form of income from employment or business or property. The wording of section 39 makes it very clear that the gain from the disposition of any property, unless specifically excluded by the *ITA*, is a capital gain unless the gain is otherwise taxed as ordinary income.

The equity argument is reinforced in the case of capital gains by the fact that capital gains are derived disproportionately by high-income individuals. The Carter Commission used statistics from the United States, where capital gains had been taxed

---

[6] For further discussion of the *Carter Report*, see Chapter 4 at heading 4.2(c) — Carter Commission's "comprehensive tax base".

for a long time, to show that capital gains tend to form a small proportion of the income reported by low-income individuals, and a large proportion of the income reported by high-income individuals. Indeed, the Commission concluded that the inclusion of capital gains in income would permit a drastic lowering of tax rates at the upper levels of income while actually improving the true progressivity of the system. In fact, as Carter predicted, the capital gains reported in Canada since tax reform in 1971 have been disproportionately concentrated in the upper-income classes. For example, in 2011, Canadians earning $250,000 or more taxable income reported 53 per cent of taxable capital gains.[7] The inclusion of capital gains, even on a preferential basis, has, therefore, contributed to the progressivity (vertical equity) of the system,[8] although the exemptions introduced into the system have reduced the impact considerably. With the "maturing" tax-free savings account program, which can be used by taxpayers, especially those in the top bracket, to avoid tax on capital gains by holding capital assets in the account, this progressivity has been further reduced.

The equity objective is arguably more important in cases where capital gains originate from "sweat capital" or human efforts (such as the sale of shares of private corporations or shares acquired under employee stock option plans). As discussed in previous chapters, remuneration for employment activities and gains from business efforts are fully taxable.

While all gains increase a taxpayer's ability to pay, this does not mean that all losses should be recognized as well. In fact, not all losses reduce the taxpayer's ability to pay. The *ITA* treats losses differently, imposing restrictions and quarantining rules. The treatment of losses is highly segregated. Losses from certain dispositions, such as "wash sales" (offsetting transactions) are not recognized because they are tax avoidance schemes. Losses from the disposition of listed personal property and personal-use property (including a principal residence) are also treated differently because the loss in value may be due to personal consumption or enjoyment.

---

[7] Canada Revenue Agency, "Income Statistics 2013 (2011 tax year)", online: <http://www. cra-arc.gc.ca/gncy/stts/gb11/pst/fnl/pdf/tbl2-eng.pdf>.

[8] These exemptions include the ones discussed at heading 10.1(c)(iii) — Achieving economic and social goals, below, as well as the exemption provided in tax-free savings accounts ("TFSAs") for all types of income (including capital gains). TFSAs are discussed in Chapter 11 at heading 11.4(a) — Tax-free savings accounts (TFSAs). As discussed in Chapter 2, all these measures are "tax expenditures", described and evaluated in an annual report published by the Department of Finance. See, e.g., Canada, Department of Finance, *Report on Federal Tax Expenditures: Concepts, Estimates and Evaluations 2017* (Ottawa: 2017). Sometimes, the effect of these "tax expenditures" on fundamental features of the tax system is not obvious. For example, the opportunity afforded even relatively affluent taxpayers to realize "tax-free" income, including capital gains in TFSAs (with no income attribution rules disrupting the multiplication of this benefit by family members) and by way of dispositions of their principal residences, raises the question of just how comprehensive the regime of taxing capital gains really is. It is another matter, however, as to how aware Canadian taxpayers are of this opportunity, which in some ways might be seen as amounting to a *de facto* renunciation of capital gains taxation.

Just as personal expenses are not deductible in computing income from a business, a loss resulting from personal consumption should not be recognized as a capital loss.

(ii) — Encouraging investment and entrepreneurship

Capital gains are taxable, but preferentially to ordinary income. Only half of capital gains are taxable and the other half are not. The reasons are primarily economic — to encourage Canadians to make investments and engage in entrepreneurship by reducing the effect of inflation, the bunching effect and the "lock-in" effect.

The *ITA* does not account for inflation in computing capital gains. The effect of inflation is more significant if the property has been owned for a long period of time with high inflation. The one-half inclusion of capital gains could conceivably be defended as a crude adjustment for inflation.

The bunching effect and lock-in effect are the result of taxing capital gains upon realization, irrespective of the length of ownership or reinvestment in other property. When the gains accrued during each year of ownership are bunched into a single gain in the year of realization, it may cause the gains to be taxed at a higher marginal rate than if they had been recognized annually over the period of accrual. This may discourage taxpayers from selling investment assets. Owners of property may even be induced by tax law to delay the sale of investment property that has appreciated in value, and, thereby, avoid making new investments even if a redeployment of the invested capital would make economic sense. They feel "locked in" by the potential tax liability. On the other hand, an owner may still sell the asset if in need of financial resources or if the asset is expected to fall in value. But the owner may still be reluctant to sell the asset merely to put its value to another use, because, in fact, the amount realized would be reduced by the amount of the tax needing to be paid. Accordingly, this lock-in effect may present a systemic or structural disincentive to the most profitable (efficient) use of investable capital. While economists do not agree on the seriousness of this impact, it seems at least intuitively plausible that adverse effects on the nation's productivity are possible. The exclusion of one-half of all gains from taxation helps reduce the disincentives to investment caused by the bunching effect and the lock-in effect.

On the other hand, the partial taxation of capital gains may encourage taxpayers to go to great lengths to arrange their affairs so that the profit is obtained in the form of a capital gain instead of ordinary income. If a tax system was neutral in its treatment of capital gains and other forms of income, there would be no tax incentive to take profits in the form of capital gains, and no need for complicated anti-avoidance measures. The Carter Commission recognized this and it is still true today. Some tax avoidance structures are designed to take advantage of the mismatch of the capital gains system and the ordinary income system. An example is borrowing to make investments in rental properties or shares. The taxpayer is able to currently deduct related interest expense in full in computing income from business or property, while the capital gain accrued to the investment is not taxable until the investment is sold and is then taxed only in half. Because the current deductions often exceed the rental or dividend income, a loss will be created and the taxpayer can use the loss to shelter income from other sources. This type of mismatch would be reduced if capital gains were not subject to differential tax treatment. Recently, in connection with the structuring of financial investments, the *ITA* has been amended to deal with "character transformation" transactions of various kinds, the effect of which may, otherwise, be to transform ordinary income into capital gains.[9]

(iii) — Achieving social and economic goals

The capital gains regime is full of special measures in order to achieve desired social and economic goals. For example, gains from donating certain securities and ecological properties to charitable organizations are exempt from tax[10] in order to encourage donations. Gains from the sale of a principal residence are exempt from tax in order to encourage home ownership. Capital gains from the disposition of "qualified small business corporation shares",[11] "qualified farm property",[12] and "qualified fishing property"[13] are taxed preferentially under the section 110.6 lifetime capital gains exemption provision to encourage savings and investment and to achieve other economic objectives.[14] Capital losses from investments in small business corporations also receive preferential treatment for this reason.[15]

(iv) — Administrative efficiency

Capital gains taxation affects every person who owns any property. A key objective of the capital gains tax scheme is to ensure that the rules can be complied with by taxpayers without excessive cost, aggravation or uncertainty. Administrative concerns underlie the design of some key features of the system, such as taxation upon disposition and deeming rules for personal-use property.

The taxation of capital gains upon disposition of property addresses two potential administrative issues: determining the amount of the gain, and liquidity (i.e., finding money to pay tax). The task of annually evaluating each and every capital property so as to assess accrued capital gains would be daunting for taxpayers and the Canada Revenue Agency (the "CRA"). On top of that, if gains were taxed on an annual accrual basis, taxpayers may not have the cash to pay the tax on "paper" gains. The realization rule gives taxpayers control over the timing of the recogni-

---

[9] Examples of character transformation transactions can be seen in *Shell Canada Ltd. v. R.*, [1999] 4 C.T.C. 313, 99 D.T.C. 5669 (Eng.), 99 D.T.C. 5682 (Fr.) (S.C.C.) [*Shell*], *Ludco Enterprises Ltd. v. Canada* (2001), [2002] 1 C.T.C. 95, 2001 D.T.C. 5505 (Eng.), 2001 D.T.C. 5518 (Fr.) (S.C.C.), and *Stewart v. R.*, [2002] 3 C.T.C. 439, 2002 D.T.C. 6969 (Eng.), 2002 D.T.C. 6983 (Fr.) (S.C.C.).

[10] *ITA*, *supra* note 1, ss. 38(a.1), (a.2).

[11] See heading 10.5(b)(i) — Lifetime capital gains exemption, below.

[12] *Ibid.*

[13] *Ibid.*

[14] As discussed in note 8, *supra*, all these measures are "tax expenditures".

[15] See heading 10.5(c) — Allowable business investment losses, below.

tion of capital gains. This is itself important in a tax system based on self-assessment. To be sure, sometimes circumstances outside the taxpayer's control will require a sale of capital property at a time that is inopportune for tax purposes. For the most part, however, the sale of property is a voluntary act, and the taxpayer is expected to be aware of the tax consequences. An example of an opportune time to sell an asset sheltering a capital gain would be when a loss has accrued on another asset. On selling both assets, the gain on one would be absorbed by the loss on the other.

The severity of universal taxation of all capital gains and the related compliance burden are significantly mitigated by the provisions related to personal-use property: the $1,000 *de minimus* rule in section 46 deems the taxpayer's proceeds of disposition ("POD") and adjusted cost base ("ACB") to be a minimum of $1,000, and paragraph 40(2)(g) deems any loss to be nil.[16] Most personal-use properties, such as furniture and automobiles, depreciate in value and produce a loss. Since such loss is deemed to be zero, taxpayers need not worry about reporting them. Therefore, taxpayers need not worry about reporting gains or loss from garage sales. The single most important personal asset that tends to appreciate in value is the family home, and gains on a family home can be sheltered by the principal residence exemption under paragraph 40(2)(b).

10.2 — "Capital gain"

(a) — Capital or income

Any gain from the disposition of property is a capital gain unless it is otherwise taxed as income. This is derived from the words in brackets in paragraph 39(1)(a).[17] Examples of property dispositions that give rise to income rather than a capital gain include the disposition of inventory (business profit) and employee stock options (employment income).

The term "property" has a broad meaning.[18] A property is a capital property if the gain or loss from its disposition is a capital gain or loss under section 39. Section 54 defines "capital property" as:

(a) any depreciable property of the taxpayer, and

(b) any property (other than depreciable property), any gain or loss from the disposition of which would, if the property were disposed of, be a capital gain or a capital loss, as the case may be, of the taxpayer;

Depreciable property "straddles" the business profit scheme and the capital gains scheme. As discussed in Chapter 9, a depreciable property is any property that is eligible for the capital cost allowance deduction under paragraph 20(1)(a) when

---

[16] There is an exception for a loss on "listed personal property", discussed at heading 10.4(e)(iii) — Listed personal property losses, below.

[17] Similarly, paragraph 39(1)(b) excludes losses from a disposition of property from capital losses if the losses are otherwise treated as losses from a regular source.

[18] See Chapter 6 at heading 6.3 — "Property".

computing profit.[19] When a depreciable property is disposed of at a gain, there will be a capital gain as well as recapture of capital cost allowance (income from business or property).

Distinguishing between business profit and capital gains is often one of the most challenging issues in tax law, especially prior to 1972 when capital gains were not taxable. As discussed below, the characterization depends on the facts and circumstances of each case. Generally speaking, it depends on whether the taxpayer is: 1) a trader who buys and sells properties in the ordinary course of business, 2) a speculator who buys property in the hope of selling it (quickly) to earn a profit, or 3) an investor who buys a property (e.g., real estate) to hold and use to earn income from business or property, or for personal use. These distinctions have produced a rich body of case law.

The characterization of the gain or loss from the disposition of a property is important for tax purposes because of the differential treatment of capital gains and losses from business profits and losses. As one would imagine, where a transaction yields a gain, the taxpayer tends to argue that the property was held as an investment and the gain is on capital account, and taxable in half. Conversely, where a transaction yields a loss, the taxpayer will argue that the property was a trading property, and the loss is from a business and deductible in full.[20]

(b) — Trading or investing

The distinction between trading and investing is often made in cases where the taxpayer is engaged in buying and selling properties on the side of his or her main line of work. In these cases, the skill and experience of the taxpayer, coupled with the frequency of the transactions, tend to lead the courts to conclude that the profits were the product of an organized business activity, namely trading.

In *Scott v. M.N.R.* (1963),[21] the Supreme Court of Canada held that a lawyer who, over a period of eight years, had purchased 149 agreements and mortgages at a discount, using both his own and borrowed money, and who had then realized a profit by holding the obligations to maturity, was a trader whose gains were income from a business. In *Forest Lane Holdings Ltd. v. M.N.R.* (1990),[22] the Federal Court — Trial Division held that a corporation carried on a business of securities trading over the two-year period in question based on the volume of transactions, the holding period of the securities, and the fact that the principal shareholder was

---

[19] See Chapter 9 at heading 9.3(b) — Depreciable property.

[20] The Minister's view is, of course, the opposite. In *Bossin v. R.*, [1976] C.T.C. 358, 76 D.T.C. 6196 (Fed. T.D.), the taxpayer had lost money on the stock market. Collier J. could not resist commenting that, if the taxpayer had made a profit, "the Minister would then, I suspect, have been making diametrically opposite arguments in this Court!" (at 371 [C.T.C.]).

[21] *Scott v. M.N.R.* (1963), [1963] C.T.C. 176, 63 D.T.C. 1121 (S.C.C.).

[22] *Forest Lane Holdings Ltd. v. M.N.R.* (1986), [1987] 1 C.T.C. 2051, 87 D.T.C. 1 (T.C.C.); affirmed [1990] 2 C.T.C. 305, 90 D.T.C. 6495 (Fed. T.D.).

an investment dealer. The taxpayer corporation's conduct was the same as an investment dealer trading on his or her own account. By contrast, in *Wood v. M.N.R.* (1969),[23] the Supreme Court of Canada held that a lawyer who, over a period of seven years, purchased 13 mortgages at a discount, using only his own money, and then realized a profit by holding the mortgages to maturity, was an investor whose gains were capital gains (which were then untaxed). The Court in *Wood* emphasized that small factual differences could change the result in these cases, and held that the smaller volume of transactions and the exclusive use of savings (as opposed to borrowings) "was consistent with the making of personal investments out of his savings and not with the carrying on of a business".[24]

Where a series of transactions are related to the taxpayer's ordinary work, this will strengthen the inference that he or she is engaged in trading rather than personal investment. In *Cooper v. Stubbs* (1925),[25] for example, a member of a firm of cotton brokers, who also purchased and sold cotton futures on his own account, carrying out about 50 transactions per year, was held to be in the business of trading in cotton futures. In *Morrison v. M.N.R.* (1927),[26] a member of a firm of grain commission merchants, who also bought and sold grain on his own account, carrying out 260 transactions in the taxation year in issue, was held to be a trader. Similarly, in *Whittall v. M.N.R.* (1967),[27] a member of a firm of stockbrokers who bought and sold corporate shares and oil and gas rights on his own account was held to be a trader.

(c) — Adventure or concern in the nature of trade

(i) — Isolated transaction

"An adventure or concern in the nature of trade" is included in the definition of "business" under subsection 248(1). The word "adventure" indicates that the dealing is isolated (or involves very few transactions) and speculative in nature. The essence of "trade" is systematic buying and selling with a view to profit. An adventure or concern *in the nature of trade* is an isolated transaction (that lacks the frequency or system of a trade) in which the taxpayer buys property with the intention of selling it at a profit, and then sells it (normally at a profit, but sometimes at a loss). Accordingly, when a taxpayer enters into an isolated transaction (or only a few transactions), he or she is not a trader. But, if the transaction was a speculative one, intended to yield a profit, it is in the nature of a business.[28]

---

[23] *Wood v. M.N.R.* (1969), [1969] C.T.C. 57, 69 D.T.C. 5073 (S.C.C.).

[24] *Ibid.* at 60 [C.T.C.].

[25] *Cooper v. Stubbs* (1925), [1925] 2 K.B. 753 (K.B.).

[26] *Morrison v. M.N.R.* (1927), [1928] Ex. C.R. 75, [1917–27] C.T.C. 343, 1 D.T.C. 113 (Can. Ex. Ct.).

[27] *Whittall v. M.N.R.* (1967), [1967] C.T.C. 377, 67 D.T.C. 5264 (S.C.C.) at 394 [C.T.C.].

[28] See *M.N.R. v. Taylor* (1956), [1956] C.T.C. 189, 56 D.T.C. 1125 (Can. Ex. Ct.) [*Taylor*], and *Regal Heights v. M.N.R.* (1960), [1960] C.T.C. 384, 60 D.T.C. 1270 (S.C.C.) [*Regal*

The courts have used a number of factors to determine whether a taxpayer was engaged in an adventure in the nature of trade. The overriding requirement is a scheme for profit making. The most important factor is the taxpayer's intention at the time of purchase of the property.[29]

(ii) — Intention on acquisition

The intention of the taxpayer at the time of the acquisition of the property is the critical factor considered by the courts in distinguishing between an adventure or concern in the nature of trade and an investment. If the taxpayer's intention was to resell the property at a profit, then the transaction is an adventure in the nature of trade. If, on the other hand, the taxpayer's intention was to hold the property as a source of regular income (or any purpose other than resale), then the transaction is an investment and any profit will be taxed as a capital gain.

How to establish a taxpayer's intention? Generally speaking, the taxpayer's oral evidence of his or her intention is self-serving and is bound to be suspect, so the courts have tended to rely primarily on the objective facts surrounding the purchase of the property, the subsequent course of dealing, and the circumstances of the sale, in order to determine whether the taxpayer acquired the property as an investment or as a speculation. These objective factors include the following:

* whether the taxpayer acquired the property with borrowed funds;

* the period of ownership of the property;

* efforts made to attract purchasers or to make the property more marketable;

* the skill and experience of the taxpayer;

* the relationship of the transaction to the taxpayer's ordinary business;

* the nature of the property, especially whether it yields regular income; and

* the circumstances of the eventual sale, especially whether it arose from something unanticipated at the time of purchase.[30]

Heights]. Property that is the subject of an adventure in the nature of trade is inventory: *Friesen v. R.*, [1995] 2 C.T.C. 369, 95 D.T.C. 5551 (S.C.C.) [*Friesen*]. The inventory of an adventure in the nature of trade must be valued at cost (s. 10(1.01)) rather than at the lower of cost or fair market value. See Chapter 8 at heading 8.8 — Inventory.

[29] See *Friesen*, *supra* note 28.

[30] Lists such as these are provided in many of the cases and by the CRA in its publications. See, e.g., Interpretation Bulletin IT-459, "Adventure or Concern in the Nature of Trade," (1980); and Interpretation Bulletin IT-218R, "Profits, Capital Gains and Losses from the Sale of Real Estate, Including Farmland and Inherited Land and Conversion of Real Estate from Capital Property to Inventory and Vice Versa," (1986), at para. 3, where the CRA lists other factors that have been used by the courts to assess intention, including feasibility of intention and the extent to which it was carried out, geographical location and zoned use of the real estate, evidence of change in intention, and the extent to which borrowed money was

Take the nature of the property as an example. When a taxpayer buys and sells property that is not for personal use and that will not yield income, there is a presumption that the taxpayer purchased the property with the intention of reselling it at a profit. In *M.N.R. v. Taylor* (1956),[31] the taxpayer purchased 1,500 tons of lead occupying 22 railway cars, which he sold at a profit. This was an isolated transaction: the taxpayer had never made a similar purchase before. The Court held that the transaction was an adventure in the nature of trade, pointing out that the taxpayer could do nothing with such an asset except sell it; he could not have acquired it for any other purpose. The same conclusion has been reached with respect to the purchase and sale of commercial quantities of toilet paper,[32] whisky,[33] sugar,[34] and sulphuric acid.[35] These assets could be turned to profit only by resale. They could not by their very nature be regarded as investments. As a result, the classification of transactions in real estate continues to be a major field of battle in the courts. Vacant land falls into this category as well. In the *Friesen* case,[36] the purchase of a tract of vacant land was held by the Supreme Court of Canada to constitute an adventure in the nature of trade.

In the case of typical investment properties, such as real estate and stocks, the determination is more challenging. These properties have the potential of generating profit when sold, and income (such as rent and dividend) prior to sale. The taxpayer's skill and experience, as well as the period of ownership and the frequency of the transactions, are relevant factors in assessing the taxpayer's intention. In *Dubé v. R.* (2005)[37] the taxpayer was a building inspector and self-employed for several years in the field of architecture. In March 2001, he purchased a building and sold it within six months to someone he had met inspecting another building. He used the profit on this sale to purchase a second building, which he again sold within six months for a profit (in March 2002) to a contractor he had met in connection with his ownership of this building. In 2002, he purchased a third building and used it as his residence and office. The Court held that the sales in 2001 and 2002 gave rise to business income because the taxpayer's primary intention was to sell the buildings rather than to keep them for rental purposes. The taxpayer testified that it became necessary to sell the buildings because the estimated repairs and

---

used and the terms of financing. GST/HST Info Sheet GI-005, "Sale of a Residence by a Builder Who Is an Individual," (2010) contains a similar list.

[31] *Taylor, supra* note 28.

[32] *Rutledge v. C.I.R.* (1929), 14 T.C. 490 (Scotland Ct. Sess.).

[33] *C.I.R. v. Fraser* (1942), 24 T.C. 498 (Scotland Ct. Sess.).

[34] *Atlantic Sugar Refineries v. M.N.R.*, [1948] C.T.C. 326 (Can. Ex. Ct.); affirmed [1949] C.T.C. 196, 49 D.T.C. 602 (S.C.C.).

[35] *Honeyman v. M.N.R.*, [1955] C.T.C. 151, 55 D.T.C. 1094 (Can. Ex. Ct.).

[36] *Friesen, supra* note 28. The characterization of the transaction as a business transaction was favourable to the taxpayer because the taxpayer wanted to recognize business losses.

[37] *Dubé v. R.* (2005), [2007] 2 C.T.C. 2437, 2007 D.T.C. 468 (Eng.) (T.C.C. [Informal Procedure]).

renovations required to turn them into rental properties were too expensive and this was only determined *after* he purchased the buildings. The Court reasoned that if the taxpayer had truly intended to retain the two buildings at issue (as opposed to selling them for a profit with a view to obtaining funds to purchase the third building), there was no doubt that the taxpayer would have inspected them himself (and determined the cost of renovations) *before* buying them, given that he had the skills and experience to do so.

The period of ownership and frequency of transactions have also been important when a taxpayer is arguing capital gains treatment because he or she wants to claim the principal residence exemption discussed at heading 10.4(d), below. While taxpayers who have owned a home for a short period of time have generally been denied capital gains treatment,[38] in at least one case, a taxpayer who owned a home for a short period of time was allowed to treat her profit as a capital gain eligible for the principal residence exemption.[39] These cases are very fact-dependent, and although the decisions are sometimes hard to reconcile, intention at the time of purchase, supported by objective evidence, has still emerged as the most important determinant.

(iii) — Secondary intention

One of the difficulties with relying on intention as a key factor in the classification of transactions is that a taxpayer may have more than one intention at the time when he or she purchases property. This fact has given rise to the "secondary intention" doctrine. If property is purchased with the primary intention of using it in some non-speculative way, but with a secondary (alternative) intention of selling it at a profit if the primary purpose proves impracticable, then such a sale for profit will likely be held to be on account of income rather than capital.[40]

---

[38] For recent examples of such cases, see *Giusti v. R.*, 2011 TCC 62, [2011] 3 C.T.C. 2016, 2011 D.T.C. 1075 (Eng.) (T.C.C. [Informal Procedure]) (a realtor bought and sold seven condominiums over eight years with holding periods ranging from 2 to 16 months); *Giguère v. R.*, 2012 TCC 309, [2013] 2 C.T.C. 2167, 2013 D.T.C. 1066 (Eng.), 2012 D.T.C. 1262 (Fr.) (T.C.C. [General Procedure]) (a police officer built and sold seven homes over five years); and *Sangha v. R.*, 2013 TCC 69, [2013] 3 C.T.C. 2143, 2013 D.T.C. 1074 (Eng.) (T.C.C. [General Procedure]) (in an isolated transaction, a house was built and sold within a year).

[39] In *Palardy v. The Queen*, 2011 TCC 108, [2011] 5 C.T.C. 2141, 2011 D.T.C. 1112 (Fr.), 2011 D.T.C. 1188 (Eng.) (T.C.C. [General Procedure]), the taxpayer owned a house for only one year and got capital gains treatment and the principal residence exemption.

[40] Note the doctrine of secondary intention is only relevant if the property is sold; it does not apply if the property is gifted. See *Staltari v. R.*, 2015 TCC 123, [2015] 5 C.T.C. 2140, 2015 D.T.C. 1130 (Eng.) (T.C.C. [General Procedure]). In *Staltari*, the taxpayer was a commercial real estate broker who had gifted ecologically sensitive land and filed his tax return on the basis that his gain was a capital gain eligible for the exemption under s. 38(a.1).

For example, in the leading case of *Regal Heights v. M.N.R.* (1960),[41] the taxpayer acquired undeveloped land with the primary intention of building a shopping centre on the site. After some development work had been done, the plan was abandoned when it was discovered that another shopping centre was to be built only two miles from the taxpayer's property. The taxpayer then sold the land at a profit. In the Supreme Court of Canada, it was held that the profit was income from a business. The trial judge had found that the taxpayer's primary intention was to develop the land into a shopping centre, but the judge had also found that there was a good chance that the shopping centre plan might not come off and that the taxpayer was aware of this and had a secondary intention to sell the land at a profit if the primary intention became impracticable. The Supreme Court of Canada accepted these findings and held that the existence of the secondary intention made the enterprise an adventure in the nature of trade.

Application of the secondary intention doctrine depends on the facts of each case. The following two cases help to define the state of mind that will qualify as a secondary intention. In *Reicher v. R.* (1975),[42] the taxpayer, who was a professional engineer, acquired land to construct an office building. The building was constructed, the taxpayer moved his offices into it, and excess space was rented to third parties. However, about a year later, the taxpayer sold the property at a profit, taking back a lease from the purchaser. The taxpayer testified that the sale and leaseback had been caused by financial difficulties that had arisen unexpectedly after the project was well underway. The Federal Court of Appeal accepted this explanation for the early sale and held that resale was not a motivating reason for the acquisition of the property; the transaction was, therefore, not an adventure in the nature of trade. A similar decision was reached in *Hiwako Investments v. R.* (1978),[43] where the taxpayer purchased a group of apartment buildings, and then sold them at a profit less than a year later. The sale had been made after it was discovered that the buildings were less profitable than anticipated, and in response to an unsolicited offer. The Federal Court of Appeal recognized that the taxpayer purchased the property for capital appreciation as well as the rental income. But this alone did not amount to a secondary intention to sell. The Court held that resale was not a motivating reason for the purchase. Therefore, the secondary intention doctrine did not apply, and the transaction was not an adventure in the nature of trade.

What *Reicher* and *Hiwako* establish is that the secondary intention to sell must have existed at the time when the property was acquired, and that it must have been "an operating motivation" or a "motivating reason" for the acquisition of the property. This language is intended to emphasize that a secondary intention does not exist merely because the taxpayer contemplates the possibility of resale of the property. That would be too strict a test, because any prudent investor would have that possi-

---

[41] *Regal Heights, supra* note 28.

[42] *Reicher v. R.* (1975), [1975] C.T.C. 659, 76 D.T.C. 6001 (Fed. C.A.) [*Reicher*].

[43] *Hiwako Investments v. R.* (1978), [1978] C.T.C. 378, 78 D.T.C. 6281 (Fed. C.A.) [*Hiwako Investments*].

bility in mind when purchasing an investment. In other words, it is not necessary for the taxpayer who claims to be an investor to show that his or her exclusive purpose was to acquire an investment. On the other hand, the secondary intention doctrine will not be satisfied unless the prospect of resale at a profit was an important factor in the decision to acquire the property.[44]

(d) — Foreign exchange

Gains or losses on foreign exchange are often incidental to other transactions. Property or services may be bought or sold by a Canadian resident in terms of a foreign currency, and the foreign exchange rate may change between the time when the obligation to pay is created and the time when payment is made. In this situation, the primary transaction is the sale or purchase of the property or services. If that transaction is on income account (e.g., a purchase of inventory or a sale of professional services), then the foreign exchange gain or loss will also be on account of income.[45] If the primary transaction is on capital account, then any foreign exchange gain or loss will also be on capital account. In *Shell Canada Ltd. v. R.* (1999),[46] the taxpayer borrowed in a weak currency at an interest rate higher than the US dollar. To protect against currency risks, the taxpayer entered into forward contracts and realized an exchange gain. The exchange gain was reported as a capital gain, while the nominal interest (which included a portion intended to compensate the lender for potential currency risks) was deducted in full. The taxpayer's characterization was upheld by the courts. The Supreme Court of Canada stated that "the characterization of a foreign exchange gain or loss generally follows the characterization of the underlying transaction".[47] Thus, "if the underlying transaction was entered into for the purpose of acquiring funds to be used for capital purposes, any foreign exchange gain or loss in respect of that transaction will also be

---

[44] The doctrine was discussed more recently in *Canada Safeway Limited v. R.*, 2008 FCA 24, [2008] 2 C.T.C. 149, 2008 D.T.C. 6074 (Eng.) (F.C.A.), where the appeal focused on whether the Tax Court had erred in applying the doctrine of secondary intention in deciding that the taxpayer's transaction was an adventure in the nature of trade. In the end, the Court confirmed the Tax Court's decision but for two different reasons. Nadon, J., writing for the majority, stated at paras. 70–71 that: "The evidence supports the inference that, from the beginning, the appellant did not want to keep its interest in the joint venture for a long period and that it intended to resell it at a profit . . . The appellant's secondary intention can be understood as a dual intention, as opposed to an alternative intention . . . Unlike the cases where the sale of the property is triggered by unexpected circumstances, such as financial difficulties or non-solicited offers to purchase, the evidence herein supports the view that the appellant always intended to resell its interest at a profit." Pelletier, J., on the other hand, disagreed with the conclusion that the taxpayer had a dual intention, writing at para. 82 that: "The fact that Canada Safeway did not acquire its co-ownership interest with the intention of holding it to produce income is apparent from the trial judge's finding of fact."

[45] See *Tip Top Tailors Ltd. v. M.N.R.*, [1957] C.T.C. 309, 57 D.T.C. 1232 (S.C.C.).

[46] *Shell*, supra note 9.

[47] *Ibid.* at para. 68.

on capital account".[48] In this case, because the debt obligations were on account of capital, the foreign exchange gain arising from the devaluation of the weak-currency loans was also received on account of capital.[49]

Where a taxpayer has made a gain or sustained a loss simply by virtue of any fluctuation in the value of foreign currency or currencies, subsection 39(2) deems the gain or loss as capital gain or loss.[50] This deeming rule applies to foreign currency gains and losses that would not otherwise be a capital gain or capital loss under the case law principles.

(e) — Election regarding Canadian securities

"Securities" typically include corporate shares and debt obligations. The classification of gains or losses from the sale of securities is generally governed by common law principles, discussed above. With respect to "Canadian securities", however, taxpayers are allowed to elect under subsection 39(4) to treat the securities as capital property.

Subsection 39(4) was enacted in 1977 to permit a taxpayer to elect capital treatment for all dispositions of Canadian securities. "Canadian security" is defined to mean shares or debt obligations of a corporation resident in Canada.[51] This election is permanent: the taxpayer is bound to accept capital treatment of dispositions of Canadian securities in future years. Capital treatment is, of course, the most favourable treatment of gains, but it may be unwelcome if losses are incurred in future years. The election is available to a resident individual and corporation except "a trader or dealer in securities",[52] who would tend to hold securities as trading assets.

---

[48] *Ibid.*

[49] As is often the case when the result of a court decision is unacceptable to the government, the result of the *Shell* case has now been reversed by statute, in this case, by the weak-currency loan rules in section 20.3 of the *ITA*. A "weak-currency loan" is defined to exist if the loan proceeds are in currency other than the final currency (the currency that the funds are to be put to use in), the debt exceeds $500,000, and the interest rate of the debt is more than two points (2 per cent) higher than the rate in the final currency. If a "weak-currency loan" exists, then the tax consequences are 1) the deduction for the interest expense on the loan is limited to the interest that would have been paid on a final currency loan (i.e., excess interest of 2 per cent or more denied); 2) all foreign exchange gains or losses are on income account (even if the loan is capital property); and 3) any interest denied in 1) can be used to reduce any foreign exchange gain (or increase any foreign exchange loss on the settlement of the debt).

[50] *ITA, supra* note 1, s. 39(1.1) recognizes capital gains or losses of individuals from foreign currency exchanges only if the total amount of gains or losses exceeds $200 each year.

[51] *Ibid.*, s. 39(6). There is an exception for "prescribed" securities, which are defined in the *Income Tax Regulations*, C.R.C., c. 945 [Regulations], reg. 6200.

[52] The terms "trader" and "dealer" are not defined in the *ITA*. In the context of subsection 39(5), the terms clearly include persons who hold themselves out to the public as dealers in shares, bonds or other securities. A private trader is also excluded from the statutory elec-

10.3 — "Disposition"

(a) — The realization principle

A gain or loss is not recognized for tax purposes until it has been realized by the disposition of the property. Accrued gains through the appreciation in value of a property are not recognized for tax purposes. The *ITA* triggers a realization of accrued gains or losses by deeming the property being disposed of in certain cases.

(b) — Meaning of "disposition"

"Disposition" is defined in subsection 248(1) for the purposes of the *ITA* as including "any transaction or event entitling a taxpayer to proceeds of disposition of property".[53] This definition points to the definition of "proceeds of disposition". A disposition is the required taxable event for taxing capital gains or recognizing capital losses.

Section 54 defines "proceeds of disposition" to include the sale price of property that has been sold and compensation for property destroyed, appropriated or damaged. It also includes mortgage settlement upon foreclosure of mortgaged property, including reductions in the liability of a taxpayer to a mortgagee as a result of the sale of mortgaged property.[54] However, an assumed obligation will only be included in a taxpayer's proceeds of disposition if it is a distinct liability that is not embedded in the cost of the asset, like needed repairs to the asset.[55]

When the definitions of "disposition" and "proceeds of disposition" are read together, it is clear that a disposition includes a sale of property, an expropriation of property for compensation, damages or injury to property covered by insurance,

---

tion: *R. v. Vancouver Art Metal Works*, [1993] 1 C.T.C. 346, 93 D.T.C. 5116 (Fed. C.A.); leave to appeal refused (1993), 160 N.R. 314n (S.C.C.).

[53] The definition goes on to list a number of specific transactions that are included or excluded. The same definition applies to disposition of depreciable property discussed in Chapter 9 at heading 9.3(e) — Proceeds of disposition.

[54] If the mortgage agreement is governed by civil law, the same rule applies to amounts arising from the foreclosure of a hypothecated property. The definition of "proceeds of disposition" also includes the principal amount of a debt's claim that has been extinguished as a result of a mortgage foreclosure or conditional sales repossession pursuant to s. 79 of the *ITA*.

[55] In *Daishowa-Marubeni International Ltd. v. R.*, 2013 SCC 29, [2013] 4 C.T.C. 97, 2013 D.T.C. 5085 (Eng.), 2013 D.T.C. 5086 (Fr.) (S.C.C.), the Court found that the assumption of absolute or contingent reforestation obligations by the purchaser of timber mill assets did not constitute proceeds of disposition to the vendor because the obligation was embedded in the cost of the assets sold and was not a distinct liability of the vendor. At para. 29, the Court compared the reforestation obligation to "needed repairs to property", which also depress the value of the asset at the time of sale, stating that "this is different from a mortgage, which . . . does not affect the value of the property it encumbers". This decision is particularly important to taxpayers in the forestry, energy and mining sectors, where obligations embedded in property are often assumed by the purchaser when a property is sold.

and the redemption or cancellation of a loan. As such, a disposition can be "voluntary" on the part of the owner, such as a sale, or involuntary, such as expropriation, loss or redemption.[56] A disposition need not involve the continued existence of the property or the acquisition of the property by someone else: destruction of property by fire, or the redemption of a debt, would lead to the disappearance of the property, yet those events are dispositions.

Because the statutory definitions of "disposition" and "proceeds of disposition" are merely inclusive, an event can be a disposition without giving rise to any proceeds of disposition. An example would be destruction or loss of a property without insurance. In general, a disposition occurs "where possession, control and all other aspects of property ownership are relinquished", even if "there is no consideration flowing to the person disposing of the property".[57] Thus, there would be a disposition if a capital property were stolen, destroyed, lost, abandoned, or confiscated without any right to compensation or insurance. In such a case, the proceeds of disposition would be zero.

(c) — Timing of disposition

The timing of a disposition determines when capital gains are taxable. The definition of "disposition" as "a transaction or event entitling the taxpayer to proceeds of disposition of property" points to the time when the taxpayer becomes "entitled" to the proceeds of disposition. As discussed in Chapter 7, the issue of when a taxpayer becomes legally entitled to receive payments is generally determined by private law. The time is generally when the taxpayer has acquired a clear and unconditional, though not necessarily immediate, right to receive an amount. When a property is sold, the time of the sale is generally determined by the transfer of title from the seller to the buyer. In the case of real property, this is often the closing date.

In the case of involuntary dispositions, subsection 44(2) deems the time at which the proceeds of disposition become receivable to be the earliest of: 1) the day the taxpayer agreed to an amount as full compensation for the property lost, destroyed, taken or sold; 2) the day the amount of compensation is finally determined by a court or tribunal; or 3) where a claim, suit, appeal or other proceeding is not taken before a tribunal or court, the day that is two years following the day of the loss, destruction or taking of the property.

---

[56] The capital gain on an involuntary disposition can be deferred if a taxpayer uses the proceeds of disposition to purchase a replacement property (s. 44). The s. 44 election is limited to the replacement of real property (business relocations) in the case of voluntary dispositions. Section 44 enables the taxpayer to elect to defer recognition of any capital gain until the replacement property is disposed of.

[57] Canada Revenue Agency, Interpretation Bulletin IT-460, "Dispositions — absence of consideration" (1980) at para. 1.

(d) — Deemed dispositions

(i) — Rationale for the deeming rules

There are several provisions in subdivision c to deem the taxpayer to have disposed of a property for tax purposes, even though the taxpayer still legally owns the property. In other words, there is no actual taxable event. The deemed disposition rules "crystalize" the inherent gain or loss in a property for specific tax purposes or delineate the income-earning use and other use of property. Deemed disposition rules create legal fictions with real tax consequences. Some common deeming rules and their rationale are briefly discussed below.

(ii) — Fair market value

The term "fair market value" is undefined in the *ITA*. Its determination is a question of fact, not law.[58] The often-quoted common law definition of fair market value is the following:

> the highest price an asset might reasonably be expected to bring if sold by the owner in the normal method applicable to the asset in question in the ordinary course of business in a market not exposed to any undue stresses and composed of willing buyers and sellers dealing at arm's length and under no compulsion to buy or sell.[59]

In other words, fair market value is the best price a vendor can obtain in an open market. When the courts hear cases with valuation issues, they hear evidence from valuation experts. Because valuation is far from an exact science, a high degree of professional judgment is involved, and experts may present different estimates of fair market value.[60] If the court finds the parties to be dealing at arm's length, the valuation may no longer be an issue.[61]

---

[58] *CIT Financial Ltd. v. R.*, [2004] 4 C.T.C. 9, 2004 D.T.C. 6573 (F.C.A.); leave to appeal refused 2004 CarswellNat 4370, 2004 CarswellNat 4371 (S.C.C.) at para. 3 [F.C.A.].

[59] *Henderson v. M.N.R.*, [1973] C.T.C. 636, 73 D.T.C. 5471 (Fed. T.D.); affirmed [1975] C.T.C. 497, 75 D.T.C. 5340 (Fed. C.A.); affirmed [1975] C.T.C. 485, 75 D.T.C. 5332 (Fed. C.A.) at para. 21 [(Fed. T.D.)]. The definition used by the CRA is similar: see Canada Revenue Agency, Information Circular IC-89-3, "Policy Statement on Business Equity Valuations" (1995) at para. 3.

[60] In *General Electric Capital Canada Inc. v. R.* (2009), [2010] 2 C.T.C. 2187, 2010 D.T.C. 1007 (Eng.) (T.C.C. [General Procedure]); additional reasons 2010 D.T.C. 1353 (Eng.) (T.C.C. [General Procedure]); affirmed (2010), [2011] 2 C.T.C. 126, 2011 D.T.C. 5011 (Eng.) (F.C.A.), a case dealing with the deductibility of a cross-border non-arm's-length loan guarantee, there was testimony from over 10 valuation experts as to what the arm's-length price for the guarantee would be for the purposes of ss. 247 and 69. The Tax Court found in favour of the taxpayer and the Federal Court of Appeal dismissed the Crown's appeal.

[61] E.g., in *Canada v. McLarty*, [2008] 4 C.T.C. 221, 2008 D.T.C. 6366 (Fr.), 2008 D.T.C. 6354 (Eng.) (S.C.C.), discussed in Chapter 8 at heading 8.7(c) — Contingent liability or amount.

(iii) — Change of use

The change of use rules under subsection 45(1) deal with situations where the use of a property is changed from an income-earning use to a non-income-earning use, such as personal, or *vice versa*. These rules deem a taxpayer to have disposed of a property for proceeds of disposition equal to fair market value when the use of the property is changed, and to have reacquired the property at a cost base equal to that fair market value. For example, if a cottage acquired primarily to earn rental income was later used primarily for recreational (personal) purposes by the owner (or *vice versa*), there would be a deemed disposition at fair market value on the change in use.[62]

In *Derlago v. R.* (1988),[63] the taxpayer rented his house to a tenant for a number of years until 1980, when he decided to demolish it and construct a new house as his personal residence. He was assessed by the Minister under subsection 45(1) for having disposed of the house for its fair market value at the time the house was demolished. The taxpayer appealed the assessment, arguing that, even though he was deemed to have disposed of the property, he was not deemed to have received any proceeds of disposition at that time. As a result, he argued that he was entitled to a reserve equal to the full amount of the deemed proceeds of disposition. In rejecting this argument, the Court noted:

> If I am to deem that the plaintiff sold his property in 1980 for a specific sum of money, I would assume, in the absence of any provision to the contrary, that he received the proceeds at the time of the disposition . . . This indicates to me, in this fictional world of taxation, that Parliament must have intended the deemed proceeds to have been received by the plaintiff because it provided for the expenditure of the proceeds by the plaintiff immediately after their creation.[64]

One reason for the deemed disposition rules under subsection 45(1) is the distinctive capital gains treatment of "personal-use property": capital gains on personal-use property that is a "principal residence" are eligible for the principal residence exemption, while capital losses on all personal-use property are not allowable. Another reason for segregating a period of primarily personal use from a period of primarily income-producing use is that CCA may not be claimed against non-in-

---

[62] When the primary use of a "housing unit" is a changed from rental (or business) use to personal use after 1984, an individual can postpone the recognition of any capital gain by making a s. 45(3) election if no CCA has been claimed personally and the property becomes the taxpayer's "principal residence". More well-known is the s. 45(2) election that is used to deem no change in use in the opposite situation: when a "housing unit" becomes primarily used to earn income from property or a business. The use of the s. 45(2) election in connection with the principal residence exemption is discussed in more detail at heading 10.4(d) — Principal residence exemption, below. Both elections are discussed in Canada Revenue Agency, Folio S1-F3-C2, "Principal Residence"

[63] *Derlago v. R.* (1988), [1988] 2 C.T.C. 21, 88 D.T.C. 6290 (Fed. T.D.).

[64] *Ibid.* at para. 11.

come-producing property, but may be claimed against some kinds of income-producing property (those that qualify as depreciable property).[65]

The distinction between non-income-producing and income-producing uses is critical for the recognition of both capital losses and CCA deductions. Other changes of use will usually make no difference. Hence, there is no deemed disposition if the use of a property is changed from one income-earning use (such as leasing a building to earn rent) to another income-earning use (converting the property into an office for the owner's business). In both cases, the property is a depreciable property for CCA purposes.

(iv) — "Crystalization" of accrued gains or losses

When a debt has been established to become a bad debt in the year, or a corporation owned by a taxpayer has become bankrupt in the year, a taxpayer may elect under subsection 50(1) to deem the bad debt or the share of a bankrupt corporation to be disposed of at the end of the year for proceeds equal to nil, and to have reacquired it immediately after the end of the year at a cost equal to nil.[66] This enables the holder of the debt or shares to "realize" the losses for tax purposes.

(v) — Departure from Canada

When a taxpayer ceases to be a resident of Canada, there is a deemed disposition at fair market value of all of the departing taxpayer's property, with certain exceptions.[67] The purpose is to tax the gains accrued while the taxpayer was resident in Canada; otherwise the gains would escape Canadian tax altogether after the taxpayer became a non-resident of Canada. This deemed disposition is often called a "departure tax" or "exit tax".

Similar rules apply to taxpayers who become Canadian residents during the year, so that the cost of their properties is the fair market value on the date of acquiring Canadian residency. The effect of this rule to ensure that capital gains accrued prior to becoming Canadian residents are not taxed in Canada.

(vi) — Death of taxpayer and inter vivos gift

When a taxpayer dies, he or she is deemed by subsection 70(5) to have disposed of each capital property immediately before death for proceeds of disposition equal to fair market value, unless the successor is the taxpayer's spouse or common-law partner.[68] There is an actual disposition on death in the sense that the deceased's

---

[65] *ITA, supra* note 1, s. 13(7) deems a similar disposition (and reacquisition) to have occurred for the purposes of the capital cost allowance ("CCA").

[66] The s. 50(1) election is discussed in detail in Canada Revenue Agency, Folio S4-F8-C1, "Business Investment Losses" [Folio S4-F8-C1] at para. 1.20 *et seq.*

[67] *ITA, supra* note 1, s. 128.1(4).

[68] Where a deceased taxpayer's property is inherited by a spouse or spouse trust, or (in the case of farming property) a child of the taxpayer, recognition of accrued gains can be post-

property passes immediately by operation of law to the personal representative (called the "legal representative" in the *ITA*), and ultimately to the deceased's successors designated by will or, if there is no will, provincial intestacy law. However, neither the legal representative nor the successors provide any proceeds of disposition and so the tax consequences of death have to be treated specifically by the *ITA*. The objective is to require the capital gains accrued during the deceased's lifetime to be recognized for tax purposes in the deceased's last taxation year (the terminal year).

The deemed disposition rule brings any taxable capital gains (or recapture of capital cost allowance) into the income of the deceased's terminal year, rather than into the income of the deceased's estate (which becomes a new taxpayer). Thus, recognition of capital gains cannot be postponed beyond the lifetime of the owner of the appreciated property. The lock-in effect caused by unrealized capital gains is, therefore, also limited to the lifetime of the owner. The successor to the capital property (the person inheriting the property) is deemed to acquire the property at its fair market value.[69]

The deemed disposition of capital property on death can be avoided by the owner giving the property away before death. But there is also a deemed disposition at fair market value on the making of an *inter vivos* gift of capital property, so that an *inter vivos* gift has the same effect as death in forcing the recognition of accrued capital gains or losses. As noted earlier, a deemed disposition on a gift of capital property is necessary to complement the deemed disposition on death.

Under paragraph 69(1)(b) of the *ITA*, where a person has made an *inter vivos* gift of property (or has made a non-arm's-length sale for inadequate consideration), the donor is deemed to have received proceeds of disposition equal to the fair market value of the property. Thus, any accrued gains (or losses) must generally be recognized by the donor at the time of the gift.[70] Under paragraph 69(1)(c), the donee of the gift is deemed to acquire the property at its fair market value, the intent being to step up the donee's cost base so that the donee never has to pay tax on the gain that was taxed at the time of the gift.[71]

---

poned through rollover provisions that are applicable to those dispositions, as well as to *inter vivos* gifts to a spouse or spousal trust or (in the case of farming property) a child. See heading 10.4(c)(iv) — Cost-basis transfers, below.

[69] *ITA, supra* note 1, s. 70(5)(b).

[70] When an individual makes a gift of property to a registered charity, he or she can claim a tax credit or deduction for the fair market value of the donation (see Chapter 12 at heading 12.5 — "Tax credits"), but, because of the deemed disposition, the donor must generally report a taxable capital gain equal to 50 per cent of the accrued capital gain on the donated property. However, as discussed at heading 10.5(b)(ii) — Charitable donations, below, for gifts of publicly-traded securities and ecologically sensitive land, none of the accrued capital gain is included in income: see ss. 38(a.1), (a.2).

[71] The language of s. 69(1)(c) does not precisely match that of s. 69(1)(b) in that s. 69(1)(c) makes no reference to a non-arm's-length sale for inadequate consideration. Accordingly, s.

The general rule, therefore, is that all accrued capital gains have to be recognized on death. As well, property cannot be passed from generation to generation by *inter vivos* gift without triggering a realization of accrued capital gains.

(vii) — Every 21st year of personal trusts

A gift of property to a trust, whether on death or *inter vivos*, gives rise to a deemed disposition just like a gift to an individual. A sale of property to a trust gives rise to the normal rules requiring recognition of any realized gain or loss, again just like a sale to an individual. Indeed, a trust is deemed to be an individual by subsection 104(2) of the *ITA*. However, once capital property has been acquired by a trust, it is sheltered for a long time from the deemed disposition on death, as a trust never dies. A trust can be made to last as long as 100 years despite the rule against perpetuities (which requires that all interests be vested within a life in being plus 21 years). Even on the termination of a trust, the distribution of capital property to the capital beneficiaries does not involve recognition of accrued capital gains.[72] The *ITA*, therefore, had to make special provision to preclude the use of a trust to postpone, for excessive periods of time, the recognition of capital gains.

Subsection 104(4) imposes, at 21-year intervals, a deemed disposition at fair market value on all capital property held by a trust. Generally, this deemed disposition occurs on the 21st anniversary of the creation of the trust, and again on the 42nd anniversary, and again on the 63rd anniversary, and so on every 21 years until the trust is terminated.[73] This deeming rule applies simply by a passage of 21 years. It differs from other deemed disposition rules that occur when there is an event or action, such as change of use, becoming a non-resident of Canada, or death.

10.4 — Computation of gain or loss

(a) — Basic method

The computation of a gain or loss is governed by subsection 40(1) of the *ITA*. It can be expressed in the following formula:

$$CG = POD - [ACB + \text{selling expenses}]$$

If the outcome is positive, that is, proceeds of disposition ("POD") exceeds the aggregate of adjusted cost base ("ACB") and selling expenses, there is a gain. If the outcome is negative, there is a loss. For example, if T sells a capital property with an ACB of $80 for POD of $100, incurring selling expenses of $5, T's gain is $15 = $100 - [$80 + $5]. If the POD were $60, T's loss would be $25.

69(1)(c) would not step up the cost base in that situation, leading to double taxation of the deemed gain.

[72] *ITA, supra* note 1, s. 107(2).

[73] This is the general rule to which there are a variety of exceptions and qualifications.

(i) — "Proceeds of disposition"

The meaning of "proceeds of disposition" was previously discussed in the context of a "disposition". The amount of proceeds of disposition is generally determined by the fair market value of the property. In some cases, the *ITA* deems the amount to be the same as the cost of the property. Some of these rules are discussed below.

(ii) — "Adjusted cost base"

The term "adjusted cost base" is defined, in section 54, differently for depreciable property and other property. In the case of depreciable property, the "adjusted cost base" is the "capital cost" of the property, the figure upon which capital cost allowance under paragraph 20(1)(a) is computed. It is essential that those two figures generally be the same so that the capital gain provisions work in harmony with the capital cost allowance provisions.[74] In the case of property other than depreciable property, the adjusted cost base is the "cost" of the property "adjusted" in accordance with section 53.

"Cost" is not defined in the *ITA*.[75] It generally means the actual cost of the property, including expenses of acquisition, such as brokerage fees, customs duties, shipping costs, sales taxes, legal costs, finder's fees and so forth, which are not otherwise deductible in computing the taxpayer's income.[76] In *Canada Trustco Mortgage Co. v. Canada* (2005),[77] the Supreme Court of Canada confirmed that, in the context of capital cost allowance provisions, "cost" is a legal concept and the

---

[74] For a discussion of CCA and the consequences of the disposition of depreciable property, see Chapter 9 at 9.3(f) — Recapture and terminal loss.

[75] When capital gains became taxable as of January 1, 1972, there was a huge transition issue: how to exempt from tax those capital gains accrued on property owned on January 1, 1972. The solution turned out to be quite complicated: *Income Tax Application Rules* ("ITARs"), R.S.C. 1985, c. 2 (5th Supp.), s. 26(3) (tax-free zone rule), and s. 26(7) (election of valuation day value). The significance of these provisions has not yet disappeared, because some taxpayers continue to own capital properties that they owned on January 1, 1972. A key concept in the transitional rules is valuation day (or "V-Day") value. The V-Day value was deemed to be the cost of property owned on January 1, 1972. The V-Day value of a property is its fair market value on December 22, 1971 for publicly-traded shares or securities and December 31, 1971 for all other capital property. ITARs, s. 26(1).

[76] In *R. v. Sterling*, [1985] 1 C.T.C. 275, 85 D.T.C. 5199 (Fed. C.A.), it was held that interest on money borrowed to purchase gold (which was not tax-deductible) was not part of the adjusted cost base of the gold. The interest payments related to the source of the funds used to make the purchase, and not directly to the cost of acquiring the property purchased. The Court stated that the word "cost" means the price that the taxpayer gives up in order to get the asset, and it does not include any expense incurred in order to put himself or herself in a position to pay that price or to keep the property afterwards.

[77] *Canada Trustco Mortgage Co. v. Canada* (2005), [2005] 5 C.T.C. 215, 2005 D.T.C. 5523 (S.C.C.) at paras. 74–76. This was the first case involving the general anti-avoidance rule in section 245 to go before the Supreme Court of Canada. For further discussion of the case, see Chapter 20.

amount paid to acquire the assets. The ordinary meaning of "cost" is the same for depreciable and non-depreciable property.

Adjustments to cost are required by section 53 by adding or subtracting an amount in specific circumstances. The purpose of these adjustments is to make the capital gains rules compatible with other provisions of the *ITA* in order to prevent double counting and to prevent gaps between the income and capital regimes. Many of the adjustments are technical in nature and have no application to the majority of capital transactions. For example, the amount of employee stock option benefit taxable under subsection 7(1) is added to the cost of the stock in order to prevent double taxation of the benefit. The amount of superficial loss that is denied recognition because of paragraph 40(2)(g) is added to the cost of the substituted property to preserve the loss for future realization.

(b) — Reserve for deferred payments

Where taxpayers dispose of a capital property for deferred payments, such as by allowing instalment payments by the purchaser, the total amount of proceeds of disposition is included in computing the gain or loss for the year of disposition. If the amount of the gain is significant and the associated tax liability is hefty, taxpayers may be in a difficult situation in terms of paying the related tax to the extent that proceeds have not actually been received in cash. Paragraph 40(1)(a) permits a deduction for a reserve for future proceeds as a relief measure.[78]

Textually, paragraph 40(1)(a) describes a mechanism for applying the reserve deduction for the year of disposition and the subsequent four years.[79] To compute the amount of gain for the year of disposition, Gain = Gain otherwise calculated - Reserve. For the following year(s), Gain = Reserve claimed in preceding year - Reserve for the current year.

---

[78] This reserve is similar in nature to the reserve for deferred payments in computing business profit under paragraph 20(1)(n); see Chapter 8 at heading 8.7(d)(iii) — Deferred payments.

[79] The reserve for deferred proceeds is expressed in subparagraph 40(1)(a)(iii) as "such amount as the taxpayer may claim . . ." These words make the reserve optional. The taxpayer is not required to claim the reserve, nor, if the taxpayer does claim the reserve, to claim the full "reasonable amount". Ordinarily, of course, the taxpayer will want to claim the maximum reserve possible, since the claim enables the taxpayer to postpone payment of some tax. But special circumstances could make it desirable not to claim the reserve (e.g., a year of exceptionally low income, or the availability of capital losses to offset the gain).

The "reserve" is the lesser of the two following amounts:

• Proportion of deferred gain, which is the amount of gain otherwise determined × deferred POD / total POD (clause 40(1)(a)(iii)(C));

• Statutory five-year limitation, which is the amount of gain otherwise determined × (4 - number of preceding years)/5 (clause 40(1)(a)(iii)(D)).[80]

Like the reserve deduction rules discussed in Chapter 8, the capital gains reserve provides technical relief when part of a gain is not realized in cash due to deferred payments. It does not reduce the amount of gain from the disposition. Therefore, when the disposition occurred in Year 1 and a reserve is deducted that year, the reserve is included in computing the gain for the following year (subparagraph 40(1)(a)(ii)).

The operation of paragraph 40(1)(a) may be illustrated by the following example:

T in Year 1 disposes of a capital property with an ACB of $100 for POD of $300, $75 of which is payable in Year 1, a further $75 is payable in Year 2, and the remaining $150 is payable in Year 10 (with interest). Since the POD is payable over 10 years, T may claim a reserve. T's gain for Years 1 to 5 would be as follows:

Year 1 (year of disposition)
Gain otherwise determined (s. 40(1)(a)(i)):

POD	$ 300	
ACB	(100)	
	$ 200	$ 200

Less reserve, which is equal to the lesser of:

— proportion of deferred gain: 200 × 225
(POD not due)/$300 (POD) =   150

— 5-year limitation: $200 × (4 - 0)/5 =   160   (150)

Capital gain for Year 1: $ 50

Year 2:
Reserve claimed in preceding year (s. 40(1)(a)(ii)) $ 150

Less: reserve, which is equal to the lesser of:

— proportion of deferred gain: $200 ×
$150/$300 = $100

---

[80] The fraction would be (4-0)/5 for the year of disposition, (4-1)/5 for the second year, (4-2)/5 for the third year, (4-3)/5 for the fourth year, and (4-4)/5 for the fifth year. Therefore, even if there is an amount of reserve allowed under the first limitation because part of POD is deferred to Year 6 and beyond, the second limitation mathematically ensures a zero reserve for the fifth year. The life of the reserve is extended to 10 years in respect of dispositions of farming property to a child: s. 40(1.1).

— 5-year limitation: 200 × (4 - 1)/5 =	120	(	100)
Capital gain for Year 2:		$	50

Year 3

Reserve claimed in preceding year	$	100

Less: reserve equal to the lesser of:

— proportion of deferred gain: $200 × $150/$300 =	$100		
— 5-year limitation: $200 × (4 - 2)/5 =	80	(	80)
Capital gain for Year 3		$	20

Year 4

Reserve claimed in preceding year (s. 40(1)(a)(ii))	$	80

Less: reserve equal to the lesser of:

— Proportion of deferred gain: $200 × $150/$300 =	$100		
— 5-year limitation: $200 × (4 - 3)/5	40	(	40)
Capital gain for Year 4		$	40

Year 5

Reserve claimed in preceding year (s. 40(1)(a)(ii))	$	40
Less: reserve equal to the lesser of:		

— Proportion of deferred gain: $200 × $150/$300 =	$100		
— 5-year limitation: $200 × (4 - 4)/5	0		0
Capital gain for Year 5		$	40

In Year 6 nothing will be reported — no reserve was claimed in the preceding year. The capital gain of $200 has now been fully recognized for tax purposes.

(c) — Special computation rules

(i) — De minimus rule for personal-use property

"Personal-use property" is defined in section 54 as property "that is used primarily for the personal use or enjoyment of the taxpayer" or of "a person related to the taxpayer". It includes such things as cottages, cars, bicycles, boats, sporting or recreational equipment, household appliances, furniture and clothing. It also includes principal residences, but the unique tax treatment of the principal residence is explained separately later. Every person in Canada has some kind of personal-use property for tax purposes. Since any gain from the disposition of any property is taxable, how can taxpayers be assured that they are not evading taxes when they do not report gains from transactions such as yard sales or gifting to relatives and friends? The $1,000 *de minimus* rule is intended to provide certainty and guidance for taxpayers.

Subsection 46(1) deems the adjusted cost base and the proceeds of disposition of personal-use property to be the higher of the actual figures or $1,000.[81] The effect of this rule is to exempt small transactions in personal-use property from the capital gains taxation. For example, Taxpayer P sells a bike, originally bought for $700, for $900. For tax purposes, P is deemed to have a $1,000 adjusted cost base and the proceeds of disposition, yielding a capital gain of zero. If, however, the sale price were $1,200, P would have a gain of $200 (actual proceeds of disposition of $1,200 - deemed adjusted cost base of $1,000).

The deeming rule affects the computation of gain or loss from the disposition of personal-use property. If the disposition gives rise to gain or loss, the gains are taxable like other gains, but the losses are subject to special stop-loss rules discussed below.

(ii) — Deemed fair market value rule

The deemed disposition rules discussed at heading 10.3(d), above, generally provide that the proceeds of disposition are deemed to be fair market value. In the case of gifting upon death or during the lifetime of the taxpayer, the donee is deemed to acquire the property at a cost equal to the deemed proceeds of disposition. Where taxpayers are deemed to have disposed of the property to themselves (such as change of use or departure from Canada), their deemed cost base is equal to the deemed proceeds of disposition.

The "fair market value" rule also apples under subsection 69(1) to transactions between taxpayers who do not deal with each other at arm's length, typically family members or related companies. The intention is to use the fair market value as a benchmark in determining the price for those transactions where the parties have the common intention to "manipulate" price to achieve tax savings.

(iii) — Transfers with non-arm's-length persons

The notion of "arm's length" refers to a relationship that is "as far away from one as the arm can reach; away from familiarity, at a distance; without fiduciary relations".[82] The determination of whether taxpayers deal at "arm's length" is also important in the application of other rules in the *ITA*.[83] Generally speaking, any dealings between strangers are presumed to be at arm's length.

---

[81] In order to preclude abuse of the $1,000 rule, there are special rules for the disposition of part of a personal-use property or part of a set of personal-use properties, which require the $1,000 limit to be prorated: ss. 46(2), (3).

[82] *The Shorter Oxford Dictionary*, 3rd ed. (Oxford University Press), definition of "at arm's length".

[83] E.g., *ITA, supra* note 1, ss. 18(4), 56(4.1), 78(1), 84.1, 118.1, 160, 212, certain definitions in ss. 248(1), 247.

For the purposes of the *ITA*, subsection 251(1) deems "related persons" not to be "dealing with each other at arm's length". "Related persons" are, in turn, listed in subsection 251(2). For tax purposes, individuals, for example, are "related" to other individuals connected by blood relationship, marriage or common-law partnership or adoption,[84] and to corporations that either they or related persons control.[85] A father, for example, is related to his daughter and his daughter's common-law partner and any corporation that the father, his daughter, or his daughter's common-law partner controls. Two corporations are related if they are controlled by the same parent corporation or if one is the parent of the other.

Unrelated parties can also be regarded as non-arm's-length parties based on the facts and circumstances of the case.[86] The criteria that courts generally use in determining whether or not a transaction is at arm's length are as follows:

1. was there a common mind that directed the bargaining for both parties to a transaction?

2. were the parties to a transaction acting in concert without separate interests? and

3. was there *de facto* control?[87]

In addition, the courts may consider whether the terms of the transactions between the parties reflect "ordinary commercial dealings", but only to "reflect on the soundness" of the conclusions after applying the three tests above.[88]

The fair market value rule applies to situations where the "transfer price" differs from the fair market value of the property, but asymmetrically to either the transferee or the transferor, not both. This is different from the gifting situation. This asymmetrical treatment can be understood as an implicit penalty for non-arm's-length transactions that deviate from the fair market value.

When a person has sold a property to a non-arm's-length purchaser at a price less than the fair market value of the property, paragraph 69(1)(b) provides that the

---

[84] *Ibid.*, s. 251(2)(a). Each of these terms is defined in s. 251(6).

[85] *Ibid.*, s. 251(2)(b).

[86] *Ibid.*, s. 251(1)(c).

[87] These tests are summarized by the CRA in Canada Revenue Agency, Folio S1-F5-C1, "Related Persons and Dealing at Arm's Length" at paras. 1.38–1.41. See, e.g., *Peter Cundhill & Associates Ltd. v. R.*, [1991] 1 C.T.C. 197, 91 D.T.C. 5085 (Fed. T.D.); affirmed [1991] 2 C.T.C. 221, 91 D.T.C. 5543 (Fed. C.A.), *Gosselin v. R.* (1996), [1997] 2 C.T.C. 2830 (T.C.C.) and *H.T. Hoy Holdings Ltd. v. R.*, [1997] 2 C.T.C. 2874, 97 D.T.C. 1180 (T.C.C.).

[88] See *R. v. Remai Estate* (2009), [2010] 2 C.T.C. 120, 2009 D.T.C. 5188 (Eng.) (F.C.A.) at para. 34; and *Petro-Canada v. R.*, [2004] 3 C.T.C. 156, 2004 D.T.C. 6329 (F.C.A.); leave to appeal refused 2004 CarswellNat 4108, 2004 CarswellNat 4109 (S.C.C.) at para. 55 [(F.C.A.))]. In *Remai*, the Federal Court of Appeal rejected the argument that the "ordinary commercial dealings" test was in addition to the three other tests. The rationale is that arm's-length parties may not always have ordinary commercial terms in their dealings.

transferor is deemed to have received proceeds of disposition equal to the fair market value. There is no corresponding step-up in the cost base of the property to the transferee. The cost of the property to the transferee is determined by the general rules, and is the price paid.

Example:

> Father owned a piece of land that he acquired at a cost of $80,000. In Year 1, he sold the land to Daughter for $100,000 while the fair market value was $120,000. Daughter then sold the property in Year 2 for $130,000. Under subparagraph 69(1)(b)(i), Father is deemed to have received proceeds of disposition equal to $120,000 and a capital gain of $40,000 ($120,000 - $80,000), but Daughter has acquired the property at a cost of $100,000 because section 69 provides no corresponding adjustment to her cost. In Year 2, when she sells the property for $130,000, she would have a capital gain of $30,000 ($130,000 - $100,000). When Father and Daughter are viewed together, they have a total of $70,000 capital gain ($40,000 + $30,000), while the actual gain accrued to the land is $50,000 ($130,000 - $80,000). There is double taxation of $20,000, the difference between the non-arm's-length transaction price and the fair market value at the time ($120,000 - $100,000). The $20,000 gain is taxed twice: once to Father and again to Daughter.

Now consider the opposite situation, which is not as common: the case of a non-arm's-length sale for consideration that is more than fair market value. Using the facts in the above example, except that, instead of selling the land to his daughter for $100,000, the father sold it for $125,000 (presumably to help the daughter minimize her future capital gains tax). In this case, section 69 contains no rule to lower the proceeds received to fair market value. Therefore, the father must report a gain of $45,000. At the same time, paragraph 69(1)(a) applies to deem the transferee to acquire the property at a cost equal to the fair market value rather than the amount paid. When the daughter sold the property in Year 2, she had a $10,000 gain. When the father and daughter are viewed together, they have a total of $55,000 capital gain ($45,000 + $10,000). There is double taxation of $5,000, which is the difference between the non-arm's-length transaction price and the fair market value at the time ($125,000 - $120,000). Again, this asymmetrical treatment of the transferor and transferee is the implicit penalty or deterrent in subsection 69(1).

(iv) — Cost-basis transfers

The general fair market value rule under subsection 69(1) is subject to exceptions provided by the *ITA* in specific circumstances. Instead of using fair market value, the transfer is deemed to occur at cost. These exceptions are called "rollovers". The effect of a rollover is to allow the transferee to kind of step into the shoes of the transferor in respect of the tax attribute of the property, so that any accrued gains or losses are realized when the transferee disposed of the property. The rollover provisions in the *ITA* are intended to encourage certain types of transfers for policy reasons (e.g., providing tax relief to families) or to postpone the taxation of gains when no economic realization has occurred (e.g., transfers of property to a corporation).

(A) — Rollovers for transfers to a spouse or common-law partner

Subsection 73(1) provides for a rollover when capital property is transferred *inter vivos* by a taxpayer to the taxpayer's spouse[89] or common-law partner,[90] or a trust for the benefit of the spouse or common-law partner.[91] Consider the following example.

> H transfers to S, his spouse, as a gift, a capital property with an adjusted cost base of $20 and a fair market value of $30.
>
> H is deemed to have disposed of the property for proceeds of disposition equal to his cost (i.e., $20). S is deemed to acquire the property at cost equal to H's proceeds of disposition.
>
> As a consequence of the rollover, H would have no capital gain. The accrued economic gain of $10 is deferred, but not foregone, because it was "embedded" in the property now owned by the transferee. When S sells the property in the future, say for $35, the capital gain will be $15 ($35 proceeds of disposition - $20 adjusted cost base).[92] This gain includes the amount accrued when the property is owned by H.

The subsection 73(1) rollover is not confined to gifts. It speaks of property "transferred". A sale from one spouse to another is also eligible for the rollover. In the event of marriage breakdown or divorce, transfers of property from one spouse or partner to another are eligible for the rollover. As mentioned below, taxpayers can opt out of the rollover by filing an election.

A similar rollover is available under subsection 70(6) for a capital property inherited by the spouse or common-law partner of the deceased taxpayer (or testamentary gifts). This rollover overrides subsection 70(5), which deems the transfer to take place for fair market value. Technically, subsection 70(6) deems the property to have been disposed of by the deceased immediately before death for proceeds of

---

[89] The term "spouse" is defined in subsection 252(3) of the *ITA* as including another individual who is a party to a void or voidable marriage with the particular individual. This definition is "inclusive": it extends the term "spouse" without defining it. Clearly, parties to a legally valid marriage are "spouses" for the purposes of the *ITA*, even though they are not part of the definition in subsection 252(3).

[90] The term "common-law partner" is defined in subsection 248(1) of the *ITA* to mean: "a person who cohabits at that time in a conjugal relationship with the taxpayer and (a) has so cohabited throughout the 12-month period that ends at that time, or (b) would be the parent of a child of whom the taxpayer is a parent".

[91] This rollover rule applies only to "qualifying transfers" as defined in subsection 73(1.01). A qualifying transfer is a transfer of property by an individual to the individual's spouse or common-law partner, or to a former spouse or common-law partner, in settlement of rights arising out of their marriage or common-law relationship. The rollover also applies on a transfer of property to a "spouse trust", which is a trust created by the taxpayer under which the spouse or common-law partner is the income beneficiary, and no person except the spouse is entitled to the capital of the trust during the spouse's or common-law partner's life.

[92] Because of the attribution rules that apply to spousal transfers, the $15 gain would attribute back to H, and H (not S) would report a taxable capital gain of $7.50. See Chapter 13 at heading 13.3(c) — Attribution of capital gains.

disposition equal to the cost amount of the property, and to have been acquired by the spouse or spouse trust for the same figure. This creates a rollover on death similar in design to that created for *inter vivos* dispositions by subsection 73(1).[93] The rollovers under subsections 73(1) and 70(6) are not mandatory. They can be elected out of by the taxpayer and the spouse or common-law partner. If the election is made, the fair market value principle under subsection 69(1) or 70(5) will apply. If no election is made, the rollover occurs automatically. In most cases, the transferor will prefer rollover treatment because it permits the postponement of tax on accrued capital gains. In some cases, however, it will be advantageous to elect out of the rollover in order to realize capital gains (to either offset capital losses or benefit from the lifetime capital gains exemption).[94]

(B) — Rollovers for transfers to child

Transfers to a child are not eligible for any rollover treatment, except where the transfer is a farming property, a fishing property or a woodlot.[95] The purpose of these rollovers is to facilitate the retention of these properties (and income sources) within a family by not realizing any accrued gains when parents transfer the property to their child. This rollover is not essentially different from the spousal rollover, although it includes a more complicated elective provision.

(C) — Rollovers regarding corporate transactions

On a transfer of property to a corporation in return for shares of the corporation, section 85 makes a rollover available. The idea is to eliminate any tax cost from the incorporation of a business, which obviously involves the transfer of business assets to the new corporation in return for shares of the corporation. The rollover is also available where property is transferred to an established corporation in return for shares of the corporation. To the extent that the transferor receives from the corporation non-share consideration, such as cash or a debt (non-share consideration is often called "boot"), there is a genuine realization of the property transferred, which should attract normal capital gains treatment. Section 85 accordingly regulates how much non-share consideration can be received without losing (or partially losing) the rollover. The section is hedged with other restrictions as well, and is elective. There are other corporate rollovers in addition to the section 85

---

[93] While the deferred capital gain will be attributed to the transferor in the case of *inter vivos* gifts, there is no attribution for the capital gain in the case of testamentary gifts.

[94] The lifetime capital gains exemption is discussed briefly at heading 10.5(b)(i) — Lifetime capital gains exemption, below. No capital loss can be created on an *inter vivos* transfer to a spouse of property that has declined in value; such a loss is a "superficial loss" (s. 54) and is deemed to be nil by s. 40(2)(g)(i).

[95] *ITA, supra* note 1, s. 70(9)–(11), 73(3)-(4). These rollovers to a child of the taxpayer will not be discussed in detail in this book. Capital gains on farming and fishing property are also eligible for the lifetime capital gains exemption. See heading 10.5(b)(i) — Lifetime capital gains exemption, below.

rollover: a section 85.1 share-for-share exchange (where one corporation takes over the shares of another in return for treasury shares of the acquiring corporation), corporate reorganizations and amalgamations under sections 86 and 87, and the winding-up of a corporation's wholly-owned subsidiary under subsection 88(1). All of these rollovers are automatic and are provided to remove tax impediments to changes in corporate structure that do not involve a genuine realization of capital assets. These rollovers are outside the scope of this book.[96]

(d) — Principal residence exemption

(i) — Tax subsidy to home ownership

Gains from the disposition of a "principal residence" are generally zero under the special rule in paragraph 40(2)(b). The effect is to exempt such gains from taxation in order to subsidize home ownership, hence the reference "principal residence exemption". The cost of this exemption to the federal government was projected to be approximately 6.8 billion in 2017.[97] It is one of the most significant tax expenditures in the *ITA*.

The principal residence exemption rule recognizes that "principal homes are generally purchased to provide basic shelter and not as an investment, and increases flexibility in the housing market by facilitating the movement of families from one principal residence to another in response to their changing circumstances".[98] It is widely accepted as a feature of the income tax system.[99] The principal residence exemption also promotes economic activities associated with home ownership, such as activities generated for builders, landscapers, interior decorators, furniture makers, home appliance makers, real estate agents, bankers, insurers, lawyers and so forth. Home ownership is also socially desirable and provides an important means of savings for retirement.

---

[96] For further discussion, see K.A. Siobhan Monaghan et al., *Taxation of Corporate Reorganizations*, 2nd ed. (Toronto: Carswell, 2012).

[97] Table 2-2 in Chapter 2 at heading 2.7(b)(ii) — Estimating the cost.

[98] Canada, Department of Finance, *Report on Federal Tax Expenditures: Concepts, Estimates and Evaluations 2016* (Ottawa: 2016) at 191, citing Hon. E.J. Benson, *Summary of 1971 Tax Reform Legislation* (Ottawa: Department of Finance, 1971); and Budget 1981.

[99] Even the Carter Commission was willing to allow an exemption for at least part of the capital gain on a taxpayer's home. The Commission recommended that there be an exemption of $1,000 gain per year, plus the value of improvements: *Carter Report*, *supra* note 2. The government's White Paper accepted the Carter recommendations (E.J. Benson, *Proposals for Tax Reform* (Ottawa: Queen's Printer, 1969)), but the final governmental decision was to exempt altogether (in most situations) any gain on the disposition of a taxpayer's "principal residence".

(ii) — Resident taxpayers

The principal residence exemption rule in paragraph 40(2)(b) applies only to individuals who are resident in Canada during that year,[100] and to gains on a housing unit (e.g., family home) that qualifies as a "principal residence" (see below) accrued while the taxpayer is a resident in Canada. A non-resident of Canada cannot claim this exemption. Gains accrued in a house prior to an individual becoming a Canadian resident or after an individual becoming a non-resident are not eligible. The meaning of "principal residence" is defined in section 54 and the key components are discussed below.

(iii) — "Housing unit"

A property that may be designated as a principal residence is referred to as a housing unit, a leasehold interest in a housing unit, and, in certain circumstances, shares of the capital stock of a cooperative housing corporation owned by the individual or personal trust. The housing unit can be outside Canada,[101] such as a condominium in Florida, a ski lodge in Austria, or a villa in the south of France. The *ITA* does not stipulate that the principal residence be in Canada. A taxpayer can own more than one housing unit. By using the word "principal" in "principal residence", the *ITA* contemplates ownership of multiple properties.[102]

The taxpayer must own the property in order to designate it as a principal residence. The notion of ownership is governed by private law, and includes sole ownership or joint ownership.[103]

Land subjacent to the housing unit is part of the property. Further, a portion of any immediately contiguous land that can reasonably be regarded as "contributing to the use and enjoyment of the housing unit as a residence" is also deemed to be part

---

[100] The meaning of "residence" is discussed in Chapter 3. A taxpayer who leaves his or her principal residence in Canada, rents it (making an election under subsection 45(2)), and who becomes non-resident for a period, cannot count the period of non-residence in reduction of the gain on a subsequent disposition of the house.

[101] Folio S4-F8-C1, *supra* note 66 at para. 2.74.

[102] However, a taxpayer can designate only one property as principal residence in any given year. The taxpayer is permitted to designate either the city house or the country cottage (in our example), but he or she cannot designate both in the same year.

[103] In the case of a co-ownership, each co-owner would determine his or her ability to designate his or her share of the property as a principal residence for the period of ownership, independently. A personal trust is also eligible for the principal residence exemption and recent changes were made to better align personal trust eligibility with direct ownership situations. The major change is to restrict the types of trusts able to make a principal residence designation for any taxation year after 2016 to: an alter ego trust, a spousal or common-law partner trust, a joint spousal or common-law partner trust, and certain trusts for the exclusive benefit of the settlor during the settlor's lifetime; a qualifying disability trust; and a trust for the benefit of a minor child (or children) of deceased parents, where the settlor is one of the parents.

of the property. However, if the total area of land under and around the principal residence exceeds half a hectare (which is approximately one acre), the excess is excluded unless the taxpayer establishes that it was necessary to the use and enjoyment.[104] In rural municipalities, there are often zoning restrictions that impose on residential land minimum lot sizes in excess of half a hectare. The courts have held that the existence of such a restriction is one way to establish whether the land in excess of half a hectare was "necessary" to the "use and enjoyment" of the housing unit as a residence. For example, in *R. v. Yates* (1986),[105] the taxpayer's property was 10 acres, and the minimum lot size was 10 acres at the date of purchase and 25 acres at the date of sale. The entire lot was considered part of the principal residence. In *Carlile v. R.* (1995),[106] the taxpayer owned a 33-acre property that was in excess of the 25-acre minimum lot size in effect from valuation day until the time of disposition. The majority of the Court found that the entire lot qualified as a principal residence because the local authority would not have authorized a partition resulting in one lot being less than 25 acres.[107]

(iv) — "Principal residence" designation

A housing unit is a principal residence in a particular taxation year if it is "ordinarily inhabited" in the year by the taxpayer or the taxpayer's spouse (or former spouse) or child, and it is "designated" by the taxpayer to be his or her principal residence for the year.[108] The principal residence designation is made in the income tax return for the year in which the property is disposed of.[109] A principal

---

[104] *ITA, supra* note 1, s. 54 "principal residence".

[105] *R. v. Yates* (1986), [1986] 2 C.T.C. 46, 86 D.T.C. 6296 (Fed. C.A.).

[106] *Carlile v. R.* (1995), [1995] 2 C.T.C. 273, 95 D.T.C. 5483 (Fed. C.A.); leave to appeal refused (1996), 203 N.R. 316 (note) (S.C.C.). The minority opinion was that, on the balance of probabilities, the partition would have been allowed, and that the property accordingly failed to qualify for the principal residence exemption.

[107] The CRA's view is that: "A municipal or provincial law or regulation may require, for example, a minimum lot size for a residential lot in a particular area that would be in excess of one-half hectare, or impose a severance or subdivision restriction with respect to a residential lot in a particular area restricting the lot from being one-half hectare or below. If such a law or regulation existed in any given year during which the taxpayer owned the property, the area that is in excess of one-half hectare would normally be part of the principal residence for that particular year." See Folio S4-F8-C1, *supra* note 66 at para. 2.35.

[108] *ITA, supra* note 1, s. 54 "principal residence".

[109] Regulations, *supra* note 51, reg. 2301. Form T2091 (or form T1255 in the case of a deceased individual) is required to be filed where a residence was not a principal residence for all years of ownership. If a property qualifies for designation for all years of ownership, the CRA now requires individuals to report the sale and designation of the property (but report no capital gain): in this case, the address of the property, the date of acquisition and the proceeds of disposition must be indicated and the designation is made by ticking a box on the capital gains schedule of the tax return (starting with the 2016 tax return). This administrative practice allows the CRA to better track an individual's use of the principal resi-

COMPUTATION OF GAIN OR LOSS

residence designation can be late-filed with penalties,[110] but making the principal residence designation is important because the *ITA* permits reassessment of tax on an unreported disposition of real estate for an unlimited period. This means that if the designation is not made (and cannot be late-filed), half of the entire gain may be taxable.[111]

When a taxpayer makes a principal residence designation, the taxpayer designates the property as his or her principal residence for all the years for which he or she claims the property as a principal residence. For each year, a taxpayer may designate only one property as a principal residence, even if the taxpayer owned and ordinarily inhabited more than one property.[112] A taxpayer may designate a property to be his or her principal residence for a particular year only if no other property has been designated for that year by the taxpayer or by the taxpayer's spouse (or by the taxpayer's unmarried children under 18). In essence, only one property can be designated for each family for a given year.

---

dence. See Canada Revenue Agency, News Release, "Reporting the Sale of Your Principal Residence for Individuals (Other Than Trusts)" (3 October 2016). (Before 2016, the CRA did not require any information to be reported.)

[110] After 2016, s. 220(3.21)(a.1) adds the principal residence designation to the list of designations that can be late-filed under subsection 220(3.2) with penalties of $100 per month late (to a maximum of $8,000).

[111] This is because the CRA is not obligated to accept a late-filed designation or election and, after 10 years, the CRA cannot accept a late designation under existing taxpayer relief legislation.

[112] Before 1982, it was possible for two spouses to each designate a property as his or her principal residence. In 1982, the definition of principal residence was amended to limit the designation to one property per family unit.

Whether a housing unit is "ordinarily inhabited" is determined on the basis of the facts in each case.[113] A seasonal residence may qualify.[114] As indicated earlier in this chapter, short-time occupancy seems to suffice in some cases but not others.[115] Sometimes a taxpayer will use a house property partly to earn business or property income. For example, a homeowner may use one room as a home office; or the homeowner may operate a daycare business in the home; or the homeowner may rent a room to a tenant; or the owner of a cottage (or other seasonal residence) may rent it for part of the year. The CRA takes the position[116] that the whole of the property still qualifies as ordinarily inhabited by the owner so long as 1) the income-producing use "is ancillary to the main use of the property as a residence";[117] 2) the taxpayer did not make structural changes to the property (to accommodate the income-producing use); and 3) the taxpayer does not claim capital cost allow-

---

[113] Folio S4-F8-C1, *supra* note 66 at para. 2.11 states its position on this matter as follows:

> The question of whether a housing unit is ordinarily inhabited in the year by a person (that is, the taxpayer, the taxpayer's spouse, common-law partner, former spouse, former common-law partner or child) must be resolved on the basis of the facts in each particular case. Even if a person inhabits a housing unit only for a short period of time in the year, this is sufficient for the housing unit to be considered ordinarily inhabited in the year by that person. For example, even if a person disposes of his or her residence early in the year or acquires it late in the year, the housing unit can be considered to be ordinarily inhabited in the year by that person by virtue of his or her living in it in the year before such sale or after such acquisition, as the case may be. If the main reason for owning a housing unit is to gain or produce income then that housing unit will not generally be considered to be ordinarily inhabited in the year by the taxpayer where it is only inhabited for a short period of time in the year. With regard to whether the main reason for owning a housing unit is to earn income, a person receiving only incidental rental income from a housing unit is not considered to own the property mainly for the purpose of gaining or producing income. However, if the main reason for owning a housing unit is to earn income but the housing unit is rented to the taxpayer's child who also ordinarily inhabits the housing unit in that year, the taxpayer could still designate that housing unit as the taxpayer's principal residence provided the other conditions are met.

[114] Folio S4-F8-C1, *ibid.*, uses a seasonal residence as an example of a residence qualifying as a principal residence in Example 1 of Appendix A.

[115] See *Ennist v. M.N.R.*, [1985] 2 C.T.C. 2398, 85 D.T.C. 669 (T.C.C.), where a taxpayer occupied a newly-purchased condominium for only 24 hours because he was transferred to another city: it was held that the condominium was not ordinarily inhabited, and the principal residence designation was denied. See also *Reicher, supra* note 42; *Hiwako Investments, supra* note 43; and the discussion of capital gains treatment and the principal residence at heading 10.2(c)(ii) — Intention on acquisition, above.

[116] Folio S4-F8-C1, *supra* note 66 at para. 2.58.

[117] In *Saccamono v. M.N.R.*, [1986] 2 C.T.C. 2269, 86 D.T.C. 1699 (T.C.C.), it was held that the taxpayer ordinarily inhabited the whole of a property that was 70 per cent rented to existing tenants when the taxpayer acquired it; the taxpayer, although occupying only 30 per cent of the property, intended to occupy the entire property.

ance on the property. If these conditions are not satisfied, then the portion of the house used for the income-producing purpose would be ineligible for principal residence status. The rest of the property, which is used as a residence, would be ordinarily inhabited by the owner and, therefore, eligible for principal residence status.

(v) — Amount of exempt gain

The amount of gain "exempt" from tax is determined under paragraph 40(2)(b), which is, essentially:

$$(A \times B / C)$$

where

A   is the amount that would be the taxpayer's gain therefrom for the year,

B   is one plus[118] the number of taxation years that end after the acquisition date for which the property was the taxpayer's principal residence and during which the taxpayer was resident in Canada,[119]

C   is the number of taxation years that end after the acquisition date during which the taxpayer owned the property whether jointly with another person or otherwise.

Expressed differently, the exempt gain is a portion of the total gain attributable to the property used as a principal residence.

---

[118] Effective for dispositions after October 3, 2016, the "one-plus" rule in the formula is available only where an individual was a resident of Canada in the year in which the property was acquired. This is intended to prevent a non-resident purchaser who later becomes a resident of Canada from benefiting from the one-plus rule. The one-plus rule is no doubt intended to deal with discontinuity in the purchase and sale of homes where, for some reason, as the principal residence exemption requires, a taxpayer does not live "in" a designated residence in a year but nevertheless has acquired it for this purpose and may be changing residences or engaged in preparatory activities to make a dwelling the taxpayer's home. That said, however, this algebraic formulation of the principal residence exemption, together with the absence of any requirement that the dwelling be inhabited throughout rather than merely "in" a taxation year, opens this rule to possible manipulation that, among other things, might include attempts to colour trading income (i.e., from buying, renovating and selling residential accommodation) as tax-free capital gains. A long-standing example of concern about the potential over-generosity of the rule to achieve its purpose of subsidizing home ownership (realizing that financing costs — mainly mortgage interest — are not deductible) is found in the continuing vigilance in CRA practice and judicial decisions regarding how much adjacent land on which a residence is located benefits from the exemption, and whether the exemption applies fully where a residence is used for an ulterior purpose, such as earning rental income.

[119] For the purpose of this rule, the year of purchase is counted as one because December 31 of that year ends after the acquisition date, even if that day is December 31. Similarly, the year of sale also "ends after the acquisition date" and is, thus, counted as a year.

$$\text{Exempt gain} = \text{Gain} \times \frac{1 + \text{\# of years designated as principal residence}}{\text{\# of years owned}}$$

Where the numerator exceeds[120] or equals to denominator, 100 per cent of the gain is exempt. The reason for including "one plus" in the numerator is to deal with the situation where the taxpayer is unable to designate the property as a principal residence for one of the years in which he or she owned it. This may arise where a previous principal residence was designated as his or her principal residence in the year that the property was purchased. The addition of one year to the numerator corrects this problem by bringing the fraction up to one, thereby cancelling out all of the gain.

Example

A house was purchased by T in Year 1 for $200,000. T cannot designate the house as her principal residence for Year 1 because she sold a condominium that year and designated the condominium as a principal residence. For Year 2 and Year 3, T designates the house as her principal residence. She sells the house in Year 3 for $230,000.

The gain otherwise determined on the house would be $30,000. The exemption portion will be 100 per cent as the fraction is (1+2)/3. In the absence of the one-plus rule, only 2/3 of the gain would be exempt from tax as she can designate the house as a principal residence for two years.

If a taxpayer owns more than one property that he or she ordinarily inhabits, he or she can designate one or more of them as principal residence, as long as only one property is designated for a given year.

If the use of a property is changed from personal use to an income-earning use, the change of use rules discussed earlier apply. After the change of use, the property cannot be designated as a principal residence.[121] However, the taxpayer is allowed to make an election under subsection 45(2) to "be deemed not to have begun to use the property for the purpose of gaining or producing income" so that the property can continue to be designated as a principal residence.[122] The designation as a prin-

---

[120] Because this formula includes "one plus" in the numerator, it will sometimes yield a numerator that is one more than the denominator. This does not mean that the *ITA* recognizes a "negative" gain for tax purposes. Textually, the gain is computed under s. 40(2)(b) to be the gain otherwise determined less the exempt gain, which is a proportion of the gain otherwise determined. If the fraction is more than 100 per cent, it produces the clumsy result that the amount to be deducted is larger than the gain. This will give a negative figure. However, s. 257 provides that the negative figure is to be treated as nil.

[121] *ITA, supra* note 1, s. 45(1)(a)(iv).

[122] The election will also prevent the taxpayer from claiming capital cost allowance in respect of the property, because reg. 1102(1)(c) excludes from the classes of depreciable property any property "that was not acquired by the taxpayer for the purpose of gaining or producing income".

cipal residence can continue for only four years,[123] to accommodate taxpayers who have to rent out their home while temporarily away.[124]

(e) — Special loss limitation rules

The *ITA* contains a number of "stop-loss" rules that deny a deduction for a capital loss in circumstances where, based on policy grounds, no deduction should be permitted. Several of the rules are based on the policy premise that no loss should be allowed where a disposition results in little or no change in the beneficial ownership of the disposed property.[125] The superficial loss rule discussed below is an example. Losses from disposition of personal-use property in general and listed personal property in particular are intended to limit recognition of losses attributable to personal consumption.

(i) — Superficial losses

A "superficial loss" is deemed to be nil under subparagraph 40(2)(g)(i). A superficial loss is defined in section 54 as a taxpayer's loss from the disposition of a property in any case where

(a) during the period that begins 30 days before and ends 30 days after the disposition, the taxpayer or a person affiliated with the taxpayer acquires a property (in this definition referred to as the "substituted property") that is, or is identical to, the particular property, and

(b) at the end of that period, the taxpayer or a person affiliated with the taxpayer owns or had a right to acquire the substituted property . . .[126]

"Superficiality" of the loss is tested by two factors: the period of time during which the property or its substitute is reacquired; and ownership by an affiliated person. The 30-day periods are arbitrary, intended to provide certainty. The definitions of "affiliated persons" and "persons affiliated with each other" are contained in subsection 251.1(1). The list of persons affiliated with a taxpayer includes the taxpayer, his or her spouse, and any corporation controlled by the taxpayer or his or

---

[123] The four-year period in which a principal residence designation continues to be available in respect of income-producing property is indefinitely extended by s. 54.1, which applies where a taxpayer has moved out of his or her home as the result of the relocation of the taxpayer's place of employment by his or her employer, and either 1) subsequently moves back into the house while still employed by the same employer or in the year immediately following the termination of his or her employment by that employer, or 2) dies during the term of employment by that employer. It also applies in the case of the relocation of the taxpayer's spouse or common-law partner by that individual's employer.

[124] The expiry of the four-year designation window does not cause a deemed disposition of the property. That will not occur until the s. 45(2) election is actually rescinded.

[125] E.g., losses are denied on a disposition of property to a tax-free savings account ("TFSA") and a registered retirement savings plan ("RRSP") (s. 40(2)(g)(iv)) and to a controlled corporation (ss. 40(2)(g)(i), 13(21.2), 40(3.3)).

[126] *ITA, supra* note 1, s. 554 "superficial loss".

her spouse. Therefore, if a taxpayer sells a property with accrued loss to his or her spouse, or his or her wholly-owned corporation, for fair market value, the loss will be a superficial loss.

The superficial loss rule prevents taxpayers from realizing losses for tax purposes without actually "divesting" the investments. Consider the example of T, who in the current year holds 100 shares in X Ltd. with an adjusted cost base of $1,000. The shares have declined in value by $600, but T does not want to get rid of them because he believes that the value of the shares will eventually rise again. However, he would like to recognize the accrued loss of $600 in order to offset capital gains from other dispositions. If it were not for the superficial loss rule, T could sell the shares for $400, triggering a $600 loss, and immediately buy another 100 X Ltd. shares for $400. That way, he would still have the same investment, while realizing the loss. Under the superficial loss rule, the loss is deemed to be nil.

The superficial loss rule does not deny the existence of the loss. It merely denies the recognition in the year of a technical disposition. The loss is preserved through being added to the adjusted cost base of the substituted property. In the above example, the ordinary cost base of the replaced shares is $400, which is adjusted under paragraph 53(1)(f) by adding the amount of superficial loss. So, the adjusted cost will be $1,000. If these shares are sold in the subsequent year for $300, T will have a loss of $700, $600 of which will be the superficial loss.

(ii) — Personal-use property losses

A loss from the disposition of personal-use property (other than "listed personal property") is deemed to be nil under subparagraph 40(2)(g)(iii). The decline in value of such property is normally the result of personal use or enjoyment, and, like other expenses of consumption, should not be recognized for tax purposes.[127] For example, where a taxpayer purchases a car for his or her personal use for $7,000 and sells it three years later for $4,000, the loss is deemed to be nil for tax purposes.

(iii) — Listed personal property losses

A listed personal property is a group of personal-use property that is listed in the definition of "listed personal property" in section 54. It includes: print, etching, drawing, painting, sculpture, or other similar work of art; jewellery; rare folio, rare manuscript, or rare book; stamp; or coin. Losses from disposition of these listed properties are not deemed to be nil, but their deduction is limited to gains on listed personal property.

The reason for this special treatment is that listed personal properties have some characteristics of investments. Like other investment assets, declines in their value would not normally be attributable to personal use, but to changing market condi-

---

[127] The same argument does not apply to *gains* on personal-use property: they are real additions to the owner's wealth and are, accordingly, taxed as capital gains (subject to the $1,000 rule, discussed at heading 10.4(c)(i) — De minimus rule for personal-use property, above.

tions. The *ITA* strikes a compromise between losses from normal investment property and losses from personal-use property. Current-year losses on listed personal property are deductible against same-year gains on listed personal property under paragraph 3(b). If losses on listed personal property exceed gains on listed personal property in a taxation year, the net loss is can be carried back three years and forward seven years, and deducted against gains on listed personal property in those years in accordance with the rules in subsection 41(2).

10.5 — Taxable capital gains and allowable capital losses

(a) — General inclusion rate

At present, 50 per cent of capital gains are taxable capital gains under paragraph 38(a), and 50 per cent of capital losses are allowable capital losses.

(b) — Special "exemptions" for taxable capital gains

(i) — Lifetime capital gains exemption

The so-called "lifetime capital gains exemption" is actually a deduction in computing an individual taxpayer's taxable income under section 110.6 (Division C). Because one-half of capital gains are included in income, the amount of the deduction is at one-half of the unused lifetime amount. The lifetime amount is capped for each taxpayer and the effect is to "exempt" taxable capital gains from taxation, hence the name.

When it was first introduced in 1985, the capital gains lifetime limit was $500,000 of capital gains and there were no restrictions on the types of dispositions and property it applied to (although the $500,000 limit was phased in over a number of years). After various amendments over the years, the lifetime exemption has been restricted to capital gains from the disposition of shares of small business corporation shares and investments in farming and fishing. As a result, the main purpose of the lifetime capital gains exemption is to encourage investment in small business corporations, farming and fishing, and to help owners of such businesses to save for retirement.

The current lifetime limits for these investments are as follows (in 2017). Capital gains from the disposition of "qualified small business corporation" ("QSBC") shares[128] are eligible for a lifetime limit of $835,176.[129] Capital gains from the

---

[128] A QSBC share must meet tests described in s. 110.6, which include a 24-month holding period and qualifying as a share of a "small business corporation" at the date of disposition. Note 134, *infra*, describes what is meant by "small business corporation".

[129] The lifetime amount for QSBC shares was increased to $800,000 in 2014 and indexed annually after that.

disposition of "qualified farm property"[130] and "qualified fishing property"[131] are eligible for an expanded lifetime limit of $1 million.[132]

(ii) — Charitable donations

In order to encourage charitable donations of certain properties (such as cultural property, ecologically sensitive land and securities), taxable capital gains from such donations are deemed to be nil.[133] In other words, the inclusion rate is zero. The *ITA* provides detailed rules defining the properties and charities eligible for this special treatment.

(c) — Allowable business investment losses

Allowable business investment losses ("ABILs") are a type of allowable capital loss, but are treated differently. An ABIL is one-half of the business investment loss. A "business investment loss" is defined in paragraph 39(1)(c) as a capital loss on the disposition of shares or debt of a "small business corporation".[134] An ABIL is fully deductible in the year against all other income of the taxpayer and does not have to be "matched" against taxable capital gains to be deductible.

The rationale for such preferential treatment of ABIL is to encourage investment in small business corporations that carry on a business in Canada, thereby creating jobs for Canadians and generating economic wealth. The theory is that, by making losses deductible against all types of income (not just taxable capital gains), the bias against risk-taking — which is inherent in the treatment of capital gains and capital losses — will be eliminated for investments in small business corporations. This treatment of ABILs complements the tax advantages accorded to the lifetime

---

[130] This includes real property used in the business of farming. An interest in a family farm partnership and shares in a family farm corporation are eligible for the exemption.

[131] This includes real property, fishing vessels, and eligible capital property used principally in a fishing business. An interest in a family fishing partnership and shares in a family farm corporation are also eligible for the exemption.

[132] The amount for qualified farming and fishing property was increased to $1 million effective 2015, and is currently not indexed.

[133] *ITA, supra* note 1, ss. 38(a.1), (a.2), (a.3), (a.4), 38.3, 38.4. In addition to realizing zero taxable capital gains, individuals can claim a tax credit in respect of the donation (corporations can claim a Division C deduction).

[134] A small business corporation is defined under s. 248(1) as a Canadian-controlled private corporation ("CCPC") that meets an "all or substantially all" asset test (90 per cent is the accepted standard): at least 90 per cent of its assets (on a fair market value basis) must either be used principally in an active business carried on primarily in Canada (by the corporation or a related corporation) or be shares or debt of other connected small business corporations. The term "active business" is defined in s. 125(7) and the term "connected" is defined in s. 186.

capital gains exemption for QSBC shares[135] and the section 44.1 rules that provide for a tax deferral when eligible small business corporation shares are sold and replaced with other eligible small business corporation shares.

---

[135] Since the preferential rules for ABILs and the lifetime capital gains exemption for QSBC shares both apply to investments in "small business corporations": the *ITA* contains rules that limit the use of one tax preference to the extent that the other is used. See ss. 110.6, 39(9).

11

OTHER INCOME AND DEDUCTIONS

11.1 — Legislative scheme

(a) — Technical design

(i) — Inclusions in income

The concept of income for tax purposes has been discussed in Chapter 4. One important feature of income is that it must have a source. Therefore, even if an amount increases a taxpayer's ability to pay, the amount is not income under paragraph 3(a) of the *Income Tax Act* (the "*ITA*")[1] unless it has a source.[2]

The wording in paragraph 3(a) contemplates that income from "other sources" may be taxable, and some of these "other sources" are specified by sections 56 to 59.1 in subdivision d of Division B of Part I of the *ITA*. In theory, amounts that are not specifically included in subdivision a (employment income), subdivision b (income from business or property), subdivision c (capital gains), or subdivision d (other income) are not necessarily free of tax. An amount could still be characterized as income "from a source" within the meaning of paragraph 3(a), in which case it would be taxable. However, the courts have shown no disposition to add new sources of income to those covered by subdivisions a, b, c, or d.[3] Therefore, for practical purposes, if an amount is not caught by these subdivisions, it is very likely that it is not taxable. For greater certainty, section 81 contains a list of items that are definitely not taxable.

---

[1] R.S.C. 1985 (5th Supp.), c. 1 [*ITA*].

[2] Because capital gains have not traditionally been considered to have a "source", paragraph 3(b) specifically includes taxable capital gains in computing income.

[3] *Canada v. Fries*, [1990] 2 C.T.C. 439, 90 D.T.C. 6662 (S.C.C.); and *Schwartz v. Canada*, [1996] 1 C.T.C. 303, 96 D.T.C. 6103 (S.C.C.) [*Schwartz*]. See also Chapter 4 at heading 4.3(d) — Unenumerated sources.

Subdivision d includes in income certain amounts that are collectively known as "other income". They generally fall into one of the following categories, some of which are explained in more detail later in this chapter:

1. Tax-deferred income, including pension income, income from registered retirement savings plans ("RRSPs"), and income from other deferred income plans;

2. Payments from contribution-based social insurance programs, such as workers' compensation and employment insurance;

3. Spousal and child support;

4. Employment-related payments, such as retiring allowances and death benefits (in excess of $10,000);[4]

5. Annuity payments and non-compete payments; and

6. Scholarships, bursaries and prizes for achievement (net of the exemption).

(ii) — Deductions

Another important feature of the concept of income under section 3 is that income is net of deductions. Income from each source (office, employment, business or property) under paragraph 3(a) is net of deductible expenses. Taxable capital gains under paragraph 3(b) are computed net of the adjusted cost base of the property and selling expenses. These deductions are inherently connected to the earning of income or capital gains. In addition, paragraph 3(c) recognizes additional expenses that are not otherwise deductible. Just like "other income" sources mentioned above, these "other deductions" are statutorily defined in sections 60 to 66.8 in subdivision e. Subdivision e amounts can be deducted from any of the income sources under paragraph 3(a) or taxable capital gains under paragraph 3(b).

Items deductible under subdivision e include the following: contributions to registered retirement savings plans ("RRSPs"); payments for spousal support;[5] the capital element of annuity payments;[6] and the deduction for pension income splitting.[7] They also include child care expenses and moving expenses that are not deductible in computing income from a business. As explained below, subdivision e deductions are policy-based deductions. As such, eligibility for each deduction is restricted based on defined criteria. Furthermore, in many cases, the maximum claim is limited to amounts determined based on underlying policies.

---

[4] See heading 11.5 — Employment-related payments, below.

[5] See heading 11.8 — Spousal and child support, below.

[6] *ITA, supra* note 1, s. 60(a).

[7] *Ibid.*, s. 60.03(1), discussed at heading 11.3 — Tax-assisted private pension plans, below.

(b) — Policy objectives

There are several policy justifications for the inclusions and deductions in subdivisions d and e. One is the ability to pay. In the absence of subdivision d, amounts such as retiring allowances[8] and non-competition payments,[9] which clearly increase the taxpayer's ability to pay, would be received tax-free under case law. Another main justification is the use of the *ITA* to achieve social and economic policy goals.[10] These goals typically include: stimulation or stabilization of the economy; income support for the retired, poor or disabled; assistance to families; mobility of Canadians; and equitable taxation of taxpayers. The use of the *ITA* as a policy instrument generally leads to a refinement of the "income" calculation by either allowing limited deductions that are otherwise denied under general principles of tax law, excluding amounts that are otherwise taxable,[11] or allowing the amounts to be taxed in the hands of a lower-income spouse or common-law partner.

For example, the moving expense deduction in section 62 helps increase the mobility of taxpayers. The scholarship exemption in paragraph 56(1)(n) reduces barriers to a university or college education. The child care expense deduction in section 63 helps reduce barriers to joining the workforce and to a university or college education. The tax assistance provided for retirement and other savings is designed to encourage Canadians to save for their retirement, as well as to accumulate capital for investment. The spousal support rules provide a subsidy to separated or divorced couples if the tax savings from the payer's deduction exceeds the tax cost to the payee.

11.2 — Public pensions

Paragraph 56(1)(a) includes in income receipts from two types of public pension programs: the federal *Old Age Security Act*[12] and similar provincial laws, and the Canada Pension Plan ("CPP") and provincial pension plans.

---

[8] See *The Queen v. Atkins*, [1976] C.T.C. 497, 76 D.T.C. 6258 (Fed. C.A.); affirming [1975] C.T.C. 377, 75 D.T.C. 5263 (Fed. T.D.) [*Atkins*].

[9] See *Fortino v. R.*, [2000] 1 C.T.C. 349, 2000 D.T.C. 6060 (Fed. C.A.) [*Fortino*], and *Manrell v. R.*, [2003] 3 C.T.C. 50, 2003 D.T.C. 5225 (Fed. C.A.) [*Manrell*], discussed in Chapter 4 at heading 4.3(d) — Unenumerated sources.

[10] See Chapter 2 at heading 2.7 — Tax expenditures.

[11] In addition, some policy goals are achieved through Division C deductions in computing taxable income or through the use of tax credits. Division C deductions and tax credits are covered in Chapter 12.

[12] R.S.C. 1985, c. O-9.

The Old Age Security program pays pensions, supplements and spouse's (or common-law partner's) allowances to persons who have reached the age of 65.[13] The basic pension is paid to all long-standing Canadian residents, but since 1989 it has been "clawed back" through the income tax system, so that pensioners with incomes in excess of $74,789 (in 2017) have to repay, in accordance with a statutory formula, all or part of the payments that they receive.[14]

The CPP (and its only provincial equivalent, the Quebec Pension Plan) also pays retirement benefits, generally to persons who have reached the age of 65.[15] The CPP differs from the Old Age Security program in two important respects. First, the CPP is contributory,[16] and benefits are paid only in respect of persons who have contributed to the CPP during their working years. Secondly, the CPP is not income-tested, and benefits are paid (and not clawed back) in accordance with the entitlement built up through contributions, regardless of the amount of other income received by the pensioner.

11.3 — Tax-assisted private pension plans

(a) — Types of plans

Section 56 of the *ITA* specifically includes payments out of the following plans in income: registered pension plans ("RPPs");[17] deferred profit sharing plans ("DPSPs");[18] registered retirement savings plans ("RRSPs");[19] and registered retirement income funds ("RRIFs").[20] RPPs and DPSPs are employer-sponsored plans, whereas RRSPs are established by individuals (and an RRIF is a continua-

---

[13] In its 1995 budget, the federal government proposed introducing an income-tested benefit for seniors, which would be tax-free. The "senior's benefit" was to come into effect in 2001 but this proposal was withdrawn in 1998.

[14] The amount that must be repaid (or "clawed back") is the lesser of the Old Age Security payments received and 15 per cent of the taxpayer's Division B income in excess of $74,789 for 2017 (s. 180.2). The amount of Old Age Security so repaid is deductible in computing the taxpayer's income (s. 60(w)).

[15] The CPP also pays disability pensions, death benefits, survivor benefits and reduced pensions to those under 65 years of age.

[16] Employee CPP contributions are matched by their employers. Self-employed taxpayers pay twice the amount paid by employees because their contributions are not so matched. An employee's CPP contributions are eligible for a tax credit (s. 118.7) and an employer's CPP contributions are deductible (s. 9). The regime for self-employed taxpayers mirrors this: one-half of their contributions are eligible for credit (s. 118.7) and the other half are eligible for a deduction (s. 60(e)).

[17] *ITA, supra* note 1, s. 56(1)(a)(i).

[18] *Ibid.*, s. 56(1)(i).

[19] *Ibid.*, s. 56(1)(h).

[20] *Ibid.*, s. 56(1)(t).

tion of an RRSP). They are all privately funded and privately organized plans, but receive public subsidy through tax assistance.

(b) — Tax assistance to retirement savings

The major form of tax assistance provided by these plans is tax deferral. Deferral occurs because contributions to the plan are presently deductible by the contributor and the amount contributed is not taxable until it is paid out to the taxpayer.[21] This deferral is "sweetened" by the tax exemption of investment earnings accumulated within the plan. As a result, the funds in the plans (both contributions and accumulated income) are not subject to tax until they are withdrawn. Because recognition of the income for tax purposes is deferred until the benefits are withdrawn from the plans (normally at retirement), the plans are often called "deferred income plans".

In addition to tax deferral, taxpayers receive tax savings if they are taxed at a lower marginal rate when funds are withdrawn from the plan, as is often the case after retirement. The first $2,000 of pension income is effectively tax-free because of the $2,000 pension credit. Further tax savings are available if pensioners split their pension income with a spouse or common-law partner who is taxed at a lower rate and is not otherwise able to use his or her pension credit. It is also possible to do this at the contribution stage under the spousal RRSP program. Under this program, a taxpayer can contribute to the RRSP of his or her spouse or common-law partner.[22] When withdrawals are made, the withdrawals are taxed in the hands of the spouse or common-law partner, except to the extent of contributions made to the plan in the year of withdrawal or the previous two years. Income splitting is also possible when pension payments are received. Under subsection 60.03(1), a pensioner can split up to 50 per cent of his or her pension income with a spouse or common-law partner for tax purposes.[23]

(i) — Benefit of tax deferral

The benefit of tax deferral occurs because of the time value of money. By deferring taxes, tax-assisted retirement savings plans allow taxpayers to invest before-tax dollars and reinvest a before-tax return, which enables them to accumulate more retirement savings than under regular methods. The amount of income that can be accumulated under such plans is, therefore, far greater than could be earned by investing after-tax dollars in an investment vehicle that was not sheltered from tax.

---

[21] As discussed in Chapter 5, s. 6(1)(a) exempts employer RPP and DPSP contributions from inclusion in employment income, and s. 8(1)(m) provides a deduction in computing employment income for employee RPP contributions. Subdivision b of the *ITA* allows an employee to deduct RPP and DPSP contributions unless they exceed the limits specified in ss. 20(1)(q) and (y), respectively.

[22] The term "common-law partner" is defined in s. 248(1) to include both common-law spouses and same-sex partners.

[23] The amount elected is included in the pension transferee's income under s. 56(1)(a.2), and deducted from the pensioner's income under s. 60(c).

Compare the situation of two taxpayers: Taxpayer A, who saves for retirement using an RRSP or RPP, and Taxpayer B, who saves for retirement outside an RRSP or RPP. Assume that they are both subject to tax at a combined federal provincial rate of 40 per cent, they can both save only $8,000 of their pre-tax salary income each year, and they can earn an annual pre-tax return of 10 per cent on their investments. At the end of 10 years, Taxpayer A would accumulate $127,496 before taxes ($8,000 × a future value factor of 15.937) whereas Taxpayer B could accumulate only $63,269 ($4,800 × 13.181). Taxpayer B's accumulation is much lower for two reasons: first, because only the after-tax amount of $4,800 ($8,000 × (1 - 40%)) could be saved each year, and, second, because the annual income earned on the investment would be only 6 per cent after taxes (10% × (1 - 40%)). Even if Taxpayer A is subject to tax at 40 per cent when she withdraws the funds from her RRSP or RPP at the end of the tenth year, she will have $76,498 ($127,496 × 60%) rather than $63,269, an increase of over $13,000 in 10 years.

The above analysis assumes that the income earned by Taxpayer B outside the RPP or RRSP is ordinary income (e.g., interest), which is taxed at full rates. The income could also be a dividend or a capital gain, both of which are taxed at preferential rates. (In reality, the income might be a mixture of the three.) Let's compare the situations of Taxpayer A and B, assuming that the amount invested earns capital gains rather than ordinary income. In this case, Taxpayer A's accumulation would be the same as before (because RRSP and RPP withdrawals are taxed as ordinary income) but Taxpayer B's accumulation would be different because the $4,800 saved each year would earn 8 per cent after taxes (rather than 6 per cent) because the effective tax rate on a capital gain is 20 per cent (1/2 × 40%). At the end of 10 years, Taxpayer B would have accumulated $69,538 ($4,800 × 14.487), which is almost $7,000 less than the $76,498 ($127,496 × 60%) that Taxpayer A will have when she withdraws the funds out of her RRSP or RPP and pays the tax. This analysis assumes that the capital gain is realized and taxed each year. If the capital gain is not realized until the end of 10 years, Taxpayer B's accumulation would initially be $76,498 before taxes ($4,800 × 15.937, because the 10% capital gain is accruing annually) but would be reduced to $70,798 after taxes (because it is taxed at the end of 10 years and the tax on the capital gain is $5,700: 20% of the $28,498 capital gain ($76,498 - (10 × $4,800 invested)). As can be seen, the tax deferral advantage is not so great with respect to income that receives preferential treatment under the *ITA*. But note, as well, that Taxpayer B's pre-tax return in this last example is the same as Taxpayer A's after-tax return from an RRSP or RPP: the amounts are both $76,498. It is the taxes of $5,700 that Taxpayer B pays at the end in this last example that make the difference! If Taxpayer B had used a tax-free savings account ("TFSA") for his annual $4,800 savings, there would have been no $5,700 tax on the investment returns and the after-tax accumulation would have been the same.[24]

---

[24] These same annual pre-tax savings ($8,000) and returns (10 per cent) are used in additional examples at heading 11.4(a) — Tax-free savings accounts (TFSAs), below. These additional examples show that accumulations under TFSAs and RRSPs will only be the same if

(ii) — Policy implications

Regarded as tax expenditures,[25] one might well question the distributional effects of the measures providing tax assistance to retirement savings vehicles. Like all deductions, these measures deliver a larger benefit to those with high incomes than to those with low incomes. Indeed, private saving for retirement is simply beyond the capacity of those whose incomes barely provide the necessities of life. A case can be made for the proposition that tax assistance for private saving should be reduced or eliminated, and the revenue saved should be directed to the enrichment of the public pensions provided by the (underfunded) CPP[26] and the (unfunded) Old Age Security program.[27] However, in view of the current desire for tax cuts (rather than increases), the steadily aging population of Canada, and other government priorities (like health care and reducing the deficit), it is obvious that private saving will continue to be the major source of retirement income for most people.[28] Measures to encourage taxpayers and their employers to make private provision for retirement during their working years, and thereby relieve the public purse from full responsibility, are easy to justify on these pragmatic grounds.

It is also possible to contest the view that tax assistance for private saving for retirement is a tax expenditure, that is, a "social program delivered through the tax sys-

---

the taxpayer's marginal rate is the same (e.g., 40 per cent) at the time of contribution and the time of withdrawal.

[25] The Ontario Fair Tax Commission described tax assistance for private retirement savings as "the biggest tax expenditure in the personal income tax system and, arguably, the most important social program delivered through the tax system": *Fair Taxation in a Changing World: Report of the Ontario Fair Tax Commission* (Toronto: University of Toronto Press, 1993) [*Fair Taxation*] at 327. The tax expenditures associated with RPPs and RRSPs (the net effect of contributions, withdrawals and the non-taxation of investment income as it accrues in the plans) "have dominated the value of tax expenditures over the period, contributing a combined 30 per cent on average of the total value of tax expenditures for years between 1991 and 2015": Canada, Department of Finance, *Report on Federal Tax Expenditures: Concepts, Estimates and Evaluations 2017* (Ottawa: 2017) [*2017 Tax Expenditures Report*] Part 4, Tax Evaluations and Research Reports, online: <https://www.fin.gc.ca/taxexp-depfisc/2017/taxexp17-eng.asp>. The net tax expenditures for 2017 were recently projected to be $26,220 million for RPPs and $16,275 million for RRSPs: *2017 Tax Expenditures Report* (*ibid.*) Part 2, Estimates and Projections (Table).

[26] The CPP will be enhanced in 2019: <https://www.canada.ca/en/services/benefits/publicpensions/cpp/cpp-enhancement.html>.

[27] The Ontario Fair Tax Commission recommended that the upper limits for the deductions for contributions to RPPs and RRSPs be reduced, and that the deductions be converted to credits: *Fair Taxation, supra* note 25 at 327–333. This has not happened.

[28] Measures recently enacted to enhance private savings include the introduction of tax-free savings accounts ("TFSAs") (in 1999) and the enactment of the *Pooled Registered Pension Plans Act*, S.C. 2012, c. 16 (in 2012). Tax-free savings accounts are discussed at heading 11.4(a), below.

tem".[29] It could be argued that, in calculating the amount of income earned each year by an individual for tax purposes, it is appropriate to set aside a portion of the income to provide for the individual's retirement. The analogy is that of the business proprietor, who sets aside a portion of the business income (depreciation charges or capital cost allowance) to allow for the wearing out of the capital assets employed in the business. It is arguable that an individual whose income is derived from his or her own effort should be permitted to make provision for the wearing out of his or her human capital — v the decline in ability and energy that will inevitably come with old age. On this basis, the provisions in the *ITA* for retirement saving are not so much a social program as tax measures to spread individual earned income over a longer period and, thereby, better measure income for tax purposes on an annual basis.[30]

(iii) — Design objectives

The ultimate purpose of the tax-assisted pension regimes is, obviously, to encourage savings for retirement. Related to this are three design objectives. The first objective is to permit individuals to have an equal amount of tax assistance irrespective of the form of retirement plan utilized. The second objective is to provide taxpayers with flexibility as to the timing of contributions to retirement plans. The third design objective (and, arguably, the most mechanical of the three) is to design a system that will allow taxpayers to achieve a targeted level of retirement income on a tax-assisted basis by setting appropriate contribution limits.

The first objective was met by integrating the contribution limits for the various types of tax-assisted retirement savings plans. Prior to 1991,[31] taxpayers who were members of the most generous defined benefit RPPs had a considerable advantage over other taxpayers. Pension reform attempted to put all types of tax-assisted retirement savings plans on equal footing. Contribution limits were adjusted so that the amounts that a member of defined benefit RPPs could save on a tax-assisted basis was no more than a taxpayer could save using a combination of a defined contribution RPP, DPSP and/or RRSP. All these measures resulted in increases in

---

[29] *Fair Taxation, supra* note 25 at 323–333.

[30] Another way of looking at it is to view the retirement savings provisions as a way of converting the income tax system into "a modified form of expenditure tax" or a "consumption tax". The provisions do this by exempting savings from tax and taxing them only on withdrawal. This was how the Carter Commission viewed these provisions: Canada, *Report of the Royal Commission on Taxation* (Ottawa: Queen's Printer, 1966) (Chairman: Kenneth Le M. Carter) [*Carter Report*], vol. 3 at 411–412.

[31] The tax reform of 1988, which made a number of fundamental changes to the tax system, also included proposals for reform of the tax-assisted pension regime: Canada, Department of Finance, *Improved Pensions for Canadians: Securing Economic Renewal* (Ottawa: Department of Finance, 1985). The pension reform proposals were originally to be enacted in 1986 at the same time as the rest of the measures of the Tax Reform of 1986 (which were actually enacted in 1988). However, because of various implementation issues, the pension reform proposals did not become law until January 1, 1991.

the tax-deductible contribution limits for defined contribution RPPs, RRSPs and DPSPs in 1991.

The second objective (flexibility) is met by allowing taxpayers to carry forward their unused RRSP contributions and permitting temporary tax-free RRSP withdrawals to purchase a home or invest in higher education.

The third design objective (tax assistance for a targeted level of retirement income) is met as follows. The current system is based on the premise that the maximum tax-assisted pension benefit should be 2 per cent per year of the average Canadian's best three years of earnings multiplied by his or her number of years of service (to a maximum of 35 years). To fund this maximum pension benefit, the maximum benefit to be accrued each year is based on the average industrial wage.[32]

The system also assumes that it takes $9 today to buy a $1 pension benefit, and this assumption creates the link between defined benefit pension plans and money purchase plans. Because of this assumption, the maximum limit for contributions to a money purchase RPP is always 9 times the maximum benefit accrual for the year. In 2017, for example, the maximum limit for contributions to a money purchase RPP is $26,230 and the maximum benefit accrual for defined benefit plans is $2,914.44 (1/9 × $26,230).[33] Only employers contribute to deferred profit sharing plans ("DPSPs"), so the maximum contribution limit for a DPSP is one-half of the RPP money purchase limit for the year, that is, $13,135 in 2017 (1/2 × $26,230). Since the maximum pension to be accrued annually is 2 per cent of earnings, it follows that another limit for RPPs and DPSPs is 18 per cent of the employee's earnings.

As mentioned earlier, RPP, DPSP and RRSP contribution limits are integrated: contributions made to one plan will reduce contributions that can be made to another plan. To make things easier for taxpayers, the system is designed so that the Canada Revenue Agency (the "CRA") calculates RRSP contribution limits for taxpayers based on contributions made to RPPs and DPSPs for the immediately preceding year (as reflected in the taxpayer's "pension adjustment") and the taxpayer's earned income in that previous year. The reason for the one-year lag is to allow the employer time to report the information to the CRA and to allow the CRA time to report the calculation to the taxpayer.[34] Because of this one-year lag, it follows,

---

[32] The maximum benefit accruals and money purchase limits for RPPs have each been indexed by the average industrial wage since 2010. See, e.g., the reference to "average wage" in the definition of the RPP "money purchase limit" in s. 147.1(1).

[33] From 2004 to 2009, the maximum benefit accruals were legislated and the money purchase limit was 9 times the maximum benefit accrual in the year. For over a decade before 2004, the maximum benefit accrual was fixed at $1,722.22. ($1,722.22 × 35 equals $60,278, which was two and one-half times the average industrial wage in the year that the amounts were originally determined. The current and historical amounts are set out on the CRA's website at <http://www.cra-arc.gc.ca/tx/rgstrd/papspapar-fefespfer/lmts-eng.html>.

[34] The CRA also provides a taxpayer's RRSP contribution limit in its "My Account" system. See <http://www.cra-arc.gc.ca/myaccount/>.

therefore, that the maximum RRSP limit is always equal to the money purchase RPP limit for the immediately preceding year. In other words, the maximum RRSP limit is $26,010 for 2017 and $26,230 for 2018.[35] It also follows that another RRSP limit is 18 per cent of the previous year's "earned income".[36]

The above discussion tells us where the numbers that the system uses for RRSPs come from. Here is how the system works for 2017.

1. Employers report a taxpayer's "pension adjustment" (defined below) for the 2016 year (the previous year) in respect of RPP and DPSP plans on the taxpayer's 2016 T4 slip in February 2017.

2. The 2016 pension adjustment is reported (but not included in income) on the taxpayer's 2016 tax return, which is due on April 30 or June 15, 2017.

3. The CRA uses the 2016 "pension adjustment" and other information reported in the taxpayer's return to calculate the taxpayer's maximum deductible RRSP contribution for 2016 and reports the amount to the taxpayer on a 2016 notice of assessment (which would normally be received within a few weeks or months of filing the 2016 return).

The terms "earned income" and "pension adjustment" ("PA") are defined later in this chapter, but it is important, at this point, to note that the purpose of the PA is to integrate tax-assisted retirement savings through the various plans. The contribution limits for RPPs, DPSPs and RRSPs are set (based on the numbers above) so that the amount that an individual who is a member of an RPP and/or DPSP can save on a tax-assisted basis is (theoretically) no greater or less than if he or she was not a member of a DPSP or RPP and could only save using an RRSP. It is the PA that ties these three systems together: the PA reflects an estimate of a taxpayer's tax-assisted retirement savings for the year using an RPP or DPSP and is deducted from the taxpayer's RRSP contribution limit for the following year. For example, if a taxpayer's 2017 RRSP contribution limit before PA was $26,010 (the maximum limit) and his or her 2017 PA (in respect of contributions to an RPP and a DPSP in that year) was $10,000, he or she could only contribute $16,010 to an RRSP in 2017.

(c) — Employer-sponsored plans

(i) — Registered pension plans (RPPs)

Registered pension plans ("RPPs") are private employer-sponsored retirement savings plans that are regulated by the CRA and by provincial pension benefit legislation, and were first introduced into the income tax legislation in 1919. Normally, both the employer and the employee contribute to an RPP, although "non-contributory" plans (to which only the employer contributes) also exist.

---

[35] The limit for 2018 is known at the time of writing (2017) because it is the 2017 RPP money purchase limit.

[36] *ITA, supra* note 1, s. 60(i).

An RPP enjoys special status under the *ITA*: contributions to an RPP by employers and employees are tax-deductible;[37] contributions by employers are not taxed to the employees as benefits from employment (subparagraph 6(1)(a)(i)); and the investment income earned by the plan is not subject to tax (paragraph 149(1)(o)). The funds accumulated and invested in an RPP on a tax-free basis only begin to be taxed when a taxpayer withdraws amounts from the plan (subparagraph 56(1)(a)(i)). In most cases, this occurs on retirement, when the taxpayer receives his or her pension income in the form of a monthly life annuity.[38] The first $2,000 of pension annuity income received from an RPP is eligible for the 15 per cent pension income credit.[39]

There are two types of RPPs: "defined benefit" plans and "defined contribution" plans (sometimes called "money purchase" plans). Some plans are a combination of these two types. In a defined benefit plan, the employer agrees to provide a "defined benefit" at retirement; the defined benefit is usually expressed as a percentage of the employee's earnings for each year of service. The earnings figure used is usually an average of earnings in the last years of service, such as the average earnings in the last three years of service. For example, if the employer agreed to provide a defined benefit of 2 per cent of earnings per year of service, and an employee had average annual earnings of $50,000 and 20 years of service, the employee's pension benefit would be $20,000. The amount required to be contributed to the plan to fund this defined benefit would be determined by an actuary, who would take into consideration such factors as the income expected to be earned on plan investments as well as employee turnover and mortality rates. The plan document would specify how the amount required to fund the defined benefit would be split between the employer and the employee. In a defined contribution (or money purchase) plan, the employer agrees to make "defined contributions" to the plan on behalf of each employee. For example, the employer might agree to contribute a certain percentage of an employee's wages or a fixed-dollar amount (the employee would usually also contribute a defined amount). In a defined contribution plan, there is no agreement or guarantee as to the amount of pension benefit that the employee will eventually receive (as is the case in a defined benefit plan); the amount of pension benefit is simply the pension annuity that can be purchased with the employee's share of the fund that has accumulated by the time of the employee's retirement. This will depend on the level of employer and employee contributions, the investment income earned on those contributions over the years to retirement, and the interest rates at the time of purchase of the pension annuity.

---

[37] *Ibid.*, s. 8(1)(m) allows an employee a deduction for his or her contribution (within limits), and s. 20(1)(q) allows an employer a deduction for his or her contribution in respect of an employee.

[38] Under most provincial pension benefit legislation, an RPP becomes vested after two years of service. Once an RPP is vested, benefits cannot be received except in the form of a life annuity on retirement.

[39] *ITA*, *supra* note 1, s. 118(3).

If an employee changes jobs, the funds to which the employee is entitled in the former employer's pension plan can be transferred directly to the new employer's pension plan (or an RRSP) on a tax-free basis.[40]

(ii) — Deferred profit sharing plans (DPSPs)

Deferred profit sharing plans ("DPSPs") are private employer-sponsored profit sharing plans. They were first introduced into the *ITA* in 1961. The *ITA* sets maximum limits on contributions by an employer and does not allow an employee to contribute. The contributions by an employer to a DPSP are not fixed like contributions to a defined contribution RPP, but fluctuate according to the employer's profitability. However, a DPSP is similar to a defined contribution (or money purchase) RPP in that the pension benefit consists simply of what can be purchased with the accumulated fund at the time of retirement or withdrawal of benefits.

The tax regime for DPSP contributions is similar to the regime for RPP contributions. Contributions by an employer to a DPSP within the limits of the *ITA* are tax-deductible to the employer (subsection 147(8)) and are not included in the employee's income as a benefit from employment. As well, the investment income earned by the plan is not subject to tax. Withdrawals from a DPSP may be made at any time (subject to any restrictions set out in the plan agreement), and when they are made, they are included in income (paragraph 56(1)(i)).

(d) — Registered retirement savings plans (RRSPs)

(i) — Definition of RRSP

Registered retirement savings plans ("RRSPs") are private retirement savings plans that can be established by individuals for their own retirement. They were first introduced into the *ITA* in 1957 to help those individuals who were not members of company pension plans. As will be explained in more detail, the *ITA* sets limits on contributions, and allows a deduction for contributions. The investment income earned by the plan is not subject to tax.

An RRSP is like a defined contribution (money purchase) RPP in that the amount of the pension annuity is not defined, but depends upon what can be purchased at the time of retirement.[41] Unlike a defined contribution RPP, however, no minimum annual contributions need be made to an RRSP. Withdrawals from an RRSP may

---

[40] These and other direct transfers of tax-assisted retirement savings are discussed at heading 11.3(e) — Direct transfers to RPPs, RRSPs and DPSPs, below.

[41] RRSPs are purchased from banks and other financial institutions. The investment can take the form of a special savings account, a term deposit or a mutual fund, or the RRSP can be self-administered, in which case it can invest in a variety of items. Investments in an RRSP are subject to restrictions: there are restrictions on the amount of investments in real estate and shares of private corporations. Service charges and investment management fees relating to RRSPs are not tax-deductible (s. 18(1)(u)).

be made at any time, and, when they are made, they are included in income.[42] The RRSP differs from the RPP and the DPSP in that only the RRSP can be established by an individual, and only that individual (or his or her spouse or common-law partner) can make contributions to the RRSP. RPPs and DPSPs, on the other hand, must be sponsored by an employer, and the employer must make contributions for the employees who are members of the plan.

As mentioned previously, RRSPs are more flexible than RPPs. While the funds in an RPP are generally locked in, as discussed below, a taxpayer is able to make temporary use of RRSP funds to buy a home or go to college or university under the rules for the RRSP Home Buyers' Plan or the RRSP Lifelong Learning Plan, respectively.

(ii) — Contributions based on earned income

If a taxpayer is not a member of an RPP or DPSP and has always contributed the maximum tax-deductible RRSP contributions[43] in previous years, his or her RRSP contribution limit is the lesser of 18 per cent of the previous year's earned income and the maximum contribution limit for the year (e.g., $26,010 in 2017).[44] In order to claim a deduction, the amount must be contributed in the year or within 60 days of the following year[45] to either the taxpayer's RRSP and/or the RRSP of the taxpayer's spouse or common-law partner.[46] (However, there is no doubling up of the taxpayer's contribution limit: the taxpayer can use this limit for his or her own RRSP or a spousal RRSP.)

Earned income is defined in subsection 146(1) of the *ITA*.[47] Its principal components are employment income, business income, and CPP, disability and spousal support payments received. Property income is not included, except for real estate rental income and certain royalty income. Business and real estate rental losses and

---

[42] *ITA, supra* note 1, s. 56(1)(h).

[43] *Ibid.*, s. 146(5) allows an individual a deduction for contributions to an RRSP (within limits). Paragraphs. 20(1)(q) and 20(1)(y) allow an employer a deduction for contributions to an RPP and DPSP, respectively (within limits). Paragraph 8(1)(m) allows an employee a deduction for his or her contribution to an RPP (within limits). Contributions in excess of these limits may deregister the plan (which will cause the funds accumulated in the plan to be immediately taxable). Subparagraph 6(1)(a)(i) states that an employer's contribution to an RPP or DPSP is not a taxable benefit.

[44] See note 35, *supra*, and accompanying text.

[45] In the case of a year that is a leap year, 60 days after the end of the year is February 29; otherwise it falls on March 1. If any deadline occurs on a weekend, the deadline is extended to the next business day: *Interpretation Act*, R.S.C. 1985, c. I-21, s. 26.

[46] *ITA, supra* note 1, s. 146(5), (5.1).

[47] The definition of "earned income" in s. 146(1) is different from the definition of "earned income" for child care expense purposes (s. 63(3)).

spousal support payments made are deducted in arriving at the net figure of earned income.[48]

These rules are best illustrated by way of an example. Assume that a taxpayer who is not a member of an RPP or DPSP earned a $50,000 salary in 2016 and paid $20,000 of deductible spousal support in that year. His 2017 RRSP contribution limit would be $5,400, which is the lesser of 18 per cent of his $30,000 earned income in 2016 (18% × [$50,000 - $20,000] = $5,400) and $26,010. If he contributed only $4,000 to his RRSP (or his spouse's RRSP) by the March 1, 2018 deadline, he would be able to carry forward his undeducted RRSP contribution room of $1,400 ($5,400 - $4,000). If, in this example, the taxpayer had not made his maximum tax-deductible RRSP contributions in previous years, the amount of his maximum deductible 2017 RRSP contribution would be increased by this so-called "undeducted RRSP contribution room".[49]

If a taxpayer is a member of an RPP or DPSP, the formula becomes more complicated. In that case, the concept of the "pension adjustment" ("PA") is used to reduce the taxpayer's RRSP contribution limits for a particular year. Omitting complications, a taxpayer's PA consists of 1) the amount of the contributions (by the employer as well as the employee) to a defined contribution RPP, plus 2) a figure derived from the benefit accrued under a defined benefit RPP, plus 3) the amount of the contributions (by the employer) to a DPSP. As explained earlier, the PA will prevent a taxpayer from achieving extra tax assistance through membership in an RPP or DPSP as well as an RRSP.

The rules we have discussed so far are in respect of the regular RRSP contributions based on earned income. In addition to making RRSP contributions based on "earned income", a taxpayer can also make contributions in respect of a retiring allowance[50] received on the termination of employment, or a "refund of premiums"[51] received on the death of a spouse or parent. RRSP contributions are commonly made in cash, but can be made using investments if a taxpayer has a self-administered RRSP. If an investment is transferred to an RRSP, the amount of the

---

[48] Child support payments paid under agreements made or varied after April 30, 1997 (or elected upon) are not taxable to the recipient or deductible to the payer and, therefore, are not relevant to the earned income calculation. The tax treatment of spousal and child support payments is discussed at heading 11.8 — Spousal and child support, below.

[49] Using the above example, but assuming that the taxpayer had undeducted RRSP contribution room from 2016 of $2,000, results in a maximum tax-deductible 2017 RRSP contribution limit of $7,400 ($5,400 from above plus $2,000). If the taxpayer still only contributes $4,000 to his RRSP for 2017, he will have a $3,400 undeducted contribution room to carry forward to future years. See the definition of unused contribution room in s. 146(1). Individuals who terminate employment after 1996 will also have added to their unused contribution room a pension adjustment reversal ("PAR"), equal to the excess of the PAs reported over the years (from their former employer's RPP or DPSP) over the termination benefit actually received.

[50] *ITA, supra* note 1, s. 60(j.1), discussed at heading 11.5(a) — Retiring allowance, below.

[51] *Ibid.* at s. 60(l), discussed at heading 11.3(d)(vi) — Tax consequences on death, below.

contribution is the fair market value of the investment, and there is a deemed disposition under section 69 at the fair market value of the investment. Accordingly, if the investment is a Canada Savings Bond or other interest-bearing security, accrued interest to the date of transfer (which has not been previously included in the taxpayer's income) must be recognized in the year of the transfer. If the investment consists of stocks or bonds that have appreciated in value, a capital gain will have to be recognized on the transfer. If the investment has gone down in value, however, the capital loss is denied.[52]

(iii) — Withdrawals

Withdrawals from a taxpayer's RRSP are generally included in the taxpayer's income in the year of withdrawal. Tax is withheld on the withdrawal,[53] and additional tax may be owing when the taxpayer's return is filed.

If a taxpayer makes a withdrawal from his or her RRSP (or receives RRSP annuity payments), and his or her spouse or common-law partner has made a contribution to the RRSP in the year of the withdrawal or the previous two years, the withdrawal will be included in the income of the spouse or common-law partner to the extent of the contributions made by this person within this period of time. For example, if a husband made a $5,000 withdrawal from his RRSP in 2017 and his wife had made contributions of $1,000 to any of her husband's RRSPs in each of the years 2015, 2016, and 2017, $3,000 would be taxed in the wife's hands (that is, the $1,000 contributed in the year of withdrawal and the previous two years) and $2,000 ($5,000 - $3,000) would be taxed in the husband's hands. This "attribution" rule limits the amount of income splitting that can be done with spousal RRSPs.[54] In order to avoid this attribution rule, the contributing spouse must stop contributing to the RRSP for three years before any withdrawal is made.

There are two exceptions to the general rule that withdrawals are included in income: the Home Buyers' Plan and the Lifelong Learning Plan. The Home Buyers' Plan assists a taxpayer to buy a home by allowing the taxpayer to withdraw up to $25,000 from his or her RRSP for this purpose without any tax.[55] Any money so withdrawn must be repaid to the RRSP in stipulated annual instalments over 15 years. In order to be considered a home buyer, neither the taxpayer nor the taxpayer's spouse or common-law partner must have owned a home in any of the five years before the year of withdrawal, and they must have repaid any previously

---

[52] *Ibid.*, s. 40(2)(g)(iv).

[53] *Income Tax Regulations*, C.R.C., c. 945 [Regulations], reg. 103. The withholding tax is lowest (10 per cent) if amounts of $5,000 or less are withdrawn at a time.

[54] If a taxpayer's RRSP is converted to a registered retirement income fund ("RRIF") (discussed at heading 11.3(d)(v), below), any RRIF payment in excess of the minimum payment amount will be included in his or her spouse's income to the extent of spousal contributions made in the year of payment or the previous two years (s. 146.3(5.1)).

[55] *ITA, supra* note 1, s. 146.01.

withdrawn amounts.[56] Contributions to an RRSP that are withdrawn under the Home Buyers' Plan within 90 days are not deductible.

The Lifelong Learning Plan operates in a manner very similar to the Home Buyers' Plan. It allows tax-free withdrawals from the RRSP of an individual, or that of his or her spouse or common-law partner, in order to finance the individual's education. Up to $20,000 can be withdrawn from RRSPs over a period of up to four years, with a maximum withdrawal in any particular year of $10,000.[57] The amounts withdrawn must be repaid to the RRSP over a 10-year period starting no later than five years after the first RRSP withdrawal. The repayment period begins earlier where the student has been out of a qualifying educational program for two consecutive years.

(iv) — RRSP annuities

If a taxpayer owns an RRSP at the end of the year in which he or she turns 71,[58] then the total value of the RRSP is included in his or her income for the year. In order to prevent this, a taxpayer must purchase either an RRSP annuity or a registered retirement income fund ("RRIF") (or a combination of the two) with the funds in the RRSP before the end of the year the taxpayer turns 71. The funds in the RRSP are transferred directly to the RRSP annuity or RRIF on a tax-free basis.[59]

RRSP annuities can be life annuities or term annuities. Life annuities may have a guaranteed term and may have joint and last survivor benefits. Term annuities must provide benefits up to age 90. If the taxpayer's spouse is younger than the taxpayer, the taxpayer may elect to have the term annuity pay benefits until the spouse reaches age 90.

(v) — Registered retirement income funds (RRIFs)

A registered retirement income fund ("RRIF") is, as has just been explained, an alternative to the RRSP annuity as the vehicle by which the RRSP pension is delivered. An RRIF is basically an extension of an RRSP and can be self-administered.[60] RRIFs pay out a minimum amount that increases each year based on a formula, but the taxpayer may withdraw any amount in excess of this minimum amount. The major differences between an RRSP annuity and an RRIF are as fol-

---

[56] Withdrawals from an RRSP made in order to purchase more suitable housing for an individual entitled to the disability tax credit available under s. 118.3(1) are not subject to the requirement that a home has not been owned with the last five years, and the withdrawals can be made by individuals related to the disabled person (s. 146.01(1)).

[57] *ITA, supra* note 1, s. 146.02(1).

[58] The age at which an individual's RPP, RRSP or DPSP is required to mature was increased from 69 to 71 effective 2007.

[59] *ITA, supra* note 1, s. 146(16).

[60] Financial institutions offering self-administered RRIFs often charge annual administration fees that are not tax-deductible (s. 18(1)(u)).

lows: 1) the RRIF provides greater tax deferral because (under the statutory formula) the RRIF payments increase over time; 2) the RRIF provides more flexibility as to investments and may be self-administered; 3) the payout under an RRIF does not depend on interest rates at the time of purchase; 4) the payout under an RRIF is more flexible, since any amount in excess of the minimum amount can be withdrawn; and 5) the payout under an RRSP annuity is guaranteed, whereas the payout under a RRIF is not.

(vi) — Tax consequences on death

The general rule is that the value of a taxpayer's RRSP, RRSP annuity or RRIF is included in the taxpayer's income in the year of death under subsection 146(8.8).[61] But if the beneficiary of the RRSP is the deceased taxpayer's spouse, the spouse will pay tax on the amounts received.[62] A rollover is available under paragraph 60(l). Any lump-sum payment received by a spouse out of a deceased taxpayer's RRSP is called a "refund of premiums", and the spouse can claim an offsetting deduction under paragraph 60(l) if the amount of the refund of premiums is contributed by the spouse to an RRSP or is used by the spouse to purchase an RRSP annuity or RRIF annuity within the year of death or within 60 days of that year. Often, because of the amount of tax that would have to be withheld on the payment of the refund of premiums to the spouse, these contributions are made by arranging for the trustee of the deceased's plan to make the transfer directly to the spouse's plan.

A similar, but more restrictive, rollover is available if the beneficiary of the deceased's RRSP is a child or grandchild who was "financially dependent" on the deceased.[63] As in the case of a refund of premiums received by a spouse, the amount included in the financially dependent child's or grandchild's hands as a refund of premiums can be offset with a deduction under paragraph 60(l) in certain circumstances. In the case of a financially dependent child or grandchild who is mentally or physically infirm, the deduction may be used for a contribution to an

---

[61] If the fair market value of the RRSP on liquidation is less than the amount included in income in the year of death, s. 146(8.92) allows the loss to be carried back to the deceased's final return. This is similar to the rule in s. 164(6) that allows a net capital loss incurred in the first taxation year of the estate to be carried back to the deceased's final return.

[62] If the spouse is not named as the beneficiary under the RRSP or RRSP annuity document, the legal representative of the deceased and the spouse can jointly elect to treat the amount as a "refund of premiums" and have the amounts taxed in the spouse's hands, so long as the spouse is entitled to at least that amount under the will (s. 146(8.1)). (It is, however, preferable to name the spouse as beneficiary under the plan in order to avoid probate fees.) In the case of an RRIF, there is no such election.

[63] According to the definition of "refund of premiums" in s. 146(1), "financially dependent" means that the child earned less than the basic personal credit amount under s. 118(1)(c) in the previous year. If the child was financially dependent because of a mental or physical infirmity, the income limit is increased (see the definition of refund of premiums in ss. 146(1) and 146(1.1)).

RRSP or a Registered Disability Savings Plan ("RDSP")[64] for the child; in the case of a financially dependent child or grandchild who is not mentally or physically infirm, the deduction is available only for the cost of the purchase of a term annuity to age 18. In the case of a child or grandchild who is 18 years of age or older and not infirm, no deduction is available.

Because a deceased's RRSP can yield a significant amount, the rules respecting a refund of premiums on death are important in estate planning. Consideration should always be given to leaving an RRSP by will to a spouse or qualifying child or grandchild so as to take advantage of the rollover. Leaving an RRSP to a qualifying child or grandchild rather than a spouse may result in future tax savings if the child is taxed at a lower rate than the spouse on payments out of the plan.

(e) — Direct transfers to RPPs, RRSPs and DPSPs

Tax-free "direct transfers" to RRSPs, RPPs and DPSPs are allowed by the *ITA*. These "direct transfers" include the following:

1. transfers from an RPP to an RPP or RRSP (subsection 147.3);

2. transfers from a DPSP to an RPP, RRSP or DPSP (subsection 147(19)); and

3. transfers from an RRSP to an RPP, RRSP or RRIF (subsection 147(16)).

The first two transfers allow a taxpayer who is terminating employment, and who is entitled to funds or benefits under the employer's RPP or DPSP, to have the funds transferred on a tax-free basis directly by the plan trustee to a new employer's plan or an RRSP.[65] The third transfer allows taxpayers with RRSPs to move their RRSPs to different financial institutions and to purchase RRSP annuities and RRIFs, all on a tax-free basis.

11.4 — Tax-assisted savings plans

(a) — Tax-free savings accounts (TFSAs)

A tax-free savings account ("TFSA") is designed to enable a taxpayer to save on a tax-free basis. TFSAs were introduced effective 2009 for Canadian residents age 18 or over, and the maximum annual contribution was $5,000 for each of the years

---

[64] The transfer of a refund of premiums to an RDSP cannot exceed the beneficiary's RDSP contribution room (lifetime maximum of $200,000) and is for deaths occurring after 2007. See heading 11.4(c) — Registered disability savings plans (RDSPs), below, for a further discussion of RDSPs.

[65] Provincial pension benefit legislation generally restricts the transfer of RPP benefits to "locked-in" RRSPs and life income funds ("LIFs", which are essentially "locked-in" RRIFs). Unlike normal RRSPs, no withdrawals can be made from a "locked-in" RRSP, and accumulated funds in a "locked-in" RRSP can only be used to purchase a life annuity (not a term annuity or RRIF). Unlike normal RRIFs, which continue to pay out benefits after age 80 (according to a formula), the funds remaining in an LIF at age 80 must be used to purchase a life annuity.

2009 to 2012, $5,500 for each of the years 2013 to 2014 and 2016 to 2017, and $10,000 for 2015. The limit increased to $5,500 in 2013 (and is still $5,500 in 2017) because contribution limits are indexed for inflation (rounded to the nearest $500). The limit was $10,000 for 2015 only because it was increased to that amount prior to a federal election, and then changed back after the election of the new government. There is an indefinite carryforward of unused TFSA contribution limit.[66] Contributions are not deductible, but income accumulates tax-free in the plan and will not be taxed when withdrawn.[67]

If a taxpayer's marginal rate is the same in the year of contribution and withdrawal, he or she will be indifferent to saving in an RRSP or TFSA. This can be illustrated by using the same example as the one used at heading 11.3(b)(i) — Benefit of tax deferral. Assume, for example, that two taxpayers are subject to tax at a combined federal provincial rate of 40 per cent, they can both save only $8,000 of their pre-tax income each year, and they can earn an annual pre-tax return of 10 per cent on their investments. The RRSP Saver saves in an RRSP and the TFSA Saver saves in a TFSA. At the end of 10 years, the RRSP Saver would accumulate $127,496 before taxes ($8,000 × a future value factor of 15.937) whereas the TFSA Saver could save and invest only $76,498 ($4,800 × 15.937). The TFSA Saver's accumu-lation is lower because only the after-tax amount of $4,800 ($8,000 × (1 - 40%)) can be saved each year. However, if the RRSP Saver is subject to tax at 40 per cent when he or she withdraws the funds at the end of the tenth year, the two taxpayers will have the same amount after taxes: $76,498 ($127,496 × 60%).

If a taxpayer's marginal rate in the year of withdrawal is projected to be higher than in the years of contribution (e.g., an individual who has just joined the workforce and expects future increases in annual earnings to push him or her into a higher tax bracket), he or she will prefer a TFSA. In the example above, if the taxpayers' marginal rate had been 25 per cent in the years of contribution and 40 per cent in the year of withdrawal, the TSFA Saver would have had a higher accumulation: this is because the RRSP Saver would still have $76,498 after the taxes (at 40 per cent) are paid on the withdrawal ($8,000 × a present value factor of 15.937 × 60%) but the TFSA Saver would have $95,622 on withdrawal ($8,000 × 15.937 × 75%), because a higher amount of $6,000 (75% of $8,000: or $8,000 × (1 - 25%) could be contributed and saved each year.

Conversely, if a taxpayer's marginal rate in the years of contribution is expected to be higher than in the year of withdrawal (e.g., on retirement), the RRSP Saver will have a higher after-tax accumulation. In the example above, if the taxpayers' mar-ginal rate is 40 per cent in the years of contribution but only 25 per cent in the year of withdrawal, the RRSP Saver will have $95,622 ($8,000 × a present value factor of 15.937 × 75%) after taxes but the TFSA Saver will only have $76,498 ($8,000 × a present value factor of 15.937 × 60%).

---

[66] *ITA, supra* note 1, s. 207.01. Like RRSPs, there is a 1 per cent per month penalty tax on overcontributions: s. 207.02.

[67] *ITA, supra* note 1, s. 146.2.

As the previous example illustrates, the after-tax accumulations of the TFSA Saver and the RRSP Saver will only be equal when the marginal rates in the year of contribution and withdrawal are equal: TFSAs offer a tax advantage to those who expect their marginal tax rate to increase in the future because of rising incomes. TFSAs offer other advantages as well. Unlike RRSPs, amounts withdrawn can be contributed back to the plan after the end of the year of withdrawal. As well, there is no spousal attribution.[68]

The tax expenditure associated with TFSAs is projected at $1,020 million for 2017.[69] While low-income taxpayers will enjoy some of this tax expenditure because TFSA withdrawals will not reduce any income-tested tax benefits or social assistance payments, it is likely that this measure will primarily benefit higher-income taxpayers.[70]

Like RRSPs, there is continued tax deferral if a TFSA is left to a spouse on death. If a spouse or common-law partner is not named as the successor on death, the TFSA will lose exempt status and any income and capital gains accrued after death will be subject to tax.[71]

(b) — Registered education savings plans (RESPs)

A registered education savings plan ("RESP") is designed to enable a taxpayer (the "subscriber") to save for the post-secondary education of a "beneficiary", who is normally, but not necessarily, the child or grandchild of the subscriber. If the beneficiary of an RESP does not attend a post-secondary institution, a substitute beneficiary can usually be named. There are two main types of RESPs: "scholarship trust" plans (which pool contributions from any subscribers) and self-administered plans (which are set up by a single subscriber). As well, "family plan" RESPs can be set up for more than one beneficiary and "joint plans" can be set up to accept contributions from more than one subscriber.

Unlike the private retirement plans discussed above, contributions to an RESP are not tax-deductible. However, like the private retirement plans, an RESP is a deferred income plan because it offers three important advantages: 1) the federal gov-

---

[68] *Ibid.*, s. 74.5(12). Like RRSPs, there is no deduction for interest on money borrowed to invest in a TFSA: s. 18(11). Unlike RRSPs, TFSAs can be used as collateral for a loan.

[69] *2017 Tax Expenditures Report, supra* note 25, Part 2, Estimates and Projections (Table), online: <https://www.fin.gc.ca/taxexp-depfisc/2017/taxexp17-eng.asp>.

[70] By 2011, TFSA participation rates for tax filers with more than $200,000 of annual income were already 58 per cent (compared to a 20 per cent participation rate for filers with less than $20,000 of annual income): see "Tax-Free Savings Accounts: A Profile of Account Holders" in Canada, Department of Finance, Tax Expenditures and Evaluations, 2012 (Ottawa: 2012) at 26, where it is also noted that: "This is consistent with the general findings on the usage of tax-assisted savings accounts in member countries of the Organisation for Economic Co-operation and Development (OECD), where participation rates generally increase with income."

[71] *ITA, supra* note 1, s. 207.02(2).

ernment provides an annual Canada education savings grant ("CESG");[72] 2) the income from investments earned within the plan is not taxed until it is distributed; and 3) when money is withdrawn from the plan and distributed to the beneficiary (who must by then be a student at a post-secondary institution), the income earned in the plan plus the amount of federal contributions are taxed as income of the beneficiary, not the subscriber. The original contributions are not taxed when they are distributed to the student because income tax has already been paid on those amounts by the contributor to the RESP.

The rules for RESPs are contained in section 146.1 of the *ITA*. There are no annual contribution limits, but the maximum CESG is paid when annual contributions are $2,500.[73] The maximum lifetime contribution limit per beneficiary is $50,000 and the maximum lifetime grant per beneficiary is $7,200.[74] Excess contributions are subject to a penalty tax of 1 per cent per month (12 per cent per year). Income earned within an RESP can accumulate on a tax-free basis for up to 25 years, but after that time the plan is deregistered.

For many years, the major disadvantage of an RESP was that the income earned inside the plan was forfeited if a beneficiary (or substitute beneficiary) did not attend a post-secondary institution. In order to make them more attractive, the *ITA* now permits a subscriber to withdraw any accumulated income under such circumstances if the RESP has been running for 10 years and each living beneficiary is at least 21 years old.[75] If the subscriber has enough contribution room, up to $50,000 of RESP income can be transferred on a tax-free basis to the RRSP of the subscriber or the subscriber's spouse. Otherwise, any RESP income so withdrawn is subject to a special 20 per cent tax under the *ITA*, as well as regular income tax. In either event, the contributions made by a subscriber are returned to him or her tax-free, and any CESG payments received by the RESP have to be repaid.[76]

---

[72] The CESG is equal to 20 per cent of RESP contributions made, to a maximum of $500 per year.

[73] 20% × $2,500 = $500 maximum CESG.

[74] The $7,200 lifetime grant limit is based on the pre-1998 $2,000 annual contribution limit and the age when CESGs normally stop (when the beneficiary is 18 years of age): $7,200 = 18 years × 20% × $2,000. If annual contributions of $2,500 are made, the $7,200 lifetime grant limit would be reached after 14 years (since 14 × $500 = $7,000). At that point total contributions would be $36,000 (14 × $2,500) and further contributions could be made (until the annuitant is 21 years of age or $50,000 lifetime contribution limit per beneficiary is reached, whichever is the earliest).

[75] These two requirements may be waived if the beneficiary is eligible for the disability tax credit.

[76] *ITA*, *supra* note 1, s. 204.94.

The government provides additional income-tested CESG and Canada Learning Bond ("CLB") payments each year for the RESPs of children of low-income families. The "means test" used for these additional payments is section 3 income.[77]

(c) — Registered disability savings plans (RDSPs)

Since 2008, a tax-assisted program called the Registered Disability Savings Plan ("RDSP") has enabled parents and others to save for a child eligible for the disability tax credit.[78] The RDSP is similar in concept to the RESP: contributions are non-tax-deductible, but the income from investments earned within the plan is not taxed until it is distributed. Like RESPs, contributions to an RDSP are eligible for a grant and there are additional income-tested grants and Canada Disability Savings Bond payments provided for low-income families.[79] As well as receiving non-deductible contributions, the *ITA* allows a tax-deferred rollover of a parent's or grandparent's RRSP on death to an RDSP of a child or grandchild.[80]

11.5 — Employment-related payments

(a) — Retiring allowance

(i) — Definition of "retiring allowance"

Retiring allowances are included in income.[81] However, unlike other types of income, retiring allowances enjoy a special tax advantage: the "eligible" portion may be contributed to an RRSP and qualify for tax deductions.

Subsection 248(1) defines a "retiring allowance" as

> an amount . . . received . . .
>
> > (a) on or after retirement of a taxpayer from an office or employment in recognition of the taxpayer's long service, or

---

[77] For additional CESG payments, see <www.canada.ca/en/employment-social-development/services/student-financial-aid/student-loan/student-grants/acesg.html>. For CLB, see <www.canada.ca/en/employment-social-development/services/student-financial-aid/education-savings/resp/resp-promoters/bulletin/2016-702.html>.

[78] *ITA, supra* note 1, s. 118.3.

[79] Contributions are limited to a lifetime maximum of $200,000 per beneficiary and can be made until the end of the year in which the child beneficiary attains 59 years of age. The Canada Disability Savings Grant ("CDSG") is equal to 100 per cent to 300 per cent of RDSP contributions (maximum: $3,500), depending on family net income. For low-income families, the Canada Disability Savings Bonds ("CDSB") provides up to an additional $1,000. Unused CDSG and CDSB room can also be carried forward to subsequent years.

[80] The amount transferred on a rollover basis cannot exceed the beneficiary's unused RDSP contribution room (lifetime maximum of $200,000). See heading 11.3(d)(vi) — Tax consequences on death, above, for a further discussion of this rollover.

[81] Retiring allowances are taxed in the year received and may be paid in instalments, although any interest element included in the instalment payment would not be a retiring allowance.

(b) in respect of a loss of an office or employment of a taxpayer, whether or not received as, on account or in lieu of payment of, damages[82] or pursuant to an order or judgment of a competent tribunal,

by the taxpayer or, after the taxpayer's death, by a dependant or a relation of the taxpayer or by the legal representative of the taxpayer.

In order to receive a retiring allowance, there must be either a "retirement" or a "loss" of office or employment. The definition of "retiring allowance" captures both the traditional "retirement" payment — a payment made "on or after retirement" in recognition of "long service"[83] — as well as compensation "in respect of a loss of an office or employment".[84] Payments made under early retirement arrangements are generally considered to be payments in respect of loss of office because early retirement arrangements are generally put in place to eliminate jobs.[85] All compensation for loss of employment — whether voluntary or involuntary — is treated as a retiring allowance. For example, most damages awards and out-of-court settlements in respect of a loss of office or employment are taxed as retiring allowances. This would include payment for general damages related to the

---

[82] Before 1978, the definition of retiring allowance did not include damages, and if the departing employee sued the employer for wrongful dismissal and recovered damages, then the damages would be received free of tax. This was because an award of damages for breach of contract (or for a tort or other cause of action) is not income for tax purposes. This was so, even though the amount of a damages award for wrongful dismissal would be computed by reference to exactly the same considerations (i.e., the amount of salary that would have been paid during a required period of notice) as would be applied to the computation of a consensual severance payment. Since court-awarded damages were free of tax, it was also held that an out-of-court settlement of a wrongful dismissal action also escaped tax. See *Atkins, supra* note 8.

[83] Payments in respect of "long service" would be determined by reference to the total number of years in an employee's career with a particular employer or affiliated employers, and would include accumulated sick leave. Based on *Harel v. Quebec (Deputy Minister of Revenue)*, [1977] C.T.C. 441, 77 D.T.C. 5438 (S.C.C.), the CRA takes the view that the payment of "accumulated sick leave credits" qualifies as a retiring allowance, but not the payment of accrued vacation pay: Canada Revenue Agency, Folio S2-F1-C2, "Retiring allowances" [Folio S2-F1-C2] at paras. 2.22, 2.24.

[84] Folio S2-F1-C2, *supra* note 83 at para. 2.24 contains a list of payments that the CRA considers to be employment income rather than a retiring allowance. The list includes accrued vacation pay, a retention bonus for reporting to work until the termination date, and amounts that represent deferred compensation. Because of the reference to "damages" in the definition of retiring allowance, a payment in lieu of earnings for a period of reasonable notice of termination is considered to be a retiring allowance when it is included in a payment of damages, but employment income when it is not.

[85] *Ibid.* at para. 2.9. The distinction between traditional retirement and payment in respect of loss of employment or office is important only if the payment is received before the date of termination. This is because s. 248(1) requires a payment in recognition of long service to be received "on or after retirement" but contains no similar restriction for a payment "in respect of a loss of an office".

loss of employment (e.g., for loss of self-respect, humiliation, mental anguish, hurt feelings, etc.), but not for personal injuries sustained before or after the loss of employment that are separate and unrelated to the loss of employment (e.g., for human rights violations, harassment during employment, or defamation after dismissal).[86]

In order to qualify a payment as a retiring allowance, there must first exist an office or employment. In *Schwartz v. Canada* (1996),[87] for example, the taxpayer entered into a contract of employment with a prospective employer, but the employer rescinded the contract before the taxpayer had actually started working for the employer. Following negotiations, the prospective employer paid the taxpayer $360,000 as damages for breach of contract. The Supreme Court of Canada held that the amount paid to the taxpayer was not a retiring allowance. The Court reasoned that, since the taxpayer was not, in fact, employed by the prospective employer at the time when the contract was rescinded, there had been no loss of employment.[88]

In *Schwartz*, there was no loss of employment because employment had not started. The more common source of doubt is whether there has been a "retirement" or "loss" of office or employment in circumstances where an employee continues to work for the same employer or an affiliate, even if it is in a different capacity or location. The CRA's answer is generally no because there is continued employment.[89] Although it is a question of fact, the CRA will consider a "retirement" or "loss" of office or employment to have occurred if there is no assurance or offer of new employment or re-employment at the time of termination.[90]

---

[86] Folio S2-F1-C2, *supra* note 83 at paras. 1.7, 1.8.

[87] *Schwartz, supra* note 1. This case is also discussed in detail in Chapter 4 at heading 4.3(d) — Unenumerated sources.

[88] To assist in determining the meaning of the term "employment", the Supreme Court in *Schwartz, supra* note 1, compared the definition of "retiring allowance" to the wording of s. 80.4(1), which requires an income inclusion in certain circumstances when an individual has received a loan by virtue of his or her "office or employment or intended office or employment". As a consequence of the distinction between "employment" and "intended employment" in s. 80.4(1), the Supreme Court drew the inference that the meaning of "employment" for purposes of the *ITA* did not include amounts related to prospective employment.

[89] Folio S2-F1-C2, *supra* note 83 at para. 2.11

[90] *Ibid.* at para. 2.12. Paragraph 2.13 also provides three examples of when retirement or loss of office or employment might occur despite continued employment. These include the situations of 1) a government employee who retires from a full-time position but obtains, through his or her own initiative, part-time employment with another department where the duties and responsibilities of the new position are unrelated to those of the former position; 2) a former employee who continues on as a corporate director (other than a director of a public company) at nominal compensation; and 3) a former employee who carries on certain administrative duties for no remuneration after the sale of the employer's business.

There is also the matter of timing. In *Serafini v. M.N.R.* (1989),[91] for example, the taxpayer continued to receive full salary and benefits and to accrue pension benefits for a 12-month period after his so-called "retirement". It was only after the 12-month period elapsed that the employee began to receive his pension benefits. The Tax Court of Canada decided that the payments during the 12-month period constituted employment income even though the employee did not perform any duties of employment. Stating that the taxpayer's situation was similar "to a preretirement leave with full pay and benefits",[92] the Court found that the date of retirement was after the end of the 12-month period.[93]

(ii) — Special treatment

A retiring allowance is included in income in the year of receipt under subparagraph 56(1)(a)(ii). However, the "qualifying" portion of the retiring allowance may be contributed to an RRSP and qualify for the deduction under paragraph 60(j.1).[94] The "qualifying" portion is $2,000 per year of service before 1996 plus an additional $1,500 for each year before 1989 for which no RPP or DPSP benefits were earned.

Consider the following example. An employee ceases employment on October 1, 2017 after working for the same employer since March 1, 1985 and receives a retiring allowance of $50,000. All his pension benefits have vested. However, because of a one-year waiting period before he could join the company pension plan, he earned no pension benefits for 1985. In this example, the "qualifying" portion is $23,500 ($2,000 × 11 years before 1996 plus $1,500 × 1 non-vested year before 1989).

---

[91] *Serafini v. M.N.R.* (1989), [1989] 2 C.T.C. 2437, 89 D.T.C. 653 (T.C.C.).

[92] *Ibid.* at 2442 [C.T.C.].

[93] The CRA's position with respect to the timing of retirement and loss of office is in line with the *Serafini* case: continued participation in a company health plan providing medical, dental and long-term disability coverage "would not, in itself, indicate that employment has not terminated, particularly if the employer's plan specifically permits former employees to be covered under the plan. However, if pension benefits continue to accrue, the accrual indicates that there is an existing employment relationship, since such benefits only accrue to employees. The fact that the employer does not require an individual to report to work is not, by itself, determinative of whether the individual has retired. For example, an individual who has been given a leave of absence for educational purposes is still an employee." See Folio S2-F1-C2, *supra* note 83 at para. 2.7.

[94] The rules respecting withholding of tax are also different for a retiring allowance than for income from employment: *ITA, supra* note 1, s. 153(1)(c); Regulations, *supra* note 53, reg. 103(4). The CRA has stated that there is no withholding requirement if the retiring allowance (or a part thereof) is paid directly to an RRSP if the payer has reasonable grounds to believe the transfer is within the deduction limits under s. 60(j.1) or ss. 146(5) or (5.1): see CRA, *Employers' Guide — Payroll Deductions and Remittances, T4001(E) Rev. 16*, Transfer of a retiring allowance (in Ch. 6 — Special payments).

This preferential tax treatment is available to both traditional retirement payments and early retirement payments. Because early retirement programs are a popular way for public- and private-sector employers to "downsize" and reduce their employee costs, this tax deduction was once very well-used. However, given that there are now relatively few employees who have worked for the same employer since before 1996 (over 20 years!), the deduction is not as important as it once was.

(b) — Death benefits

Death benefits are included in income under s. 56(1)(a)(iii) of the *ITA*. The term "death benefits" is defined in s. 248(1) as amounts received "on or after the death of an employee in recognition of the employee's service in an office or employment . . ." The definition goes on to exclude the first $10,000 received and to allocate the $10,000 tax-free limit first to the employee's spouse. If any of the $10,000 limit remains, and payments are received by other taxpayers (e.g., the employee's children), the limit is allocated to others in proportion to the payments received by them. The first $10,000 tax-free amount is technically not a death benefit.

11.6 — Income separated from capital

(a) — Annuities

An annuity is a contract to receive a periodic payment and is usually purchased from a life insurance company. (The owner of the annuity contract is called the "annuitant".) There are two basic types of annuities: "life annuities" and "term annuities". A "life annuity" is an annuity that is paid for the remainder of the annuitant's life or his or her spouse's life. A "term annuity", on the other hand, has a fixed term (i.e., the annuity will be paid for a fixed number of years only). A life annuity can also have a "guaranteed term" (i.e., payments will be guaranteed for a fixed number of years even if the annuitant dies before the end of that period). A life annuity can also have "joint and last survivor benefits", in which case the amount will be paid until the later of the dates of death of the annuitant or his or her spouse (i.e., the "last survivor's" date of death). The amount of the annuity that can be purchased for a certain dollar amount (e.g., $100,000) varies, depending upon interest rates and, if it is a life annuity, the age of the taxpayer (and his or her spouse, if the annuity has joint and last survivor benefits).

The income portion of an annuity payment is included in income in the following manner: first, the entire amount of the annuity payment is included in income (s. 56(1)(d)) and then the capital element of the annuity payment is deducted (s. 60(a)), since the capital element is a return of the annuitant's invested after-tax capital. These rules apply only to annuities purchased with after-tax funds. Pension annuities and RRSP annuities, on the other hand, are fully taxed. There is no capital amount to deduct because they are purchased with tax-sheltered retirement savings.[95]

---

[95] See heading 11.3 — Tax-assisted private pension plans, above.

(b) — Non-compete payments

In reaction to the court's narrow interpretation of the source concept, Parliament often amends the *ITA* by adding a specific rule. For example, there were two decisions that encouraged taxpayers selling shares of a corporation carrying on a business to structure the transactions and settlements to include non-compete payments received under a restrictive covenant. The first decision was *R. v. Fortino* (2000),[96] in which the Court held that non-compete payments received by shareholders were tax-free because they did not constitute income from a source. *Fortino* was followed by a second decision, *Manrell v. R.* (2003),[97] which addressed whether such payments could be taxed as proceeds of dispositions of property resulting in a capital gain. In *Manrell*, the Court held that the payments were tax-free because the right to compete was not "property". This is why section 56.4 of the *ITA* was proposed in 2003 and enacted in 2013 (retroactive to October 7, 2003), to overrule the case law. Under this provision, a non-competition payment is characterized as income except to the extent that all or part of the payment can reasonably be shown to represent proceeds of disposition, giving rise to capital gains.

11.7 — Miscellaneous amounts

(a) — Scholarships, bursaries and awards

Paragraph 56(1)(n) includes scholarships, bursaries and awards in income, net of the scholarship exemption available under subsection 56(3). A full exemption is available for most scholarships and bursaries received in connection with a post-secondary program if the student is a full-time student.[98] Subsection 56(3.1) stipulates that the scholarship exemption applies only to awards that can reasonably be regarded as being received in connection with the student's enrolment in a qualifying program and, in the case of a part-time student, limits the scholarship exemption to the total of the tuition fees and the cost of program-related materials.[99] The intent of the subsection 56(3.1) is to ensure that the subsection 56(3) exemption is not being used to re-characterize employment income as tax-free income.

Scholarships and bursaries received in connection with enrolment in an elementary or secondary school program are also eligible for a full exemption.[100] By doing this, the federal government has made an odd tax policy choice: to use the tax system to reduce the barriers to private schools, rather than increasing provincial trans-

---

[96] *Fortino, supra* note 9.

[97] *Manrell, supra* note 9.

[98] See Canada Revenue Agency, Folio S1-F2-C3, "Scholarships, Research Grants and Other Education Assistance".

[99] This limitation for part-time students does not apply to taxpayers eligible for the disability tax credit.

[100] This is effective 2007. Before 2007, such scholarships were only eligible for a $500 exemption.

fer payments to provide more direct funding to the public school and post-secondary education systems.

Awards are exempt from tax if they are received in connection with the production of a literary, dramatic, musical or artistic work.[101] In any other case, the exemption is only $500.

(b) — Employment insurance

Benefits provided under the federal *Employment Insurance Act*[102] are included in income under 56(1)(a)(iv) of the *ITA*. The benefits are paid to all Canadians who are eligible because of unemployment but are "clawed back" through the income tax system, so that recipients with incomes in excess of $64,125 (2017) have to repay some of the benefits they receive.[103] Paragraph 60(n) allows a deduction for this repayment.

(c) — Workers' compensation and social assistance payments

Workers' compensation and social assistance[104] payments are included in income under paragraphs 56(1)(v) and (u). The amounts are not taxed, however, because they are deducted in computing taxable income under paragraph 110(1)(f). The section 56 inclusion serves an important purpose because, as we shall see in Chapter 12, section 3 income (rather than taxable income) is used as a "means test" for various income-tested tax refundable credits (the refundable GST credit,[105] the Canada child benefit,[106] the working income tax benefit,[107] and the refundable medical expense credit[108]), as well as claims for dependants by others[109] and the age credit.[110] As discussed earlier, income (rather than taxable income) is also used

---

[101] Awards that reimburse personal or living expenses, and expenses that are otherwise deductible in computing income and expenses, do not qualify: s. 56(3).

[102] S.C. 1996, c. 23.

[103] When the income of the recipient exceeds 1.25 times the maximum yearly insurable earnings (1.25 × $51,300 in 2017), the general rule is that the lesser of 30 per cent of the excess income or 30 per cent of the benefits must be repaid.

[104] Social assistance payments are payments made by the federal, provincial and municipal governments to assist low-income taxpayers. The federal "guaranteed income supplement" and "spouse's allowance" benefits that low-income seniors receive are examples. Welfare payments are another example. The only social assistance payments that are specifically excluded from income are payments for foster care (s. 81(1)(h)).

[105] *ITA, supra* note 1, s. 122.5.

[106] *Ibid.*, s. 122.6.

[107] See Chapter 12 at heading 12.5(h) — Refundable credits.

[108] *Ibid.*

[109] *ITA, supra* note 1, ss. 118(1)(a), (b), (c.1), (d).

[110] *Ibid.*, s. 118(2). These credits are discussed further in Chapter 12 at heading 12.5 — Tax credits.

to determine how much of a taxpayer's Old Age Security[111] and employment insurance ("EI") payments must be "clawed back" and repaid. Section 56 includes the payments for this purpose, but paragraph 110(1)(f) (a deduction after the net income) excludes the payments from taxable income, which is the basis for computing tax. Therefore, these payments are not subject to tax.

What is the rationale for excluding these payments from taxable income? There is a good argument for taxing these payments because they increase the recipient's ability to pay tax.[112] In the case of workers' compensation payments, there is the additional argument that, since the premiums that employers pay are tax-deductible, the payments received by former employees should be taxable. The main argument against taxing these payments is that the net cost to the government would be the same: since the level of assistance is predetermined, any amount of tax payment must be covered by an increase in the assistance payment. The Government of Canada treats the non-taxation of social assistance and workers' compensation as a tax expenditure, valued at $1.065 billion for 2017.[113]

11.8 — Spousal and child support

(a) — Definitions

Subsection 56.1(4) of the *ITA* contains the following definitions of support amount and child support amount:

> "support amount" means an amount payable or receivable as an allowance on a periodic basis for the maintenance of the recipient, children of the recipient or both the recipient and children of the recipient, if the recipient has discretion as to the use of the amount, and
>
> > (a) the recipient is the spouse or common-law partner or former spouse or common-law partner of the payer, the recipient and payer are living separate and apart because of the breakdown of their marriage or common-law partnership and the amount is receivable under an order of a competent tribunal or under a written agreement; or
> >
> > (b) the payer is a natural parent of a child of the recipient and the amount is receivable under an order made by a competent tribunal in accordance with the laws of a province.

---

[111] See heading 11.2 — Public pensions, above.

[112] Workers' compensation payments were initially excluded from income (see s. 81(1)(h), as it read before 1982) until 1982, when the current inclusion-deduction system for these payments became effective (s. 56(1)(v)). The Carter Commission recommended that workers' compensation and social assistance payments be subject to tax: *Carter Report*, *supra* note 30.

[113] The $1.065 billion figure reported above is the sum of three projections for 2017 contained in the *2017 Tax Expenditures Report*, *supra* note 25, Part 2, Estimates and Projections (Table), online: <https://www.fin.gc.ca/taxexp-depfisc/2017/taxexp17-eng.asp>: $190 million for the Guaranteed Income Supplement and spouse's allowance benefits, $215 million for social assistance payments, and $660 million for worker's compensation benefits.

"child support amount" means any support amount that is not identified in the agreement or order under which it is receivable as being solely for the support of a recipient who is a spouse or common-law partner or former spouse or common-law partner of the payer or who is a parent of a child of whom the payer is a natural parent.[114]

To constitute a "support amount" in the case of breakdown of a marriage or common-law partnership, payments must satisfy the following requirements: 1) the payments must be an "allowance" (discussed below); 2) the payments must be made "on a periodic basis" (a lump-sum payment is not deductible);[115] 3) the payer and recipient must be "living separate and apart" from each other; and 4) the payments must be made under the terms of either a court order or a "written agreement". In the case where there has been no marriage or common-law partnership between the payer and the recipient, but the payer is the parent of a child of the recipient, a "support amount" must also be an "allowance", made "on a periodic basis", and the payer must have been living "separate and apart" from the recipient. However, the definition is more restrictive than that for a marriage or partnership breakdown: the payments must have been made under a court order; a written agreement will not suffice for such payments, let alone anything less formal.

In order for a payment to constitute an "allowance", the recipient must have "discretion as to the use of the amount". As a result, payments made directly to third parties for the benefit of the spouse (or former spouse) or children are excluded from the definition of support amount, because in that case the recipient would have no "discretion as to the use of the amount". Common examples of third-party payments include payment of rent, mortgage payments,[116] tuition fees, and dental and counselling expenses. Subsections 56.1(2) and 60.1(2) create an exception to the general rule by deeming a third-party payment to be an "allowance payable on a

---

[114] *ITA, supra* note 1, s. 56.1(4).

[115] See *McKimmon v. R.*, [1990] 1 C.T.C. 109, 90 D.T.C. 6088 (Fed. C.A.), in which the Court distinguished between a periodic payment that is an allowance and a payment made as an instalment of a capital amount. Some of the criteria listed by the Court in *McKimmon* are summarized in Canada Revenue Agency, Folio S1-F3-C3, "Support Payments" [Folio S1-F3-C3] at para. 3.44: a lump-sum payment covering periodic payments that are in arrears will be considered to be a periodic payment; it will, therefore, be deductible to the payer and taxable to the recipient in the year of payment. Because of our graduated system of tax, a single lump sum received on account of periodic payments in arrears may be taxed at a higher rate than the periodic payments would have been. To ameliorate this result, the *ITA* now contains averaging rules that adjust the tax rate on retroactive lump-sum payments to the amount that would have been owed if the periodic payments had been received when they were due. To this amount is added the interest at the prescribed rate for the late payment of the taxes: ss. 110.2, 120.3.1.

[116] *Gagnon v. R.*, [1986] 1 C.T.C. 410, 86 D.T.C. 6179 (S.C.C.) allowed such an amount to be deducted as an allowance; the result was reversed by the enactment of former s. 56(12), which required that the recipient have "discretion as to the use of the amount" in order for the amount to be deductible. This requirement is now contained in the definition of "support amount" in s. 56.1(4).

periodic basis" and deeming the recipient to "have discretion as to the use of that amount" if the order or written agreement provides that these subsections "shall apply". These provisions allow third-party payments to be treated as "support amounts" if the payer and the recipient so agree and the payments are paid pursuant to a court order or written agreement (if applicable) that refers to subsections 56.1(2) and 60.1(2).

Payments made before a written agreement or court order has come into existence are deemed to have been "paid and received thereunder" if the agreement or order so provides and the payments are made in the year that the agreement or order is made or in the previous year.[117] This allows taxpayers to make payments that qualify for the deduction-inclusion treatment and still have some time to negotiate a written agreement or obtain a court order. Because a right to support is considered to be property, legal and accounting expenses incurred by the recipient to establish, defend or collect support amounts are deductible under section 9 of the *ITA*.[118]

(b) — Deduction-inclusion system

Payments for the support of a spouse or former spouse are deductible by the payer under paragraph 60(b), and must be included in the income of the recipient under paragraph 56(1)(b).[119] These rules do not apply to child support payments required to be made under agreements or orders made or varied after April 30, 1997 (or orders in place before May 1, 1997 if the payer and the recipient so elect). Payments made pursuant to such orders will not be taxable in the hands of the recipient and will not be deductible in the hands of the payer.[120]

---

[117] *ITA, supra* note 1, s. 56.1(3), 60.1(3).

[118] *Nadeau v. MNR*, 2003 FCA 400, 2003 D.T.C. 5736, [2004] 1 C.T.C. 293 (F.C.A.) contains a good summary of the basis for deducting legal and accounting fees under s. 9: the cases have consistently held that the right to support, once established, is "property" within the meaning of s. 248(1), and a pre-existing right to a support amount can arise from a written agreement, a court order or family law. For greater certainty, Folio S1-F3-C3, *supra* note 115, provides a list of deductible and non-deductible legal and accounting fees in paras. 3.78-3.84, but not the basis for the deduction.

[119] Earned income for RRSP purposes is reduced by support amounts paid and deducted from income under s. 60(b), and increased by support amounts received and included in income under s. 56(1)(b). See paras. (b) and (f) of the definition of earned income in s. 146(1).

[120] *ITA, supra* note 1, s. 60(b) (deduction) and 56(1)(b) (inclusion) contain the formula "A - (B + C)" to describe the payments that they cover. Amount "A" in the formula is the total of "support amounts" (i.e., spousal and child support payments) paid and received during the year when the payer and recipient were living separate and apart. Amount "B" in the formula is the total of "child support amounts" that became receivable during the year under an agreement or order made or varied after April 30, 1997 (or orders in place before May 1, 1997 if the payer and the recipient so elect). (See the definition of "commencement day" in s. 56.1(4).) Amount "C" in the formula is the total of all "support amounts" included or deducted in a previous year. The net result of the formula is that all support amounts are

(c) — Policy objectives

The full deductibility of payments for spousal and child support is an anomaly, because the payments have no connection to the earning of income. In an intact family, they are consumption expenses that are not deductible against any source of income. It is, therefore, odd that the payments should be deductible when a family has broken up. Once deductibility is allowed, however, it is sound tax policy to require the recipient to report the payments and pay income tax on them. Otherwise, the income represented by the payments would escape tax altogether.

So why was the deduction-inclusion introduced in the first place and why was it modified in 1997?

The deduction-inclusion system was introduced into the *ITA* in 1942 with the avowed purpose of providing a subsidy to split families to assist with the additional expenses of maintaining two households.[121] The system was based on the premise that the payer is usually in a higher tax bracket than the recipient; when that is the case, the diversion of some income from the payer to the recipient creates an income split that reduces the total amount of tax that is payable.[122] The subsidy provided by the deduction-inclusion system is the difference between the cost in foregone revenue caused by the payer's deduction and the amount of revenue raised by the recipient's inclusion. The Government of Canada treats the subsidy as a tax expenditure with a projected value of $80 million for 2017.[123] Since this figure excludes provincial taxes, which in the aggregate amount to about 50 per cent of federal tax, the combined federal-provincial tax expenditure was about $1.2 million in 2017 ($80 million × 1.5 = $1.2 million).

If the universe unfolded as it should, this subsidy would be reflected in a higher level of support payments: the deductibility of the payments for the higher-income payer should enable the lower-income payee to negotiate, or obtain in court, a higher level of support than could be provided if the payments were not deductible, and that higher level of support should more than offset the tax that the recipient would become liable to pay. The tax benefit will not, however, be shifted forward to the recipient if the amount of support is fixed without regard for the tax consequences to payer and recipient. And, in those cases where the recipient is in the same (or a higher) tax bracket as the payer, the deduction-inclusion system produces no tax benefit.[124]

---

deductible by the payer and included in the income of the recipient, except for child support payments (described in B) and support amounts received in the year but included in income in a prior year.

[121] The legislative history is related in *Thibaudeau v. Canada*, [1995] 1 C.T.C. 382, 95 D.T.C. 5273 (S.C.C.) [*Thibaudeau*] at paras. 143, 144, 147.

[122] See Chapter 13.

[123] *2017 Tax Expenditures Report, supra* note 25, Part 2, Estimates and Projections (Table), online: <https://www.fin.gc.ca/taxexp-depfisc/2017/taxexp17-eng.asp>.

[124] If the recipient's income-tested refundable credits (such as the GST credit and the Canada child benefit) are being reduced because of the inclusion of taxable support payments,

In *Thibaudeau v. Canada* (1995),[125] a recipient of child support payments challenged the validity of former paragraph 56(1)(b), the provision that required her to include the payments in her income. She argued that paragraph 56(1)(b) was a violation of the equality guarantee in section 15 of the *Canadian Charter of Rights and Freedoms* (the "*Charter*"),[126] because paragraph 56(1)(b) discriminated against separated custodial parents by forcing them to pay the tax on support payments. The Supreme Court of Canada, by a majority, rejected the argument and upheld paragraph 56(1)(b). The Court held that the provision should not be assessed in isolation from paragraph 60(b) (which is the matching deduction for the payer spouse) and the family law system, under which support orders and agreements are made. The deduction-inclusion system resulted in a reduction of tax for the majority of separated couples. While it was the payer who received the benefit of the deduction, the deduction increased the payer's ability to pay support. While it was the recipient who suffered the tax burden, the family law system required that the tax burden be taken into account in fixing the amount of support, so that the amount should be grossed up to fully compensate the recipient for the additional tax liability. In Thibaudeau's case, the family court had taken her additional tax liability into account, but it appeared that the liability had been underestimated and that the gross-up for tax was, therefore, insufficient.[127] In deciding against Thibaudeau, the Court held that this deficiency should be remedied by a review of the support order by the family court. Although some separated custodial parents did not benefit from the deduction-inclusion system, as a group custodial parents did benefit.[128] Therefore, the *ITA* did not discriminate against them, and there was no breach of equality rights under section 15 of the *Charter*.

---

the recipient's marginal tax rate should include the rates at which these payments are being phased out. Income-tested refundable credits are discussed in Chapter 12 at heading 12.5(h) — Refundable credits.

[125] *Thibaudeau, supra* note 121. The principal majority opinion was written by Gonthier J. Short concurring opinions were written by Sopinka J., with whom La Forest J. agreed, and by Cory and Iacobucci JJ. Dissenting opinions were written by McLachlin and L'Heureux-Dubé J.

[126] *Canadian Charter of Rights and Freedoms* [*Charter*], s. 15, Part I of the *Constitution Act, 1982*, being Schedule B to the *Canada Act 1982* (U.K.), 1982, c 11.

[127] The Court did not consider the question, upon which no evidence seemed to have been led, as to how much lower the support order would have been if the deduction in s. 60(b) did not exist. Without some estimate of this, it is not apparent, merely from the inadequacy of the tax gross-up, that Thibaudeau was worse off than she would have been in a world without the deduction-inclusion system.

[128] Justices McLachlin and L'Heureux-Dubé dissented primarily on the grounds that the family law system could not be relied upon to shift the tax benefit forward to the custodial spouse. By conferring the benefit of the deduction on the non-custodial spouse and imposing the burden of the tax on the custodial spouse, the *ITA* was discriminatory. A subsequent study of 708 cases of court-ordered child support contained in a Department of Justice database found that 77 per cent of the recipients would be better off under the reforms made to family law and tax rules after *Thibaudeau* (and 23 per cent of the them would be worse

Although Thibaudeau lost the court battle, she won the war against the deduction-inclusion system for child support. The Government of Canada, in consultation with the provinces, announced its intention to reform the child support system within months of the *Thibaudeau* decision. These reforms are now law: they include the introduction of a no deduction-no inclusion system for child support agreements or orders made or varied after April 30, 1997 (discussed above), guidelines for calculating the child support to be paid (to reduce legal costs and improve the fairness and consistency of amounts awarded), and improvements in the enforcement of court-ordered child support.

11.9 — Moving expenses

(a) — Deduction

Section 62 allows a deduction for "moving expenses". The definition of moving expenses includes travel costs, transportation and storage of household effects, temporary lodging and meals, the costs of selling an old residence, and the legal expenses of buying a new residence. The deduction is only available if the move was within Canada, was 40 kilometres or more, and was caused by a change in the location of the taxpayer's work (or, in the case of a student, a change of university).[129] The deduction can be taken from income from employment at the new location or income from business at the new location or scholarships or research grants at the new location (paragraph 62(1)(c)). Any excess of deductible expenses over qualifying income can be carried forward for one year (paragraph 62(1)(d)).

The deduction for moving expenses is available only for expenses that were not reimbursed by the taxpayer's employer. Chapter 5 makes the point that the rules allowing an employer to reimburse an employee for moving expenses on a tax-free basis are far more generous than the rules in section 62, which allow an employee to deduct only those expenses listed in subsection 62(3).[130] As a result, it is better for an employer to reimburse a taxpayer for non-deductible moving expenses than to pay the taxpayer an allowance for the same amount. For example, if an employee is reimbursed for a $15,000 loss on the sale of a house, the reimbursement need not

---

off): Glenn Feltham & Alan Macnaughton, "The New Child Support Rules and Existing Awards: Choosing the Best Tax and Family Law Regime" (1996) 44 Can. Tax J. 1265 at 1285.

[129] See the definition of "eligible relocation" in s. 248(1).

[130] The restricted list of moving expenses is set out in s. 62(3) and discussed in Canada Revenue Agency, Folio S1-F3-C4, "Moving Expenses". The rules state that a taxpayer deducting moving expenses must include any reimbursement or allowance received in respect of those expenses in his or her income in order to deduct the expenses (s. 62(1)(g)). Typically, however, any employer-reimbursed expenses would simply be left off the list of moving expenses to be deducted in the employee's tax return, whereas any allowances would automatically be included in his or her income under s. 6(1)(b). Paragraph 62(1)(g) ensures that employer-reimbursed expenses are not deducted.

be reported because it not considered to be employment income.[131] However, if the taxpayer's employer pays the taxpayer a $15,000 allowance in respect of this loss, the allowance would have to be reported as employment income,[132] but no amount would be deductible as a moving expense because a loss on the sale of a house is not one of the deductible moving expenses listed in subsection 62(3). In the second case, the taxpayer would report $15,000 of income for tax purposes, whereas, in the first case, the taxpayer would have nothing to report. This is an anomalous result.

(b) — Policy objectives

Moving expenses incurred to start a new job or education at a new location are generally considered to be personal expenses, or, at most, mixed expenses, and are not deductible. In order to promote mobility of Canadians within Canada and to recognize the dual nature of moving expenses, section 62 specifically allows the deduction. The conditions and limitations of this deduction reflect these policy objectives. Expenses related to relocation for purely personal reasons are not deductible. The amount of deduction is tied to the income derived from employment, business, or scholarship at the new location.

11.10 — Child care expenses

(a) — Deduction

Subsection 63(3) defines "child care expenses" as expenses incurred to enable the taxpayer (or a supporting person) to perform duties of an office of employment, to carry on a business, to carry on research or to attend a designated educational institution. In order to qualify, the services must be provided by someone other than a person who is the child's parent, a dependant claimed by the taxpayer, or a related person who is under 18 years of age. The amount that can be claimed for boarding school or camp is also restricted.[133] In essence, child care expenses represent large out-of-pocket costs to families and, as defined above, might not be incurred except to enable parents to work outside the home.

The section 63 deduction is subject to three important limitations: 1) only the lower-income parent can generally claim the deduction; therefore, the deduction cannot be claimed at all if one parent has no income;[134] 2) the deduction cannot

---

[131] Note that one-half of any reimbursement of housing losses in excess of $15,000 is included in a taxpayer's income. See Chapter 5 at heading 5.6(e)(i) — Housing loss.

[132] *ITA, supra* note 1, s. 6(1)(b).

[133] See the definition of child care expenses in s. 63(3) and Canada Revenue Agency, Folio S1-F3-C1, "Child Care Expense Deduction".

[134] *ITA, supra* note 1, s. 63(1)(b). There are some exceptions to this rule to meet the case where both incomes are equal (in which case a joint election determines eligibility) (s. 63(2.1)), and where the lower-income person is separated from the taxpayer, infirm, confined to a bed or wheelchair, in prison or attends a secondary school or a designated educational institution (in these cases, the higher-income parent may claim a deduction) (s. 63(2)).

generally exceed two-thirds of the "earned income" of the lower-income parent, which is defined to include income from an office or employment, income from a business, and income from grants and training allowances;[135] and 3) the deduction cannot generally exceed $8,000 per child under the age of seven and $5,000 per child between the ages of 7 and 16, inclusive.[136]

(b) — Policy objectives

The deduction for child care expenses can be seen as a tax expenditure designed to assist parents with the costs of child care and to lower a barrier to the entrance of women to the workforce. This special deduction is necessary because, as discussed in Chapter 8,[137] child care expenses have been traditionally regarded as personal or living expenses that are not deductible as income-earning expenses.

As a tax expenditure, section 63 is open to criticism. Although it treats employed and self-employed taxpayers equally, it possesses the fundamental disadvantage of all deductions: it delivers a larger benefit to high-income earners than to low-income earners, and no benefit at all to persons without taxable income. Other policy instruments, such as direct provision of daycare services, or direct subsidization of low-income parents, might be more effective uses of the amount of revenue foregone by section 63. If the tax system is to be a vehicle of assistance, section 63 would be better targeted as a tax credit, especially a credit that was refundable and income-tested (or vanishing).[138]

Moreover, because the amount of deduction under section 63 is limited, the deduction cannot fully offset the cost of child care incurred by full-time working parents. In *Symes v. Canada* (1993),[139] the Supreme Court of Canada held that section 63 was the legislative response to help women enter the workforce and it was not necessary for the Court to reconsider whether child care expenses were business expenses in light of the fact that women are an important part of the workforce. In this case, the taxpayer argued that her section 15 right under the *Charter*[140] was infringed by the *ITA* to the extent that section 63 prevented her from fully deducting her child care expenses as business expenses under section 9. The Court split along

[135] See s. 63(1)(e) for the earned income limitation and s. 63(3) for the definition of "earned income". This definition of earned income is different than the one used for the "earned income" RRSP contribution. The RRSP definition is contained in s. 146 and is discussed at heading 11.3(d)(ii) — Contributions based on earned income, above.

[136] There is no deduction for the care of a child after the year of his or her 16th birthday, except in the case of a child with a mental or physical infirmity (s. 63(3) definition of "eligible child"). If a child is eligible for the disability credit (s. 118.3), the annual limit is $11,000 (rather than $8,000 or $5,000) (see s. 63(3) definition of "annual child expense amount").

[137] See Chapter 8 at heading 8.4(a)(iii) — Expenses enabling taxpayers to work.

[138] See Chapter 12 at heading 12.5(h) — Refundable credits.

[139] *Symes v. Canada* (1993), [1994] 1 C.T.C. 40, 94 D.T.C. 6001 (S.C.C.) [*Symes*], discussed further in Chapter 8 at heading 8.4(a)(iii) — Expenses enabling taxpayers to work.

[140] *Charter, supra* note 126, s. 15.

gender lines on this issue. The majority (all the male judges) rejected the taxpayer's argument that the section 63 restrictions had a disproportionate impact on women: although women were more likely to bear the social costs of child care, there was no evidence that women were more likely to bear the financial costs of child care; and the restrictions affected only the financial costs of child care. The majority reasoned that section 63 did not draw a distinction on the basis of sex and it did not have an adverse effect upon women.[141] As to the social costs that were born by women disproportionally, the majority regarded it to be "very real", but nonetheless something that "exists outside of the *Income Tax Act*".[142]

---

[141] *Symes, supra* note 139 at paras. 135–144.

[142] *Ibid.* at para. 143.

12

TAXABLE INCOME AND TAX FOR INDIVIDUALS

12.1 — Tax for individuals

(a) — Computation of tax payable

The computation of tax payable under Part I of the *Income Tax Act* (the "*ITA*")[1] by resident individuals involves the determination of 1) "income for the year" under section 3; 2) "taxable income" under subsection 2(2); 3) "tax payable" under section 117; 4) "tax credits" under sections 118 to 122.71 and 126 to 127.41; and 5) the "alternative minimum tax" under section 127.5. In addition, Canadian provinces and territories levy income taxes on individuals.

Chapters 3 to 11 of this book have discussed the concept of residence and the computation of income from each of the sources; dispositions of capital property; "other income"; and subdivision e deductions. This chapter first revisits section 3 in order to contextualize the discussion of "taxable income" and highlight certain policy objectives of the scheme of taxing individuals. It then discusses the other key elements mentioned above.

(b) — Legislative scheme and policy rationale

(i) — Revenue-raising scheme

The *ITA* provides a clear roadmap for computing Part I tax for resident individuals: Division A (section 2) creates the individual's income tax liability; Division B provides rules for computing income; Division C allows deductions in computing taxable income; Division D applies to the computation of taxable income earned by non-residents; and Division E stipulates tax rates and specifies tax reliefs and subsidies in the form of tax credits.[2] In cases where the tax payable under Division E is

---

[1] R.S.C. 1985 (5th Supp.), c. 1 [*ITA*].

[2] Corporations compute their tax liability using the same roadmap and, in many cases, under the same rules in Division E: subdivision a applies to individuals, subdivision b applies to corporations, and subdivision c applies to all taxpayers.

"too low" from a policy perspective, Division E.1 requires certain individuals to pay an "alternative minimum tax" ("AMT").

The overall purpose of this legislative scheme is to define the tax liability of resident individuals in a manner that advances the policy objectives of the *ITA*. One objective is to tax individuals based on the "ability to pay" principle. The notion of horizontal equity is expressed through section 3 and provisions that determine the computation of income and taxable income. The objective of vertical equity is achieved through the progressive rate structure under section 117. In addition to raising revenue in an equitable and efficient manner, the *ITA* is used as a major instrument of social and economic policy. Many of the subdivision e deductions, Division C deductions, and tax credits are intended to meet certain social and economic goals. The policy concern with respect to the integrity of the tax base and effectiveness of tax expenditure measures underlies the design of some elements of the scheme, such as the AMT.

(ii) — Technical design of tax expenditure measures

As discussed in Chapter 2, the *ITA* is the biggest spending document in Canada. The scheme for taxing individuals is replete with tax expenditures, many of which have been discussed in earlier chapters. Each stage of determining a taxpayer's tax liability involves some tax expenditure provisions. It is, thus, important to appreciate the deliberate policy rationale for each technical design choice.

In general, tax expenditures that are somewhat related to the earning of income, or can be linked to an income-earning source or activity, are located in rules governing the computation of income in subdivisions a to c of Division B. Examples are the exclusions from employee benefits under subsection 6(1) and the principal residence exemption under paragraph 40(2)(b). Tax expenditures in subdivision e, such as child care expenses and moving expenses, are somewhat associated with income-earning and, thus, recognized as "other deductions" in computing a taxpayer's income under section 3. Tax expenditures that are more driven by personal circumstances (e.g., age, disability, illness) or private decisions that have social implications (e.g., charitable donations) are provided in the form of tax credits and taken into account at the final stage of computing tax liability. Tax expenditures in the nature of a "negative income tax" or "poverty relief" also take the form of tax credits even though they have little to do with reducing tax payable: these measures simply rely on the tax system to deliver funds to low-income families.

The choice of designing a tax expenditure as a deduction in computing income or taxable income, or as a deduction in computing tax payable (i.e., a tax credit), has significant policy implications. The value of a tax expenditure in the form of a deduction in computing the tax base is determined by the applicable marginal tax rate. The higher the tax rate, the higher the amount of tax saved. For example, the federal tax saving arising from a $100 deduction would be $33 for a taxpayer in the highest bracket, $15 for a taxpayer in the lowest tax bracket, and nil for a person who has no taxable income. This is the so-called "upside-down" effect of tax deductions. In contrast, a tax credit reduces the taxpayer's tax payable dollar for dollar. The upside-down effect erodes the progressivity of the tax system. A tax credit is preferred, as it delivers the same amount of tax savings irrespective of the taxpayer's income level. This is one of the reasons that the tax reform of 1988 converted personal exemptions (which were deductions in computing taxable income under Division C) to credits under Division D. Almost all of the credits in sections 118 to 118.9 are set at the rate for the lowest bracket so that the tax savings are the same for all taxpayers.

12.2 — Net income

(a) — Role of section 3

Section 3 is the closest the *ITA* comes to defining "income". The amount of income under section 3 is the basis for computing taxable income. It is a net amount, in that current-year losses and subdivision e amounts are deducted from the aggregated income from various sources and taxable capital gains. Such net income is intended to correspond to a taxpayer's economic income, which is used in designing tax credits in Division E.

(b) — Aggregation of income from all sources

Paragraph 3(a) requires income to have a "source", and paragraph 3(b) specifically includes taxable capital gains from the disposition of property. Therefore, if an individual is employed part-time, carries on a business, and owns some investments, he or she must first compute his or her income or loss from each of the employment, business and property. He or she must add the income from each source under paragraph 3(a) and recognize the losses separately under paragraph 3(d). If he or she sells some capital assets and has capital gains and/or losses, he or she must compute the amount of taxable capital gain and/or allowable capital losses. If he or she has both taxable capital gains and allowable capital losses, the losses are offset against the taxable captain gains.

Paragraph 3(c) then aggregates the income amounts from each source and the net taxable capital gains from all dispositions of property, and allows subdivision e deductions.

(c) — Subdivision e deductions

Subdivision e deductions are not otherwise deductible in computing income under paragraph 3(a) or (b). They are allowed as deductions for social policy reasons.[3] Many of the expenditures eligible for a subdivision e deduction are somewhat related to earning income. In addition to the previously mentioned moving expenses and child care expenses, others include expenses of appealing a tax assessment (paragraph 60(o)) and contributions to tax-deferred savings plans (various paragraphs of section 60). These expenditures reduce the taxpayer's economic income for the year. It, thus, makes sense to deduct them in computing income under section 3(c).

---

[3] Subdivision e deductions are discussed in Chapter 11.

(d) — Loss for the year

(i) — Allowable capital losses

Allowable capital losses are "quarantined" in the sense that they can only be deducted against taxable capital gains under paragraph 3(b). To the extent that the allowable capital losses exceed taxable capital gains, there will be no income arising from paragraph 3(b), and the excess is eligible for carryover to other years as a Division C deduction. Losses from the disposition of a listed personal property ("LPP") are further restricted: they can only be deducted against gains from the disposition of an LPP in the year or carried over to other years under section 41.[4]

The restriction on the deductibility of allowable capital losses stands in contrast to the treatment of losses from office, employment, business or property, which are deductible against ordinary income as well as taxable capital gains. The restriction on the deductibility of allowable capital losses also stands in contrast to the treatment of taxable capital gains. A taxable capital gain must be recognized in the year that it is derived, whereas an allowable capital loss is not necessarily deductible in the year that it is sustained. The asymmetrical treatment of gains and losses has been described as creating "a bias against risk-taking". What is the reason for this distinction? The answer is that it is an attempt to reduce the advantage of the realization basis of capital gains taxation. Capital gains that have accrued on a property do not have to be recognized for tax purposes until they are realized by the sale or other disposition of the property. This enables tax on capital gains to be postponed until a time of the taxpayer's choosing (a disposition usually being a voluntary act). If there were no restriction on the deductibility of capital losses, a taxpayer could dispose of a property with accrued losses and obtain an immediate deduction despite the fact that the taxpayer was continuing to hold other properties upon which gains had accrued but had not been realized. By restricting the deductibility of capital losses, the *ITA* reduces the incentive to postpone the realization of capital gains and diminishes the ability of taxpayers to manipulate their capital gains income.

(ii) — Loss from an office, employment, business or property

Paragraph 3(d) allows a taxpayer to deduct his or her loss for the year from an office, employment, business or property. This deduction is made against income from all other sources as well as taxable capital gains, derived in the same taxation year. For example, assume taxpayer X has income from employment of $20,000 (included under paragraph 3(a)) and a taxable capital gain of $10,000 (included under paragraph 3(b)). If, in the same year, X has incurred a business loss of $30,000, X may deduct (under paragraph 3(d)) the amount of the loss from the combined amount under paragraphs 3(a) and 3(b), resulting in a total income of nil ($20,000 + $10,000 - $30,000 = zero) under paragraph 3(e).

---

[4] As discussed in Chapter 10 at heading 10.4(e)(iii) — Listed personal property losses, s. 41 allows LPP losses to be carried back three years and carried forward seven years against net LPP gains.

(iii) — Allowable business investment losses (ABILs)

Paragraph 3(d) also allows a taxpayer to deduct an allowable business investment loss ("ABIL") for the year. An ABIL is one-half of the business investment loss. A "business investment loss" is defined in paragraph 39(1)(c) as a capital loss on the disposition of shares or debt of a small business corporation.[5] An ABIL is, therefore a special type of allowable capital loss that is treated differently from other allowable capital losses — it is fully deductible against all other income of the taxpayer. In other words, it does not have to be "matched" against taxable capital gains to be deductible.

The rationale for such preferential treatment of an ABIL is to encourage investment in small business corporations that carry on a business in Canada, thereby creating jobs for Canadians and generating economic wealth. The theory is that, by making losses deductible on the same basis that capital gains are included, the bias against risk-taking — which is inherent in the asymmetrical treatment of capital gains and capital losses — will be eliminated for investments in small business corporations. This treatment of losses complements the tax advantages accorded to capital gains on the sale of small business corporation shares.[6]

12.3 — Taxable income

(a) — Purposes of Division C deductions

The purpose of Division C is to refine the tax base as computed under section 3 by allowing a deduction for certain amounts that are not deductible in computing income. The Division C deductions applicable to individuals generally fall into one of the following categories:

- Tax subsidies, such as the lifetime capital gains exemption under section 110.6 and the deduction in respect of employee stock options under paragraph 110(1)(d) or (d.1);[7]

- Incorporation of tax treaty exemptions, such as paragraph 110(1)(f) allowing a taxpayer to exclude income exempted from Canadian taxation under a tax treaty;

- Technical rules that are part of a delivery mechanism to achieve a specific policy objective. For example, the deduction for social assistance payments

---

[5] A small business corporation is defined under s. 248(1) of the *ITA, supra* note 1, as a Canadian-controlled private corporation ("CCPC") that meets an "all or substantially all" asset test (90 per cent is the accepted standard): at least 90 per cent of its assets (on a fair market value basis) must either be used principally in an active business carried on primarily in Canada (by the corporation or a related corporation) or be shares or debt of other connected small business corporations. The term "active business" is defined in s. 125(7) and the term "connected" is defined in s. 186.

[6] The most important of these is the lifetime capital gains exemption under s. 110.6.

[7] See Chapter 5 at heading 5.7 — Employee stock options.

under paragraph 110(l)(f) "neutralizes" the inclusion of such payments in the recipient's income under subsection 56(1) so that such payments are not taxed;[8] and

- Tax relief provisions, such as the loss carryover rules under section 111 and the part-year resident rule under section 114.[9]

Some Division C deductions are discussed in other chapters. This chapter will, thus, focus on loss carryovers.

(b) — Loss carryovers

(i) — General policy

The loss carryover rules under section 111, and the rules under section 3 in respect of current-year losses, are consistent in that they, subject to specific exceptions, permit taxpayers to offset losses from one business or another source of income against profits from another. One exception is that capital losses cannot offset profits from a source of income. A second exception is that losses from a part-time farming business are restricted under section 31.[10] Both restrictions are reflected in the section 111 loss carryover rules.

(ii) — Non-capital losses

The point has been made that, when a taxpayer incurs a loss in a year from a non-capital source, the loss is deductible under paragraph 3(d). If the positive income for the year is not sufficient to offset the loss, the taxpayer will have no income pursuant to paragraph 3(f). The taxpayer's deficit for the year (the excess of the current loss over the current income) is the taxpayer's "non-capital loss" for the year under subsection 111(8). For example, where a taxpayer who, in a taxation year, had employment income of $50,000, a taxable capital gain of $9,000 and a business loss of $80,000, the taxpayer would have a non-capital loss for that year of $21,000 ($50,000 + $9,000 - $80,000 = $21,000).

In computing a taxpayer's taxable income for a year (the loss-utilization year), the question is whether a non-capital loss is eligible for deduction under section 111. Paragraph 111(1)(a) provides as follows:

> For the purpose of computing the taxable income of a taxpayer for a taxation year, there may be deducted such portion as the taxpayer may claim of the taxpayer's
>
> > (a) non-capital losses for the 20 taxation years immediately preceding and the 3 taxation years immediately following the year;

---

[8] For further discussion, see Chapter 11 at heading 11.7(c) — Workers' compensation and social assistance payments.

[9] See Chapter 3 at heading 3.5(a) — Part-year residents.

[10] See Chapter 6 at heading 6.6(d) — Farm losses.

The effect of this provision is that a non-capital loss sustained in a given year (the loss-generation year) can be carried back 3 years and forward 20 years from the loss-generation year.

Paragraph 111(1)(a) is confusing at first, until one realizes that it is drafted from the standpoint of the loss-utilization year, as opposed to the loss-generation year. From the standpoint of the loss-generation year, the loss may be carried back 3 years and forward 20 years. From the standpoint of the loss-utilization year, a non-capital loss would be available as a deduction if it were incurred in the 3 years immediately following (from which it would have been carried back) or in the 20 years immediately preceding (from which it would have been carried forward).

Paragraph 111(1)(a) allows the deduction of "such portion as the taxpayer may claim" of the non-capital loss for a year.[11] This language gives the taxpayer discretion as to whether or not to deduct an available non-capital loss in a particular year, and discretion to deduct only a portion of the loss in a particular year.[12] This makes it possible for the taxpayer to allocate the loss as advantageously as possible over the years of highest income (which will usually result in the highest tax refund). Of course, holding on to a non-capital loss in anticipation of future high income involves the risk that the income may not materialize before the expiry of the 20-year carryforward period, in which case the loss could be wasted.

The policy rationale for the carryover of non-capital losses is to provide relief to taxpayers whose income fluctuates from year to year. If losses in "bad years" cannot offset income in "good years", even though the taxpayer may end up with no net profit overall, he or she has to pay tax on the income in the good years, which, of course, violates the ability to pay principle. However, indefinite carryover of losses involves significant costs in respect of record keeping and recalculating taxable income of previous years in the case of loss carryback. The current 20-year carryforward limitation was extended from the previous 10-year period, which may help make the Canadian tax system more accommodating to business realities and more competitive internationally. The 3-year carryback period has remained unchanged, largely due to administrative concerns.

---

[11] When a taxpayer decides to carry a non-capital loss back to a previous taxation year, this involves reopening the taxpayer's tax liability for the previous year. In the usual case, the taxpayer will have filed a return for that year; the Minister will have issued an assessment; and the taxpayer will have paid the tax due for the year. In order to deduct a loss carryback in a previous year, the taxpayer files a form entitled "Request for Loss Carryback" with the CRA, to claim the deduction. If the request is in order, the Minister reassesses the taxpayer for the previous year (employing that year's rules), and then sends the taxpayer a refund of the tax which, as a result of the new deduction, will be shown to have been overpaid. (Interest on the refund is payable only from the time that the loss is claimed: s. 164(5)(d).)

[12] *ITA, supra* note 1, s. 111(3) provides that the amount of a loss that may be deducted in a particular year is reduced by amounts that have been deducted in previous years.

(iii) — Net capital losses

If, in a taxation year, a taxpayer incurs allowable capital losses that exceed the taxpayer's taxable capital gains in that year, the non-deductible excess of the allowable capital losses is described by the *ITA* as the taxpayer's "net capital loss" for the year under subsection 111(8). Our previous example was a taxpayer who, in a taxation year, has $50,000 of business income and a taxable capital gain of $9,000. If he had an allowable capital loss of $80,000 (instead of a business loss of $80,000), he would have a net capital loss for the year of $71,000 ($80,000 - $9,000).

A net capital loss is not deductible in the year in which it is incurred, because the taxpayer has no more taxable capital gains against which the loss could be applied. This is so even if, as in our example, the taxpayer does have positive income other than taxable capital gains in the same year. However, paragraph 111(1)(b) provides that a net capital loss for a particular year may be carried backward three years and forward indefinitely (over the lifetime of the taxpayer). The deduction of such carried-over net capital loss is still subject to the same restrictions on deductibility: it is deductible only against taxable capital gains of the year into which the net capital loss has been carried. It is the existence of this restriction that explains why the carryforward period is not restricted to 20 years, as it is for a non-capital loss. In the year of death of a taxpayer and the immediately preceding year, subsection 111(2) removes the restriction on deductibility. In those two years, net capital losses (as well as allowable capital losses incurred in the year of death) are deductible against income from all sources.[13] The reason for the more generous treatment of the last two years is that the year of death is the end of the carryforward period, and any losses not deducted by then would be wasted.

In other respects, the rules for the carryover of a net capital loss are similar to the rules for a non-capital loss. In particular, the taxpayer has discretion as to the year or years to which the loss is carried, and whether to deduct only a portion of the loss in a particular year.

(iv) — ABILs

The hybrid nature of ABILs is reflected in the manner in which they can be carried forward. By virtue of the definition of "net capital loss" under subsection 111(8), ABILs can be carried forward like non-capital losses, but only for 10 years. ABILs remain part of a taxpayer's non-capital losses in the year in which they are sustained and in the following 10 years. If they are not utilized within the 10-year period, they become net capital losses subject to the same limitations applicable to net capital losses.

---

[13] This deduction against all sources of income is reduced to the extent that the taxpayer has claimed the lifetime capital gains exemption claims: see the reference in ss. 111(2)(b)(iii) to s. 110.6.

(v) — Farm losses and restricted farm losses

A "farm loss" is defined in subsection 111(8) as the non-deductible portion of the taxpayer's loss for the year from a farming or fishing business. Farm losses can be carried back 3 years and forward 20 years pursuant to paragraph 111(1)(d). A "restricted farm loss" is defined in subsection 31(1.1). It is the amount of a part-time farmer's farming loss that is non-deductible for a particular year by virtue of the formula in subsection 31(1) of the *ITA*.[14] Under paragraph 111(1)(c), restricted farm losses can be carried back 3 years and forward 20 years but only against farming income.

Farm losses are, thus, treated the same as other business losses. The restriction on recognition of part-time farmers' losses is consistent in computing income under section 3 and taxable income under subsection 2(2).

12.4 — Tax rates

(a) — Progressive

The rates of tax payable by an individual are set out in subsection 117(2), which employs a graduated rate structure, with the following five brackets (for 2017):

Federal Tax Bracket	Rate
First $45,916	15%
Over $45,916 up to $91,831	20.5%
Over $91,831 up to $142,353	26%
Over $142,354 up to $202,800	29%
Over $202,800	33%

The rate structure is progressive because the marginal rate[15] for each bracket is progressively higher. The definition of each bracket changes each year due to indexation for inflation. The 33 per cent top bracket was introduced in 2016, along with the 20.5 per cent rate for the second bracket. Before 2016, only four brackets existed (15 per cent, 22 per cent, 26 per cent and 29 per cent) and, except for the lowest bracket, the rates had been the same since 2000 (the current 15 per cent dates from 2006).

The progressive rate structure under subsection 117(2) is different from a "flat" rate system under which the same rate applies irrespective of the amount of the taxable income so that the rate remains constant as a proportion of income. The progressive rate structure is the opposite of a regressive rate structure under which the rates increase as income decreases. There is no personal income tax system in the world that adopts such nominal regressive rates. However, if one examines the effect of

---

[14] *ITA, supra* note 1, s. 31 is discussed in Chapter 6 at heading 6.6(d) — Farm losses.

[15] A marginal rate is the applicable rate of tax at each bracket level, while the rate that is applicable to the taxpayer's total taxable income is called the average or effective rate.

the tax burden or the incidence of a tax (i.e., the economic burden of paying taxes), the income tax payable by individuals is the only progressive tax in Canada.

From a historical perspective, the tax rate structure has been significantly flattened since the 1988 tax reform. For example, in 1987, there were nine brackets with rates ranging from 16 per cent (on taxable income exceeding $1,320) to 34 per cent (on taxable income exceeding $63,347); in 1974, there were 12 brackets with rates ranging from 18 per cent (on taxable income exceeding $533) to 47 per cent (on taxable income exceeding $63,960). As a result, the *ITA* has become less progressive over the years.

(b) — Indexing for inflation

Section 117.1 provides for the annual indexing of tax brackets and fixed-dollar credits. The inflation factor that is used is the annual increase in the Consumer Price Index ("CPI") for the period ended on September 30 of the previous year (i.e., the increase for the 12-month period ended September 30, 2016 for 2017 tax brackets and credits.[16]

Indexing for inflation is intended to compensate for the erosion in the value of the dollar due to inflation. Without indexing, one of the characteristics of a progressive tax system is that, when an individual's income rises, his or her tax liability rises more than proportionately, and when the increased income pushes the individual into the next tax bracket, this is called "bracket-creep". The increase in the rate of tax that is caused by inflation is exacerbated if fixed-dollar credits against tax are not indexed for inflation, and this is why most fixed-dollar credits are also indexed by section 117.1.

12.5 — Tax credits

(a) — Nature of tax credits

A tax credit reduces a taxpayer's tax payable dollar by dollar. As mentioned above, the tax reform of 1988 converted personal exemptions (which were deductions from taxable income) to credits to avoid the upside-down effect of deductions. Almost all credits under sections 118 to 118.95 are set at the rate for the lowest bracket so that the tax savings are the same for all taxpayers except those who have little or no income. A standard (non-refundable) tax credit has no meaning if the taxpayer does not otherwise have any tax payable. To use a tax credit to provide social assistance requires a credit to be refundable (i.e., worth something even if no tax is owing) and income-tested.

---

[16] Indexation was first introduced in 1974 when s. 117.1 of the *ITA* was enacted to cause the tax system to be indexed by the annual change in the CPI. From 1986 to 1999, an amendment to s. 117.1 excluded the first 3 per cent of the annual increase in the CPI from the indexing formula but full indexing was restored in 2000. There have also been amendments to the *ITA* to increase brackets and credits to amounts in excess of annual indexing.

(b) — Technical design

As tax expenditures, tax credit provisions need to be carefully drafted to capture the desired scope and level of the tax subsidy or relief in order to achieve the desired policy purpose. For example, the amount of most of the personal credits is calculated by multiplying the eligible amount by 15 per cent (the rate in the lowest tax bracket).[17] Most eligible amounts and the income limits change each year because they are indexed for inflation.[18] Administrative rules, such as verification of the eligible activity or expenditure, are necessary to ensure a tax credit measure can be administered fairly and efficiently.

Eligibility for a tax credit varies from one credit to another. The majority of the tax credits require an eligible expenditure be made by the taxpayer. Examples are the tuition tax credit or charitable tax credit. Some personal credits are available to all individuals without requiring any specific expenditure be made. The refundable tax credits are transfers from the government to the individuals. Instead of being linked to an expenditure, they are linked to the income of the taxpayer's family: the credits are phased out when family income reaches a certain level.

Most of the credits are non-refundable, which means that, if the taxpayer pays no tax, the credit cannot be claimed. However, many of the credits exist because a spouse or a common-law partner or a child has no income. In such circumstances, the *ITA* treats the family as a unit in designing the tax credits. Examples are the spouse or common-law partner credit, the spouse equivalent (or eligible dependant) credit amount, the caregiver credit and the disable/infirm dependant credit. If the spouse or dependant has income over a certain threshold, these credits cannot be claimed. Similarly, the medical expense and charitable donation credits can be claimed by either spouse or common-law partner, and the medical expenses of dependant children can be claimed by parents. In the case of education credits, the *ITA* provides for the transfer of certain unused credits.[19]

(c) — Personal credits

The personal credits under paragraph 118(1)[20] are available to all individual taxpayers in amounts that vary depending on the taxpayer's spousal or common-law

---

[17] The term "appropriate percentage" is used to determine the amount of tax credit. This term is defined in s. 248(1) as "the lowest percentage referred to in s. 117(2)".

[18] The limits for the charitable donation and pension income credits are not indexed.

[19] *ITA, supra* note 1, s. 118.3(2) allows the disability credit to be transferred from anyone that the taxpayer has claimed as dependant (or could have claimed had his or her income not been as high). Section 118.8 permits any unused age, pension, mental or physical impairment, and tuition credits to be transferred to a spouse. Similarly, s. 118.9 allows the unused tuition credits to be transferred to a parent or grandparent. Students also have the option of carrying forward unused tuition, education and textbook credits to a future year when they might owe tax.

[20] For 2017, the indexed personal credit amounts are as follows: basic personal, $11,635; spouse or common-law partner, $11,635* (reduced by dependant's income); spouse

partner status and the number and type of dependants supported.[21] The credits for dependants recognize the importance of family in Canadian society and provide some relief to the caring of family members.

The basic personal credit serves an important purpose — it relieves individuals with no or low income from paying tax under the *ITA*. For 2017, this credit is 15 per cent of $11,635. This means that an individual is subject to tax only when his or her taxable income exceeds the basic personal amount. It, thus, helps ensure that individuals in the bottom of the lowest income bracket pay little if any income tax. This makes sense, as individuals who have no disposable income after paying the basic cost of living cannot be expected to be willing or able to pay income taxes.

The spousal credit is available to a taxpayer who, at any time in the taxation year, was a married person or a person in a "common-law partnership" and supported his or her spouse or "common-law partner". For the 2017 taxation year, the spousal credit is 15 per cent of the amount (if any) by which $11,635 exceeds the spouse or common-law partner's income for the year. If the spouse's income exceeds $11,635, he or she cannot be claimed as a dependant but t the spouse can claim his or her own basic personal credit of $11,635. If the spouse's income is nil, on the other hand, the taxpayer can claim the full spousal $11,635 credit as well as his or her own $11,635 basic personal credit. Because the tax relief for supporting a spouse is structured as a credit at 15 per cent, the disincentive for a spouse or common-law partner to earn income is relatively low compared to the pre-1988 system of personal exemptions. Structured as an exemption (deduction), the pre-1988 tax relief was computed using the taxpayer's top marginal rate, thereby effectively taxing any income earned by the lower-income spouse at that higher rate (rather than 15 per cent), thereby discouraging a spouse from earning income.

(d) — Education-related credits

Education is not only important to the development of the individual receiving the education, but also to his or her family and the community as a whole. Canada's future economic, social and political development is correlated to the level and

---

equivalent/eligible dependant, $11,635* (reduced by dependant's income); infirm dependant age 18 or older, $6,883 (reduced by dependant's income over $16,163); disability, $8,113; disability amount supplement under 18, $4,732 (reduced by child/attendant care expenses over $2,772); and age, $7,225 (reduced by 15% of taxpayer's income over $36,430) (* see note 21, *infra*).

[21] The proposed Canada Caregiver Credit ("CCC"), which replaces the pre-2016 "family caregiver credit", increases the amounts marked with an asterisk (*) in note 20, *ibid.* by $2,151 (for 2017) if the dependency is by reason of mental or physical infirmity. (The $2,151 enhancement is already included in the infirm dependant amount of $6,883.) In the case of a child under 18 years of age, the infirmity must be expected to continue for a prolonged and indefinite duration and the child must need significantly more assistance compared to children of the same age in order to qualify for the CCC enhancement to the spousal equivalent/eligible dependant claim (e.g., by a single parent) or for a separate CCC claim of $2,151 (in 2017). The CCC was proposed in the 2017 federal budget.

quality of education of Canadians. Education generally helps develop better citizens, productive workers, and leaders in technology and innovation. Given the rising cost of post-secondary education in Canada, the *ITA* has provided a number of relief measures in the form of tax credits, including a tuition credit (section 118.5) and a credit for interest on student loans (section 118.62).[22] In recognition of the fact that students often do not earn enough income to take advantage of the credits, the *ITA* allows unused tuition credits earned in the year to be transferred to a spouse (section 118.8), parent or grandparent (section 118.9).[23] As well, all unused education-related credits can be carried forward by the student (section 118.61).[24] To be eligible for the credits, the student must be enrolled at a qualifying educational institution (e.g., typically a university, college or other educational institution providing post-secondary courses) on a full-time or part-time basis. The eligibility for the tuition credit is extended to individuals residing in Canada near the Canada-U.S. border and commuting to a post-secondary educational institution in the United States. Since 2011, the tuition credit has been extended to cover occupational, trade or professional examination fees, such as bar admission examination fees for law students (paragraph 118.5(1)(d)).

These tax credits can be justified not only on the basis of social and economic objectives, but also on the basis of technical tax policy. The cost of education is in the nature of investment in human capital. However, unlike investment in physical or financial assets, the cost of which is recovered through the capital cost allowance ("CCA") system or the non-taxation of return of capital, the cost of an investment in human capital cannot be recovered for tax purposes. The earnings of educated taxpayers are fully taxable without any deduction for the cost of education. Educational expenses are not considered as incurred for income-earning purposes and are, thus, not deductible in computing income from employment or business. The effect of the education-related tax credits is to correct the asymmetrical treatment of investment in business and financial capital and investment in human capital. As such, the *ITA* makes education a joint private and public investment in recognition of the fact that education benefits the students, their families, and society as a whole.

---

[22] Before 2017, an education tax credit and a post-secondary textbook credit were allowed under subsection 118.6). The education and textbook credits were abandoned in favour of increased direct expenditures on post-secondary education starting in 2017.

[23] Unused tuition credits (and, before 2017, education and textbook credits) earned in the year can be transferred to a spouse or common-law partner (s. 118.8) or parent or grandparent (s. 118.9), but the amount transferred cannot exceed $5,000 (before multiplying by 15 per cent) minus the amount that is needed to reduce the student's tax to nil after applying most other tax credits available to the student (with the exception of the medical expense credit, the charitable tax credit and the dividend tax credit). See ss. 118.81, 118.92.

[24] Unused tuition credits can be carried forward indefinitely. The credit for student loan interest can be carried forward for five years.

(e) — Charitable gifts credit

Section 118.1 provides for a three-tier charitable gifts credit: credit for the first $200 of donations is computed by using the standard percentage of 15 per cent; the credit for the balance of donations is computed at the top rate of 33 per cent (to the extent that the taxpayer has taxable income taxed in the 33 per cent bracket) with the remainder computed at the rate of 29 per cent. Such a three-tier system clearly indicates Parliament's intent to encourage more charitable giving, especially by high-income earners, as it was thought that having the entire credit at 15 per cent would be a disincentive for donors in the two top tax brackets.

To be eligible for the credit, donations must be made to registered charities and registered athletic associations. Eligible charitable donations are limited to 75 per cent of net income.[25] Donations can be carried forward for five years. There is also a one-year carryback in the year of death. A one-time "first-time donor's super credit" is available to encourage new donors: a "first-time donor" is entitled to a credit equal to 40 per cent (rather than 15 per cent) of the first $200 of donations, and 54 per cent (rather than 33 per cent or 29 per cent) of the excess (up to $1,000).[26]

The main policy justifications for the charitable donation credit and super credit are to encourage private support to charitable organizations that provide important social goods and services, such as education, culture, poverty relief and religion. Through these tax credits, the government subsidizes the production of these goods and services, but giving taxpayers the right to choose the charitable organizations or activities they wish to support.

(f) — Tax credits as relief measures

(i) — Medical expenses

The medical expense credit under section 118.2 provides relief to taxpayers who sustain extraordinary medical expenses on their own account or on account of certain dependants. The types of medical expenses that qualify for the credit are carefully defined in paragraphs 118.2(2)(a) to (u) and are intended to exclude amounts paid for medical or dental services provided purely for cosmetic purposes. The credit is available where the qualifying expenditures exceed the lesser of 3 per cent of the individual's net income or $2,268 (in 2017). In the case of amounts paid for the medical expenses of the taxpayer, the taxpayer's spouse and minor children, it is the taxpayer's net income that is used for this calculation. Medical expenses for

---

[25] There is no 75 per cent net income limit for gifts to Her Majesty (such as universities or hospitals) or gifts of certified cultural property. There is also no 75 per cent net income limit for gifts in the year of death or the previous year.

[26] An individual will qualify as a "first-time donor" if neither the individual nor his or her spouse or common-law partner has claimed a donation tax credit after 2007. The one-time credit applies to donations of money made from March 21, 2013 to December 31, 2017. The maximum donation claim per couple is $1,000 in respect of only one taxation year from 2013 to 2017.

any other dependant (e.g., a child who is 18 or older) are subtotalled separately and reduced by the lesser of the 3 per cent of the dependant's net income and $2,268 (in 2017).

There are several policy justifications for this credit. The health care of Canadians is recognized as a public good through the public funding of medical services. Providing public support through tax credits to individuals who have to pay involuntary, necessary medical and dental expenses is a natural extension of the line of thinking that underlies Canada's public health care system. The challenge lies in the design of the credit to cover only those expenses that need to be subsidized. Another policy justification (and challenge) is the equitable tax treatment of individuals who are not covered by tax-subsidized, employer-provided private health plans.[27]

(ii) — Dividend tax credit

The dividend tax credit under section 121 (discussed in Chapter 14) provides relief from double taxation of income earned through Canadian corporations.

(iii) — Foreign tax credit

The foreign tax credit under section 126 provides relief to taxpayers from international double taxation of income earned from foreign countries. As briefly explained in Chapter 3, such income is included in the resident taxpayer's income. Since the foreign-source country generally taxes the same income as well, Canada cedes its jurisdiction to tax such income through section 126 so that the income is not subject to double taxation. The credit under section 126 is limited to the amount of foreign tax paid as long as it does not exceed the amount of income tax computed under the *ITA*.

(g) — Behaviour-inducing tax credits

The *ITA* provides a number of tax credits aimed at altering taxpayer behavior, including the first-time home buyers' tax credit (section 118.05), and the volunteer firefighter tax credit (section 118.06). The social and economic importance of home ownership underlies the principal residence exemption provision as well as the first-time home buyers' tax credit. And, of course, who can argue against having more volunteer firefighters?

While well-intended, the effect of these credits is often poor. The public transit pass credit in section 118.02, for example, was terminated after June 30, 2017 because evidence showed that that money would be better spent directly investing in public transit.

---

[27] The benefit relating to employer-provided private health care plans is not a taxable benefit federally: s. 6(1)(a)(i). It is a taxable benefit for Quebec income tax purposes.

(h) — Refundable credits

As noted already, a non-refundable tax credit provides little help for those whose incomes are so low that they are outside the tax system altogether or are unable to enjoy the full benefit. The effect is regressive. These regressive features can be eliminated by making the credit "refundable" — the government pays the individuals who qualify for the credit but who have insufficient income to employ (or fully employ) the credit as an offset to their tax liability. A refundable tax credit can also be designed to target low-income individuals or families (i.e., income-tested) and used as a means of delivering tax-free social assistance.

Most of the credits under the *ITA* are neither refundable nor income-tested.[28] The four credits below are the exceptions: they are both refundable and income-tested based on family (net) income (taxpayer and co-habiting spouse). Except for the Canada child benefit, each of them has maximum tax-free benefits and income thresholds that are indexed to inflation each year. The Canada child benefit tax-free benefits and income thresholds will not be indexed until 2020.

(i) — GST/HST credit

The GST/HST credit under section 122.5 is designed to compensate low-income individuals and families for the fact that a sales tax is a regressive tax. The credit is subject to an income test: it starts to reduce when the family income for the previous year reaches a stipulated (indexed) threshold. The amount of the credit (which is calculated by a formula based on the size of the family) is reduced by 5 per cent of the family income for the previous year above the threshold, so that it eventually vanishes altogether. The credit is paid quarterly.

(ii) — Refundable medical expense supplement

The refundable medical expense supplement under section 122.51 is designed to give some additional relief for medical expenses to low-income working individuals. It is available to taxpayers who have a minimum level of income from employment or business in the year ($3,514 in 2017) and begins to vanish at the rate of 5 per cent of family income when family income reaches a stipulated threshold. The credit is paid annually when a tax return is filed.

(iii) — Working income tax benefit

The working income tax benefit ("WITB") under section 122.7 is designed to offset costs incurred by low-income workers 19 years of age or older. The WITB is equal to 25 per cent of employment and business income over $3,000 (with indexed maximum amounts for individuals and families), with an additional supplement for individuals eligible for the disability tax credit. The credit is phased out at a rate of 15 per cent of net income in excess of a stipulated (indexed) threshold and is generally not available to full-time students. The WITB is paid annually when a tax return is

---

[28] However, there are two credits that are income-tested but not refundable: the age credit allowed to persons 65 and older and the medical expense credit.

filed, but taxpayers can apply to have 50 per cent of the WITB paid in advance on a quarterly basis.

(iv) — Canada child benefit

The Canada child benefit ("CCB")[29] under sections 122.6 to 122.63 is designed to support low-income families with children, and is the most generous of the four refundable credits. The CCB is available to an "eligible individual" (typically a parent)[30] in respect of a "qualified dependant". A qualified dependant at any time is defined in section 122.6 as a person who at that time: (a) has not attained the age of 18 years; (b) is not a person in respect of whom a marriage credit was claimed by the person's spouse or common-law partner, and (c) is not a person in respect of whom a special allowance under the *Children's Special Allowances Act*,[31] is payable for the month that includes that time (e.g., a child under foster care).

The CCB is determined based on the number and age of each qualified dependant (child) and the eligible individual's family income for the previous year. The maximum benefit is: $6,400 per year ($533 per month) for each child under the age of 6; $5,400 per year ($450 per month) for each child aged 6 to 17; plus an additional $2,730 per year for each child qualifying for the disability tax credit. Eligible individuals with up to $30,000 in family income receive the maximum benefit. As family income increases, the benefit is phased out at various rates depending on the number of children and the level of family income.

---

[29] The Canada child benefit program replaced the Universal Child Care Benefit ("UCCB"). The UCCB was introduced to apply as of July 1, 2006. The UCCB was similar to the post-World War II universal Family Allowance program that was discontinued when the tax-free income-tested Canada child tax benefit program commenced in 1992. The UCCB was paid to all families (it was not income-tested) and the payments were taxable in the hands of the lower-income parent.

[30] To qualify as an "eligible individual" in respect of a qualified dependant at any time, the individual must at that time: (a) reside with the qualified dependant; (b) either be the parent who primarily fulfils the responsibility for the child's "care and upbringing"[30] and who is not a "share-custody parent" in respect of the child, or be the "share-custody parent" of the child; (c) be resident in Canada; (d) not be an employee of a foreign country; (e) either be, or have a "co-habiting spouse or common-law partner who is, a Canadian citizen or a permanent resident within the meaning of subsection 2(1) of the *Immigration and Refugee Protection Act*, S.C. 2001, c. 27 ("*IRPA*"), a temporary resident within the meaning of the *IRPA*, who was resident in Canada throughout the preceding 18-month period, a protected person within the meaning of the *IRPA*, a member of a class defined in the *Humanitarian Designated Classes Regulations*, or an Indian within the meaning of the *Indian Act*, R.S.C. 1985, c. I-5. Where the child resides with his or her female parent, that female parent is presumed to be the parent who primarily fulfils the responsibility for the child's care and upbringing. As a result, the dependant's female parent will most often be the eligible individual who receives the child tax benefit payment. The presumption does not apply in such circumstances as where the female parent declares in writing to the Minister that the male parent, with whom she resides, is the eligible individual.

[31] S.C. 1992, c. 48, Schedule.

12.6 — The alternative minimum tax

(a) — Rationale

As discussed in previous chapters, the *ITA* is replete with tax expenditure provisions, providing various tax preferences. As many of the tax preferences are available only to wealthy individuals, higher-income taxpayers are sometimes able to avail themselves of sufficient tax preferences to reduce their tax liability to an extremely low figure. Indeed, it became apparent in the mid-1980s that tax preferences enabled a few wealthy individuals to escape the bite of tax altogether. The ensuing public protest caused the enactment in 1986 of the alternative minimum tax ("AMT") under section 127.5.

The AMT is "alternative" because taxpayers must calculate both the amount of their AMT and their "ordinary tax", and then pay whichever figure is greater. The rate of the AMT is 15 per cent (the rate applicable to the lowest tax bracket in section 117), which combines with the lowest provincial tax to yield a combined rate of approximately 20 to 25 per cent. The AMT differs from ordinary income tax in that it is calculated on a broader tax base (one that excludes many tax preferences) than the ordinary income tax. However, if the AMT is payable, the amount by which it exceeds the ordinary income tax is available as a credit against ordinary income tax in any of the following 10 years. In most cases, therefore, the AMT will not be an additional tax liability, but rather an early payment of a future tax liability.

The political appeal of the AMT can be easily understood, but its tax policy rationale is less easy to fathom. If the tax preferences that are excluded from the AMT base are unfair, then surely the appropriate response is to repeal them. Since it is the policy of the government to retain the provisions, why should some taxpayers be precluded from using them? In any case, the AMT applies to few taxpayers and raises little revenue, so that it is of little practical importance.

(b) — Computation of the AMT

There are four steps involved in determining the amount of the AMT. First, a taxpayer must recalculate his or her taxable income based on the peculiar rules under section 127.52. This process basically involves the calculation of taxable income in the normal way, followed by the adding back into income of those deductions considered to be tax preferences. For example, a taxpayer who had reported a taxable capital gain would be required to add 30 per cent of the capital gain back into his or her taxable income for the purposes of the AMT, so that 80 per cent (rather than 50 per cent) is applicable. Once this "adjusted taxable income" has been calculated, the next step is that the taxpayer is allowed to deduct a "basic exemption" of $40,000 from the adjusted taxable income. The $40,000 exemption ensures that only upper-income taxpayers making extensive use of tax preferences will be subjected to the AMT. The third step is to apply the rate of 15 per cent to the figure determined by the previous calculations. Finally, taxpayers are permitted to deduct certain credits from the amount of tax thus far determined. However, many credits that would otherwise be available are not available for the purposes of the AMT on the ground that they are tax preferences.

Having derived the amount of the AMT, the taxpayer must now compare this figure to the ordinary tax otherwise payable, and pay the greater of the two amounts. Only where the amount of the AMT exceeds the amount of tax calculated in the ordinary way is the taxpayer obliged to pay the AMT. If the taxpayer must pay the AMT rather than his or her ordinary tax, the amount by which the AMT exceeds the ordinary tax may be carried forward for up to 10 years and used as a credit against tax in any year where ordinary tax payable exceeds the AMT. For example, if in Year 1 a taxpayer has calculated $30,000 of ordinary tax, and $36,000 of AMT, the taxpayer must pay the higher figure of $36,000. However, the $6,000 difference between ordinary tax and AMT may be carried forward for up to 10 years. If in Year 2 the taxpayer's ordinary tax payable is $40,000 and his or her AMT is only $30,000, the $6,000 carried forward from the previous year may be applied to reduce the tax liability for Year 2 to $34,000.

The five steps for the calculation of AMT are summarized in Table 12-1, which follows.

Table 12-1
Taxable income

Step 1	+/- Adjustments (a)	
	Adjusted taxable income	
Step 2	($40,000 Exemption)	
	Net amount	
Step 3	× 15% Rate	
	Minimum tax before minimum tax credits	
Step 4	(Minimum tax credits) (b)	
	Minimum tax	
Step 5	Compare to basic federal tax and use the greater (c)	

Notes:

(a) *The adjustments to taxable income include*

   Additions

      Losses due to CCA or interest/carrying charges on rental, leasing, film and videotape properties

      Losses due to resource deductions

30% of the excess of capital gains over capital losses for the year[32]

60% of the stock option deduction[33]

Losses from united partnerships

Home relocation loan deduction[34]

Losses from partnerships in which the taxpayer is a passive partner

Losses from tax shelters

Resource-related deductions

Deductions

30% of business investment losses for the year

Dividend gross-up

(b) *The credits exclude*

Credits transferred from others

Pension and dividend tax credits

Political tax credit

Investment tax credit

(c) *There is a similar calculation for most provinces.*

12.7 — Provincial taxes

Canadian provinces and territories also levy income taxes.[35] Most provinces have progressive rate structures similar to the federal structure. Some provinces have made the progression steeper for provincial purposes, allowing credits against provincial tax for low-income taxpayers, and imposing a provincial surtax on high-income taxpayers. As can be seen below, Ontario has five brackets: the first two

---

[32] The purpose of the 30 per cent add back is to include 80 per cent of the capital gain in AMT income (80% = 50% + 30%). When the taxable capital gains fraction was 3/4, the entire capital gain was included in AMT income. However, when the fraction changed to one-half, including the entire capital gain was thought to be too severe: 80 per cent was a compromise.

[33] The stock option deduction is normally 50 per cent of the stock option benefit. The purpose of the 60 per cent add back is to reduce the stock option deduction from 50 per cent to 20 per cent of the stock option benefit ([100% - 60%] × 50% = 20%), thereby resulting in 80 per cent of the stock option benefit being included in AMT income. When the stock option deduction was 25 per cent of the stock option benefit, the entire deduction was added back. However, when the fraction was changed to one-half, including the entire stock option benefit was thought to be too severe: like the treatment of capital gains, *ibid.*, 80 per cent was a compromise.

[34] *ITA*, *supra* note 1, s. 110(1)(j). The March 22, 2017 federal budget proposed to repeal s. 110(1)(j) for 2018 and subsequent years.

[35] See Chapter 1 at heading 1.3(f) — Provincial income tax statutes.

brackets are indexed and cover almost equal amounts of taxable income. The third bracket was the top tax bracket until 2012, when a fourth indexed bracket was added for 2012 and 2013: 12.16 per cent on income in excess of $500,000 in 2012, changing to 13.16 per cent on income in excess of $509,000. In 2014, the fourth bracket was changed to 12.16 per cent on income over $150,000 up to $220,000 and a new fifth bracket of 13.16 per cent on income over $220,000 was added. Because these top two brackets have not been indexed, the rates and brackets in Ontario in 2017 are as follows:

Ontario Tax Bracket	Rate
First $42,401	5.05%
Over $42,401 up to $84,404	9.15%
Over $84,404 up to $150,000	11.16%
Over $150,000 up to $220,000	12.16%
Over $220,000	13.16%

In order to obtain an individual's total combined federal and provincial tax rate, the provincial rates have to be added to the federal rates. For example, the highest combined federal-provincial rate of tax in Ontario in 2017 is 53.53 per cent, a figure that includes the 33 per cent federal top rate, the 13.16 Ontario top rate, and two Ontario surtaxes.[36] In Alberta, on the other hand, the highest combined rate is 48 per cent (the 33 per cent federal top rate and the 15 per cent Alberta top rate) and in British Columbia, the highest combined rate is 47.70 per cent (the 33 per cent federal top rate plus the 14.70 per cent top British Columbia rate). The rate structures in Alberta and British Columbia are progressive but there are no surtaxes.

When provinces levy surtaxes, they are calculated on provincial tax, not income.[37] The taxpayer first determines the amount of his or her federal tax, and then calculates provincial tax and then adds the provincial surtax (or surtaxes) to yield the full tax liability. Surtaxes make the rate structure more progressive, which could also be done through the creation of additional tax brackets. Replacing surtaxes by building additional tax brackets would make the actual rates of provincial tax more transparent to taxpayers, and would make it harder for governments to hide tax increases by changing surtaxes. Changing the rate schedule is considered to be a reform of the tax system, whereas introducing or changing a surtax is considered to be a more temporary measure.[38]

---

[36] That is, 53.53% = 33% plus 1.56 × 13.16%. The provincial surtaxes are 20 per cent and 36 per cent and are levied as follows in 2017: 20 per cent of Basic Ontario Tax over $4,556 plus 36 per cent of Basic Ontario Tax over $5,831. Basic Ontario tax is Ontario tax after deducting most tax credits except the dividend tax credit.

[37] *Ibid.*

[38] There are no federal surtaxes at present, but there was a high-income surtax from 1991 to 2000 (it was 5 per cent of basic federal tax over $15,500 in 2000) and a general federal surtax in effect from 1986 to 1999 that applied to all taxpayers (the rate varied between 1.5 per cent, 3 per cent and 5 per cent, depending on the year): s. 180.1. The general federal surtax was introduced as a temporary measure to reduce the deficit and was to be removed

Since 2001 (when tax on income ("TONI") was introduced), indexing for inflation has been slightly different for provincial purposes than for federal purposes. In other words, while tax brackets (and credits and other limits) started out the same in 2000, they have changed since then because of the different approaches to indexation taken by the various provinces. Some provinces index by the national or provincial CPI, some use a modified index, and some have not indexed at all since 2000 or 2001. Ontario, Manitoba, Alberta, British Columbia, and the three territories, for example, use each province's/territory's CPI for indexation, rather than the national CPI.

---

when the GST was introduced. Although the GST was introduced in 1991, the state of the federal deficit discouraged previous federal governments from removing this surtax. In 1999, the general surtax was reduced to 1.5 per cent of basic federal tax and eliminated for low- and middle-income taxpayers. In 2000, it was removed completely.

13

INCOME SPLITTING

13.1 — Whose income?

Previous chapters have discussed two of the crucial questions that an income tax law must answer, namely: what items are taxable and how is income computed? This chapter deals with another crucial question, namely: whose income is it?

Ordinarily, of course, the question "whose income is it?" is easily answered. Income is taxed to the person who earns and receives it, by providing personal services as an employee, by carrying on a business, or by virtue of owning property. However, in some instances the question requires further analysis, both in terms of technical rules and tax policy. One major instance arises in the context of the family. Family members often make gifts to each other and share economic resources, and some family members (often parents) exercise some control over the economic and personal lives of others (children). Related to this context is the use of family-controlled corporations and trusts as intermediaries between the legal owner and the income. High-income individuals may use such legal arrangements to shift income to corporations and/or lower-income earners of the family to minimize tax. Another instance arises in the business world when related corporate taxpayers enter into transactions with each other to gain maximum after-tax profit for the entire corporate group. In such instances, the corporations may have a shared economic interest in shifting income to corporate taxpayers that have deductions or are taxed at lower rates.

Tax law generally relies on private law for determining who is the owner of income. Should tax law ignore the formal legal arrangements in certain circumstances to protect the integrity of the tax system? If so, what are those circumstances?

13.2 — Legislative scheme

(a) — Technical rules

(i) — Choice of tax unit and rates

The choice of tax unit and rate structure "invites" taxpayers to "legally" shift income to related persons for tax purposes. The *Income Tax Act* (the "*ITA*")[1] taxes each person separately and taxes individuals at progressive rates. As explained in Chapter 12, the first dollar of taxable income is currently taxed at 15 per cent and this rate rises as income rises (currently to a maximum of 33 per cent). The net result is that, as taxable income rises, tax liability also rises, both in absolute terms and as a percentage of income. The progressive rate structure encourages high-income individuals to shift income to low-income family members or to entities taxed at lower rates, such as corporations. This effort is often referred to as the "splitting" of income.

For example, if a child owns property in his or her own right, the income from the property is included in the child's taxable income and reported on the child's tax return. The child is eligible for the basic personal credit, which effectively exempts the first $11,635 (in 2017) of income from tax.[2] The applicable tax rate will be determined by the child's taxable income. The *ITA* does not lump the child's income together with the parents', even though parents and children are obviously members of a single household. Because the marginal rate varies from one individual to another, depending upon the individual's income bracket, a family whose

---

[1] R.S.C. 1985 (5th Supp.), c. 1 [*ITA*].

[2] See Chapter 12 at heading 12.5 — Tax credits.

entire income is taxed to one member — say, the father — would usually pay a higher overall tax than a family with the same income but divided evenly among all the family members.

As discussed in Chapter 14, a taxpayer's income can be earned through a corporation or trust. A corporation computes its tax liability separately from its owners (the shareholders) and pays tax at a rate lower than the rate of individual shareholders. For example, if a taxpayer operates a business as a sole proprietor and earns $500,000 in 2017, the income is subject to tax at progressive rates (with a top combined federal-provincial rate of over 53 per cent applying to income over $220,000 in Ontario).[3] If the business is operated through a corporation, the tax rate applicable to the entire income is 15 per cent in Ontario.[4] In addition, a taxpayer can "split" the income by having family members as shareholders and "sprinkling" dividends among them. "There is nothing in the [corporate statute] or at common law that prohibits this dividend allocation technique."[5] It was, therefore, not surprising that the 2017 federal budget promised a review of the use of private corporations to achieve what may be considered undue tax avoidance. In July 2017, the Department of Finance issued a consultation paper describing the government's concerns and its proposed responses, as well as draft legislation limiting income sprinkling and the use of the lifetime capital gains exemption effective for 2018 and subsequent years.[6]

---

[3] See Chapter 12 at heading 12.7 — Provincial taxes.

[4] On income eligible for the small business deduction, the federal tax rate is 10.5 per cent and the provincial tax rate in Ontario is 4.5 per cent

[5] *McClurg v. M.N.R.*, [1991] 1 C.T.C. 169, 91 D.T.C. 5001 (S.C.C.) [*McClurg*] at para. 14. Iacobucci J. of the Supreme Court of Canada stated in *Neuman v. Minister of National Revenue*, [1998] 3 C.T.C. 177, 98 D.T.C. 6297 (S.C.C.) [*Neuman*] at para. 63: "[T]axpayers can arrange their affairs in a particular way for the sole purpose of deliberately availing themselves of tax reduction devices in the *ITA*." That, he explained, included the use of "corporate structures which exist for the sole purpose of avoiding tax".

[6] See the consultation paper, Department of Finance, Canada, "Tax Planning Using Private Corporations" (18 July 2017) [July 2017 consultation paper], online: <http://www.fin.gc.ca/activty/consult/tppc-pfsp-eng.asp>, and the draft legislation, online: <http://www.fin.gc.ca/drleg-apl/2017/ita-lir-0717-eng.asp>. As discussed at heading 13.5 — Kiddie tax, below, the draft legislation proposes to limit income sprinkling using dividends by adding a reasonableness test and expanding the tax on split income (the so-called "kiddie tax"), which will no longer just apply to minors. Legislative proposals relating to the use of the lifetime capital gains exemption are also briefly discussed at heading 13.5. The consultation paper discusses the draft legislation as well as possible measures to eliminate the tax deferral advantage that results when after-tax business earnings are invested in passive investments inside a corporation rather than outside a corporation on which it is seeking input. This tax deferral advantage is discussed further in Chapter 14 at heading 14.3 — Private corporations.

(ii) — Specific income splitting rules

The *ITA* contains a number of rules that specifically permit family members, especially spouses, to split income. For example, transfers of capital property can be done on a cost (or rollover) basis between spouses or common-law partners.[7] Other examples include the deduction for a contribution to a registered retirement savings plan ("RRSP") for a spouse or common-law partner,[8] the pension-income splitting rules,[9] and the exemption of tax-free savings account ("TFSA") withdrawals from the anti-income splitting rules discussed below.[10]

(iii) — Anti-income splitting rules

Income splitting is possible because the *ITA* generally relies on private law to determine the ownership of income. A taxpayer can, therefore, use legally effective arrangements and structures to allocate income to a spouse, child or other family member.

In certain circumstances, however, the *ITA* prevents income splitting by ignoring these legal arrangements and taxing the person that actually earns the income. These rules include the following:

- attribution of income that formally belongs to a spouse or minor child to the taxpayer who loaned or transferred the income-producing property to the spouse or child or to a trust for the spouse's or child's benefit (sections 74.1 and 74.3);

- attribution of capital gains from the disposition of property loaned or transferred to a spouse or a spouse trust (sections 74.2 and 74.3);

- imputation of income at the prescribed interest rate to a taxpayer who transfers property to a corporation for the purpose of splitting income with a spouse or child (section 74.4);

- assignment of income from the person who formally receives the payment to the taxpayer who actually "earns" it (i.e., subsection 56(2)); and

- a special tax on "split income" at the top rate (the so-called "kiddie tax") when certain types of income, such as dividends from a private corporation, are earned by minor children (section 120.4).[11]

---

[7] See Chapter 10 at heading 10.4(c)(iv)(A) — Rollovers for transfers to a spouse or common-law partner.

[8] See Chapter 11 at heading 11.3(b) — Tax assistance to retirement savings.

[9] *Ibid.*

[10] *ITA, supra* note 1, s. 74.5(12): see Chapter 11 at heading 11.4(a) — Tax free savings accounts (TFSAs).

[11] Other rules preventing income splitting include: limitations on deductions for compensation paid to family members (such as ss. 67 and 18(1)(h), discussed in Chapter 8); restrictions for "personal services businesses", which effectively "pierce the corporate veil" in the

The statutory "anti-split" rules have become increasingly complicated over the years, as more and more loopholes have gradually been plugged. As a result, they now add considerable complexity to the *ITA*. Some anti-avoidance rules even have their own anti-avoidance rules to ensure that they are not abused by crafty tax planning. For example, subsection 74.5(11) provides that the attribution rules do not apply to a transfer or loan of property "where it may reasonably be concluded that one of the main reasons for the transfer or loan" was to use the attribution rules to reduce the tax on the income or capital gain derived from the property. In addition, the general anti-avoidance rule ("GAAR") under section 245 is potentially applicable to income splitting transactions, especially where the transaction was designed to circumvent the application of any specific anti-avoidance rules.[12]

(b) — Policy issues

(i) — Progressivity of individual taxation

The personal income tax system is the only element of the Canadian tax structure that is truly progressive. It allocates the tax burden among Canadians on the basis of the ability to pay and helps redistribute income to achieve equity. Income splitting allows high-income earners to reduce their tax liability, resulting in the overall reduction of progressivity of the tax system. If progressivity is justified, controlling income splitting is undeniably an important policy objective.

(ii) — Fairness and integrity of the system

"Fairness" is a fundamental notion of tax policy. It certainly encompasses fair treatment of individual taxpayers. It is true that the *ITA* does not treat all taxpayers equally, owing to administrative and other policy reasons. "Opportunities of tax avoidance are not equal, for it clearly has little practical meaning to salaried and wage-earning taxpayers from whom tax is deducted at source . . ."[13] The *ITA* explicitly removes the tax advantages of using corporations by employees.[14] Owners of businesses and investments have more opportunities to split income. However, both fairness and the integrity of the tax system are undermined if the tax liability of certain taxpayers is "dependent upon the taxpayer's sophistication at manipulating a sequence of events to achieve a patina of compliance with the apparent pre-

---

case of incorporated employment income (i.e., s. 125(7), which denies the small business deduction, and s. 18(1)(p), which limits the expense deductions); and substitution of fair market value for the transfer price in non-arm's-length transactions (s. 69(1), discussed in Chapter 10 at heading 10.4(c)(iii) — Transfers with non-arm's-length persons).

[12] One example is *Lipson v. R.*, [2009] 1 C.T.C. 314, 2009 D.T.C. 5015 (Eng.), 2009 D.T.C. 5016 (Fr.) (S.C.C.), which is discussed in more detail in Chapter 17.

[13] Canada, *Report of the Royal Commission on Taxation* (Ottawa: Queen's Printer, 1966) (Chairman: Kenneth Le M. Carter) [*Carter Report*], vol. 3, Appendix A at 542.

[14] See Chapter 14 at heading 14.3(c)(iii) — CCPCs as incorporated employees.

requisites for a tax deduction".[15] Taxpayers who use devices and schemes to minimize their tax burden shift the tax burden to other taxpayers.

On the other hand, individual taxpayers have the right to arrange their affairs to minimize their tax. As the Supreme Court noted in *Canada Trustco Mortgage Co. v. Canada* (2005), the preservation of "certainty, predictability and fairness" for individual taxpayers is considered a "basic tenet of tax law".[16] In *Neuman*, Iacobucci J. warned that courts should not be "quick to embellish" tax avoidance provisions in the *ITA*, but should await "precise and specific" measures from legislators to combat any perceived "mischief".[17]

(iii) — Treatment of the family

The *ITA* does not regard the family as a taxation unit. As explained above, this creates income splitting opportunities between spouses and between parents and children. If the family were the taxation unit, there would be less tax incentive to split income among family members. Many jurisdictions remove the most obvious temptation to income splitting by aggregating for tax purposes the incomes of spouses (or common-law partners). The Carter Commission's recommended family unit went one step further by including children's income in the aggregation.[18] Canada has rejected these approaches, but the *ITA* recognizes the family in limited instances, such as the spousal rollover rules.[19]

It may be argued that income splitting has some positive social implications. It may be an incentive for property owners to share their property with their spouses, common-law partners and children, and this might contribute in some small way to a more equitable distribution of wealth, especially to women, who often lack the same opportunity to accumulate wealth as men. The anti-splitting rules may have the effect of discouraging substantial intra-family gifts by taxing the income or capital gains from the gifted property in the hands of the transferor.

13.3 — Attribution rules

(a) — Nature and scope

(i) — Tax "fictions"

Generally, income from property is treated for tax purposes as owned by the owner of the property and is taxed to that person, at his or her rate. The "attribution rules" under sections 74.1 to 74.4 change the general rule: the income or capital gain that

---

[15] *The Queen v. Bronfman Trust*, [1987] 1 C.T.C. 117, 87 D.T.C. 5059 (S.C.C.).

[16] *Canada Trustco Mortgage Co. v. R.*, [2005] 5 C.T.C. 215, 2005 D.T.C. 5523 (S.C.C.) at para. 61.

[17] *Neuman, supra* note 4 at para. 63.

[18] *Carter Report, supra* note 13, vol. 3, ch. 10.

[19] See Chapter 2 at heading 2.5 — Tax unit.

belongs to one person is deemed for tax purposes to belong to another person.[20] The income or gain is "attributed" to that other person. The attribution rules apply only to property transferred or loaned, directly or indirectly, by a taxpayer to a spouse or common-law partner or a related minor.[21]

Assume that A and B are common-law partners and A is the high-income earner. A gives $1,000 cash to B, and B invests the money in a bond that earns $100 interest every year. The interest income is taxed to A under section 74.1, even if it is legally received by B. The same rule applies if B were a five-year-old daughter of A. In the case of capital gains, however, as discussed further below, section 74.2 applies only to transfers (and loans) to a spouse or common-law partner.

The attribution rules are tax "fictions" in that the attributed income or gain "belongs to" the transferor only for tax purposes. For all other purposes, the transfer is perfectly valid and the transferee is the legal owner. In essence, they treat the transferor as if the property had not been transferred.

(ii) — Spouse, common-law partner or related minor

The attribution rules in sections 74.1 to 74.5 apply only to the immediate members of a taxpayer's family: spouse, common-law partner or related minor.[22] The attribution will end in the event of the termination of the spousal or common-law relationship, or the death of either party, or the permanent departure from Canada of the transferor. Where spouses or common-law partners are living separate and apart because of a breakdown of their marriage or common-law partnership, subsection 74.5(3) provides that attribution of income under section 74.1 is suspended for as long as the separation continues.[23] If the marriage is ended by divorce, the attribution rules will cease to apply.

This chapter uses the term "related minor" as a shorthand for "a person who was under 18 years of age" and who "does not deal with the individual [transferor] at arm's length, or is the niece or nephew of the individual [transferor]".[24] A niece or nephew of a taxpayer is not "related" to the taxpayer under section 251(2),[25] but is

---

[20] Note, however, that s. 160 makes both parties liable, and empowers the Minister to assess both parties. Presumably, this power would be invoked only if the tax could not be collected from the owner of the property.

[21] The term "related minor" is used in this chapter as a shorthand for minors who are either related (for tax purposes) to the taxpayer or are the taxpayer's nieces or nephews.

[22] *ITA, supra* note 1, s. 56(4.1), discussed at heading 13.4(d) — Interest-free or low-interest loans, below, may apply to attribute income from loans to other non-arm's-length individuals made for income splitting purposes.

[23] The spousal RRSP attribution rules are also suspended (s. 146(8.3)), but attribution of capital gains can only be suspended if a joint election is made (s. 74.5(3)(b)).

[24] See wording of s. 74.1(2) and definition of "designated person" in s. 74.5(5)(b), which is used in ss. 74.3 to 74.5 of the *ITA, supra* note 1.

[25] As discussed in Chapter 10 at heading 10.4(c)(iii) — Transfers with non-arm's-length persons, related persons are deemed not to deal at arm's length (s. 251(1)(a)) and individuals

brought into the attribution rules as if he or she was related. A transfer (or loan) to a minor is, thus, subject to the attribution rules if the minor transferee is the transferor's child, grandchild, brother, sister, niece or nephew.[26]

(iii) — "Transfer" or "loan" directly or indirectly

The attribution rules apply to income transferred or loaned by a taxpayer to a spouse or common-law partner or a related minor. A "transfer" typically includes a gift or sale. Gifts are the primary targets of these rules. A sale for fair market value is exempted from the attribution rules. A "loan" is specifically added to overrule court decisions that a loan was not a transfer for purposes of the attribution rules.[27]

Indirect transfers and loans are specifically covered by the attribution rules. Indirect transfers refer to transfers accomplished through intermediaries.[28] The *ITA* specifically deals with "back-to-back transfers and loans", in which it is the intervention of a third-party individual that masks the transfer of property to a spouse, common-law partner or related minor. For example, Partner A could give Blackacre to a third party, who in turn gives the property to Partner B. Or, A could give Blackacre to a third party, who in turn gives Greenacre to B. In both these examples, there is no direct transfer or loan from A to B, but the third party is playing a purely intermediary role in what is, in substance, a gift from A to B. Both cases are specifically provided for by subsection 74.5(6), which treats the transactions as if the property had been given directly by A to B.

(iv) — Exception for fair market value transactions

The attribution rules do not apply to a transfer of property for fair market value under subsection 74.5(1). The reason for the exemption is that, if fair market value has been paid by the transferee spouse, common-law partner or related minor, then

---

are "related" for tax purposes to individuals connected by blood, marriage or adoption (s. 251(2)(a)). Minor individuals connected by blood would include a taxpayer's sibling or child (or other descendant) but not a niece, nephew or cousin (s. 251(6)). See also Canada Revenue Agency, Folio S1-F5-C1, "Related Persons and Dealing at Arm's Length".

[26] Attribution of income from a related minor will continue for so long as the transferor remains a resident of Canada and the transferee remains under the age of 18. In the taxation year in which the transferee attains the age of 18, attribution ceases. The death of either the transferor or the transferee will also bring the attribution to an end.

[27] See *Dunkelman v. M.N.R.*, [1959] C.T.C. 375, 59 D.T.C. 1242 (Can. Ex. Ct.); *Oelbaum v. M.N.R.*, [1968] C.T.C. 244, 68 D.T.C. 5176 (Can. Ex. Ct.). Because an interest-free loan was held to be outside the attribution rules, interest-free loans became a common method of avoiding the attribution rules. The lender would derive no income from the money lent, because no interest was payable. The borrowing spouse or minor would invest the borrowed money in income-producing investments, and the resulting income would not be attributed back to the lender. In this way, a diversion of income was achieved.

[28] E.g., *Naiberg v. M.N.R.* (1969), 69 D.T.C. 361, [1969] Tax A.B.C. 492 (Can. Tax App. Bd.), where attribution was applied to a complex scheme involving transfers of property among three married couples.

the transferor has simply substituted another potentially income-producing asset for the one transferred; there is no income splitting and the transaction is outside the mischief of the attribution rules. However, paragraph 74.5(1)(a) stipulates that the consideration must be at least equal in value to the property transferred, and paragraph 74.5(1)(b) stipulates that, if the consideration includes indebtedness, the purchaser must be obliged to pay a commercial rate of interest and must actually regularly pay the interest. These stipulations ensure that artificial sales for inadequate consideration or for consideration in the form of an interest-free debt cannot be used as devices to divert property income from the "vendor" to a "purchaser" who is a spouse,[29] common-law partner or a related minor.

There is a similar exemption for loans at a commercial rate of interest. Subsection 74.5(2) exempts a loan if the loan is made at a commercial rate of interest and if the borrower actually regularly pays the interest. The reason for this exemption is that, if the debt bears interest, the lender has acquired an income-producing asset (the debt) for the money lent; there is no income splitting and the transaction is outside the mischief of the attribution rules.

(b) — Income from transferred or loaned property

The attribution rules under section 74.1 apply only to income or loss from a property transferred or loaned by the taxpayer to a spouse or common-law partner or a related minor. In addition to income derived from the transferred or loaned property, these rules apply to income from a "substituted property". As such, if the transferee sells the transferred property and reinvests the proceeds of sale, the attribution rules continue to cling to the new investments. Income from the new investments will be attributed in the same way as if the investments were the original subjects of the transfer or loan.[30]

Section 74.1 does not attribute income from a business. The characterization of income earned from the transferred property is, thus, crucial. The transfer of an apartment building (yielding property income) will attract attribution, while the transfer of an apartment hotel (yielding business income) will not.[31] This gap in the attribution rules may be explained on the basis that income from a business does not flow automatically from the ownership of property, but requires activity on the

---

[29] In the case of a spouse or common-law partner, s. 74.5(1)(c) adds the further requirement that, on the sale, the transferor must have elected against the s. 73(1) rollover.

[30] However, if the recipient of property to which the attribution rules apply invests the income yielded by the transferred property, the income yielded by the investments representing the income ("income on income" or "second generation income") is not attributed. Investments that represent income from the transferred property are neither property transferred nor property substituted therefor. For the same reason, interest on interest that is allowed to accumulate is also not attributed. This is recognized by in Canada Revenue Agency, Interpretation Bulletin IT-511R, "Interspousal and certain other transfers and loans of property" (1994) at para. 6.

[31] For the distinction between business and property income, see Chapter 6 at heading 6.3(b) — Property income distinguished from business income.

part of the transferee (or his or her employees). In view of the difficulty of apportioning the transferee's income from the business between the assets transferred and the transferee's own efforts, the *ITA* does not attribute any of the income from the business.[32]

(c) — Attribution of capital gains

Where a property is transferred or loaned to a spouse or common-law partner, capital gains or losses realized by the transferee from disposition of the property are attributed to the transferor pursuant to section 74.2.[33] If the transferee is a related minor, this provision does not apply.[34] In other words, while the attribution of income under section 74.1 covers loans and transfers to both spouses or common-law partners and children, the attribution of capital gains under section 74.2 is limited to transfers to a spouse or common-law partner.[35]

What are the technical and policy justifications for attributing capital gains from a spouse or common-law partner, but not a child? Technically, although these rules appear incoherent when viewed on a stand-alone basis, they make sense when viewed as part of the scheme of the *ITA* that deals with intra-family transfers. You may recall that the tax treatment of the initial transfer from the taxpayer to a spouse or common-law partner and a child is different: a transfer to the former qualifies for a "rollover" under subsection 73(1), but a transfer to a child does not. In the absence of an attribution, a taxpayer could transfer a property with accrued gains to a spouse or common-law partner and divert not only the gains accrued after the transfer, but also the gains accrued prior to the transfer. That would be a complete shift of the transferor's tax liability to the transferee spouse or common-law partner. On a transfer to a child, because capital gains must be accrued to the transferor by virtue of subsection 69(1), and the child is deemed to acquire the property at its fair

---

[32] There is a rule, however, that deems income (that would otherwise be business income) earned by a limited partner in a limited partnership or a passive partner in a partnership to be property income: s. 96(1.8). This rule was introduced when it became popular to transfer businesses such as hotels and nursing homes to partnerships and then sell them as passive partnership investments, which would otherwise be exempt from the attribution rules.

[33] The attribution of capital gains to a spouse generally ends when the income attribution ends: on death or divorce (when the taxpayer is no longer a spouse) or departure from Canada (when the taxpayer is no longer resident in Canada): see the preamble to ss. 74.1 and 74.2. However, if there is a marital breakdown and spouses are living separate and apart, income attribution will automatically be suspended but capital gains will not. Both spouses must jointly elect to suspend capital gains attribution. If the separation is ended by reconciliation, the attribution rules will return to force. See ss. 74.5(3) and (4).

[34] This is because s. 74.1(2), like s. 74.1(1), applies only to income or loss from property, and there is no equivalent of s. 74.2 applicable to transfers to minors.

[35] However, capital gains and losses on the transfer of farming or fishing property from a taxpayer to his or her child are attributed to the transferor under section 75.1, but this is a special case (explained in note 36, *infra*). In general, there is no attribution of capital gains or losses on a transfer to a minor.

market value at the time of the transfer, only gains accrued after the transfer are shifted to the child.[36]

Conceptually, the capital gains attribution rule reflects the recognition of the marital unit as a tax unit in respect of property transfers, but not the unit of parents and children. In the case of transfers between spouses or common-law partners, the *ITA* effectively ignores the transfers. No real tax consequences arise until the property finally leaves the marital unit. For example, Partner A buys a rental property in Year 1 for $20,000 and earns $3,000 rental income (characterized as income from property) each year. In Year 1, A includes the rent in his income. In Year 2, A gives the property to his partner, B, when the fair market value is $21,000 and B receives the $3,000 rent. The accrued $500 gain is not taxable to A because of the rollover, and B is deemed to have bought the property at a cost equal to $20,000. The $3,000 rental income is attributed to A under section 74.1. When B sells the property in Year 3 for $24,000, the $4,000 capital gain is attributed to A (so is any rental income earned prior to the sale). Consequently, as far as tax law is concerned, the outcome is exactly the same as if A has owned the property until the sale in Year 3.

In contrast, a child is treated by the *ITA* as a separate taxpayer. Transfers of property (other than farming or fishing property or a woodlot) between a parent and his or her child are treated like fair market value gifts to total strangers. Income from the property transferred is attributed to the parent under section 74.1 because of anti-avoidance concerns: the assumption is that the parent exercises *de facto* control over the income received from the investment of the property until the child turns 18 years of age. Taxation of capital gains generally occurs only when the property is disposed of. Because the attribution ceases in the year of the minor's 18th birthday, a minor could avoid attribution of capital gains very easily, by not disposing of the transferred property until January 1 of the year he or she turns 18. One way of precluding this result would be to provide for a "deemed disposition" of the transferred property at fair market value immediately before that time. But the policy decision was evidently taken not to introduce that much complexity into the system. The result is that the *ITA* makes no provision for attribution of capital gains derived by a transferee-minor when logic would dictate that it should. When the rule was designed in 1972, very few minors earned capital gains. At that time, there were very few mutual funds that would allow investors to invest to earn capital gains annually on a diversified portfolio of growth investments. The situation is quite different today, and investing in growth mutual funds that earn capital gains is one of the main ways that parents can income split with their minor children.

---

[36] In the case of farming property, fishing property and woodlots, there is a rollover on a transfer from the taxpayer to his or her child under s. 73(3), and that is the special case in which there is attribution of capital gains and losses (s. 75.1).

(d) — Transfers or loans to a trust

Transfers of property to a trust are subject to the attribution rules if the beneficiary of the trust is a spouse, common-law partner or related minor of the settlor. As mentioned above, the attribution rules specifically include "indirect transfers" through the use of a trust. As such, the interposition of a trust between the transferor and the transferee will not avoid the application of these rules.[37] Section 74.3 provides for specific rules to backstop the basic attribution rules. Simply explained, where the trust's property income is paid or payable to a spouse, common-law partner or related minor, subsection 74.1(1) or (2) applies. Where the trust's capital gains are paid or payable to a spouse or common-law partner, section 74.2 applies. This is so, even if the payment is the exercise of a discretionary power by the trustee. Where income is not paid or payable to beneficiaries, it is generally taxed in the trust at the top marginal rate.

In addition, the trust income may be attributed to the settlor under subsection 75(2). This provision operates to attribute to the settlor income or taxable capital gains from property transferred to a trust in which a settlor has reserved to himself or herself a power to revoke the trust, or a power to change the beneficiaries, or a power to direct or veto dispositions of the trust property. Attribution occurs regardless of who are the beneficiaries of the trust; subsection 75(2) is not confined to trusts for spouses and related minors. The idea is that a settlor should not be able to divert taxable income away to the beneficiaries of a trust while continuing to retain substantial control over the trust.

(e) — Transfers or loans to a corporation

Transfers or loans to a corporation are subject to section 74.4 if the transferor's spouse, common-law partner or a related minor is a "specified shareholder" (generally speaking, owning 10 per cent or more of the shares)[38] and "one of the main purposes of the transfer or loan may reasonably be considered to be to reduce the income of the individual [transferor] and to benefit [a spouse, common-law partner or related minor of the transferor]".[39] This "main purpose test" involves an inquiry into the intention of the transferor at the time of making the transfer or loan to the corporation. This inquiry injects into section 74.4 an element of uncertainty that is absent from the other attribution rules; the other rules simply rely on the objective legal effect of the transfer or loan.

---

[37] The pre-1985 rules were not sufficiently specific to provide clear answers to all the attribution issues raised by trusts for the benefit of spouses and minors.

[38] Before s. 74.4 was introduced in 1985, the prevailing view was that the existing attribution rules did not apply in such situations, but that s. 56(2) might apply. See heading 13.4(b) — Indirect payment, below.

[39] *ITA, supra* note 1, s. 74.4.

The amount of income attributable to the transferor is stipulated to be the amount that is derived by applying the prescribed quarterly interest rate[40] to the value of the property transferred or loaned.[41] This imputation rule overcomes the problem, from the standpoint of the *ITA*, arising from corporate law, which does not require dividends to be paid annually. If the spouse, common-law partner or minor does not receive dividends, there will be income to be attributed under the attribution rules in section 74.1. In effect, subsection 74.4 treats the spouse, common-law partner and minor to have received fictitious income from the corporation, which legally owns the transferred or loaned property and then attributes such income to the transferor.[42]

Section 74.4 exempts a transfer or loan to a small business corporation, which is as a Canadian-controlled private corporation with all or substantially all of its assets used in an active business carried on primarily in Canada.[43] This exemption reflects the policy of the attribution rules to apply to income from property, and not income from a business.

13.4 — Income diversion

(a) — Overview

The attribution rules of sections 74.1 through 74.5 are designed to stop income splitting by the transfer of income-producing property from a high-income taxpayer to his or her spouse, common-law partner and related minor.

They do not apply to transfers of property to other non-arm's-length persons (such as parents, adult children or siblings). Neither do these attribution rules apply to transactions that do not involve a transfer or loan of "property". The rules discussed below are intended to address some of the income diversion arrangements. As with the attribution rules, the income diversion rules override the legally effective arrangements in allocating the income to its "rightful" owner.

---

[40] The prescribed rate is set quarterly under the *Income Tax Regulations*, C.R.C., c. 945, reg. 4301.

[41] This is the maximum amount to be taxed in the transferor's hands. If consideration is received that is not shares or debt, this is deducted from the value of the property transferred or loaned before applying the prescribed rate: see definitions of "outstanding amount" and "excluded consideration" in s. 74.4(1). If the transferor (or lender) has received dividends on the shares (or interest income on the debt), the amount of the interest and the grossed-up amount of the dividends is deducted in computing the amount that s. 74.4 attributes: see ss. 74.2(2)(e), (f).

[42] The attributed figure is reduced by the amount of any grossed-up dividends that are subject to kiddie tax in the hands of a minor for whose benefit the transfer or loan was made. This is because the kiddie tax is another anti-avoidance rule that imposes a penalty on income splitting. Kiddie tax is discussed at heading 13.5, below.

[43] *ITA, supra* note 1, s. 248(1).

(b) — Indirect payment

The first general rule precluding diversion of income from high-income earners to lower-income earnings is subsection 56(2) which provides:

> A payment or transfer of property made pursuant to the direction of, or with the concurrence of, a taxpayer to some other person for the benefit of the taxpayer or as a benefit that the taxpayer desired to have conferred on the other person . . . shall be included in computing the taxpayer's income to the extent that it would be if the payment or transfer had been made to the taxpayer.

It is useful to view this provision as having four conditions that must be met in order for it to apply:

1. there is a payment or transfer of property to a person other than the taxpayer;

2. the payment or transfer is at the direction of or with the concurrence of the taxpayer;

3. the payment or transfer is for the taxpayer's own benefit or for the benefit of some other person upon whom the taxpayer wishes to have the benefit conferred; and

4. the payment or transfer would have been made to the taxpayer if it had not been made to that other person.[44]

When subsection 56(2) applies, it will render diversions of income by a taxpayer to another person ineffective. For example, an employee might direct the employer to pay all or part of the employee's salary to a creditor of the employee. Or a creditor might direct the debtor to make payments of interest to the creditor's mother. Or a consultant might bill clients (for work done by the consultant) in the name of a company controlled by the consultant. All of these arrangements are perfectly legal and effective for other purposes, but subsection 56(2) makes them ineffective for tax purposes because they meet the four conditions.[45] These arrangements will not shift the tax liability away from the person who is entitled to the source of the income. In each case, the taxpayer would have to report the income, even though he or she did not actually receive it.

The application of subsection 56(2) to situations involving shareholders receiving dividends was considered by the Supreme Court of Canada in *McClurg v. Canada*

---

[44] Adapted from the list of conditions set out by Cattanach J. in *Murphy v. R.*, [1980] C.T.C 386, 80 D.T.C. 6314 (Fed. T.D.). This list has been applied by the courts in dealing with the application of s. 56(2) in subsequent cases.

[45] The taxpayer must have "desired" to confer a benefit on the recipient. Where there is no evidence of such a desire, as where a company transferred a property to Father at the direction of Son for a price that Son did not realize was less than fair market value, s. 56(2) does not apply: *Ascot Enterprises v. R.* (1995), [1996] 1 C.T.C. 384, 96 D.T.C. 6015 (Fed. C.A.).

(1990)[46] and *Neuman v. R.* (1998).[47] In *McClurg*, the taxpayer and an associate had incorporated a company to operate a truck dealership. The corporation had three classes of shares, two of which were held entirely by the taxpayer and his associate. The third class was held entirely by the taxpayer's wife and the wife of his associate. The articles of incorporation contained a discretionary dividend clause that entitled each class of shares to dividends only at the discretion of the directors. The taxpayer and his associate, who were the sole directors, exercised their power under this clause to declare a dividend of $10,000 only on the class of shares held by the wives. The corporation accordingly paid this dividend to the wives, and paid nothing to the taxpayer and his associate, who held the other classes of shares. In assessing the taxpayer's income, the Minister applied subsection 56(2) and attributed to him a portion of the dividend that had been paid to the taxpayer's wife. The Supreme Court of Canada, by a majority, held that the dividend payment in *McClurg* escaped attribution under subsection 56(2). According to Dickson J. for the majority, the exercise by the directors of their power under the discretionary dividend clause in the company's articles of incorporation should not be regarded as a payment caught by subsection 56(2). Had no dividend been declared, the income would have remained in the corporation; it would not have gone to the taxpayer. Because this fourth and last condition in subsection 56(2) was not met, the provision did not apply. Subsection 56(2) was, therefore, blocked by the corporate veil, and the discretionary dividend clause was held to be successful in diverting income away from the higher-income taxpayer to his lower-income spouse.

In *McClurg*, Dickson J., made a puzzling reference to the fact that the taxpayer's wife had been active in the business: he described the dividend payment to her as a "legitimate *quid pro quo*" for what she had contributed.[48] Since a dividend is income from property — the return on the capital invested in the company by the shareholder — it seems odd to characterize it as a *quid pro quo* for services performed for the company. This statement also seemed irrelevant to the *ratio decidendi* in the case: had no dividend been declared, the income would have remained in the corporation and would not necessarily have gone to the taxpayer. This issue of the relevance of the contribution made to the company by the shareholder was subsequently settled in the *Neuman* case. In *Neuman*, unlike *McClurg*, the recipient wife had made no contribution to the company other than her subscription to the shares on which the dividend was paid, and it was held that subsection 56(2) did not apply.[49]

---

[46] *McClurg, supra* note 5.

[47] *Neuman, supra* note 5.

[48] *McClurg, supra* note 5 at para. 44.

[49] *Neuman, supra* note 5. The facts of *Neuman* arose before 1985, when s. 74.4 was added to the *ITA*. Section 74.4 would now attribute to the husband an amount of income determined by the formula in that section, unless the corporation qualifies as a "small business corporation" throughout the year.

In *Ferrel v. R.* (1999),[50] the Federal Court of Appeal considered applying subsection 56(2) to a situation where a trust was set up to earn business income, and found that it did not apply. In *Ferrel*, management fees were paid to a trust by a holding company controlled by the taxpayer and in which the trust also owned shares. The beneficiaries of the trust were the taxpayer's children. The taxpayer, the trust and the company had entered into an agreement under which the trust (through the taxpayer) provided services to the company in return for a management fee. In *Ferrel*, the court cited the Supreme Court of Canada's dictum in *Neuman* that was cited earlier in this chapter.[51]

(c) — Assignment of income

Subsection 56(4) attributes income to the taxpayer where the taxpayer has assigned the rights to receive income to a person with whom the taxpayer is not at arm's length. For example, an author might assign a right to royalties to his or her child (whether or not that child is a minor); the royalty income will be attributed back to the author by virtue of subsection 56(4).

(d) — Interest-free or low-interest loans

Subsection 56(4.1) applies to non-arm's-length loans that bear little or no interest and where the borrower invests the loan in an income-producing property, but only when "it may reasonably be considered that one of the main reasons for making the loan . . . was to reduce or avoid tax".[52] It attributes the income from the property to the lender.

Interest-free or low-interest loans extended by a taxpayer to his or her spouse or common-law partner and a related minor are governed by the income attribution rules under section 74.1. Subsection 56(4.1) differs from 74.1 in three important respects. First, subsection 56(4.1) applies only where the lender of the money had a tax avoidance reason for the loan; if the loan can be explained by a non-tax avoidance reason, then subsection 56(4.1) will not apply. Subsection 74.1 does not have such a purpose test. Second, subsection 56(4.1) applies to transactions that divert income to *any* non-arm's-length individual and not just to spouses, common-law partners and related minors. For example, subsection 56(4.1) will catch a loan to an adult child. Third, subsection 56(4.1) applies only to loans and not to outright gifts. As a result, a loan to an adult child of the taxpayer would be caught by subsection 56(4.1), while an outright gift to an adult child is neither caught by that section nor by any other provision of the *ITA*.[53] This has led one commentator to argue that

---

[50] *Ferrel v. R.* (1999), [1999] 2 C.T.C. 101, 99 D.T.C. 5111 (Fed. C.A.) [*Ferrel*].

[51] See the statement in *Neuman, supra* note 17 and accompanying text. The same statement was cited in *Ferrel, ibid.* at para. 1.

[52] *ITA, supra* note 1, s. 56(4.1).

[53] A sale in return for a non-interest-bearing promissory note probably also avoids the section, because a sale on deferred payment terms has not in the past been treated as a loan for tax purposes: W. Goodman, Tax Column (1988) 9 Est. & Tr. J. 77 at 79.

subsection 56(4.1) favours the wealthy, who can "afford parting irrevocably with their capital by making gifts rather than loans to their children".[54]

13.5 — Kiddie tax

The decline in the number of two-spouse, one-income families, the increasing use of private corporations and the case law principles discussed earlier in this chapter have each influenced the most recent addition to the anti-income splitting rules: the tax on split income in section 120.4. This tax eliminates the advantage of several income splitting strategies, the most common of which is having family members as shareholders of a private corporation and "sprinkling" dividends among them. If spouses or common-law partners earn similar incomes, they each pay tax at similar rates and there is less scope for income splitting between them. As a result, the diversion of income to minor children became the target of tax planning strategies and it was for this reason that the tax on split income currently enacted under section 120.4 is confined to minors and commonly referred to as a "kiddie tax". Since 2000, when section 120.4 first became effective, the definition of split income subject to kiddie tax has been amended three times to deal with specific arrangements involving minors. More recently, draft legislation released in July 2017 and effective 2018 includes proposals to amend section 120.4 to expand the definition of "specified individuals" subject to kiddie tax to include individuals over 18 years of age (such as children, spouse and others) as well as to expand the definition of split income.[55]

Section 120.4, as enacted, imposes a special tax at the top rate (currently 33 per cent) on "split income" (as defined) received by minor children who are "specified individuals" (section 120.4) but it ceases to apply effective January 1 of the year of the taxpayer's 18th birthday. No tax credits can be claimed against the "kiddie tax" except for the dividend tax credit or foreign tax credit, if applicable. The tax is similar to what is paid by an *inter vivos* trust: it is at the top rate with no personal tax credit. The rationale is that the tax is intended to equal the tax that the parent

---

[54] *Ibid.*

[55] It is proposed that dividends received by such individuals over 18 years of age will be split income to the extent the dividend is in excess of a reasonableness test. For family members age 25 or over, the reasonableness test is proposed to be based on what an arm's-length party would have agreed to pay considering labour and capital contributions and previous returns and remuneration. For family members age 18 to 24, the reasonableness test will be more restrictive (presumably because, according to page 21 of the July 2017 consultation paper, *supra* note 6, dividends paid to family members in this age group present particular advantages as they "may have lower-income levels for a variety of reasons, including due to post-secondary studies or being at an early stage of a career"). If the individual is under the age of 25, income on split income is also proposed to be split income (under the current rules, second-generation income was not included). Additional changes for capital gains are discussed in note 61, *infra*. For further details, see the July 2017 consultation paper and draft legislation, referred to in note 6, *supra*.

who is taxable in the highest tax bracket would have paid on the income if not for the income split.

The five planning arrangements it currently targets are as follows:

1.   The first arrangement is similar to the one that we saw in *McClurg* and *Neuman*:[56] an arrangement where a trust established for a minor child's benefit owns shares of a private corporation paying dividends. These arrangements allow dividend income to be diverted to a minor, with substantial savings in tax. The grossed-up private corporation dividends are split income.

2.   The second arrangement is where a trust established for a minor child's benefit owns an interest in a partnership earning business income by providing property[57] or services to a related entity — or any entity if a person related to the child (e.g., a parent) is actively engaged on a regular basis in providing the property or services. An example of a related entity arrangement is as follows: the trust for the child of a lawyer may be a partner in a limited partnership that provides services to the parent's law firm. The partnership will buy services on behalf of the law firm and then sell them to the law firm, charging a management fee with a markup (generally 15 per cent).[58] The markup is retained as a profit in the limited partnership, allocated to each trust that is a partner, and is taxed in the hands of the child by having the trust make the income paid or payable to the child.[59] The income paid or payable to the child is split income.

3.   The third arrangement is similar to the second: it is where a trust established for a minor child's benefit (rather than a partnership) operates a business that earns its income from property or services provided to a related entity — or any entity if a person related to the child (e.g., a parent) is actively engaged on a regular basis in providing the property or

---

[56] *McClurg, supra* note 5; *Neuman, supra* note 5.

[57] The words "property or" are applicable to taxation years that begin after December 20, 2002, which means that kiddie tax applies to income from property provided to a related entity (as well as services) after that effective date. Examples include 1) rental income earned by a partnership (or trust) owning real estate that is rented to a related entity, and 2) interest income earned by a partnership (or trust) loaning money to a related entity. Note that income earned on property provided to other entities would not be subject to kiddie tax but might be subject to the normal attribution rules under ss. 74.1(2), 74.3.

[58] A markup of 15 per cent is generally not challenged by the Canada Revenue Agency.

[59] The use of a limited partnership is an improvement over a management corporation because it avoids the imposition of corporate income taxes on the income to be diverted to family members, while allowing the family members to maintain limited liability status similar to that which they would have as shareholders of a corporation. See Chapter 14.

services. This was the type of arrangement used successfully in *Ferrel*.[60] The income paid or payable to the child is split income.

4.   The fourth arrangement is where the minor child (or a trust established for his or her benefit) owns shares of a private corporation and the minor child receives a shareholder benefit under section 15, such as a loan from a private corporation that triggers a taxable benefit to the shareholder under subsection 15(2). The subsection 15(2) benefit is split income.

5.   The fifth arrangement is where the minor child (or a trust established for his or her benefit) owns shares of a private corporation and the minor child sells the shares to a non-arm's-length person and pays little or no tax because of the lifetime capital gains exemption. In the case of dispositions on or after March 22, 2011, the capital gain is deemed to be a dividend from a private corporation, which is grossed up and included as split income.[61]

The kiddie tax does not apply to dividend income earned on shares of public corporations, interest income, employment income or capital gains. The kiddie tax also does not apply to minors who have no Canadian resident parent, to income from property inherited from a deceased parent, or to income from property inherited from persons other than a parent if the minor is a full-time student at a post-secondary institution or is eligible for the disability credit.[62]

---

[60] *Ferrel, supra* note 50.

[61] *ITA, supra* note 1, s. 120.4(4) deems the capital gain to be a private corporation dividend, and s. 120.4(1)(a) includes the deemed dividend in split income. The July 2017 draft legislation, *supra* note 6, proposes to have this rule (deeming capital gains on non-arm's-length transfers to be dividends) apply to those 18 and older. In addition, it is proposed that if dividends received on shares are split income, the taxable capital gain on any other disposition of shares will be "split income" and, therefore, the lifetime capital gains exemption ("LCGE") will not apply. It is also proposed that the LCGE will not apply to capital gains realized or accrued before an individual reaches the age of 18 or accrued while shares are held in family trusts.

[62] Because only "specified individuals" are subject to kiddie tax, the kiddie tax only applies to minors who are resident in Canada and have a parent who is resident in Canada. Because "split income" does not include "excluded amounts", income and capital gains earned from inherited property are not included in split income. The exclusion always applies if the property is inherited from a parent. In any other case (e.g., property inherited from grandparent), the exclusion will apply if the minor is enrolled at a post-secondary institution or is eligible for the disability tax credit.

14

INCOME EARNED THROUGH PRIVATE CORPORATIONS, PARTNERSHIPS AND TRUSTS

14.1 — Taxable persons and their income

Individuals often carry on business activities or hold investment assets through corporations, partnerships or trusts. Possibly the most important policy issues and challenges faced by our tax system today are created by the taxation of income earned through these legal vehicles and arrangements.

At a general level, the *Income Tax Act* (the "*ITA*")[1] treats each corporation as a person and a taxpayer in respect of its income. It treats trusts as "individuals" and, thus, "taxpayers" — effectively as "persons" independent of the "settlor" from whom the trust acquired the property and the "beneficiaries" from whom the property is administered. When the *ITA* refers to a trust, it is understood to be referring to the trustee of the trust (and others who act in a similar representative and administrative capacity with respect to property for the benefit of others, but not including persons who are considered to be agents for trust beneficiaries in an arrangement sometimes described as a "bare trust"). Some public commercial trusts are subject to rules in the *ITA* that effectively assimilate them and their beneficiaries to the kind and degree of taxation associated with corporate income taxation. These are the so-called "specified investment flow-through" trusts ("SIFTs"), which were designed to prevent tax avoidance through the use of income trusts. The *ITA* does not treat partnerships as taxable persons but, instead, taxes partners on their share of income of the partnership.

As discussed in Chapter 13, the legal separation of income and its owners offers opportunities for income splitting, and the use of corporations offers opportunities for tax deferral because corporate income is taxed at lower tax rates and is not taxable to a shareholder until distributed as dividends. When individuals pay tax at progressive rates and the top personal rate is much higher than the corporate tax rate, income splitting and tax deferral, if left uncontrolled, threaten the integrity of progressive taxation of personal income. From the outset of income taxation in Canada in the *Income War Tax Act, 1917*,[2] through to the present, there is a pervasive thread of "putting Humpty Dumpty" back together again — in more prosaic terms, overcoming the separation of income from its owners.

This formidable challenge is readily apparent in several simple examples. What happens if the proprietor of a small business decides that the business should be conducted by a corporation the proprietor owns? Should the manner in which the business is conducted have a tax effect? After all, from a practical, functional, eco-

---

[1] R.S.C. 1985 (5th Supp.), c. 1 [*ITA*].

[2] S.C. 1917, c. 28 [*IWTA 1917*].

nomic point of view, the proprietor actually conducts the business. A corporation is simply a legal construct, a fiction of sorts that, for a variety of very good reasons, the law recognizes as a person distinct from its shareholder owners. But a corporation cannot actually do anything. When the corporation earns income, in an economic or constructive sense, it is the proprietor who is compensated. But the tax law treats a shareholder as a different person from the corporation the shareholder owns. What if the corporate tax rate is less than the rate at which the proprietor, as a direct income earner, would have been taxable? When the corporation pays its income to the shareholder, to what degree should it be taxed? Is the same income being taxed twice? Should it be? Should the corporation and the shareholder somehow be combined (or recombined) for tax purposes to reflect their economic unity despite their legal separateness? How can this be accomplished without upsetting the private law applecart that respects their separateness?

Another example is a trust, a much-misunderstood legal creature in Canadian tax law. Trusts are commonly used by individuals to make disciplined, systematic provision for family members by setting aside income-generating wealth to provide for their medical health, to fund the education of children, to look after loved ones after an individual's death, and the like. But what is a trust? A trust is not a "thing" or a "person". It is simply an obligation. A trust lacks personality of any kind, even in private law. It is an obligation undertaken by a person, called the "trustee", to hold and administer property that belongs to another person (called the "settlor") that has been set aside for purposes that the settlor has orchestrated to provide for the interests of others, called "beneficiaries".[3] There are a number of fundamental, obvious questions. Is the settlor relieved of income tax responsibilities on the settled property simply because he or she has decided to set aside the property with the instructions for its use and administration typically found in a deed of trust? Is this arrangement more or less the same as the settlor, without these arrangements, simply deciding to set aside property and spend the income arising from it on those he or she wishes to benefit — like a bank account that the settlor uses for particular purposes? If yes, then why should the *ITA* tax the income differently?

These are very difficult questions, all emanating from a very simple conviction that individuals should be free to use corporations or trusts as their alter egos in commercial and investment arrangements, but they should not use these alter egos to reduce their tax liability. Since 1917, large swaths of the Act have been dedicated to overcoming, even ignoring, the legal separation of income from its owners without actually overturning the private law that has created the legal fictions of corporations and trusts that enable this separation. The *ITA* also accepts the "fiscal" separateness of corporations when they exist primarily for commercial purposes, and this is typically the case with public corporations and private corporations carrying on business in Canada. But the *ITA* also provides incentives for this separation by

---

[3] It is a "non-recourse" obligation of the trustee provided, generally, the trustee acts responsibly (i.e., does not commit negligent or illegal acts). This means that the trustee's own property is not required to be used to satisfy the objectives of the trust, but only the property set aside by the settlor to achieve the settlor's objectives.

taxing corporations more lightly on business income, tolerating the deferral of taxation, and allowing income splitting in many situations.

This chapter provides a brief overview of these policy and technical issues. The
focus is on the taxation of individuals in their capacity as shareholders, partners or
settlors/beneficiaries, not the taxation of the corporation, partnership or trust. The
goal is to offer a sense of how and why the *ITA* (as we know it) is so consumed
with restoring the economic or fiscal unity of shareholders and corporations, partners and the income activities carried on together via partnerships, and settlors and
beneficiaries. This tendency of the tax law is not accidental. It has been, and continues to be, a seminal feature of Canadian income taxation to balance the need to
respect the legal fictions that separate income from its ultimate owners (individuals) and the means by which income is earned, and the need to preserve the progressive taxation of personal income.

Given the complexity of the subject matter, our approach is to use selective but not
uncommon examples to explain the major policy concerns and the technical design
features. This approach is not meant to be complete or comprehensive; we try to
simplify without oversimplifying. Our hope is to reveal the "system" in the "tax
system" free of the opacity and distractions engendered by focusing on the "detail".
The *ITA* taxes "persons" (section 2) on their income (section 3) accounted for qual-
itatively and by location (section 4). That is the frame or the tax structure. The rest,
as one of us might say, is "plumbing". But none of this works without knowing
who the taxable person is in relation to the income. And that question, and the
subtlety of the answers, lie at the very heart of the income taxation in Canada.

14.2 — Framework for taxing individuals

(a) — Individuals as taxpayers

The *ITA* ultimately is about taxing the income of natural persons who use their
resources to pay for "goods" they consume collectively ("public goods"). While
they might not see it quite this way, citizens decide through the political process on
the "kind of society" they want. Taxation is the way to pay for it. In this way, the
tax system is a reflection of the choices people make. The *ITA* reflects who we are
as Canadians.[4] Not surprisingly, therefore, the basic architecture of the Act is concerned with establishing: 1) who are the individuals liable to tax; 2) what is their
income for tax purposes; and 3) how much tax should be paid? As discussed in
Chapter 2, the policy objectives are to raise revenue in a fair and efficient manner.
Equity and fairness are hallmarks of the system.

When an individual earns income through a corporation, partnership or trust, an
imperative reasonable starting point may be to tax such income at a level (or rate)

---

[4] J. Li & S. Wilkie, "Celebrating the Centennial of the Income War Tax Act, 1917: Canada
The Future by the Light of 100 Candles" in J. Li, J.S. Wilkie & L. Chapman, eds., *Income
Tax at 100 Years: Essays and Reflections on the Centennial of the Income War Tax Act*
(Toronto: Canadian Tax Foundation) [forthcoming in 2017] at 1:1.

that is comparable to the situation where the income is earned directly by the individual. This expectation is an outgrowth of the notion of tax neutrality — individuals are free to use different legal vehicles or arrangements to conduct their business or investment activities, but the ultimate tax burden on the income should not be distorted or changed by such private choices. Of course, the tax system can decide if it is in its (and our collective) interests to foster differences in order to promote business and other activities that enrich all of our economic circumstances. Further, the *ITA* can even "distort" private choices by nudging taxpayers in the direction of making some economic choices rather than others. For example, the *ITA* encourages innovation or job creation by providing "tax breaks". There are many choices Canadians might make, which are reflected in the tax system. Indeed, interpreting the *ITA* often involves discovering latent statutory purpose — which manifests larger social and economic objectives — as we will see in the next chapter.

The *ITA* provides a basic framework for taxing individuals who are shareholders, partners and beneficiaries: 1) Division A of Part I (i.e., section 2) charges the individual as the taxpayer in respect of such income; 2) Division B requires the taxpayer to include dividends (subdivision h), income or loss from a partnership (subdivision j) and income distributed by a trust (subdivision k) in computing his or her income for purposes of section 3; and 3) as part of the total taxable income, dividends, partnership income and beneficiary's income are taxed at progressive rates (Divisions C and E).

Because a corporation is a "person" under private law and is treated as a taxpayer under the *ITA*, the Act needs to "reconcile" the tax paid by a corporation and the tax payable by the shareholder to prevent so-called "double taxation" of income earned through corporations. To achieve that goal, the *ITA*, effectively, treats the corporate tax as a withholding tax and allows individual shareholders to credit such tax against his or her personal tax (s. 121). Because income earned through a partnership or trust is taxed only once (in the hands of partners, beneficiaries or trusts), there is no need to prevent double taxation of such income.

(b) — Measuring ability to pay

One of the overarching themes of the *ITA* is to measure an individual's income as much as possible to reflect his or her ability to pay. From the outset of Canadian income tax there has been an undercurrent of the "conscription of wealth". The idea that higher-income individuals were expected to contribute to the war effort (just as able-bodied but generally lower-income individuals were called upon to fight) was the setting, if not entirely the reason, for the introduction of the 1917 *Income War Tax Act*.[5]

The measurement of ability to pay is key to the integrity and fairness of the system. As such, if income earned through private corporations or trusts is not taken into account and not rationalized in a deliberate manner with how their shareholders and beneficiaries are taxed, the integrity and fairness of the system may be undermined.

---

5 *IWTA 1917, supra* note 2.

And it is always possible that too much rather than too little tax might be paid. The idea of integrating the taxation of corporations and their shareholders can be found in subsection 3(4) of the *Income War Tax Act, 1917*,[6] which permitted the attribution of undistributed corporate earnings to individual shareholders. A notion of "fiscal unity" seems to underlie the design of this early provision, as well as the subsequent evolution of the rules governing the taxation of income, particularly income earned through private corporations.[7]

In principle, because the *ITA* treats each individual as a taxation unit and applies progressive rates to an individual's income, high-income individuals can minimize their taxes by "splitting" income with lower-income family members for tax purposes, without giving up actual control over the income. Income splitting also can be achieved through the use of family corporations, trusts and partnerships. For example, it is possible for a family corporation created by parents to issue shares for nominal value to their children and pay dividends on those shares. Similarly, a parent can transfer income-producing property to a trust or partnership for the benefit of his or her children. To prevent income splitting or shifting in such situations, the *ITA* generally "ignores" the effect of the legal separation of the income from the parent while the children are minors: this is the purpose and effect of the attribution and kiddie tax rules discussed in Chapter 13.

The *ITA* has a more tempered response to losses. Measuring an individual's ability to pay also entails addressing losses. Because a corporation is a separate taxpayer, losses are recognized at the corporate level and are not distributed or attributed to shareholders.[8] But corporate losses normally affect the value of corporate shares and are effectively realized by a shareholder when the shares are disposed of (as a capital loss, which is one-half deductible, generally only against taxable capital gains).

In contrast, losses of partnerships are allocated to partners annually, since partnerships do not have a separate taxable personality but are simply, for tax and non-tax purposes, a specific kind of association among the persons who are the taxpayers. But where the *ITA* perceives an absence of risk-taking, it denies the allocation losses until the partner (typically a limited partner) can be said to actually be taking risk (e.g., through financial commitments to the loss-making enterprise).

In the case of trusts, income earned by a trust may be taxed to the beneficiaries if distributed, but otherwise is taxable at the trust level. The *ITA* does not allow the distribution of losses to beneficiaries directly.[9]

---

[6] *Ibid.*, s. 3(4).

[7] S. Wilkie, "Three Spirits of Canadian Corporate Income Tax: The Relic, the Remnant, and the Reflection" in Li, Wilkie & Chapman, *supra* note 4 at 8:1.

[8] That is why some taxpayers delay incorporation until their business earns a profit, which they can accomplish on a rollover basis using a s. 85 election. This is discussed briefly in Chapter 10 at heading 10.4(c)(iv)(C) — Rollovers regarding corporate transactions.

[9] The *ITA* does facilitate the indirect distribution of losses by permitting trusts to retain otherwise distributable income (to be "sheltered" with the losses that it has sustained) and

(c) — Income earned through corporations, partnerships and trusts

The *ITA* takes the legal status or relationships in private (non-tax) law as a given or a starting point in determining the tax consequences flowing from private law. In cases where corporations or trusts are used to carry on business or commercial activities, the *ITA* treats the corporations or trusts as separate "taxable persons" and even offers tax incentives to encourage socially desirable investments and activities, such as research and development and job creation.

On the other hand, when corporations or trusts are largely the alter egos of their legal owners or beneficiaries, the *ITA* adopts various measures to remove the fiscal effect of using corporations and trusts to defer taxation, or to split or shift income. One group of these rules "integrates" the corporation's tax with the shareholder's personal tax when the corporate income is distributed to shareholders as a dividend. Another group of rules seeks to tax undistributed corporate income at a level comparable to the top marginal personal tax rate to prevent tax deferral and income splitting. This second set of rules generally applies to income from investments or from personal services (i.e., incorporated employment income).

Trusts, particularly personal trusts, may be used to hold shares of family corporations, shares of other corporations, other financial assets, and tangible property, functioning almost like private investment funds. Like a corporation, a trust legally separates the original owner of the property (the "settlor") and the income earned from such property. Further, the trust income is earned for the benefit of the beneficiaries of the trust, which may or may not include the settlor. Trusts are, thus, flexible legal constructs to achieve income shifting and income splitting. The *ITA* taxes the income of the trust at the top marginal personal tax rate if the income is not distributed to beneficiaries in order to prevent income splitting.[10]

When individuals carry on business activities through a partnership, because a partnership is not a separate legal person, there is no "legal separation" of the partnership's income and the partner's income. The *ITA* provides rules that allow the "flow-through" of the partnership's income or loss to the partners, and prevent partnerships from being used as tax-avoidance vehicles.

---

then to make non-taxable distributions of capital to the beneficiaries (which reduce the tax cost of a beneficiary's trust interest in a commercial trust setting). The effect is similar to distributing the losses to the beneficiaries and is another example of how, in so many respects, the *ITA*'s complexity results from its attempts to combine the incomes of separate taxpayers to reflect their economic unity.

[10] In the case of both corporations and trusts, there is an intergenerational aspect to consider. Corporations have perpetual existence; their undistributed income is not taxable, possibly, for a long time. The *ITA* addresses this with provisions that discourage the retention of undistributed investment income. In the case of trusts, akin to the "Rule Against Perpetuities", the *ITA* limits the intergenerational tax-free transfer of wealth. See heading 14.5(d)(iv) — Deemed disposition of property.

14.3 — Private corporations

(a) — Nature of corporations

A corporation is a legal fiction or creature of statute. Under the federal or provincial corporate law, a corporation is a legal person and separate from its shareholders. The shareholders have no proprietary interest in the corporation's underlying assets, that is, assets acquired by the corporation with the funds raised by issuing shares (or borrowing money or retaining after-tax earnings). What the shareholders own are shares in the corporation, which are a quite different kind of asset. Similarly, the liabilities of the corporation are its alone, and they must be satisfied out of the assets of the company. The personal assets of the shareholder are not at risk. This is known as "limited liability". This is contrasted to a sole proprietorship or partnership business where the proprietor or partners are personally liable to satisfy the liabilities incurred by the business. So, in a legal sense, a corporation is a person, capable of owning assets and earning income.

For policy reasons, corporations are treated differently, depending on whether they are public corporations, and, if they are private corporations, whether they are Canadian-controlled private corporations ("CCPCs"), and whether their income is from carrying on business (technically, an "active business") or not. Private corporations offer opportunities for the selective and self-interested separation of income from its economic owners. The same effect occurs with public corporations but their "publicness" generally means that they cannot be easily used by their shareholders to accomplish ulterior, highly personal planning objectives. Generally speaking, public corporations are presumed to be genuine business entities and are not used primarily by shareholders to avoid progressive personal income tax. The same presumption applies to CCPCs earning business income, but, generally, not to CCPCs earning investment income or that are "incorporated employees".

(b) — Canadian-controlled private corporations (CCPCs)

A "Canadian-controlled private corporation" is "a private corporation that is a Canadian corporation other than a corporation . . . controlled, directly or indirectly in any manner whatever, by one or more non-resident persons, by one or more public corporations . . . or by any combination thereof . . ."[11] A CCPC is, essentially, a private corporation that is owned and controlled by Canadian residents.

Canadians use CCPCs to conduct genuine business and commercial activities, as well as to defer and save personal income taxes. One tax advantage of using CCPCs is the lower rate of tax on business income. The federal corporate tax rates have been lowered in recent years to be internationally competitive. The general rate is currently 15 per cent and the special CCPC rate is currently 10.5 per cent for

---

[11] *ITA, supra* note 1, s. 125(7). This definition is drafted in the negative sense: A corporation is a CCPC if it is not a public corporation and is not controlled by a public corporation or non-resident person. Subsection 89(1) defines the terms of "private corporation", "public corporation" and "Canadian corporation".

the first $500,000 of Canadian business income. Meanwhile, the graduated personal tax rates are 15 per cent, 20.5 per cent, 26 per cent, 29 per cent and 33 per cent. The 33 per cent top rate was added in 2016, but as long as the corporate income is not distributed as dividends to individual shareholders, none of the higher personal tax rates will apply, resulting in the deferral of tax. This deferral of tax means that more after-tax business earnings can be invested in passive investments if the after-tax business income is earned (and retained) inside a corporation than if the income is earned outside a corporation and taxed at graduated rates.

Income splitting is another possible tax advantage. The income earner's family members can subscribe shares of a corporation and receive dividends from the corporation. It is, perhaps, rare for a private corporation to be owned by the "breadwinner" alone. Because of the increasing use of private corporations to earn business income, there was increasing use of these three tax reduction strategies: deferral, income splitting, and the use of the lifetime capital gains exemption. It was, therefore, not surprising that the 2017 federal budget promised a review of the use of private corporations, nor that, in July 2017, the Department of Finance issued a consultation paper describing the government's concerns and its proposed responses as well as draft legislation containing measures that limit the use of private corporation dividends to split income and the use of the lifetime capital gains exemption effective for 2018 and subsequent years. The consultation paper discusses all of the government's concerns as well as possible measures to eliminate the tax deferral advantage that results when after-tax business earnings are invested in passive investments inside a corporation rather than outside a corporation.[12]

Converting ordinary income into capital gains can be achieved through the use of private corporations, and the rules for incorporated small businesses encourage this outcome. Instead of receiving dividends from a corporation, a shareholder can dispose of the shares and have a capital gain. Capital gains are taxed more favorably (currently one-half of capital gains is taxable). More importantly, capital gains from the disposition of qualified small business corporation ("QSBC") shares are eligible for a section 110.6 lifetime capital gains exemption of $835,716 (in 2017).

(c) — "Fiscal unity" of CCPCs and their shareholders

(i) — Notion of "fiscal unity"

The *ITA* treats a corporation as a separate taxpayer in general, but it seeks to treat a corporation and its shareholders as a single economic and taxpaying unit in certain

---

[12] See Department of Finance, Canada, "Tax Planning Using Private Corporations" (18 July 2017) [July 2017 consultation paper], online: <ttp://www.fin.gc.ca/activty/consult/tppc-pfsp-eng.asp>, and the July 18, 2017 draft legislation, online: <http://www.fin.gc.ca/drleg-apl/2017/ita-lir-0717-eng.asp>. As discussed at heading 13.5 — Kiddie tax, the draft legislation proposes to limit income sprinkling using dividends by adding a reasonableness test and expanding the tax on split income (the so-called "kiddie tax"), which will no longer just apply to minors. Legislative proposals relating to the use of the lifetime capital gains exemption are also briefly discussed at heading 13.5.

respects. Since as early as 1917, there has been an inextricable link between the personal and corporate income tax regimes in taxing income ostensibly earned by corporations, particularly private corporations and especially CCPCs. This "fiscal unity" idea is reflected in the treatment of dividends received by individuals from corporations — that is, the "integration" of corporate and personal tax — to achieve a degree of taxation that approximates the tax that would have been paid by individual shareholders had they earned the income directly.

The fiscal unity treatment is deferred when CCPCs earn business income. This deferral is the way in which the *ITA* recognizes corporations as quintessentially vehicles for carrying on business, and the limited liability principle as important in encouraging entrepreneurs to take risks and raise capital. The success of business corporations contributes to the success of the Canadian economy in terms of innovation, risk-taking and job creation. As an added incentive, the *ITA* provides a special, lower CCPC tax rate for business income. This rate is often called the "small business" rate because it results from what the *ITA* calls the "small business deduction" ("SBD"). Currently, the SBD applies to a CCPC's Canadian business income up to $500,000 per year.

(ii) — Dividends received by individuals

Individuals receiving dividends from Canadian corporations, including CCPCs, must include the amount of dividends in computing their income.[13] Assuming that the dividends are paid out of corporate after-tax income, the *ITA* effectively allows an individual shareholder to "deduct" from tax the amount of corporate tax "borne" by the dividends. The mechanism for achieving this effect is complex, consisting of dividend gross-up rules and tax credit rules.[14] Two corporate tax rates are assumed and indicated by distinguishing dividends as "eligible dividends" (dividends paid out of income taxed at the general corporate tax rate) and dividends other than eligible dividends (non-eligible dividends). Public corporations and CCPCs earning business income over the small business deduction limit ($500,000) pay tax at the general rate and can pay eligible dividends to shareholders.

Conceptually, the gross-up rate for eligible dividends is 38 per cent (which assumes the corporate tax rate is almost 28 per cent) and 17 per cent for non-eligible divi-

---

[13] *ITA, supra* note 1, ss. 12(1)(j), 82(1)(a), 82(1)(a.1).

[14] Underpinning the design of the gross-up and dividend tax credit systems are the concepts of "corporations resident in Canada", "taxable dividends", "eligible dividends" and "dividends other than eligible dividends" (non-eligible dividends). A corporation is resident in Canada by reason of incorporation under Canadian laws (federal or provincial) or having its central and management control in Canada. Section 89(1) defines "taxable dividends" to mean all dividends except for dividends that are exempt from tax, such as capital dividends. Subsection 89(14) defines a dividend as an "eligible dividend" if the corporation designates it as such when it is paid. Eligible dividends can be designated by public and private corporations.

dends (which assumes the corporate tax rate is almost 15 per cent).[15] The amount of dividend actually received plus the gross-up amount are included in the shareholder's taxable income and taxed at the marginal rate. Then, the gross-up amount is "credited" against personal income tax.[16] In the end, dividends are taxed at a level that is comparable to the amount of income earned directly by the individual. The following two tables illustrate the dividend gross-up and credit mechanism and how it achieves the "fiscal unity" objective by taxing the individual at the same level, whether or not the income is earned through a corporation or directly by himself or herself.

As well as illustrating the "fiscal unity" objective, these tables also show the deferral advantage, enjoyed by those earning business income earned in a private corporation, that is the concern and subject of the Department of Finance's July 2017 consultation paper. If the amount available for dividend, which is in the third line of each table ($72 in Table 14-1 and $85 in Table 14-2), is retained and invested in passive investments in the corporation rather than being paid out as a dividend, much more can be invested than the after-tax amount of $47 ($100 minus $53) that

---

[15] These corporate rates are combined federal-provincial rates, and the provincial corporate rates are assumed because they vary across provinces and territories. The higher rate of 28 per cent includes a 15 per cent federal rate and a 13 per cent provincial rate. The lower rate of 15 per cent includes a 10.5 per cent rate with the SBD and an assumed 4.5 per cent rate. This book rounds the assumed corporate tax rate figures used to design the gross-ups upwards to 28 per cent (38/138 = 27.5 per cent for eligible dividends) and 15 per cent (17/117 = 14.5 per cent for non-eligible dividends). The actual 2017 combined weighted average rates across Canada are now even lower than those used to design these two gross-ups: they are 26.7 per cent and 14.4 per cent. See July 2017 consultation paper, *supra* note 12 at 8.

A CCPC can designate eligible dividends only to the extent of its general-rate income pool ("GRIP") amount at the year-end, and a public corporation cannot designate eligible dividends if it has a low-rate income pool ("LRIP") at the time of the dividend payment. These rules exist to ensure that dividends paid from "low-rate" income (e.g., income that has benefited from the SBD) have the lower 17 per cent non-eligible dividend gross-up and tax credit; excess eligible dividend designations are subject to a penalty tax. A CCPC's GRIP account includes any eligible dividends received (say, from a public corporation) as well as 72 per cent of any business income that has not benefitted from the SBD (because the general rate on business income is 28 per cent and, therefore, only 72 per cent is left to pay dividends) and is not investment income, and is reduced by eligible dividends paid. As illustrated in Tables 14-1 and 14-2, the system assumes that the amount of the gross-up is fully credited against the shareholder's personal income tax.

[16] The combined federal-provincial dividend tax credit is presumed to equal the gross-up. In provinces where the provincial corporate tax rates and/or the provincial portion of the dividend tax credit are not the assumed amounts, there will be under-credit and over-credit situations. It is beyond the scope of this book to explain the details of this imputation system. For further discussions, see David Duff & Geoffrey Loomer, *Taxation of Business Organizations in Canada* (Toronto: LexisNexis, 2015) at 232–267; and Paul Bleiwas & John Hutson, *Taxation of Private Corporations and Their Shareholders*, 4th ed. (Toronto: Canadian Tax Foundation, 2010) at 18:1–18:26.

can be invested if the income is distributed to the shareholder (or earned directly outside a corporation) and taxed at the top personal rate of 53 per cent. This is the deferral advantage or benefit.

Table 14-1: Eligible Dividends Compared to Earning Income Directly

	Taxpayer earns business income directly ($)	Corporation earns business income and pays dividends ($)
Income	100	100
Less Corporate tax at combined 28% general rate (15% federal plus 13% provincial)		(28)
Dividends paid by corporation		72
Dividend gross-up: $72 × 38%		28
Amount included in income		100
Personal income tax (53% combined rate)	53	53
Less Dividend tax credit equal to the gross-up		(28)
Net tax payable by individual	53	25
Total corporate and personal tax	53	53 (28 + 25)

Table 14-2: Non-eligible Dividends Compared to Earning Income Directly

	Taxpayer earns business income directly ($)	CCPC earns business income and pays dividends ($)
Income	100	100
Less Corporate tax at combined 15% small business rate (10.5% federal plus 4.5% provincial)		(15)
Dividends paid by corporation		85
Dividend gross-up: $85 × 17%		15
Amount included in income		100
Personal income tax (53% combined rate)	53	53
Less Dividend tax credit equal to the gross-up		(15)
Net tax payable by individual	53	38
Total corporate and personal tax	53	53

(iii) — CCPCs as incorporated employees

Corporations are business entities, but not all businesses deserve the low corporate rates and tax deferral treatment available to the business income in Tables 14-1 and 14-2 when it was earned through a corporation. Perhaps not all businesses contribute to the success of the Canadian economy in terms of innovation, risk-taking and job creation. The underlying assumption is that, in these situations, the legal separation of the income and its ultimate owner (the shareholder) does not warrant the income to be taxed at a corporate tax rate, which is lower than the shareholder's marginal personal tax rate, allowing an indefinite deferral of personal income tax. Additional taxes are, therefore, imposed at the corporate level to mimic the top marginal personal tax rate when the business involves earning investment income or when the business is considered to be that of an "incorporated employee". It is in these two situations that the *ITA* has restored the fiscal unity of the shareholder and the corporation by restricting tax deferral benefits to "active" businesses of CCPCs. The *ITA* draws a line between an "active business", a "specified investment business" and a "personal service business" by providing definitions of these terms in subsection 125(7). These two other types of businesses must generally have more than five full-time employees to be considered to be "active businesses".

A personal services business ("PSB") is a business carried on by a corporation that, in essence, does nothing more than offer the services of a shareholder-employee of the corporation on terms that are substantially similar to those that would exist if the shareholder-employee were simply an employee of the person paying for those services.[17] An example would be where Ms. X is a computer programmer and the sole shareholder of X Ltd. and X Ltd. provides services to a law firm with Ms. X doing the actual work. In the absence of the PSB rules, the income earned by X Ltd. would enjoy more liberal deduction rules with respect to expenses (because it is a corporation carrying on a business) as well as a lower rate of taxation when the income is earned. Unless X Ltd. pays dividends to Ms. X, any personal tax on dividends would be deferred indefinitely.

Under the PSB rules, the *ITA* treats the incorporated employee income like an employment income. Paragraph 18(1)(p) of the *ITA* denies the deduction of expenses incurred in gaining or producing income from a PSB, except to the extent of the salary and benefits paid to employees and other expenses that would be deductible by an employee. It treats the corporation as if it were an employee in terms of deductibility of expenses. Furthermore, the income of a personal services business is taxed at a special rate of 33 per cent,[18] which is the same as the 33 per cent top marginal rate for personal income. These rules leave such corporations little choice but to pay wages equal to the pre-tax profits. Otherwise, the income would be excessively taxed: 33 per cent at the corporate level and again at the shareholder level as an eligible dividend with a dividend tax credit, which only compensates for combined federal-provincial tax at the general rate.[19]

---

[17] *ITA, supra* note 1, s. 125(7).

[18] The *ITA* computes the 15 per cent general and 10.5 per cent small business rates by providing reductions from a higher 28 per cent basic rate. PSB income does not qualify for these rate reductions: the 33 per cent federal corporate rate on PSB income is computed as the basic rate of 28 per cent plus a 5 per cent additional tax under s. 123.5. When combined with provincial taxes, the PSB rate would be something like 46 per cent (33 per cent federal plus 13 per cent assumed provincial).

[19] The system for eligible dividends assumes a combined federal provincial general rate is 28 per cent (15 per cent + 13 per cent), whereas the combined federal provincial PSB rate would be something like 46 per cent, *ibid*.

(iv) — CCPCs earning investment income other than Canadian dividends

A specified investment business is a business whose main purpose is to earn income from investment (e.g., interest, dividends, rent or royalties). Depending on the type of investment income, the *ITA* provides for different mechanisms for removing the tax deferral advantage. It is not eligible for the lower rate of taxation.

A CCPC's investment income other than Canadian dividends is subject to an additional tax of 10 2/3 per cent.[20] This brings the federal rate to 38 2/3 per cent[21] (higher than the top personal rate of 33 per cent). Part of this tax (30 2/3 per cent) is refunded to the corporation when taxable dividends are paid out to shareholders, so that the net corporate tax is 8 per cent.[22] The high initial rate of corporate income tax (before the "dividend refund") acts as an incentive to pay dividends to shareholders. The goal is to allow little or no tax deferral to taxpayers who incorporate their portfolio. In the example illustrated by Table 14-3, below, there is a small deferral because the shareholder is at a top rate of 53 per cent and the combined federal provincial rate is 51.67 per cent. But note that, like PSB income, the income is excessively taxed: in this case, integration does not quite work because a non-eligible dividend has a dividend tax credit that only compensates for the low small business rate of tax (a combined federal-provincial corporate rate of 15 per cent as per Table 14-2) and the 21 per cent net corporate rate on investment income is higher. Initially, slightly less is paid (51.67 per cent versus 53 per cent) but when income is flowed through slightly more is eventually paid (56 per cent versus 53 per cent).

---

[20] *ITA, supra* note 1, s. 123.3.

[21] Like PSB income, investment income does not qualify for the rate reductions for business income described in note 18, *supra*. The corporate tax on investment income is the basic corporate rate of 28 per cent plus the 10 2/3 per cent additional tax under s. 123.3.

[22] Technically, the refund is tracked through the corporation's "refundable dividend tax on hand" ("RDTOH") account. This account keeps track of the amount of refundable dividend tax available to a corporation. It is a cumulative, ongoing account. In simple terms, it is credited with 30 2/3 per cent of the "aggregate investment income" and Part IV tax, and reduced by dividend tax refund claimed. Aggregate investment income is income from property (except for dividends from taxable Canadian corporations) and taxable capital gains minus net capital losses. Part IV tax is also added to the RDTOH account. Part IV tax is a special, refundable tax on private corporations that receive dividends from other corporations: its function is similar to the refundable taxes on aggregate investment income. It is not a "real" tax because it is refunded to the corporation when dividends are paid to its shareholders. The RDTOH is reduced by the amount of dividend refund received, so that only the amount of refundable taxes that have not been refunded remain in the account.

426

Table 14-3: Interest Income Earned Directly or Through a CCPC

	Taxpayer earns the income directly ($)	Taxpayer earns the income through a CCPC ($)
Interest income	100	100.00
Less: Corporate tax at combined 51.67% rate (28% basic federal plus 10 2/3% additional refundable tax and 13% provincial)		(51.67)
After-tax cash		48.33
RDTOH available for dividend refund		30.67
Dividend distribution including dividend refund ($48.33 + $30.67)		79.00
Net corporate tax: $51.67 - $30.67 = $21		
Shareholder's dividends received		79.00
Dividends gross-up		13.50
Total taxable income		92.50
Personal income tax (53% combined rate)	53	49
Less Dividend tax credit equal to gross-up		(14)
Net tax payable by individual	53	35
Total corporate and personal taxes	53	56 (21 + 35)

(v) — Private corporations earning Canadian dividends

Taxable dividends received by one corporation from another corporation in Canada are generally "tax-free" to prevent cumulative taxation of corporate income at the corporate levels.[23] CCPCs are eligible to receive tax-free dividends. However, in order to discourage individuals from using CCPCs to hold shares and defer tax on the dividends, a special refundable tax of 33 1/3 per cent of the dividends applies.[24] This tax is refunded to the private corporation when it pays dividends to the shareholders. The anti-deferral and integration goals can be seen in Table 14-4, below:

---

[23] These dividends are technically included in computing income under s. 82, but fully deducted in computing taxable income under s. 112(1).

[24] *ITA, supra* note 1, s. 186, which is in Part IV of the *ITA*. This tax is often referred to as "Part IV tax". The tax is refundable and is payable by all private corporations, not just CCPCs. This means that a private corporation that is not a CCPC will also have an RDTOH account. However, that account will include only the Part IV tax on inter-corporate dividends, not any refundable 30 2/3 per cent Part I tax. Ironically, private corporations that are not CCPCs are subject to the lower general business rate on other kinds of investment income, and Canadian shareholders of such private corporations enjoy a deferral of tax on income from property (other than Canadian dividends) and taxable capital gains. A CCPC is defined in s. 125(7) and is required to be a Canadian corporation (which is defined in s. 89(1)).

Table 14-4: Eligible Dividends Earned Directly or Through a Private Corporation

	Taxpayer earns income directly ($)	Taxpayer earns income through a private corporation ($)
Eligible dividends	100	100.00
Part I corporate tax (no Part I tax or additional refundable tax as dividends are not aggregated investment income)		0.00
Part IV tax		(38.33)
After-tax cash		61.67
RDTOH available for dividend refund		38.33
Dividend distribution (including dividend refund)		100.00
Net corporate tax ($38.33 - $38.33) = 0		
Shareholder's dividends received	100	100
Dividends gross-up	38	38
Total taxable income	138	138
Personal income tax (53% combined rate)	73.14	73.14
Less Dividend tax credit equal to gross-up	(38.00)	(38.00)
Net tax payable by individual	35.14	35.14
Total corporate and personal tax	35.14	35.14

(vi) — CCPCs earning capital gains

The "fiscal unity" idea applies to capital gains as well. The taxable portion is treated as investment income, subject to the additional refundable tax of 10 2/3 per cent (see above). The tax-free portion is "preserved" as "tax-free" through a special capital dividend account that is available to all private corporations.[25] Out of that account, the corporation can elect (by filing a special form) to pay capital dividends to the shareholders. Capital dividends are tax-free in the hands of the shareholders. If a CCPC earns a $200 capital gain, the taxable capital gain of $100 would be subject to the same regime as the $100 of interest income in Table 14-3 and the total taxes on the $200 capital gain would be exactly the same as in Table 14-3 when it is earned directly and through a CCPC. The tax-free $100 would be received tax-free when it is earned directly and (provided a capital dividend election is filed) through a CCPC.

---

[25] *ITA, supra* note 1, s. 83(2).

(d) — Tax incentives for CCPCs earning active business income

Where a CCPC carries on an active business in Canada and incurs expenditures on research and development, the *ITA* provides for generous subsidies.[26] Shareholders of such CCPCs enjoy the benefit of tax deferral as well as the lifetime capital gains exemption and special deduction rules of allowable business investment losses.[27]

14.4 — Partnerships

(a) — Nature of partnerships

As with corporations, the *ITA* defers to private law for the definition of partnerships. Under provincial partnership legislation, a partnership is defined as "the relation that subsists between persons carrying on business in common with a view to profit",[28] and has no separate legal person status. In private law, a partnership is in between a joint venture and a corporation. In the case of "joint ventures" each co-venturer carries on its own business and shares revenue and expenses, but not income. A partnership is simply a way of conducting a business in much the same way as would be the case for an incorporated business, but without the limited liability protection that comes from incorporation. In other words, through a partnership, partners conduct the business jointly, own the business property jointly and share in the resulting income or loss.[29] The partnership rules in the *ITA* are a reac-

---

[26] *Ibid.*, ss. 125, 127.

[27] See Chapter 12 at heading 12.2(d) (iii) — Allowable business investment losses (ABILs).

[28] E.g., Ontario *Partnership Act*, R.S.O. 1990, c. P.5, as amended, s. 2. The definition of a partnership at common law is not entirely clear, and each of the partnership statutes enacted in each common law jurisdiction (following the model of the English Act) supply this definition as well as associated rules. The civil law position is similar to the common law, although the civil code does accord more legal personality to a partnership than does the common law: John E.C. Brierley & Roderick A. Macdonald, eds., *Quebec Civil Law: An. Introduction to Quebec Private Law* (Toronto: Emond Montgomery, 1993) at 667. Although partners normally share profits (or losses), the sharing of profits (or losses) is normally neither a necessary nor a sufficient characteristic of a partnership: *Cox and Wheatcroft v. Hickman* (1860), 11 E.R. 431, 8 H.L. Cas. 268 (H.L.) and Ontario *Partnership Act* (*ibid.*), s. 3.

[29] Property used by a partnership is owned in law by the individual partners. Liabilities incurred by a partnership are owed in law by the individual partners and may have to be satisfied out of the personal assets of the partners, except in the case of "limited partners" whose liability typically would be limited to the amounts invested by them in the partnership, including undistributed partnership income to which they are entitled and in respect of which they would have paid tax according to their allocated shares. The limitation on liability enjoyed by limited partners generally is the consequence of provincial legislation that provides for the creation of limited partnerships and the consequences for the partners of being partners in a partnership with this status. This law — provincial statute law — does not "create" a partnership; a partnership exists or not, as the case may be, according to whether persons conduct themselves in a fashion warranting this determination under the law (i.e., they carry on business in common with a view to profit and share in that profit (or

tion to this form of business association, rather than a tax-originated direction on how to conduct business.

Section 96 of the *ITA* attempts, on the one hand (with certain limited exceptions in section 96), to tax the partners as if they conducted the business separately (though together), while at the same time creating the computational fiction of a partnership as a "person".[30] The net income or loss of the partnership is allocated to the partners. As such, the partnership is a "conduit" or "flow-through" vehicle. This flow-through characteristic makes partnerships attractive vehicles for flowing out or shifting losses. The flow-through characteristic also applies to the character and source of income or loss of the partnership. For example, eligible dividends received by a partnership are allocated to the partners as eligible dividends.

(b) — Income or loss from partnerships

A partner's income from a partnership is computed in two steps: first at the partnership level, and then allocated to the partner. As a tax accounting unit, a partnership computes its income or loss each year as if it were "a separate person resident in Canada" (paragraph 96(1)(a)). It must recognize all revenues and take all deductions that would be applicable to a separate person resident in Canada that uses the calendar year as a fiscal period.[31] For example, a partnership engaged in providing services must recognize its revenues on an accrual basis and deduct expenses incurred for income-earning purposes, such as interest and wages to employees.

---

income) from their common enterprise). A limited partnership is first a partnership, engrafted on which, by legislation, are distinctions among the general and limited partners that confine limited partners' liability for partnership obligations (for which general partners are generally liable and that may be satisfied by all their property) essentially as long as they are passive (i.e., as long as they do not participate in running the partnership business). In that sense, limited partners are a little bit like creditors or, using a corporate analogy, preferred shareholders. Their "equity" participation in the partnership business and, consequently, their responsibility for it is limited to the capital they have invested by subscribing for units or interests in the partnership and allowing for their allocated income shares, on which they are taxed, to actually be retained by the partnership to fund its business.

[30] There are other examples in the *ITA* that use the fictitious personality of partnerships, but in most cases it is directed to administering the Act (i.e., having a computational focus to determine allocated income of a partnership on a source-by-source basis, and, in the case of the withholding tax rules, to give a "person" who can be invested with administering the withholding tax). Also, a partnership does not file a tax return, but it does have to file an annual "information return" setting out the income of the partnership and details of the partners who are entitled to a share of the income (*Income Tax Regulations*, C.R.C., c. 945, reg. 229).

[31] A non-calendar year is only allowed if none of the partners are individuals, professional corporations, or partnerships: s. 249.1(1)(b)(ii). If all the partners are corporations other than professional corporations, the partnership may have a non-calendar year-end; however, the ability to defer income by selecting a different partnership year-end has been eliminated for corporate partners with a 10 per cent or greater interest due to the requirement to accrue stub period income under s. 34.2.

A partnership's income or loss is then allocated among the partners in accordance with their shares in the partnership (paragraph 96(1)(f)). Each partner is then obliged to report his or her share of the partnership income or loss as part of his or her income for the year. The allocation of partnership income will generally be defined in the partnership agreement. However, if the principal reason for the allocation may reasonably be considered to be for the purpose of reducing or postponing tax (i.e., achieving income splitting or shifting), the share of each partner is deemed to be the amount that is "reasonable" in the circumstances.[32] Similarly, if non-arm's-length persons agree to allocate partnership income in a manner that is not reasonable with regard to the partners' contributions of property, work performed and other factors, the share of income is deemed to be the amount that is "reasonable" in the circumstances.[33]

The income of each individual partner retains the source characterization that it had when it was derived by the partnership. Accordingly, the appropriate share of income that was business income in the partnership is treated as business income in the hands of the partner; property income remains property income; and taxable capital gains remain taxable capital gains. This means that the individual partner is subject to the rules applicable to each source of income. For example, a partner's share of partnership dividends from taxable Canadian corporations is grossed up and eligible for the dividend tax credit in the partner's hands. As another example, although the partnership's business income will be a net figure from which all deductions that were applicable at the partnership level have been taken, the individual partner may have further deductions if he or she incurred expenses personally to earn the partnership income (for example, by using a personal automobile in the business or by attending a business conference). As another example, if an individual partner incurred an allowable capital loss in his or her private investments, the loss will be deductible against his or her share of any taxable capital gains derived by the partnership.

(c) — Loss of limited partners

A limited partnership is a special type of partnership and often has been used to flow out deductions and losses to passive investors as a financing device for the partnership business. Part of the return to partners for their investments is the "tax recovery" arising from applying partnership losses to reduce their taxable incomes, but the *ITA* severely limits this possibility through various rules, including specific "tax shelter" rules that are partly compliance-based reporting and disclosure rules and partly loss limitation rules.

Provincial limited partnership statutes allow the creation of a "limited partnership", in which a "limited partner" (or partners) has limited liability like that of a shareholder in a corporation, and a "general partner" (usually a corporation with no as-

---

[32] *ITA, supra* note 1, s. 103(1).

[33] *Ibid.*, s. 103(1.1). There is no principal purpose test in the case of non-arm's-length partners.

sets) has unlimited liability. However, the limited partner must be an entirely passive investor: participation in the management of the business exposes the limited partner to the same liability as a general partner. The use of limited partnerships for tax shelters resulted in restrictions for these partnerships[34] years before the more specific "tax shelter" rules were introduced.

Why are losses restricted for limited partners? Partners, even limited partners, would expect to share losses in the same way as they would share income. And for a long time, the *ITA* has included some basic limitations on this possibility: losses reduce a partner's adjusted cost base, and when a limited partner's adjusted cost base became negative (because, for example, his or her cumulative losses exceeded his or her investment in the partnership), the negative balance was (and still is) taxable as a capital gain[35] (which is not the case for general partners). However, the use of limited partnerships as after-tax financing devices and tax shelter vehicles resulted in the *ITA* being amended to further restrict losses, because of the various ways by which limited partners were being effectively relieved of any risk on their invested capital through collateral transactions involving sponsors that put them in the same position as if they had not invested capital (and yet, getting the benefit of loss allocations as if they had a genuine capital investment). In other words, a limited partner's nominal investment in the partnership was essentially "given back" to him or her via these collateral arrangements. As a result, any allocation of a partnership's losses to such limited partner would, in effect, amount to shifting losses of the investment of an equity partner to the limited partner whose closest commercial equivalent would be a lender. The limited partner rules under subsections 96(2.1) to (2.4) and paragraph 111(1)(e) were introduced and grew to address this type of situation.

The limited partner rules provide an example of the *ITA* using specific provisions to protect the integrity of income measurement where private law arrangements are used to shift losses. They apply not only in respect of limited partners in the commercial law sense, but also in respect of partners whose lack of involvement in the management of the business of the partnership puts them in an equivalent position. The amount of losses allocated to such partners is limited by the partner's at-risk amount (i.e., generally, his or her net investment in the partnership).[36]

---

[34] The limited liability partnerships ("LLPs") used by lawyers and accountants are not limited partnerships and are exempted from these restrictions. Paragraphs 40(3.14)(a) and 96(2.4)(a) exclude a partner of an LLP from the definition of "limited partner" for the purposes of the negative adjusted cost base rules and "at-risk" rules discussed.

[35] *ITA*, *supra* note 1, ss. 40(3), (3.1).

[36] The rules in this regard in ss. 96(2.1), 96(2.2) and related provisions are supplemented by the at-risk adjustment rules in s. 143.2, which are related to the tax shelter reporting rules in s. 237.1 and are concerned with limiting taxpayers' access to tax benefits that would otherwise arise under the *ITA* from their expenditures that constitute "tax shelter investments" (143.2(1)), where it is determined that the taxpayers are not "at risk" for those investments.

(d) — Partnership interest

A partner's capital investment in a partnership generally represents his or her share of equity interest in the partnership, which determines his or her entitlement to share in the income or loss of the partnership. This is analogous to a shareholder's interest as a shareholder in a corporation. Just as would a shareholder, a partner acquires an interest in a partnership by subscribing for it, that is, by contributing capital in money and property to the partnership in return for an interest in the underlying business evidenced by the partnership interest. As in the case of shares, the participation in the business represented by a partnership interest is defined by its terms relative to other partnership interests, of equal, superior or inferior rank.

As capital property, partnership interest can be disposed of at a gain or loss. The adjusted cost base of partnership interest is typically the original investment, plus or minus certain adjustments under paragraph 53(1)(e) or 53(2)(c). These adjustments are designed to make sure that the amount of income or loss allocated to a partner is not recognized again as capital gain or capital loss if the partner disposes of the partnership interest.

Paragraph 53(1)(e) provides for various additions to be made, and paragraph 53(2)(c) provides for deductions from the cost figure. Under paragraph 53(1)(e), a main addition is that any amount of partnership income from a prior year to which the partner is entitled (which is included in the partner's income already) is not subject to double taxation by increasing the value of the partner's interest in the firm.[37] Similarly, under paragraph 53(2)(c), the partner's share of any losses generated by the partnership in a prior year must be deducted from the partner's adjusted cost base, as these amounts will also have been reported under section 96.[38] If subsection 53(2) deductions exceed (on a cumulative basis) the original cost of the interest and all subsection 53(1) additions, the adjusted cost base of the partnership interest will be a negative amount. As indicated earlier, a negative adjusted cost base will result in an immediate capital gain for a passive or limited partner, but not a partner actively involved in the partnership.[39]

14.5 — Trusts

(a) — Nature of trusts

A trust exists when the legal ownership, management and control of property is vested in one person or persons (a "trustee") while enjoyment of the property "belongs" to another person or persons (a "beneficiary"). Broadly, the legal formula-

---

[37] In order to avoid double taxation, the partner adds to the adjusted cost base the partner's share of the partnership's full capital gain (not just the one-half portion that is a taxable capital gain): s. 53(1)(e)(i)(A).

[38] The other major deduction from the adjusted cost base of the partnership interest, provided for by paragraph 53(2)(c), is the value of any distribution (or "drawings") of capital or income that the partner has received from the partnership.

[39] *ITA, supra* note 1, ss. 40(3), 53(1)(a), 40(3.1)–(3.2).

tion by which this division between the management and enjoyment of property is accomplished entails legal title to the trust property being with the trustee while equitable (or beneficial) "ownership" of the trust property belongs to the beneficiary. The trustee is obligated to the contributor of the property (i.e., the "settlor") and implicitly to the beneficiaries to administer the property for their benefit. The separation of legal and beneficial ownership of property, coupled with the manner in which the property and income arising from it are administered and the reasons that the arrangement is implemented, are the hallmarks of a trust. In essence, trusts are legal obligations undertaken by the trustee to manage the property for the beneficiaries.

The fragmentation of the ownership and enjoyment of property and resulting income is a core feature of a trust — the separation of owners of property from the means by which the property is used to earn income. The *ITA* addresses when this separation is acceptable to have tax outcomes consistent with the separation, and when that is not the case. When the *IT* wants to overcome this separation, it does so through a variety of provisions that may attribute income from the settled property to its original owner and otherwise police the circumstances in which there is a sufficiently genuine and enduring separation that the tax outcomes ordinarily caused by it may be accepted.

Trusts are classified into several categories, based on whether the settlor is alive at the time the trust is created, whether the powers of the trustee are discretionary, whether the beneficiary is a spouse, or whether the purpose of the trust is personal or commercial. In very general terms, a main distinction for tax purposes is whether a trust is employed to achieve personal or family objectives (a personal trust), or is a means by which a commercial venture or enterprise is arranged and conduced (a commercial trust). The *ITA* treats commercial trusts in much the same manner it does corporations earning business income.[40]

(b) — Personal trusts

A personal trust is defined as a testamentary or *inter vivos* trust in which the beneficiaries did not purchase their interests from the trust or from anyone who had made a contribution to the trust.[41] The term "commercial trust" is not defined in the *ITA*

---

[40] In fact, a "specified investment flow-through" ("SIFT") trust is treated exactly like a corporation (as are SIFT partnerships). A SIFT trust is a public trust (with public unit holders) and a SIFT partnership is a public partnership (with public partner investors). SIFT trusts originated as investment vehicles created to earn income from deductible payments by corporations, such as interest and royalties, which reduced the corporations' incomes. In many cases, the holders of interests in these investment vehicles were, and are, non-taxable deferred income plans. These "income trusts" were considered to account for a significant reduction in the tax base. Taxing them and their interest holders — partners and beneficiaries — as if they were corporations with shareholders effectively restores to the corporate business income tax base the amounts that otherwise the deductible charges would deplete. See Part IX.1 (SIFT Partnerships) and sections 122 and 122.1.

[41] *ITA, supra* note 1, s. 248(1).

but is generally used to refer to a trust that is not a personal trust. The most common examples of commercial trusts are publicly-traded mutual funds (which own a portfolio of securities) and real estate investment trusts ("REITS") which own a portfolio of real estate). Unless otherwise stated, we focus on the taxation of personal trusts, which are sometimes referred to as family trusts and are resident in Canada.

Personal trusts can be discretionary or non-discretionary trusts. The trust document (or will) sets out the powers and the obligations of the trustee of a trust. Many trusts will allow the trustee some discretion as to the amounts to be paid to beneficiaries or, perhaps, the date of the termination of the trust. In a non-discretionary trust, the payment of income and capital to beneficiaries is set out in the terms of the trust, and there is no flexibility. If a trustee has some discretion as to whether or not to pay income or capital to a particular beneficiary, the trust is called a discretionary trust. Discretionary trusts are more useful for tax and estate planning than non-discretionary trusts.

Personal trusts can be testamentary or *inter vivos*. A testamentary trust is created "as a consequence of the death of an individual."[42] An *inter vivos* (or living) trust is created by a living person (called the "settlor"). Most testamentary trusts are created by will, which, of course, becomes operative only on the death of the testator or testatrix (who is the settlor). If an individual dies without a will, the personal representative administers and distributes the deceased's property to the successors. Until the property is distributed, the personal representative holds the property in trust.

Family trusts have the settlor's spouse, common-law partner or children as beneficiaries. A "spousal trust" enjoys special treatments under the *ITA*, namely a rollover when property is transferred to the trust, and an exemption from the 21-year deemed disposition rule discussed below.[43] In a spousal trust, only the spouse is entitled to the income[44] from the property arising in his or her lifetime, and other beneficiaries (such as children) are not entitled to the use of the capital until the spouse's death. If the trustee has a power to encroach on the capital for the benefit of the spouse, the trust would still qualify as a spousal trust. But if the trustee has a power to allocate income or capital to anyone other than the spouse during the

---

[42] *Ibid.*, s. 108(1). An *inter vivos* trust is defined as a trust other than a testamentary trust.

[43] The rollover rules are discussed in Chapter 10 at heading 10.4(c)(iv)(A) — Rollovers for transfers to a spouse or common-law partner, and the deemed disposition rule is discussed at heading 14.5(d)(iv) — Deemed disposition of property, below.

[44] The word "income" in the definition of a spousal trust in ss. 70(6) and 73(1) means income in the trust accounting sense, not the tax sense (s. 108(3)). It is not necessary, therefore, for the spouse to be entitled to capital gains. Accordingly, capital gains realized by a spousal trust will be subject to tax in the hands of the trust unless the gains are paid or made payable to the spouse beneficiary. This tax rule is often forgotten or not understood.

lifetime of the spouse, the existence of that power would "taint" the trust for tax purposes.[45]

(c) — Trusts taxed as "fiscally transparent"

The *ITA* recognizes the separateness but also, in a manner of speaking, the opacity or transparency of trusts in a regime dedicated to taxing income associated with them.[46] Income distributed by a trust to the beneficiaries is taxed to the beneficiaries as if the beneficiaries had earned the income in terms of the character and source. Income that is not distributed to the beneficiaries is taxable to the trust as if the trust is an individual.[47]

Like a partnership, a trust is a tax accounting unit and computes the net income or loss each year. It is the net income that is distributed to beneficiaries. Unlike a partnership, however, losses are not distributed, although it may be possible in some cases to "convert" those losses to non-taxable capital distributions by the trust's application of those losses to "shelter" otherwise taxable income. But the formative tax accounting issue is more difficult for trusts; partners generally know their entitlements, provided for in a partnership agreement. Often, however, trust beneficiaries cannot count on receiving anything, or at least anything at regular intervals. Trust distributions are often made according to the exercise by a trustee of discretionary authority provided in a deed of trust. The *ITA* is not so harsh as to tax persons on amounts they not only do not receive, but have no enforceable entitlement to get. But that reality does not displace the fact that property has been set aside and is generating income. Who should pay the tax?

In principle, tax should be paid, essentially, by everyone interested in the property, as contributor and beneficiary. But without a predetermined exercise of discretion, how is that to happen? The *ITA* treats trusts as taxable persons, taxable on the income they nominally earn unless it is distributed to beneficiaries who then become the taxable persons in some respects as if they had received the income directly. In result, by making a trust a taxable person, the *ITA* is able to hold somebody accountable as a taxpayer even though the settlor, who set up the trust, no longer owns the settled property, and the beneficiaries have not received, and may never actually receive, any trust distributions. The *ITA* composes and joins together all the interested parties in the arrangement and makes the trust, via the trustee, the taxable person as the trustee's alter ego.

Technically speaking, there are questions that need to be contended with. Double taxation is one. And when income is distributed, should it retain its character as the trust is considered to have received it? This might matter if the character of the income matters for other purposes in the *ITA* to avoid unwarranted taxation, such as the foreign tax credit provisions or how income earned by corporations is taxed

---

[45] A tainted trust is, of course, perfectly valid: it simply loses the benefit of the spousal trust's tax privileges, which include a rollover.

[46] *ITA*, *supra* note 1, ss. 104–108 (subdivision k of Division B).

[47] *Ibid.*, s. 104(2).

when distributed to their shareholders. To make the questions even harder, what is the right response when a trust is "non-discretionary" (i.e., the beneficiaries have "fixed interests", as is commonly the case in a commercial contrasted with a personal trust)? Are the same concerns present about having a taxable person to hold accountable as the taxpayer of first instance?

(d) — Trusts taxed as individuals

(i) — Trusts as fictional individuals

Subsection 104(2) of the *ITA* says a trust shall be deemed to be an individual. This means that the computation of income, taxable income, tax payable and tax credits of a trust are similar to those of a real individual. However, the *ITA* also provides several specific rules that modify the treatment of this fictional individual in cases where it can be used to undermine the progressive taxation of personal income through income splitting or shifting.

(ii) — Tax rates and credits

Individuals are taxed at progressive rates under section 117 of the *ITA*. In the absence of specific rules, treating each trust as an individual would mean that a high-income person can avoid paying tax at the top rate by either 1) "multiplying" himself or herself through the creation of multiple trusts, each of which reports income in the lowest bracket, or 2) shifting income to a spouse or children who are in lower-income brackets. The *ITA* contains several rules to prevent such outcome.

All trusts (other than a qualified disability trust and a "graduated rate estate") are taxable only at the top marginal rate, currently 33 per cent.[48] This rule removes the tax advantage of progressive graduated rates and income splitting from most trusts. Before 2016, all testamentary trusts were taxed at graduated rates, but the graduated rates are now restricted to an estate arising on the death of an individual for the 36 months after death.[49] Restricting graduated rates to the first 36 months of an estate became necessary because taxpayers had been motivated to establish trusts in their wills as income splitting vehicles for their family members.

Unlike individuals, trusts are not eligible for personal credits in respect of specific personal circumstances.[50] To further remove the tax advantage of using multiple trusts, subsection 104(2) provides that, where there are a number of trusts in which 1) substantially all the property of the various trusts has been received from one person, and 2) the various trusts are conditioned so that the income thereof accrues or will ultimately accrue to the same beneficiary, or group or class of beneficiaries,

---

[48] *Ibid.*, s. 122(1)(a). A SIFT trust is also excluded from this rule, since it is taxed under s. 122(1)(b) at rates applicable to corporations.

[49] See definition of "graduated rate estate" in s. 248(1).

[50] *ITA, supra* note 1, s. 122(1.1).

the Minister has the power to lump all the trusts together and tax all of the income as the income of a single trust.[51]

Income splitting is specifically permitted when a trust is created to benefit disabled persons. A qualified disability trust is not subject to the top rate of taxation to assist families to use trusts to accumulate income for beneficiaries who are disabled. Further, an election can be made in respect of "preferred beneficiaries" (individuals eligible for the credit for mental or physical impairment or the disability tax credit)[52] to have income that is not paid or payable to beneficiaries taxed in the hands of beneficiaries.[53] As a result, such income is not taxed at the top rate, but the rate applicable to the beneficiaries. In other words, income splitting is permitted as a tax relief measure.

(iii) — Computation and designation of income

As a fictional individual, a trust must determine its income and taxable income for tax purposes. In addition, as a fiscal conduit, a trust can deduct the amount of income that is taxable to the beneficiary.[54] As such, the trust is taxable only on income that is earned in a taxation year and not paid or payable to a beneficiary[55] and income that is designated to be taxable to the trust.[56] Because losses are not flowed to beneficiaries, the designations enable a trust to designate income or capital gains that are paid or payable to beneficiaries as taxable income of the trust in order to offset the losses.[57]

(iv) — Deemed disposition of property

Since capital gains are taxable only upon disposition of capital property, and individuals are deemed to dispose of their capital property upon death, triggering a realization of capital gains for tax purposes, a family trust can be used to hold capital property indefinitely, thereby avoiding tax on the accrued capital gains. To prevent such tax deferral, subsection 104(4) provides for a periodic deemed disposi-

---

[51] This does not prevent taxpayers from setting up different trusts for different beneficiaries: see *Mitchell v. M.N.R.* (1956), 56 D.T.C. 521, 16 Tax A.B.C. 99 (Can. Tax App. Bd.). In *Mitchell*, the settlor had four children and he created a separate trust for each of them. It was held that, because the beneficiary of each trust was different, the multiple trust rule in s. 104(2) was inapplicable (s. 104(2) was s. 63(2) at that time). After this decision, until the enactment of s. 122(1) in 1971, the use of separate *inter vivos* trusts for children became a popular means of income splitting.

[52] For the criteria, see *ITA*, *supra* note 1, ss. 118.3(1)(a), (b).

[53] *Ibid.*, s. 108(1) "preferred beneficiary".

[54] *Ibid.*, s. 104(6)(b).

[55] This assumes that the income is not subject to a preferred beneficiary election of an infirm or disabled beneficiary.

[56] *ITA*, *supra* note 1, s. 104(13.1) or (13.2).

[57] Effective 2016, this designation is actually restricted to losses: s. 104(1.3.3) states that a s. 104(13.1) or (13.2) election will be invalid if the trust's income is greater than nil.

tion and reacquisition at fair market value of all capital property held by a trust, thereby forcing the trust to recognize for tax purposes all accrued capital gains and losses.[58] For trusts other than spousal trusts, alter ego trusts, and joint spousal trusts, the deemed disposition occurs every 21 years.[59] Spousal trusts, alter ego trusts, and joint spousal trusts are not subject to these deemed dispositions during the lifetime of the spouse or settlor beneficiaries (as the case may be),[60] but there is a deemed disposition on the death of these persons and (if the trust continues) every 21 years thereafter.[61]

(e) — Income of beneficiaries

(i) — Income and character flow-through

As a fiscally transparent vehicle, a trust does not pay tax on the income that is distributed to beneficiaries. A beneficiary includes the amount in computing his or her income under subsection 104(14) or (15). Technically, the *ITA* regards income as distributed if it is "payable" to a beneficiary.[62] Income is "payable" if it is "paid" in the year, or if not actually paid but the beneficiary "was entitled in that year to enforce payment thereof".[63]

The tax character of income received from a trust is income from property that is an interest in the trust (paragraph 108(5)(a)). However, certain amounts may retain their tax character if a designation is made to that effect by the trust; the designation is elective but often advantageous for various reasons. The designations include all or part of any: 1) dividends from Canadian corporations received by the trust[64] so that the beneficiary can then take advantage of a dividend tax credit; 2)

---

[58] In the case of depreciable property, the deemed disposition is required by s. 104(5), and, of course, it may also cause a recapture of capital cost allowances.

[59] The 21-year periods are measured from the creation of the trust, or, in the case of trusts in existence at the beginning of 1972, from January 1, 1972 (s. 104(4)(b), (c)). In 1991, ss. 104(5.3)–(5.7) were enacted, which enabled a trust with at least one "exempt beneficiary" (a family member only one generation removed from the settlor, e.g., a child of the settlor) to elect to postpone the deemed disposition until the death of the exempt beneficiary. This election is not available after 1998 (s. 104(5.3)). Trusts that made the election had a deemed disposition on January 1, 1999 of any property they owned on that date (s. 104(5.3)(a)(i)).

[60] *ITA, supra* note 1, ss. 104(4)(a)(iii), (iv).

[61] *Ibid.,* ss. 104(4)(b), (c).

[62] *Ibid.,* s. 104(6)(b).

[63] *Ibid.,* s. 104(24). If a beneficiary is an infant or minor and cannot enforce payment solely for that reason, the income is still deemed to be payable to the beneficiary. In addition, certain amounts paid by a trust to third parties for the benefit of beneficiaries may be considered as income payable to a beneficiary (s. 105(1)). Typical expenses are the cost of tuition fees, medical expenses, clothing and holidays, but not general household expenses. See Canada Revenue Agency Technical Interpretations in 1993 and 1997 on this issue (Document Nos. 9233505 and 9722465, respectively).

[64] *ITA, supra* note 1, ss. 104(19), (20).

capital gains realized by the trust[65]so that the beneficiary can take advantage of the preferential treatment of capital gains; and 3) foreign-source income received by the trust[66] so that the beneficiary may claim a foreign tax credit.

As discussed earlier in this chapter, in cases where a trust has sustained losses, the losses are not distributed to beneficiaries, but the trust can elect to designate income paid to beneficiaries as its own taxable income, which is then sheltered by the losses. Such treatment of a trust's losses turns a trust into a tax shelter: the trust holds back income that is otherwise distributable (and taxable to a beneficiary); it offsets its losses against such income so that the income is not taxable; and it capitalizes the "sheltered" income. In a subsequent year, the trust distributes the sheltered income as a capital distribution, which is not taxable to a beneficiary but, instead, reduces the beneficiary's adjusted cost base of its interest in the trust.[67] The overall effect is to convert what otherwise would have been income into a capital gain when the basis goes negative or the reduced basis is otherwise recovered on a disposition of the interest. Given trust law, this character transformation is not entirely strange because, as a trust law matter, income loses its income source when held over into another fiscal period and becomes part of the accumulated trust capital.

(ii) — Special rules for capital gains

The tax treatment of capital gains will often reflect a difference between the concept of income for tax purposes and the concept of income for trust accounting purposes. Taxable capital gains are, of course, income for tax purposes, but they are capital for trust accounting purposes (unless the trust instrument provides otherwise). Accordingly, capital gains that are earned by a trust will not normally be payable to the income beneficiary of the trust, but will be added to the capital of the trust. Even if all of a trust's income (for trust accounting purposes) is payable each year to an income beneficiary, capital gains will not be payable to the income beneficiary. Capital gains will ultimately be payable to the capital beneficiary, but not until the time comes to distribute the capital of the trust. It follows that capital gains earned by a trust in a taxation year will often not be payable to a beneficiary in the year, and will, therefore, be treated for tax purposes as accumulating income of the trust. If so, the trust will be obliged to report the capital gains as its income.

If capital gains are payable to a beneficiary, a designation under subsection 104(13.2) can be made to have them taxed in the trust. If capital gains are not payable to a beneficiary, a preferred beneficiary election may be available (in re-

---

[65] *Ibid.*, ss. 104(21), (21.2).

[66] *Ibid.*, ss. 104(22), (22.1).

[67] The beneficiary's ACB is relevant when he or she disposes of an interest in a trust. Section 107 contains the rules that apply to the disposition of a capital interest in a trust. (s. 106 contains the rules that apply to the disposition of income interests and is the subject of Canada Revenue Agency, Folio S6-F2-C1, "Disposition of an Income Interest in a Trust").

spect of an infirm or disabled beneficiary) to have the capital gains taxed in the beneficiary's hands.

(f) — Income attributed to the settlor

Under general circumstances, a property transferred by a settlor to a trust is legally owned by the trust for the benefit of beneficiaries. For tax purposes, any income from the property legally belongs to the fictional individual, not the settlor. However, in certain circumstances, income earned by the trust or the beneficiary may be attributed to the settlor to prevent income splitting or shifting.

Where a person transfers (or loans) property to a trust, and the income from the property is payable by the trust to the transferor's spouse, or to a related minor, then the income will be attributed to the transferor (or lender) under subsection 74.1(1) (in the case of the spouse) and subsection 74.1(2) (in the case of the minor). If the transferred property is disposed of by the trust, and if any capital gain is payable to the transferor's spouse, then the capital gain will be attributed to the transferor under subsection 74.2(1). There is no attribution of capital gains if the beneficiary is a related minor. Income accumulating in a trust for the ultimate benefit of a spouse or related minor is not subject to attribution (see section 74.3) and is, thus, taxed to the trust.

If a trust is a revocable trust within the meaning of subsection 75(2), any income (or loss) from property transferred to the trust by the settlor, as well as any taxable capital gains (or allowable capital losses) from the disposition of the transferred property, may be attributed to the settlor. The same treatment applies to any substituted property. This treatment does not apply to property transferred to the trust by the settlor in a fair market value commercial or commercial-like exchange.[68] A revocable trust is a trust where property is held on condition "(a) that it or property substituted therefor may (i) revert to the person from whom the property or property for which it was substituted was directly or indirectly received (in this subsection referred to as 'the person'), or (ii) pass to persons to be determined by the person at a time subsequent to the creation of the trust, or (b) that, during the lifetime of the person, the property shall not be disposed of except with the person's consent or in accordance with the person's direction".[69] In essence, in a revocable trust, the settlor has reserved to himself or herself a power to revoke the trust, or a power to change the beneficiaries, or a power to direct or veto dispositions of the trust property, or a reversionary interest in the trust property. No separate fictional individual is deemed to exist for tax purposes.

---

[68] See *Canada v. Sommerer*, 2012 FCA 207, 2012 D.T.C. 5126 (F.C.A.).

[69] *ITA, supra* note 1, s. 75(2).

15

TAX ADMINISTRATION AND ETHICS

15.1 — Legislative scheme

(a) — Statutory provisions

Divisions I and J of Part I and Part XV of the *Income Tax Act* (the "*ITA*")[1] provide rules for returns, assessments, payments, appeals and enforcement. In addition, subsection 221(1) provides the Governor in Council with the authority to make all necessary regulations relating to the administration and enforcement of the *ITA*.

---

[1] R.S.C. 1985 (5th Supp.), c. 1 [*ITA*].

These regulations are effected by Order in Council. Sections 200 to 238 of the *Income Tax Regulations* (the "Regulations")[2] provide details on information returns.

The statutory provisions are organized so that they follow in a logical, temporal sequence: section 150 of the *ITA* requires taxpayers to file annual tax returns; section 151 requires taxpayers to estimate their tax payable; section 152 authorizes the Minister to assess the returns; sections 153 to 160 provide procedures for payment of tax; sections 161 and 161.1 deal with interest on tax debts; sections 162 to 163.2 spell out penalties for failure to file returns, or making false statements in returns by the taxpayer or a third party; section 164 deals with refunds to be paid by the Minister; sections 165 sets forth procedures for filing objections to assessment; and sections 169 to 180 address issues related to appeals to the Tax Court of Canada and Federal Court of Appeal. The temporal organization makes sense because tax procedure inevitably follows a time sequence, given that each tax obligation is determined based on a tax period, with a subsequent possibility of reassessment by the Canada Revenue Agency (the "CRA"), the taxpayer's appeal of the reassessment, and ultimate determination of tax liability for the period. Naturally, not every taxpayer would be involved in each possible step in the procedure. Most individual taxpayers' involvement is limited to filing a tax return and either making a payment to the government or receiving a tax refund.

Sections 220 to 244 regulate matters related to the Minister's duty, collection of taxes, record keeping, the Minister's powers to obtain information and duty to keep taxpayer information confidential, solicitor-client privilege, as well as offences and punishment. The *ITA* does not positively spell out the legal rights of taxpayers. The CRA publishes a Taxpayers' Bill of Rights on its website.[3] The *ITA* imposes various obligations on the Minister and his or her delegates, which can be understood as creating rights for taxpayers. By and large, the *ITA* is heavy on duties and obligations and light on legal rights.

Other than the third-party liabilities imposed under sections 163.1 and 163.2, the *ITA* is silent on professional ethics.

(b) — Self-assessment

(i) — "Voluntary" compliance

Instead of direct assessment by the CRA of each taxpayer's tax liability, the *ITA* implements a self-assessment system. Many of the provisions mentioned above are designed to ensure that self-assessment works. Taxpayers file annual tax returns and estimate their tax payable on the returns. The CRA reviews the return and issues a notice of assessment correcting computational errors. This assessment is final unless the Minister reassesses it within the specified period of time. In a sense, the compliance with the *ITA* is "voluntary". To ensure compliance, however, the

---

[2] C.R.C., c. 945 [Regulations].

[3] CRA website: <http://www.cra-arc.gc.ca/E/pub/tg/rc4418/rc4418-11e.pdf>.

ITA contains a number of "carrots" and "sticks" to encourage compliance or punish non-compliance.

(ii) — "Carrots"

There is a general buy-in to the idea of paying income taxes in Canada, as there has been no serious political attempt to abolish them. And yet, it is naïve to believe that people enjoy sharing their hard-earned income with the government by paying taxes. Most taxpayers regard it as their legal obligation to pay taxes, and appreciate the fact that failure to comply attracts serious consequences. The *ITA* entices taxpayers to file tax returns through a number of measures. One is to link the receipt of a tax refund to filing tax returns: subsection 164(1) provides the statutory authority for the making of refunds of overpaid tax, interest, and penalties by the Minister, as long as the taxpayer's return of income has been made within three years from the end of the year.[4] Another measure is to link the taxpayer's reported income to his or her eligibility for certain tax subsidies, such as deduction of contributions to an RRSP or qualification for refundable tax credits. Low-income taxpayers who have no tax payable are encouraged to file in order to establish their entitlement to the GST/HST credit, the child tax benefit, and any refundable provincial credits.

In recognition of the fact that individuals may not have the best accounting records for their various income sources, the *ITA* and the Regulations require the payers of certain types of income[5] and trusts and partnerships to prepare information returns. These returns must state the amount of income paid to the taxpayer during the year. A copy of the return must be provided to the taxpayer and the CRA. The linchpin of the information returns and tax returns is the taxpayer's social insurance number, which is used as a tax filing number. The confidentiality of taxpayer information is protected under section 241 of the *ITA*.

To ease the pain of tax payment or motivate tax filing, the *ITA* makes the tax payable by most individuals deducted at source throughout the year. Because the source withholding tends to result in an over-deduction of taxes, a tax refund can generally be expected soon after a tax return is filed.

(iii) — "Sticks"

As explained in more detail below, non-compliance is punishable by civil and/or criminal penalties. The *ITA* authorizes the CRA to audit a taxpayer's books and records, to make an assessment and reassessment of the taxpayer's tax payable, and to levy interest and penalties. Through the use of information technology, the CRA has tremendous capacity to identify incorrect reporting on tax returns through utilizing the information reported by third parties as well as information obtained through other sources, including foreign governments. Once a tax debt is established, the CRA has the power and means to enforce collections.

---

[4] In the case of individuals and testamentary trusts, the CRA, at its discretion, may refund tax if the return is filed within 10 years after the end of the year: s. 164(1.5).

[5] E.g., salary and taxable benefits, dividends, interest and pensions.

(c) — Purpose and rationale

The primary goal of the *ITA* is to generate revenue in a fair and equitable manner. The legislative scheme governing tax administration serves that goal by ensuring that taxes are collected efficiently and fairly. The substantive rules in the *ITA* mean little if they cannot be complied with by taxpayers or administered by the CRA at a reasonable cost.

The main rationale for self-assessment is cost-effectiveness. From the government's perspective, self-assessment is cost effective because it delegates the determination of tax to taxpayers, the task of collecting taxes to the payers of income (primarily employers), and the task of reporting correct amounts of income to employers and financial institutions (with less motivation to cheat than taxpayers). From the taxpayers' perspective, however, there can be significant compliance cost involved, including both time and money. While many taxpayers prepare their own returns and those of family members, many others pay a fee to a professional preparer.

Another rationale for self-assessment is to give taxpayers a sense of autonomy and self-control. Even though many taxpayers approach the annual filing deadline with some trepidation, it is unlikely that they would prefer a direct assessment system in which their tax liability is determined by the CRA. That may also be one of the reasons that many other democratic countries use self-assessment. Perhaps the annual ritual of filing a tax return reminds taxpayers to be mindful of what their government is doing with their tax dollars and to be more engaged citizens.

15.2 — Compliance by taxpayers

(a) — Filing of tax returns

Pursuant to subsection 150(1) of the *ITA*, every individual who is liable to pay tax in a particular taxation year must file a tax return for that year. In most cases, the obligation to file a tax return applies only if the individual has received enough income to become liable to pay tax. However, the Minister has the power, under subsection 150(2), to demand the filing of a return by an individual who is not liable to pay tax. Corporations must file returns whether or not they are liable to pay tax. The return is in a form prescribed by the Minister. It not only reports all relevant income, deduction, and credit amounts with supporting documentation, it also provides an estimate of the amount of the tax payable or tax refund.

Returns by individuals must generally be filed no later than April 30 of the following year. The deadline is extended to June 15th if the taxpayer (or his or her spouse or common-law partner) has income from a business. Corporate returns must be filed within six months of the end of the taxation year, which is the corporation's fiscal period. Individuals may file a return by mailing it or by e-file or Netfile (using approved software). Corporations with gross revenues in excess of $1 million must generally e-file their returns. As well, all professional preparers may only "paper file" up to 10 personal and 10 corporate returns annually; all additional returns must be e-filed.

(b) — Payment of tax

Payment of unpaid tax must accompany a taxpayer's income tax return pursuant to section 156.1. An assessment by the Minister also generates an obligation to pay the unpaid part of the amount assessed. In general, however, most taxes are paid either by way of withholding at source or instalments.

(i) — Withholding at source

Taxpayers receiving income from employment or office have their tax withheld at source. Under section 153, the employer must deduct the tax payable by an employee from each payment of remuneration and remit the tax deducted to the government. The amounts of tax deducted during the year are often too high, for example, because they do not take account of all the deductions or credits to which the taxpayer is entitled. To obtain a tax refund, the taxpayer needs to file a return. The Minister has no obligation to pay the refund unless a return is filed.

Section 227 establishes penalties for failure by an employer to withhold tax at source, and for failure to remit to the government any tax that was withheld; the delinquent employer is liable for the amount that should have been withheld or remitted, plus penalties and interest. Where a corporation has failed to withhold or remit tax, section 227.1 imposes personal liability on the directors of the corporation, subject to a defence of due diligence. The employee is also liable for tax that was never withheld, but the employee is not liable for tax that was withheld but not remitted to the CRA.[6]

(ii) — Instalments

The general rule is that an individual who derives income from which tax has not been withheld at source (for example, income from business or property) must pay tax by quarterly instalments[7] and pay any balance due on April 30 of the following year.[8] The instalment requirement applies only if the individual's total federal and provincial tax liability, apart from tax withheld at source, exceeds $3,000. It, thus, removes the obligation to pay tax in instalments for most individuals who derive income primarily from employment.

---

[6] *Lalonde v. M.N.R*, [1982] C.T.C. 2749, 82 D.T.C. 1772 (T.R.B.).

[7] Tax instalments are payable quarterly, approximately two weeks before the end of each quarter, on March 15, June 15, September 15, and December 15 of each year. The amounts are determined by a formula based on taxes payable for the current year and two prior years. Farmers and fishermen do not pay quarterly instalments. They must pay a single instalment of two-thirds of their liability (provided it exceeds $3,000) on or before December 31, and the balance on or before April 30 of the following year: s. 155.

[8] The general rule in s. 157(1) is that corporations are required to pay tax in 12-monthly instalments throughout the taxation year, subject to a similar $3,000 exemption.

(c) — Interest

Under section 152 and 161, interest is charged on late and overdue taxes. In some cases, the amount of interest can be significant and even exceed the amount of taxes owed. The interest is computed by reference to the "prescribed rate" of interest. This rate is set quarterly and consists of the average yield on 90-day treasury bills sold in the first month of the previous quarter, rounded up to the nearest percentage point, plus 4 percentage points.[9] The prescribed rate of interest on tax refunds payable to individuals, but not corporations, is the same treasury-bill rate plus 2 (instead of 4) percentage points.

(d) — Records and books

Sections 230 and 230.1 set out requirements for keeping adequate books of account and records for tax purposes. These books and records must generally be retained for six years and ready for inspection by the CRA.

15.3 — Assessment and enforcement by the Minister

(a) — Notice of assessment

The Minister is required by subsection 152(1) to assess the tax payable by the taxpayer. This task must be accomplished "with all due dispatch".[10] When the return is received by the CRA at one of its taxation centres, it is checked to ensure that the

---

[9] Regulations, *supra* note 2, reg. 4301.

[10] The courts have given a flexible meaning to the phrase "with all due dispatch", defining it as meaning no more than a reasonable period, bearing in mind that the purpose of the provision is primarily to protect the taxpayer: see *Ficek v R.*, 2013 FC 502, 2013 D.T.C. 5104 (Eng.), [2013] F.C.J. No. 556 (Fed. T.D.) citing *J. Stollar (also cited as Stoller) Construction v. M.N.R.*, [1989] 1 C.T.C. 2171, 89 D.T.C. 134 (T.C.C.) and *Hillier v. Canada (Attorney General)*, 2001 FCA 197, [2001] 3 CTC 157 (Fed. C.A.) on this point. In *Ficek*, the Court held in favour of the taxpayer: it was established that the reason for the 18-month delay in the assessment of the taxpayer's 2010 return until the completion of the 2010 audit of a charity tax shelter (which had issued invalid receipts in the past) was a CRA Taxation Office program designed to discourage participation in this and similar shelters, and this was not a valid reason for delay. (Note that a 2013 federal budget proposal, which has since been enacted, is apt to discourage participation in such shelters as it will allow the CRA to collect 50 per cent of disputed taxes, interest or penalties when a taxpayer objects to an assessment related to a charitable donation tax shelter.) In other earlier cases, the courts accepted as valid assessments issued after quite lengthy delays: e.g., *Hutterian Brethren Church of Wilson v. R.*, [1979] C.T.C. 1, 79 D.T.C. 5052 (Fed. T.D.); affirmed [1980] C.T.C. 1, 79 D.T.C. 5474 (Fed. C.A.) (15 months); *Lipsey v. M.N.R.*, [1984] C.T.C. 675, 85 D.T.C. 5080 (Fed. T.D.) (2 years); and *Weih v. M.N.R.*, [1988] 2 C.T.C. 2013, 88 D.T.C. 1379 (T.C.C.) (15 months). The limits of tolerance were exceeded by a six-year delay in *Stollar*: in that case the Court vacated the assessment. An assessment will not be vacated for failure to assess with all due dispatch unless the taxpayer goes through the objection and appeal process described at headings 15.4(a) — Administrative appeals, and 15.4(b) — Appeal to the Tax Court of Canada, below: *R. v. Ginsberg*, [1996] 3 C.T.C. 63, 96 D.T.C. 6372 (Fed. C.A.).

arithmetic is correct, that all required documentation has been supplied, and that the return is, on its face, in order. This process may involve obtaining more information from the taxpayer, and may result in additions to or subtractions from the income reported by the taxpayer. When the process is complete, a notice of assessment is issued: any tax still owing must be paid "forthwith" under section 158, and any overpaid taxes will be refunded.

(b) — Examination and audit

After the notice of assessment has been issued, some returns undergo a more thorough examination. Such examination involves cross-checking the information returns provided by third parties against the taxpayer's return.

A small number of returns are selected for audit. The audit program is mainly directed at those categories of taxpayers who are most likely to have under-reported their income. Wage and salary earners are rarely audited because their income is readily cross-checked against information returns filed by employers. Taxpayers such as self-employed individuals, corporations, and trusts are the most likely candidates for audit.

By virtue of section 231.1, auditors have the power to inspect the taxpayer's books and records, and to enter business premises without a warrant, and to require the owner or manager of the premises to provide "all reasonable assistance" and to answer "all proper questions". A warrant is required to enter the taxpayer's dwelling without the consent of the occupant. Section 231.2 empowers the Minister to demand information or documents from the taxpayer and from others. Most audits result in an upward adjustment of the taxpayer's tax liability.

(c) — Reassessment

A notice of reassessment is issued following an examination or audit. A taxpayer may also request reassessment when he or she discovers an error in the return after receiving the notice of assessment, or wishes to carry back some losses to reduce the taxable income of a previous taxation year. A reassessment typically includes interest on overdue taxes and may also include civil penalties.

Under subsection 152(4), the period of reassessment for individual returns is three years from the date of mailing of the original assessment (the period is four years for corporations other than Canadian-controlled private corporations). Outside the normal reassessment period, the Minister cannot reassess the taxpayer. In some circumstances, however, the taxpayer may wish to waive the time limit by filing a waiver so that more evidence or information can be produced to obtain a more favorable outcome.[11] The time limit does not prevent the Minister from refunding overpaid taxes or waiving interest or penalties in cases of taxpayer hardship.[12]

---

[11] *R. v. Canadian Marconi Co.*, [1991] 2 C.T.C. 352, 91 D.T.C. 5626 (Fed. C.A.); leave to appeal refused (1992), 139 N.R. 395 (note) (S.C.C.).

[12] *ITA*, *supra* note 1, s. 164(1.5), 152(4.2), 220(3.1) or (3.4).

Neither does it prevent the Minister from reassessment in cases of taxpayer misrepresentation or fraud.[13]

(d) — Collection

Section 222 establishes a 10-year limitation period for the collection of taxes unpaid. It was introduced in response to the Supreme Court of Canada decision in *Markevich v. Canada* (2003),[14] which limited the collection of federal taxes to the six-year limitation period set out in the *Crown Liability and Proceedings Act*[15] because there was no specific limitation period set out in the *ITA*.

Section 224 enables the Minister to effect collection of taxes and other amounts owing under the *ITA* by way of garnishment. The Minister can use the garnishment procedure when the Minister has knowledge or suspects that a third party, such as the taxpayer's employer, is liable to make a payment to the taxpayer who owes taxes. In other words, the Minister has the power to garnish the taxpayer's wage without a court order.

By virtue of section 225, the Minister may certify that a taxpayer's tax has not been paid and direct that the taxpayer's goods and chattels be seized. Such certification and direction must be preceded by 30 days' notice by registered mail addressed to the taxpayer's last known place of residence, but no court order is required to effect seizure.

(e) — Confidentiality of taxpayer information

The confidentiality of taxpayer information is critical to promoting honesty and truthfulness in taxpayers' reporting of their incomes and the integrity of the tax administration. Therefore, section 241 prohibits the use or release of "taxpayer information" by an "official". Taxpayer information includes information of any kind relating to one or more taxpayers that was obtained by or on behalf of the Minister for the purposes of the *ITA*. An official refers to a person in the service of the Crown or a person formerly in the service of the Crown.

The prohibition is subject to a large number of exceptions, such as information related to criminal proceedings or legal proceedings relating to the administration or enforcement of the *ITA*. Accordingly, income tax returns may be subpoenaed, and officials are free to testify or otherwise release taxpayer information in such proceedings.[16] Furthermore, section 241 provides that taxpayer information may be released where an individual is in imminent danger; the information is required in

---

[13] *Ibid.*, ss. 152(4.3), (4.4).

[14] *Markevich v. Canada* (2003), [2003] 2 C.T.C. 83, 2003 D.T.C. 5185 (S.C.C.).

[15] R.S.C. 1985, c. C-50.

[16] The phrase "legal proceedings relating to the administration or enforcement of this Act" has received a broad interpretation by the courts. In *Slattery (Trustee of) v. Slattery*, [1993] 2 C.T.C. 243, 93 D.T.C. 5443 (S.C.C.), the Supreme Court of Canada held that, in a bankruptcy initiated by the Minister of National Revenue, proceedings by the trustee in bank-

formulating government policy; the information is needed for the enforcement or administration of various federal or provincial laws; or the taxpayer concerned has given his or her consent.

15.4 — Dispute resolution

(a) — Administrative appeals

Taxpayers who disagree with a notice of assessment can contact the CRA for an explanation. Many disputes of a minor nature are resolved informally without recourse to the formal process of objection.

The formal means of initiating an administrative appeal from an assessment (or reassessment) is by serving a notice of objection on the Minister pursuant to section 165. The deadline is the later of one year after the filing-due date and 90 days from the mailing of the notice of assessment for individuals and 90 days from the mailing of the notice of assessment for corporations. The Minister has the discretion to extend the deadline.[17] There is no prescribed form of notice of objection, but subsection 165(1) requires the form to set out "the reasons for the objection and all relevant facts". The taxpayer will be contacted and given an opportunity to make representations during this process. At the end of the process, the Minister will decide whether to confirm, vary or vacate the assessment, and will notify the taxpayer of the decision.

(b) — Appeal to the Tax Court of Canada

If the Minister's decision under section 165 is not acceptable to the taxpayer, he or she has the right of appeal to the Tax Court of Canada ("TCC") under section 169.[18] The appeal must be initiated within 90 days from the day of the mailing of the Minister's notice of objection decision.

There are two alternative procedures at the TCC: the informal procedure and the general procedure. The informal procedure can be used by the taxpayer for cases where the amount of tax and penalties in issue is no more than $12,000, the amount of loss in issue is no more than $24,000, or only interest is in issue. Under this procedure, the taxpayer may appear in person or be represented by an agent who need not be a lawyer; no special form of pleadings or other formalities are required; the Court is not bound by technical rules of evidence; costs may not be awarded against the taxpayer; and judgment must generally be rendered within 60 days. The

---

ruptcy for the recovery of assets were proceedings concerning the administration of the *ITA* within the meaning of s. 241(3).

[17] *ITA, supra* note 1, s. 166.2(1).

[18] The Court replaced the Tax Review Board (T.R.B.) in 1983, which in turn replaced the Tax Appeal Board (T.A.B.) in 1971.

decision of the Court is final and no further right of appeal is available. However, the decision is subject to judicial review by the Federal Court of Appeal.[19]

The general procedure is used in all other cases, including cases where the amount of tax or loss in issue is less than the prescribed amounts for the informal procedure but the taxpayer has not elected for the informal procedure. Under the general procedure, a taxpayer may not be represented by a non-lawyer; the proceedings are more formal; costs may be awarded against the taxpayer; and there is no time limit on the rendering of judgment. The decision of the TCC is subject to appeal to the Federal Court of Appeal, and from there (with leave) to the Supreme Court of Canada.

The foregoing appeal procedures apply only to those cases that originate as an objection by a taxpayer to an assessment. Prosecutions of taxpayers who are alleged to have evaded tax in violation of the penal provisions of the *ITA* are a different matter entirely. The TCC has no jurisdiction over criminal matters. As discussed below, prosecutions occur in the courts of the provinces in accordance with the procedure laid down by the *Criminal Code*.[20]

(c) — Burden of proof

(i) — Taxpayer's onus

Under the self-assessment system, once the taxpayer has reported his or her income by filing a tax return, the Minister has the power to assess the taxpayer by fixing the quantum and tax liability. The process of assessment includes the initial assessment, reassessment, and confirmation at the end of the administrative appeals.[21] In making the assessment, the Minister can rely on available facts or assumed facts.

When the taxpayer appeals the Minister's assessment to the TCC, there is a trial in which both sides adduce evidence on issues of fact and make submissions on issues of law. It has been held by the Supreme Court of Canada in *Johnston v. M.N.R.* (1948)[22] that the burden of proof lies on the taxpayer to establish that the factual findings[23] upon which the Minister based the assessment were wrong. In that case, the Minister's position that the taxpayer did not support his wife was sustained on the ground that the taxpayer had not discharged the onus of proving that he did support his wife. The taxpayer's burden of proof does not require the taxpayer to

---

[19] See s. 28 of the *Federal Court Act*, R.S.C. 1985, c. F-7, which permits review of the decisions of federal tribunals for breach of the rules of natural justice, error of law, or perverse error of fact.

[20] R.S.C. 1985, c. C-46 [*Criminal Code*].

[21] See *R. v. Anchor Pointe Energy Ltd.*, [2007] 4 C.T.C. 5, 2007 D.T.C. 5379 (Fed. C.A.); leave to appeal refused 2008 CarswellNat 76, 2008 CarswellNat 77 (S.C.C.) [*Anchor Pointe*] at para. 33 [(Fed. C.A.)].

[22] *Johnston v. M.N.R.* (1948), [1948] C.T.C. 195, 3 D.T.C. 1182 (S.C.C.).

[23] The doctrine is sometimes expressed with reference to the Minister's rulings of law as well as his or her findings of fact, but there can be no burden of proof on issues of law.

rebut every imaginable set of facts that would justify the Minister's assessment. The Court in *Johnston* made clear that the Minister was under a duty to disclose to the taxpayer the findings upon which the assessment was based, and it was only those findings that the taxpayer came under a duty to rebut. The standard of proof that must be satisfied by the taxpayer is, of course, the civil standard of the balance of probability.

A variety of reasons have been suggested for imposing the burden of proof on the taxpayer. One is the wording of subsection 152(8), which provides, rather cryptically, that an assessment is "deemed to be valid and binding notwithstanding any error, defect or omission in the assessment". A second reason is that the taxpayer is the appellant, who ought to affirmatively establish the propositions upon which he or she relies. A third reason, perhaps the most persuasive one, is that the taxpayer has the best access to the facts.

(ii) — Shifting of the burden to the Minister

The courts have emphasized the principle that "the burden of proof put on the taxpayer is not to be lightly, capriciously or casually shifted".[24] However, the courts also recognize that there are instances where the shifting of the burden may be warranted. An example is where the pleaded assumptions of facts are "exclusively or peculiarly within the Minister's knowledge and that the rule as to the onus of proof may work so unfairly as to require a corrective measure".[25] Fairness would require the burden be shifted if a fact is solely within the knowledge of the Crown.

The taxpayer's onus to demolish the Minister's assumptions is met if the taxpayer establishes a *prima facie* case that the Minister's assumptions are wrong. Once the taxpayer establishes a *prima facie* case, then the burden shifts to the Minister to prove its assumptions on a balance of probabilities.[26] In *Canderel Ltd. v. R.* (1998),[27] in the course of finding that the taxpayer was entitled to deduct tenant inducement payments in the computation of profit under section 9, the Supreme Court of Canada stated:

> On reassessment, once the taxpayer has shown that he has provided an accurate picture of income for the year, which is consistent with the Act, the case law, and well-accepted business principles, the onus shifts to the Minister to show either that the figure provided does *not* represent an accurate picture, or that another method of computation would provide a *more* accurate picture.[28]

---

[24] *Orly Automobiles Inc. v. Canada*, 2005 FCA 425, [2005] G.S.T.C. 200 (Fed. C.A.) at para. 20.

[25] *Anchor Pointe, supra* note 21 at para. 36, citing Bowman J. in *Holm v. Canada*, [2003] 2 C.T.C. 2041, 2003 D.T.C. 755 (T.C.C.) at para. 20.

[26] *Newmont Canada Corporation v. The Queen*, [2012] 6 C.T.C. 72, 2012 D.T.C. 5138 (Fed. C.A.).

[27] *Canderel Ltd. v. R.* (1998), [1998] 2 C.T.C. 35, 98 D.T.C. 6100 (S.C.C.), discussed in Chapter 6 at heading 6.4(b) — Question of law.

[28] *Ibid.* at para. 53.

In cases involving the general anti-avoidance rule "(GAAR")" in section 245, the Supreme Court of Canada clearly stated in *Canada Trustco Mortgage Co. v. Canada* (2005)[29] that the burden is on the Minister to establish that there was abusive tax avoidance in the sense that it cannot be reasonably concluded that a tax benefit would be consistent with the object, spirit, or purpose of the provisions relied upon by the taxpayer.

If the taxpayer appeals the imposition of penalties under section 163 or 163.2, the Minister bears the burden to establish the facts justifying the assessment of the penalty.[30] Similarly, the Minister bears the burden of proof in cases where the taxpayer appeals an assessment issued by the Minister outside the normal three-year time limit on the ground of misrepresentation or fraud on the part of the taxpayer.[31]

(iii) — Criminal offences

Where a taxpayer is prosecuted for a criminal offence under section 238 or 239 of the *ITA*, the prosecution is conducted in the provincial court system under the rules of criminal procedure of the *Criminal Code*.[32] In a criminal case, the burden of proving all elements of the offence charged rests on the Crown, and the standard of proof is proof beyond a reasonable doubt.[33]

(d) — Settlement

The CRA is willing, in certain circumstances, to settle a dispute with a taxpayer, and many such settlements are, in fact, made. Typically, of course, each side gives up some part of what had originally been claimed in return for a similar compromise by the other side.

It is essential that both sides be bound by a settlement agreement. In *Smerchanski v. M.N.R.* (1976),[34] the Supreme Court of Canada held that a taxpayer, who had agreed to waive a right of appeal from an assessment as part of a settlement agreement, could not later change his mind and exercise that right of appeal. But, in *Cohen v. R.* (1980),[35] the Federal Court of Appeal held that a settlement agreement, under which the Minister agreed to assess a taxpayer's profit as a capital gain while the taxpayer agreed not to object to other assessments, could not bind the Minister.

---

[29] *Canada Trustco Mortgage Co. v. Canada* (2005), [2005] 5 C.T.C. 215, 2005 D.T.C. 5523 (S.C.C.), discussed in Chapter 17 at heading 17.3(a)(ii) — Canada Trustco.

[30] This special burden is confined to the facts that justify the imposition of a penalty under s. 163 or 163.2. The burden of establishing that the underlying assessment of tax is wrong remains with the taxpayer. *De Graaf v. R.*, [1985] 1 C.T.C. 374, 85 D.T.C. 5280 (Fed. T.D.).

[31] *M.N.R. v. Taylor*, [1961] C.T.C. 211, 61 D.T.C. 1139 (Can. Ex. Ct.).

[32] *Criminal Code*, supra note 20.

[33] *Medicine Hat Greenhouses v. R.*, [1981] C.T.C. 141, 81 D.T.C. 5100 (Alta. C.A.); leave to appeal refused 38 N.R. 180 (S.C.C.).

[34] *Smerchanski v. M.N.R.* (1976), [1976] C.T.C. 488, 76 D.T.C. 6247 (S.C.C.).

[35] *Cohen v. R.* (1980), [1980] C.T.C. 318, 80 D.T.C. 6250 (Fed. C.A.).

"The Minister has a statutory duty to assess the amount of tax payable on the facts as he finds them in accordance with the law as he understands it"; it followed that an agreement by the Minister to assess otherwise than in accordance with law would be "illegal".[36] The Court accordingly upheld the Minister's assessment, even though it did not comply with the agreement, and even though the taxpayer had complied with his part of the agreement.

The effect of the *Smerchanski* and *Cohen* cases is that the taxpayer is bound by a settlement agreement, but the Minister is not.[37] Of course, a settlement of litigation that was implemented by a formal entry of judgment would then have the force of a court judgment, which is binding on both parties. However, in *Galway v. M.N.R.* (1974),[38] the Federal Court of Appeal refused an application for a consent judgment to implement the terms of a settlement agreement between the Minister and a taxpayer. According to the Court, the Minister has no power to assess in accordance with a "compromise settlement", and the Court should not sanctify an *ultra vires* act. The Minister's duty is to assess in accordance with the law, and the only kind of settlement that the Court would be prepared to implement by a consent judgment, would be one in which the parties were agreed on the application of the law to the facts.[39]

The attitude of the Federal Court of Appeal in *Cohen* and *Galway* is arguably far too rigid and doctrinaire. If the Minister were really unable to make compromise settlements, he or she would be denied an essential tool of enforcement. The CRA has limited resources and it is not realistic to require the Minister to insist on every last legal point, and to litigate every dispute to the bitter end. Most disputes about tax are simply disputes about money that are inherently capable of resolution by compromise. Presumably, the Minister would agree to a compromise settlement only on the basis that it offered a better net recovery than would probably be achieved by continuance of the litigation. It seems foolish to require the Minister to incur the unnecessary costs of avoidable litigation in the name of an abstract statutory duty to apply the law.[40]

---

[36] *Ibid.* at 319 [C.T.C.].

[37] See also *Consoltex Inc. v. R.*, [1997] 2 C.T.C. 2846, 97 D.T.C. 724 (T.C.C.).

[38] *Galway v. M.N.R.* (1974), [1974] C.T.C. 454, 74 D.T.C. 6355 (Fed. C.A.).

[39] See David W. Smith, "Reassessments, Waivers, Amended Returns, and Refunds" Income Tax Enforcement, Compliance, and Administration, 1988 Corporate Management Tax Conference (Toronto: Canadian Tax Foundation, 1988) 8:1, 8:14. As Smith points out, some compromises are possible within this doctrine. An issue of valuation could be compromised because value is a matter of opinion. Where there are several issues of law in dispute, a compromise could be achieved by the Minister accepting the taxpayer's position on some issues, while maintaining his or her own position on others. What cannot be compromised is a single issue to which there can only be one answer, e.g., is a particular profit a capital gain or ordinary income? In that case, the Minister cannot make a compromise settlement of the "split-the-difference" kind.

[40] Compare the ruling in *Optical Recording Laboratories v. Canada*, [1990] 2 C.T.C. 524, 90 D.T.C. 6647 (Fed. C.A.), where it was held that the Minister did have the power to nego-

(e) — Remission order

As a general principle, liability for tax under the *ITA* does not depend upon administrative discretion. The *ITA* allows the Minister with discretion to provide relief from the deadlines and interest and penalties in the case of taxpayer hardship, but none of these rules authorize any change in the liability to pay tax.[41] However, taxes may be remitted to a taxpayer pursuant to a remission order. Such order is authorized by section 23 of the *Financial Administration Act*, which provides that

> The Governor in Council, on the recommendation of the Treasury Board, whenever he considers it in the public interest, may remit any tax, fee or penalty.[42]

Remission orders are issued sparingly in order to provide relief in cases of hardship or to correct a particular perceived injustice. For example, complex provisions of the *ITA* may have unexpectedly produced double taxation; a taxpayer may have been misled by the CRA; or a taxpayer may have fallen ill and lost the financial capacity to meet a tax liability. Taxpayers must request relief. Although the power of remission is exercised by the Governor in Council on the recommendation of the Treasury Board, in practice, it is the CRA that normally makes recommendations to the Treasury Board. Remission orders are published.[43]

(f) — Rectification

Unintended tax outcomes resulting from certain transactions may be rectified or corrected by taxpayers by obtaining an equitable remedy — rectification. At common law, rectification is granted if, by mistake, the terms of a written instrument do not accord with the true agreement between the parties. The rectified documents often enable the taxpayer to obtain the intended tax result. In *Juliar v. Canada (Attorney General)* (2000),[44] for example, a rectification order was granted based on the intention of the parties to avoid the immediate tax consequences of an unanticipated deemed dividend. The taxpayers had intended that their holding company be transferred to a new holding company under the rollover provisions of subsection 85(1) without triggering immediate tax consequences. However, to obtain the

---

tiate postponed-payment arrangements with a taxpayer who was unable to pay in full. This power stemmed from the Minister's authority over "the management of taxes".

[41] For example, the *ITA* permits the Minister to extend the deadline for filing a return (s. 220(3)); reassess an income tax return beyond the normal reassessment period if requested by an individual (s. 152(4.2)); accept various late-filed, amended or revoked elections (ss. 220(3.2) to 220(3.7); and waive or cancel penalties or interest (s. 230(3.1). See Canada Revenue Agency, Information Circular IC-07-1R1, "Taxpayer Relief Provision" (2017).

[42] R.S.C. 1985, c. F-11, s. 23.

[43] They are published in Part II of the *Canada Gazette* and reported by commercial tax services. Remission orders are also required to be reported to the House of Commons in the Public Accounts.

[44] *Juliar v. Canada (Attorney General)*, [2000] 2 C.T.C. 464, 99 D.T.C. 5743 (Ont. S.C.J.); affirmed [2001] 4 C.T.C. 45, 2000 D.T.C. 6589 (Ont. C.A.); leave to appeal refused (2001), 272 N.R. 196 (note) (S.C.C.).

rollover, the transferor cannot take back debt in excess of a certain amount, and that was exactly what the taxpayers did. The taxpayers were not aware of the undesired tax consequences until the transaction was audited by the CRA. The taxpayers applied to the Ontario Superior Court of Justice for a rectification order. At common law, four requirements must be met before a rectification order is granted: a prior agreement; common intention; a document that properly records the intention of the parties; and a common or mutual mistake. The CRA contested the application on the basis that the taxpayers had not initially intended to acquire shares. The Court, however, disagreed with the CRA and granted the rectification order on the ground that the taxpayer's intention was to avoid immediate tax consequences.

In a self-assessment system, it makes sense to provide taxpayers with an opportunity to correct innocent mistakes that have significant adverse tax implications. However, there are also policy concerns if seeking rectification orders becomes a way of fixing aggressive tax plans that are uncovered by audit, or a way of doing retroactive tax planning. Unlike the rectification remedy at common law, which corrects documentation that is in error because it does not reflect the true intention of the parties involved, a rectification order sought for tax purposes affects the interest of a third-party — the CRA. The parties involved in the relationship may have the common intention to minimize taxes. It is possible that a rectification order is not used to rectify the transaction back to its intended form, but instead to replace the intended transaction with a new one to achieve tax objectives. It, thus, makes sense for the CRA to contest rectification orders in such situations.

15.5 — Penalties

(a) — Civil penalties

Sections 162, 163 and 163.2[45] provide civil penalties for a variety of delinquent acts and omissions, including (for example) the late filing of a tax return, the failure

---

[45] *Guindon v. Canada*, [2015] 3 S.C.R. 3, [2015] 6 C.T.C. 1, 2015 D.T.C. 5086 (S.C.C.) concerned a lawyer, Guindon, with little expertise in tax matters who provided a legal opinion on a charitable donation scheme without reviewing the legal documents. She was also president of the charity that participated in the scheme and she signed charitable donation slips. The scheme involved timeshare units that never existed and a trust that was never settled. The Minister of National Revenue assessed her for advisor penalties under s. 163.2 for statements she made in donation receipts, which it was alleged she knew or would reasonably be expected to have known could be used by taxpayers to claim an unwarranted tax credit. The Minister's assessment was upheld at all levels of appeal. The appeal to the Supreme Court of Canada was cast as a constitutional case in an effort to use the *Charter* (*Canadian Charter of Rights and Freedoms*, Part I of the *Constitution Act, 1982*, being Schedule B to the *Canada Act 1982* (U.K.), 1982, c 11) to overcome what were argued to be draconian penalties that were essentially criminal in nature so as to invoke *Charter* protections, even though they were included in the *ITA* as civil penalties relating to the administration of the Act. Colouring the presentation of the case was multiplication of penalties by the number of opinions given, which was argued to be excessive. The Court declined to conclude that the penalties were criminal and, consequently, the *Charter* did not save the tax-

to file a return, the repeated failure to file a return, the failure to provide information on a prescribed form, the failure to report an item of income, the making of a false statement or an omission in a return, and the misrepresentation of another person's tax matters by a third party.

The acts and omissions that are the subject of civil penalties may also be the subject of criminal penalties under sections 238 and 239. The civil penalties are imposed on taxpayers by the Minister as part of the assessment process, and so when a criminal charge is laid against a taxpayer, the taxpayer has usually already been assessed for the applicable civil penalty. When this is the case, any punishment imposed on conviction for the criminal offence is in addition to the civil penalty. (The criminal court would, of course, take the civil penalty into account in fixing the punishment.) The decision to prosecute in such a case involves a judgment by the CRA and the Department of Justice that the civil penalty is an inadequate punishment for the taxpayer's conduct. In the unusual case where the taxpayer has not been assessed for a civil penalty at the time when the criminal charge is laid, then the punishment imposed on conviction for the criminal offence is the exclusive sanction, and no civil penalty can be imposed for the same conduct.[46]

(b) — Criminal prosecutions

Sections 238 and 239 make tax evasion a criminal offence. Section 238 makes it an offence to fail to file a tax return or to break various other provisions of the *ITA*. The section 238 offences are ones of strict liability, that is to say, there is no requirement of *mens rea* (a guilty mind), although a taxpayer may be exculpated by proving that he or she acted with due diligence. Section 239 makes it an offence to falsify records or to evade compliance or payment in other ways. These offences require *mens rea* as an essential ingredient.

The special investigations division of the CRA investigates suspected cases of tax evasion, and when it obtains evidence, it prepares the case for prosecution. The *ITA* provides officials of the CRA with investigatory powers. In the earlier discussion of audits, we noted the power conferred by section 231.1 to enter business premises without a warrant, and to enter a dwelling-house with a warrant, in order to inspect the books and records of a taxpayer. We also noticed the power conferred by section 231.2 to demand documents or information. These powers are available to an investigator as well as to an auditor. Where material has not been surrendered voluntarily or cannot be found, section 231.3 empowers a judge to issue a search warrant authorizing the investigator to search premises for evidence and seize evidence. Where all these measures have apparently not yielded full information, section 231.4 authorizes an "inquiry" to be held by a "hearing officer", who is ap-

---

payer. It seems trite to say that advisers who advise beyond their competence and without undertaking the work for which they are engaged expose themselves to significant penalties for their failures, which amount to failures to contribute responsibly to the self-enforcement system that underlies the *ITA*.

[46] *ITA, supra* note 1, ss. 238(3), 239(3).

pointed by the Tax Court of Canada, and who has the power to compel the attendance of witnesses and the giving of testimony under oath. Where the CRA considers that there is sufficient evidence to justify the preferring of a criminal charge, it will hand over the case to the Department of Justice for criminal prosecution in accordance with the *Criminal Code*.[47]

15.6 — Tax practice and ethics

(a) — Roles of tax practitioners

Lawyers and accountants share the practice of taxation. Tax practice involves work in four principal areas: compliance, dispute resolution, planning and tax policy.

Compliance is the preparation of the client's income tax return or any other form that must be filed with the CRA. A lawyer may be instructed to prepare the return or form, although this task is almost always entrusted to an accountant. The lawyer may be instructed to provide advice to the client or the client's accountant on a tax or non-tax legal issue arising in the preparation of the return or form. In this role, the lawyer is primarily a legal advisor. However, if controversy is anticipated, the lawyer may advise on strategies to avoid the controversy, which may give rise to ethical issues.

A controversy or dispute with the CRA typically starts when the Minister issues an assessment or reassessment that rejects a position taken on the client's income tax return. The lawyer may be instructed to prepare and file a notice of objection or to prepare and file an appeal to the TCC, or to represent the client as counsel at hearings before CRA officials or courts.[48] In this context, the tax lawyer serves as advocate. Because the government is generally represented by lawyers, especially in court proceedings, the lawyer's duty to the client is paramount.

The bulk of most tax practitioners' time is spent on tax planning and advice. Planning is a field in which accountants as well as lawyers play an important role, but the provision of legal advice on some difficult issues and the drafting of legal documents can only be undertaken by lawyers. As a planner, the tax lawyer is an advisor and not an advocate. Planning differs from compliance and advocacy in that planning looks to the future rather than the past. The tax practitioner may be instructed to provide advice on how to structure a proposed transaction so as to minimize or defer the tax liability arising from the transaction, or the tax practitioner may be instructed to provide more general advice as to the most favourable way to organize and operate a client's business or personal investments. He or she may provide an opinion on the tax benefits of a transaction and advise the client about the risks that such benefits will be realized. He or she may also need to seek an advance ruling from the CRA on the tax consequences of certain transactions. In addition, a tax

---

[47] *Criminal Code, supra* note 20.

[48] Accountants as well as lawyers engage in advocacy before CRA officials and in the "informal procedure" of the Tax Court. Only lawyers can appear in the "general procedure" of the Tax Court and in the Federal Court of Appeal and the Supreme Court of Canada.

practitioner may be involved in designing, developing and marketing "tax products" or "tax shelters".

In advising clients on tax matters, the lawyer is often required to provide a legal opinion. A legal opinion is typically a lawyer's expression of his or her judgment as to how the legal issues considered would be resolved if presented for decision to the appropriate legal forum. It is different from a one-sided work of advocacy. The client can best make his or her decision if the opinion is balanced and reasoned. A legal opinion may be prepared only for the client's eyes or prepared for third parties as well. In the former, the lawyer owes the client all of the duties previously discussed in the context of the lawyer's role as an advisor. If the lawyer prepares an opinion that will be relied upon by third parties, due diligence requires a higher standard of care because the lawyer has access to information that may be available to the client but not to the third parties.

An advance tax ruling is a written statement issued by the CRA to the taxpayers that interprets the law and applies it to a specific set of assumed facts. It is often used when the client desires greater certainty about the tax consequences of the proposed transactions. In some cases, such as complex corporate reorganizations or tax shelters, obtaining a ruling is critical to the client.

Many tax practitioners participate in tax policy formulation by serving as a paid lobbyist, speaking in public forums, serving as a member of a tax reform commission, or making submissions or commentary on draft legislation.

(b) — Importance of tax ethics

Tax practice involves ethical issues that are common to all lawyers and accountants, as well as some issues unique to tax. For example, when the tax practitioner learns that the CRA has made a mistake, should he or she inform the CRA? If a client's previous returns contain wrong information, should the tax practitioner advise the client to report the mistake to the CRA? If the government has over-refunded the client, should the tax practitioner advise the client to keep the refund? The nature of the *ITA*'s penalty provisions is primarily administrative or regulatory, not criminal, as they are designed to ensure compliance by punishing non-compliance. In light of that, how should a tax lawyer advise the client about "voluntary" compliance with the *ITA*, the right against self-incrimination, the principle of unjust enrichment, or the right against unreasonable search or seizure? Lawyers working as Crown counsel face particular considerations in tax cases, especially in cases where the taxpayer is not represented by counsel in the informal procedures before the TCC. Crown counsel has an overriding duty to be "fair", not to win or lose.[49] But what constitutes "fair" in tax litigation, civil or criminal?

---

[49] *R. v. Boucher*, [1955] S.C.R. 16 (S.C.C.) at 23-24: "It cannot be over-emphasized that the purpose of a criminal prosecution is not to obtain a conviction, it is to lay before a jury what the Crown considers to be credible evidence relevant to what is alleged to be a crime. Counsel have a duty to see that all available legal proof of the facts is presented: it should be done firmly and pressed to its legitimate strength but it must also be done fairly. The role of

Ethical behaviour is important to the tax system, the administration of justice, the client and the practitioner. Tax practitioners are specialists. It often takes years to acquire the necessary level of knowledge, skill and wisdom to render sophisticated tax advice. Such level of expertise generally commands the trust of clients and the confidence of the public. The reputation of a lawyer is of paramount importance to clients, to other members of the profession, and to the judiciary. "Reputation is the cornerstone of a lawyer's professional life."[50] The same is true for accountants.

The price to be paid for unethical behaviour is high. No tax practitioner would wish to be associated with tax evasion, be disciplined for professional misconduct, or be a defendant in a civil lawsuit. Even if a lawyer is acquitted or not disbarred, his or her reputation may be irreversibly damaged. More importantly, the public interest is not well served if confidence is lost in tax professionals and the system.

The proper functioning of the self-assessment system largely depends on the involvement of well-trained tax practitioners. It could be said that the tax system relies on tax lawyers and other professionals acting as "gatekeepers".

15.7 — Ethical regulation

When acting as tax advisors, lawyers and accountants owe the clients the duty to disclose, the duty of confidentiality and the duty to avoid conflicts of interest. However, because of the different professional roles of lawyers and accountants, there are some notable differences in the scope of responsibilities of these two professions.

The practice of law, as distinct from the practice of tax, is preserved exclusively for lawyers. Only lawyers are involved in tax litigation and the preparation of legal documents that create rights and obligations between parties and that have tax consequences. Only lawyers can prepare legal opinions. As an advocate, a lawyer is subject to the strict obligation of loyalty to the client and must present the client's position in the best possible light. The lawyer is a "legal fighter" or "a knight in armour" (whether or not shining) for the client. When acting as an advocate, "the lawyer must treat the court or tribunal with courtesy and respect and must represent the client resolutely, honourably and within the limits of the law".[51] The solicitor-client privilege applies only to communications between a client and a lawyer.

---

prosecutor excludes any notion of winning or losing; his function is a matter of public duty than which in civil life there can be none charged with greater personal responsibility. It is to be efficiently performed with an ingrained sense of the dignity, the seriousness and the justness of judicial proceedings." These comments were found to apply to Crown counsel who appear at the Tax Court: see *Rainforth v. R.*, [2007] 3 C.T.C. 2229, 2007 D.T.C. 523 (T.C.C.) at para. 62.

[50] *Hill v. Church of Scientology of Toronto*, [1995] 2 S.C.R. 1130 (S.C.C.) at para. 118.

[51] Canadian Bar Association, *Code of Professional Conduct* (adopted by Council, August 2004 and February 2006, amended Resolution 09-02-M), online: <http://www.cba.org/CBA/activities/code> [*CBA Code*, ch. IX.

The accounting profession enjoys a statutory monopoly in the performance of the audit of public companies. The price to be paid for this monopoly is the preservation of independence. The provision of non-audit services, such as tax advice, to an audit client may create a conflict with the duty of independence. This is particularly true when accountants are involved in designing and promoting tax-planning products aimed at exploiting perceived loopholes in the law in order to generate "tax savings". Since the corporate scandals associated with the collapse of such companies as Enron and WorldCom, accountants have been subject to much public scrutiny and regulation.[52]

While some countries, such as the United States, have published a code of conduct for tax practitioners,[53] Canada has not.

By and large, tax practitioners in Canada have served their clients and the public well. In recent years, however, there has been increasing attention to ethical issues. Tax lawyers have been sued by their clients[54] and by third parties who have relied on a tax opinion in making investment decisions.[55] "Tax schemes" devised by lawyers have been considered "shams" by courts.[56] Minimum standards of tax practice are imposed by Parliament through third party penalty provisions. Respected members of the tax profession have opined on ethical standards and the duties of tax practitioners.[57]

---

[52] For further discussion, see Robert James Hogan & Frédéric Brassard, "Standards of Practice and Duties of Tax Advisors in the Post Enron Environment" in *Report of Proceedings of the Fifty-Fourth Tax Conference Convened by the Canadian Tax Foundation (2002)* (Toronto: Canadian Tax Foundation, 2003) 34:1.

[53] United States, IRS Circular 230 establishes standards in various areas, including minimum levels of accuracy for tax return advice given to clients, the diligence required of practitioners, prohibition on representation of conflicting interests, and minimum quality standards for tax shelter opinions. See L. Chapman, et al., "The Evolving Nature of Tax Practice" in *Report of Proceedings of the Fifty-Seventh Tax Conference Convened by the Canadian Tax Foundation (2005)* (Toronto: Canadian Tax Foundation, 2006) 2:1.

[54] E.g., *Strother et al. v. 3464920 Canada Inc. et al.*, [2007] 4 C.T.C. 172, 2007 D.T.C. 5273 (S.C.C.) [*Strother*], discussed at heading 18.7(d) — The *Strother* case, below.

[55] E.g., *Cannon v. Funds for Canada Foundation* (2012), 2012 ONSC 399, [2012] 3 C.T.C. 132 (Ont. S.C.J.); additional reasons 2012 CarswellOnt 7212 (Ont. S.C.J.); leave to appeal refused 2012 CarswellOnt 13625 (Ont. Div. Ct.) [*Cannon*], discussed at heading 18.9(c) — Third parties, below.

[56] E.g., *Faraggi c. R.*, [2009] 3 C.T.C. 77, (sub nom. *2529-1915 Québec Inc. v. R.)* 2009 D.T.C. 5585, 2004 D.T.C. 6523 (F.C.A.).

[57] E.g., Chapman, *supra* note 53 at 2:1–22; Hogan & Brassard, *supra* note 52 at 34:1–47; Sheldon Silver, "Ethical Considerations in Giving Tax Opinions" in *Report of Proceedings of the Forty-Sixth Tax Conference Convened by the Canadian Tax Foundation (1994)* (Toronto: Canadian Tax Foundation, 1995) 36:1–16; and Bruce Russell, "Avoiding Evasion: Tax Advisers' Professional Responsibilities" in *Report of Proceedings of the Fifty-Sixth Tax Conference Convened by the Canadian Tax Foundation (2004)* (Toronto: Canadian Tax Foundation, 2005) 35:1–10.

(a) — Professional regulation

Ethical standards for tax practitioners, as for all practitioners, are regulated primarily by the profession and, to a much lesser extent, by government. In addition, tax practitioners owe fiduciary duties to the client under common law. The main goal of ethical regulation is to protect the public interest.

(i) — Lawyers

A lawyer's conduct is governed by the lawyer's regulating law society and the court. The Rules of Professional Conduct of the provincial bar[58] impose a duty of competence, a duty of *honesty* and *candour*, a duty of *confidentiality*, and the duty of *loyalty*.[59] Like other lawyers, tax lawyers are subject to the disciplinary sanctions under the Rules of Professional Conduct for "professional misconduct" or "for conduct unbecoming a lawyer".[60]

As an officer of the court, a lawyer's conduct in legal proceedings may affect the administration of justice, and the courts have authority to exercise some control over counsel when necessary to protect their process. "Inherent jurisdiction of the court includes the authority to control the process of the court, prevent abuses of process, and ensure the machinery of the court functions in an orderly and effective manner."[61] In exercising its jurisdiction, the court may remove counsel from the record or refuse to grant counsel's application for withdrawal.[62] The Supreme Court of Canada describes the court's authority to regulate a lawyer's conduct as "preventive — to protect the administration of justice and ensure trial fairness" — and the law society's disciplinary role as "reactive", and considers both roles necessary to ensure effective regulation of the profession and protect the process of the court.[63]

In reality, perhaps the more powerful enforcement weapon lies with a client who can terminate the professional relationship with a lawyer, or even bring a civil action against the lawyer for breach of fiduciary duties.[64]

---

[58] E.g., Law Society of Upper Canada (LSUC), Rules of Professional Conduct (June 2009), online: <www.1suc.on.ca/media/rpc.pdf> [LSUC Rules]. See also *CBA Code, supra* note 51. Similar rules are found in the rules of professional conduct or codes of the ethics applicable to other tax professionals.

[59] *LSUC Rules, supra* note 58, rr. 2.01–2.04.

[60] *Ibid.*, r. 6.11.

[61] *The Queen v. Cunningham*, [2010] 1 S.C.R. 331 (S.C.C.) at para. 18.

[62] *Ibid.*

[63] *Ibid.* at para. 35.

[64] There are a number of applications for certification of a class action, such as *Cannon, supra* note 55, discussed at heading 18.9(c) — Third parties, below. The plaintiffs alleged that the lawyer negligently prepared a tax opinion leading them to believe that they could both support the charity and reduce their tax liability, and that the lawyer failed to exercise the care and skill to be expected of a reasonably competent tax solicitor.

(ii) — Accountants

The Code of Professional Conduct for Chartered Professional Accountants ("CPAs") focuses on serving the public interest. The CPA Code of Professional Conduct ("CPA Code") states that:

> It is a hallmark of a profession that there is a voluntary assumption, by those who comprise it — the members of the profession of ethical principles which are aimed, first and foremost, at serving the public interest and, second, at achieving orderly and courteous conduct within the profession. It is to these purposes that the CPA Code is directed.[65]

The CPA Code is derived from five fundamental principles of ethics: professional behaviour, integrity and due care, objectivity, professional competence and confidentiality.[66]

(b) — Statutory control

The *ITA* imposes civil penalties on tax professionals under section 163.2. Also, a tax practitioner may be liable to a penalty if he or she files false or misleading information with the Minister in respect of an application for an identification number for a tax shelter (subsection 237.1(7.4)). A tax practitioner may be liable to a penalty in the context of the filing of an information return or a return regarding a reportable transaction (subsection 237.3(8)). These provisions constitute a minimum standard of conduct for tax practitioners. They are disciplinary rules rather than aspirational goals.

An information reporting requirement for aggressive tax avoidance transactions is set out in section 237.3 of the *ITA*.[67] Filing the required information does not in any way mean that the general anti-avoidance rule ("GAAR") will apply. However, if full and accurate disclosure is not made, the Minister may impose a late-filing penalty and may redetermine the tax consequences as if the GAAR was deemed to apply, ignoring the misuse and abuse test in subsection 245(4). If the reporting obligation is satisfied after the filing date, and any late-filing penalty and interest is paid, the Minister may allow the tax benefit (where all other requirements of the *ITA* are satisfied). Persons who fail to fully satisfy their reporting obligations may be jointly and severally liable for the penalty, subject to a limitation for advisors and promoters and a due diligence defence.

Section 237.3 imposes a reporting obligation on 1) the person for whom a tax benefit could result from an avoidance transaction or series, 2) any person who enters

---

[65] Chartered Professional Accountants of Ontario, "CPA Code of Professional Conduct", online: <https://media.cpaontario.ca/stewardship-of-the-profession/pdfs/CPA-Ontario-Code-of-professional-conduct.pdf> at 1.

[66] *ibid.* at 2–4.

[67] The rules apply in respect of avoidance transactions entered into after 2010, or that are part of a series of transactions that commenced before 2011 and is completed after 2010. The information return is due on June 30th of the year following the calendar year in which the reportable transaction occurred.

into an avoidance transaction for the benefit of the particular person, and 3) any "advisor" or "promoter" who is entitled to a fee in circumstances described in the definition of "reportable transaction" in subsection 237.3(1). However, as long as one party files the properly completed report on time, no penalties are owing to any party. A "reportable transaction" is an "avoidance transaction", or a transaction that is part of a "series"[68] of transactions that includes an avoidance transaction, if, at any time, any two of three "hallmarks" exist in respect of that avoidance transaction or series. The first hallmark is that the tax advisor is being paid based, at least in part, on the dollar value of the tax benefit. The second hallmark is that the tax advisor requires that the transaction(s) remain confidential. The third hallmark is that the taxpayer or the advisor obtains "contractual protection", which is also defined in subsection 237.3(1).[69]

(c) — Common law principles

(i) — Fiduciary duties

The very basis of the lawyer-client relationship is that the lawyer will use his or her special skills to act in the best interests of the client. This relationship has all the core characteristics of a fiduciary relationship: 1) the lawyer has scope for the exercise of some discretion or power; 2) the lawyer can unilaterally exercise that discretion or power so as to affect the client's legal or practical interests, and 3) the client is particularly vulnerable to or at the mercy of the lawyer holding the discretion or power.[70] As Binnie J. stated in *Strother v. 3464920 Canada Inc.* (2007), "fiduciary duties provide a framework within which the lawyer performs the work and may include obligations that go beyond what the parties expressly bargained for".[71] The core of fiduciary duty is loyalty.

The Supreme Court of Canada has also emphasized that courts will enforce fiduciary duties in the context of all professional advisory relationships:

> The very existence of many professional advisory relationships, particularly in specialized areas such as law, taxation and investments, is premised upon full disclosure by the client of vital personal and financial information that inevitably results in a

---

[68] The terms "avoidance transaction" and "series" are taken from the GAAR, which is discussed in detail in Chapter 17.

[69] Quebec has a similar but different regime. It requires mandatory disclosure of all transactions providing a tax benefit of at least $25,000 or a reduction of income of at least $100,000 if either 1) the adviser requires the taxpayer to respect a confidentiality agreement with regard to third parties, or 2) the remuneration of the adviser is contingent, in whole or in part, upon the realization of the tax benefit. Voluntary preventative disclosures can also be filed to avoid the possibility of GAAR penalties. Taxpayers and promoters of transactions to which the GAAR applies are subject to penalties unless the taxpayer has filed a mandatory or voluntary preventative disclosure of the transaction with Revenue Québec. The prescribed form is at <http://www.revenuquebec.ca/en/sepf/formulaires/tp/tp-1079_di.aspx>.

[70] *Frame v. Smith* (1987), 42 D.L.R. (4th) 81 (S.C.C.) at 99.

[71] *Strother, supra* note 54 at para. 34.

"power-dependency" dynamic . . . [T]he type of disclosure that routinely occurs in these kinds of relationships results in the advisor's acquiring influence which is equivalent to a discretion or power to affect the client's legal or practical interests . . . In the advisory context, the advisor's ability to cause harm and the client's susceptibility to be harmed arise from the simple but unassailable fact that the advice given by an independent advisor is not likely to be viewed with suspicion; rather it is likely to be followed.[72]

Why is it important to impose fiduciary duties on tax practitioners? The answer lies in public interest. The public interest is served by protecting "the integrity of the administration of justice"[73] and by maintaining public confidence in tax professionals. It is in the public interest to have truth ascertained by an adversarial judicial system that "function[s] clearly and without hidden agendas".[74] It is important for the law to foster public confidence in lawyers and other professionals in order to preserve a trustworthy image of the judicial system as a whole.

There are other competing values underlying fiduciary law. These include the freedom of the client to secure the counsel of his or her choice, the need for mobility in the legal profession, and the need for lawyers to serve multiple clients. But public confidence in the judicial system prevails over all these other values.[75]

(ii) — Loyalty to client and avoidance of conflict of interest

The fiduciary relationship between the tax lawyer and his or her client is associated with certain duties, such as the duties of care, confidentiality, disclosure and loyalty. Loyalty is the core of fiduciary duties: the lawyer must act in the best interests of the client. The judgment as to what the client's best interests are is, of course, entrusted to the lawyer. So, how can the lawyer know if his or her duty of loyalty has been fulfilled? "The law's solution is to require that the fiduciary's judgments be made in a 'sterile' environment, where even the slightest appearance of impropriety is not tolerated."[76] The parameters of the sterile environment are largely drawn along the line of the conflict of interest rules. These rules build a zone of protection around the possibility of disloyalty. They prevent the fiduciary from being in situations where the duty of loyalty is in danger of being breached.

The term "conflict of interest" was defined by the Supreme Court of Canada in *R. v. Neil* (2002)[77] as an interest that gives rise to a "substantial risk that the lawyer's

---

[72] *Hodgkinson v. Simms*, [1994] 3 S.C.R. 377, 95 D.T.C. 5135 (S.C.C.) at para. 61.

[73] *Strother*, *supra* note 54 at para. 34, citing *MacDonald Estate v. Martin*, [1990] 3 S.C.R. 1235 (S.C.C.) [*MacDonald*].

[74] *R. v. Neil* (2002), 2002 SCC 70, [2002] 3 S.C.R. 631 (S.C.C.) at para. 24.

[75] *MacDonald*, *supra* note 73 at 1265 (per Cory J.). As McLachlin J. noted in her dissenting decision in *Strother*, *supra* note 54 at para. 140, there is also a public interest in lawyers' ability to serve multiple clients.

[76] R. Valsan & L. Smith, "The Loyalty of Lawyers: A Comment on *3464920 Canada Inc. v. Strother*" (2008) 87 Can. Bar. Rev. 247 at 263.

[77] *Neil*, *supra* note 74.

representation of the client would be materially and adversely affected by the lawyer's own interests or by the lawyer's duties to another current client, a former client, or a third person". This definition contemplates two kinds of conflicts:

1. A conflict of the lawyer's self-interest and the lawyer's duty to act in the best interests of the client (self-interest and duty conflict). This may occur when the lawyer's personal interests may have an impact on the substance of the advice given to the client, leading in turn to situations that could prejudice the client's own interest. Fiduciary law prohibits the tax adviser from abusing his or her position to reap a personal gain.

2. A conflict of the lawyer's duty to different clients (duty-to-duty conflict). The lawyer's duty to provide candid and proper legal advice to one client is in conflict with his or her duty of confidentiality to another client.

The conflict of interest definition above emphasizes "substantial risk" or the appearance of substantial risk, not necessarily "actual conflict". "Conflict" means that the two things point in opposite directions. In the case of conflict of self-interest and duty, the conflict arises merely because the two things (i.e., self-interest and duty to the client) point in opposite directions. The lawyer's personal interest could have an impact on the substance of the advice provided, thereby creating a situation that could prejudice the client's own best interests. The lawyer must, therefore, avoid being in a situation of conflict.

In the case of duty-to-duty conflict, the rules are not concerned with clients' business interests, but with their interests in even-handed legal representation. The business interests of two clients in the same industry or in the same marketplace may be adverse, but that alone does not create a risk of impairment in even-handed legal presentation. As Binnie J. remarked in *Strother*:

> The clients' respective "interests" that require the protection of the duty of loyalty have to do with the practice of law, not commercial prosperity. Here the alleged "adversity" between concurrent clients related to business matters. This is not to say that commercial interests can never be relevant ... However, commercial conflicts between clients that do not impair a lawyer's ability to properly represent the legal interests of both clients will not generally present a conflict problem. Whether or not a real risk of impairment exists will be a question of fact.[78]

The ability to serve multiple clients is important in tax practice. The skills of tax lawyers and accountants often take years to develop. They are entitled to make a living by offering their services to multiple clients who compete commercially within a given industry as long as their legal interests are not in conflict.

The rules against conflicts exist to protect the client's interest, and not to condemn the professional. The cardinal rule for lawyers to follow is to avoid being in the situation of conflict. The way out of a conflict is to disclose the conflict of interest. With the client's consent, the lawyer can continue to serve the client notwithstanding such conflict.

---

[78] *Strother, supra* note 54 at para. 55.

(d) — The Strother case[79]

The *Strother* case is interesting. The facts of this case provide students with a glimpse into tax practice involving tax shelters and the associated ethical issues. By a narrow margin of five judges to four, the Supreme Court of Canada provided some clarification on the scope of the lawyer's duty of loyalty.

(i) — Facts and issues

The facts of the case are as follows. Monarch was a corporation in the business of selling tax-assisted production services funding ("TAPSF") investments, which were tax shelter investments in the Canadian film industry. Mr. Strother, a tax lawyer and partner in Davis & Co. ("Davis"), had special expertise in the structuring of these investments. He also had expertise in obtaining favourable advance tax rulings in connection with these tax shelters, which was an important precondition for selling them. Monarch was a client of Strother and Davis. Effective October 1996, Monarch had a written retainer that prohibited Strother and Davis from acting for others in relation to TAPSF investments (with limited exceptions). In the mid-1990s, Monarch paid Davis more than $5 million in legal fees in connection with the $13 million of profits from the sale of TAPSF investments. Strother was the highest billing Davis partner, with the fees from Monarch representing more than half of his billings.

In November 1996, the federal government announced the introduction of the matchable expenditures rules ("MER"). These rules meant that Monarch's TAPSF structure would no longer work after October 1997. Strother advised Monarch that he did not have a "fix" to avoid the effect of this legislation. In 1997, Monarch sought Strother's advice about what could be done to salvage their business, but Strother suggested that they defer that discussion until 1998. Strother's advice was candid and consistent with the advice given by other tax professionals at that time. By the end of October 1997, Monarch's business was winding down and its written retainer with Strother and Davis was terminated at the end of 1997.

In late 1997 or early 1998, Darc, a former employee of Monarch, approached Strother to discuss another structure that took advantage of an exception in the new rules. Strother drafted an advance tax ruling request and submitted it to Revenue Canada in March 1998. Strother and Darc had agreed in January 1998 that, if a favourable ruling was granted, Strother would receive 55 per cent of the first $2 million of profit of Sentinel (the corporate entity used to promote the tax shelters) and 50 per cent thereafter.

After terminating the written retainer at the end of 1997, Monarch verbally retained Strother and the firm to continue to do work for Monarch in 1998 and 1999. Monarch executives testified that they met with Strother several times in 1998 and asked him what business opportunities might be available in light of the new tax rules. Strother did not at any time advise them that there might be a "way around"

---

[79] *Strother, supra* note 54.

the new rules. Nor did he advise Monarch of the favourable ruling Sentinel received after it was issued in October 1998.

In August 1998, Strother told Davis about a possible conflict of interest. Davis's managing partner told Strother that he would not be permitted to own any interest in Sentinel. Effective March 1999, Strother resigned from the firm. In April 1999, he became a 50 per cent shareholder of Sentinel.

By September 2001, when tax law was changed to eliminate the advantages of schemes used by Sentinel, Sentinel and its affiliates had reaped profits of almost $130 million and Strother's share in profits was estimated to be $32 million.

After learning of Sentinel's tax ruling in early 1999, Monarch sued Strother and Davis for breach of fiduciary duty, but never continued its film tax shelter business.

The British Columbia Court of Appeal held that Strother had conflicts of interest — a conflict between the interests of his two clients (Monarch and Darc/Sentinel) and a conflict between his own personal financial interests and those of Monarch — and ordered Strother to disgorge to Monarch all profits derived from Sentinel and its affiliates. The majority of the Supreme Court of Canada held that Strother breached his fiduciary duty to Monarch but ordered him to disgorge only the profits made during the period of conflict.

(ii) — Majority judgment

The majority of the Court found that Strother owed fiduciary duties to Monarch in addition to the duties stipulated in the post-1997 oral retainer. A core fiduciary duty is the duty of loyalty, an element of which is the avoidance of conflicts of interest.

According to Binnie J., who authored the majority decision, Strother breached his duty when he took a personal financial interest in the Darc/Sentinel venture during the critical period when Monarch was looking to him for advice about what tax-assisted business opportunities were open. Binnie J. stated:

> The difficulty is not that Sentinel and Monarch were potential competitors. The difficulty is that Strother aligned his personal financial interest with the former's success ... Strother put his personal financial interest into conflict with his duty to Monarch. The conflict compromised Strother's duty to "zealously" represent Monarch's interest (Neil, para. 19), a delinquency compounded by his lack of "candour" with Monarch "on matters relevant to the retainer" (*ibid.*), i.e., his own competing financial interest.[80]

As a client, Monarch was entitled to candid and complete advice from a lawyer who was not in a position of conflict. Strother's personal interest in Monarch's competitor "gave Strother a reason to keep the principals of Monarch in the dark, in breach of his duty to provide candid advice on his changing views of the potential for film production services tax shelters". In Binnie J.'s view, Strother breached his duty to Monarch twice. The first breach occurred when he failed "to revisit his 1997 advice in 1998 at a time when he had a personal, undisclosed financial inter-

---

[80] *Ibid.* at para. 67.

est in Sentinel". The second breach happened "when he did not advise Monarch of the successful tax ruling when it became public on October 6, 1998".[81]

Unlike "used car salesmen or pawnbrokers whom the public may expect to operate on the basis of 'didn't ask, didn't tell'", the lawyers' relationship with clients is one of "trust and confidence".[82] Strother owed Monarch a duty of disclosure:

> Why would a rainmaker like Strother not make rain with as many clients (or potential clients) as possible when the opportunity presented itself (whether or not existing retainers required him to do so)? The unfortunate inference is that Strother did not tell Monarch because he did not think it was in his personal financial interest to do so.[83]

According to Binnie J., Strother could not rely on his duty of confidentiality to Darc as a defense for such breach:

> Of course, it was not open to Strother to share with Monarch any confidential information received from Darc. He could nevertheless have advised Monarch that his earlier view was too emphatic, that there may yet be life in a modified form of syndicating film production services expenses for tax benefits, but that because his change of view was based at least in part on information confidential to another client on a transaction unrelated to Monarch, he could not advise further except to suggest that Monarch consult another law firm. Moreover, there is no excuse at all for Strother not advising Monarch of the successful tax ruling when it was made public in October 1998 . . . I therefore conclude that Davis (and Strother) failed to provide candid and proper legal advice in breach of the 1998 retainer.[84]

Acting for clients with competing commercial interests does not, by itself, impair a lawyer's ability to properly represent the legal interests of both clients in an even-handed way:

> There is no reason in general why a tax practitioner such as Strother should not take on different clients syndicating tax schemes to the same investor community, notwithstanding the restricted market for these services in a business in which Sentinel and Monarch competed. In fact, in the case of some areas of high specialization, or in small communities or other situations of scarce legal resources, clients may be taken to have consented to a degree of overlapping representation inherent in such law practices, depending on the evidence. The more sophisticated the client, the more readily the inference of implied consent may be drawn. The thing the lawyer must not do is keep the client in the dark about matters he or she knows to be relevant to the retainer.[85]

Whether or not a conflict of interests exists is a question of fact. It existed in the *Strother* case because "Strother could not with equal loyalty serve Monarch and

---

[81] *Ibid.* at para. 70.

[82] *Ibid.* at para. 42.

[83] *Ibid.* at para. 70.

[84] *Ibid.* at para. 47.

[85] *Ibid.* at para. 55.

pursue his own financial interest".[86] Binnie J. also found that the impact of Strother's breach on Monarch's interest (i.e., in obtaining proper legal advice) was "material and adverse". He noted:

> While it is sufficient to show a possibility (rather than a probability) of adverse impact, the possibility must be more than speculation . . . That test is met here, for the reasons already discussed. Once the existence of Strother's personal financial interest in Sentinel was established, it was for Strother, not Monarch, to demonstrate the absence of any material adverse effect on Monarch's interest in receiving proper and timely legal advice . . .[87]

On the question of remedies, the majority held that Strother was required to account to Monarch for the profits that he acquired from the moment of the initial breach until the time when the solicitor-client relationship ended. Davis was not in breach but was vicariously liable pursuant to the B.C. *Partnership Act*.[88]

(iii) — Dissenting judgment

The dissenting decision, authored by McLachlin J., took a much narrower approach to determining the scope of duties owed by Strother to Monarch and the existence of conflict of interest. The Chief Justice opined that fiduciary duties should be "molded to" the contractual terms.[89] The investigation of a possible conflict of interest should be limited to the provisions of the retainer agreements. She found that there was no conflict between what Strother agreed to do for Monarch and what he was doing for Darc and himself with Sentinel. She also found no conflict between Strother's personal interest and what he agreed to do for Monarch under the retainer. The Chief Justice's approach "would be destructive of a basic underlying principle of the fiduciary relationship".[90]

(iv) — Summary of key points

Based on the majority decision in *Strother* and other cases, the principles governing conflict of interest can be summarized as follows:

- The terms of a retainer contract between a lawyer and the client specify the concrete services to be performed by the lawyer, but they are not exhaustive of the duties owed to the client. Fiduciary law imposes on the lawyer fiduciary duties that may not have been expressly included in the retainer.

- Fiduciary responsibilities include the duty of loyalty, of which an element is the avoidance of conflicts of interest.

---

[86] *Ibid.* at para. 70.

[87] *Ibid.* at para. 61.

[88] R.S.B.C. 1996, c. 348.

[89] *Strother*, *supra* note 54 at para. 141.

[90] Valsan & Smith, *supra* note 76.

- The rules against conflicts are strict, but they do not require lawyers to have superhuman abilities; they require the careful exercise of judgment, something that can always be demanded of a professional.

- It is always possible to be candid without disclosing confidential information.

- As a fiduciary, a lawyer's duty is to avoid situations where he or she has, or potentially may develop, a conflict. However, this rule does not prevent the lawyer from acting for multiple clients. A lawyer can represent multiple clients with conflicting business interests as long as the lawyer can provide even-handed representation to both clients.

- There is always a way out of conflict: either by taking the necessary steps to remove the conflict or by obtaining informed consent to it. Informed consent requires disclosure. "The client cannot be taken to have consented to conflicts of which it is ignorant."[91]

15.8 — Duty to the client

(a) — The lawyer-client relationship

The lawyer-client relationship is governed by both contract and fiduciary law. When a client retains a lawyer, the scope of the retainer is governed by contract. In this contract, the parties determine the scope of the services the lawyer is to perform and other contractual terms of the engagement. In addition, the lawyer-client relationship is "overlaid with certain fiduciary responsibilities, which are imposed as a matter of law".[92] As discussed in more detail above, the engagement letter or retainer contract generally describes "what" it is that the lawyer must do on behalf of the client. The fiduciary obligation indicates "how" the lawyer must do it: the lawyer must act in the best interests of the client at all times. To act in the best interests of the client at all times is at the heart of the lawyer's fiduciary obligation and underscores the rules of professional conduct.

(b) — Competence

All lawyers owe their clients the duty of competence. A "competent lawyer" means "a lawyer who has and applies relevant skills, attributes, and values in a manner appropriate to each matter undertaken on behalf of a client including . . . knowing general legal principles and procedures and the substantive law and procedure for the areas of law in which the lawyer practices . . ."[93]

Tax lawyers are held out as lawyers possessing special knowledge and skills in tax law. A client is, thus, entitled to assume that the tax lawyer has the ability and capacity to deal adequately with tax matters to be undertaken on the client's be-

---

[91] *Strother, supra* note 54 at para. 55.

[92] *Ibid.* at para. 34.

[93] LSUC Rules, *supra* note 58, r. 2.01(1).

half.[94] In some situations, this will require that the client be referred to a more expert lawyer.

(c) — Honesty and candour

"When advising clients, a lawyer shall be honest and candid."[95] This rule requires that the advice be "open and undisguised, clearly disclosing what the lawyer honestly thinks about the merits and probable results".[96] The lawyer has the duty to disclose to the client any material information within his or her mandate in order to adequately equip the client to properly instruct the lawyer. It also requires the lawyer "to inform the client promptly of the facts, but without admitting liability, upon discovering that an error or omission has occurred in a matter for which the lawyer was engaged and that is or may be damaging to the client and cannot readily be rectified".[97] In other words, if the mistake may be harmful to the client's interest, the lawyer must promptly inform the client of the mistake.

This duty also requires a lawyer to disclose any conflict of interest.[98] If a client is kept in the dark, the advice given cannot be, by nature, candid.

(d) — Confidentiality and privilege

Rules of professional conduct require that the lawyer must hold in strict confidence all information about the client's affairs that was acquired as the result of the professional relationship.[99] This duty of confidentiality covers not only confidential communications, but also all information that the lawyer obtains relating to the representation of the client.

This duty is of fundamental importance, as lawyers cannot advise to the best of their abilities unless the client shares with them crucial information without reserve. Keeping such information confidential helps foster such open communication. At common law, the scope of the duty is defined broadly:

> Whether founded on contract or equity, the duty to preserve confidentiality is unqualified. It is a duty to keep the information confidential, not merely to take all reasonable steps to do so. Moreover, it is not merely a duty not to communicate the information to a third party. It is a duty not to misuse it, that is to say, without the consent of the former client to make any use of it or to cause any use to be made of it by others otherwise than for his benefit.[100]

---

[94] *Ibid.*

[95] *Ibid.*, r. 2.02.

[96] *Ibid.*, LSUC Commentary on r. 2.02.

[97] *CBA Code*, *supra* note 51, ch. III, Commentary 11.

[98] LSUC Rules, *supra* note 58, r. 2.04.

[99] *Ibid.*, r. 2.03.

[100] *Bolkiah v. KPMG*, [1999] 1 All E.R. 517 (U.K H.L.) at 527.

Confidential information may be disclosed only with the consent of the client or in the rare cases where disclosure is required by law.[101]

In addition to the duty of confidentiality, lawyers must be mindful of privilege.[102] Solicitor-client evidentiary privilege protects the client's information by prohibiting the state from compelling the lawyer to disclose confidential communications between the lawyer and the client. It is restricted in scope to those communications treated as confidential by the client. The client can waive the claim of privilege under section 232 of the *ITA*. This privilege is related to the lawyer's role as an officer of the court charged with facilitating the administration of justice. It is not extended to communications between an accountant and the client.

Solicitor-client privilege applies only in the context of controversies and serves only to limit the information that can be extracted from the lawyer about communications between him or her and the client. It is different from the ethical duty of confidentiality, which precludes only voluntary disclosure by a lawyer. If a court or tribunal orders disclosure, the lawyer must disclose the information, unless the information is protected by the solicitor-client privilege.

(e) — Loyalty

Loyalty is fundamental to the lawyer-client relationship. "As a general principle, a lawyer has a duty to give undivided loyalty to every client."[103] The Supreme Court of Canada described the duty in *Strother* as follows: "A fundamental duty of a lawyer is to act in the best interest of his or her client to the exclusion of all other adverse interests, except those duly disclosed by the lawyer and willingly accepted by the client."[104] This is a fiduciary duty that goes beyond what the parties expressly bargain for.[105]

(f) — Ethical considerations in practice

(i) — Compliance

In considering ethical issues surrounding compliance, it is important to remember that the integrity of the system depends upon an honest self-assessment. The CRA cannot audit more than a tiny proportion of the returns filed, and relies heavily on the information supplied by the taxpayer. In these circumstances, compliance is quite unlike litigation, where each position advanced by a lawyer on behalf of the client is opposed by a lawyer on behalf of an opponent, and ruled upon by a judge. The reality of compliance is that positions taken in a tax return can easily be buried

---

[101] LSUC Rules, *supra* note 58, r. 2.03(2)–(5).

[102] The *Quebec Charter of Human Rights and Freedoms*, R.S.Q., c. C-12, s. 9 extends this privilege to a client's information communicated to professionals bound by a professional secrecy law, including accountants.

[103] LSUC Rules, *supra* note 58, r. 2.03.

[104] *Strother, supra* note 54 at para. 34.

[105] *Ibid.*

and immunized from any scrutiny short of an (unlikely) audit. In these circumstances, the tax lawyer's ethical duty of honesty and candour requires him or her to counsel adequate disclosure.

The lawyer's duty is to advise the client as to the law and the consequences arising from a violation of the law. The decision as to whether to file on a timely basis is the client's. Because the statutory obligation to file a tax return is regulatory in nature, and not to gather evidence as part of the criminal investigation (although this may be the result), a lawyer cannot advise the client not to file on the basis of avoiding self-incrimination.

In providing a legal opinion as to a position to be taken on a return, the lawyer should frankly disclose his or her opinion as to whether a debatable and defendable position is likely to be sustained in court if challenged by the CRA, and, if not, whether there is sufficient support for the position (a reasonable basis) to enable it to be asserted at all, but with adequate disclosure to the CRA. There is no reason that lawyers cannot advise taxpayers to resolve honest doubts in their own favour, provided the circumstances are adequately disclosed. If the client wishes to file a false return, the lawyer can advise the client on how the return should be filed, but how the client ultimately files is the client's own decision. A lawyer must never knowingly assist in or encourage any dishonesty, fraud, or criminal or illegal conduct, or instruct a client on how to violate the law. If the client refuses to follow the advice, the lawyer should resign from the engagement.

Since the duty to comply with tax law rests with the taxpayer, a tax lawyer's duties are derivative. Nevertheless, the practitioner who either prepares a client's return or advises a taxpayer is liable for the so-called "preparer" penalty under subsection 163.2(4). The preparer penalty is applicable to tax return preparers or advisors who counsel or assist others in making false statements or who are wilfully blind to obvious "errors" when preparing, filing, or assisting a taxpayer in filing a return. It could also be applicable in situations where the tax preparers or advisors "assent to or acquiesce in" the making of a false statement. The standard applied is "culpable conduct".[106]

A "good faith reliance" defence is available under subsection 163.2(6). It provides that the preparer penalty will not apply if the advisor relied in good faith on information provided by or on behalf of the client. This good faith reliance defence can be claimed "when the information used by the advisor or tax return preparer is not on its face, clearly false, or obviously unreasonable to a prudent person or does not raise obvious questions in the mind of the advisor or tax return preparer".[107] For example, it could apply when a new client provides a list of expenses that appear to relate to the client's business and seem to be reasonable but turn out to be fabricated.

---

[106] *ITA*, *supra* note 1, s. 163.2(1).

[107] See Canada Revenue Agency, Information Circular IC-01-1, "Third Party Civil Penalties" (2001) at para. 35.

A second third-party civil penalty, the so-called "planner penalty" under subsection 163.2(2), applies to those who prepare, promote or sell tax shelters or tax-shelter-like plans or arrangements that contain false statements. The "good faith" reliance defence does not apply if the advisor is involved in the promoting or selling of a tax shelter arrangement[108] and there is no maximum penalty.

(ii) — "Aggressive" tax planning

Aggressive tax planning deals with the "grey" area of tax law: it is not illegal in the sense of tax fraud, but it is not clearly consistent with the spirit of the law. There are different shades of grey. If, in the judgment of the tax practitioner, a tax planning scheme, if challenged, is more likely than not to prevail in court, then it is clearly ethical to advise the client to undertake the scheme (or help the client to implement the scheme).[109] The notion of "more likely than not" indicates that there may be some risk of being wrong or some room for different conclusions, but a court will likely uphold the scheme.

If the tax practitioner advises a client not to carry out the tax planning scheme because it fails the "more likely than not" threshold, he or she can still assist the client with the transaction as long as there is a reasonable and defendable basis for that position. The lawyer has no obligation to disclose the scheme to the CRA. The public policy reasons for opposing aggressive tax planning are not sufficiently specific and powerful to overcome the lawyer's duty to act in the interests of the client.

In the "big lie" cases, where the lawyer is presented with a clearly fraudulent scheme, the lawyer's choice is straightforward — the client must be advised that his or her conduct is fraudulent. If the client persists in it, the lawyer should withdraw from the representation. The lawyer also should be on guard against becoming the tool or dupe of an unscrupulous client.[110]

(iii) — Legal opinion

Some good practices to follow in the preparation of opinions are as follows:[111]

- Communicating clearly in writing with the client regarding the terms of the engagement.

- Establishing the facts, determining which facts are relevant, and evaluating the reasonableness of any assumptions or representations. It is not enough to simply rely on the information provided by the client: the material facts and cir-

---

[108] See *ITA*, *supra* note 1, s. 163.2(7) and the definition of "excluded activity" in s. 163.2(1).

[109] For further discussion, see Chapman, *supra* note 53; Silver, *supra* note 57.

[110] LSUC Rules, *supra* note 58, r. 2.02(5) states: "When advising a client, a lawyer shall not knowingly assist in or encourage any dishonesty, fraud, crime, or illegal conduct, or instruct the client on how to violate the law and avoid punishment."

[111] See Chapman, *supra* note 53; Hogan & Brassard, *supra* note 52; Silver, *supra* note 57; Russel, *supra* note 57.

cumstances upon which the opinion is based should be independently obtained or verified to avoid legal liability.[112]

• Making reasonable inquiry about the issues critical to the matter in respect of which an opinion is being given. These issues should not be assumed away. Examples are valuation issues and timing and dating issues. Many tax consequences turn on valuation, and, generally, the tax practitioner will turn to a qualified appraiser. In some cases, due diligence requires the tax practitioner to identify factors that may affect the fair market valuations. Similarly, the timing of a transaction affects the tax consequences. A tax practitioner must examine documentation that raises difficult timing and dating issues and may, in some circumstances, need to conduct an independent investigation in order to avoid rendering any opinion that would be misleading.

• Documenting and demonstrating that all relevant legal issues have been researched and analyzed and the legal conclusions are backed up by appropriate due diligence.

• Relating the applicable law to the relevant facts. The "law" includes not only the specific provisions of the *ITA* directly applicable to the issue, but also the general anti-avoidance rule ("GAAR") and judicial doctrines. A GAAR analysis is crucial in legal opinions about tax planning in general, and aggressive tax planning or tax shelters in particular. In light of the growing body of jurisprudence and the general shift toward contextual and purposive interpretation, lawyers need to do a sophisticated legal analysis about whether a proposed tax structure violates the object and spirit of the relevant provisions of the *ITA* or the *ITA* read as a whole.

• Arriving at a conclusion supported by the law and facts. Since the term "opinion" connotes a lawyer's conclusion as to the likely outcome of an issue if challenged and litigated, the lawyer should, if possible, state his or her opinion of the probable outcome on the merits of each material tax issue. The lawyer may also need to opine on the position that the CRA is likely to take on the issue, and to set forth the risks associated with the proposed tax structures.

(iv) — Advocacy and litigation

When acting as an advocate, a lawyer will face situations in which the lawyer and the client differ as to the advisability of disclosure of confidences and secrets. Examples of such situations are where a lawyer learns that his or her client has provided false information to the CRA; a lawyer discovers errors made by his or her client or by the CRA that favour the client; or the lawyer becomes aware of the fact

---

[112] A U.S. court has held that "when a law firm knows or has good reason to know that the factual description of a transaction provided by another is materially different from the actual transaction, it cannot escape liability simply by including in an opinion letter a statement that its opinion is based on provided facts". Canadian courts may share this view. See Chapman, *supra* note 53; Silver, *supra* note 57.

that his or her client has not complied with the tax law. In these situations, the duty to keep a client's information confidential may be in conflict with the lawyer's duty of honesty and candour. If the lawyer feels strongly about disclosure and the client disagrees, what course may (must) the lawyer pursue? Clearly, lawyers should not make false information or advise clients in doing so. If they do, they may be subject to the third-party civil penalties, as well as disciplinary action by the provincial law society to which they belong.[113] But there are no rules requiring the lawyer to reveal confidential information in these circumstances.

(v) — Advising multiple clients

The issue of a conflict of interest may arise in circumstances involving tax planning for more than one person. Examples are cases where a lawyer provides advice as to the organization (or reorganization) of a business for two or more clients or where a lawyer mediates a disputed issue between two or more clients. Similarly, where a lawyer acts as an estate planner, often both spouses approach the lawyer together to ask for assistance in planning their estates. Sometimes the client is accompanied by a potential beneficiary, such as a child.

Conflicts of interest may also exist when the lawyer has clients who are business competitors or have adversarial financial interests. The law requires that there be informed consent by the parties to the concurrent representation. Informed consent by a client requires disclosure. In *Neil*, the Supreme Court of Canada stated:

> The bright line is provided by the general rule that a lawyer may not represent one client whose interests are directly adverse to the immediate interests of another current client — *even if the two mandates are unrelated* — unless both clients consent after receiving full disclosure (and preferably independent legal advice), and the lawyer reasonably believes that he or she is able to represent each client without adversely affecting the other.[114]

As discussed earlier, the duty to disclose does not, however, require a lawyer to disclose confidential information concerning one client to another.

In some cases, the duty of confidentiality and duty of undivided loyalty may mean that the lawyer cannot act for more than one client. This is the case where the tax advice is crucial to the success of the business transactions. In the case of *Strother*, for example, the Supreme Court of Canada recognized that the new tax shelter structure created for Sentinel was confidential and Strother could not disclose it to Monarch. Instead, the Court suggested that Strother should have advised Monarch that there may be "a way around the new rules" and to consult another lawyer. The proprietary nature of the tax advice implies an exclusive relationship between the tax advisor and the client.[115]

---

[113] Under LSUC Rules, *supra* note 58, r. 2.02, "a lawyer shall not knowingly assist in or encourage any dishonesty, fraud, crime, or illegal conduct, or instruct the client on how to violate the law and avoid punishment".

[114] *Neil, supra* note 74 at para. 29.

[115] See Hogan & Brassard, *supra* note 52.

15.9 — Duty to other parties

(a) — Tribunal

In litigation, where the lawyer is representing a client in a dispute with the Minister, there do not seem to be any ethical issues that are unique to the tax context. In tax litigation, as in other litigation, the lawyer's duties of honesty and candour require that the lawyer be scrupulous and never mislead his or her opponent or the court by misstating the facts or the law, or by failing to inform the court of a relevant authority. The failure to inform the court of a relevant authority is a breach of legal ethics, even if the authority is adverse to the client and has been overlooked by the opponent's lawyer. This is an example where the lawyer's obligation to the system trumps or mitigates his or her duty of loyalty to the client.

Within these constraints, a lawyer is free to urge on behalf of the client any position that is fairly arguable, even if the lawyer believes that position to be unmeritorious. In the role of an advocate (as opposed to an adviser), the lawyer is not asserting his or her opinion as to the correct legal position, but is simply submitting arguments on behalf of the client. The lawyer leaves to the court the task of evaluating the strengths of the competing arguments, and determining what is the correct legal position.

A lawyer working at the Department of Justice and representing the Crown at the Tax Court of Canada, particularly in a self-represented appellant case, is expected to assist judges in determining the correctness of an assessment, not to win every case.[116]

(b) — The CRA

Tax practice differs from other types of law practice in that the opposing party is always the government, which, through the CRA, assumes a variety of roles with respect to the lawyer. Overall, the relationship between the CRA on the one hand, and the lawyer and client on the other hand, is adversarial or potentially adversarial. The CRA also assumes a quasi-judicial role in issuing rulings in response to taxpayers' requests for guidance in particular situations and in hearing taxpayer appeals from an assessment (or reassessment). Although the CRA is not technically a "tribunal", one would expect a lawyer to treat the CRA with an appropriate level of candour, fairness, courtesy and respect.

Lawyers may represent a client in a controversy with the CRA at the stage of audit, administrative appeal within the CRA, or in the courts. In this context, the lawyer serves as an advocate. Candour towards the tribunal and the duty of confidentiality to the client are critical to the lawyer's role as an advocate.

(c) — Third parties

Tax lawyers sometimes render opinions that affect third parties or the public at large. This is typically the case when third-party investors rely on a legal opinion in

---

[116] *Faibish v. The Queen*, 2008 TCC 241, 2008 D.T.C. 3554 (T.C.C.) at para. 31.

making their investment decisions. For example, investors may agree to participate in a corporate reorganization only when a lawyer has provided a legal opinion on the tax consequences of the proposed transactions.

Canadian courts have ruled that a corporate lawyer may owe a duty of care to an investor in the corporation by which the lawyer has been retained.[117] The lawyer may be held liable for negligence or fraudulent misrepresentation or for breach of the fiduciary duty of care. Both ethical and liability considerations may force tax practitioners to adopt a reasonably elevated standard of care in rendering their opinions.[118]

In *Cannon v. Funds for Canada Foundation* (2012),[119] the plaintiff applied to certify a class action suit against a number of defendants, including the promoter of a tax shelter involving charitable donations (the "Gift Program") and a tax lawyer for providing a "Comfort Letter". The plaintiff and many others participated in the Gift Program by making donations, the deduction of which was denied by the CRA. The tax lawyer was accused of "negligent misrepresentation". The tax lawyer admitted on cross-examination in court that the Comfort Letter was prepared by him with the intention that it would be included in the Gift Program materials that would be given to potential donors to show that it was a *bona fide* program. In certifying the class action, the Court found that: "[I]n providing the Comfort Letter, his biography and his photograph for use in the marketing brochure and as part of the sales pitch for the Gift Program, [the lawyer] knowingly brought himself into direct proximity with Cannon and Class members. The only purpose of the Comfort Letter was to help [the Promoter] sell the Gift Program."[120] The Court further noted that "it was foreseeable that a donor would rely on the Comfort Letters and it was entirely reasonable that he or she would do so".[121]

(d) — Duty to the system

Traditionally, the ethical obligations of tax lawyers do not differ much from the ethical obligations of other lawyers. The same rules of professional conduct apply to the practice of tax law. In recent years, however, there has been a trend in Canada and elsewhere to impose additional obligations on tax practitioners, who by virtue of their expertise, are viewed as gatekeepers for the tax system.

---

[117] E.g., *Filipovic v. Upshall*, 1998 CarswellOnt 2305, [1998] O.J. No. 2256 (Ont. Gen. Div.); additional reasons 1998 CarswellOnt 4286 (Ont. Gen. Div.); affirmed 2000 CarswellOnt 2163 (Ont. C.A.), in which it was held that the lawyers stood in a sufficient relationship of proximity with the plaintiffs to engender a duty of care on their part. It required the lawyers to carry out their duties in a reasonable, professional and competent manner, and with the utmost good faith.

[118] Silver, *supra* note 57 at 36:8.

[119] *Cannon, supra* note 55.

[120] *Ibid.* at para. 549.

[121] *Ibid.* at para. 550.

Well-educated tax professionals who understand the policies and principles under-lying our tax system, as well as the ethical standards of their profession, have an edge over others in light of recent developments. Their in-depth knowledge of the *ITA* and case law will enhance their ability to advise clients while advancing the integrity of the tax system. Ideally, they can end up "doing well and doing good at the same time".[122] Some leaders of the tax profession recognize that the "legal profession is not simply a business; it is a calling. It is more than a vocation; it is a public trust".[123]

---

[122] Eliot Freidson, *Professionalism: The Third Logic* (Chicago: University of Chicago Press, 2001) at 197–222, discussing the "soul" of professionalism.

[123] Chapman, *supra* note 53 at 18, citing Irwin Cotler's address to the Canadian Bar Association, "The Constitutional Revolution, the Courts, and the Pursuit of Justice", August 15, 2005.

16

STATUTORY INTERPRETATION

16.1 — Introduction

This chapter discusses how to interpret the provisions of the *Income Tax Act* (the "*ITA*").[1] Statutory interpretation is an important issue in income tax law because tax liability is created solely by statute. The *ITA* is the primary tax statute. The goal of statutory interpretation is to find the meaning of words in a statutory provision in relation to particular facts. The process of statutory interpretation involves the determination of the meaning of a statutory provision, the characterization of facts for tax purposes, and the application of the appropriate meaning to the facts. Statutory interpretation is more challenging in tax avoidance cases and is discussed in Chapter 17.

Establishing the meaning of words is often challenging because it is rare for a word to have a single meaning. Taxpayers may rely on one meaning and the government may prefer a different meaning. Taxpayers rarely go to court with clear cases. Why waste time and money? Whether a judge takes a liberal or restrictive interpretation can have fundamental implications for our tax system. Even the notions of "liberal" and "restrictive" to describe the consequences of statutory interpretation are not determinative. "Liberal" or "restrictive" are measured with reference to what standard?

16.2 — Overview of statutory interpretation

(a) — Scope and responsibility

Before considering the elements of statutory interpretation in greater detail, it is important to establish a clear view of the objective, and the main limitations of this fundamentally legal exercise. Construing tax law with reference to general law lies at the heart of applying the *ITA* in all its dimensions. The focus of this exercise is the application of private and public law generally in relation to particular "tax law" that exists to achieve various tax policy purposes we touch on in Chapter 1. Accordingly, in considering the meaning of words, it is useful to reflect more broadly on why we care about the meaning of words in the tax context. That animates our entire approach to interpreting the *ITA*, and marks the line between mechanical and thoughtful statutory interpretation.

The purpose for which words were chosen by the legislature, and the context, in the law and more generally, that gave rise to the enactment of the legislation in which

---

[1] R.S.C. 1985 (5th Supp.), c. 1 [*ITA*].

the words are textually used, necessarily influence and even condition their meaning in the tax context. Moreover, the textual meaning of words as items of language is also influenced by constructions beyond the immediacy of a tax statute. Tax law is accessory to the private law — the law of business associations, commercial law, torts, and all the other disciplines of the law — that attaches its own meanings to words that are used both in ordinary speech and in the specialized tax environment. As this chapter reveals, Canadian tax law has evolved, albeit somewhat haltingly and not always in a straightforward manner, to recognize explicitly three reference points for construing a tax provision: text, context and purpose of the legislation, or the "TCP" approach. Pointedly, this articulation of the undercurrents of statutory interpretation has most recently been exposed in judicial reasoning of the scope and significance of the "general anti-avoidance rule" ("GAAR") in section 245 of the *ITA*. Subsection 245(4) requires a determination of the alignment of a tax outcome arising from the application of the *ITA* apart from the GAAR and the underlying expectations of the Act that, if not taken into account, would result in an "abuse" of the *ITA* or a "misuse" of its provisions — which the Supreme Court of Canada says is one test and not two.[2]

The TCP approach is key to the application of the GAAR. More importantly, it is inherent in any intelligent analysis of the provisions of the *ITA*, apart from the GAAR. This, possibly, is what courts mean when they assert, as they commonly do, that the GAAR is a remedy of last resort in the *ITA*.[3] So it should be if the exercise of understanding the provisions of the *ITA* in a thoroughly legal exercise of construing those provisions has already taken account, as it should, of: the "what" — what words are used and what do they ordinarily mean (i.e., what does the "text" say?); the "why" — why is the provision using those words as the medium for achieving some sort of objective (i.e., what is its "purpose"?); and the "how" — how are the words used in the provision and how is the provision used in the *ITA* with that purpose in mind (i.e., what is the "context" in the *ITA* in which the words are used?).

Any analysis of a statute should entail the above elements. Indeed, as a general matter of interpreting human language (not just the meaning of the *ITA* or any law), words always have the meaning that is most suitable for them, taking account of the circumstances in which they are used — even in ordinary speech. It is hard to imagine this truism being less "true" in a specialized environment such as tax law, which creates its own ecosystem of words and concepts to achieve the ulterior objectives tax law exists to serve.

This important feature of statutory interpretation — fundamentally, an inquiry into the meaning of words — is captured in the reasons of Justice Rothstein in

---

[2] *Canada Trustco Mortgage Co. v. Canada* (2005), [2005] 5 C.T.C. 215, 2005 D.T.C. 5523 (S.C.C.) [*Canada Trustco*].

[3] E.g., see the reasons of Rothstein J. in *Copthorne Holdings Ltd. v. The Queen* (2011), [2011] 3 S.C.R. 721, [2012] 2 C.T.C. 29, 2012 D.T.C. 5006 (Fr.), 2012 D.T.C. 5007 (Eng.) (S.C.C.) [*Copthorne*].

Copthorne Holdings Ltd. v. The Queen (2011). Notable is the importance the Court attaches to the elements of "text", "context" and "purpose" in "normal" statutory interpretation, as well as the extended exercise in determining whether a statutory construction fulfils the "object and purpose" of the *ITA* and does not entail "abuse" or "misuse". Justice Rothstein captured the essence of the interpretive exercise this way (with our emphasis added to illustrate the steps of interpretation):

> [65] The most difficult issue in this case is whether the avoidance transaction was an abuse or misuse of the Act. *The terms "abuse" or "misuse" might be viewed as implying moral opprobrium regarding the actions of a taxpayer to minimize tax liability utilizing the provisions of the Income Tax Act in a creative way. That would be inappropriate.* Taxpayers are entitled to select courses of action or enter into transactions that will minimize their tax liability (see *Duke of Westminster*).

> [66] *The GAAR is a legal mechanism whereby Parliament has conferred on the court the unusual duty of going behind the words of the legislation to determine the object, spirit or purpose of the provision or provisions relied upon by the taxpayer.* While the taxpayer's transactions will be in strict compliance with the text of the relevant provisions relied upon, they may not necessarily be in accord with their object, spirit or purpose. In such cases, the GAAR may be invoked by the Minister. The GAAR does create some uncertainty for taxpayers. *Courts, however, must remember that s. 245 was enacted "as a provision of last resort"* (*Trustco*, at para. 21).

> [67] A court must be mindful that a decision supporting a GAAR assessment in a particular case may have implications for innumerable "everyday" transactions of taxpayers. . . . Because of the potential to affect so many transactions, the court must approach a GAAR decision cautiously. *It is necessary to remember that "Parliament must . . . be taken to seek consistency, predictability and fairness in tax law"* (*Trustco*, at para. 42). As this Court stated in *Trustco*:

>> Parliament intends taxpayers to take full advantage of the provisions of the *Income Tax Act* that confer tax benefits. Indeed, achieving the various policies that the *Income Tax Act* seeks to promote is dependent on taxpayers doing so. [para. 31]

> . . . . .

> [69] *In order to determine whether a transaction is an abuse or misuse of the Act, a court must first determine the "object, spirit or purpose of the provisions . . . that are relied on for the tax benefit,* having regard to the scheme of the Act, the relevant provisions and permissible extrinsic aids" (Trustco, at para. 55). The object, spirit or purpose of the provisions has been referred to as the "legislative rationale that underlies specific or interrelated provisions of the Act" (V. Krishna, *The Fundamentals of Income Tax Law* (2009), at p. 818).

> [70] *The object, spirit or purpose can be identified by applying the same interpretive approach employed by this Court in all questions of statutory interpretation — a "unified textual, contextual and purposive approach"* (*Trustco*, at para. 47; *Lipson v. Canada*, 2009 SCC 1, [2009] 1 S.C.R. 3, at para. 26). *While the approach is the same as in all statutory interpretation, the analysis seeks to determine a different aspect of the statute than in other cases. In a traditional statutory interpretation approach the court applies the textual, contextual and purposive analysis to determine what the words of the statute mean. In a GAAR analysis the textual, contextual and purposive analysis is employed to determine the object, spirit or purpose of a*

provision. Here the meaning of the words of the statute may be clear enough. The search is for the rationale that underlies the words that may not be captured by the bare meaning of the words themselves. However, determining the rationale of the relevant provisions of the Act should not be conflated with a value judgment of what is right or wrong nor with theories about what tax law ought to be or ought to do.
[emphasis added]⁴

The Supreme Court's reasons in the *Copthorne* case also illuminate another important but frequently misunderstood aspect of interpreting the *ITA*. In remarking on the connotations of the GAAR, the Court went out of its way essentially to say that interpreting the *ITA* is a legal and not a moral exercise. The same point was made by Justice Sharlow, even more directly, in *Canadian Imperial Bank of Commerce v. The Queen* (2013):

[1] In quantifying a taxpayer's tax liability under the *Income Tax Act*, R.S.C. 1985, c. 1 (5th Supp.), is it ever necessary to evaluate the morality of the taxpayer's conduct? As a matter of general principle, the answer should be no. The *Income Tax Act* is intended to raise revenue for the use of the federal government. It also contains provisions intended to facilitate the distribution of social benefits according to standards established by Parliament, or to encourage or discourage certain industries or commercial practices in the public interest as perceived by Parliament from time to time. But nothing in the *Income Tax Act* expressly permits or requires the Minister of National Revenue, or the Courts, to apply the *Income Tax Act* differently depending upon the morality of the taxpayer's conduct.

[2] Indeed, it has long been accepted in Canada that a taxpayer who conducts an illegal business, or a business conducted unlawfully, is taxable on the profits of that business on the same principles as any other business, except to the extent that a different result is required by a specific provision of the *Income Tax Act*. Similarly, the Courts have consistently rejected the notion that the *Income Tax Act* should be interpreted or applied more generously for a taxpayer whose conduct meets a sufficiently high moral standard.⁵

To understand the scope of, but also the responsibility engaged by, statutory interpretation — understanding the meaning of words in the context in which and for the purpose they were used — it is important to look inward at the law to guide the interpretive exercise.⁶ When Justices Rothstein and Sharlow disavow morality as a

---

⁴ *Ibid.* at paras. 65–70.

⁵ *Canadian Imperial Bank of Commerce v. The Queen* (2013), 2013 FCA 122, [2013] 4 C.T.C. 218, 2013 D.T.C. 5098 (Eng.) (F.C.A.) at paras. 1–2.

⁶ The scholarship of Lon Fuller (concerning contract interpretation and damages law in relation to parties' reasonable expectations), Ronald Dworkin (concerning legal integrity), and John Prebble and Zoë Prebble (concerning morality and tax avoidance) is particularly instructive in forming and informing perceptions about how the law, including the tax law, as typically understood is infused with inferences and judgements about what the law means and how it should be interpreted and applied; see the references to their thinking in particular in J. Scott Wilkie, "Transfer Pricing Aspects of Intangibles: The License Model" in Michael Lang, Alfred Storck & Raffaele Petruzzi, eds., *Transfer Pricing in a Post-BEPS World* (Wolters Kluwer, Eucotax Series, 2016) ch. 3, nn 1, 18. Even where the tax law is not di-

determinant of what the law means or how it should be applied, they mean an exogenous moral standard. They are not saying that the morality of civil society that ultimately is framed in the law is not relevant. In fact, they are saying, though not in so many words, that the law is a reflection of moral judgments, which, once made and articulated in the *ITA* and other law, are not to be second-guessed, because it may be convenient to do so, by moral justifications that do not reflect the political choices — the social welfare choices — that tax law exists to support. In other words, the morality of a provision is found in the words of the *ITA*, in the determination of what the words "mean" and where a more exhaustive examination is required according to the *ITA*'s object and spirit; and the morality of a taxpayer's behavior or conduct in relation to the *ITA* is to be determined by expectations that the law itself — the *ITA* itself — actually speaks to. As Justice Sharlow effectively says, the *ITA* establishes the applicable "moral standard". The exercise of statutory interpretation — understanding the meaning of words in the *ITA* — yields the awareness of that moral standard and how it is meant to be satisfied in the tax environment.

Discovering the meaning of words lies at the heart of tax law. Words do not reveal their meaning by themselves, and words — alone, in phrases and sections, and collected as the entire *ITA* — have the meanings that are suitable for the tax context in which they are used. This influences all elements of the process of statutory interpretation. It is so fundamental to the practice of tax law that both in and outside the GAAR context, it must be understood as the jumping off point for all the more particular manifestations of statutory interpretation discussed below.

(b) — Evolution of statutory interpretation approaches

(i) — Judicial doctrines

Rules of statutory interpretation are found in case law, as statutory interpretation is very much the province of the judiciary. The *ITA* does not contain a general interpretation rule. Parliament is generally reluctant to tell judges how to interpret legislation. In fact, even when Parliament has spoken on the issue of interpretation, its instructions are often ignored.[7]

The present state of the law on statutory interpretation continues to evolve, although, particularly in relation to the GAAR, the Supreme Court of Canada has offered substantial direction for a coherent theory and related guidance. The Supreme Court of Canada historically has often been split in its decisions where statutory interpretation is a prominent consideration in difficult applications of the *ITA*, making it a fascinating and, indeed, paramount area of study for students.

---

rectly concerned, these scholars provide insightful points of reference to understanding when the Act is not simply a book of rules but rather a system, some might say the embodiment of a fiscal ecosystem, all of the elements of which need to be considered and understood to make good sense of any of them. See also, generally, Lon L. Fuller, *The Morality of Law*, revised ed. (New Haven and London: Yale University Press, 1964, 1969).

[7] Ruth Sullivan, *Statutory Interpretation* (Concord, ON: Irwin Law, 1997) at 27.

Canadian courts have adopted various approaches to the interpretation of the *ITA*. Chronologically speaking, more or less, these include the strict interpretation, the "plain meaning," and the so-called "modern rule" or the "textual, contextual and purposive" approach. The general trend has been to move from a literal, formalistic approach to a more liberal, substantive approach that, in the GAAR context particularly, has evolved to be the TCP approach that we discussed at the outset of this chapter. Even so, it is important for students of tax law to understand the various manifestations and stages of the development of the evolved state of statutory interpretation. Vestiges of formalism and literalism are still present,[8] influenced in part by the strictures and dictates of the private law, and possibly a less-than-fully-expansive understanding of the texture of these ways of interpreting the *ITA*.

(ii) — Strict interpretation

The old rule that tax legislation must be interpreted strictly is perhaps best articulated in a *dictum* of the House of Lords in *Partington v. Attorney General* (1869):

> ... as I understand the principle of all fiscal legislation, it is this: if the person sought to be taxed comes within the letter of the law he must be taxed, however great the hardship may appear to the judicial mind to be. On the other hand, if the Crown, seeking to recover the tax, cannot bring the subject within the letter of the law, the subject is free, however apparently within the spirit of the law the case might otherwise appear to be.[9]

Under this approach, if the language of the statute is not literally apt to catch the transaction at issue, then it escapes. There is a presumption that, if there is doubt or ambiguity in provisions that levy a tax, the ambiguity should be interpreted in favour of the taxpayer. From the taxpayers' perspective, strict interpretation could be a double-edged sword. It not only leads to a narrow (strict) interpretation of charging provisions in a taxing statute, it also leads to a narrow interpretation of relieving provisions, such as exemptions or deductions. For example, in *Whitthum v. Minister of National Revenue* (1957),[10] the taxpayer was denied a medical expense

---

[8] See, e.g., *Veracity Capital Corporation v. Canada (National Revenue)*, 2017 BCCA 3, [2017] 3 C.T.C. 104, 2017 D.T.C. 5005 (B.C. C.A.) [*Veracity*]; *The TDL Group Co. v. R.*, 2016 FCA 67, [2017] 3 C.T.C. 71, 2016 D.T.C. 5075 (F.C.A.) [*TDL*]; *Inter-Leasing, Inc. v. Ontario (Revenue)*, 2014 ONCA 575, [2014] 6 C.T.C. 153 (Ont. C.A.); reversing 2013 ONSC 2927, [2013] 6 C.T.C. 21, 2013 D.T.C. 5124 (Eng.) (Ont. S.C.J.); additional reasons 2014 CarswellOnt 13697 (Ont. C.A.); leave to appeal refused *Ontario (Minister of Revenue) v. Inter-Leasing, Inc.*, 2015 CarswellOnt 2996, 2015 CarswellOnt 2997 (S.C.C.) [*Inter-Leasing*]; *Husky Energy Inc. v. Alberta*, 2012 ABCA 231, [2012] 6 C.T.C. 202, 2012 D.T.C. 5132 (Eng.) (Alta. C.A.); leave to appeal refused 2013 CarswellAlta 265, 2013 CarswellAlta 266 (S.C.C.) [*Husky*]; *595710 British Columbia Ltd. v. The Queen*, 2016 TCC 288, [2017] 3 C.T.C. 2155, 2017 D.T.C. 1004 (T.C.C. [General Procedure]).

[9] *Partington v. Attorney General* (1869), L.R. 4 H.L. 100 (U.K. H.L.) [*Partington*] at 122, per Lord Cairns.

[10] *Whitthum v. Minister of National Revenue* (1957), 57 D.T.C. 174, 17 Tax A.B.C. 33 (T.A.B.).

deduction for the expense of a full-time attendant for his spouse. The Act allowed this deduction only if a person was "necessarily confined by reason of illness . . . to a bed or wheelchair". The Court found that his wife did not qualify because she was confined to a "rocking chair".

The strict approach to constructing taxing statutes is one of the principles established by the House of Lords in *Inland Revenue Commissioners v. Duke of Westminster* (1935).[11] These principles have been profoundly influential in Canada today. The facts in this case are straightforward. The Duke of Westminster had a number of household servants. The then British *Income Tax Act* did not allow a deduction of wages of household servants, but allowed a deduction of annual payments made in pursuance of a legal obligation other than remuneration of servants (i.e., similar to modern-day "annuities" or "pensions"). The Duke accordingly entered into deeds of covenant with each of his servants, under which he undertook to pay each of them annual sums for a period of seven years. The payments were to be made irrespective of whether any services were performed by the promisee, and were without prejudice to the promisee's entitlement to remuneration if he or she did perform any services to the promisor. However, it was established by evidence that the understanding between the Duke and his servants was that they would rest content with the provision made for them by deed, and would not assert any right to remuneration. In this way, the Duke converted his non-deductible wages obligation into deductible annuity obligations. The issue was whether the "annual payments" under the covenants fell within the meaning of this term as used in the tax statute.

In ruling in favour of the Duke, the majority of the House of Lords articulated the following key principles:

1. A tax statute is to receive a strict or literal interpretation;
2. A transaction is to be judged not by its economic or commercial substance but by its legal form;
3. A transaction is effective for tax purposes even if it has no business purpose, having been entered into solely to avoid tax; and
4. Taxpayers are entitled to arrange their affairs to minimize their tax liability.

The principle of strict interpretation was articulated by Lord Russell of Killowen. He quoted *Partington* and stated: "The subject is not taxable by inference or by analogy, but only by the plain words of a statute applicable to the facts and circumstances of his case."[12] In this case, the meaning of the terms "annuity" and "salary" were given their literal meaning. None of the law lords made any inquiry about the purpose or spirit of the legislation relied upon by the Duke to claim the deduction for annuities. One could imagine that, among other things, the legislation was intended to encourage employers to provide income support to retired employees.

---

[11] *Inland Revenue Commissioners v. Duke of Westminster* (1935), [1936] A.C. 1 (H.L.) [*Duke of Westminster*].

[12] *Ibid.* at 24.

The principle of "form over substance", that is, to characterize the Duke's relationship with his servants in accordance with the rights and obligations in the deed of covenant, not its real commercial substance or purpose, was crucial to the Duke's success in court. There was no doubt that the deeds were legally effective in that all legal formalities had been carried out. Nor were the deeds shams: the Duke had covenanted to pay the annuities for seven years, and had, thereby, assumed the risk of having to continue to pay an annuitant who had stopped working for him or who had insisted upon additional remuneration for working for him. Of course, the understanding that the faithful retainers would continue to work for him, and would do so without extra charge, virtually eliminated this risk. But the risk was genuinely assumed, and none of their lordships regarded the deeds as shams. The form of the transaction (i.e., the "annuity contract") was, thus, regarded as the "substance" of the transaction. Lord Atkin, the sole dissenter, was the only law lord who found the device unsuccessful in avoiding tax. For Lord Atkin, "the substance of the transaction was that what was being paid was remuneration".[13] But for the other law lords, the legal form of the transactions was controlling and the Duke was entitled to deduct the payments. The substance doctrine was rejected because it involved substituting "the uncertain and crooked cord of discretion" for "the golden and straight metwand of the law".[14]

However, it needs to be recognized in this connection, and more generally, that judicial decisions reflect all of the circumstances in which legal issues arise to be decided. Specifically, decisions like the *Duke of Westminster* case need to be understood according to the social and cultural norms of the environment in which they were decided — compared to the environment in which the outcomes of those cases are held up to have rigid and incontrovertible doctrinal significance. Without recanting at all from the focus of statutory interpretation on legal substance, it must be recognized that decisions of the courts — and, indeed, we would say the architecture of legislation including the precision with which it is drafted — inevitably are influenced according to a law-based approach by the larger environment for which the law is a framework for conduct.[15] The strict interpretation of tax statutes reflects some outdated presumptions about tax law. Traditionally, tax law in England was compared to criminal law and the confiscation of property.[16] This tradition has been followed in Canada.[17] As a result, if the meaning of words of a tax

---

[13] *Duke of Westminster, supra* note 11 at 24–25.

[14] *Ibid.* at 19–20.

[15] See Assaf Likhovski, "Tax Law and Public Opinion: Explaining IRC v. Duke of Westminster" in John Tiley, ed. *Studies in the History of Tax Law*, vol. 2 (Oxford: Hart, 2006); and Assaf Likhovski, "The Duke and The Lady: Helvering v. Gregory and the History of Tax Avoidance Adjudication" (2004) 25 Cardozo Law Review 953.

[16] Robert Stevens, *Law and Politics: The House of Lords as a Judicial Body, 1800–1976* (Chapel Hill: University of North Carolina Press,1978) at 170–71.

[17] Warren Grover & Frank Iacobucci, *Materials on Canadian Income Tax*, 5th ed. (Toronto: Richard de Boo Publishers, 1981) at 62–65, cited by Estey J. in *Stubart Investments Ltd. v. R.*, [1984] C.T.C. 294, 84 D.T.C. 6305 (S.C.C.) [*Stubart*] at para. 57.

statute is doubtful, the doubt must be resolved against the government and in favour of the taxpayer, as it is for criminal law. This strict interpretation was aimed at protecting the taxpayer's property rights from government claims that were not clearly prescribed in advance. In other words, it was "not only legal but moral to dodge the Inland Revenue".[18]

In recent times, however, taxes have begun to be viewed somewhat differently. True, the immediate economic effect of paying a criminal fine or a tax may be similar, as the payer parts with property in both cases. However, a criminal fine is assessed in order to punish wrongdoing, whereas a tax is collected to apportion the costs of government among those who presumably benefit from it. As explained in Chapters 1 and 2, the main purpose of an income tax is to raise revenue, but subsidiary objectives are also pursued. Estey J. recognized the *ITA*'s fiscal and economic objectives in *Stubart Investments Ltd. v. R.* (1984):

> Income tax legislation, such as the federal Act in our country, is no longer a simple device to raise revenue to meet the cost of governing the community. Income taxation is also employed by government to attain selected economic policy objectives. Thus, the statute is a mix of fiscal and economic policy.[19]

(iii) — Modern rule

Stubart is a landmark case that signaled the change towards a more purposive interpretation of the *ITA*. Estey J. held that the "modern rule" applied to taxing statutes, just like it did to other statutes:

> The words of an Act are to be read in their entire context and in their grammatical and ordinary sense harmoniously with the scheme of the Act, the object of the Act, and the intention of Parliament.[20]

In evaluating the significance of *Stubart*, including as a precursor of, if not a catalyst for, the GAAR, it is important to recall what was in issue in the case. Very briefly, a corporate reorganization of sorts had taken place, ostensibly to shift income from one entity to the another commonly controlled loss-making entity, essentially to achieve a measure of practical corporate tax consolidation that the *ITA* does not afford. This was arranged by transferring the profitable business' assets to the loss-making company, which appointed the former owner to carry on the business for it. Everything involved in running the business stayed the same functionally, from one vantage as if the transaction had not taken place, but resulting in tax savings by offsetting income and loss of two different corporations. There were

---

[18] John Willis, "Statute Interpretation in a Nutshell" (1938) 16 Can. Bar Rev. 1 at 26, cited by Estey J. in *Stubart, supra* note 17 at para. 58. (Willis was referring to *Levene v. Inland Revenue Commissioners*, [1928] A.C. 217 (U.K. H.L.) at 227.)

[19] *Stubart, supra* note 17 at para. 55. In *Québec (Communauté urbaine) v. Notre-Dame de Bonsecours (Corp.)* (1994), [1995] 1 C.T.C. 241, 95 D.T.C. 5091 (Fr.), 95 D.T.C. 5017 (S.C.C.) [*Notre-Dame*] at para. 33, the Supreme Court of Canada also recognized that a taxing statute "serves other purposes and functions as a tool of economic and social policy".

[20] *Stubart, supra* note 17 at para. 61.

some errors allegedly made in implementing the reorganization, which the tax authorities contended made the transaction incomplete and, accordingly, should have invalidated its effect — that, in their view, exposed it to be nothing more than an insubstantial tax play.

The Supreme Court upheld the effectiveness of what might be regarded as a highly formal transaction to achieve an objective not available simply by applying the *ITA* in a straightforward way. The Court effectively characterized the alleged shortcomings as administrative imperfections that did not reach the core of the transaction. This context is important in understanding what the Court's articulation of the "modern rule" really means. The case, in this light, also might usefully be consulted to anticipate, and evaluate, the reasonable scope and effect of the GAAR.

In *Stubart*, the "modern rule", with its emphasis on statutory purpose and context, arose from — and sustained — a highly formalistic transaction undertaken only to secure a tax benefit. The Supreme Court, with this sensitivity, focused on the legal substance of the arrangements — essentially asking what the parties set out to do. How they achieved it, according to the evidence, aligned sufficiently with the legal implications of their chosen organizational and commercial course to warrant recognition according the *ITA*'s accessory application to the underlying private law constructs. That was the issue before the Court, and that is what the outcome of that case is directed to. In reaching its conclusion, the Court essentially combined various doctrinal notions critical of anti-tax avoidance, cutting to the heart of the relationship between the law and an evidence-based examination of the nature of the taxpayers' relations, regardless of the form or nomenclature adopted by them to describe and document what they were doing.

The modern rule differs from the traditional strict interpretation by requiring statutory provisions to be interpreted in a broader context and in harmony with the object and spirit of the legislation. One year after the *Stubart* decision, the *Interpretation Act*[21] was enacted, codifying the modern rule. Section 12 of the *Interpretation Act* provides: "Every enactment is deemed remedial, and shall be given such fair, large and liberal construction and interpretation as best ensures the attainment of its objects."[22]

Why did the Court feel the need to reject the strict interpretation in *Stubart*? Estey J. attributed part of the reason to the changing role of tax law: "the introduction of [tax] exemptions and allowances was the beginning of the end of the reign of the strict rule."[23] He also regarded the replacement of strict interpretation with purposive interpretation as a blow to tax avoidance and a way of reducing legislative complexity. According to Justice Estey, purposive interpretation would "reduce the attraction of elaborate and intricate tax avoidance plans, and reduce the rewards to

---

[21] R.S.C. 1985, c. I-21.

[22] *Ibid.*, s. 12.

[23] *Stubart, supra* note 17 at para. 59.

those best able to afford the services of the tax technicians"[24] and "reduce the action and reaction endlessly produced by complex, specific tax measures aimed at sophisticated business practices, and the inevitable, professionally guided and equally specialized taxpayer reaction".[25]

(iv) — Plain meaning

The so-called "plain meaning" approach to statutory interpretation means that the court must apply the clear and unambiguous meaning of provisions of the *ITA* without the need to resort to the general object and spirit of the provision. For example, McLachlin J. (as she then was) stated in *Shell Canada Ltd. v. Canada* (1999):

> [I]t is well established in this Court's tax jurisprudence that a searching inquiry for either the "economic realities" of a particular transaction or the general object and spirit of the provision at issue can never supplant a court's duty to apply an unambiguous provision of the Act to a taxpayer's transaction. Where the provision at issue is clear and unambiguous, its terms must simply be applied.[26]

In a number of cases, including *Canada v. Antosko* (1994),[27] *Singleton v. Canada* (2001)[28] and *Ludco Enterprises Ltd. v. Canada* (2001),[29] the Supreme Court, while reiterating the modern rule of statutory interpretation, clearly limited the relevance of legislative purpose or intent to instances where the legislative provision is ambiguous. In these three cases, as well as others, the Court did not find the provision at issue ambiguous and, thus, felt no need to go beyond its plain meaning. In essence, the plain meaning approach is not much different from that of "strict interpretation".

The *Antosko* case[30] was one of the first post-*Stubart* cases in which the Supreme Court of Canada formulated the plain meaning approach. In that case, as an attempt to rehabilitate a failing company, the taxpayer acquired, for a nominal consideration from a provincial government agency, some debt obligations (a debenture and promissory notes) that had been issued by the company to the agency (which had been lending money to the company). The taxpayer also acquired the shares of the company, and became responsible for running the business. The tax issue arose when the company made interest payments on the debt obligations to the taxpayer. The taxpayer reported the full amount of the interest income for tax purposes, but

---

[24] *Ibid.* at para. 56.

[25] *Ibid.* at para. 66.

[26] *Shell Canada Ltd. v. Canada* (1999), [1999] 4 C.T.C. 313, 99 D.T.C. 5669 (S.C.C.) [*Shell*] at para. 40. See also Chapter 8 at heading 8.9 — Interest expense.

[27] *Canada v. Antosko* (1994), [1994] 2 C.T.C. 25, 94 D.T.C. 6314 (S.C.C.) [*Antosko*].

[28] *Singleton v. R.*, [1996] 3 C.T.C. 2873, 96 D.T.C. 1850 (T.C.C.); reversed [1999] 3 C.T.C. 446, 99 D.T.C. 5362 (Fed. C.A.); affirmed (2001), [2002] 1 C.T.C. 121, 2001 D.T.C. 5533 (S.C.C.) [*Singleton*], discussed in Chapter 8 at heading 8.9 — Interest expense.

[29] *Ludco Enterprises Ltd. v. Canada* (2001), [2002] 1 C.T.C. 95, 2001 D.T.C. 5505 (S.C.C.), discussed in Chapter 8 at heading 8.9 — Interest expense.

[30] *Antosko, supra* note 27.

claimed a deduction for the portion of the interest that had accrued prior to the transfer of the debt obligation from the provincial agency to the taxpayer. The deduction was authorized by the language of subsection 20(14) of the *ITA*, which provided that, on the transfer of a debt obligation, any unpaid interest accrued to the date of the transfer was to be included in the transferor's income, and deducted from the transferee's income. In this case, the transferor, being an agency of the provincial government, was exempt from tax, so that it did not report or pay tax on the interest accrued up to the date of transfer. The Minister took the position that it was contrary to the object and spirit of the *ITA* to allow the transferee taxpayer to deduct the accrued interest in the circumstances of this case, when the transferor was not taxable on the interest. The Supreme Court of Canada rejected the Minister's argument and allowed the taxpayer to take the deduction. Iacobucci J., who wrote for the Court, held that the taxpayer was entitled to rely upon the terms of the statute, which clearly entitled the transferee of a debt obligation to a deduction for the interest accrued to the date of transfer. Where the words of the statute were "clear and plain", and where the legal and practical effect of the taxpayer's transaction brought the taxpayer within the words of the statute, then the statute had to be applied according to its terms regardless of the object and purpose of the provision.

The decision in *Antosko* is sound in that intolerable uncertainty would be introduced into the *ITA* if clear language in detailed provisions of the *ITA* were to be routinely qualified by unexpressed exceptions derived from a court's view of the object and purpose of those provisions. However, *Antosko* may go too far in implying that one can rely on plain meaning *to the exclusion* of legislative purpose. After all, language can never be interpreted independently of its context, and legislative purpose is part of the context. It would seem to follow that consideration of legislative purpose may not only resolve patent ambiguity, but may, on occasion, reveal ambiguity in apparently plain language.[31]

The plain meaning approach may be thought, sometimes, to result in an interpretation that contradicts fundamental principles of income tax law. For example, in *Friesen v. R.* (1995),[32] the issue was whether vacant land held in an adventure or concern in the nature of trade constituted "inventory" for purpose of subsection 10(1) of the *ITA*. If the land was inventory, the taxpayer could deduct the accrued but unrealized loss by writing down the value of the land under the lower of the fair market value and cost valuation method permitted by subsection 10(1). Subsection 248(1) defines "inventory" to mean "a description of property the cost or value of which is relevant in computing a taxpayer's income from a business for a taxation year". The majority of the Supreme Court of Canada held that the plain meaning of the definition in subsection 248(1) is that an item of property need only be relevant to business income in a single year to qualify as inventory, because the key word

---

[31] *Pigott Project Management Ltd. v. Land-Rock Resources Ltd.*, [1996] 1 C.T.C. 395 (S.C.C.) at 404, per Cory J. for the majority.

[32] *Friesen v. R.* (1995), [1995] 2 C.T.C. 369, 95 D.T.C. 5551 (S.C.C.). For more discussion on inventory, see Chapter 8 at heading 8.8 — Inventory.

used in the definition is "a", not "the" (as argued by the Minister). As a result, the taxpayer could deduct the paper loss. This result was contrary to the fundamental principle of realization in income tax law, and had to be overruled by amendment to subsection 10(1) and the introduction of subsection 10(1.01).

(v) — Textual, contextual and purposive interpretation

The "textual, contextual and purposive" ("TCP") principle was adopted by the Supreme Court in *Canada Trustco Mortgage Co. v. Canada* (2005):

> The interpretation of a statutory provision must be made according to a textual, contextual and purposive analysis to find a meaning that is harmonious with the Act as a whole. When the words of a provision are precise and unequivocal, the ordinary meaning of the words plays a dominant role in the interpretive process. On the other hand, where the words can support more than one reasonable meaning, the ordinary meaning of the words plays a lesser role. The relative effects of ordinary meaning, context and purpose on the interpretive process may vary, but in all cases the court must seek to read the provisions of an Act as a harmonious whole.[33]

This TCP principle is, in essence, a restatement of the "modern rule". There is no coincidence that the Court articulated this principle in *Canada Trustco*, its first GAAR case. It is now clear that the approach applies generally to interpreting any provision of the *ITA*.[34] The Supreme Court of Canada emphasized, however, the importance of textual interpretation when the statutory provisions are highly technical. For example, the Court stated in *Canada Trustco*:

> There is no doubt today that all statutes, including the *Income Tax Act*, must be interpreted in a textual, contextual and purposive way. However, the particularity and detail of many tax provisions have often led to an emphasis on textual interpretation. Where Parliament has specified precisely what conditions must be satisfied to achieve a particular result, it is reasonable to assume that Parliament intended that taxpayers would rely on such provisions to achieve the result they prescribe.[35]

The Court recognizes the importance of certainty, predictability and fairness, and taxpayers' right to legitimately minimize taxation.

16.3 — Interpreting provisions of the ITA

(a) — Textual meaning

The fundamental task in statutory interpretation is to establish the meaning of words used by Parliament in the statute. Therefore, statutory interpretation begins with the words of the *ITA*. This is the case under all of the above-discussed doctrines of statutory interpretation.

---

[33] *Canada Trustco, supra* note 2 at paras. 10, 11.

[34] E.g., *Placer Dome Canada Ltd. v. Ontario (Minister of Finance)*, 2006 SCC 20, 2006 D.T.C. 6532 (Eng.) (S.C.C.) [*Placer Dome*] at para. 111; and *Imperial Oil Ltd. v. R.* (2006), [2007] 1 C.T.C. 41, 2006 D.T.C. 6660 (Fr.), 2006 D.T.C. 6639 (Eng.) (S.C.C.) [*Imperial Oil*].

[35] *Canada Trustco, supra* note 2 at para. 11.

Words often have multiple meanings, both in their everyday usage and their legal usage. Some words in the *ITA* are defined by Parliament, some are "terms of art", and the majority are common words. There are some interpretation conventions about which meaning takes precedence.

(i) — Statutory meaning

Subsection 248(1) and other sections of the *ITA* define the meaning of certain words and phrases. Statutory meaning takes precedence over the ordinary meaning. In fact, in interpreting the *ITA*, one should always refer first to the statutory definitions.

There are three types of statutory definitions in the *ITA*: exhaustive, inclusive and deemed. The Act uses the word "means" or "is" to indicate an exhaustive definition. For example, an "individual" "means a person other than a corporation".[36] A "taxation year" for individuals "is . . . a calendar year".[37] An exhaustive definition is a complete definition and is the most authoritative.

The *ITA* uses the word "includes" to indicate an inclusive definition. For example, a person is defined under subsection 248(1) to include "any corporation." An inclusive definition is not complete; it simply specifies a specific meaning to be added to the ordinary meaning of the defined word or phrase. Thus, the ordinary meaning is implicitly included. Because individuals are generally understood to be persons, they are implicitly included in the definition of "persons" so that both individuals and corporations are taxed as "persons" under the Act.

The *ITA* uses the phrase "shall be deemed" in defining some concepts. For example, under paragraph 70(5)(a), a taxpayer shall be deemed to have disposed of each of his or her capital property and received proceeds of disposition therefore equal to the fair market value of the property immediately before his or her death. The deemed meaning is often artificial or even counterintuitive, but it is useful in achieving a particular legislative purpose. The deemed disposition rule under paragraph 70(5)(a) ensures that capital gains (or losses) are realized and taxed in the year of death.

(ii) — Ordinary, technical or legal meaning

The ordinary meaning of words is their ordinary, everyday meaning or idea conveyed by the word. It is often the meaning found in dictionaries. In the absence of statutory definitions or overriding legal meanings, it makes sense to interpret words used in the *ITA* according to their ordinary meaning. "Most taxpayers are not (and likely have no desire to be) learned in the law."[38] In assessing their income tax

---

[36] *ITA, supra* note 1, s. 248(1).

[37] *Ibid.*, s. 249(1).

[38] *Will-Kare Paving & Contracting Ltd. v. R.*, [2000] 3 C.T.C. 463, 2000 D.T.C. 6467 (S.C.C.) [*Will-Kare*] at para. 39, per Binnie J. (dissenting).

liability, it is the everyday meaning of words to which these taxpayers refer. Drafters of the statute can be presumed to have adopted such meaning in the statute.

However, where a word has a technical or legal meaning, the technical or legal meaning should be preferred to the ordinary and grammatical meaning, especially where such an interpretation is justified by the statutory context in which the word appears. In *Will-Kare Paving & Contracting Ltd. v. R.* (2000),[39] the issue was whether the words "goods for sale", when used for purposes of two tax incentives (the investment tax credit and accelerated capital cost allowance), have their ordinary meaning or their legal meaning. The Court held that, although the word "sale" has an everyday meaning, its settled legal meaning as established under private commercial law prevails. The legal meaning was more consistent with the purpose of the two tax incentive provisions.

(b) — Context

(i) — Statutory context

Words must be interpreted within the context in which they are used. This is particularly important when a word has more than one meaning, or the meaning is ambiguous. The context includes the particular section of the *ITA* in which the word is used (immediate context), other related sections of the Act and the Act as a whole. The presumption underlying contextual analysis is that the provisions of the *ITA* work together towards a common purpose and are internally coherent, consistent and logical.[40]

Very often, the immediate context is sufficient to establish the ordinary meaning. For example, the meaning of the phrase "other benefits of any kind whatever" in paragraph 6(1)(a) of the *ITA* is apparently broad, but its scope is limited by its immediate context to mean economic benefits received in respect of employment. In other cases, the broader context as established by the scheme of the *ITA* and permissible extrinsic aids must be examined.

The *ITA* is structured to address five basic questions: 1) who is liable to tax; 2) what is income and whose income is it; 3) when is tax payable; 4) how much is payable by a taxpayer; and 5) how is the tax collected. Each provision of the *ITA* has a purpose. For example, the purpose might be to accurately measure economic income, to provide a subsidy to taxpayers for engaging in a particular activity in a specific way, or to exclude or defer certain items from income for a variety of reasons. Depending on the policy objective to be met, a provision of the *ITA* can be a "technical" provision that answers the five questions above, a "tax expenditure" provision that provides relief to taxpayers for social or economic reasons, or an "anti-avoidance" provision that ensures the integrity of the technical provisions and the tax expenditure provisions. In interpreting the *ITA*, it is important to be aware

---

[39] *Ibid.*

[40] See Ruth Sullivan, *Sullivan and Driedger on the Construction of Statutes*, 4th ed. (Markham, Ont.: Butterworths, 2002) at 261–262.

of the type of the provision to be interpreted, and to apply the proper policy analysis when necessary.

As evidenced by paragraphs 3(a) and 3(b), the *ITA* has two separate schemes for income and capital. The scheme for income applies to income or loss from office, employment, business, property and other income. Under this scheme, income or loss is recognized in full and a loss can offset income from any source as well as a taxable capital gain. In contrast, capital is a source of income, but not income *per se*. The notion of capital can be understood as "tax-paid funds"[41] and the return of capital is not income. Income derived from capital (such as interest, rent, royalty or dividends) is taxable under the income scheme as income from property. The capital scheme recognizes 50 per cent of the capital gain or capital loss for tax purposes in the event of a disposition of a capital property; capital losses are quarantined in that they cannot offset income from a source.

The income scheme and the capital scheme intersect for several types of capital properties: one example is a depreciable property and another is a share. In the case of depreciable property used to earn income from property or income from a business, the *ITA* deals with the income aspect of the purchase by permitting a deduction for capital cost allowance ("CCA"), and the capital aspect by recognizing the capital gain from the disposition of the property. The two schemes intersect at the point of cost by explicitly excluding a loss from the disposition of a depreciable property as a "capital loss" under paragraph 39(1)(b). This is because any loss on a depreciable property is recognized in full under the CCA rules in the income scheme. In the case of a share, a shareholder will generally realize the economic profits accumulated within a corporation by receiving a dividend (which is taxed as income from property) and/or disposing of the share to realize a gain (which is taxed under the capital scheme). But when a corporate distribution is made to redeem a share, the *ITA* deals with the capital aspect by allowing only the "paid-up capital" ("PUC") of the shares to be returned to the shareholder on capital account and tax-free. The *ITA* deals with the income aspect by treating any excess amount as a dividend. The differential treatment of capital gains and dividends, and whether a corporate distribution constitutes a return of PUC, have given rise to tax planning opportunities known as "surplus stripping" and a fair amount of tax controversy.

Within the income tax scheme, there are sub-schemes for different types of income. For example, the *ITA* deals with employment income differently from business income. As explained in Chapters 5 to 9, income from employment is taxed largely on a gross basis. Expenses incurred by employees are not deductible in computing income from employment unless it is explicitly permitted by section 8. In contrast, expenses incurred by businesses are generally deductible unless the *ITA* says otherwise. Another example is the different treatment of "active" income and "passive" income in the case of private corporations. Active income is eligible for tax subsi-

---

[41] See *Copthorne, supra* note 3.

dies in the form of the small business deduction and manufacturing and processing credits, whereas passive income is subject to anti-deferral rules (see Chapter 14).[42]

The scheme of the *ITA* is important in establishing the purpose or intent of the provisions of the Act.[43] In *Imperial Oil*, LeBel J. gave significant weight to the legislative scheme in interpreting paragraph 20(1)(f) of the *ITA*.[44]

(ii) — Historical context

The historical context of a statutory provision is often very telling about the purpose of the provision. Clear examples are some recent provisions enacted to override a specific court decision, such as section 245 (in reaction to *Stubart*),[45] section 20.3 (in reaction to *Shell Canada*),[46] section 67.6 (in reaction to *65302 British Columbia Ltd.*)[47] and section 56.4 (in reaction to *Fortino* and *Manrell*).[48]

(c) — Legislative purpose and intent

(i) — Growing relevance

The legislative purpose or intent is an important element of the "textual, contextual and purposive" interpretation. Ideally, courts interpret the meaning of a provision to best reflect its underlying purpose and the intention of Parliament.[49] In practice, however, it may be difficult to discern statutory purpose and/or legislative intent by simply reading the *ITA*. As such, the extent to which legislative purpose or intent affects the outcome of statutory interpretation largely depends on the willingness of the courts to go beyond the "plain meaning" of the text of a specific provision.

Since the *ITA* rarely expressly states the purpose or intent of a particular provision, such intent or purpose must be discerned from materials intrinsic to the *ITA* (e.g., the text of the particular provision and scheme of the Act), materials extrinsic to the *ITA* (such as legislative history and other statutes) or resorting to canons of statutory interpretation (such as presumptions).

---

[42] The separate regime of taxing active and passive income also applies to foreign corporations controlled by Canadian residents. For more discussion, see J. Li, A. Cockfield & J.S. Wilkie, *International Taxation in Canada: Principles and Practices*, 3rd ed. (Markham, Ont.: LexisNexis, 2014).

[43] See *Canada Trustco, supra* note 2 at para. 10: "The relative effects of ordinary meaning, context and purpose on the interpretive process may vary, but in all cases the court must seek to read the provisions of an Act as a harmonious whole."

[44] *Imperial Oil, supra* note 34 at para. 17.

[45] *Stubart, supra* note 17.

[46] *Shell, supra* note 26.

[47] *65302 British Columbia Ltd v. R.*, [2000] 1 C.T.C. 57, 99 D.T.C. 5799 (S.C.C.) [*65302 BC*].

[48] *Fortino v. R.*, [2000] 1 C.T.C. 349, 2000 D.T.C. 6060 (Fed. C.A.); and *Manrell v. R.*, [2003] 3 C.T.C. 50, 2003 D.T.C. 5225 (Fed. C.A.).

[49] *Imperial Oil, supra* note 34 at para. 17

(ii) — Purpose or intent

The terms "purpose" and "intent" were used interchangeably in *Canada Trustco*[50] and *Mathew v. Canada* (2005).[51] According to *Imperial Oil*,[52] however, the distinction between "purpose" and "intention" is apparently important. LeBel J. (writing for the majority) referred to the intention of Parliament in enacting paragraph 20(1)(f), whereas Binnie J. (writing for a three-justice minority) focused on the "purpose" of subsection 20(1) in general. LeBel J. framed the question as follows:

> In the end, the question is still whether s. 20(1)(f) was intended by Parliament to apply to the appreciation or depreciation of the obligation, in which case the calculation would be analogous to the computation of a capital gain, or whether it was intended to apply to an income expense or, more accurately, a point-in-time expense that would, but for that section, be a payment on account of capital.[53]

Binnie, J. was uncomfortable with the reliance on unexpressed legislative intention:

> My colleague concludes that s. 20(1)(f) is designed "to address a specific class of financing costs arising out of the issuance of debt instruments at a discount" (para. 67). Such a narrow focus, as stated earlier, is nowhere expressed in the Act, although it would have been a simple thing to say so if that was Parliament's intent.[54]

Given that the purpose of subsection 20(1) was to encourage "companies to raise capital by allowing them to deduct virtually all costs of borrowing", Binnie J. opined that interpreting paragraph 20(1)(f) more broadly "advance[s] Parliament's purpose whereas the conclusion reached by my colleague would act as a deterrent".[55]

The Court provided no principled basis for determining "purpose" or "intent". As can be seen from above, the term "intent" is often used to refer to the meaning that Parliament would have given to a specific provision in a given fact situation, whereas the term "purpose" is broader and more dynamic by allowing the Court to address issues that were not totally anticipated by the drafters. It is debatable whether Parliament's actual intention can be clearly established, especially in cases where there are new problems that were unanticipated by the drafters of the statute. Nonetheless, the textual, contextual and purposive principle requires the textual interpretation to be consistent with the intention of Parliament.

In some cases, there may be more than one legislative intent or purpose. For example, the Court in *Notre Dame* (1994) found that the purpose of the statute as a whole was to raise revenue, but it also "serves other purposes and functions as a

---

[50] *Canada Trustco, supra* note 2 at para. 74.

[51] *Mathew v. Canada* (2005), [2005] 5 C.T.C. 244, 2005 D.T.C. 5538 (S.C.C.) [*Mathew*].

[52] *Imperial Oil, supra* note 34.

[53] *Ibid.* at para. 56.

[54] *Ibid.* at para. 102.

[55] *Ibid.* at para. 103.

tool of economic and social policy".[56] In this particular case, the taxing statute also pursued "a secondary policy of exempting social works".[57] This secondary policy goal was advanced by giving a broader interpretation of the exemption provision at issue.

(iii) — Inferences from the text

Legislative intent or purpose can be inferred from the text of the provisions, the absence of specific rules, and legislative context. The text and the scheme of the *ITA* sometimes indicate the purpose of a provision, at least at a general level. For example, paragraph 6(1)(a) uses extremely broad language to convey the intention of taxing various forms of compensation for employment.

In *Imperial Oil*,[58] LeBel J. referred to the text of paragraph 20(1)(f) and the scheme of the *ITA* before reaching his conclusion that paragraph 20(1)(f) was not intended to allow the taxpayer to deduct foreign exchange losses associated with a debt issued in a foreign currency. Legislative context is helpful in establishing the purpose or rationale of the impugned provisions in the GAAR cases discussed in Chapter 17.

Inferences about statutory purpose may be made from the absence of specific provisions. In *Canada Trustco*, for example, the Court found that the purpose of the CCA provisions "emerges clearly from the scheme of the CCA provisions within the Act as a whole",[59] which did not limit CCA deductions to amounts bearing real financial risk or "economic cost". The Court stated:

> The applicable CCA provisions of the Act do not refer to economic risk. They refer only to "cost". Where Parliament wanted to introduce economic risk into the meaning of cost related to CCA provisions, it did so expressly, as, for instance, in s. 13(7.1) and (7.2) of the Act, which makes adjustments to the cost of depreciable property when a taxpayer receives government assistance.[60]

---

[56] *Notre-Dame, supra* note 19 at para. 34. In this case, the question arose whether an old age home was entitled to a full exemption from Quebec's municipal property tax. There was no doubt that 11 per cent of the home, which was a shelter section in which the residents received special care, qualified for the exemption. The question was whether the remaining 89 per cent of the home, which consisted of apartments, also qualified for the exemption. Since the language of the exemption did not provide a clear answer, the Supreme Court of Canada had to settle the question in favour of the taxpayer by reference to the purpose of the provision.

[57] *Ibid.* at 250 [C.T.C.].

[58] *Imperial Oil, supra* note 34.

[59] *Canada Trustco, supra* note 2 at para. 74.

[60] *Ibid.* at para. 75.

Similarly, in *65302 British Columbia Ltd.*, the Court found the lack of a specific provision prohibiting the deduction of fines and penalties to be an indication of Parliament's intent to permit their deduction.[61]

In the context of the GAAR, however, this "implied exclusion" doctrine has limited application, as it contradicts the nature of a GAAR analysis. The Court made it clear in *Copthorne* that, when the Minister invokes the GAAR, he is conceding that the words of the statute do not cover the impugned transactions at issue, and relying on the underlying rationale or purpose of the legislation to support his position.[62]

(iv) — Relevance of extrinsic materials

Extrinsic materials sometimes shed light on the purpose or rationale of a provision of the *ITA*. These are viewed as "interpretive aids" and can only be used with caution. In *Imperial Oil*, LeBel J. expressed this point by saying that he "would be loath to rely on one" and "will return to the text of the statute itself" to infer legislative purpose.[63] The extrinsic materials referred to by the Supreme Court in tax cases include the following:

- Technical Notes issued by the Department of Finance to explain the introduction of or amendments to a provision (referred to in *Canada Trustco, Mathew,* and *Imperial Oil*);[64]

- The interpretive practice adopted by the Minister. In *Placer Dome*, LeBel J. stated: "It is well established that in resolving doubt about the meaning of a tax provision, the administrative practice and interpretation adopted by the Minister, while not determinative, are important factors to be weighed."[65] But when the administrative practice changed, the new practice was considered to reflect the ambiguity that inheres in the statute itself and "cannot be relied upon as an interpretive tool except to support the view that the statutory definition falls short of being clear, precise and unambiguous".[66] In *Imperial Oil*, LeBel J. found the Minister's practice (i.e., allowing certain foreign exchange losses to be deducted as expenses) "troubling" and did not give it much weight.[67]

- Other statutes may define the meaning of a term that may be relevant to the interpretation of the *ITA*. In *Will-Kare*, the meaning of "sale" under the *Sale of*

---

[61] *65302 BC, supra* note 47 at para. 63. He also regarded the design of the tax collection system to be based on self-assessment as evidence of Parliament's intention to allow the deduction of all income-earning expenses, including fines and penalties (para. 57).

[62] *Copthorne, supra* note 3 at paras. 108–111.

[63] *Imperial Oil, supra* note 34 at para. 57.

[64] *Canada Trustco, supra* note 2; *Mathew, supra* note 51; *Imperial Oil, supra* note 34.

[65] *Placer Dome, supra* note 34 at para. 10.

[66] *Ibid.* at para. 40.

[67] *Imperial Oil, supra* note 34 at para. 59.

Goods Act, 1893 was adopted for the purposes of the Act.[68] In *Copthorne*, the meaning of "stated capital" in the Alberta *Business Corporations Act* and the *Canada Business Corporations Act* was relevant to interpreting the meaning of "paid-up capital" in the *ITA*.[69]

- Academic texts sometimes help the courts identify legislative purpose. In each of its recent decisions, the Supreme Court has cited some texts, including earlier editions of this book.

- Case law in other countries. As Canada is a common law jurisdiction, Canadian courts draw inferences from the case law of other common law jurisdictions, particularly the U.K., the United States and Australia. One of the most important common law principles in Canadian tax law — the *Duke of Westminster* principle — is derived from a British decision.[70]

(v) — Presumptions

In certain cases, it may be necessary to impute legislative intent when the "actual" intention is difficult to discover. The Supreme Court has relied on a number of canons of statutory construction or presumptions. These include the following:

- The presumption against a Parliamentary intention to encourage violations of other laws. In *65302 British Columbia Ltd.*, Bastarache J, writing for the dissent, was persuaded by the presumption and Iacubocci J. was not, but both found it relevant.[71]

- The presumption against tautology. LeBel J. stated in *Placer Dome*: "A court should avoid adopting an interpretation that renders any portion of a statute meaningless or redundant and, in this case, the presumption against tautology carries considerable weight."[72]

- The presumption in favour of the taxpayer in cases where application of the ordinary principles of interpretation does not resolve the issue. In *Placer Dome*, LeBel J. emphasized that this is a residual presumption only. "Any doubt about the meaning of a taxation statute must be reasonable, and no recourse to the presumption lies unless the usual rules of interpretation have been applied, to no avail, in an attempt to discern the meaning of the provision at issue."[73]

There may be more than one intention that can be inferred from the text of the *ITA*, extrinsic materials and the above presumptions and, in the case of differing inten-

---

[68] *Will-Kare, supra* note 38 at para. 59.

[69] *Copthorne, supra* note 3 at para. 76.

[70] *Duke of Westminster, supra* note 11.

[71] *65032 BC, supra* note 47 at paras. 9–13 (Bastarache J.) and paras. 52, 68 (Iacobucci J.).

[72] *Placer Dome, supra* note 34 at paras. 3, 43–46.

[73] *Ibid.* at para. 24.

tions, the court must decide which intention is the overriding one. Thus far, the intention derived from the scheme of the *ITA* tends to override others. In *65302 British Columbia Ltd.*, for example, five out of seven justices of the Supreme Court favoured Parliamentary intention to permit the deduction of fines and penalties based on the scheme of the Act over the presumption against Parliamentary intention to encourage violations of other laws.[74]

(d) — Navigating between text and purpose

(i) — Special characteristics of tax statutes

One factor that is intrinsic and unique to the *ITA* is its high-level technical detail, precision and complexity. The Supreme Court stated in *Canada Trustco* and subsequent decisions that the text of the *ITA* has often been given "greater emphasis" in the interpretation "because of the degree of precision and detail characteristic of many tax provisions".[75] The Court further stated that clear, precise and unequivocal words play a dominant role because taxpayers are entitled to certainty in planning their affairs.[76] LeBel J. stated:

> The interpretive approach is thus informed by the level of precision and clarity with which a taxing provision is drafted. Where such a provision admits of no ambiguity in its meaning or in its application to the facts, *it must simply be applied*. Reference to the purpose of the provision "cannot be used to create an unexpressed exception to clear language." . . . Where, as in this case, the provision admits of more than one reasonable interpretation, greater emphasis must be placed on the context, scheme and purpose of the Act. Thus, legislative purpose may not be used to supplant clear statutory language, but to arrive at the most plausible interpretation of an ambiguous statutory provision.[77]

In the meantime, the Court also acknowledges that statutory context and purpose may reveal or resolve latent ambiguities of apparently clear statutory language.[78]

The fact of the matter is that the *ITA* is an intimidating statute to interpret. Since its introduction in 1917, the Act has been amended constantly and grown to be a gigantic statute, occupying thousands of pages and weighing more than a kilogram.[79] The statutory language has become more technical and detailed. Many provisions are drafted in a formulaic style. The following passage, written over 60 years ago, succinctly describes the state of complexity of the *ITA* today:

> In my own case the words of such an act as the Income Tax, for example, merely dance before my eyes in a meaningless procession: cross-reference to cross-reference, exception upon exception — couched in abstract terms that offer no handle to

---

[74] *65302 BC, supra* note 47.

[75] *Canada Trustco, supra* note 2 at para. 21.

[76] *Ibid.*

[77] *Ibid.* at para. 23.

[78] *Ibid.* at para. 10.

[79] *Ipsco Inc. v. R.*, [2002] 2 C.T.C. 2907, 2002 D.T.C. 1421 (T.C.C.) [*Ipsco*] at para. 26.

seize hold of — leave in my mind only a confused sense of some vitally important, but successfully concealed, purport, which it is my duty to extract, but which is within my power, if at all, only after the most inordinate expenditure of time. I know that these monsters are the result of fabulous industry and ingenuity, plugging up this hole and casting out that net, against all possible evasion; yet at times I cannot help recalling a saying of William James about certain passages of Hegel: that they were no doubt written with a passion of rationality; but that one cannot help wondering whether to the reader they have any significance save that the words are strung together with syntactical correctness.[80]

The complexity of the statute attracts different reactions from reasonable and well intentioned judicial minds:

> Legislation weighing more than a kilogram does not have much room in it for liberal, general interpretation, particularly when the road to the resolution of a specific issue is well-marked and the voyage is undertaken in accordance with a detailed map and a handy guidebook.[81]

> It is quite true that as the articulation of a statute increases, the room for interpretation must contract; but the meaning of a sentence may be more than that of the separate words, as a melody is more than the notes, and no degree of particularity can ever obviate recourse to the setting in which all appear, and which all collectively create.[82]

It is important to note that the traditional approach to statutory interpretation is, in part, responsible for the increasing complexity of the *ITA*. Under strict interpretation or the plain meaning approach, taxpayers are entitled to benefit from any ambiguity in the legislation or unintentional glitches in the law that they (or their tax advisors) find by applying a literal reading of the law, until the ambiguity or glitches are addressed through legislation. New provisions of the *ITA* are drafted to be as detailed and airtight as possible. The *ITA* can only become inexorably longer and more complicated as Parliament must overturn decision after decision by statutory amendment. As the *ITA* becomes more detailed and complex, it breeds more aggressive tax planning and leaves less room for "liberal" interpretation, causing yet more amendments. The cycle perpetuates itself.

It is also important to keep in mind the fact that, despite its size and complexity, the *ITA* is just like any other statute. It has objectives and a legislative scheme. At a general level, the *ITA* has a well-structured scheme designed to meet its various social and economic policy objectives. Each provision of the *ITA* constitutes part of a coherent whole. As such, the common law presumption against tautology and the presumption of coherence and consistency make good sense in interpreting the *ITA* as well as other statutes.

---

[80] Learned Hand, "Thomas Walter Swan" (1947) 57 Yale L.J. 167 at 169.

[81] *Ipsco, supra* note 79 at para. 26.

[82] *Halvering v. Gregory*, 69 F.2d 809 (2nd Cir., 1934) at 810-811.

(ii) — Common law mentality

While income tax law is statutory law, its interpretation is a matter of common law. With the exception of those trained in the Quebec civil law system, judges generally possess the so-called "common law mentality". A great common law judge is described as the person "who has the intelligence to discern the best rule of law for the case at hand and then the skill to perform the broken-field running through earlier cases that leaves him free to impose that rule".[83] To the mindset of a common law judge, the key questions are "what is the most desirable resolution of this case?" and "how can any impediments to the achievement of that result be evaded?"[84] This mindset is often not appropriate in statutory interpretation. The judge must work with the text produced by Parliament, not common law broken-field running toward the end zone of good policy.[85] The precision and specificity of the language of the *ITA* represent the starkest contrast to the traditional common law mindset. The frequent amendments to the *ITA* to specifically overrule the common law do little to encourage judges to adjust their mindset to work with the legislative purpose and intent.

This inherent challenge for common law judges in working with the tax statute may explain some judicial interpretation practices. One is the judicial preference for getting the "right result" in a given case (which often means that the taxpayer gets the benefit of the doubt in case of any ambiguity in the text) over finding the purpose of the text or the intention of Parliament. For example, in determining whether strike pay is taxable in *R. v. Fries* (1990), Sopinka J. wrote the shortest decision in the Supreme Court's recent history (72 words), stating:

> We are not satisfied that the payments by way of strike pay in this case come within the definition of "income . . . from a source" within the meaning of section 3 of the *Income Tax Act*. In these circumstances the benefit of the doubt must go to the taxpayers.[86]

The context and purpose of section 3 are not mentioned and the clear wording — "from a source inside or outside Canada, including, without restricting the generality of the foregoing, the taxpayer's income for the year from each office, employment, business and property" — was ignored.

A second judicial practice is to follow a precedent or common law principle instead of giving a purposive interpretation of the statutory provision. For example, in *Tsiaprailis v. R.* (2005),[87] the issue was whether a lump-sum settlement received by the taxpayer from her employer's insurer under a disability policy must be in-

---

[83] Antonin Scalia, "Common-Law Courts in a Civil-Law System: The Role of United States Federal Courts in Interpreting the Constitution and Laws" in Amy Gutman, ed., *A Matter of Interpretation: Federal Courts and the Law* (Princeton, N.J.: Princeton University Press, 1997) at 9.

[84] *Ibid.* at 13.

[85] *Ibid.*

[86] *R. v. Fries*, [1990] 2 C.T.C. 439, 90 D.T.C. 6662 (S.C.C.).

[87] *Tsiaprailis v. R.*, [2005] 2 C.T.C. 1, 2005 D.T.C. 5119 (S.C.C.).

cluded in her income under paragraph 6(1)(f). Charron J. (writing for the majority) held that settlements were taxable and to conclude otherwise would "render the surrogatum principle meaningless".[88] The context and purpose of paragraph 6(1)(f) are not even mentioned.

The doctrine of precedent at common law poses a significant challenge to the movement towards a more purposive interpretation of the *ITA*. Reversing a precedent is a step not to be lightly taken and is done only in exceptional cases. In *Canada v. Craig* (2012),[89] the Supreme Court took such a step in overruling its decision in *Moldowan v. The Queen* (1978)[90] that interprets section 31 of the *ITA* in respect of farm losses:

> The *Moldowan* approach to the combination question is incorrect and it is appropriate for this Court to revisit this aspect of the interpretation of s. 31. Section 31(1) provides two distinct exceptions to the loss deduction limitation. A judge-made rule that reads one of them out of the provision cannot stand.[91]

The introduction of the GAAR signals Parliament's intent to reverse some of the common law traditions on statutory interpretation. As discussed further in Chapter 17, the GAAR has led to a more contextual and purposive interpretation of the *ITA*.

(iii) — Divergent theories about the role of judges

In traditional common law, the judges make the law and interpret the law. In statutory law, it takes two branches of the government — the legislature and the courts — to make and interpret the law. In income tax law, the administrative agency (the Canada Revenue Agency, or "CRA") also plays an important role in not only administering the law, but also interpreting it, as its views are one source of interpretive aid. The *ITA* is, perhaps, the most pervasive federal statute on the books, and has become an important governmental tool for influencing many aspects of modern Canadian life. As such, it is not surprising that there are divergent views on the role of the courts in giving meaning to the text of the *ITA*.

The textual, strict interpretation approach is closely associated with the restrictive theory of statutory interpretation and the doctrine of Parliamentary supremacy. Judges want no or minimal role in the making of tax law. McLachlin J. states in *Shell*:

> The Act is a complex statute through which Parliament seeks to balance a myriad of principles. This Court has consistently held that courts must therefore be cautious before finding within the clear provisions of the Act an unexpressed legislative intention . . . Finding unexpressed legislative intentions under the guise of purposive

---

[88] *Ibid.* at para. 16.

[89] *Canada v. Craig*, [2012] 5 C.T.C. 205, 2012 D.T.C. 5115 (Eng.), 2012 D.T.C. 5116 (Fr.) (S.C.C.) [*Craig*].

[90] *Moldowan v. The Queen* (1977), [1977] C.T.C. 310, 77 D.T.C. 5213 (S.C.C.).

[91] *Craig, supra* note 89 at para. 32.

interpretation runs the risk of upsetting the balance Parliament has attempted to strike in the Act.[92]

Iacobucci J. makes a similar point in *65302 British Columbia Ltd.*:

> The law of income tax is sufficiently complicated without unhelpful judicial incursions into the realm of lawmaking. As a matter of policy, and out of respect for the proper role of the legislature, it is trite to say that the promulgation of new rules of tax law must be left to Parliament.[93]

This narrow view of the role of the courts is problematic. While easy cases do exist, for the most part the disputes that reach the courtroom involve ambiguous statutory language. If judges simply interpret with the use of a dictionary or with reference to the ordinary plain meaning of the words, they can certainly resolve the particular dispute. However, it is highly questionable whether they have discharged the duty imposed on them. Chief Justice McLachlin writes about the changing role of the judges:

> Resolving disputes is still the primary and most fundamental task of the judiciary. But for some time now, it has been recognized that the matter is not so simple. In the course of resolving disputes, common law judges interpreted and inevitably, incrementally, with the aid of the doctrine of precedent or *stare decisis*, changed the law. The common law thus came to recognize that while dispute resolution was the primary task of the judge, the judge played a secondary role of lawmaker, or at least, law-developer. In the latter part of the twentieth century, the lawmaking role of the judge has dramatically expanded. Judicial lawmaking is no longer always confined to small, incremental changes. Increasingly, it is invading the domain of social policy, once perceived as the exclusive right of Parliament and the legislatures.[94]

The Chief Justice's view of a more active role for judges in general stands in contrast to her restrictive view of the judicial role in tax cases. Since the *ITA* is, arguably, one of the most important instruments of social policy in Canada, a more purposive interpretation of the *ITA* is more consistent with her vision of the role of judges.

The doctrine of legislative supremacy provides the conceptual basis for statutory interpretation, as it means how much, if any, policymaking discretion is left for those interpreting and implementing the legislature's statutes. It supports both the strict, textual interpretation and the more liberal, purposive interpretation. The strict textual interpretation reflects the value of this doctrine: the legislature is supreme and it enacts laws into statutory text. Judges are the "honest agents" of the legisla-

---

[92] *Shell, supra* note 26 at para. 43.

[93] *65302 BC, supra* note 47 at para. 62.

[94] "The Role of Judges in Modern Society: Remarks of the Right Honourable Beverley McLachlin, P.C.", The Fourth Worldwide Common Law Judiciary Conference, Vancouver, British Columbia (5 May 2001), online: <http://www.scc-csc.ca/judges-juges/spe-dis/bm-2001-05-05-eng.aspx>.

ture and "carry out decisions they do not make."[95] Under such a theory, judicial discretion to make law is suspect in statutory interpretation.

A more liberal and purposive interpretation of statutes also finds support in the legislative supremacy doctrine. It was argued that "purposive interpretation . . . better accords with the principle of legislative supremacy",[96] and "intelligent judicial cooperation" is important in a Parliamentary democracy in the "fulfillment of the aims and objects of parliament".[97] The Supreme Court of Canada recognizes this view in *Mathew*:

> To resolve the dispute arising from the combined operation of s. 18(13) and s. 96 of the *Income Tax Act*, it is necessary to determine Parliament's intention in enacting these provisions by interpreting them purposively, in light of their context.[98]

Chief Justice McLachlin acknowledges that judges play "a secondary role of lawmaker, or at least, law-developer".[99] The cooperative relationship between Parliament and the courts is particularly important in certain areas of tax law where it is inherently difficult for Parliament to use precise language in the statute in order to achieve its legislative goals.

16.4 — Characterization of facts

(a) — Importance of characterization

The starting point for applying the *ITA* is to know what the Act is being applied to. This sounds simple and obvious, perhaps, but it is surprising how many tax analyses take this formative step for granted. Characterization of facts is foundational. Much of tax practice is concerned with "the facts", and most tax avoidance controversies are mostly fundamentally factual, despite the fact that often-extensive consideration of the meaning of the law is almost as would be entailed in a reference case.

Characterizing — that is inferring or understanding — "the facts" engages a range of legal considerations. It is grounded not only in tax law but also private law, as well as evidence-based inquiries into what taxpayers did regardless of how they may have recorded their arrangements.[100] How to characterize a transaction for tax

---

[95] See, e.g., Frank H. Easterbrook, "The Supreme Court, 1983 Term — Foreword: The Court and the Economic System, (1984) 98 Harv. L. Rev. 4 at 60; and Frank H. Easterbrook, The Role of Original Intent in Statutory Construction, (1988) 11 Harv. J.L. & Pub. Policy 59 (arguing that an honest agent will look only to statutory language in discharging her responsibilities).

[96] Willis, *supra* note 18 at 14.

[97] J.A. Corry, "Administrative Law and the Interpretation of Statutes" (1936), 1 U.T.L.J. 286 at 289.

[98] *Mathew*, *supra* note 51 at para. 40.

[99] McLachlin, *supra* 94.

[100] See, e.g., *Continental Bank of Canada and Continental Bank Leasing Corporation v. The Queen* (1994), [1995] 1 C.T.C. 2135, 94 D.T.C. 1858 (T.C.C.); additional reasons 1994 Car-

purposes is important because different types of transactions attract different tax treatment. For example, in the *Duke of Westminster* case payments under an "employment contract" were not tax-deductible, but payments under an "annuity contract" were. The nearly unlimited range of transactions must be categorized in terms of the provisions of the *ITA*. The Act necessarily has a limited number of terms, many of which are imported into it with their meaning established in private law (e.g., contracts, property, etc.). The challenge is whether the legal rights and obligations created under private law should be respected for tax purposes.

Very often, the legal rights and obligations created in private law are determinative for tax purposes. Unless the legal relationship is a sham or invalid, in most cases, the legal forms must inevitably be controlling. The courts would assume an extraordinary power if, for taxation purposes, they could ignore such basic matters as the obligations of a deed of covenant, the legal and beneficial ownership of property, and the separate legal personalities of different companies. Therefore, the courts will not disregard genuinely created legal relationships. Indeed, tax law would become intolerably uncertain if courts felt unconstrained by the legal form of the taxpayer's arrangements, and felt free to impose tax on a different basis.

Characterization of facts is obviously a different question from whether the *ITA* should be given a strict or a purposive interpretation. But the two questions are intimately related. Under a regime of strict interpretation, the courts are less likely to read the *ITA* as authorizing an inquiry that goes beyond a legal form and substance than they are under a regime of purposive interpretation. Under a regime of purposive interpretation, a purposive constructive of the legal arrangements may be more appealing.

---

swellNat 2669 (T.C.C.); affirmed [1996] 3 C.T.C. 14, 96 D.T.C. 6355 at 6368 (Fed. C.A.); affirmed [1998] 4 C.T.C. 77, 98 D.T.C. 6501 (S.C.C.); reversed (1996), [1997] 1 C.T.C. 13, 96 D.T.C. 6355 (Fed. C.A.); reversed [1998] 4 C.T.C. 119, 98 D.T.C. 6505 (S.C.C.) [*Continental Bank*]. The T.C.C. decision was appealed to and ultimately upheld by the Supreme Court of Canada, but is cited here for Tax Court Chief Justice Bowman's incisive legal analysis, notably at 1869–1871 [D.T.C. (T.C.C.)], where what some might have called an "economic substance" inquiry is configured more thoughtfully as an inquiry into the "legal substance" of the arrangements underlying the application of the *ITA* — in other words, the correspondence between the manner in which the taxpayers formulated their arrangements and evidence as to what they expected of each other and, therefore, what the essence of their arrangement was. If the "form" of the arrangement and the manner in which the parties evidently performed it — relied on it — would align, then that is "the transaction"; if not, the inquiry must rely on evidence as to the parties dealings, not as an economic exercise but to discover their legal arrangements. For the importance of inquiring into the "legal substance" of taxpayers' arrangements, see also *The Queen v. GlaxoSmithKline Inc.* (2012), [2012] 3 S.C.R. 3, [2013] 1 C.T.C. 99, 2012 D.T.C. 5147 (Eng.), 2012 D.T.C. 5148 (Fr.) (S.C.C.) [*GlaxoSmithKline*], notably at paras. 52–58, in which the Supreme Court of Canada effectively anticipates the possibility that the formal written contracts in a transfer pricing case might not fully reflect all the contractual relations that mattered for the application of the *ITA*.

(b) — Legal rights and obligations created in private law

(i) — Form versus substance

The *Duke of Westminster* case indicates that the success of the Duke's tax avoidance plan depended upon the Court's willingness to characterize the agreements entered into with his servants as annuity contracts rather than employment contracts — possibly more accurately to respect the private law formulations of these arrangements, their "legal substance", provided that the parties to those arrangements were actually behaving in a fashion consistent with those arrangements despite other legal formulations that conceivably could have and indeed formerly had had the same economic outcome. The Court's acceptance of the legal form (annuity) rather than the commercial substance (employment) was critical to the success of the plan. In so doing, however, the Court was not inventing a characterization. As is clear, the Court probed the legal arrangement adopted by the parties despite economically equivalent alternate legal formulations, and enforced the deeds. The Court understood that the gardener's employment was the context in which the Duke visited his largesse, a little like a pension of sorts, on the gardener. But, what the Court enforced is what the Court saw, after taking account of the relevant evidence.

In tax law, form matters, not for its own sake, but as a foundation on which the tax law then applies. The firmness of that undoubtedly is influenced by the facts, the discovery of which is a legal and not an economic exercise, and also the legal culture at the time when decisions about the effectiveness of tax planning are being made.[101]

Similarly, in the *Stubart* case,[102] the Court accepted the legal forms (sale and agency agreement), although the commercial substance of the arrangement was that Stubart had not divested itself of the business. While testing the effectiveness of taxpayers' transactions in a tax avoidance context may be described as evaluating the form in relation to the substance, as we point out, what is actually being undertaken is a thorough inquiry according to the law into the effectiveness, and then fiscal effectiveness, of taxpayers' arrangements. This is what Chief Justice Bowman aptly referred to as "legal substance" in the *Continental Bank* case.[103]

(ii) — Substance over form

While the courts should not freely disregard the taxpayer's legal relationships in general, this does not mean that the courts should always be bound by such relationships, especially where the actual legal relationships were different from legal

---

[101] It is important to bear this in mind in deciding how readily decisions in a particular circumstance at a particular time may apply to different circumstances or at a different time.

[102] *Stubart, supra* note 17.

[103] *Continental Bank, supra* note 100 [(T.C.C.)].

substance[104] or "true character".[105] Expressing the idea more colourfully, "calling a horse a dog does not make the horse a dog".[106] On the other hand, if it is a dog, the fact that one might not like the breed makes it no less a dog.

There are some examples where the courts find the legal form mischaracterizes the legal substance.[107] In general, however, "[r]echaracterization is only permissible if the label attached by the taxpayer to the particular transaction does not properly reflect its actual legal effect".[108] In determining whether the "label" (i.e., the legal relationships existing between parties to a transaction as evidenced by the words of the documents used to label the transaction) reflects the actual legal rights and obligations agreed to by the parties, the courts may examine the actions taken by the parties. In *Backman v. R.* (2001),[109] for example, a "partnership" was found not to exist because the evidence did not show that the parties intended to carry on business with a view to profit.

(iii) — Legal underpinnings of tax law

The search for "substance" — whether in the facts or the law — does not entail an inquiry outside the law or the substitution of extra-legal considerations for the law in force. As mentioned in discussing the evolution and the varieties of statutory interpretation, it should be remembered that taxpayers and tax law exist within the legal system. The legal system is replete with constructions — fictions — essential for orderly and predictable behavior by and among citizens, institutions and even nations. Perhaps the inquiry and the struggle by adjudicators to square their "substance"-oriented reactions to circumstances with legal doctrine and statutory provi-

---

[104] *Ibid.*, per Bastarache J. [(S.C.C.)].

[105] *Purdy v. Minister of National Revenue*, [1985] 1 C.T.C. 2294, 85 D.T.C. 254 (T.C.C.).

[106] *Gillette Canada Inc. v. The Queen*, [2001] 4 C.T.C. 2884, 2001 D.T.C. 895 (T.C.C. [General Procedure]); affirmed [2003] 3 C.T.C. 27, 2003 D.T.C. 5078 (Fed. C.A.).

[107] E.g., a contract for independent services was recharacterized as a contract of employment (see *CCLI (1994) Inc. v. The Queen*, [2006] 4 C.T.C. 2001, 2006 D.T.C. 2695 (Eng.) (T.C.C. [General Procedure]); reversed in part [2007] 4 C.T.C. 19, 2007 D.T.C. 5372 (Eng.) (F.C.A.) at para. 26 [(T.C.C.)]); a "retiring allowance" was recharacterized as consideration for the surrender of a share (see *Milne v. R.*, [1994] 2 C.T.C. 2190 (T.C.C.)); consulting fees were recharacterized as payments for goodwill (see *Bowens v. R.*, [1994] 2 C.T.C. 2404, 94 D.T.C. 1853 (T.C.C.); affirmed [1996] 2 C.T.C. 120, 96 D.T.C. 6128 (Fed. C.A.)); and a lump-sum payment made by a lessee to a lessor was characterized as income rather than capital on the basis that its substance was a prepayment of rent, causing the lessor to agree to receive (and pay tax on) a lower rate of rent (see *Front & Simcoe Ltd. v. Minister of National Revenue*, [1960] C.T.C. 123, 60 D.T.C. 1081 (Can. Ex. Ct.)).

[108] *Shell*, *supra* note 26 at para. 39.

[109] *Backman v. R.* (2001), [2001] 2 C.T.C. 11, 2001 D.T.C. 5149 (S.C.C.). The Court stated at para. 25: "[T]o ascertain the existence of a partnership the courts must inquire into whether the objective, documentary evidence and the surrounding facts, including what the parties actually did, are consistent with a subjective intention to carry on business in common with a view to profit."

sions including the GAAR — which entails analysis that is "substantial" in the legal sense whether to determine facts, understand law or test the alignment of facts as disclosed by evidence and the law — is best understood as Chief Justice Bowman explained it in the *Continental Bank* case:[110]

> So far as the broader question of substance versus form is concerned, we should at least be clear on what we are talking about when we use the elusive expression "substance over form". Cartwright, J. (as he then was) said in *Dominion Taxicab Assn. v. M.N.R.*, 54 DTC 1020 at p. 1021:
>
>> It is well settled that in considering whether a particular transaction brings a party within the terms of the Income Tax Acts [sic] its substance rather than its form is to be regarded.
>
> His Lordship did not elaborate but in light of other authorities I do not think that his words can be taken to mean that the legal effect of a transaction is irrelevant or that one is entitled to treat substance as synonymous with economic effect. The true meaning of the expression is, I believe, found in the judgment of Christie, A.C.J.T.C.C., in *Purdy v. M.N.R.*, 85 DTC 254 at p. 256, where he said:
>
>> It must be borne in mind that in deciding questions pertaining to liability for income tax the manner in which parties to transactions choose to label them does not necessarily govern. What must be done is to determine what on the evidence is the substance or true character of the transaction and render judgment accordingly.
>
> Viscount Simon in delivering the judgment of the House of Lords in *Commissioners of Inland Revenue v. Wesleyan and General Assurance Society* (1948), 30 T.C. 11, said at page 25:
>
>> It may be well to repeat two propositions which are well established in the application of the law relating to Income Tax. First, the name given to a transaction by the parties concerned does not necessarily decide the nature of the transaction. To call a payment a loan if it is really an annuity does not assist the taxpayer, any more than to call an item a capital payment would prevent it from being regarded as an income payment if that is its true nature. The question always is what is the real character of the payment, not what the parties call it.
>
> In *Front & Simcoe Ltd. v. M.N.R.*, 60 DTC 1081, Cameron, J., said at page 1085:
>
>> In *Simon's Income Tax*, Second Ed., Vol. 1, p. 50, the author, after referring to a number of decisions, states:
>>
>>> The true principle, then, is that the taxing Acts are to be applied in accordance with the legal rights of the parties to a transaction. It is those rights which determine what is the "substance" of the transaction in the correct usage of that term. Reading "substance" in that way, it is still true to say that the substance of a transaction prevails over its nomenclature.

These observations highlight the essence of the interpretive exercise — discovering by construction what the law is and what it means in relation to the facts. Relieved

---

[110] *Continental Bank*, *supra* note 100 at paras. 83-86. [(T.C.C.)].

of the colour of the *Duke of Westminster* mantra that taxpayers are entitled to arrange their affairs to pay as little tax as the law permits — which is not the fiscal equivalent of "anything goes" — the inherent "legally substantial" ground of statutory interpretation is revealed. This is the case even where the sham doctrine is thought not to apply in the absence of deceit akin to the criminal law's *mens rea*. Similarly, Justice Rothstein's implied instruction in the *GlaxoSmithKline* case[111] to inquire into legal arrangements — contractual dealings — that might exist apart from the obvious written contracts is a polite reminder that the dealings with which the *ITA* contends have to be discovered and evaluated in relation to relevant evidence — and this is not the same thing as an "economic substance" or "economic reality" test overriding the law.

A recent expression of the judicial respect for the legal underpinnings of the *ITA*, or legal substance as we call it, even in the context of a tax avoidance inquiry, is found in Justice Sharlow's reasons in the Federal Court of Appeal's decision in the *Garron Trust* case, more formally St. Michael Trust Corp., as Trustee of the Fundy Settlement and of the Summersby Settlement.[112] Fundamentally, this case concerned whether to respect the residence of two offshore trusts employed as part of a tax plan to freeze the value of shares of a Canadian corporation and then dispose of them free of Canadian tax relying on the gains article of the Canada-Barbados Income Tax Convention.[113] The systematic deference of the trustee to the settlor of the trusts was found to so undermine the independence of the trustee that the trusts were found to be Canadian residents, relying on an adaptation of the corporate tax residence test of "central management and control". However, in outlining the qualities of independence that were missing in the administration of these trusts by the trustee, Justice Sharlow effectively sheds light, not only in the immediate situation but more generally, on the kind of respect for legal constructions that courts expect — that the *ITA* expects — for tax consequences planned by taxpayers to prevail.

In summarizing, in a relatively benign descriptive way, what might be called the "bad" facts in paragraph 66 of her reasons, Justice Sharlow implicitly indicates what would have been persuasive "good" facts. The Court was working within the expectations of the legal arrangements undertaken by the parties: What is a trust? What are the roles and responsibilities of a trustee? What does it mean to settle a trust, to part with ownership of property in favour of others? These are the questions that evidently underlie the factual analysis. Despite the obvious connotation

---

[111] *GlaxoSmithKline, supra* note 100.

[112] *Garron Family Trust (Trustee of) v. R.*, 2010 FCA 309, [2011] 2 C.T.C. 7, 2010 D.T.C. 5189 (Eng.) (F.C.A.); affirmed [2012] 3 C.T.C. 265, 2012 D.T.C. 5063 (Eng.), 2012 D.T.C. 5064 (Fr.) (S.C.C.). The Federal Court of Appeal upheld the Tax Court of Canada's decision, and later the Federal Court of Appeal's decision was not disturbed by the Supreme Court of Canada.

[113] Agreement Between Canada and Barbados for the Avoidance of Double Taxation and the Prevention of Fiscal Evasion with Respect to Taxes on Income and on Capital, 22 January 1980, E102234 — CTS 1980 No. 29 [Canada-Barbados Income Tax Agreement].

of tax avoidance — the continuing economic interest of the settlor in the settled property — the Court did not defer to economic substance or economic realities as some sort of supervening force to displace the law. To the contrary, the Court tested the circumstances disclosed by the evidence with reference to what the law expects, what frames its legal constructions?

A trust is an obligation undertaken by a person, the trustee, to hold and administer property formerly belonging to another person, the settlor, for the benefit of persons the settlor directs are to benefit, the beneficiaries. The same economic effect could be achieved by a disciplined settlor who simply segregated income-generating property informally (e.g., in a separate account), and made payments, gifts, from time to time to persons intended to benefit. In that case, all of the tax consequences associated with the ownership of the property would be those of the property owner; the income on the informally segregated property would be that of its owner. The law of trust, as the tax law accommodates it, expects a real legal separation of the settlor from the property. The test of whether that expectation is satisfied works within the law of trust, and determines whether, according to evidence gathered and tested as the law provides, the circumstances align with the law's expectation. That is not a substance over form analysis. Equally, it is not a displacement of the law, formal or not, by economic realities. It is a determination, rather, of what the law is and whether what the law supposes would occur did, in fact, occur.

Was Justice Sharlow telegraphing an indomitable and slavish adherence to form for form's sake? No, she was not. Was she taking for granted that the law is the framework within which a taxpayer's conduct should be evaluated? Yes, she was.

As formalistic as the gardener's arrangements in the *Duke of Westminster* case may seem, the employment context in which the gardener, a long-time employee, realized the Duke's benefaction did not transform the deeds according to their terms into something else. Many things with different legal characteristics are or may seem economically equivalent. But most are themselves creatures of the law. Testing their effectiveness is an exercise in applying the law; it is not a moral, spiritual, economic or political exercise, even though applying the law thoughtfully ought to yield conclusions that are consistent both with what taxpayers did and what the "object and spirit" or purpose of the law is discovered or revealed to be. When there seems to be misalignment is when those charged with interpreting the law need to work a little harder.

(c) — Economic substance

The economic substance doctrine has been applied by courts in the United States and, to lesser extent, in the U.K. to attack aggressive tax avoidance transactions. The U.S. courts have long held that if a business transaction has no value except to create tax losses, then it can be disallowed by the government. "Otherwise, tax lawyers could just move symbols around pieces of paper, and their clients would never pay taxes."[114] The United States has now codified the economic substance doctrine[115] and U.K. has adopted the GAAR.[116]

(i) — No recharacterization of "bona fide" legal relationships

The shift towards the plain meaning approach was accompanied by a more explicit recognition of "legal" substance and virtual rejection of the "economic" substance doctrine. For example, McLachlin J. stated in *Shell*:

> . . . this Court has never held that the economic realities of a situation can be used to recharacterize a taxpayer's bona fide relationships. To the contrary, we have held that, absent a specific provision of the Act to the contrary or a finding that they are a sham, the taxpayer's legal relationships must be respected in tax cases . . .[117]

The principle in *Shell* is, therefore, that *bona fide* legal relationships created by the taxpayer cannot be recharacterized to reflect the economic realities. Since this principle applies only to "*bona fide* legal relationships", it is necessary to make a normative inquiry into whether or not such relations are created *bona fide*. The Court has not provided any guidelines for such inquiry. In fact, there seem to have been no cases in which the Court found the taxpayer's relationships not to be *bona fide*. The *Shell* principle resonates well with the *Duke of Westminster* principles. The substance of a taxpayer's legal relationships, especially those created with professional advice, is generally consistent with the form of the legal arrangements.

In cases where the tax avoidance purpose is achieved through a series of transactions or multiple legal steps, the *Shell* principle requires each transaction or step to

---

[114] D.C. Johnston, "A Tax Shelter, Destructed," *New York Times* (13 July 2003).

[115] In March 2010, this test was codified as section 7701(o) of the U.S. *Internal Revenue Code*. To meet the U.S. economic substance test, a transaction must change a taxpayer's economic position in a meaningful way, ignoring any tax benefits. To demonstrate a meaningful change in economic position, the taxpayer must rely on such factors as business or regulatory realities, the fact that the transaction was imbued with tax-independent considerations and that the transaction was not shaped solely by tax avoidance features that have meaningless labels attached. A taxpayer can also rely on profit potential to prove economic substance, but only if the present value of the reasonably expected pre-tax profit from the transaction is substantial in relation to the present value of the expected net tax benefits that would be allowed if the transaction were respected. The notion of "pre-tax profit" refers to profit before considering the tax benefits. In computing the pre-tax profit, transaction fees and other expenses must be taken into account as expenses. It is interesting to observe that in *Altria Group, Inc. v. United States* (2010), U.S. courts found transactions similar to those in *Canada Trustco* lacked economic substance and denied the taxpayer the tax benefits of ownership (i.e., the depreciation deduction associated with the cost of acquiring the assets).

[116] The U.K. GAAR legislation is set out in Part 5 of FA 2013 and Schedules 43 to 43C to that Act.

[117] *Shell, supra* note 26 at paras. 39–40. For an excellent overview of the form over substance doctrine, see Chief Justice Bowman's decision in *Continental Bank, supra* note 100 [(T.C.C.)].

be characterized separately without looking at the overall purpose or effect of these transactions.

(ii) — Potential relevance of economic substance of transactions

In applying the GAAR, the economic substance of the transaction may be relevant. In the *Canada Trustco* case,[118] the Supreme Court of Canada referred to the statement by the Department of Finance "that the provisions of the Act are intended to apply to transactions with real economic substance".[119] The Court has not provided much guidance on the scope of "economic substance" and the circumstances in which economic substance prevails.

Some provisions of the *ITA* explicitly require an examination of the economic substance or business reality of the transactions, or so it might be said. Examples are section 67 and former subsection 69(2) ("reasonable in the circumstances") and subsection 247(2) ("terms or conditions . . . that would have been made between persons dealing at arm's length"). In such cases, the courts are not limited by the formalistic, *Singleton* approach, and consider the impugned transactions in light of the economic and business reality of the transactions, including other related contracts and arrangements.[120]

But being aware of the facts to which the law applies — which is what the application of the law always involved — does not mean that the law is being interpreted or applied according to economic substance. It's being applied to what happened, but what happened is not necessarily self-evident either factually or in terms of the meaning of relevant legislative provisions. That's where an evidence-based application of the law comes into play. There is nothing particularly unusual about this.

---

[118] *Canada Trustco, supra* note 2.

[119] Canada, Department of Finance, *Explanatory Notes to Legislation Relating to Income Tax* (Ottawa: June 1988) at 464-465. The Supreme Court of Canada quoted the above paragraph in *Canada Trustco, supra* note 2 at paras. 48–49.

[120] See, e.g., *GlaxoSmithKline, supra* note 100. In this case, the taxpayer entered into two separate contracts with its foreign related companies: a licence agreement to obtain the rights to use certain intangible property, including the brand name Zantac for the drug, and a supply agreement to purchase ingredients for making the drug. The issue was whether the price paid for the ingredients was excessively high and, thus, not "reasonable in the circumstances" within the meaning of former subsection 69(2). The Minister did not challenge the rate of royalty under the licence agreement and applied the *Singleton* test (*Singleton, supra* note 28) in singling out the supply agreement in reassessing the taxpayer. The Minister's position was upheld by the Tax Court of Canada, but overturned by the Federal Court of Appeal and the Supreme Court of Canada. The Supreme Court stated at para. 44: "Because s. 69(2) requires an inquiry into the price that would be reasonable in the circumstances had the non-resident supplier and the Canadian taxpayer been dealing at arm's length, it necessarily involves consideration of all circumstances of the Canadian taxpayer relevant to the price paid to the non-resident supplier. Such circumstances will include agreements that may confer rights and benefits in addition to the purchase of property where those agreements are linked to the purchasing agreement."

However, commentaries on statutory interpretation in the tax area, especially in the context of the GAAR, have sometimes resulted in distractions associated with doctrinal distinctions possibly without any differences "in substance".

(d) — Purpose of transactions

(i) — Primary purpose

The business purpose test can be used as an anti-avoidance rule — where a transaction lacks a primary business (or non-tax) purpose, the intended tax result of the transaction is denied.[121] Before *Stubart*,[122] there had been occasional cases in which Canadian courts had applied a business purpose test in order to defeat artificial tax avoidance schemes, but these cases ran against the general current of authority, which remained faithful to the *Duke of Westminster* case.[123]

The *Duke of Westminster* case was an authority for the proposition that there was no business purpose test in tax jurisprudence. In that case, the deeds of covenant that the Duke entered into with his servants were effective for tax purposes, despite the fact that they had been brought into existence solely to avoid tax. The deeds of covenant were not characterized as employment contracts despite the fact that the beneficiary of the deeds was in service to the Duke and continued to work during the term of the deeds, and the legal culture of the time distinguished between contracts of service and other legal arrangements. The legal arrangements were construed and applied as the rights and obligations between the parties existed, despite

---

[121] In the United States, a business purpose test has been adopted by Courts as either a stand-alone anti-avoidance doctrine or part of the economic substance doctrine. Under this doctrine, tax benefits with respect to a transaction are not allowable if the transaction does not have economic substance or lacks a business purpose. Whether a taxpayer has a substantial business (or non-tax) purpose for entering into a transaction is determined on the basis of objective facts, such as whether the transaction was structured and implemented to make a profit. In the U.K., a business purpose test has been applied by the House of Lords to a "step transaction". In *Furniss v. Dawson* (1984), [1984] A.C. 474 (U.K. H.L.), the House of Lords charged the vendor of property with a capital gain, although the capital gain had actually been received by a company owned and controlled by the vendor that was incorporated in the Isle of Man (a tax haven). Their lordships held that the transaction was to be regarded as a sale and purchase between two U.K. parties, which was the commercial reality. The intermediate step of transferring the property to the controlled Isle of Man company (which then sold the property to the true purchaser) had been undertaken solely to divert the capital gain to the Isle of Man and avoid its recognition in the U.K. Their lordships held that this "inserted step", because it had "no business purpose apart from the deferment of tax", was to be disregarded for tax purposes. The business purpose test of *Furniss v. Dawson* has been confined to "step transactions", or "composite transactions", as they are known in the U.K. Even so, the case obviously constitutes a radical change in the approach of the House of Lords to artificial tax avoidance schemes. As Lord Roskill noted in *Furniss v. Dawson* at 515, the *Duke of Westminster* case, *supra* note 11, was now seriously undermined in the U.K.

[122] *Stubart, supra* note 17.

[123] *Duke of Westminster, supra* note 11.

the reason for the arrangement and its context, taking account of evidence that the deeds were performed according to their terms. As noted earlier, economically equivalent outcomes may have quite different legal formulations. But that, in itself, is not a reason for disregarding the legal arrangements undertaken by taxpayers if the taxpayers have actually respected those arrangements.

The relevance of the business purpose test in Canada was fully argued before the Supreme Court of Canada in the *Stubart* case. Counsel for the Minister argued that the transfer of assets between the two subsidiaries should be disregarded for tax purposes on the ground that it lacked any business purpose other than the avoidance of tax. Estey J. for the majority of the Supreme Court of Canada reviewed the American, English and Canadian authorities, and rejected the business purpose test for Canada: "I would therefore reject the proposition that a transaction may be disregarded for tax purposes solely on the basis that it was entered into by a taxpayer without an independent or *bona fide* business purpose."[124] In other words, courts had no power to disregard a transaction for tax purposes simply because the transaction lacked an independent business purpose.

Parliament enacted the GAAR in 1988, principally in response to the *Stubart* decision. A "non-tax purpose" test has now been codified into the GAAR. Even according to the GAAR, the absence of a non-tax purpose is insufficient, itself, to disregard a tax outcome. This might be sufficient to invoke the GAAR — to establish the existence of an "avoidance transaction" — but whether the GAAR applies is determined by whether the *ITA* or its provisions have been abused or misused.

Outside the GAAR, the business purpose doctrine was rejected in *Stubart*. Some decisions of the Courts, in the absence of countervailing factual or legal arguments presented to them, may seem surprisingly respectful of formalism.[125] It is important to understand, however, that the *Duke of Westminster* case, in the present environment, is capable of being construed in a more refined way that is not as respectful of form as might too frequently be perceived.[126]

(ii) — Step transactions

When a taxpayer takes multiple steps to achieve the overall result, an issue may arise as to the overall purpose of the transactions and whether each step is examined separately. Outside the GAAR, the prevailing law is illustrated by the decision in the *Singleton* case.[127] The taxpayer was a partner of a law firm and had at

---

[124] *Stubart, supra* note 17 at para. 55.

[125] See *Veracity, supra* note 8; *TDL, supra* note 8; *Inter-Leasing, supra* note 8; *Husky, supra* note 8.

[126] As noted earlier, good tax planning may be seen as planning to avoid the tax that should not be paid, not to avoid the tax that should be paid.

[127] *Singleton, supra* note 28.

least $300,000 in his capital account at the firm before October 27, 1988. On October 27, 1988, he did the following transactions:

- Borrowed $298,750 from a bank and used the house he was going to purchase as a mortgage;

- Paid $300,000 (the $298,750 borrowed money along with $1,250 of his own money) into the taxpayer's capital account at the firm;

- Received a $300,000 cheque from the firm and deposited it into his personal bank account;

- Issued a cheque of $300,000 drawn on his personal bank account to pay for the purchase of the house.

The exact sequence of the above transactions was disputed. Unfortunately, it is the sequencing of the transactions that determines the outcome of the case.

The issue was whether the taxpayer could deduct the interest paid on the money borrowed from the bank under paragraph 20(1)(c) of the *ITA*. The Minister denied the interest deduction on the ground that the borrowed money was used to finance the purchase of the house (an ineligible use of the borrowed money). Bowman J. of the Tax Court of Canada upheld the Minister's assessment. He took a "realistic" view of the transactions and concluded that, on October 27, 1988, the borrowed money was channeled through the firm and immediately went to the taxpayer for the purchase of the house. He remarked:

> On any realistic view of the matter it could not be said that the money was used for the purpose of making a contribution of capital to the partnership. The fundamental purpose was the purchase of a house and this purpose cannot be altered by the shuffle of cheques that took place on October 27, 1988.[128]

Bowman J. added that the steps of the transaction were "conterminous and interdependent". Even if the legal validity of the steps was accepted and the tax motivation treated as irrelevant, he concluded that "... one is still left with the inescapable factual determination that the true economic purpose for which the borrowed money was used was the purchase of a house, not the enhancement of the firm's income earning potential by a contribution of capital."[129]

Bowman J.'s decision was overruled by the majority of the Federal Court of Appeal and the Supreme Court of Canada. Major J., writing for the majority of the Supreme Court, held that the taxpayer was entitled to deduct the interest expense. Paragraph 20(1)(c) of the *ITA* requires, among other conditions, that *the borrowed money be used for the purpose of earning non-exempt income from a business or property* and that a direct link be drawn between the borrowed money and an eligible use. Investment in the firm by paying into the capital account is an "eligible use". Given that the taxpayer had at least $300,000 of his own money in the law firm and he was free to use his own money or borrowed money to finance the

---

[128] *Ibid.* at para. 30 [(T.C.C.)].

[129] *Ibid.* at para. 16 [(T.C.C.)].

business of his law firm, Major J. found a direct link between the borrowed money and financing the law firm. He stated:

> In reviewing what the respondent did, it is clear that the relevant cheques were deposited and honoured. There is no suggestion that the transaction was a sham. Giving effect to the legal relationships in this case, it is clear that the respondent used the borrowed funds to refinance his capital account.[130]

Major J. further stated that the characterization of the use of the funds is not altered by the fact that the transactions occurred on the same day.[131]

Despite the way the Supreme Court reasoned its outcome, it is interesting to reflect on what actually occurred. At one level — a level that was not controlling for the Supreme Court — the case could be portrayed as a borrowing to purchase a personal residence, on which interest would not be deductible. But more was going on; the taxpayer's circumstances, as they transpired, created for him two borrowing needs, one to fund his professional practice and the other to buy a house. Had fortune allowed these events to take place according to a more fortuitous sequence, the case might not have arisen. As noted, the case essentially concerned whether the sequence of transactions should affect their results where, had they occurred in a different order — that is, had the taxpayer known when he bought his house that he would also need to borrow working capital for his professional practice — the contested issue would not have arisen. Even more penetrating, the further question is whether the accidental, unplanned ordering of transactions deprived the taxpayer of securing an outcome that, quite clearly, the *ITA* could fairly accommodate, namely a business borrowing on the one hand (interest on which would be deductible), and a personal borrowing on the other (interest on which would not be deductible). Recalling earlier discussions on statutory interpretation, can it be said that the result in this case is entirely in keeping with the legal substance of the arrangements and a thoughtful, contextual and purposive construction of the *ITA* in the circumstances? Maybe in less benign circumstances, but they were not present in this case. The outcome in this case gives effect to a textual, contextual and purposive interpretation of the *ITA*, avoiding a perversion of the outcome intended by the Act (which would arise from an excessively formalistic application of the law).

As discussed further in Chapter 17, in cases where the GAAR is invoked, however, the primary purpose of each transaction in a "series of transactions" and the overall result of the series are relevant.

(e) — Sham

As alluded to earlier in this chapter, legal relationships are ignored if they amount to a sham. In Canada, the sham doctrine has been occasionally applied by courts to

---

[130] *Ibid.* at para. 32 [(S.C.C.)].

[131] *Ibid.* at para. 34 [(S.C.C.)]: "In my respectful opinion, it is an error to treat this as one simultaneous transaction. In order to give effect to the legal relationships, the transactions must be viewed independently."

defeat blatant, artificial tax structures. A "sham" was defined in the *Snook v. London & West Riding Investments Ltd.* (1967) case as

> . . . acts done or documents executed by the parties to the "sham" which are intended by them to give to third parties or to the court the appearance of creating between the parties' legal rights and obligations different from the actual legal rights and obligations (if any) which the parties intend to create.[132]

The *Snook* definition makes clear that a sham always involves an element of deceit. A transaction is not a sham merely because it is artificial, contrived, or lacking in an independent business purpose.[133] There is no sham where the legal formalities accurately reflect the true relationship between the parties. In the *Duke of Westminster* case, for example, the deeds of covenant entered into by the Duke with his servants were *bona fide* instruments under which the Duke genuinely undertook an enforceable obligation to pay the annuities. The deeds were not deceptive and, therefore, could not be regarded as shams.[134]

Persistently, a sham is considered generally to require deliberate deceit by a taxpayer akin to the *mens rea* standard of the criminal law, even though it is possible to conduct a more objective construction that infers the requisite deceit from the incompatibility of a taxpayer's conduct with how that conduct is portrayed. This doctrine allows the court to ignore the "façade" created by the taxpayer, and to impose tax in accordance with the true facts. If an entire transaction is a sham, the transaction will be completely ineffective. For example, parties may create false documentation for the sale of an asset when no such sale occurred (the motive could be to create a capital loss for the pretended vendor). If only part of the transaction was a sham, then the transaction will be effective in accordance with the actual rights and liabilities created. For example, if an asset is actually sold for $1, but the parties inserted a figure of $150 for consideration in the documentation (perhaps to increase the purchaser's capital cost allowance deduction), the tax consequences would be determined based on the actual consideration of $1.

Canadian courts have adopted the *Snook* definition of "sham",[135] but have applied it sparingly. In the *Stubart* case, the Court concluded that there was a genuine sale of assets and agency agreement between the sister corporations. There was no sham because there was no attempt to create "a false impression" for tax purposes: the "appearance" was "precisely the reality", and fully enforceable obligations were

---

[132] *Snook v. London & West Riding Investments Ltd.* (1967), [1967] 2 Q.B. 786 (C.A.) at 802.

[133] From time to time the word "sham" is broadened to include any artificial tax avoidance transaction: see, e.g., the *obiter dictum* in *Bronfman Trust v. R.*, [1987] 1 C.T.C. 117, 87 D.T.C. 5059 (S.C.C.) at para. 53.

[134] *Duke of Westminster*, *supra* note 11.

[135] See *Minister of National Revenue v. Cameron* (1972), [1974] S.C.R. 1062, [1972] C.T.C. 380, 72 D.T.C. 6325 (S.C.C.); and *Stubart*, *supra* note 33.

genuinely created. The deceit that is "the heart and core of a sham" was entirely absent.[136]

Faraggi v. R. (2008)[137] and *Antle v. R.* (2010)[138] are cases that apply the sham doctrine. The Tax Court's decision in *Faraggi* offers some support for seeing a sham as sustaining an objective connotation, to be inferred objectively from the circumstances without the need for a finding of subjective deceit. In *Faraggi*, the taxpayer and his partner, Mr. Langlois, were lawyers specialized in corporate and tax law. They applied their expertise to creating an elaborate tax plan.[139] Rip J.

---

[136] *Stubart, supra* note 33.

[137] *Faraggi v. R.* (2007), [2008] 1 C.T.C. 2425, 2007 D.T.C. 911 (Fr.), 2008 D.T.C. 3245 (Eng.) (T.C.C. [General Procedure]); affirmed 2008 FCA 398, [2009] 3 C.T.C. 77, 2009 D.T.C. 5023 (Eng.) (F.C.A.); leave to appeal refused 2009 CarswellNat 1153 (S.C.C.) [*Faraggi*].

[138] *Antle v. R.*, 2010 D.T.C. 5172 (Eng.) (F.C.A.); affirming (2009), [2010] 4 C.T.C. 2327, 2009 D.T.C. 1305 (Eng.) (T.C.C. [General Procedure]); leave to appeal refused 2011 CarswellNat 5822 (S.C.C.); reconsideration / rehearing refused 2012 CarswellNat 172, 2012 CarswellNat 173 (S.C.C.); leave to appeal refused 2011 CarswellNat 1491, 2011 CarswellNat 1492 (S.C.C.); reconsideration / rehearing refused 2012 CarswellNat 183, 2012 CarswellNat 184 (S.C.C.) [*Antle*].

[139] *Faraggi, supra* note 137 at para. 2, 3, where Rip J. describes the plan as follows:

> The plan contemplated using newly formed corporations with nominal assets to subscribe for shares in other newly formed corporations and then create [capital dividend account] CDA through a combination of share subscriptions, redemption of shares, capital gains by sale of shares and purported elections under subsection 83(2) of the *Income Tax Act* ("Act"), among other things. Then, through another sequence of share subscriptions and share redemptions, third parties at arm's length to the appellants would receive capital dividends.
>
> In short, after the "creation" of capital gains several corporations would make elections under subsection 83(2) of the Act and declare tax-free dividends on classes of preferred shares. Near the end of the exercise the aggregate CDAs of these corporations would find their way to an appellant corporation. A third-party corporation would subscribe for shares in an appellant corporation. These shares would have a nominal par value, say $0.01 per share, and a high redemption amount, say $1,000 per share. The third-party corporation would pay $1,210 per share and an appellant corporation would redeem the share for $1,000, electing under subsection 83(2) of the Act that the deemed dividend of $999.99 (subsection 84(1) of the Act) be paid out of the appellant company's capital dividend account. The third-party corporation would then have a capital dividend account and pay its shareholders, after making its own subsection 83(2) election, $1,000 tax-free. Before the transaction, the third-party corporation had no amount in a capital dividend account and could only pay its shareholders a taxable dividend of $1,210; the tax rate in Quebec for individual shareholders was 41.87 per cent. After the transaction the shareholders received $1,000 tax-free; the third-party corporation effectively paid $210 for the tax-free $1,000 dividend. The effective cost to the third-party corporation and its shareholders for the $1,000 dividend was 21 per cent, an economic saving of 20.87 per cent.

found the scheme to be a sham — a common intention to deceive was present in each step of the series of transactions. These two sophisticated lawyers "concocted the scheme and controlled the corporate appellants to effect transactions that were shams and abuses of provisions of the Act. All the appellants knew the score."[140]

In *Antle*, the taxpayer employed a tax planning strategy known as a "capital property step-up" in order to shelter the capital gains arising on the sale of shares of a private Canadian corporation to an arm's-length Canadian purchaser. Pursuant to this strategy, he transferred his shares on a tax-deferred basis to a trust that had been settled in Barbados. Shortly afterwards, the trust sold the shares at fair market value to the trust's sole beneficiary, the taxpayer's wife, who then sold the shares to the purchaser. The key to the strategy was that the gain on the sale of the shares was realized by the trust and the trust then sought to rely on an exemption under the Canada-Barbados Treaty.[141] The Minister reassessed the taxpayer on the primary basis that the trust had not been validly constituted. The Minister also took the position that, even if the trust had been validly constituted, the arrangement was a sham and should not be respected for Canadian tax purposes. As a further alternative, the Minister invoked the GAAR to deny any tax benefit otherwise available.[142]

The Tax Court found that the taxpayer did not truly intend to settle the shares in trust with the trustee and to relinquish control of the shares or the money resulting from the sale. The taxpayer simply signed the requisite documents on the advice of his professional advisors with the expectation that, by doing so, he would avoid tax in Canada. As such, the trust was not validly constituted because it lacked certainty of intention and certainty of subject matter. On appeal, the Federal Court of Appeal agreed with the conclusion of the Tax Court that the trust had not been validly constituted. While not strictly necessary to decide the appeal, the Court found that the trust constituted a sham on the basis that the trust deed did not reflect the true arrangement between the parties involved. The Court noted that the intent or state of mind required in order for there to be a sham need not go so far as to give rise to the common law tort of deceit or criminal intent to deceive. It suffices that the parties to a transaction present it as being different from what they know it to be. In this case, both the taxpayer and the trustee knew with absolute certainty that the latter had no discretion or control over the shares. Yet both signed a document saying the opposite. Nothing more was required in order to hold that the trust was a sham.[143]

The taxpayer corporations created by Faraggi and Langlois were assessed on the basis that they earned a profit of $4.6 million and $8.1 million, respectively, in their 1987 taxation years, from carrying on businesses of selling fictitious CDAs to third parties. The taxpayers' appeal to the Tax Court was dismissed with costs.

[140] *Ibid.* at para. 96.

[141] Canada-Barbados Income Tax Agreement, *supra* note 113.

[142] *Antle, supra* note 138.

[143] *Ibid.*

17

TAX AVOIDANCE

17.1 — Introduction

In the modern world, virtually everything a taxpayer does takes into account tax consequences. Tax planning leads to tax avoidance. Tax avoidance "is not a dirty word"[1] and is not illegal. If left uncontrolled, however, aggressive tax planning amounts to "gaming" the tax system and offends fundamental tax policies. The key is to draw the line between legitimate tax planning and tax avoidance considered to be offensive — an outcome and associated taxpayer conduct that is more than simply avoiding the payment of tax that need not be paid within the expectations of the tax system. In theory, the line should be drawn on the basis of whether the avoidance transaction violates Parliament's legislative intent or purpose. The standard for making this determination has crystallized in the statutory interpretation discipline we have already discussed in Chapter 16, taking account together of legislative "text", "context" and "purpose" — the "TCP" approach. In practice, however, the line-drawing is often difficult because the legislative intent or purpose of a provision may be unclear.

Tax avoidance is one of the most difficult topics in income tax law. It involves, and indeed overlaps with, a variety of complex issues, including statutory interpretation, the availment of tax incentives in the *Income Tax Act* (the "*ITA*"),[2] the scope and effectiveness of the general anti-avoidance rule ("GAAR") itself and in relation to various specific anti-avoidance rules, the role of the judiciary and common law principles. Because tax avoidance is intimately connected to the broader exercise of discerning and understanding the meaning of the *ITA*, this chapter is better read together with Chapter 16.

---

[1] *Canada Trustco Mortgage Co. v. Canada*, [2003] 4 C.T.C. 2009, 2003 D.T.C. 587 (T.C.C.); affirmed [2004] 2 C.T.C. 276, 2004 D.T.C. 6119 (Fed. C.A.); affirmed [2005] 5 C.T.C. 215, 2005 D.T.C. 5523 (S.C.C.) [*Canada Trustco*] at para. 57 [(T.C.C.)].

[2] R.S.C. 1985 (5th Supp.), c. 1 [*ITA*].

(a) — Taxpayers' right to tax planning

The *Duke of Westminster* case[3] established a principle that taxpayers are entitled to arrange their affairs to minimize the amount of tax payable. This is found in the often-quoted words of Lord Tomlin:

> Every man is entitled if he can to order his affairs so as that the tax attaching under the appropriate Acts is less than it otherwise would be. If he succeeds in ordering them so as to secure this result, then, however unappreciative the Commissioners of Inland Revenue or his fellow taxpayers may be of his ingenuity, he cannot be compelled to pay an increased tax. This so-called doctrine of "the substance" seems to me to be nothing more than an attempt to make a man pay notwithstanding that he has so ordered his affairs that the amount of tax sought from him is not legally claimable.[4]

According to Wilson J. in *Stubart Investments Ltd. v. R.* (1984): "Lord Tomlin's principle is far too deeply entrenched in our tax law for the courts to reject it in the absence of clear statutory authority."[5] Even the GAAR does not reject this principle — it only attenuates it.[6]

That said, it bears repeating that Lord Tomlin's famous *dictum* has a relevant context, not only in the rest of his speech, but in the implications of the pertinent private law to which evidently highly prescriptive tax law was accessory, as well as the fiscal culture of the time. It would be wise to keep such context in mind; it may affect the readiness with which that *dictum* would be applied in any present case as if it were tantamount to a statutory provision.[7]

The courts in the U.K. and elsewhere began to realize their important role in controlling avoidance. For example, the House of Lords decided that it was time to move away from the *Duke of Westminster* doctrines.[8] In *Furniss v. Dawson* (1984), Lord Roskill opined:

> The ghost of the *Westminster* case . . . has haunted the administration of this branch of the law for too long. I confess that I had hoped that that ghost might have found

---

[3] *Inland Revenue Commissioners v. Duke of Westminster* (1935), [1936] A.C. 1 (H.L.) [*Duke of Westminster*].

[4] *Ibid.* at 19.

[5] *Stubart Investments Ltd. v. R.* (1984), [1984] C.T.C. 294, 84 D.T.C. 6305 (S.C.C.) [*Stubart*] at para. 55. In *Québec (Communauté urbaine) v. Notre-Dame de Bonsecours (Corp.)* (1994), [1995] 1 C.T.C. 241, 95 D.T.C. 5091 (Fr.), 95 D.T.C. 5017 (S.C.C.), the Supreme Court of Canada also recognized that a taxing statute "serves other purposes and functions as a tool of economic and social policy" (para. 33).

[6] *Canada Trustco, supra* note 1 at para. 13.

[7] See Chapter 16 at heading 16.2(b)(ii) — Strict interpretation.

[8] E.g., *W.T. Ramsay Ltd. v. Inland Revenue Commissioners* (1981), [1982] A.C. 300 (H.L.) [*W.T. Ramsay*] at 326, per Lord Wilberforce:

> While the techniques of tax avoidance progress and are technically improved, the courts are not obliged to stand still. Such immobility must result either in loss of tax, to the prejudice of other taxpayers, or to Parliamentary congestion or (most likely) to

quietude with the decisions in *Ramsay* and in *Burmah*. Unhappily it has not. Perhaps the decision of this House in these appeals will now suffice as exorcism.[9]

(b) — Tax avoidance

(i) — Distinguished from tax evasion

Tax "avoidance" must be distinguished from tax "evasion". Evasion involves a deliberate breach of the *ITA*, by, for example, failing to file a return, failing to report all taxable income, deducting non-existent expenses, or concealing or falsifying other relevant information. Evasion is illegal, and is subject to both civil and criminal penalties under the *ITA*. The process of audit, investigation, search, seizure and prosecution is described in Chapter 15.

Avoidance differs from evasion in that it is legal. It does not involve fraud, concealment, or any other illegal measure. What it does involve is the ordering of one's affairs in such a way as to reduce the tax that would otherwise be payable. Avoidance presupposes that the taxpayer has a choice as to the ordering of his or her affairs, and the taxpayer chooses the course that would minimize tax liability. Where the course of tax minimization is taken for predominantly personal or business reasons, with tax saving only a subsidiary consideration (or otherwise a natural consequence of the accessory application of the *ITA* to private law forms and patterns of conduct that taxpayers actually implement and follow as the general law would expect), then the taxpayer's action can hardly be objected to, and, indeed, it may not be appropriate to describe it as "avoidance" at all.

(ii) — Unacceptable tax avoidance

Tax avoidance can be distinguished as acceptable and unacceptable, depending on whether the outcomes and/or behaviors are compatible with the *ITA*. If the avoided tax is tax that a taxpayer ought not to pay in light of how it conducts itself, it is generally acceptable. In this regard, tax planning involves avoiding the tax that taxpayers should not pay, not avoiding the tax that they should pay.[10] An example of acceptable tax avoidance is the avoidance of tax that the *ITA* signals by its provisions and encompassing context. For instance, a taxpayer transfers a business to a family-owned corporation on a tax-deferred basis in order to defer tax and split income with family members who are shareholders and employees of the corporation. When this offers commercial or personal advantages, as well as tax advan-

---

both. To force the courts to adopt, in relation to closely integrated situations, a step by step, dissecting, approach which the parties themselves may have negated, would be a denial rather than an affirmation of the true judicial process. In each case the facts must be established, and a legal analysis made: legislation cannot be required or even be desirable to enable the courts to arrive at a conclusion which corresponds with the parties' own intentions.

[9] *Furniss v. Dawson*, [1984] A.C. 474 (H.L.) at 513, per Lord Scarman.

[10] We attribute this way of expressing the distinction to a view known to have been held by the late David A. Ward, one of Canada's pre-eminent tax lawyers.

tages, the taxpayer successfully navigates various provisions of the *ITA* (such as attribution rules and income splitting rules discussed in Chapter 13) that essentially describe when avoided tax is a "norm" and not impugnable tax avoidance.

Another way of detecting undue tax avoidance is to ask whether the return or profit realized by a taxpayer from a particular course of conduct or transaction is mostly, if not entirely, attributable to the "saved tax". Justice Rothstein, sitting as a justice of the Federal Court of Appeal, expressed the test this way in the *OSFC Holdings* case.[11]

When a taxpayer orders his or her affairs primarily to avoid or reduce tax in the sense that the point of the arrangement is only to avoid tax, and there is no reasonable possibility of benefit apart from tax that is not paid, then, potentially, there is a true case of tax avoidance. This becomes a consideration, either concerning the GAAR or, more generally, the interpretation of the *ITA* according to the textual, contextual and purposive interpretation standard, for highly structured financial transactions the effect of which may be to transform the character of income and otherwise to "arbitrage" tax savings that are the main, if not exclusive, source of financial return to the parties.

(c) — Tax planning

(i) — Goals

The ultimate goal of tax avoidance is a reduction in tax liability. This can be achieved in several ways, including: deferral, changing of the characterization of a transaction, or shifting income or loss to another taxpayer.

"Deferral" involves the postponement of the payment of a tax liability.[12] The extent of tax savings depends on the time value of money. Taxpayers can structure their transactions to take advantage of the timing rules by advancing deductions or postponing the recognition of income. For example, taxpayers can postpone the recognition of income by structuring their affairs to earn it through a corporation, which is taxed separately from its shareholders (and often at a lower rate) and is not required to distribute dividends every year. Individuals can also take advantage of the tax incentives provided in the form of tax deferrals, such as savings for retirement in the form of registered retirement savings plans ("RRSPs").[13]

---

[11] *OSFC Holdings Ltd. v. R.*, [2001] 4 C.T.C. 82, 2001 D.T.C. 5471 (Fed. C.A.); leave to appeal refused 2002 CarswellNat 1388, 2002 CarswellNat 1389 (S.C.C.) [*OSFC Holdings*]. While the *OSFC Holdings* case has been succeeded by subsequent GAAR cases, the most recent (*Copthorne*, also by Justice Rothstein as a justice of the Supreme Court of Canada) reflects undertones of the approach Justice Rothstein took in the *OSFC Holdings* case: *Copthorne Holdings Ltd. v. The Queen* (2011), [2011] 3 S.C.R. 721, [2012] 2 C.T.C. 29, 2012 D.T.C. 5006 (Fr.), 2012 D.T.C. 5007 (Eng.) (S.C.C.) [*Copthorne*].

[12] For further discussion of deferral, see Chapter 1 at heading 1.6(e) — Tax deferral.

[13] See Chapter 12 at heading 11.3 — Tax-assisted private pension plans.

In tax law, character matters. It is not "bad" to adopt a particular legal formulation to achieve an economic outcome that it is possible to achieve adopting a difference legal formulation. An investment in a corporation made by subscribing for shares is not the same as lending it money, unless possibly, but rarely if ever, the *ITA* specifically establishes an equivalence of tax purposes or provides for recharacterization.[14] When an economic transaction can be characterized differently for tax purposes, it is natural that taxpayers will opt for the preferentially taxed category. Often, a key issue in evaluating whether avoided tax amounts to "tax avoidance" is whether the taxpayers actually did what they purported to do. Does the evidence of their conduct align with the description of it as documentation would otherwise suggest?[15] An example is the "incorporated employee", which takes the form of a corporation providing services while, in effect, the shareholder/employee of the corporation provides services to a "client" in a manner no different from those of an employee of the "client".[16]

Shifting income from a highly-taxed person to a less-heavily-taxed family member naturally achieves tax savings without causing the reduction of economic income of the family unit.[17] The *ITA* contains "attribution" rules that establish when this may, nevertheless, be permissible and effective. Shifting losses in a reverse direction equally achieves a reduction of the overall tax liability of the economic unit; equally, the *ITA* and related judicial decisions may also have something to say about that. Shifting losses from a stranger (arm's-length party) has been considered in several GAAR cases, including *Mathew v. Canada* (2005)[18] and *MacKay v. R.* (2008).[19] Shifting losses within a corporate family to effect what amounts to *de facto* consolidation of the group otherwise not provided for directly in the *ITA* is looked on more favourably; an example is the *Stubart* case.[20] The reason is that these transactions produce a tax outcome that is not inconsistent with the proper use

---

[14] E.g., *ITA, supra* note 2, s. 258(3) deeming dividends on term preferred shares to be interest.

[15] See *Continental Bank of Canada and Continental Bank Leasing Corporation v. The Queen* (1994), [1995] 1 C.T.C. 2135, 94 D.T.C. 1858 (T.C.C.); additional reasons 1994 CarswellNat 2669 (T.C.C.); affirmed [1996] 3 C.T.C. 14, 96 D.T.C. 6355 at 6368 (Fed. C.A.); affirmed [1998] 4 C.T.C. 77, 98 D.T.C. 6501 (S.C.C.); reversed (1996), [1997] 1 C.T.C. 13, 96 D.T.C. 6355 (Fed. C.A.); reversed [1998] 4 C.T.C. 119, 98 D.T.C. 6505 (S.C.C.) and *The Queen v. GlaxoSmithKline Inc.* (2012), [2012] 3 S.C.R. 3, [2013] 1 C.T.C. 99, 2012 D.T.C. 5147 (Eng.), 2012 D.T.C. 5148 (Fr.) (S.C.C.), discussed in Chapter 16 at heading 16.4(1) — Importance of characterization, note 100.

[16] See Chapter 14 at heading 14.3(iii) — CCPCs as incorporated employees.

[17] See Chapter 13.

[18] *Mathew v. Canada* (2005), [2005] 5 C.T.C. 244, 2005 D.T.C. 5538 (S.C.C.) [*Mathew*].

[19] *MacKay v. R.* (2008), [2008] 4 C.T.C. 161, 2008 D.T.C. 6238 (Fed. C.A.); leave to appeal refused 2009 CarswellNat 19, 2009 CarswellNat 20 (S.C.C.) [*MacKay*].

[20] *Stubart, supra* note 5.

of private law forms and the way in which groups commonly account for their financial results for non-tax purposes.

Achievement of any or all of these goals is possible because of inconsistencies and gaps that exist within the *ITA*; tax expenditure provisions; the creativity and aggressiveness on the part of taxpayers and their advisors; and judicial attitudes towards tax avoidance. Whether any of these goals collide with the *ITA*'s expectations is determined by carefully considering the Act's provisions in light of their legislative context and purpose and, possibly most importantly, the facts of a case. Tax avoidance cases are usually, if not almost always, about the facts. The meaning of the *ITA*'s provisions, of course, is important, but determining whether taxpayers' conduct does or does not comport with those provisions and the underlying private law very much entails close attention to the facts — what, how and why a taxpayer did what it did.

(ii) — Using a tax relief provision

Taking advantage of a relief provision of the *ITA* is technically a form of tax avoidance, although it is clearly acceptable. Indeed, Parliament wants many tax relief schemes to be used by taxpayers in order to achieve the desired policy objectives. In effect, Parliament invites taxpayers to be its agents, to undertake expenditures of various kinds to achieve social, economic and political objectives, rather than doing these things directly itself. For example, a person may give to charity, or to a political party, or contribute to an RRSP, in order to increase credits or deductions allowed by the *ITA*. These credits and deductions are available for the very purpose of encouraging private provision for charitable objects and political parties and saving for retirement. One can argue about the wisdom of the statute's policy, but one can hardly question the moral right of a taxpayer to do what the statute manifestly approves. In addition to tax expenditure provisions, the *ITA* contains "favourable" treatment of certain transactions, such as inter-spouse transfers of property, corporate rollovers, etc. Naturally, there is nothing wrong when a taxpayer engages in these transactions.

Canada's tax treaties also provide tax relief in the form of exemptions or reductions to residents of treaty countries. Because Canada does not have a treaty with every country, notably tax haven countries, residents in non-treaty countries sometimes structure transactions in order to formally qualify for treaty relief. This is called "treaty shopping". Treaty shopping can also be used by taxpayers to take advantage of different levels of tax relief under different treaties. Not all treaty shopping is abusive. In some recent cases,[21] Canadian courts have held that treaty shopping does not violate the GAAR. However, the recent international project on base ero-

---

[21] See *MIL (Investments) S.A. v. R.*, [2006] 5 C.T.C. 2552, 2006 D.T.C. 3307 (T.C.C.); affirmed [2007] 4 C.T.C. 235, 2007 D.T.C. 5437 (Fed. C.A.) [*MIL (Investments)*].

sion and profit shifting ("BEPS") and proposed amendments to the *ITA* have attempted to address treaty abuse.[22]

(iii) — Tax-efficient structures

A common type of avoidance transaction is to use a more tax-efficient structure in arranging one's economic affairs when the *ITA* treats economically similar transactions differently. For example, because the *ITA* treats the cost of financing (i.e., dividends and interest) differently, the taxpayer might take advantage of the interest deduction through debt financing rather than equity financing. Because business income earned by a sole proprietor is taxable at progressive rates, but business income earned through a corporation is taxable at a lower rate, the very decision to incorporate a business often entails a choice between these two tax treatments. Similarly, a corporation's decision to retain profit to enhance the value of its shares rather than to distribute the profits to shareholders by way of dividends leads to different tax treatment because capital gains are taxed differently from dividends. In these cases, it is difficult to argue that avoidance of tax by simply using a more tax-efficient structure is offensive.

A more aggressive type of avoidance involves the use of intermediate steps to achieve the desired result. These steps may not have any stand-alone significance. They may be entirely unnecessary to achieving the taxpayer's objectives apart from facilitating the avoidance of tax, which, in effect, amounts to a self-generated tax expenditure enforced on the tax system by the taxpayer (i.e., the taxpayer creates an elective tax subsidy to itself at the amount of tax that would have been payable but was not paid). Or, these steps may even be purely formalistic and not evidently followed, or their demands as legal constructs not respected, by the taxpayer. For example, a person who tries to take the retained earnings out of a closely held corporation as a capital gain or return of capital (including capital "manufactured" in the course of the extraction transaction) instead of a dividend may be prevented

---

[22] OECD/G20 Base Erosion and Profit Shifting Project, *Preventing the Granting of Treaty Benefits in Inappropriate Circumstances, Action 6 — 2015 Final Report*; *ITA, supra* note 2, ss. 212(3.2)–(3.94) (back-to-back loan arrangement rules).

from doing so by various rules designed to prevent "surplus stripping"[23] and will need to go through various other steps to avoid the specific rules.[24]

(iv) — Tax arbitrage

Tax arbitrage takes advantage of the different tax treatment of similar economic transactions or different tax schemes for taxing income and capital gains. The transactions in *Ludco Enterprises Ltd.* (2001)[25] (an investment in shares of offshore companies) and *Stewart v. R.* (2002)[26] (an investment in rental properties) are examples of arbitrage. These transactions are designed to take advantage of the different treatment of capital gains and income from property and the different timing rules for the deduction of interest expense and the realization of capital gains.

---

[23] These rules include ss. 55(2), 84(2) and (3), 84.1, 212.1, 212.3 and 245(2) of the *ITA*, *supra* note 2, as well as proposed amendments to s. 84.1 and new s. 246.1, which are contained in the July 18, 2017 draft legislation, online: <http://www.fin.gc.ca/drleg-apl/2017/italir-0717-eng.asp>. It is a fair debate whether the *ITA* reflects an underlying principle against "surplus stripping". See Justice Rothstein's reasons in *Copthorne*, *supra* note 11. Many believe that there is no such principle, and point in particular to the case of *Collins & Aikman Products v. Canada*, 2010 FCA 251, [2011] 1 C.T.C. 250, 2010 D.T.C. 5164 (Eng.) (F.C.A.) as justification for this profound conclusion. It is doubtful that such a principle exists, taking into account the history of the *ITA* as it has come to grips with the separation of owners of income from its underlying sources. Moreover, a careful readying of Justice Rothstein's reasons may indeed validate a conclusion that surplus stripping is antithetical to the *ITA*. However, these manifestations of this antithesis — the principle against surplus stripping — lie in particular provisions of the *ITA* such as those listed at the beginning of this note, which are to be construed according to their text, context and purpose.

[24] Surplus stripping was the issue in *McNichol v. R.*, [1997] 2 C.T.C. 2088, 97 D.T.C. 111 (T.C.C.) [*McNichol*]. It was the very first case to apply the GAAR. A holding company ("Holdco"), owned by four shareholders, sold its only asset, which was an office building. After all tax-free distributions had been made to the shareholders, the company was left with cash of approximately $318,000. Since the company had no business and no other reason for existence, the natural next step would be for the shareholders to wind the company up. However, because subsection 84(2) provides that, on the winding-up of a company, the property distributed to shareholders in excess of the paid-up capital is deemed to be a taxable dividend, this would have forced each of the four shareholders to report and pay tax on a dividend of $79,500 ($318,000 divided by 4). In order to avoid this result, the four shareholders found a purchaser for the shares. The purchaser was an arm's-length inactive company and agreed to purchase all the shares of Holdco for $300,000. The purchaser company had virtually no assets (it had a bank account with $63 in it) and borrowed the $300,000 purchase price from a bank. Then, as soon as the transaction closed, the purchasing company repaid the loan using Holdco's cash and was left with a profit of $18,000, which was the difference between the value of Holdco's assets and the purchase price. The four shareholders of Holdco each received $75,000, which constituted a capital gain for each of them. Before the application of the GAAR, two of the shareholders paid no tax and the other two shareholders paid only a small amount of tax because of the lifetime capital gains exemption.

[25] *Ludco Enterprises Ltd.* (2001), [2002] 1 C.T.C. 95, 2001 D.T.C. 5505 (S.C.C.) [*Ludco*].

[26] *Stewart v. R.* (2002), [2002] 3 C.T.C. 439, 2002 D.T.C. 6969 (S.C.C.) [*Stewart*].

When the current full deduction of expenses (typically interest expense) exceeds the current income (from rent or dividends), the resulting loss can be used to shelter income from other sources. Overall, the taxpayer will derive a profit if the investment property appreciates in value each year, but the capital gains are only partially taxed. Because interest expense is deductible on a current basis and the recognition of capital gains is deferred until the property is sold, this mismatch results in tax savings. The fact that interest is normally deductible in full and capital gains are partially tax-free further increases the tax savings.

The *Shell Canada Ltd. v. Canada* (1999)[27] case is another example. In this case, the taxpayer, through weak-currency loans and forward contracts, achieved a current deduction of interest expense payable at a higher-than-normal rate (to compensate for risks associated with a weak currency), while at the same time realizing capital gains from the forward arrangements that covered these risks. In effect, the taxpayer's capital gain was equal to the excess interest expense. Mismatching was involved in *Shell* because the gains were taxed at the end of the term of the loan, while interest expense was deducted on a current basis. Additional tax savings were available in this case because the capital gains offset the taxpayer's capital losses.

From time to time the *ITA* responds to particular kinds of tax arbitrage that, for example, have the effect of changing the character of income from ordinary income to capital gains;[28] generating credit for foreign tax that, taking account of differences between the Canadian and foreign tax systems, might not ultimately have been paid to the foreign government;[29] and transforming payments of a particular kind that would be subject to non-resident withholding tax under Part XIII of the *ITA* into nondescript contractual payments not captured by any of the withholding tax categories.[30] In some cases, these changes will have been prompted by judicial decisions that declined to find untoward tax avoidance. Others have been inspired by regular attention by Canada's revenue and finance officials to the *ITA*'s responsiveness to changing patterns of taxpayer behavior that expose interstices in the Act.[31]

---

[27] *Shell Canada Ltd. v. Canada* (1999), [1999] 4 C.T.C. 313, 99 D.T.C. 5669 (S.C.C.) [*Shell*].

[28] E.g., *ITA*, *supra* note 2, ss. 84.1, 212.1.

[29] E.g., *ibid.*, s. 126(4.11) enacted in response to transactions such as those in *4145356 Canada Ltd. v. R.*, 2011 TCC 220, [2011] 4 C.T.C. 2207, 2011 D.T.C. 1171 (T.C.C. [General Procedure]).

[30] E.g., *ITA*, *supra* note 2, s. 212(1)(b)(ii) enacted in response to *Lehigh Cement Ltd. v. R.*, [2010] 5 C.T.C. 13, 2010 D.T.C. 5081 (Eng.) (F.C.A.); leave to appeal refused 2010 CarswellNat 4035, 2010 CarswellNat 4036 (S.C.C.) [*Lehigh*].

[31] See, e.g., *Collins v. The Queen*, 2009 TCC 56, [2009] 3 C.T.C. 2206, 2009 D.T.C. 1055 (Eng.) (T.C.C. [General Procedure]); reversed [2010] 3 C.T.C. 100, 2010 D.T.C. 5028 (Eng.) (F.C.A.); leave to appeal refused 2010 CarswellNat 5845, 2010 CarswellNat 5846 (S.C.C.).

(v) — Tax shelters

A "tax shelter" can be simply described as an investment vehicle that "shelters" income from taxes. When used in a general sense, it includes a tax-favoured investment that is clearly sanctioned by the *ITA*, such as an RRSP, a tax-free savings account ("TFSA") or other registered plan. It can also describe tax arbitrage transactions or schemes designed to "trade" or "manufacture" tax attributes (e.g., a tax deduction or exemption). At a technical level, however, a "tax shelter" is defined to be an investment that can be written off over four years and must be registered for tax purposes under section 237.1 of the *ITA*. This chapter uses the term "tax shelter" in its general sense.

Tax shelters are not illegal. Some tax shelters, such as RRSPs or TFSAs, are totally legitimate in that they involve tax-favoured investments clearly sanctioned by the *ITA*. Arbitrage-based transactions, such as those in *Shell*, *Ludco*, and *Stewart*,[32] have been sanctioned by the Supreme Court. As discussed in more detail below, however, the tax shelter transaction in *Mathew*[33] was found to be "abusive" under the GAAR.

(vi) — Anti-avoidance karate

"Anti-avoidance karate" is a term coined by Lord Walker of Gestingthorpe to refer to a situation in which taxpayers attempt to use a statutory anti-avoidance provision to their advantage.[34] One example of this is the *Mathew* case, in which the taxpayers attempted to take advantage of the "stop-loss" rule in subsection 18(13) to acquire the loss of another taxpayer. As the Supreme Court stated in *Mathew*:

> Section 18(13) preserves and transfers a loss under the assumption that it will be realized by a taxpayer who does not deal at arm's length with the transferor . . . To use these provisions to preserve and sell an unrealized loss to an arm's length party results in abusive tax avoidance under s. 245(4).[35]

Another example is *Lipson v. R.* (2008),[36] in which the taxpayers turned an attribution rule under subsection 74.1(1)[37] on its head and used it as part of a scheme to obtain interest deductions. Not surprisingly, the Court ruled against the taxpayers in both *Mathew* and *Lipson*.

(d) — Moral implications

Tax avoidance is not universally condemned, as witnessed by the famous *dictum* of Lord Tomlin in the *Duke of Westminster* (1935) case: "Every man is entitled if he

---

[32] *Shell, supra* note 27; *Ludco, supra* note 25; *Stewart, supra* note 26.

[33] *Mathew, supra* note 18.

[34] Lord Walker, "Ramsay 25 Years On: Some Reflections on Tax Avoidance" (2004) L.Q.R. 412 at 422.

[35] *Mathew, supra* note 18 at para. 58.

[36] *Lipson v. R.* (2008), [2009] 1 C.T.C. 314, 2009 D.T.C. 5015 (S.C.C.) [*Lipson*].

[37] See Chapter 13 at heading 13.3 — Attribution rules.

can to order his affairs so as that the tax attaching under the appropriate Acts is less than it otherwise would be".[38] Expressed that way, there is a tendency to intuit an underlying assumption that the tax laws are confiscations of private property, interferences with the natural order of the free market, and violations of civil liberty: the oppressed taxpayer is morally entitled to get around tax laws if it can be done legally. However, as discussed earlier, even that *dictum* — a mantra of sorts to many planners and taxpayers — is capable of a much more refined understanding that pays due respect both to the relevant private law that framed the Duke's obligations to his gardener and to the ever-important tax law culture of the time. As the barometers and controllers of the law's relevant elasticity, judges' construction of the law is contextualized by private law and tax culture.[39]

Morality should not be used as some sort of controlling, stand-alone principle to detect and proscribe tax avoidance. Canadian courts are loathe to impose an exogenous moral standard in applying the *ITA*.[40] However, it is important to realize that the law — including the tax law — implicitly expresses norms and expectations of conduct of citizens that define the boundaries of a civil society. How people choose to live and interact with others (whether individuals, legal constructions like corporations that host collective conduct, or institutions) are moral determinations. Morality inheres in the law that is enacted or otherwise exists to organize and guide how people interact with each other. As explained in Chapter 16, tax provisions encase a variety of underlying social welfare and economic decisions that might be regarded as expressing the moral choices adopted collectively by a country's citizens. Discerning statutory purpose with reference to text and context is, in that sense, always an exercise in giving voice to morality as an intrinsic element of, and a force within, the law, but not to supplant the law.

There is certainly room for lively debate, despite the determination of the Federal Court of Appeal that morality is not a factor affecting how the *ITA* applies.[41] There is a more nuanced view of what it means to invoke morality in the construction of a tax statute. On the one hand, the law hosts moral judgments of the society whose law it is. In this respect, every attempt to apply the law, including tax law, implicitly engages and enforces moral judgments that law digests and expresses, sometimes even in very mundane ways. On the other hand, as the Federal Court of Appeal might have meant, exogenous moral judgments or reactions to particular outcomes should not supplant the law, or essentially justify discarding or overwriting the law to suit the view of the moment. To the extent that an outcome is to be criticized, the criticism must come from within the law. This makes the discipline of statutory interpretation generally, and the application of the GAAR in particular, demanding but essential.

---

[38] *Duke of Westminster*, *supra* note 3 at 19, *supra* note 4 and accompanying text..

[39] For more discussion, see Chapter 16 at heading 16.2(b)(ii) — Strict interpretation.

[40] *Canadian Imperial Bank of Commerce v. Canada*, 2013 FCA 122, [2013] 4 C.T.C. 218, 2013 D.T.C. 5098 (Eng.) (F.C.A.) at para. 1.

[41] *Ibid.*

(e) — Policy implications

In terms of tax policy, aggressive tax avoidance results in loss of tax revenue, inequity in sharing the tax burden among taxpayers, and a threat to the integrity of the system. The exact amount of revenue lost is estimated to be in the billions, and this is why section 237.3 of the *ITA* requires the reporting of certain types of aggressive transactions to enable the Canada Revenue Agency (the "CRA") to improve its enforcement efforts.[42]

The lost tax revenue presumably shifts the burden onto other taxpayers through the need to maintain tax rates at higher levels than would otherwise be needed. The equities of the situation are further impaired by the fact that, generally speaking, opportunities for tax avoidance are unavailable to those whose income is derived from employment, which is reported by their employer and for which there are limited deductions; only those with substantial investment or business income are usually able to profit from tax avoidance.

It has been suggested that widespread tax avoidance may lead to a deterioration of tax morality, in that taxpayers who see others avoiding taxes legally and are unable to do the same may feel justified in resorting to illegal methods; this kind of attitude is, of course, fatal to the system of self-assessment. It may also be said that tax avoidance leads to a substantial expenditure of effort by lawyers, accountants and administrators, which is economically unproductive.[43]

17.2 — Anti-avoidance rules

(a) — Identifying unacceptable tax avoidance

The *ITA* contains rules to deny certain tax results sought by taxpayers through tax planning. Other than the GAAR, these rules are "specific" anti-avoidance rules ("SAARs") because they counter specific types of avoidance transactions. Examples are anti-income shifting rules,[44] stop-loss rules,[45] and capital gains and surplus stripping rules.[46] Some SAARs are designed to override what might be perceived or described to be the "form over substance" doctrine,[47] to recognize the notion of "economic profit" or "substance",[48] and transfer pricing.[49] Some SAARs were in-

---

[42] Section 237.3 of the *ITA* was proposed in 2010 and enacted in 2013. For a further discussion of these rules, see Chapter 15 at heading 15.7(b) — Statutory Control.

[43] Canada, *Report of the Royal Commission on Taxation* (Ottawa: Queen's Printer, 1966) (Chairman: Kenneth Le M. *Carter*) vol. 3, Appendix A includes a public policy analysis of tax avoidance.

[44] E.g., *ITA, supra* note 2, ss. 56(2)–(5), 74.1–75.1, 95(6), 120.4.

[45] E.g., *ibid.*, ss. 40(2)(g)(i), 18(13) and many other provisions.

[46] E.g., *ibid.*, ss. 55, 84, 84.1, 212.1, 212.3.

[47] See those listed in the first sentence of note 23, *supra*.

[48] E.g., *ibid.*, s. 126(7).

[49] *Ibid.*, s. 247.

troduced to curtail abuse in the area of tax shelters. The GAAR targets transactions that fall outside the scope of any SAARs and result in an abuse of the provisions of the *ITA*.

Anti-avoidance rules have been proposed or introduced in reaction to unsatisfactory court decisions or uncovered undue avoidance transactions. For example, the GAAR was enacted after the *Stubart* decision,[50] although the GAAR may be seen as a being in the nature of a codification of the Supreme Court's approach in that case, taking account of the remarkable similarity between Justice Estey's relevant principles of statutory interpretation and the TCP approach that many years later the Supreme Court expressed as the overarching expression of the GAAR's significance and how it should be applied.[51] Section 20.3 of the *ITA* deals with weak-currency loans and was introduced in response to the Supreme Court decision in *Shell*;[52] subsection 10(1.01) prohibits taxpayers from using the "lower of cost and fair market value" inventory method for a business that is an adventure or concern in the nature of trade, and was introduced in response to the Supreme Court decision in *Friesen v. R.* (1995);[53] section 56.4 ensures that a payment for a non-competition covenant is included in taxable income, and was introduced in response to the Federal Court of Appeal decisions in *Fortino v. R.* (2000) and *Manrell v. R.* (2003).[54] Other examples are section 31, which restricts the use of farming as a tax shelter;[55] and Regulations 1100(11) to (14),[56] which do not allow taxpayers to increase or create a rental loss with capital cost allowance.[57] Alternative minimum tax ("AMT") rules[58] add back losses created by using certain tax shelters.

---

[50] *Stubart, supra* note 5.

[51] *Canada Trustco, supra* note 1.

[52] *Shell, supra* note 27.

[53] *Friesen v. R.* (1995), [1995] 2 C.T.C. 369, 95 D.T.C. 5551 (S.C.C.), discussed in Chapter 8 at heading 8.8(c)(i) — Valuation methods.

[54] *Fortino v. R.*, [2000] 1 C.T.C. 349, 2000 D.T.C. 6060 (Fed. C.A.); and *Manrell v. R.*, [2003] 3 C.T.C. 50, 2003 D.T.C. 5225 (Fed. C.A.).

[55] See Chapter 6 at heading 6.6(d) — Farm losses.

[56] *Income Tax Regulations*, C.R.C., c. 945, regs. 1100(11)–(14).

[57] See Chapter 9 at heading 9.3(h)(i) — Rental property. Other examples include s. 40(3.1), which provides that, if the adjusted cost base of the partnership interest of a limited partner is negative, the negative amount will be a capital gain; s. 96(2.2), which limits the business or property losses by a limited partner to the extent of the partner's "at-risk" amount in the partnership in the year; s. 96(1.8), which deems the income of a business (such as the running of a hotel or a nursing home) earned by a limited partner in a limited partnership or a passive partner in a partnership to be property income for the purposes of the attribution rules.

[58] See Chapter 12 at heading 12.6 — The alternative minimum tax.

(b) — Specific anti-avoidance rules

The history of SAARs testifies to the fact that tax law is like a game that can be described as follows:

> The government has the first move, in which it must determine the content of the law. The taxpayer then determines her transactions. The government has the pen; the taxpayer has the plan. Given this game, the taxpayer has a distinct advantage over the government, because the taxpayer acts with complete knowledge of the government's decisions while the government can only guess at the taxpayer's decisions. One-way [anti-avoidance] rules level the playing field by reducing the taxpayer's ability to take advantage of the situation.[59]

A common feature of SAARs is that they are highly technical and detailed. Each rule needs to clearly define the scope of the offensive transaction or problem and specify how the tax benefit that would otherwise be available is to be denied in a manner that does not offend other tax policies or interfere with the operation of other provisions of the *ITA*. Some judges have openly complained about this drafting style. For example, Mogan J. referred to the definition of "term preferred shares" (which is part of the anti-avoidance scheme in respect of after-tax financing transactions) as follows:

> The definition of "term preferred shares" is prolix in the extreme. The persons who drafted that definition did not practise any economy of words or language. One may ask how many members of Parliament understood the definition when it was made law by amendment to the Act ... It is so detailed; so particularized; so long and tedious and excessive in its use of language.[60]

SAARs can be effective in "shutting down" a specific type of avoidance transaction. However, without a GAAR, SAARs are not effective in preventing similar types of avoidance transactions. To some extent, the highly specific description of the problematic transactions may function as a blueprint for tax planning, as taxpayers can then structure their transactions on the basis of the literal meaning of the provisions. This is particularly true when the courts adhere to the literal interpretation of the *ITA* and refuse to examine the economic substance or business purpose of the transactions. For example, in *Stubart*,[61] Estey J. relied on the number and variety of the SAARs that were in existence at the time to buttress his conclusion that the Court of its own motion should not create a business purpose test that had not been enacted by Parliament. Since none of the SAARs caught the situation in *Stubart*, he reasoned that the Court should not assume the power to disregard genuine legal arrangements simply because of their tax avoidance motivation. The lesson that the Department of Finance drew from the reasoning in *Stubart* was that the *ITA* ought to include a GAAR, which would cover such a broad range of tax avoid-

---

[59] David A. Weisbach, "Costs of Departures from Formalism: Formalism in the Tax Law," (1999) 66 U. Chi. L. Rev. 860 at 878.

[60] *Citibank Canada v. R.*, [2001] 2 C.T.C. 2260, 2001 D.T.C. 111 (T.C.C.); affirmed [2002] 2 C.T.C. 171, 2002 D.T.C. 6876 (Fed. C.A.) at para. 29 [(T.C.C.)].

[61] *Stubart, supra* note 5.

ance activity that an unforeseen device such as that employed in *Stubart* would not fall through the cracks again.

The enactment of the GAAR has not stopped the introduction of new SAARs. New SAARs allow the government to immediately stop the offensive schemes instead of living with the uncertainty of relying on the GAAR.

Some interesting issues arise about the relationship between a SAAR and the GAAR. As discussed below, the GAAR is a measure of last resort that can be invoked to control avoidance transactions that are otherwise successful. If an avoidance scheme does not work independently of the GAAR, there is no need to invoke the GAAR.[62] If no SAAR applies to a particular avoidance transaction, the GAAR may apply. The GAAR can also apply to avoidance transactions that circumvent the application of a SAAR (as in the case of *Copthorne*)[63] or use a SAAR to achieve tax avoidance results (e.g., *Lipson*).[64]

When a SAAR is introduced to close a previously existing loophole, the taxpayer that took advantage of the loophole may not be able to argue that the loophole was previously intended by Parliament. In other words, a new SAAR may not be used to block the application of the GAAR on the grounds that the SAAR covers a situation that was not specifically prohibited. As the Court stated in the *Duncan (Water's Edge)* (2002) case: "The amendment demonstrates that Parliament moved as quickly as it could to close the loophole exploited by the appellants precisely because the result achieved was anomalous having regard to the object and spirit of the relevant provisions of the Act."[65] As discussed below, whether the GAAR can be applied to close the pre-existing loophole depends on the finding of whether an avoidance transaction frustrates the legislative purpose or rationale.

(c) — The GAAR

(i) — Section 245

Section 245 was introduced into the *ITA* in 1988 and amended once in 2005 with retroactive effect to 1988.[66] The current text reads as follows:

(1) In this section,

---

[62] *Geransky v. The Queen*, [2001] 2 C.T.C. 2147, 2001 D.T.C. 243 (T.C.C.) [*Geransky*] at para. 25.

[63] *Copthorne*, *supra* note 11.

[64] *Lipson*, *supra* note 36.

[65] *Water's Edge Village Estates (Phase II) Ltd. v. Canada*, [2002] 4 C.T.C. 1, 2002 D.T.C. 7172 (Fed. C.A.); affirming *Duncan v. Canada*, [2001] 2 C.T.C. 2284, 2001 DTC 96 (T.C.C.) at para. 47 (Fed. C.A.) [*Duncan (Water's Edge)*]. Leave to appeal to the Supreme Court of Canada was refused 2003 CarswellNat 707, 2003 CarswellNat 708 (S.C.C.).

[66] A similar provision is found in provincial tax statutes (e.g., Ontario *Corporations Act*, R.S.O. 1990, c. C40, s. 5) and the federal *Excise Tax Act*, R.S.C. 1985, c. E-15, s. 274 (imposing the Goods and Services Tax). In 2010, a second amendment was made, which was

"tax benefit" means a reduction, avoidance or deferral of tax or other amount payable under this Act or an increase in a refund of tax or other amount under this Act or an increase in a refund of tax or other amount under this Act, and includes a reduction, avoidance or deferral of tax or other amount that would be payable under this Act but for a tax treaty or an increase in a refund of tax or other amount under this Act as a result of a tax treaty;

"tax consequences" to a person means the amount of income, taxable income, or taxable income earned in Canada of, tax or other amount payable by or refundable to the person under this Act, or any other amount that is relevant for the purposes of computing that amount;

"transaction" includes an arrangement or event.

(2) Where a transaction is an avoidance transaction, the tax consequences to a person shall be determined as is reasonable in the circumstances in order to deny a tax benefit that, but for this section, would result, directly or indirectly, from that transaction or from a series of transactions that includes that transaction.

(3) An avoidance transaction means any transaction

(a) that, but for this section, would result, directly or indirectly, in a tax benefit, unless the transaction may reasonably be considered to have been undertaken or arranged primarily for bona fide purposes other than to obtain the tax benefit; or

(b) that is part of a series of transactions, which series, but for this section, would result, directly or indirectly, in a tax benefit, unless the transaction may reasonably be considered to have been undertaken or arranged primarily for bona fide purposes other than to obtain the tax benefit.

(4) Subsection (2) applies to a transaction only if it may reasonably be considered that the transaction

(a) would, if this Act were read without reference to this section, result directly or indirectly in a misuse of the provisions of any one or more of

(i) this Act,

(ii) the *Income Tax Regulations*,

(iii) the Income Tax Application Rules,

(iv) a tax treaty, or

(v) any other enactment that is relevant in computing tax or any other amount payable by or refundable to a person under this Act or in determining any amount that is relevant for the purposes of that computation; or

(b) would result directly or indirectly in an abuse having regard to those provisions, other than this section, read as a whole.

---

not retroactive: to change the phrase "mailing of the notice" to "sending of the notice" in subsection 245(6). The text of this subsection is not included in the excerpt below.

(5) Without restricting the generality of subsection (2), and notwithstanding any other enactment,

> (a) any deduction, exemption or exclusion in computing income, taxable income, taxable income earned in Canada or tax payable or any part thereof may be allowed or disallowed in whole or in part,
>
> (b) any such deduction, exemption or exclusion, any income, loss or other amount or part thereof may be allocated to any person,
>
> (c) the nature of any payment or other amount may be recharacterized, and
>
> (d) the tax effects that would otherwise result from the application of other provisions of this Act may be ignored,

in determining the tax consequences to a person as is reasonable in the circumstances in order to deny a tax benefit that would, but for this section, result, directly or indirectly, from an avoidance transaction . . .[67]

(ii) — Legislative context and purpose

Section 245 is a Parliamentary response to the *Stubart* decision.[68] It gives the government and courts a statutory basis to combat abusive tax avoidance. As remarked by the Honourable Donald Bowman, former Chief Justice of the Tax Court of Canada:

> I think that GAAR stems from two factors. First, it stems from the fact that people who draft legislation have finally thrown up their hands and said that no matter how specific we get, we cannot plug every loophole, so we need this sort of general rule to fill in the gaps. Second, the attitude of the courts — *Stubart* being an example — is that we are going back to strict construction, and the *Duke of Westminster* is alive and well. Therefore, the government figures that many schemes will succeed unless we have some sort of general anti-avoidance rule.[69]

Unlike SAARs that are located in various parts of the *ITA* to address specific issues, section 245 is in Part XVI and is applicable only after all of the other provisions of the Act, including SAARs, have been exhausted. While SAARs and most other provisions of the *ITA* are drafted in highly technical, airtight language dictating specific consequences, the GAAR is a broadly drafted provision. It is intended to negate the specific consequences of unacceptable tax arrangements that otherwise would be permissible under a literal interpretation of other provisions of the *ITA*. In spite of its special character, section 245 is just one provision of the *ITA* and, as such, it should be interpreted textually, contextually and purposively, like any other provision of the Act.

The text of section 245, and the historical context in which it was enacted, clearly indicate that the GAAR is intended to counter avoidance transactions that result in

---

[67] *ITA*, *supra* note 2, s. 245.

[68] *Stubart*, *supra* note 5.

[69] A. Meghji & J.S. Wilkie, "A Fireside Chat with the Chief Justice of the Tax Court of Canada — The Honourable Donald G.H. Bowman with Al Meghji and J. Scott Wilkie" (2010) 58 (supp.) Can. Tax J. 29 at 35.

a misuse or abuse of a specific provision of the *ITA* or provisions of the Act read as a whole. In *Canada Trustco*, the Supreme Court accepted the government's statement about the purpose of the GAAR:

> The new section 245 . . . is intended to prevent abusive tax avoidance transactions or arrangements but at the same time is not intended to interfere with legitimate commercial and family transactions. Consequently, the new rule seeks to distinguish between legitimate tax planning and abusive tax avoidance and to establish a reasonable balance between the protection of the tax base and the need for certainty for taxpayers in planning their affairs.[70]

Establishing a reasonable balance between the public interest in protecting the tax base and the private interest in minimizing one's tax liability requires some limitations on the *Duke of Westminster* principles. Taxpayers' right to tax minimization is to be limited to "legitimate tax planning". According to the Supreme Court, the principle that emphasizes textual interpretation is attenuated[71] and replaced by a "textual, contextual and purposive" interpretation. Whether the principle of "form over substance" is constrained by the GAAR remains unclear.

(d) — The role of the GAAR

(i) — A "shield", not "sword"

The GAAR is a measure of last resort.[72] The courts have been extremely cautious in applying the GAAR. Some earlier GAAR decisions have described the GAAR as an "extreme sanction",[73] an "ultimate weapon",[74] a "heavy hammer",[75] or a "blunt instrument".[76] In *Lipson* (2008), however, LeBel J. clarified that the "GAAR is neither a penal provision nor a hammer to pound taxpayers into submission."[77] The GAAR functions as a shield, not a sword. It is used to ensure the "object, spirit and purpose", not just the words, of the provisions relied upon by the taxpayer are complied with. There are no reported cases in which the Minister has invoked the GAAR as a charging provision to create a tax liability.

As a shield, the GAAR protects the tax base from avoidance transactions that are designed either to "fall within" the technical application of a SAAR or a tax relief

---

[70] *Canada Trustco, supra* note 1 at para. 15.

[71] *Ibid.* at para. 13.

[72] *Ibid.* at para. 21; *Copthorne, supra* note 11 at para. 66.

[73] *Jabs Construction Ltd. v. R.*, [1999] 3 C.T.C. 2556, 99 D.T.C. 729 (T.C.C.) at para. 48, per Bowman J.

[74] *Hill v. R.*, [2003] 4 C.T.C. 2548, 2002 D.T.C. 1749 (T.C.C.) at para. 63, per Miller J.

[75] *Canada Trustco, supra* note 1 at para. 58 [(T.C.C.)].

[76] *CIT Financial Ltd. v. R.*, [2004] 1 C.T.C. 2232, 2003 D.T.C. 1138 (T.C.C); reconsideration/rehearing refused [2004] 1 C.T.C. 2992, 2003 D.T.C. 1545 (T.C.C); affirmed [2004] 4 C.T.C. 9, 2004 D.T.C. 6573 (Fed. C.A.); leave to appeal refused 2004 CarswellNat 4370, 2004 CarswellNat 4371 (S.C.C.) at para. 30 [(T.C.C.)], per Bowman J.

[77] *Lipson, supra* note 36 at para. 52.

(including a tax expenditure) provision in order to obtain a tax benefit; or to "fall outside" the technical application of a charging provision to avoid the tax liability imposed by such provision. In the case of a SAAR or tax relief provision, the GAAR negates the tax benefit that is otherwise permitted by the technical provision. In the case of a charging provision, the GAAR backstops the application of the charging provision.

In terms of the consequences of the application of the GAAR, the GAAR merely denies the tax benefit of an avoidance transaction and allows the Minister to assess the tax consequences to the taxpayer "as is reasonable in the circumstances".[78] Consequently, the GAAR applies to discourage taxpayers from taking the chance that they might get away with abusive tax avoidance transactions. It does not impose any penalty (other than interest for the taxes owing). There is no downside risk to the taxpayer. The cost of failure is not much more than a loss of the tax benefit sought. The taxpayer is in no worse position than not having undertaken the transaction in the first place.[79]

(ii) — Not about "right" or "wrong"

The moral and policy implications of abusive tax avoidance might have motivated Parliament in enacting the GAAR, but that does not mean that the interpretation of the GAAR involves a value judgment of what is right or wrong. As Rothstein J. states, writing for the unanimous court in *Copthorne* (2012):

> In a GAAR analysis the textual, contextual and purposive analysis is employed to determine the object, spirit or purpose of a provision. Here the meaning of the words of the statute may be clear enough. The search is for the rationale that underlies the words that may not be captured by the bare meaning of the words themselves. *However, determining the rationale of the relevant provisions of the Act should not be conflated with a value judgment of what is right or wrong nor with theories about what tax law ought to be or ought to do.* [emphasis added][80]

The GAAR analysis must be anchored in the statutory provisions of the *ITA*, not in any overarching tax policy or tax theory that is not supported by the provisions. This is consistent with the role of the GAAR as a shield, not a sword. In practice,

---

[78] A draft version of s. 245 (in Canada, Department of Finance, *The White Paper: Tax Reform 1987* (Ottawa: 18 June 1987) [*1987 White Paper*]) stipulated that the tax consequences should be designed "ignoring the transaction". This phrase is not in the current version, but there is no doubt that, in most cases, the reasonable tax consequences will be constructed by ignoring the transaction. For example, if the deeds of covenant entered into by the Duke in the *Duke of Westminster* case, *supra* note 3, were caught by the GAAR, this would result in the payments made to the servants becoming non-deductible, as if the deeds did not exist. The Duke would be no worse off than if he had not entered into the covenants in the first place.

[79] Penalties are imposed under similar tax legislation in the United States, Australia, New Zealand and some other countries.

[80] *Copthorne*, *supra* note 11 at para. 70.

however, some GAAR decisions point to the existence of a judicial "smell test".[81] For example, seemingly similar transactions are treated differently in different decisions. Sometimes, the same judge may take a different approach in a seemingly similar case. There are also examples of Tax Court judges who have ruled universally in favour of (or against) the application of the GAAR in all decisions during the period 1997 to 2010.[82]

(iii) — Not to fill all legislative gaps

The GAAR cannot be used to fill in all the gaps left by Parliament in the *ITA*. As Bowman J. stated so clearly in *Geransky v. R.* (2001):

> . . . The *Income Tax Act* is a statute that is remarkable for its specificity and replete with anti-avoidance provisions designed to counteract specific perceived abuses. Where a taxpayer applies those provisions and manages to avoid the pitfalls the Minister cannot say "Because you have avoided the shoals and traps of the *Act* and have not carried out your commercial transaction in a manner that maximizes your tax, I will use GAAR to fill in any gaps not covered by the multitude of specific anti-avoidance provisions".[83]

What constitutes a legislative gap or loophole? It may mean a legislative omission or oversight. For example, the loophole identified in *R. v. Imperial Oil* (2004) was the failure of Parliament to deal with the consequences of different corporate year-ends in defining the term "investment allowance", which reduces "taxable capital" under Part I.3 of the *ITA*.[84] A loophole may also mean a gap between the various schemes of the *ITA* in dealing with a specific issue, such as the gap between the capital cost allowance ("CCA") system and the partnership rules, which the taxpayers in *Duncan (Water's Edge)* (2002)[85] and *Mathew* (2005)[86] exploited. According to the Court in *Duncan (Water's Edge)*, the taxpayers "exploited what can only be seen as an obvious loophole which allowed them to deduct a cost in excess of $4 million for a computer which had a value of some US$7,000 when it first became

---

[81] Hon. Donald G.H. Bowman et al., "GAAR: Its Evolution and Application," in *Report of Proceedings of the Sixty-First Tax Conference Convened by the Canadian Tax Foundation (2009)* (Toronto: Canadian Tax Foundation, 2010) 2:1–22 at 2:16: "The first thing that is absolutely certain, in my view, is that whether you win or lose a GAAR case depends on the judge you get in the first instance . . . I think that there continues to be a certain visceral element — people inelegantly call it the smell test, the olfactory factor, the gut reaction."

[82] For an empirical study, see J. Li & T. Hwong, "The GAAR in Action: An Empirical Exploration of Tax Court of Canada Cases (1997–2010) and Judicial Decision Making" (2013) 61:2 Can. Tax J. 321.

[83] *Geransky, supra* note 62 at 42.

[84] *Imperial Oil Ltd. v. R.*, [2004] 2 C.T.C. 190, 2004 D.T.C. 6044 (Fed. C.A.) [*Imperial Oil*]. Both these terms are defined in s. 181.2 of the *ITA*. Before 2006, these terms were important for the computation of large corporation tax, now repealed, which was the subject of this case.

[85] *Duncan (Water's Edge), supra* note 65.

[86] *Mathew, supra* note 18.

depreciable property under the Act".[87] A loophole is often revealed when the government plugs it through a legislative amendment. For example, section 245 was amended in 1998 to explicitly include regulations and tax treaties as taxing statutes that may be abused.

Clearly, a seeming gap in the *ITA*, more casually and unflatteringly a "loophole", cannot be merely illusory on the basis of reading a statutory provision literally without regard to the context and purpose. Under the GAAR and a textual, contextual and purposive interpretation of the *ITA*, some loopholes turn out to be "free space" designed by Parliament for the courts to fill, while others do not. For example, the GAAR applied in *Duncan (Water's Edge)*, but it did not apply in *Imperial Oil*.[88] As Miller J. correctly states in *Antle v. R.* (2010), "taking advantage of the loophole in and of itself is not abusive: one must analyze whether in so doing, there has been a frustration of the object, spirit and purpose of the provisions in play."[89]

(e) — Minister's discretion

The GAAR has evolved since its introduction. Along the way, criticism of the potential breadth and vagueness of the GAAR's controlling concepts has yielded to a clearer understanding of its scope as it has been applied by courts and consequently refined. It should be noted, however, that the provision does not take the easy route of leaving the issue to the discretion of the Minister.[90] In practice, of course, much will depend upon the CRA's interpretation of, and its policies with respect to its application of, the GAAR. The CRA's GAAR committee, comprised of officials from Finance and Justice as well as from the CRA, helps standardize the application of the GAAR. The committee reviews all files where the GAAR might apply, including requests by taxpayers for advance rulings and referrals from the CRA's audit division, and decides whether to issue a GAAR-based ruling or reassessment.

Needless to say, the CRA's decisions that emerge from this careful process will not be decisive. The ultimate forum of interpretation remains the courts. The taxpayer can use the objection and appeal process to secure a review by a court of any determination made by the Minister under the GAAR, and the court will not be obliged to defer to the Minister's findings of fact or law or to the Minister's decision as to

---

[87] *Duncan (Water's Edge), supra* note 65 at para. 45 [(Fed. C.A.)]. The taxpayers sought to deduct a terminal loss based on the $4 million cost.

[88] *Duncan (Water's Edge), supra* note 65; *Imperial Oil, supra* note 84.

[89] *Antle v. R.*, 2010 D.T.C. 5172 (Fed. C.A.); affirming [2010] 4 C.T.C. 2327, 2009 D.T.C. 1305 (T.C.C.); leave to appeal refused 2011 CarswellNat 5822; reconsideration / rehearing refused 2012 CarswellNat 172, 2012 CarswellNat 173 (S.C.C.) at para. 102 [(T.C.C.)].

[90] It is worthwhile to note that the Minister was granted broad discretionary powers to counter tax avoidance. See, e.g., C. Campbell & R. Raizenne, "The 1917 Income War Tax Act: Origins and Enactment" in J. Li, J.S. Wilkie & L. Chapman, eds., *Income Tax at 100 Years: Essays and Reflections on the Centennial of the Income War Tax Act* (Toronto: Canadian Tax Foundation) [forthcoming in 2017] at 2:1.

the tax consequences. There is a growing body of GAAR jurisprudence that sheds light on the application of the GAAR.

17.3 — Application of the GAAR

(a) — Judicial guidelines

(i) — Guidelines

Although the GAAR was enacted in 1988, it took 17 years for the first GAAR case to be heard by the Supreme Court of Canada. At the time of writing, there had been only four GAAR cases heard by the Court: *Canada Trustco* (2005), *Mathew* (2005), *Lipson* (2009), and *Copthorne* (2012). The Court was unanimous in holding that the GAAR applied in *Mathew* and *Copthorne*, and did not apply in *Canada Trustco*. It was split in *Lipson*. These cases serve as guideposts for determining whether an avoidance transaction is subject to the GAAR. The Court also provides the following set of guidelines for the interpretation and application of the GAAR.

1. Three requirements must be established to permit application of the GAAR:

    (1) A *tax benefit resulting from a transaction* or part of a series of transactions (s. 245(1) and (2));

    (2) that the transaction is an *avoidance transaction* in the sense that it cannot be said to have been reasonably undertaken or arranged primarily for a *bona fide* purpose other than to obtain a tax benefit; and

    (3) that there was *abusive tax avoidance* in the sense that it cannot be reasonably concluded that a tax benefit would be consistent with the object, spirit or purpose of the provisions relied upon by the taxpayer.

2. The burden is on the taxpayer to refute (1) and (2), and on the Minister to establish (3).

3. If the existence of *abusive tax avoidance* is unclear, the benefit of the doubt goes to the taxpayer.

4. The courts proceed by conducting a unified textual, contextual and purposive analysis of the provisions giving rise to the tax benefit in order to determine why they were put in place and why the benefit was conferred. The goal is to arrive at a purposive interpretation that is harmonious with the provisions of the Act that confer the tax benefit, read in the context of the whole Act.

5. Whether the transactions were motivated by any economic, commercial, family or other non-tax purpose may form part of the factual context that the courts may consider in the analysis of abusive tax avoidance allegations under s. 245(4). However, any finding in this respect would form only one part of the underlying facts of a case, and would be insufficient by itself to establish abusive tax avoidance. The central issue is the

proper interpretation of the relevant provisions in light of their context and purpose.

6.   Abusive tax avoidance may be found where the relationships and transactions as expressed in the relevant documentation lack a proper basis relative to the object, spirit or purpose of the provisions that are purported to confer the tax benefit, or where they are wholly dissimilar to the relationships or transactions that are contemplated by the provisions.

7.   Where the Tax Court judge has proceeded on a proper construction of the provisions of the *Income Tax Act* and on findings supported by the evidence, appellate tribunals should not interfere, absent a palpable and overriding error.[91]

(ii) — Canada Trustco

This case involved a factually complex but conceptually straightforward type of leveraged lease. The Court summarized the facts as follows:

> Briefly stated, on December 17, 1996, the respondent, with the use of its own money and a loan of approximately $100 million from the Royal Bank of Canada ("RBC"), purchased trailers from Transamerica Leasing Inc. ("TLI") at fair market value of $120 million. CTMC [*Canada Trustco*] leased the trailers to Maple Assets Investments Limited ("MAIL") who in turn subleased them to TLI, the original owner. TLI then prepaid all amounts due to MAIL under the sublease. MAIL placed on deposit an amount equal to the loan for purposes of making the lease payments and a bond was pledged as security to guarantee a purchase option payment to CTMC at the end of the lease. These transactions allowed CTMC to substantially minimize its financial risk. They were also accompanied by financial arrangements with various other parties, not relevant to this appeal.[92]

Canada Trustco treated $120 million as the capital cost of depreciable property and deducted CCA. The Minister invoked the GAAR in denying the CCA deductions and took the position that the cost of the trailers should be the "economic cost" as opposed to the "legal cost".

The Tax Court found an avoidance transaction that gave rise to a tax benefit, but no "misuse" or "abuse" on the grounds that the transactions amounted to an ordinary sale leaseback and fell within the spirit and purpose of the CCA scheme. It is to be noted that the Tax Court made a fundamental and, we suggest, highly probative and influential factual determination after considering the evidence before it: despite the significance of the tax benefit — itself under the GAAR an agnostic determination and not a judgment that availing of the benefit is somehow "bad" — the transaction had an overarching commercial significance and was in line with normal business conduct (i.e., to secure the financing return to the bank).

The Federal Court of Appeal affirmed the Tax Court's decision. At the Supreme Court, the sole issue was whether the transactions were abusive.

---

[91] *Canada Trustco, supra* note 1 at para. 66.

[92] *Ibid.* at para. 3.

The Crown argued that 1) the object and spirit of the CCA provisions is "to provide for the recognition of money spent to acquire qualifying assets to the extent that they are consumed in the income-earning process"; and 2) the circular sale lease-back transaction involved "no real risk" and the taxpayer did not actually spend $120 million to purchase the trailers. Because the taxpayer created a "cost for CCA purposes that is an illusion" without incurring any "real" expense, the arrangement contravened the object and purpose of the CCA provisions and constituted abusive tax avoidance. The Crown framed the economic substance argument as follows:

> In this case, the pre-ordained series of transactions misuses and abuses the CCA regime because it manufactures a cost for CCA purposes that does not represent the real economic cost to CTMC of the trailers . . . *There was no risk at all that the rent payments would not be made.* Even the $5.9 million that CTMC apparently paid in fees was fully covered as it, along with the rest of CTMC's contribution of $24.9 million in funding, will be reimbursed when the $19 million bond pledged to CTMC matures in December 2005 at $33.5 million.[93]

In contrast, Canada Trustco relied on the Tax Court's finding that the transaction was a profitable commercial investment and fully consistent with the object and spirit of the *ITA* and, thus, not abusive. The Supreme Court agreed with the Tax Court's decision, providing the following analysis:

> Textually, the CCA provisions use "cost" in the well-established sense of the amount paid to acquire the assets. Contextually, other provisions of the Act support this interpretation. Finally, the purpose of the CCA provisions of the Act, as applied to sale-leaseback transactions, was, as found by the Tax Court judge, to permit de-duction of CCA based on the cost of the assets acquired. This purpose emerges clearly from the scheme of the CCA provisions within the Act as a whole. The appellant's argument was not that the purpose of these provisions was unclear, but rather that the GAAR ought to override their accepted purpose and effect, for reasons external to the provisions themselves.
>
> The appellant suggests that the usual result of the CCA provisions of the Act should be overridden in the absence of real financial risk or "economic cost" in the transaction. However, this suggestion distorts the purpose of the CCA provisions by reducing them to apply only when sums of money are at economic risk. The applicable CCA provisions of the Act do not refer to economic risk. They refer only to "cost". Where Parliament wanted to introduce economic risk into the meaning of cost related to CCA provisions, it did so expressly, as, for instance, in s. 13(7.1) and (7.2) of the Act, which makes adjustments to the cost of depreciable property when a taxpayer receives government assistance. "Cost" in the context of CCA is a well-understood legal concept. It has been carefully defined by the Act and the jurisprudence. Like the Tax Court judge, we see nothing in the GAAR or the object of the CCA provisions that permits us to rewrite them to interpret "cost" to mean "amount economically at risk" in the applicable provisions. To do so would be to invite inconsistent results. The result would vary with the degree of risk in each case. This

---

[93] *Ibid.* at para. 70.

would offend the goal of the Act to provide sufficient certainty and predictability to permit taxpayers to intelligently order their affairs . . .[94]

Overall, the Supreme Court's analysis of subsection 245(4) in the context of this case is disappointing. In terms of statutory interpretation, a "textual, contextual and purposive" interpretation of the concept of "cost" was effectively reduced to a "textual" interpretation. The Court drew a negative inference from the fact that Parliament introduced economic risk into the meaning of cost in some provisions of the *ITA* (e.g., subsections 13(7.1) and (7.2), which adjust the cost of depreciable property when a taxpayer receives government assistance). In terms of characterizing facts, the Court continued to embrace the "form over substance" or "legal substance" doctrine in constructing the facts:

> Here the documents detailing the transaction left no uncertainty as to the relationships between the parties. CTMC paid $120 million to TLI for the equipment, partly with borrowed funds and partly with its own money. Having become the owner of the equipment, it leased it to MAIL. MAIL then subleased it back to the vendor, TLI. The relationships between the parties as expressed in the relevant documentation were not superfluous elements; they were the very essence of the transaction.[95]

The Court also stated that the economic substance of transactions may be relevant under a GAAR analysis, but it must be considered in relation to the proper interpretation of the specific provisions that are relied upon for the tax benefit. Of course, it is correct to ground the GAAR analysis, including the economic substance of the avoidance transactions, in the provisions of the *ITA*. However, a highly textual interpretation of statutory provisions and formalistic characterization of facts would render the GAAR largely meaningless.

(iii) — Mathew

The Supreme Court heard this case together with *Canada Trustco*. The *Mathew* case involved transactions designed to transfer business losses from a bankrupt corporation to investors by way of a partnership.[96] Standard Trust was in the business of lending money on the security of mortgages of real property. At the time of bankruptcy, Standard Trust's assets included a portfolio of mortgage loans ("the STIL II portfolio") with a total cost of $85 million and a fair market value of $33 million. The related accrued losses of $52 million were of no value to Standard Trust because of its insolvency. In order to maximize the amount realized by Standard Trust on liquidation, the liquidator devised the following plan to sell the portfolio without triggering the $33 million of losses:

- Standard Trust incorporated a wholly-owned subsidiary.

---

[94] *Ibid.* at paras. 74, 75.

[95] *Ibid.* at para. 77.

[96] *Mathew*, *supra* note 18.

- Standard Trust entered into a partnership with the subsidiary ("partnership A"). The interests of Standard Trust and its subsidiary in partnership A were 99 per cent and 1 per cent respectively.

- The STIL II portfolio was transferred to partnership A.[97]

- The liquidator carried out an intensive campaign to market Standard Trust's 99 per cent interest in partnership A and, after difficult and protracted negotiations, eventually sold it to OSFC Holdings Ltd.

- OSFC assigned its partnership interest to a general partnership ("partnership B").

- OSFC retained an interest in partnership B but sold interests in the partnership to a number of individuals and entities (the taxpayers in the *Mathew* case).

- On the eventual sale or writedown of the STIL II portfolio, partnership B allocated the portfolio losses to its partners, including the taxpayer, who claimed their proportionate shares of the losses as a deduction against their own incomes.

As a result of these transactions, Standard Trust's accrued losses of $52 million were transferred to various arm's-length taxpayers through the use of subsection 18(13) and the partnership vehicle. The Minister reassessed the taxpayer by invoking the GAAR and denied the deduction of his share of the Partnership B losses.

The Tax Court and Federal Court of Appeal found that the facts in this case were essentially the same as those in *OSFC Holdings Ltd. v. R.* (2001)[98] and, following the decision of the majority in *OSFC Holdings*, dismissed the taxpayer's appeal. At the Supreme Court, the first two GAAR requirements, namely the existence of a tax benefit and an avoidance transaction, were conceded. As in *Canada Trust*, the only issue before the Court was whether the avoidance transactions are abusive within the meaning of subsection 245(4).

The taxpayer argued that he was entitled to deduct the losses because of the wording of subsection 18(13) and section 96. Subsection 18(13) is a stop-loss rule: when a property is transferred to a partnership and the transferor does not deal at arm's length with the partnership, the transferor cannot recognize the loss from the disposition and the loss is added to the cost of the property to the partnership. Section 96 allows a partner to claim his share of the loss (or income) of the partnership. Neither provision explicitly restricts the claim of the losses.

---

[97] The plan relied on s. 18(13) to disallow the $52 million of losses realized on the transfer and add the denied losses to the cost of the portfolio to the partnership so that it would continue to be $85 million.

[98] *OSFC Holdings, supra* note 11. The Federal Court of Appeal ruled against the taxpayer and held that the transactions constituted an abuse of the provisions of the *ITA* read as a whole.

Applying a textual, contextual and purposive approach to the abuse analysis, the Supreme Court acknowledged that a literal reading of subsection 18(13) and section 96 as stand-alone provisions would allow the deduction of the losses. The real question is, however, whether these provisions can apply in conjunction to allow the taxpayer to claim losses that originated with the original transferor. These two provisions must be purposively construed in relation to each other and in the context of other provisions of the *ITA* that address the transfer of losses. According to the Court, the legislative context "suggests that Parliament would not likely have intended arm's length parties to be able to buy losses generated by s. 18(13)."[99] Without resorting to extrinsic materials, the Court found that the purpose of the loss-sharing rules in section 96 "is to promote an organizational structure that allows partners to carry on a business in common in a non-arm's length relationship"[100] and that the purpose of subsection 18(13) is "to prevent a taxpayer who is in the business of lending money from claiming a loss upon the superficial disposition of a mortgage or similar non-capital property".[101] The Court went on to say that the combined effect of subsection 18(13) and section 96 is not to allow taxpayers to preserve and transfer unrealized losses to arm's-length parties. The Court held that allowing the taxpayer to deduct the losses would frustrate the purpose of these rules, and that the transaction was not of the type contemplated by Parliament. The following facts were considered relevant:

- The losses originated from the failure of a third party (Standard Trust).

- Partnership A served as a "holding vehicle" for the unrealized losses that Standard Trust planned from the outset to sell to arm's-length parties.

- Partnership B was relatively passive; its purpose was simply to realize and allocate the tax losses without any other significant activity.

- Even though the partners of partnership B paid substantial amounts to acquire their partnership interests and sought to minimize their exposure to risk, these facts cannot negate the above conclusions.

- Neither partnership A nor partnership B ever dealt with real property, apart from the original mortgage portfolio from Standard Trust.

- Standard Trust was never in a partnership relationship with either OSFC or any of the taxpayers.

- The purported non-arm's-length relationship between partnership A and Standard Trust was vacuous and artificial.

The Court attempted to ground its abuse analysis in a contextual and purposive interpretation of the provisions. However, it is unclear why the Court took a broader and more purposive interpretation of the relevant provisions in this case,

---

[99] *Mathew, supra* note 18 at para. 50 [(S.C.C.)].

[100] *Ibid.* at para. 52 [(S.C.C.)].

[101] *Ibid.* at para. 53 [(S.C.C.)].

but not the CCA provisions in *Canada Trustco*. The Court might have been influenced by the fact that the transactions in *Mathew* were more artificial, lacking any air of commerciality, and could be packaged as tax shelters, whereas the transactions in *Canada Trustco* were found to be profitable commercial transactions. But the goal of both avoidance transactions was to generate a tax attribute: the deduction of losses in *Mathew* and the deduction of CCA in *Canada Trustco*. The nature of the impugned provisions in *Mathew* might also have been a factor, because it is easier to identify an abuse of a specific anti-avoidance rule.

(iv) — Lipson

The facts of the Lipson case[102] can be described as "*Singleton* with a spousal twist" because the transactions undertaken by Mr. and Mrs. Lipson were similar to those in the *Singleton* case.[103]

- On April 24, 1994, the taxpayers entered into an agreement to purchase a house for $750,000 with a closing date of September 1, 1994.

- On the day before the closing date, Mrs. Lipson borrowed $562,500 from a bank and used the money to purchase certain shares that Mr. Lipson held in a family company. Mrs. Lipson did not have enough income to pay the interest on this loan (the "share loan") and the bank would not have lent it to her on an unsecured basis but for the fact that Mr. Lipson had agreed to repay the loan in its entirety the following day.

- On the closing date, the proceeds from the sales of the shares were used to pay for the purchase of the house.

- The next day, the Lipsons mortgaged the house (the "house loan") and used the money to repay Mrs. Lipson's original share loan.

These transactions were designed to enable Mr. Lipson to deduct the interest expenses in respect of the "house loan". They relied on the following provisions of the *ITA*:

- Subsection 73(1) allows a transfer of property between spouses on a rollover basis. As a result, the shares were transferred to Mrs. Lipson without triggering any immediate capital gain to Mr. Lipson.

- Section 74.1 attributes any income or loss from property transferred from one spouse to another back to the transferor for tax purposes. Any income or loss earned by Mrs. Lipson from the shares acquired from her husband was deemed to be Mr. Lipson's.

---

[102] *Lipson, supra* note 36.

[103] *Singleton v. R.,* [1996] 3 C.T.C. 2873, 96 D.T.C. 1850 (T.C.C.); reversed [1999] 3 C.T.C. 446, 99 D.T.C. 5362 (Fed. C.A.); affirmed (2001), [2002] 1 C.T.C. 121, 2001 D.T.C. 5533 (S.C.C.). This case is discussed in Chapter 16 at heading 16.4(d)(ii) — Step transactions.

- Paragraph 20(1)(c) permits the deduction of interest on money borrowed for the purpose of earning income from a property. The shares in the Lipson family company were income-producing property. Interest on the share loan was, thus, deductible.

- Subsection 20(3) allows a deduction for interest on money borrowed to repay previously borrowed money if the interest on the original loan is deductible. Because the Lipsons used the house loan to repay the share loan, the interest on the house loan was, thus, deductible.

Mr. Lipson deducted the interest on the house loan pursuant to paragraph 20(1)(c) and reported the taxable dividends on the shares as income. The Minister disallowed the interest expenses by relying on the GAAR. At trial, the parties conceded that the transactions were avoidance transactions for purposes of the GAAR. As in *Canada Trustco* and *Mathew*, the sole issue before the Court was whether the transactions resulted in an abuse or misuse. The Tax Court applied the GAAR, holding that the "overall purpose" of the transactions was to make interest on the house loan deductible, and that resulted in a misuse of the relevant provisions of the *ITA*. The Federal Court of Appeal upheld that decision.

The Supreme Court was unanimous that *Singleton*-type planning remains acceptable under the GAAR, but split on the application of the GAAR to the spousal twist. The majority of the Court (4:3), in reasons written by LeBel J., held that the "spousal twist" was abusive because the Lipsons turned to the anti-avoidance rules to obtain the tax savings. The dissent, written by Binnie J., held that the transactions did not result in an abuse of those provisions, but fulfillment of them. Preventing spouses from reducing their tax burden through non-arm's-length transactions by deeming them abuse would give the GAAR too large a field of operation. Rothstein J. disagreed with both LeBel J. and Binnie J. on the ground that the specific anti-avoidance rule in section 74.5 should be applied instead of the GAAR.

This split decision speaks to the uncertainty about the application of the GAAR. It also reveals the philosophical divide among the justices. According to LeBel J., one cannot read the GAAR out of the *ITA* based on concerns for certainty in tax planning. The GAAR "may introduce a degree of uncertainty into tax planning, but such uncertainty is inherent in all situations in which the law must be applied to unique facts".[104] Binnie J. called the majority's concerns for the GAAR "apocalyptic", and expressed concern for the future of the still-viable *Duke of Westminster* principle: "The GAAR is a weapon that, unless contained by the jurisprudence, could have a widespread, serious and unpredictable effect on legitimate tax planning."[105] According to the majority, however, "Binnie J. essentially guts the GAAR and reads it out of the *ITA* under the guise of an exercise in legal interpretation."[106]

---

[104] *Lipson, supra* note 36 at para. 52.

[105] *Ibid.* at para. 55.

[106] *Ibid.* at para. 52.

(v) — Copthorne

The facts in the *Copthorne* case[107] are as follows. Copthorne Holdings Ltd. was a Canadian company and member of a corporate group controlled by Li Ka-Shing and his son, Victor Li. By a series of transactions in 1993 and 1994, Copthorne sold the shares in its Canadian subsidiary, VHHC Holdings Ltd., to its non-resident parent company, Big City B.V. As a result, the two Canadian companies became "sister" corporations. The sister corporations were then amalgamated by a "horizontal" amalgamation. Had they remained as a parent and subsidiary when they amalgamated (a "vertical" amalgamation), the $67,401,279 of paid-up capital ("PUC") of the shares of VHHC Holdings would have been cancelled by virtue of subsection 87(3) of the *ITA*. In 1995, following further internal restructuring transactions, the amalgamated corporation redeemed a large portion of its shares and paid out the aggregate PUC attributable to the redeemed shares to its non-resident shareholder. That payment was not reported as taxable dividend to the shareholder but, instead, as a return of capital free of Canadian withholding tax. The Minister applied the GAAR and reduced the PUC of the shares and treated the excess payment as a taxable dividend. Copthorne was assessed for failure to withhold tax on the dividends. The Minister considered the transaction by which the parent and subsidiary became sister corporations to have circumvented certain provisions of the *ITA* in an abusive manner.

The key issues in this case were the meaning of "series of transactions" and abuse. The Tax Court found that all elements necessary to apply the GAAR had been established: the tax benefit occurred when the preservation of the $67,401,279 PUC was returned to shareholders on a tax-free basis; obtaining such tax benefit was the primary purpose of the series of transactions, which included the avoidance transaction (the 1993 share sale transaction); and the avoidance transaction misused provisions, including subsection 87(3). The Federal Court of Appeal affirmed the judgment of the Tax Court, but on slightly different grounds. The Supreme Court of Canada upheld the lower courts' judgments.

The Supreme Court decision in *Copthorne* reinforces and consolidates principles enunciated in *Canada Trustco*, *Mathew* and *Lipson*. For the first time, the Court provides some clear guidance on the appropriate methodology for the interpretation of taxing statutes and the unique methodology to be used when the GAAR is in play. The *Copthorne* decision will be discussed throughout the rest of this chapter.

(b) — Tax benefit

The first step in applying the GAAR is to determine whether there is a tax benefit arising from a transaction, or from a series of transactions of which the transaction is part. A "tax benefit" is defined in subsection 245(1) as including not only the avoidance or reduction of tax, but also the deferral of tax and an increase in a refund of tax. A tax benefit may be the result of the deduction of an expense or losses, the exclusion of income, the time value of money from deferral, the avoid-

---

[107] *Copthorne*, *supra* note 11.

ance of a tax, obtaining tax relief under a tax expenditure provision, or using a tax-efficient structure to recharacterize or shift income.

There are some important principles guiding the determination of whether a tax benefit exists. The determination is a factual one.[108] As such, the Minister will initially make a determination on the basis of the available information or assumptions of facts. The taxpayer has the onus of refuting the Minister's determination. The court will decide whether the taxpayer has met the burden of proof.

The existence of a tax benefit *may be* established by comparison with an alternative arrangement or a benchmark.[109] The Court stated in *Canada Trustco*:

> For example, characterization of an amount as an annuity rather than as a wage, or as a capital gain rather than as business income, will result in differential tax treatment. In such cases, the existence of a tax benefit might only be established upon a comparison between alternative arrangements.[110]

If a comparison approach is used, the alternative arrangement must be one that might reasonably have been carried out but for the existence of the tax benefit.[111] In *Copthorne*, a vertical amalgamation was the alternative arrangement that was reasonable except for the difference in how PUC was treated under the *ITA*. It should be noted, however, that a comparative analysis is not really necessary in *Copthorne* because the tax benefit in this case was the avoidance or reduction of Canadian withholding tax on dividends imposed by subsection 212(2) of the *ITA*, which clearly falls within the statutory definition of "tax benefit". The avoidance of the application of a charging provision, such as subsection 212(2), *prima facie* gives rise to a tax benefit.

The magnitude of the tax benefit is not relevant,[112] even though about half of the GAAR cases involve assessments exceeding $1 million.[113] The person who obtains the tax benefit does not necessarily have to be the person who undertook or ar-

---

[108] *Canada Trustco, supra* note 1 at para. 19.

[109] For example, in *McNichol, supra* note 24, the shareholders of a corporation sought to distribute the funds in the corporation in a manner other than by way of dividend. That manner resulted in an arrangement producing capital gains that were eligible for the lifetime capital gains exemptions. The Tax Court found that there was a tax benefit: "There is nothing mysterious about the subsection 245(1) concept of tax benefit. Clearly a reduction or avoidance of tax does require the identification in any given set of circumstances of a *norm* or *standard* against which reduction is to be measured." (para. 20). In *Evans v. R.* (2005), [2006] 2 C.T.C. 2009, 2005 D.T.C. 1762 (T.C.C.) [*Evans*], Bowman J. also had no difficulty finding the tax benefit to be the tax otherwise payable on dividends. He said (at para. 17): "I think there was a tax benefit. Had Dr. Evans simply received a dividend of over $267,000 from 117679 he would have paid tax on it."

[110] *Canada Trustco, supra* note 1 at para. 20.

[111] *Ibid.* at para. 35.

[112] *Ibid.*, para. 19.

[113] Li & Hwong, *supra* note 82.

ranged the transaction in question. In *Mathew*, for example, Mr. Mathew did not undertake the avoidance transaction.

The threshold for finding a tax benefit has been set relatively low. In the majority of cases, the existence of a tax benefit is not controversial and the GAAR analysis moves to the next question — was the transaction giving rise to the tax benefit an "avoidance transaction" under subsection 245(3)?

(c) — Avoidance transaction

The function of subsection 245(3) "is to remove from the ambit of the GAAR transactions or series of transactions that may reasonably be considered to have been undertaken or arranged primarily for a non-tax purpose".[114] According to this provision, an avoidance transaction is any transaction that results in a tax benefit and is not undertaken primarily for a *bona fide* non-tax purpose. An avoidance transaction may produce a tax benefit on its own, or operate as part of a series of transactions that produces a tax benefit. The characterization of a transaction as an avoidance transaction, thus, requires the application of a non-tax purpose test to a specific transaction as well as a "result test" to either a specific transaction alone or a series of transactions that includes the transaction.

Whether a transaction is characterized as an avoidance transaction is a factual determination falling within the jurisdiction of the Tax Court. In the absence of a palpable and overriding error, the Tax Court's decision cannot be overruled by the appellate court. A high premium is, thus, paid for meticulous documentation during the designing and execution of a tax plan and careful presentation of the facts at the Tax Court.

(i) — "Transaction" and "series of transactions"

Subsection 245(1) extends the meaning of "transaction" to include an "arrangement or event". The ordinary meaning of this term is broad. It includes a contract, agreement, exchange, or transfer between two or more persons that establishes a legal obligation. The extended definition does not mean that a transaction can be taken apart in order to isolate its business and tax purposes. In *Canadian Pacific* (2002),[115] the Federal Court of Appeal rejected the Minister's position that the taxpayer's act of denominating the debentures in Australian dollars was in and of itself a transaction, separate from the borrowing transaction:

> The words of the Act require consideration of a transaction in its entirety and it is not open to the Crown artificially to split off various aspects of it in order to create an avoidance transaction. In the present case, the Australian dollar borrowing was one complete transaction and cannot be separated into two transactions by labelling the designation in Australian dollars as a separate transaction.[116]

---

[114] *Canada Trustco, supra* note 1 at para. 21.

[115] *R. v. Canadian Pacific Ltd.*, [2002] 2 C.T.C. 197, 2002 D.T.C. 6742 (Fed. C.A.); reconsideration/rehearing refused [2002] 2 C.T.C. 150 (Fed. C.A.) [*Canadian Pacific*].

[116] *Ibid.* at para. 26

The concept of "series of transactions" is important in a GAAR analysis because sophisticated tax planning structures often involve more than one transaction. Pursuant to paragraph 245(3)(b), a tax benefit may be the result of a series of transactions that includes one transaction (a "step transaction") that fails to meet the non-tax purpose test. In other words, "where a series of transactions would result in a tax benefit, that tax benefit will be denied unless the primary objective of each transaction in the series is to achieve some legitimate non-tax purposes".[117]

What constitutes a "series of transactions"? At common law, a series of transactions involves a number of transactions that are "pre-ordained in order to produce a given result" with "no practical likelihood that the pre-planned events would not take place in the order ordained".[118] Subsection 248(10) extends the meaning of "series of transactions" to include "related transactions or events completed in contemplation of the series". The Supreme Court stated in *Canada Trustco* that "contemplation" in subsection 248(10) should be interpreted "not in the sense of actual knowledge" but in the broader sense of "because of" or "in relation to" the series.[119] The phrase can be applied to events either before or after the avoidance transaction.

The decision in *Copthorne* reaffirmed that "contemplation" in subsection 248(10) should be read both prospectively and retrospectively. In *Copthorne*, the tax benefit resulted from the 1995 redemption of shares. However, it was found that this transaction satisfied the non-tax purpose test and was, thus, not an avoidance transaction. The sale and amalgamation transactions in 1993 and 1994 were part of a series of transactions. However, these transactions themselves did not result in a tax benefit. The taxpayer argued that the redemption transaction that resulted in the tax benefit was not part of the series because subsection 248(10) should not be read retrospectively. The Court rejected this argument:

> The text and context of subsection 248(10) leave open when the contemplation of the series must take place. Nothing in the text specifies when the related transaction must be completed in relation to the series. Specifically, nothing suggests that the related transaction must be completed in contemplation of a subsequent series. The context of the provision is to expand the definition of a series which is an indication against a narrow interpretation.[120]

The Court further stated that each case must be decided on its own facts. The length of time between the series and the related transaction may be a relevant consideration in some cases, as would intervening events taking place between the series and the completion of the related transaction. Although the "because of" or "in relation

---

[117] Canada, Department of Finance, *Explanatory Notes to Legislation Relating to Income Tax* (Ottawa: June 1988).

[118] *Craven v. White*, [1989] A.C. 398 (U.K.H.L.) at 514, per Lord Oliver; see also *W.T. Ramsay, supra* note 8. The Supreme Court endorsed the test for a series of transactions in *Canada Trustco, supra* note 1 at para. 25.

[119] *Canada Trustco, supra* note 1 at para. 26.

[120] *Copthorne, supra* note 11 at para. 54.

to" test does not require a "strong nexus", it does require more than a mere possibility or a connection with an extreme degree of remoteness.[121]

(ii) — Result test

As discussed above, subsection 245(3) makes it clear that the identified tax benefit may be the result of a single transaction or a series of transactions. To be characterized as an avoidance transaction, the transaction in issue must meet the non-tax purpose test, but not necessarily the result test. A transaction lacking a primary non-tax purpose may operate alone to produce the tax benefit or as a step transaction in a series to produce the tax benefit. As illustrated in *Copthorne*,[122] if a transaction that results in a tax benefit (e.g., the 1995 redemption transaction) cannot be linked to a transaction that lacks a primary non-tax purpose (the 1993 share sale transaction), there will be no avoidance transaction and the GAAR will not apply. In *Copthorne*, the link was established by treating the transactions as part of a series under subsection 248(10).

While the taxpayer in *Copthorne* was not successful in its attempt to de-link the transaction that produced the result and the transaction that failed the non-tax purpose test, the taxpayer in *MIL (Investments)* (2007)[123] was. The tax benefit in this case was the claim of a treaty exemption under the *Canada-Luxembourg Tax Treaty*[124] in respect of capital gains from the disposition of shares of a Canadian mining company. A key condition for the treaty exemption is that the non-resident's share ownership does not exceed 10 per cent. Initially, MIL was a resident of the Cayman Islands, a country that had no tax treaty with Canada. It held over 29 per cent of the shares of a Canadian mining company, Diamond Fields Resources ("DFR"). DFR discovered the Voisey Bay nickel find. In June 1995, Inco agreed to acquire DFR and effected a share exchange on a tax-free basis with MIL. After the share exchange, MIL held less than 10 per cent of the shares of DFR and Inco. In July 1995, MIL moved its residence to Luxembourg. In August and September 1995, MIL sold its Inco and DFR shares, realizing a gain. In August 1996, MIL sold its remaining DFR shares, realizing a gain of almost $430 million. MIL claimed treaty exemption, which was available if a resident of Luxembourg owned less than 10 per cent of shares of a Canadian mining company. The Minister invoked the GAAR to deny the treaty exemption for the 1996 sale. (The 1995 sales were not assessed by the Minister.) The Tax Court concluded that the GAAR did not apply. The 1996 sale (which resulted in the tax benefit) was considered only after the death of a key DFR employee in October 1995, and, hence, it met the

---

[121] *Ibid.* at para. 47.

[122] *Copthorne, supra* note 11.

[123] *MIL (Investments), supra* note 21.

[124] Convention Between the Government of Canada and the Government of the Grand Duchy of Luxembourg For the Avoidance of Double Taxation and the Prevention of Fiscal Evasion with respect to Taxes on Income and on Capital, 10 September 1999 (entered into force 17 October 2000).

primary non-tax purpose test and was not an avoidance transaction on its own. Further, the 1996 sale was not part of the series of transactions that included the relocation of residence to Luxembourg and the share exchange transactions that reduced MIL's share ownership in FDR to below 10 per cent, on the ground that the death of the key employee, which helped trigger the 1996 sale, bore no relationship to the series of transactions as conceived by the taxpayer in June, 1995. The Court concluded that the sale could not be included in that series because of a mere possibility of a future potential sale of any shares.

In *MIL (Investments)* the Tax Court stated:

> There must be a strong nexus between transactions in order for them to be included in a series of transactions. In broadening the word "contemplation" to be read in the sense of "because of" or "in relation to the series", the Supreme Court [in *Canada Trustco*] cannot have meant mere possibility, which would include an extreme degree of remoteness. Otherwise, legitimate tax planning would be jeopardized, thereby running afoul of that Court's clearly expressed goals of achieving "consistency, predictability and fairness".[125]

As previously mentioned, the Supreme Court in *Copthorne* explicitly rejected the proposition that there be a "strong" nexus, but it did accept that subsection 248(10) does require more than a mere possibility or a connection with an extreme degree of remoteness.[126] The Court stated that each case must be decided on its own facts, and the length of time between the series and the related transaction may be relevant in some cases, as would intervening events taking place.

If there is a series that results, directly or indirectly, in a tax benefit, it will be caught by subsection 245(3) as an avoidance transaction unless each transaction within the series could reasonably be considered to have been undertaken or arranged primarily for *bona fide* non-tax purposes.

(iii) — Non-tax purpose test

Having determined that a transaction or series of transactions resulted in a tax benefit, the next question is whether the primary purpose of the transaction or any transaction in the series was to obtain the tax benefit, as opposed to achieving some *bona fide* non-tax purposes. Subsection 245(3) excludes a transaction from being an "avoidance transaction" if it "may reasonably be considered to have been undertaken or arranged primarily for *bona fide* purposes other than to obtain the tax benefit".[127]

"Non-tax purpose" is obviously broader than "non-business purpose". Section 245 does not use the phrase "business purpose", which was the controlling concept under the *1987 White Paper* version of section 245.[128] The main difficulty with the

---

[125] *MIL (Investments)*, *supra* note 21 at para. 65.

[126] *Copthorne*, *supra* note 11 at para. 47.

[127] *ITA*, *supra* note 2, s. 245(3).

[128] *1987 White Paper*, *supra* note 78.

phrase "business purpose" is that "many legitimate transactions are carried out for non-tax reasons, such as family, personal, or investment reasons, that cannot be characterized as business reasons".[129] The non-tax purpose test is able to accommodate all purposes other than tax avoidance.[130]

Subsection 245(3) uses the words "reasonably" and "primarily" to suggest an objective and comparative inquiry. It gives primacy to the objective facts available to an outside observer, as opposed to the evidence as to the taxpayer's subjective intention. It requires "an objective assessment of the relative importance of the driving forces of the transaction."[131] The word "primarily" indicates a comparative evaluation in cases where a transaction has both a non-tax and a tax purpose. Some factors that are relevant in this assessment include:

- a quantitative comparison of the tax and the non-tax advantages of the transaction;

- steps involving transitory, short-term arrangements;

- whether "tax drove the deal"; and

- why one method of accomplishing the transaction was chosen over another.

A comparison of the amount of the estimated tax benefit and the estimated business earnings may be relevant to the determination of the primary purpose of a transaction. In *Duncan (Water's Edge)*,[132] a group of taxpayers purchased a 93.5 per cent interest in an American partnership ("Klink") on December 20, 1991 for $320,000. Klink held a capital asset, a mainframe computer with a fair market value of US$7,000, which was leased to a third party for profit. Klink acquired the computer in 1981 for US$3.7 million. On December 20, 1991, Klink contributed the computer to a partnership in British Columbia in return for a 50 per cent interest in the partnership. The taxpayers purportedly tried to lease the obsolete computer in a foreign market. In computing its income for 1991, Klink treated the computer as a depreciable property and claimed a large terminal loss under subsection 20(16) as a result of the disposition of the computer to the B.C. partnership. The terminal loss deduction led to a net loss of $4.4 million in Klink. The taxpayers claimed their share of the loss against their incomes. The taxpayers accepted that they received a tax benefit, but argued that the transactions were undertaken for a purpose other than to obtain this tax benefit. Noël J. found that "the quest for the tax benefit was the only reason why the transactions unfolded as they did".[133] He contrasted the value of the tax loss in the hands of the taxpayers with the income earning pros-

---

[129] Brian J. Arnold & James R. Wilson, "The General Anti-Avoidance Rule — Part 2" (1988) 36:5 Can. Tax J. 1123 at 1155.

[130] Nevertheless, the test is really nothing more than "an expanded version of the business purpose test". *Ibid.* at 1159.

[131] *Canada Trustco, supra* note 1 at para. 28.

[132] *Duncan (Water's Edge), supra* note 65.

[133] *Ibid.* at para. 36 [(Fed. C.A.)].

pects of the obsolete computer, noting that the former was much larger. He found that the difference between the cost of the Klink partnership interest (i.e., $320,000) and the value of the computer (i.e., US$7,000) indicated that, first and foremost, the taxpayers paid to acquire a tax loss.

Steps involving transitory short-term arrangements are very common in tax planning transactions. For example, a taxpayer may create a corporation or partnership (to effect a purchase or sale of an asset) and then eliminate or sell its interest in the entity after a short period of time when the objective of the tax plan is achieved. In *MacKay* (2008),[134] a bank was planning to foreclose on its interest in a shopping centre. The taxpayers, who were real estate developers, agreed to purchase the shopping centre from the bank for $10 million in order to access the losses. The series of transactions undertaken to do this was similar to the series in *Mathew*,[135] and was as follows:

- On November 5, 1993, the bank incorporated a wholly owned subsidiary and formed a partnership with this subsidiary: the subsidiary was the general partner and the bank was the limited partner.

- On November 23, 1993, the bank assigned its $16 million mortgage receivable to the partnership in exchange for 10,000 limited partnership units. The transaction was structured to fall within subsection 18(13) so that the bank was denied the loss on the transfer of the mortgage to the partnership and the $6 million denied loss was added to the adjusted cost base of the mortgage inside the partnership.

- The partnership foreclosed on the mortgage and acquired the shopping centre (cost base: $16 million plus interest and foreclosure expenses; fair market value $10 million).

- On December 29, 1993, the taxpayers became general partners in the partnership by purchasing 2,000 partnership units for $2 million.

- On December 30, 1993, the partnership redeemed the bank's limited partnership units for $8.6 million, using the money the bank had lent to the partnership. The bank ceased to be a partner of the partnership.

- On December 31, 1993 (the partnership's year-end), the partnership wrote down the cost base of the shopping centre to its then fair market value ($10 million) under subsection 10(1),[136] resulting in a $6 million loss.

The tax benefit was found to be the transfer of tax losses through the partnership to the taxpayers. The primary purpose of the transactions undertaken by the bank (i.e., becoming a partner of the partnership at the outset, transferring the mortgage re-

---

[134] *MacKay, supra* note 19.

[135] *Mathew, supra* note 18.

[136] *ITA, supra* note 2, s. 10(1.01), which was introduced in 1995, did not prevent this. These transactions took place before its effective date.

ceivable to the partnership before any of the respondents became partners, and remaining a partner for more than 30 days after the transfer) was to obtain the tax benefit. "Nothing in the record suggests that the non-tax business objectives of the respondents required those steps to be taken."[137]

When evidence indicates that "the tax benefit drove the deal",[138] a primary tax purpose can be established. In *Canada Trustco*, the taxpayer hired a consultant to put together a tax plan that provided very attractive returns by generating CCA deductions. Miller J. found that "this was a profitable investment in a commercial context, but such a finding does not outweigh the primary purpose of obtaining the tax benefit from the investment . . ."[139]

When there is a legitimate non-tax objective for undertaking a transaction and there are alternative methods of achieving that objective, the use of a most tax-efficient method does not necessarily make the transaction an avoidance transaction.[140] "Subsection 245(3) . . . does not permit a transaction to be considered to be an avoidance transaction because some alternative transaction that might have achieved an equivalent result would have resulted in higher taxes."[141] But the taxpayer has the onus to prove the existence of a *bona fide* non-tax purpose. In *Copthorne*, the taxpayer failed to show why the sale of VHHC Holdings shares to Big City was required for the purposes of simplifying the corporate structure and other non-tax purposes.

In the case of a series of transactions, the primary purpose of *each* transaction in the series must be assessed. If one transaction in a series fails the non-tax purpose test, an avoidance transaction is found so that the tax benefit arising from the series may be denied under the GAAR. This is apparent from the wording of s. 245(3).

---

[137] *MacKay, supra* note 19 at para. 22.

[138] *Canada Trustco, supra* note 1 at para. 57.

[139] *Ibid.* at para. 57.

[140] See, e.g., *Evans, supra* note 109, where the taxpayer used a series of transactions to take advantage of the s. 110.6 lifetime capital gains exemption in respect of qualified small business corporation shares and the s. 74.5(1)(b) exemption from the attribution rules to remove corporate surplus almost tax-free. Bowman J. found that the primary purpose of the series of surplus stripping transactions was to put the corporate funds in Dr. Evans' hands. The method chosen was one designed to enable him to do so at the least tax cost. Similarly, in *Spruce Credit Union v. R.*, [2013] 1 C.T.C. 2096, 2012 D.T.C. 1295 (T.C.C.); additional reasons [2014] 4 C.T.C. 2227, 2014 D.T.C. 1063 (Eng.) (T.C.C. [General Procedure]); affirmed [2014] 6 C.T.C. 1, 2014 D.T.C. 5079 (Eng.) (F.C.A.), Boyle, J. (T.C.C.) found that the primary purpose of the payment of a dividend to member credit unions (which was tax-free under s. 112) was to provide them with funds to pay for a credit union assessment. Following *Copthorne, supra* note 11, Boyle, J stated, at para. 71, "that tax considerations may play a primary role in a taxpayer's choice of available structuring options to implement a transaction or series of transactions without necessarily making the transaction itself primarily tax motivated". Unlike, *Copthorne*, there was no extra transection included in the series that was primarily for tax purposes

[141] *Canadian Pacific, supra* note 115 at para. 10.

Conversely, if each transaction in a series was carried out primarily for *bona fide* non-tax purposes, there will be no avoidance transactions, and, thus, the GAAR cannot be applied to deny a tax benefit. There is no need for every transaction in the series to be an avoidance transaction.

This question is important, as many tax-planning schemes involve a series of transactions that is carefully planned: everything is supposed to work like clockwork. Even if the primary purpose of the series is not tax avoidance, a particular transaction in the series may still constitute an avoidance transaction. The GAAR may, thus, apply to deny the tax benefit if the avoidance transaction is abusive under subsection 245(4).

(d) — Abuse or misuse

(i) — Analytical approach

The analysis under subsection 245(4) is the key and most difficult issue in the application of the GAAR. It was the only issue before the Supreme Court in *Canada Trustco, Mathew*, and *Lipson*. A tax avoidance transaction is subject to the GAAR only if it may reasonably be considered that the transaction would result directly or indirectly in a misuse of the provisions of a taxing statute or an abuse having regard to those provisions read as a whole.

The wording of subsection 245(4) refers to both "misuse" and "abuse" in the English version, and only "abus" in the French version. The Supreme Court has found the concept of "abuse" broad enough to include "misuse" and has adopted a single unified approach.[142] The Supreme Court has endorsed the following two-step approach to the abuse analysis:

1. A court must determine the "object, spirit or purpose of the provisions . . . that are relied on for the tax benefit, having regard to the scheme of the Act, the relevant provisions and permissible extrinsic aids".[143] The object, spirit or purpose of the provisions can be referred to as the "legislative rationale that underlies specific or interrelated provisions of the Act";[144] and

2. A court must consider whether the transaction falls within or frustrates the identified purpose or rationale.

According to the Supreme Court, Parliament intends to seek consistency, predictability and fairness in tax law and intends taxpayers to take full advantage of the provisions of the *ITA* that confer tax benefits. Therefore, the GAAR can only be applied to deny a tax benefit "when the abusive nature of the transaction is

---

[142] *Canada Trustco, supra* note 1 at para. 43.

[143] *Ibid.* at para. 55.

[144] *Copthorne, supra* note 11 at para. 69.

clear".[145] The Minister must clearly demonstrate that the transaction is an abuse of the *ITA*, and the benefit of the doubt is given to the taxpayer.

(ii) — Establishing object, spirit or purpose

The abuse analysis must be rooted in a textual, contextual, and purposive interpretation of the provisions relied on for the tax benefit. The goal is to search for the rationale that underlies the words and that may not be captured by the bare meaning of the words themselves.[146] In non-GAAR cases, the goal is more on establishing the meaning of the statutory provisions. A court involved in a GAAR analysis has the "unusual duty" of going behind the words of the legislation to determine the object, spirit or purpose of the provision or provisions relied on by the taxpayer.[147]

The text of the provisions is the starting point. In GAAR cases, the text generally does not literally preclude a tax benefit. If it does, there is no need to resort to the GAAR. And yet, the text is important in shedding light on what the provision was intended to do. For example, the provision at issue in *Copthorne* is subsection 87(3) of the *ITA*, which reads:

> (3) Subject to subsection 87(3.1), where there is an amalgamation or a merger of 2 or more Canadian corporations, in computing at any particular time the paid-up capital in respect of any particular class of shares of the capital stock of the new corporation,
>
> > (a) there shall be deducted that proportion of the amount, if any, by which the paid-up capital, determined without reference to this subsection, in respect of all the shares of the capital stock of the new corporation immediately after the amalgamation or merger exceeds the total of all amounts each of which is the paid-up capital in respect of a share (*except a share held by any other predecessor corporation*) of the capital stock of a predecessor corporation . . .[148]

Subsection 87(3) provides that, where two or more corporations are amalgamated, the PUC of the shares of the amalgamated corporation does not exceed the total of the PUC of the shares of the amalgamating corporations. The parenthetical clause ensures that the PUC of the shares of an amalgamating corporation held by another amalgamating corporation (as in the case of an amalgamation of a parent and subsidiary) is cancelled. In other words, in a horizontal amalgamation of sister corporations, the PUC of the amalgamated corporation is the aggregate of the PUC of the shares of the amalgamating corporations, whereas in a vertical amalgamation of a parent and subsidiary, the PUC of the shares of the subsidiary is cancelled in determining the PUC of the amalgamated corporation. What does the text say about the purpose or intent? The Supreme Court found that this provision is concerned with limiting the PUC of shares of an amalgamated corporation. Because PUC can be withdrawn from a corporation on a tax-free basis, the intent is to limit PUC such

---

[145] *Ibid.* at para. 50.

[146] *Ibid.* at para. 70.

[147] *Ibid.* at para. 66.

[148] *ITA, supra* note 2, s. 87(3).

that it is not inappropriately increased merely through the device of an amalgamation. Therefore, the parenthetical clause is intended to limit the PUC of the shares of the amalgamated corporation to the PUC of the shares of the amalgamating parent corporation.

The contextual interpretation of a provision involves the consideration of other related sections of the *ITA* as well as permissible extrinsic aids. Contextual consideration is particularly important in cases where multiple provisions are relied on by taxpayers. The *Mathew* case is an example.[149] Even in cases where a single provision was identified as the impugned provision, a contextual interpretation helps identify the legislative rationale. In *Copthorne*, the Court considered the PUC scheme of the *ITA*, including subsections 84(3) and 89(1), the principle of taxing each corporation as a separate entity under section 2, the capital gains scheme, the "*in rem*" nature of PUC, stop-PUC rules, and the implied exclusion principle (*"unius est exclusion alterius"*). The contextual considerations led the Court to conclude that "one rationale for subsection 87(3) is that payments to shareholders from an amalgamated corporation on a share redemption should not be taxable as a deemed dividend, only to the extent that such payments reflect investment made with tax-paid funds. The objective of this exemption is to recognize PUC as a return of capital to shareholders."[150]

The purposive interpretation aims at ascertaining what the impugned provisions are intended to achieve. Since it is rare for the text or context of the provision to explicitly state its purpose, inferences must be drawn from the text, context, and extrinsic aids. Judicial guidance on this issue is just beginning to emerge. The *Canada Trustco* decision relied on the CCA scheme as evidence of its finding that the purpose of the CCA provisions is to permit deduction of CCA based on the cost of the assets acquired.[151] The *Mathew* decision refers to no extrinsic evidence or careful analysis of the context before finding the purpose of subsections 96(1) and 18(13).[152] In *Lipson*, the purpose of section 74.1 was found by LeBel J. to be preventing spouses from reducing tax by taking advantage of their non-arm's-length status on the transfer property between themselves,[153] but by Binnie J. to be permitting the attribution of income or loss back to the transferor spouse.[154] The methodology and analysis in *Copthorne* have been the most sophisticated. After a careful textual and contextual consideration, the Court concluded that subsection 87(3) serves the purpose of preserving the PUC of amalgamating corporations (the wording without the parenthetical portion), but the parenthetical portion serves the purpose of precluding corporations from preserving the PUC of the shares of a sub-

---

149 *Mathew, supra* note 18.

150 *Copthorne, supra* note 11 at para. 112.

151 *Canada Trustco, supra* note 1.

152 *Mathew, supra* note 18.

153 *Lipson, supra* note 36 at para. 32.

154 *Ibid.* at para. 81.

sidiary in a vertical amalgamation because the PUC of the subsidiary reflects investment of the same tax-paid dollars as in the parent corporation.[155]

Legislative purpose or rationale is not the same as general tax policy. According to the Supreme Court, the "search for an overarching policy . . . that is not anchored in a textual, contextual and purposive interpretation of the specific provisions that are relied upon for the tax benefit would run counter to the overall policy of Parliament that tax law be certain, predictable and fair, so that taxpayers can intelligently order their affairs".[156] The Court stated in the *Copthorne* decision:

> What is not permissible is basing a finding of abuse on some broad statement of policy, such as anti-surplus stripping, which is not attached to the provisions at issue. However, the tax purpose identified in these reasons is based upon an examination of the PUC sections of the Act, not a broadly stated policy. The approach addresses the rationale of the PUC scheme specifically in relation to amalgamation and redemption and not a general policy unrelated to the scheme under consideration.[157]

(iii) — Finding abuse

The second step in the abuse analysis considers whether an avoidance transaction falls within or frustrates the identified purpose or rationale of the provisions. More specifically, a transaction is abusive where 1) it achieves an outcome the statutory provision was intended to prevent; 2) it defeats the underlying rationale of the provision; or 3) it circumvents the provision in a manner that frustrates or defeats its object, spirit or purpose.[158]

In *Lipson* and *Mathew*, the taxpayer used a specific anti-avoidance rule (SAAR) (section 74.1 in *Lipson* and subsection 18(13) in *Mathew*) to achieve tax avoidance, and the transaction was, thus, abusive. In *Copthorne*, the Court found that the sale of VHHC Holdings shares to Big City was undertaken to protect $67,401,279 of PUC from cancellation. This avoidance transaction circumvented the parenthetical words of subsection 87(3) and, as part of the series, achieved a result that subsection 87(3) was intended to prevent (i.e., making a payment ostensibly as a tax-free return of capital in excess of the tax-paid amount of an investment).

The lack of economic substance in an avoidance transaction does not necessarily mean that the transaction is abusive.[159] "Motivation, purpose and economic substance are relevant under subsection 245(4) only to the extent that they establish whether the transaction frustrates the purpose of the relevant provisions."[160] On the other hand, courts cannot look at a document or transaction in isolation from any

---

[155] *Copthorne, supra* note 11.

[156] *Canada Trustco, supra* note 1 at para. 42.

[157] *Copthorne, supra* note 11 at para. 118.

[158] *Canada Trustco, supra* note 1 at para. 45; *Lipson, supra* note 36 at para. 40; *Copthorne, supra* note 11 at para. 72.

[159] *Canada Trustco, supra* note 1 at para. 57.

[160] *Ibid.* at paras. 57–60; *Lipson, supra* note 36 at para. 38, per LeBel J.

context to which it properly belongs. The artificiality or vacuity of avoidance transactions is an underlying factor in the abuse analysis in cases such as *Mathew* and *Copthorne*.

In cases where the series of transactions at issue resulted in more than one tax benefit, "the individual tax benefits must be analyzed separately, but always in the context of the entire series of transactions and bearing in mind that each step may have an impact on the others, in order to determine whether any of the provisions relied upon for each tax benefit was misused and abused".[161] For example, the majority in *Lipson* found that the tax benefit conferred on Mrs. Lipson by paragraph 20(1)(c) and subsection 20(3) (i.e., the entitlement to deduct the interest) did not result in a misuse or abuse of these provisions. The tax benefit conferred by subsection 73(1) and section 74.1, namely the rollover and attribution of income or loss, results in an abuse because "a specific anti-avoidance rule is being used to facilitate abusive tax avoidance".[162]

(e) — Reasonable consequences

If the GAAR applies to a transaction, subsection 245(5) provides for the tax consequences: the tax benefits that would flow from the abusive transactions will be denied. The court must determine whether these consequences are reasonable in the circumstances. In *Lipson*, LeBel J. considered it reasonable to disallow the interest deduction in computing the income or loss attributable to Mr. Lipson so that only the dividend was attributable. In *Mathew* and *Copthorne*, the tax benefit sought by the taxpayer was denied. There are no penalties under the GAAR.

(f) — Developing GAAR jurisprudence

The GAAR is about drawing a line between acceptable tax planning and abusive tax avoidance. The generally-worded section 245 delegates the line-drawing task to the courts. The courts have provided some guidance through an evolving body of jurisprudence. Overall, judicial uncertainty is a reality. At the same time, the application of the GAAR is increasingly grounded in statutory interpretation. Facts matter in GAAR cases. The existence of "tax benefit" and an "avoidance transaction" are questions of fact, and the taxpayer bears the burden of proof. Less than a third of the GAAR cases at the Tax Court were resolved when the taxpayer successfully refuted these questions. The other cases moved on to the misuse or abuse stage, which is primarily a statutory interpretation exercise. After the Supreme Court of Canada decision in *Canada Trustco*, Tax Court judges paid more attention to "contextual and purposive" interpretation. With the additional guidance from the Supreme Court of Canada in *Copthorne*, this trend is expected to continue.

A quick survey of the GAAR jurisprudence indicates some emerging patterns

---

[161] *Lipson*, *supra* note 36 at para. 40, per LeBel J.

[162] *Ibid.* at para. 42.

1. In terms of the type of transactions, the GAAR has been found to apply to:

    * loss transfers (*Mathew, MacKay*);

    * synthetic losses (*Triad Gestco Ltd. v. R.* (2012))[163] and *1207192 Ontario Ltd. v. R.* (2012);[164]

    * surplus stripping (*McNichol* (1997), *Desmarais v. R.* (2006));[165]

    * the duplication of PUC (*Copthorne*);

    * spousal rollover and mortgages (*Lipson*); and

    * inter-provincial tax arbitrage in the "Quebec shuffle" (*OGT Holdings* (2009)),[166] but not the "Ontario shuffles" (*Husky Energy Inc. v. Alberta* (2012)[167] and *Canada Safeway Inc. v. Alberta* (2012)).[168]

2. The GAAR has been found not to apply to other types of transactions such as:

    * sale leaseback (*Canada Trustco*);

    * surplus stripping plus income splitting (*Evans*);

    * treaty shopping (*MIL Investments*);

    * tiered financing (*Univar Canada Ltd. v. R.*);[169]

    * interest-coupon stripping (*Lehigh*);

    * capital gain stripping or hybrid asset and share sales (*Geransky*); and

    * the recognition of terminal loss (*Landrus v. R.* (2009)).[170]

---

[163] *Triad Gestco Ltd. v. R.* (2012), [2013] 1 C.T.C. 202, 2012 D.T.C. 5156 (Fed. C.A.).

[164] *1207192 Ontario Ltd. v. R.* (2012), [2013] 1 C.T.C. 1, 2012 D.T.C. 5157 (Fed. C.A.); leave to appeal refused 2013 CarswellNat 11395, 2013 CarswellNat 11394 (S.C.C.).

[165] *Desmarais v. R.* (2006), [2006] 3 C.T.C. 2304, 2006 D.T.C. 2376 (T.C.C.).

[166] *OGT Holdings Ltd. v. Québec (Sous-ministre du Revenu)*, 2009 QCCA 191, 2009 D.T.C. 5048 (Que. C.A.); leave to appeal refused 2009 CarswellQue 8756, 2009 CarswellQue 8757 (S.C.C.).

[167] *Husky Energy Inc. v. Alberta* (2012), 2012 ABCA 231, [2012] 6 C.T.C. 202, 2012 D.T.C. 5132 (Eng.) (Alta. C.A.); leave to appeal refused 2013 CarswellAlta 265, 2013 CarswellAlta 266 (S.C.C.).

[168] *Canada Safeway Inc. v. Alberta* (2012), 2012 ABCA 232, 2012 CarswellAlta 1300, [2012] 5 C.T.C. 243, 2012 D.T.C. 5133 (Eng.) (Alta. C.A.); leave to appeal refused 2013 CarswellAlta 246, 2013 CarswellAlta 247 (S.C.C.).

[169] *Univar Canada Ltd. v. R.*, [2006] 1 C.T.C. 2308, 2005 D.T.C. 1478 (T.C.C.).

[170] *Landrus v. R.* (2009), [2009] 1 C.T.C. 2009, D.T.C. 3583 (T.C.C.); affirmed [2009] 4 C.T.C. 189, 2009 D.T.C. 5085 (Fed. C.A.).

3. In terms of tax attributes, the GAAR was found to apply to transactions that involve:

    - tax attribute trading (*Mathew*, *McKay*);

    - tax attribute importation (*Duncan* (*Water's Edge*));

    - tax attribute exportation (*OGT Holdings*, *Antle*); and

    - tax attribute double counting (*Copthorne*).

4. The GAAR was not found to apply in transactions that created a tax attribute (*Canada Trustco*, *Lehigh*) or realized a tax attribute (*Landrus*).

Some factors that have been alleged as indicators of abusive tax avoidance have been rejected as significant or relevant by the courts. Examples include the complexity of transactions and the involvement of indifferent third parties (*Canada Trustco*) and transactions designed to "work like clockwork" (*Evans*). In *Evans*, Bowman J. remarked:

> I do not think that it can be said that there is an abuse of the provisions of the *Act* where each section operates exactly the way it is supposed to. The Crown's position seems to be predicated on the view that since everything worked like clockwork there must have been an abuse. The answer to this position is, of course, that if everything had not worked like clockwork we would not be here.[171]

Similarly, a taxpayer's motivation to minimize tax is irrelevant. For example, LeBel J. stated in *Lipson* that an avoidance purpose is needed to establish a violation of the GAAR when subsection 245(3) is in issue, but is not determinative in the subsection 245(4) abuse analysis.[172] The lack of economic substance is not, on its own, the basis for finding abuse.[173] The potential loss of tax revenue is not a factor in GAAR decisions. However, a concern with the relative ease with which the market can duplicate an avoidance transaction may underlie the decisions in *Mathew*, *Lipson* and *Copthorne*.

The common features of the three Supreme Court decisions in *Mathew*, *Lipson* and *Copthorne* include: a series of transactions designed to produce a tax benefit; a specific anti-avoidance rule relied upon to obtain the benefit (that is, anti-avoidance karate transactions); and both the Tax Court and Federal Court of Appeal ruling in favour of applying the GAAR. *Copthorne* is different from *Mathew* and *Lipson* in that the transactions involved no third parties and were completed entirely among members of the Copthorne corporate group. *Canada Trustco* can be distinguished from these three cases by the fact that the transactions were profitable commercial transactions and the impugned provision was one that defined the tax base, and was not an anti-avoidance rule.

---

[171] *Evans, supra* note 109 at para. 29.

[172] *Lipson, supra* note 36 at para. 38.

[173] *Canada Trustco, supra* note 1 at para. 60.

At the time of writing, there are no GAAR cases that deal with the abuse of a charging provision (i.e., a provision that creates a tax liability, such as subsections 2(1) or 2(3) of the *ITA*). In existing GAAR cases, the impugned provision that was relied upon by the taxpayer to obtain a tax benefit was generally a tax deduction/exemption provision (e.g., paragraph 20(1)(a) in *Canada Trustco*), a rollover or other relief provision, or a SAAR (e.g., the parenthetical phrase in subsection 87(3) in *Copthorne*). In many cases, the taxpayer's transaction is designed to "technically comply" with the provision in order to obtain a tax benefit. The Minister relies on the GAAR to deny the tax benefit. This may lead one to argue that the precondition for the application of the GAAR is a technical compliance with an impugned provision. If there were no technical compliance with an impugned provision, there would not be any tax benefit (e.g., a tax deduction would not be available), and, as such, there would be no "avoidance transaction" for the purpose of the GAAR.

INDEX

Financial statements, *see also* Generally accepted accounting principles (GAAP)
- balance sheet, Appendix A
- income statement, Appendix B
- samples, Appendix C

Flat taxes, *see* Tax rates

Foreign affiliates, *see* Non-residents

Foreign exchange, 10.2(d)

G

GAAP, *see* Generally accepted accounting principles

GAAR, *see* General anti-avoidance rule (GAAR)

GST, *see* Good and Services Tax

Gambling winnings, 4.3(d)

General anti-avoidance rule (GAAR)
- abusive tax avoidance, 17.2(c)(ii)
- • misuse or abuse test, 17.3(d)
- • reasonable consequences, 17.3(e)
- • result test, 17.3(c)(ii)
- • vs legitimate tax minimization, 17.1(b)(i)
- application of, 17.3
- • avoidance transaction, 17.3(c)
- • judicial guidelines, 17.3(a)
- • non-tax purpose test, 17.3(c)(iii)
- • series of transactions, 17.3(c)(i)
- • tax benefit, 17.3(b)
- avoidance transaction defined, 17.2(c)(i)
- • series of transactions defined, 17.3(c)(i)
- • tax benefit, 17.2(b)
- case law, 17.3(f)

- • *Canada Trustco*, 17.2(c)(ii), 17.3(a)(ii)
- • *Copthorne*, 17.2(d)(ii), 17.3(a)(v)
- • *Lipson*, 17.2(d)(i), 17.3(a)(iv)
- • *Mathew*, 17.3(a)(iii)
- general, 17.2(c)(ii)
- interpretation guidelines, 17.3(a)(i)
- introduction of, 17.2(d)(i)
- measure of last resort, 20.4(b)
- minister's discretion and role of courts, 17.2(e)
- misuse or abuse, 17.3(d)
- no down-side risk for taxpayers, 17.2(d)(i)
- not to fill loop-holes in Act, 17.2(d)(iii)
- primary purpose
- • constraint of Duke of Westminster principle, 17.2(c)(ii)
- • last resort measure, 17.2(d)(i)
- • prevent abusive tax avoidance, 17.2(c)(ii)
- section 245, 17.2(c)(i)

Generally accepted accounting principles (GAAP), *see also* Profit
- accrual method, 6.5(c)(ii)
- amortization, 6.5(d)
- capital assets, 6.5(c)(i)
- cash method, 6.5(d)(i)
- deferral, 6.5(c)(ii)
- defined, 6.5(c)
- depreciation, 6.5(d)
- interpretative aids only, 6.5(c)
- inventory, 6.5(c)(i)
- matching principle, 6.5(d)(ii)
- use of, 6.5(c)
- well-accepted business principles and, 6.3(c)